CONTENTS I

Model Chart	4
Engine	5
Valve Adjustment	21
The Ignition System	51
Spark Plugs	61
The Cooling System	73
The Fuel System	86
Carburetor Adjustment	98
The Clutch	112
The Gearbox	130
The Propeller Shaft	154
The Rear Axle	161
The Rear Road Springs	183
The Steering Gear	187
The Hydraulic Dampers	218
The Braking System	222
The Electrical System	262
Electrical Trouble Shooting	298
Wiring Diagrams	301
Lubrication	306
General Data	313
18GB Section	337
Contents II	340
Driver's Handbook	431

MODEL CHART

MODEL	SERIAL NUMBERS FOR:	DESCRIPTION	COMMENCING	FINISHING
MGB Tourer GHNB (through 1967)	Three Main Bearing Engines	Without Overdrive — Without Crankcase Emission Control	18GUH101	18GUH31121
		With Overdrive — Without Crankcase Emission Control	18GRUH101	18GRUH31050
		Without Overdrive — With Crankcase Emission Control	18GAUH101	18GAUH17500
		With Overdrive — With Crankcase Emission Control	18GARUH101	18GARUH16071
	Five Main Bearing Engines	Without Overdrive — With Crankcase Emission Control	18GBUH101	18GBUH91200
		With Overdrive — With Crankcase Emission Control	18GBRUH101	18GBRUH74528
	Car (On Body)	Smaller Fuel Pump	GHN3-101	GHN3-44438
		Larger Fuel Pump	GHN3-44439	GHN3-138400
		Banjo Type Rear Axle	GHN3-101	GHN3-123715*
		Tube Type Rear Axle	GHN3-132923	ON
	Body		MGB-101	MGB-110292
MGB Tourer GHN4 (1968 ON)	Five Main Bearing Engines (Except U.S.A.)	New Fascia — All Synchronized 4-Speed Transmission (Optional) All Synchronized 4-Speed Transmission With Overdrive (Optional) Fully Automatic 3-Speed Transmission (BW35)	18GD101	ON
	Five Main Bearing Engines (U.S.A.)	New Fascia — All Synchronized 4-Speed Transmission (Optional) All Synchronized 4-Speed Transmission With Overdrive (Optional) Fully Automatic — 3-Speed Transmission (BW 35) Exhaust Emission Control System	18GF101	ON
	Car (On Body)	Tube Type Rear Axle — Larger Fuel Pump	GHN4-138401	ON
	Commission (Except U.S.A.)		G23N-101F	ON
	Commission (U.S.A.)		GU23N-101F	ON
	Body (Except U.S.A.)		MGB-110401	ON
	Body (U.S.A.)		MGBU-101	ON
MGB GT GHD3 (through 1967)	Five Main Bearing Engines	SAME AS MGB TOURER GHN3 EXCEPT: Three Main Bearing Engine NOT USED.	18GBU101	ON
	Car (On Body)	Tube Type Rear Axle — Larger Fuel Pump	GHD3-71933	GHD3-139471
	Body		GBD-101	GBD-21777
MGB GT GHD4 (1968 ON)	Five Main Bearing Engines (Except U.S.A.)	SAME AS MGB TOURER GHN4	18GD101	ON
	Five Main Bearing Engines (U.S.A.)	SAME AS MGB TOURER GHN4	18GF101	ON
	Car (On Body)	Tube Type Rear Axle — Larger Fuel Pump	GHD4-139472	ON
	Commission (Except U.S.A.)		G23D-101P	ON
	Commission (U.S.A.)		GU23D-101P	ON
	Body (Except U.S.A.)		GBD-22001	ON
	Body (U.S.A.)		GBUD-500101	ON

*GHN3-123716 to GHN3-132922 — either type of axle fitted during production.

ENGINE

The M.G. (Series MGA) overhead-valve engine is built in unit construction, with an 8 in. single-plate dry clutch.

The valves are set in line in the detachable cylinder head and are operated by rockers and push-rods from the camshaft in the left-hand side of the engine. Oil seals are fitted to the valves and there is the normal provision for clearance adjustment. The camshaft, running in three steel-backed white-metal bearings, is chain driven. The oil pump, distributor and engine revolution indicator are driven from the camshaft; each component has its own drive shaft.

The solid-skirt pistons are of aluminium alloy with anodized finish, and carry three compression rings and a slotted oil control ring. The piston pins are clamped in connecting rods, which have steel-backed indium-lead renewable big-end bearings. Three steel-backed white-metal renewable bearings support the forged-steel counterbalanced crankshaft. The thrust is taken by special washers at the center main bearing. The renewable element full-flow oil filter is secured to the right-hand side of the engine.

A centrifugal water pump and fan are driven from the crankshaft by belt.

Two semi-down draft S.U. carburetors are supplied with fuel by an electric high-pressure S.U. pump. Air enters the carburetors through twin filters.

An eccentric-type oil pump inside the crankcase is driven from the camshaft by a short vertical shaft. Oil is drawn into the pump through a strainer and is delivered through crankcase drillings to a non-adjustable plunger-type relief valve located at the rear of the engine on the left-hand-side. From the relief valve the oil passes through an internal oil pump to the main filter. From the filter the oil passes to the main, big-end and camshaft bearings. The connecting rod ends are drilled and supply oil to the cylinder walls.

From the rear camshaft bearing oil passes through the block and a drilling in the rear rocker shaft bracket to lubricate the rockers, returning to the sump via the push-rod holes.

Two grooves in the front camshaft journal register with small holes in the camshaft thrust plate as the camshaft turns, allowing a small amount of oil for chain and wheel lubrication to pass into the timing case twice in each revolution of the camshaft. A drain is provided to return oil from the timing case to the sump.

The filter bowl is filled with oil at full pressure which passes through the element into the annular space around the centre bolt and from there into the main oil gallery.

Engine in Car

Many portions of the engine can be attended to without calling for its removal from the chassis. These obviously include craburetion, ignition, head, valve assembly, accessories, etc. All of the components discussed ahead of the section "Removing Engine & Gearbox" can be so handled. Operations which call for complete removal of the power unit are discussed following this section.

Oil Pressure

Under normal running conditions the oil pressure in the MGA-1600 engine should not drop below 30 pounds per square inch. Approximately 10 psi should be shown when the engine is idling. In the MGB, a minimum of 50 psi should be shown on the gage at normal road speed and 15 psi at idle.

Should there be a noticeable drop in pressure, the following points should be checked:
1. That there is a good supply of the correct grade of oil in the engine sump.
2. That the strainer in the sump is clean and not choked with sludge.
3. That the bearings, to which oil is fed under pressure, have the correct working clearances. Should the bearings be worn and the clearances excessive, the oil will escape more readily from the sides of the bearings, particularly when the oil is warm and becomes more fluid. This will cause a drop in pressure on the gauge as compared with that shown when the bearings are in good order.

The automatic relief valve in the lubrication system deals with an excessive oil pressure when starting from cold. When hot the pressure drops as the oil becomes more fluid.

Should the oil filter become blocked, two relief valves in the filter blow off to enable the oil to by-pass the filter and pass direct into the main gallery.

Continuous cold-running and unnecessary use of the mixture control are often the cause of serious oil dilution by fuel with a consequent drop in pressure.

Particular attention is called to the recommended change of oil every 3,00 miles.

THE M.G. (Series "MGA") ENGINE

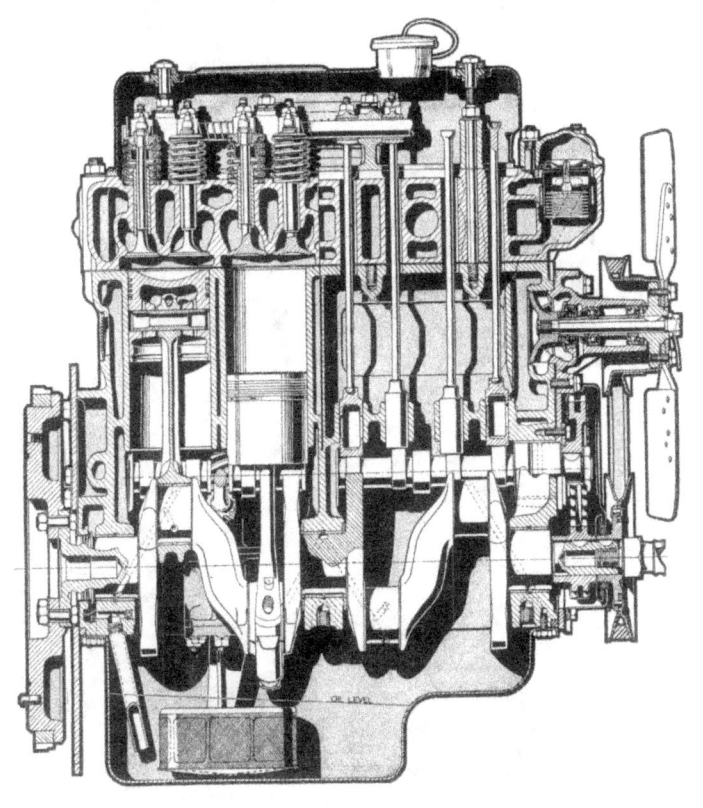

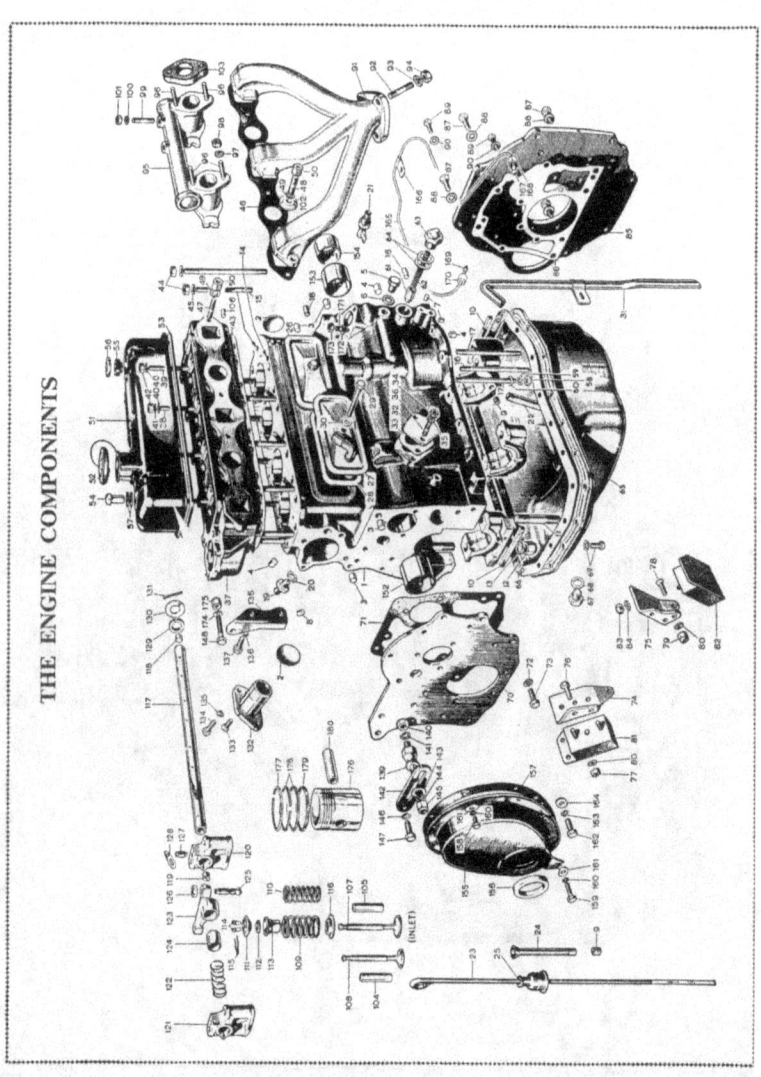

THE ENGINE COMPONENTS

KEY TO THE ENGINE COMPONENTS

No.	Description
1.	Block assembly—cylinder.
2.	Plug—core hole.
3.	Plug—oil gallery.
4.	Plug—taper—crankcase oil hole.
5.	Plug—screwed—transverse oil hole.
6.	Plug—plug.
7.	Plug—oil relief valve hole.
8.	Plug—oil filter boss.
9.	Plug—redundant dipper boss (and rear main bearing cap).
10.	Joint—front/rear main bearing cap.
11.	Stud—main bearing cap.
12.	Nut—main bearing cap stud.
13.	Washer—spring.
14.	Stud (long)—cylinder head.
15.	Stud (short)—cylinder head.
16.	Stud (long)—oil pump.
17.	Stud (short)—oil pump.
18.	Dowel—gearbox mounting plate.
19.	Union—oil gauge pipe.
20.	Washer—union.
21.	Tap—water drain.
22.	Pipe—drain—rear bearing cap.
23.	Dipper rod.
24.	Tube—dipper rod.
25.	Dust cap.
26.	Cover—side—rear.
27.	Cover—side—front—with elbow.
28.	Joint—side covers.
29.	Set strip—side covers.
30.	Washer—set screw.
31.	Pipe—vent with clip—crankcase.
32.	Plate—cylinder block blanking—N/S.
33.	Joint—blanking plate.
34.	Nut—blanking plate stud.
35.	Washer—blanking plate stud.
36.	Stud—L/H side crankcase blanking plate.
37.	Cylinder head.
38.	Stud—rocker bracket—short.
39.	Stud—rocker bracket—long.
40.	Washer—stud.
41.	Washer—spring—stud.
42.	Nut—rocker bracket studs.
43.	Joint—head to block.
44.	Nut—cylinder head stud.
45.	Washer—stud.
46.	Joint—manifold to head.
47.	Stud—exhaust manifold to head.
48.	Stud—manifolds to head.
49.	Washer—spring.
50.	Nut—stainless steel.
51.	Cover assembly—rocker gear.
52.	Cap—oil filler and cable.
53.	Joint—cover to head.
54.	Cap nut—cover.
55.	Bush—rubber—capnut.
56.	Cap washer—bush.
57.	Washer—packing—cover stud.
58.	Nut—oil pump stud.
59.	Washer—spring.
60.	Washer—plain.
61.	Valve—oil relief.
62.	Spring—relief valve.
63.	Cap nut—relief valve.
64.	Washer—cap nut.
65.	Reservoir—oil.
66.	Joint—oil reservoir.
67.	Plug—drain.
68.	Washer—drain plug.
69.	Set screw—reservoir (with captive washer).
70.	Plate—front mounting.
71.	Joint—plate to block.
72.	Washer—spring.
73.	Set screw—plate to block.
74.	Bracket—front R.H.
75.	Bracket—front L.H.
76.	Screw—R/H bracket to mounting plate.
77.	Nut—R/H bracket to plate screw.
78.	Screw—countersunk—L/H bracket to plate.
79.	Nut—countersunk screw.
80.	Washer—spring.
81.	Mounting—R/H—front.
82.	Mounting—L/H—front.
83.	Nut—engine mounting to bracket.
84.	Washer—spring.
85.	Plate—gearbox mounting.
86.	Joint—plate to block.
87.	Set screw—plate to block.
88.	Lock washer—set screw.
89.	Set screw—plate to block.
90.	Lock washer—set screw.
91.	Manifold—exhaust.
92.	Stud—exhaust pipe flange.
93.	Washer.
94.	Nut.
95.	Manifold—induction.
96.	Stud—carburetter.
97.	Washer—spring.
98.	Nut—carburetter stud.
99.	Stud—inlet manifold (accelerator abutment bracket).
100.	Washer—spring.
101.	Nut—inlet manifold stud.
102.	Yoke—manifold.
103.	Washer—carburetter insulating.
104.	Guide—valve—exhaust.
105.	Guide—valve—inlet.
106.	Plug—oil hole.
107.	Valve—inlet.
108.	Valve—exhaust.
109.	Spring—valve (outer).
110.	Spring—valve (inner).
111.	Cup—valve spring.
112.	Packing ring—valve.
113.	Shroud—valve guide.
114.	Cotters—valve.
115.	Circlip—cotter.
116.	Collars—valve spring (bottom).
117.	Shaft.
118.	Plug—plain.
119.	Plug—screwed.
120.	Bracket—tapped hole.
121.	Bracket—plain.
122.	Spring—rocker shaft spacing.
123.	Rocker.
124.	Bush.
125.	Screw—tappet adjusting.
126.	Locknut—screw.
127.	Screw—tappet-locating.
128.	Plate—locking—locating screw.
129.	Washer—double coil.
130.	Washer—plain.
131.	Split pin.
132.	Housing—distributor.
133.	Screw—to block.
134.	Screw—distributor to housing.
135.	Washer—spring—screw.
136.	Bracket—dynamo—rear.
137.	Screw—bracket to crankcase.
138.	Washer—spring.
139.	Adjusting link pillar.
140.	Nut—pillar to front plate.
141.	Washer.
142.	Adjusting link.
143.	Washer—plain.
144.	Washer—spring.
145.	Nut—link to pillar.
146.	Washer—spring,—link to dynamo.
147.	Screw—link to dynamo.
148.	Bolt—dynamo to bracket.
152.	Liner—front camshaft bearing.
153.	Liner—centre camshaft bearing.
154.	Liner—rear camshaft bearing.
155.	Cover complete—crankcase (front).
156.	Felt ring.
157.	Joint—crankcase front cover.
158.	Set screw—cover to engine plate.
159.	Set screw—cover and plate to bearing cap.
160.	Washer—spring.
161.	Washer—plain.
162.	Set screw—cover and plate to crank case.
163.	Washer—spring.
164.	Washer—set screw.
165.	Pipe—ignition control.
166.	Clip—pipe.
167.	Nipple.
168.	Nut—carburetter e.d.
169.	Olive—distributor end.
170.	Nut—distributor end.
171.	Stud—tachometer pinion housing.
172.	Washer—housing stud.
173.	Nut—housing stud.
174.	Washer—dynamo bolt.
175.	Nut—dynamo bolt.
176.	Piston assembly.
177.	Ring—compression—first.
178.	Ring—compression—second and third.
179.	Ring—scraper.
180.	Gudgeon pin.

THE ENGINE LUBRICATION SYSTEM

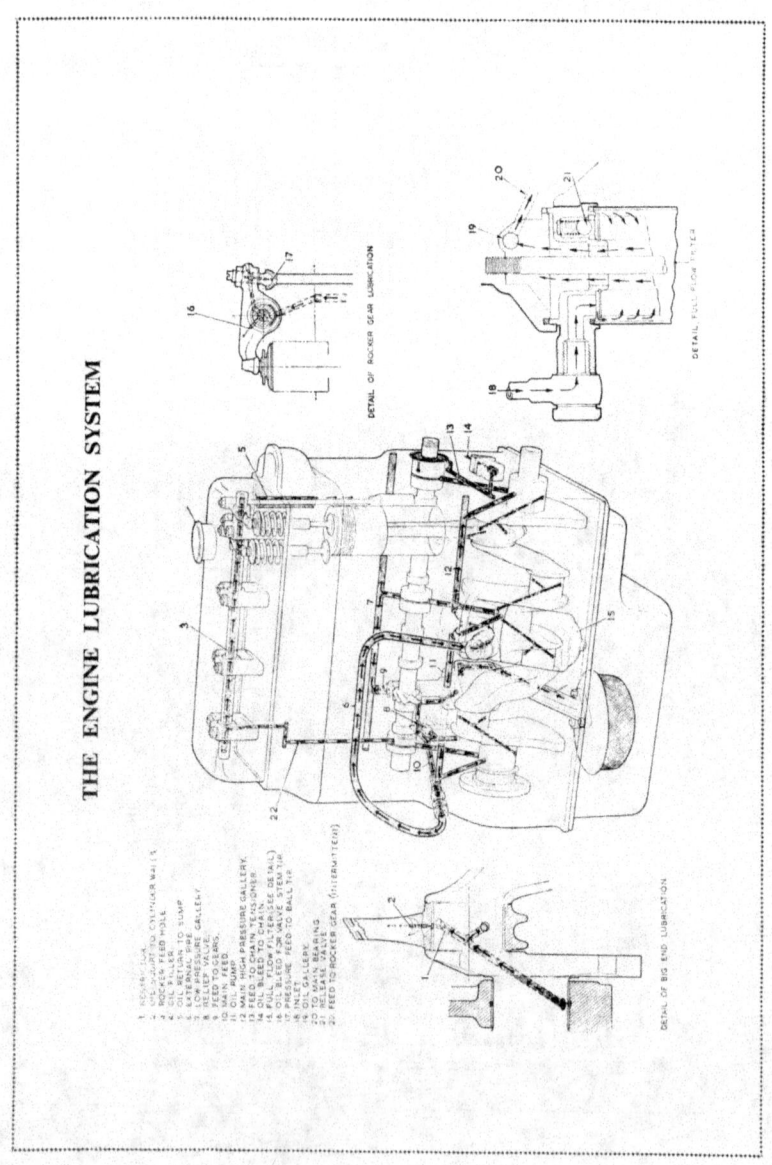

Oil Pressure Relief Valve

The non-adjustable oil pressure relief valve is situated at the rear of the left-handed side of the cylinder block and is held in position by a domed hexagon nut sealed by two fiber washers. The relief valve spring maintains a valve cup against a seating machined in the block.

The valve should be examined to ensure that the cup is seating correctly and that the relief spring has not lost its tension. The latter can be checked by measuring the length of the spring. To give correct relief pressure of 75 to 80 lb. per sq. in. this should not be less than 3 in. Fit a new cup and spring if necessary.

Removing and Replacing the Water Pump

The water pump is of the centrifugal impeller type and is mounted on a common spindle with the fan in a casting bolted to the front of the cylinder block.

The water pump and fan assembly is attached to the front of the cylinder block by four bolts and may be withdrawn and serviced.

If the gasket is damaged as the pump body is withdrawn from the cylinder block, ensure that all traces of it are removed before a new gasket is fitted and the pump replaced.

Removing and Replacing the Carburetors

1. Release the spring clips and detach the breather hose from the air cleaner and rocker cover.
2. Disconnect the fuel supply pipe at the rear carburetor banjo union.
3. Remove the split pin and flat washer and release the mixture cable and clevis pin from the mixture control linkage and release the mixture outer cable abutment from its bracket.
4. Detach the throttle return spring and release the throttle cable.
5. Unscrew the union nut and disconnect the ignition vacuum control pipe from the rear carburetor.
6. Remove the nut and flat washer to release the vent pipe from the top of each float-chamber.
7. Remove the four nuts securing the carburetor flanges and withdraw the carburetors and air cleaners as an assembly.

Replacement is a reversal of the above procedure.

Removing and Replacing the Manifolds

1. Remove the air cleaners and carburetors as detailed above.
2. Remove the nut, bolt and washers securing the exhaust pipe to the steady bracket on the rear engine plate.

3. Release the distributor vacuum advance pipe and, if fitted, the heater pipe, from the manifold.
4. Remove the three exhaust pipe to manifold clamp bolts and spring washers and release the pipe.
5. Six studs and nuts secure the manifolds to the cylinder head. The four center nuts have large washers enabling them to secure both the inlet and exhaust manifolds. The two remaining nuts, one at each end of the manifolds, have smaller washers and secure the exhaust manifold only.

Replacement of manifolds is a reversal of these instructions. Use a new gasket.

Removing and replacing the Rocker Assembly
1. Drain the cooling system. One drain tap is at the base of the radiator and the other is at the rear of the engine on the right hand side. If anti-freeze mixture is being used it should be drained into a suitable clean container and carefully preserved
2. Release the breather pipe from the front of the rocker cover.
3. Slacken the clamping nut and withdraw the throttle cable from the lever and outer cable abutment. Unscrew the two nuts and lift off the rocker cover, taking care not to damage the cork gasket or lose the washers and rubber seals. Notice that under the right-hand rear rocker stud nut is a special locking plate. Unscrew the eight rocker-shaft bracket fixing nuts gradually, a turn at a time until all load has been released.

4. NOTE: It is necessary to drain the radiator and slacken the seven external cylinder head securing nuts because four of the rocker-shaft bracket fixing nuts also secure the cylinder head, and if the seven external cylinder head fixing nuts are not slackened distortion may result and water find its way from the cooling system into the cylinders and sump.

5. Completely unscrew the eight rocker shaft bracket nuts and remove the rocker assembly, complete with brackets and rockers. Withdraw the eight push-rods, storing them carefully so that they may be replaced in the same positions. To dismantle the rocker shaft assembly, first remove the grub screw which locates the rocker shaft in the rear rocker mounting bracket and remove the split pins, flat washers and spring washers from each end of the shaft. Slide the rockers, brackets and springs from the shaft.

6. Unscrew the plug from the front end of the shaft and clean out the oilways.

Reassembly and replacement is a reversal of the above procedure, replacing the rockers and springs in their original positions on the shaft. Remember to replace the rocker cover with the vent pipe to the front. Check that the two cap nut rubber bushes and the rocker cover cork gasket are undamaged; if they are found to be faulty, fit new ones or oil leaks may result.

Removing and Replacing the Cylinder Head Assembly

1. Drain the water from the cooling system.
2. Remove the top water hose. Remove the three thermostat housing securing nuts and washers and remove the housing and thermostat.
3. Remove the air cleaners and carburetors.
4. Remove the inlet and exhaust manifolds.
5. Remove the rocker assembly and remove the seven external cylinder head nuts at the same time. Withdraw the push-rods, keeping them in the order of their removal.
5. Detach the high-tension cables and remove the spark plugs, taking care not to damage the porcelain insulators. If fitted, remove the heater hose from the water valve on the right-hand side of the cylinder head by slackening the retaining clip.
6. Unscrew the thermal transmitter from the front of the cylinder head and release the conductor from its supporting clip.
7. Slacken the clips and disconnect the hoses from the water pipe on the left-hand side of the cylinder head and remove the pipe. Release the ignition vacuum control pipe from the rear cylinder head stud and remove the cylinder head. **Break the cylinder head joint by levering it at one end, then lift up the head evenly.**

Refitting the Cylinder Head
1. Make sure that the surfaces of both the cylinder head and the cylinder block are clean. It will be noticed that the cylinder head gasket is marked 'FRONT' and 'TOP' to assist in replacing it correctly with the copper side uppermost. Having slipped the gasket over the studs, next lower the cylinder head into position. Replace the vacuum control pipe clip and fit the seven cylinder head external nuts finger-tight.
2. Replace the push-rods in the position from which they were taken.
3. Replace the rocker assembly and securing nuts, finger-tight.
4. Tighten the 11 cylinder head nuts, a turn at a time, in the order given in the illustration.
5. Tighten the four rocker assembly nuts.

Reassembly continues in the reverse order to the dismantling procedure.

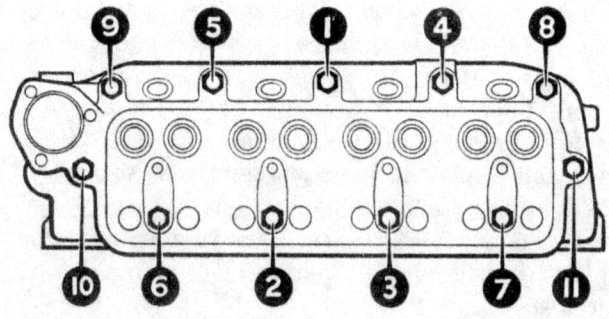

Removing and Replacing Valves
1. Remove the cylinder head.
2. Remove the valve circlip. Compress the double valve springs, using special tool 18G45 or a suitable spring compressor, and remove the two valve cotters. Release the valve springs and remove the compressor, valve spring cap, shroud, inner and outer springs, and bottom collar.
3. Remove the valve packing ring from the cotter groove and withdraw the valve from the guide.
4. Keep the valves in their relative positions when removed from the head to ensure replacement in their original valve guides. The exhaust valve heads are concave and are smaller in diameter than the inlet valves.

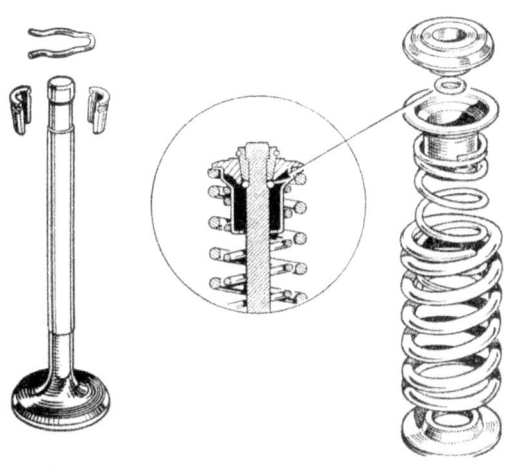

*Parts of the valve assembly, **showing the** valve, cotters, circlip, bottom collar, double valve springs, shroud, packing ring, and spring cap. The inset shows the valve packing ring fitted correctly at the bottom of the cotter groove below the cotters*

To replace the valves place each valve into its guide and fit the bottom collars, inner and outer valve springs, shrouds, and caps. Compress the valve springs and push a new synthetic rubber packing ring over the tip of the valve stem down to the bottom of the cotter groove. Refit the two valve cotters and remove the compresor. Replace the valve circlip.

NOTE: Do not fit old valve packing rings, or oil sealing may suffer. The rings are fitted more easily if they have been soaked in clean engine oil for a short period before using.

Decarbonizing
1. Remove the cylinder head.
2. Withdraw the valves.
3. Remove the cylinder head gasket and plug the water-ways with a clean rag.

If special equipment is not available for decarbonizing it will be necessary to scrape the carbon deposit from the piston crowns, cylinder block and cylinder head, using a blunt scraper.

A ring of carbon should be left round the periphery of the piston crown and the rim of carbon round the top of the cylinder bore should not be touched. To facilitate this, an old piston ring can be sprung into the bore so that it rests on top of the piston.

THE CYLINDER HEAD COMPONENTS

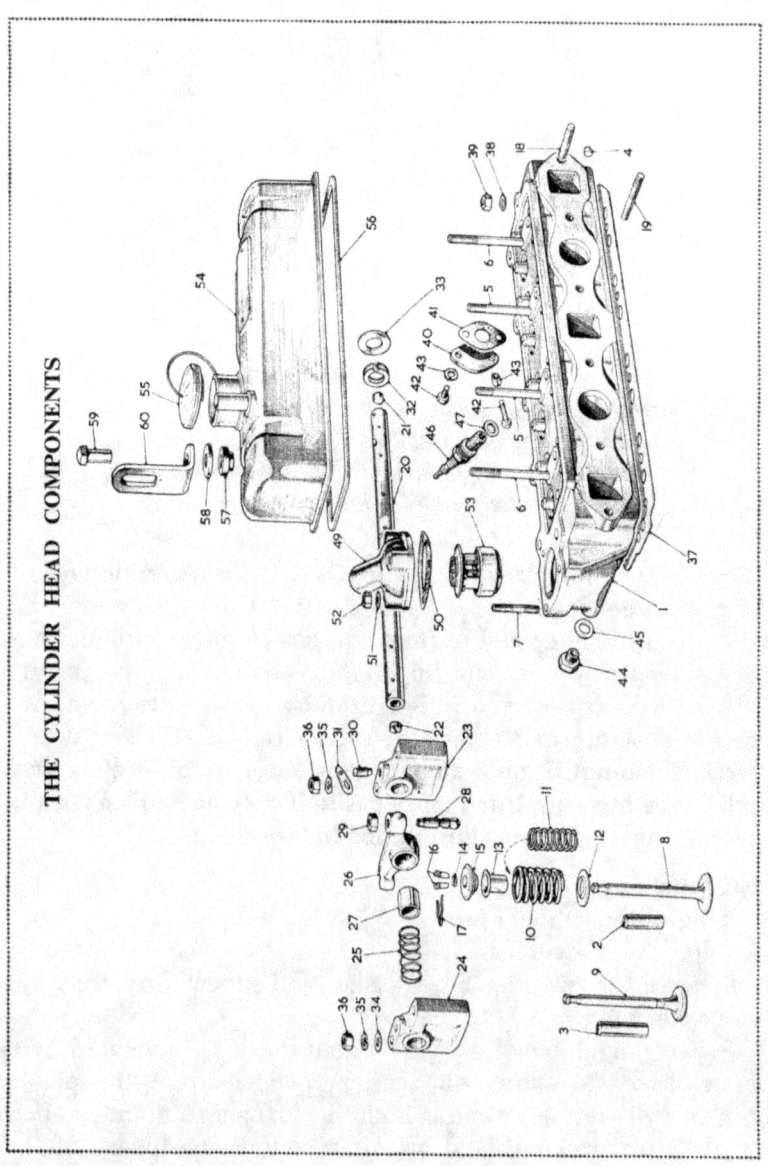

KEY TO THE CYLINDER HEAD COMPONENTS

No.	Description
1.	Cylinder head assembly—with guides.
2.	Guide—inlet valve.
3.	Guide—exhaust valve.
4.	Plug—oil hole.
5.	Stud—short—rocker bracket.
6.	Stud—long—rocker bracket.
7.	Stud—water outlet elbow to head.
8.	Valve—inlet.
9.	Valve—exhaust.
10.	Spring—outer—valve.
11.	Spring—inner—valve.
12.	Collar—valve spring.
13.	Shroud—valve guide.
14.	Ring—valve packing.
15.	Cup—valve spring.
16.	Cotter—valve (halves).
17.	Circlip—valve cotter.
18.	Stud—exhaust manifold to head.
19.	Stud—inlet and exhaust manifold to head.
20.	Shaft—valve rocker—plugged.
21.	Plug—plain—valve rocker.
22.	Plug—screwed—valve rocker.
23.	Bracket—tapped—rocker shaft.
24.	Bracket—plain—rocker shaft.
25.	Spring—rocker spacing.
26.	Rocker—valve—bushed.
27.	Bush—valve rocker.
28.	Screw—adjusting—tappet.
29.	Nut—tappet adjusting screw.
30.	Screw—locating—rocker shaft.
31.	Plate—lock—locating screw.
32.	Washer—double-coil rocker shaft.
33.	Washer—rocker shaft.
34.	Washer—plain—rocker shaft stud.
35.	Washer—spring—rocker shaft stud.
36.	Nut—rocker bracket stud.
37.	Joint washer—cylinder head.
38.	Washer—cylinder head nut.
39.	Nut—cylinder head stud.
40.	Plate—blanking—heater outlet elbow.
41.	Joint washer blanking plate.
42.	Screw—plate to cylinder head.
43.	Washer—spring—screw.
44.	Plug—thermal transmitter boss.
45.	Washer—plug.
46.	Plug—sparking.
47.	Gasket—steel—plug.
48.	Elbow—outlet—water.
49.	Joint washer—elbow.
50.	Washer—plain—stud in cylinder head.
51.	Nut—stud.
52.	Thermostat.
53.	Cover—valve rocker.
54.	Cap and cable—oil filler.
55.	Washer—oil filler cap.
56.	Joint washer—valve rocker cover.
57.	Bracket—engine sling.
58.	Bush—rubber—cover.
59.	Washer—cup.
60.	Nut—cap—rocker cover.

The cylinder head is next given attention. The spark plugs must be cleaned and adjusted. Clean off the carbon deposit from the valve stems, valve ports and combustion spaces of the cylinder head. Remove all traces of carbon dust with compressed air and then thoroughly clean with kerosene or solvent.

Fit a new cylinder head gasket when replacing the head if the old has been damaged, noting that the gasket is marked to indicate the top face and the front end.

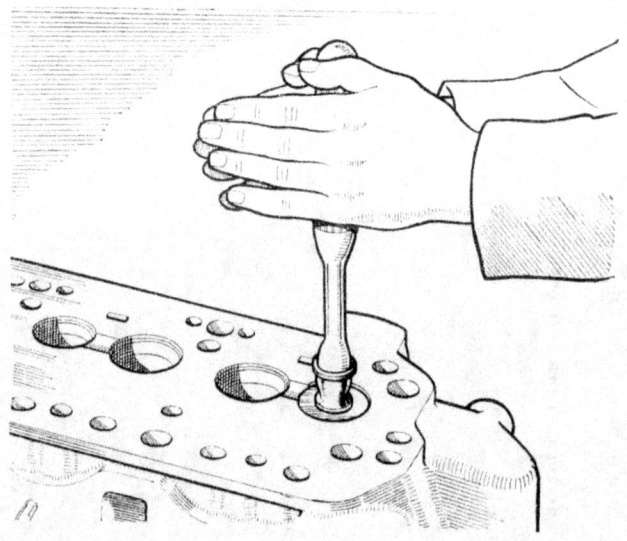

Grinding Valves
1. Remove the valves.
2. Each valve must be cleaned thoroughly and carefully examined for pitting. Valves in a pitted condition should be refaced with a suitable grinder or new valves should be fitted. If valve seats show signs of pitting or unevenness they should be trued by the use of a suitable grinder or special cutter. When using a cutter, care must be exercised to remove only as much metal as is necessary to ensure a true surface.
3. When grinding a valve onto its seat the valve face should be smeared lightly with a fine or medium grade carborundum paste and then lapped in with a suction grinder. Avoid the use of excessive quantities of grinding paste and see that it remains in the region of the valve seat only.

4. A light coil spring placed under the valve head will assist considerably in the process of grinding. The valve should be ground to its seat with a semi-rotary motion and occasionally allowed to rise by the pressure of the light coil spring. This assists in spreading the paste evenly over the valve face and seat. It is necessary to carry out the grinding operation until a dull, even, matt surface, free from blemish, is produced on the valve seat and valve face.

5. On completion, the valve seat and ports should be cleaned thoroughly with a rag soaked in kerosene or solvent, dried, and then thoroughly cleaned by compressed air. The valves should be washed similarly and all traces of grinding paste removed.

Fit a new oil seal when refitting the valves and ensure that the chamfered side of the seal is downwards.

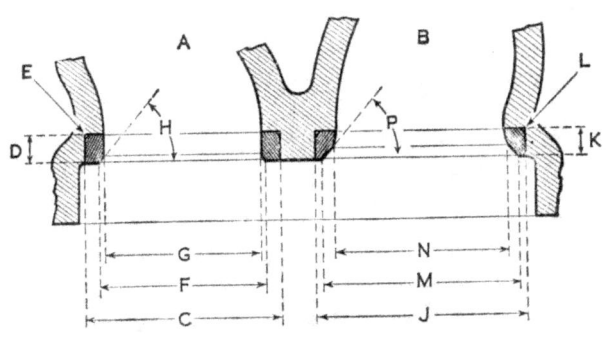

Fig. A.1

Valve seat machining dimensions

Exhaust (A)
- C. 1·437 to 1·438 in.
  (36·5 to 36·52 mm.).
- D. ·186 to ·188 in.
  (4·72 to 4·77 mm.).
- E. Maximum radius ·015 in.
  (·38 mm.).
- F. 1·286 to 1·288 in.
  (32·20 to 32·71 mm.).
- G. 1·165 to 1·175 in.
  (29·59 to 29·84 mm.).
- H. 45°.

Inlet (B)
- J. 1·530 to 1·531 in.
  (38·86 to 38·88 mm.).
- K. ·186 to ·188 in.
  (4·72 to 4·77 mm.).
- L. Maximum radius ·015 in.
  (·38 mm.).
- M. 1·487 to 1·507 in.
  (37·77 to 38·27 mm.).
- N. 1·302 to 1·322 in.
  (33·07 to 33·57 mm.).
- P. 45°.

Fitting Valve Seat Inserts

Should the valve seatings become so badly worn or pitted that the normal workshop cutting and refacing tools cannot restore them to their original standard of efficiency, special valve inserts can be fitted.

The seating of the cylinder head must be machined to the dimensions given in Fig. A.1   Each insert should have an interference fit of .0025 to .0045 in. and must be pressed and not driven into the cylinder head.

After fitting, grind or machine the new seating to the dimensions given in Fig. A.1   Normal valve grinding may be necessary to ensure efficient valve seating.

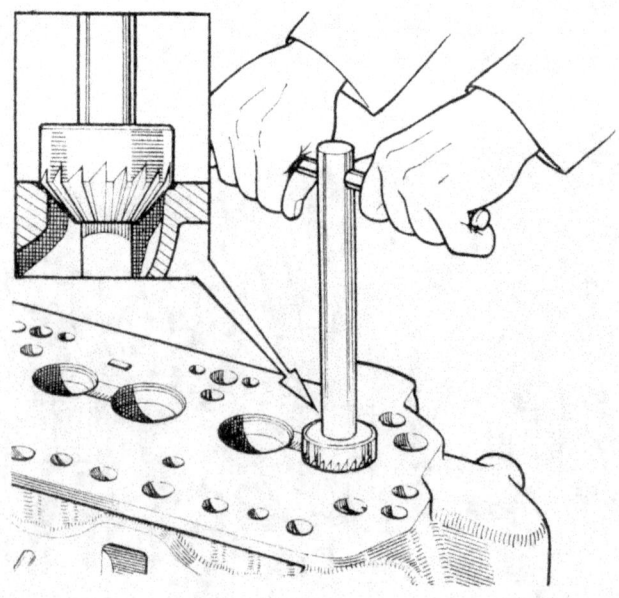

Removing and Replacing Valve Guides
1. Remove cylinder head.
2. Remove the appropriate valve and springs. Rest the cylinder head with its machined face downwards on a clean surface and drive the valve guide downwards into the combustion space with a suitable-sized drift. This should take the form of a hardened steel punch 9/16 in. in diameter and not less than 4 in. in length, with a locating spigot 5/16 in. diameter machined on one end for a length of 1 in. to engage the bore of the guide.
3. When fitting new valve guides, these should be pressed in from the top of the cylinder head. The inlet valve guides must

be inserted with the end having the largest chamfer at the top, and the exhaust valve guides should have their counterbored ends at the bottom. The valve guides should be driven into the combustion spaces until they are 5/8 in. above the machined surface of the valve spring seat.

Removing and Replacing Tappets
1. Remove the carburetors and the rocker cover.
2. Remove the manifolds.
3. Disconnect the high-tension leads from the spark plug.
4. Remove the rocker assembly and withdraw the push-rods, keeping them in their relative positions to ensure their replacement onto the same tappets. Release the breather pipe and remove the tappet covers and lift out the tappets, also keeping them in their relative positions.

New tappets should be fitted by selective assembly so that they just fall into their guides under their own weight when lubricated.

Assembly is a reversal of the above procedure, but care should be taken to see that the tappet cover joints are oiltight and that the rockers are adjusted to give the correct valve clearance.

Adjusting Valve Rocker Clearances

If the engine is to give its best performance and the valves are to retain their maximum useful life, it is essential to maintain the correct valve clearance. Accordingly it is recommended that the clearances be checked at regular intervals and any necessary adjustments made.

For the correct valve rocker clearance refer to '**GENERAL DATA**'. The engine has been designed to operate with this clearance and no departure from it is permissible. An additional .001 in. must be allowed when the engine is cold.

Provision for adjusting the valve clearance is made in the rocker arm by an adjustable screw and locknut.

The rocker adjusting screw is released by slackening the hexagon locknut with a box or end wrench while holding the screw against rotation with a screwdriver. The valve clearance can then be set by carefully rotating the rocker screw while checking the clearance with a feeler gauge. This screw is then re-locked by tightening the hexagon locknut while again holding the screw against rotation.

It is important to note that while the clearance is being set the tappet of the valve being operated upon is on the back of its cam, i.e. opposite to the peak.

As this cannot be observed accurately, the rocker adjustment is more easily carried out in the following order, and this also avoids turning the engine over more than is necessary:

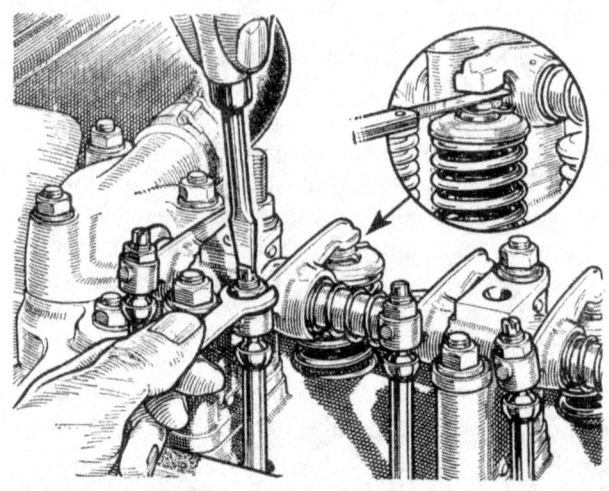

Adjust No. 1	rocker with	No. 8	valve fully open.
”	No. 3	”	”	No. 6	”	”	”
”	No. 5	”	”	No. 4	”	”	”
”	No. 2	”	”	No. 7	”	”	”
”	No. 8	”	”	No. 1	”	”	”
”	No. 6	”	”	No. 3	”	”	”
”	No. 4	”	”	No. 5	”	”	”
”	No. 7	”	”	No. 2	”	”	”

Checking Valve Timing

1. Set No. 1 cylinder inlet valve to .060 in. (.021 in. for the MGB) clearance with the engine cold, and then turn the engine until the valve is about open.

2. The indicating notch in the flange of the crankshaft pulley should then be opposite the longest of the three pointers on the timing cover, i.e. the No. 1 valve should be about to open on its compression stroke.

Do not omit to reset the inlet valve clearance to the recommended clearance (see 'GENERAL DATA') when the timing check has been completed. The clearance of .060 in. is necessary to bring the opening position of the valve to T.D.C. It is not possible to check the valve timing accurately with the normal running valve clearance.

Removing and Replacing the Timing Chain Cover
1. Drain the cooling system and remove the radiator.
2. Slacken the generator attachment bolts and remove the belt.
3. Bend the tab on the starting dog nut locking washer. Unscrew the starting dog nut and remove the locking washer.
4. Pull off the crankshaft pulley.
5. The timing cover is secured by nine bolts. Each bolt has a shakeproof washer and a plain washer. Remove all nine bolts with their washers and remove the timing cover.

Care should be taken not to damage the timing cover gasket. If it is damaged, clean the face of the cover flange and the front engine mounting plate and fit a new gasket when reassembling. The felt washer situated in the timing cover should also be renewed if necessary.

It should be noted that the oil thrower, which is located behind the crankshaft pulley, is fitted with its concave side facing away from the engine.

Replacement of the timing cover is a reversal of the above procedure.

If a rubber seal is fitted fill the annular groove between the lips with grease. Lubricate the hub of the pulley and push it into the seal, at the same time turning it to avoid damaging the felt

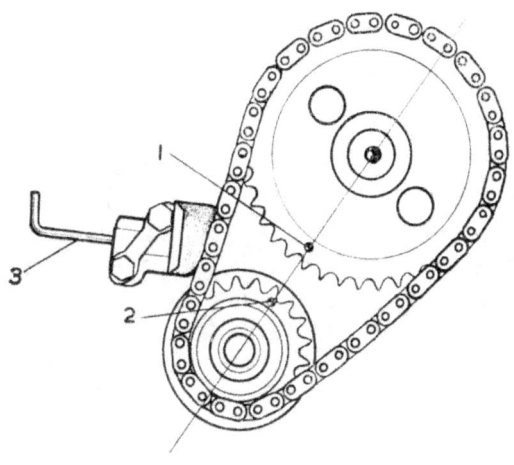

Crank the engine until the timing dimples (1) and (2) are opposite each other before removing the timing chain and chain wheels. The chain tensioner is retracted into the unloaded position by turning the Allen key (3) in a clockwise direction

or the lips of a rubber seal. Slide the pulley onto the shaft with the keyway in line with the key in the crankshaft. Turn the cover as necessary to align the set screw holes with those in the crankcase, taking care not to strain the cover against the flexibility of the seal.

Insert the set screws and tighten up.

Refit and tighten the pulley securing screws.

Removing and Replacing the Timing Chain

1. Remove the timing cover and oil thrower.
2. Unlock and remove the camshaft chain wheel nut and remove the nut and lock washer. Note that the locating tag on the lock washer fits into the keyway of the camshaft chain wheel.
3. The camshaft and crankshaft chain wheels may now be removed, together with the timing chain, by easing each wheel forward, a fraction at a time, with suitable small levers.
4. As the crankshaft gear wheel is withdrawn care must be taken not to lose the gear packing washers immediately behind it. When reassembling replace the same number of washers as was found when dismantling, unless new camshaft or crankshaft components have been fitted which will disturb the alignments of the two gear wheels. To determine the thickness of washers required, place a straight-edge across the sides of the camshaft wheel teeth and measure with a feeler gauge the gap between the straight-edge and the crankshaft gear. Subtract .005 in. from the feeler gauge reading and add the resultant thickness of crankshaft gear packing washers.

When replacing the timing chain and gears, set the crankshaft with its keyway at T.D.C., and the camshaft with its keyway approximately at the one o'clock position when seen from the front. Assemble the gears into the timing chain with the two marks on the gear wheels opposite to each other. Keeping the gears in this postion engage the crankshaft gear keyway with the key on the crankshaft and rotate the camshaft until the camshaft gear keyway and key are aligned. Push the gears onto the shafts as far as they will go and secure the camshaft gear with the lock washer and nut.

Replace the oil thrower, concave side forward, and the remaining components.

Timing Chain Tensioner

Commencing at Engine No .259, a timing chain tensioner, is fitted to the engine front mounting plate and secured by two bolts and a locking plate.

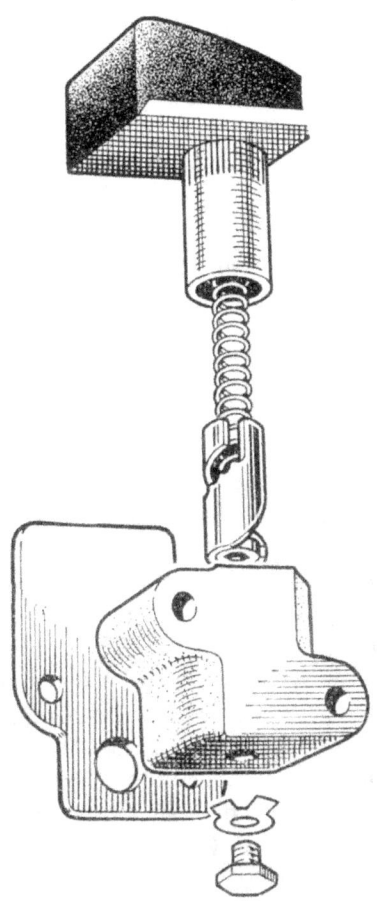

Also fitted are a modified camshaft locating plate and a camshaft timing gear in which the rubber tensioner ring is deleted. The timing chain now receives lubrication via the tensioner slipper and not as previously by an injection of oil from the camshaft locating plate. The chain tensioner cannot be fitted to earlier vehicles.

1. Before removing the assembly from the engine, unlock the tab washer and remove the bottom plug from the tensioner body. Insert a 1/8 in. Allen key to engage the cylinder and turn the key clockwise until the rubber slipper is compeltely free of spring pressure. Between a half and one full turn is all that is necessary.

2. Unlock and remove the bolts to release the chain tensioner assembly and the backplate.

3. Withdraw the plunger and slipper assembly from the tensioner body and engage the lower end of the cylinder with the Allen key. Turn the key clockwise, holding the key plunger securely until the cylinder and springs can be withdrawn from inside the plunger.

4. The components should be cleaned thoroughly in solvent and the .125 in. diameter inlet oil hole in the spigot and the .040 in. outlet oil hole in the slipper should be cleaned with compressed air before reassembling.

When the tensioner is in operation and the engine is running, oil from the lubrication system enters the spigot on the back face under pressure and lubricates the bearing surface through a hole in the slipper pad. The pad is held against the chain by spring and oil pressure.

Should the chain stretch with use, the slipper plunger rises and the limiting peg, bearing on the top of the helical slot, rotates the cylinder until the next recess in the lower edge of the slot comes into line with the limiting peg and prevents the plunger returning to its original position and allowing the chain to become slack again.

When assembling, insert the spring in the plunger and place the cylinder on the other end of the spring. Compress the spring until the cylinder enters the plunger bore, engaging the helical slot with the peg in the plunger. Hold the assembly compressed in this position and engage the Allen key. Turn the cylinder clockwise until the end of the cylinder is behind the peg and the spring is held compressed. Withdraw the key and insert the plunger assembly in the body. Replace the backplate and secure the assembly to the cylinder block.

When the timing chain is in position the tensioner is released for operation by inserting the key and turning it clockwise, allowing the slipper head to move forward under spring pressure only.

Secure the bolts with the locking plate; replace the bottom plug and lock with a tab washer.

Removing Engine and Gearbox—MGA

1. Drain oil from the engine and gearbox.
2. Mark the propeller shaft and rear axle drive flange and disconnect the propeller shaft from the axle.
3. Mark the hand brake cable operating lever and splined shaft to assist replacing the lever in its original position.
4. Remove the clamping nut and bolt from the lever and prise the lever from the splined shaft.
5. **Remove** the nuts, bolts and spring washers and withdraw

the reinforcement bracket from inside the propeller shaft tunnel.
6. Remove both seats and frames, the floor covering from the toeboards, floorboards and gearbox cover, floorboards and toeboards, the gear lever knob and the propeller shaft and gearbox covers.
7. Disconnect the speedometer drive cable.
8. Remove the banjo bolt to release the flexible supply pipe from the clutch slave cylinder.
9. Detach the hood from its hinges
10. Drain the water from the radiator and disconnect and remove the top and bottom water hoses. Remove the three bolts with spring and flat washers, securing each side of the radiator, and withdraw the radiator.
11. Remove the carburetors.
12 Disconnect the engine revolution indicator drive from the left-hand side of the engine Release the exhaust pipe from the exhaust manifold and from the steady bracket on the engine rear mounting plate.
13. Unscrew the thermal transmitter from the cylinder head and release the conductor from its support clip.
14. Disconnect the flexible oil gauge pipe from the union at the rear of the cylinder block on the right-hand side.
15. Disconnect the cables from the generator, ignition coil, distributor, and starter motor. Remove the gearbox remote control assembly from the gearbox extension.
16. Place a rope sling around the power unit and attach the lifting tackle. Arrange the sling so that the unit may be lifted slightly and moved forward, and finally lifted from the frame at a sharp angle with the front considerably higher than the rear.
17. Take the weight of the unit, release the engine from the two front mounting rubbers and remove the rubbers. Remove the nut, bolt and spring washer to release the gearbox from the mounting bracket on the frame cross-member.

Replacement is a reversal of the above instructions, not forgetting to refill the engine and gearbox with oil.

Modified Power Unit (1500)

A new power unit, having the type designation 15GD, is fitted from Car No. 61504 and to certain earlier cars.

The engine incorporates the various modifications made to the 15GB unit and has the starter motor placed higher on the gearbox mounting plate.

Modifications have also been made to the gearbox to the propeller shaft to the gearbox cover, and to the right-hand toeboard, so that neither the engine, the gearbox, nor the propeller

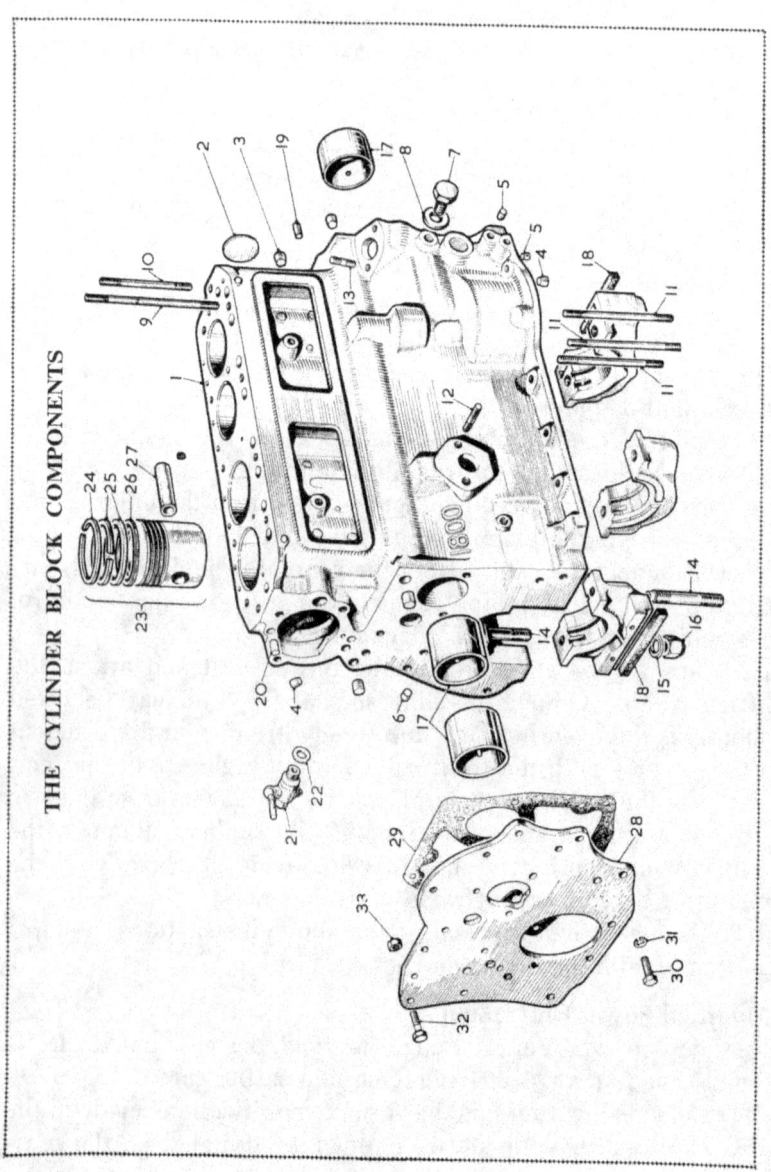

KEY TO THE CYLINDER BLOCK COMPONENTS

No.	Description
1.	Cylinder block assembly.
2.	Plug—welch—large.
3.	Plug—crankcase oil gallery.
4.	Plug—taper—crankcase oil hole.
5.	Plug—oil relief valve vent hole.
6.	Plug—chain tensioner oil feed.
7.	Plug—oil hole—screwed.
8.	Washer—screwed plug.
9.	Stud—cylinder head—long.
10.	Stud—cylinder head—short.
11.	Stud—oil pump—short.
12.	Stud—crankcase vent pipe clip.
13.	Stud—tachometer spindle housing.
14.	Stud—main bearing cap.
15.	Washer—plain—main bearing stud.
16.	Nut—main bearing stud.
17.	Liner—camshaft bearing.
18.	Joint—front and rear main bearing cap.
19.	Dowel—gearbox mounting plate.
20.	Dowel—water pump.
21.	Tap—drain—cylinder block.
22.	Washer—drain tap.
23.	Piston assembly—standard H.C.
24.	Ring—compression—top—standard.
25.	Ring—compression—2nd and 3rd standard.
26.	Ring—scraper—standard.
27.	Pin—gudgeon.
28.	Plate—engine mounting.
29.	Joint—washer—mounting plate.
30.	Screw—mounting plate to crankcase.
31.	Washer—spring—screw.
32.	Bolt—engine mounting bracket to front plate R.H. top.
33.	Nut—bolt.

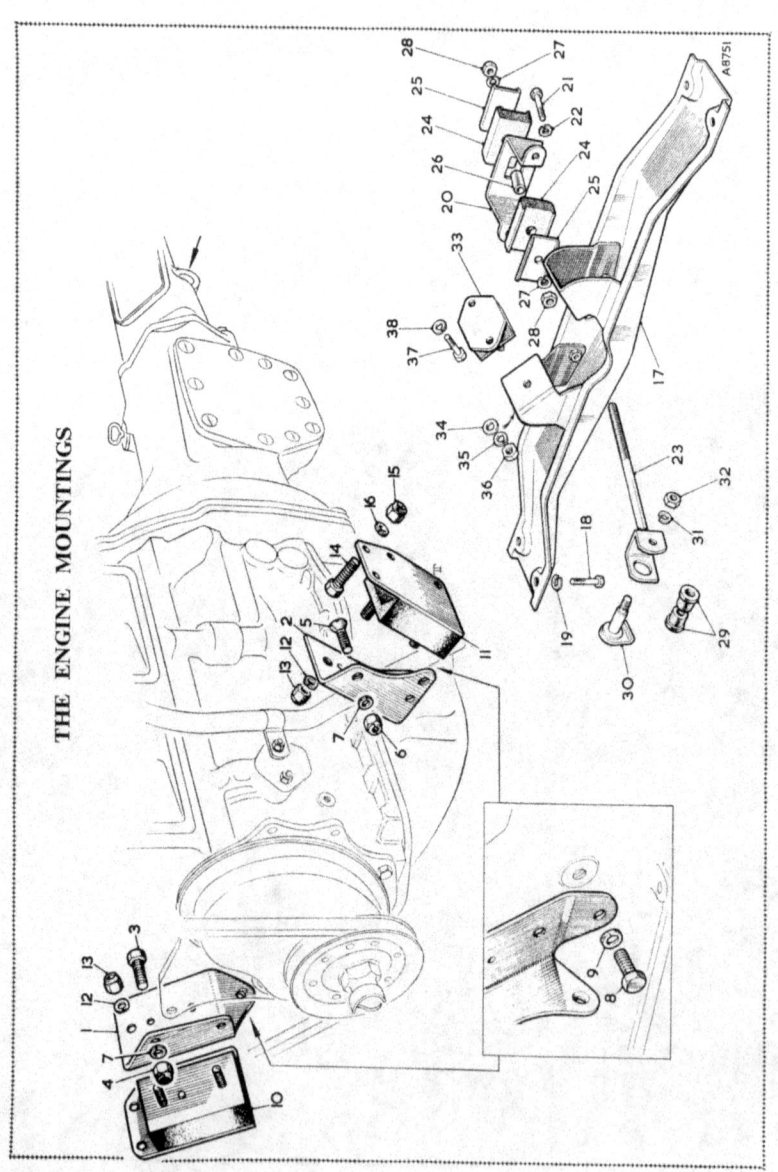

KEY TO THE ENGINE MOUNTINGS

No.	Description
1.	Bracket—front engine mounting R.H.
2.	Bracket—front engine mounting L.H.
3.	Screw—bracket to mounting plate—R.H.
4.	Nut for screw.
5.	Screw—bracket to mounting plate—L.H.
6.	Nut for screw.
7.	Washer—spring.
8.	Screw—bracket to block.
9.	Washer—spring.
10.	Rubber—front engine mounting—R.H.
11.	Rubber—front engine mounting—L.H.
12.	Washer—spring—mounting to bracket.
13.	Nut—mounting to bracket.
14.	Screw—mounting and coil bracket to frame bracket.
15.	Nut for screw.
16.	Washer—spring.
17.	Cross-member assembly—rear mounting.
18.	Screw—cross-member to frame.
19.	Washer—spring.
20.	Bracket—engine stay-rod.
21.	Screw—bracket.
22.	Washer—spring.
23.	Stay-rod—engine.
24.	Buffer—stay-rod.
25.	Plate—buffer.
26.	Distance tube for stay-rod.
27.	Washer—spring—stay-rod.
28.	Nut—stay-rod.
29.	Bush—shouldered—gearbox rear extension.
30.	Pin—stay-rod.
31.	Washer—spring stay-rod pin.
32.	Nut—stay-rod pin.
33.	Mounting—engine—rear.
34.	Washer—plain—rear mounting to cross-member.
35.	Washer—spring—rear mounting to cross-member.
36.	Nut—rear mounting to cross-member.
37.	Screw—rear mounting to gearbox.
38.	Washer—spring.

shaft is interchangeable with those previously fitted.

The above changes involve alterations to the procedure for power unit removal and replacement.

Follow the instructions given, but note that the propeller shaft need not be disconnected from the rear axle flange. When the floorboards, toeboards, gearbox cover, and propeller shaft cover have been removed mark the propeller shaft and gearbox flanges and disconnect the propeller shaft from the gearbox.

Removing and Replacing the Engine—MGB

The engine may be removed from the car on its own or together with the gearbox. Where the gearbox is to be serviced the complete power unit should be removed as the fixed chassis cross-member prevents the gearbox from being withdrawn with the engine in the car.

1. Drain the oil from the engine and coolant from the radiator. Disconnect the batteries.
2. Remove the hood, the radiator and diaphram assembly and the air cleaners and carburetors.
3. Disconnect the exhaust pipe flanges and then remove the heat shield and the inlet and exhaust manifolds.
4. Disconnect and remove the coil and its bracket from the front engine mounting, the external oil filter, and the starter motor.
5. Disconnect and remove the thermal transmitter, the distributor cap and plug leads, the oil pressure gauge union, the heat control cable and heater inlet and outlet hoses, and the revolution indicator drive.
6. Take the weight of the engine and support the gearbox.
7. Remove the screws and nuts securing the front mounting brackets to the frame brackets and the gearbox clutch housing to the engine mounting plate. Free the exhaust pipe bracket attached to the lower flange of the gearbox clutch housing and tie it to one side.
8. Pull the engine forward until the clutch is clear of the first motion shaft and then lift the engine from the car. It will be necessary to lift both the engine and gearbox a little at a time and gently ease the engine forward to allow sump to clear the front cross-member and then disengage the clutch and first motion shaft.

Replacement is a reversal of the removal sequence. After refitting the engine fill the sump with fresh oil.

Removing and Replacing the Power Unit

Prepare the engine for removal as described in paragraphs (1) to (6) above and then proceed as follows:

1. Drain the oil from the gearbox.
2. Disconnect and remove the propeller shaft and disconnect the speedometer pinion drive.
3. Remove the clutch slave cylinder from the clutch housing and tie it to one side.
4. Remove the screws securing the rear cross-member to the chassis frame and allow the gearbox to rest on the fixed body cross-member.
5. Remove the engine stay-rod from the gearbox and the screws securing the rear mountings to the gearbox. Withdraw the rear cross-member and engine stay-rod.
6. Remove the gear lever from the tower and the rubber cover from the tunnel.
7. Ease the assembly forward until it is clear of the fixed cross-member and then tilt the assembly and lift it from the car.

Replacement is a reversal of the removal sequence. After refitting refill the engine and gearbox with fresh oil.

Removing and replacing the Sump and Oil Pump Strainer
1. Drain the oil from the engine sump.
2. Remove the bolts and withdraw the sump from the crankcase.
3. To remove the oil strainer, remove the two bolts securing it to the pump cover.
4. The strainer may be dismantled for cleaning by removing the center nut and bolt and the two delivery pipe flange bolts. Note that there is a locating tongue on the side of the cover which must be positioned correctly when replacing. Remember also to replace the distance tube.
5. Clean out the sump and strainer with solvent or kerosene and a stiff brush; never use a rag.

When refitting the sump to the engine give particular attention to the sealing gaskets for the crankcase which fit into recesses in the crankcase. If the gaskets are in good condition and have not been damaged during removal of the sump they may be used again, but it is always advisable to fit new ones. Before fitting new gaskets, remove all traces of the old ones from the sump and crankcase faces. Smear the faces of the crankcase joint with grease and fit the two halves of the large gasket. Lift the sump into position on the crankcase, insert the 19 bolts and tighten them evenly.

Removing and Replacing Main and Big-End Bearings
Unless the bearing journals are badly worn the big-end bearings may be renewed without removing the crankshaft. To renew the main bearings it is necessary to withdraw the crank-

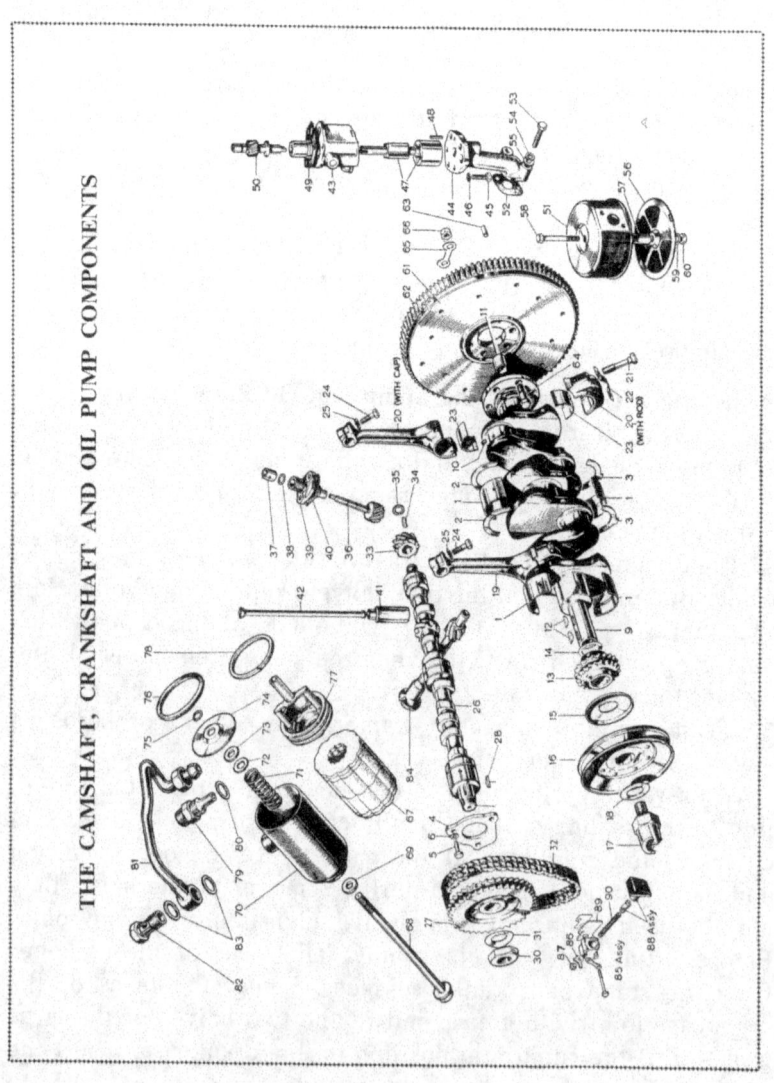

THE CAMSHAFT, CRANKSHAFT AND OIL PUMP COMPONENTS

KEY TO THE CAMSHAFT, CRANKSHAFT AND OIL PUMP COMPONENTS

No.	Description
1.	Bearing—main—standard.
2.	Thrust washer—upper.
3.	Thrust washer—lower.
4.	Plate—camshaft locating.
5.	Screw—plate to engine.
6.	Washer—spring—plate screw.
9.	Crankshaft.
10.	Restrictor—oil.
11.	Bush—first-motion shaft.
12.	Key—gear/fan pulley.
13.	Gear.
14.	Washer—gear packing.
15.	Oil thrower—front.
16.	Pulley—crankshaft fan.
17.	Nut—starting dog.
18.	Lock washer—nut.
19.	Rod and cap—Nos. 1 and 3.
20.	Rod and cap—Nos. 2 and 4.
21.	Set screw—cap.
22.	Lock washer.
23.	Bearings—standard.
24.	Screw—gudgeon pin clamp.
25.	Spring washer—screw.
26.	Camshaft.
27.	Gear—camshaft.
28.	Key—gear.
29.	Tensioner ring—gear.
30.	Nut—gear.
31.	Lock washer—nut.
32.	Chain—camshaft timing.
33.	Gear—tachometer drive.
34.	Key—gear.
35.	Spring ring.
36.	Pinion—tachometer drive.
37.	Oil seal—pinion.
38.	Retaining ring.
39.	Housing pinion.
40.	Joint washer—housing.
41.	Tappet—valve.
42.	Push-rod.
43.	Body and plug.
44.	Cover.
45.	Set screw.
46.	Spring washer.
47.	Shaft—driving—with rotors.
48.	Dowels—cover.
49.	Joint—pump to block.
50.	Spindle—oil pump driving.
51.	Body complete—oil strainer.
52.	Joint—strainer to pump.
53.	Set screw—strainer to pump.
54.	Spring washer.
55.	Plain washer.
56.	Cover—oil strainer.
57.	Distance-piece—cover.
58.	Bolt—cover.
59.	Washer—shakeproof.
60.	Nut—cover bolt.
61.	Flywheel.
62.	Ring—starter.
63.	Dowel—clutch.
64.	Bolt—flywheel to crankshaft.
65.	Lock washer—bolt.
66.	Nut—bolt.
67.	Element—oil filter.
68.	Bolt—centre.
69.	Washer—sealing—small.
70.	Container.
71.	Spring.
72.	Washer.
73.	Washer—felt.
74.	Pressure plate.
75.	Circlip.
76.	" O " ring.
77.	Valve assembly.
78.	Washer—sealing—large.
79.	Adaptor—oil filter connection.
80.	Joint washer—pipe to crankcase.
81.	Pipe assembly—filter to crankcase.
82.	Screw—banjo union.
83.	Washer—banjo union screw.
84.	Spindle—distributor drive.
85.	Tensioner—timing chain.
86.	Lock washer—plug.
87.	Plug—body.
88.	Slipper head and cylinder.
89.	Back-plate—body.
90.	Spring.

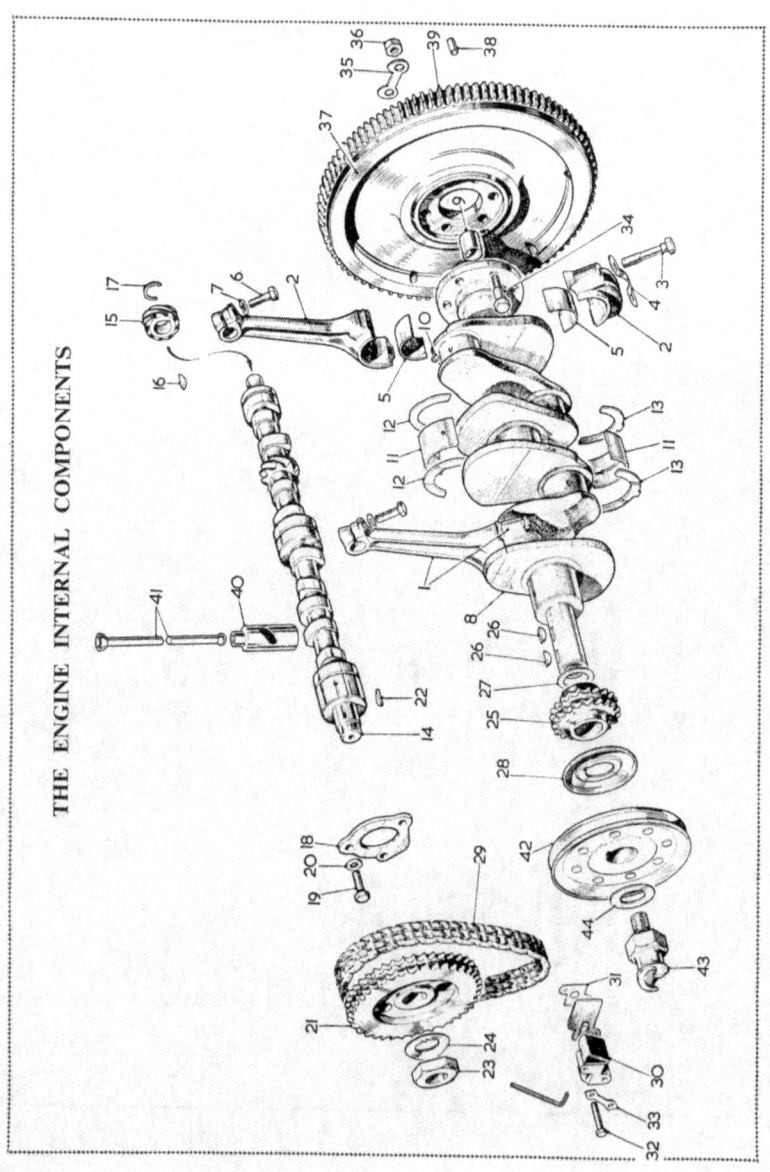

KEY TO THE ENGINE INTERNAL COMPONENTS

No.	Description	No.	Description	No.	Description
1.	Connecting rod and cap—Nos. 1 and 3 cylinders.	16.	Key—tachometer gear	31.	Joint washer—tensioner.
2.	Connecting rod and cap—Nos. 2 and 4 cylinders.	17.	Ring—spring—tachometer gear.	32.	Screw—tensioner to crankcase.
3.	Screw—cap.	18.	Plate—camshaft locating.	33.	Washer—lock—screw.
4.	Washer—lock—screw.	19.	Screw—locating plate to crankcase.	34.	Bolt—flywheel to crankshaft.
5.	Bearing—connecting rod—standard.	20.	Washer—lock—screw.	35.	Washer—lock—bolt.
6.	Screw—connecting rod clamping.	21.	Gear—camshaft.	36.	Nut—bolt.
7.	Washer—spring—screw.	22.	Key—camshaft gear.	37.	Flywheel.
8.	Crankshaft.	23.	Nut—camshaft gear.	38.	Dowel—clutch to flywheel.
9.	Bush—1st motion shaft.	24.	Washer—lock-nut.	39.	Ring gear—starting.
10.	Plug.	25.	Gear—crankshaft.	40.	Tappet.
11.	Bearing—main—standard.	26.	Key—crankshaft gear and pulley.	41.	Push-rod.
12.	Washer—thrust—upper.	27.	Washer—packing—crankshaft gear.	42.	Pulley—crankshaft.
13.	Washer—thrust—lower.	28.	Thrower—oil—front—crankshaft.	43.	Nut—starting.
14.	Camshaft.	29.	Chain—timing.	44.	Washer—lock—starting nut.
15.	Gear—tachometer driving.	30.	Tensioner—chain.		

shaft. Liners are used both for the main and the big-end bearings, which are of the shimless type and therefore non-adjustable.

Big-End Bearings
1. Drain the engine oil and remove the sump.
2. As the bearings are of the shimless type it is essential that no attempt should be made to adjust bearings which are worn. Always fit new bearings in place of worn parts. If the crankshaft journals are found to be in a worn condition it is advisable to fit a reground crankshaft, complete with main and big-end bearings.
3. Both the big-end and main bearings liners are located in the bearing housings by a small tag on one side of each half-bearing; it should be noted that the bearings are fitted so that the tags come on the same joint edge of the bearing housing although on opposite corners.
4. To detach the big-end bearings, bend down the locking strips so that the bolts may be removed. Remove the connecting rod caps and extract the bearings. Care should be taken to see that the bearing journals are thoroughly cleaned before installing new bearings. No scraping is required, as the bearings are machined to give the correct diametrical clearance of .0016 in.

Main Bearings
Remove the flywheel and clutch, the timing chain, the sump and strainer, and the rear engine mounting plate.
2. Remove the self-locking nuts securing the main bearing caps to the cylinder block and two bolts securing the front cap to the front engine bearer plate.
3. Note that thrust washer is fitted on each side of the center main bearing to take the crankshaft end-thrust. These thrust washers each consists of two semicircular halves, one having a lug which is located in a recess in the detachable half of the bearing and the other being plain.
4. When fitting new bearings no scraping is required as the bearings are machined to give the correct diametrical clearance of .005 in.
5. In the case of a 'run' bearing it is always essential to clean out thoroughly all the oilways in the crankshaft and block, wash out the engine sump with solvent or kerosene and clean the oil pump and sump strainer to ensure that no particles of metal are left anywhere in the lubricating system. The rear main bearing cap horizontal joint surfaces should be thoroughly cleaned and lightly covered with Wel-Seal or an equivalent sealing

compound before the cap is fitted to the cylinder block. This will ensure a perfect oil seal when the cap is bolted down to the block. Replace each main bearing and cap, replacing the thrust washers in their correct positions at the center main bearing with the oil grooves towards the bearing. Refit the locking strip or locking plates to each bearing cap and bend them to lock the bolts after tightening. Note that the two bolts securing the front main bearing cap to the front bearer plate are locked by a common plate.

Removing and Replacing Pistons and Connecting Rods
1. Remove the cylinder head. Drain and remove the sump and oil strainer.
2. The pistons and connecting rods must be withdrawn from the top of the cylinder block.
3. Unlock and remove the big-end bolts and remove the bearing caps. Release the connecting rod from the crankshaft.
4. Withdraw the piston and connecting rod from the top of the cylinder block and refit the bearing cap. The big-end bearing caps are offset, and the caps on the big-ends in Nos. 1 and 3 cylinders are interchangeable when new, as are those for Nos. 2 and 4 cylinders. When used parts are replaced after dismantling it is essential that they should be fitted in their original positions. In order to ensure this, mark the caps and connecting

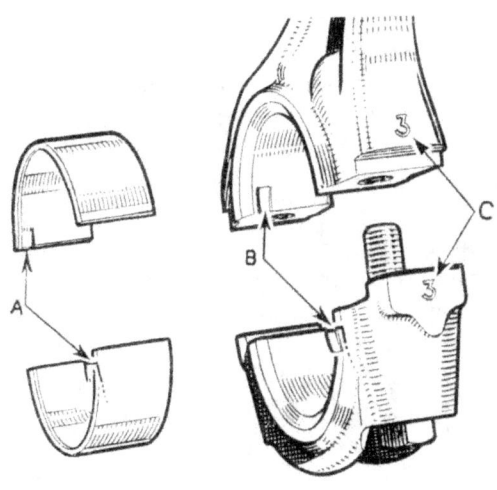

The connecting rod big-end bearing locating tags (A) *and grooves* (B). *The figures* (C) *indicate the cylinder from which the rod and cap were removed*

rods on their sides which are fitted together with the number of the cylinder from which each was taken

Replacement of the piston and connecting rod is a direct reversal of the above, but the piston ring gaps should be set at 180° to each other.

If the piston rings have been removed from the piston they must be replaced.

It is essential that the connecting rod and piston assemblies should be replaced in their own bores and fitted the same way round, i.e. with the piston pin clamp screw on the camshaft side of the engine. The piston crowns are marked 'FRONT' to assist correct assembly to the connecting rods.

Refit the big-end bearings in their original positions.

Dismantling and Reassembling Piston and Connecting Rod Assemblies

1. The piston pin is rigidly held in the split little-end of the connecting rod by a clamp bolt engaging the central groove of the pin.
2. Before the piston and pin can be dismantled from the connecting rod it is necessary to remove the clamp screw. To enable the assembly to be held in a vice for this operation without damage, holding plugs should be inserted in each end of the pin.
3. Unscrew the pin clamp and remove it completely.
4. Push out the pin.

IMPORTANT—Attention must be given to the following points when assembling the piston to the connecting rod:

1. That the piston fitted the correct way round on the connecting rod. The crown of the piston is marked 'FRONT' to assist this, and the connecting rod is fitted with the pin clamp screw on the camshaft side.
2. That the pin is positioned in the connecting rod so that its groove is in line with the clamp screw hole.
3. That the clamp screw spring washer has sufficient tension.
4. That the clamp screw will pass readily into its hole and screw freely into the threaded portion of the little-end and also that it will hold firmly onto the spring washer.

Fitting Piston Pins

A certain amount of selective assembly must be used when fitting new pins. They must be a thumb-push fit for three-quarters of their travel, to be finally tapped in with a raw-hide mallet. This operation should be carried out with the piston and pin cold, i.e. at ambient air temperature.

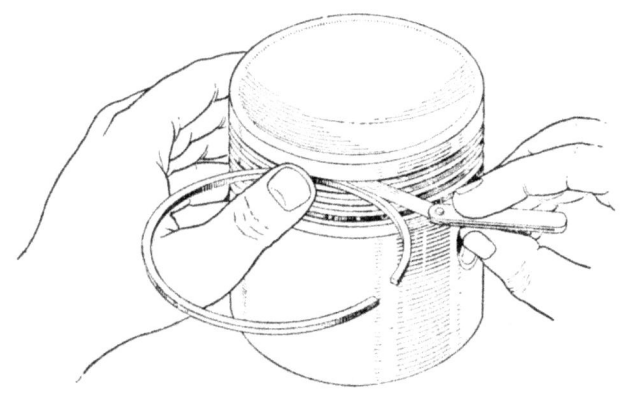

Removing and Replacing Piston Rings

If no special piston ring expander is available, use a piece of thin steel such a smoothly ground hacksaw blade or a disused .020 in. (.50 mm) feeler gauge.

1. Raise one end of the ring out of its groove. Insert the steel strip between the ring and the piston. Rotate the strip around the piston, applying slight upward pressure to the raised portion of the ring until it rests on the land above the ring grooves. It can then be eased off the piston.
2. Do not remove or replace the rings over the piston skirt, but always over the top of the piston.
3. Before fitting new rings, clean the grooves in the piston to remove any carbon deposit. Care must be taken not to remove any metal or sideplay between the ring and the groove will result, with consequent excessive oil consumption and loss of gas tightness.
4. The cylinder bore glazing should be removed before fitting new rings to a worn bore.
5. When refitting the rings note that the second and third compression rings are tapered and marked with the letter 'T' (top) for correct reassembly.

New rings must be tested in the cylinder bore to ensure that the ends do not butt together. The best way to do this is to insert the piston approximately 1 in. into the cylinder bore and push the ring down onto the top of the piston and hold it there in order to keep the ring square with the bore. The correct ring gap is .008 to .013 in.

Piston Sizes and Cylinder Bores

In addition to the standard pistons there is a range of four oversize pistons available for service purposes.

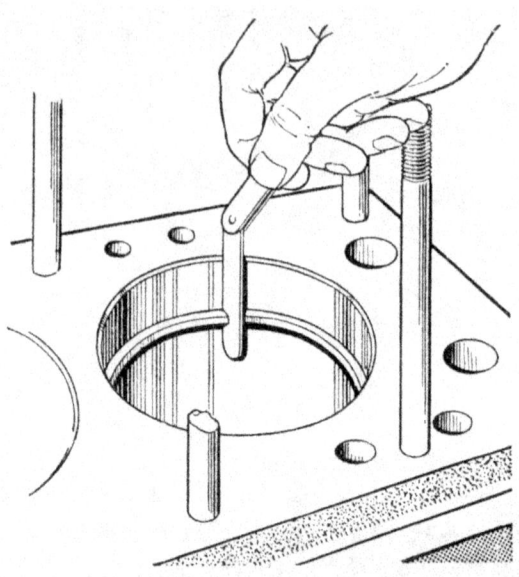

Oversize pistons are marked with the actual oversize dimensions enclosed in an ellipse. A piston stamped .020 is only suitable for a bore .020 in. larger than the standard bore; similarly pistons with other markings are only suitable for the oversize bore indicated.

The piston markings indicate the actual bore size to which they must be fitted, the requisite running clearance being allowed for in the machining.

After reboring an engine, or whenever fitting pistons differing in size from those removed during dismantling, ensure that the size of the piston fitted is stamped clearly on the top of the cylinder block alongside the appropriate cylinder bore.

Pistons are supplied in the sizes indicated in the table.

Piston marking	Suitable bore size
Standard	2.8757 in.
	2.8760 in.
Oversize +.010 in.	2.8857 in.
	2.8860 in.
+.020 in.	2.8957 in.
	2.8960 in.
+.030 in.	2.9057 in.
	2.9060 in.
+.040 in.	2.9157 in.
	2.9160 in.

Removing and Replacing the Camshaft

1. Disconnect the battery.

2. Remove the inlet and exhaust manifold assembly.
3. Remove the push-rods and take out the tappets.
4. Remove the timing cover, timing chain and gears.
5. Disconnect the vacuum advance unit pipe from the distributor and take out the two bolts with flat washers securing the distributor to the housing. Do not slacken the clamping plate bolt or the ignition timing setting will be lost.
6. Withdraw the distributor.
7. Take out the bolt securing the distributor housing to the cylinder block. Using one of the tappet cover bolts as an extractor screwed into the tapped end of the distributor drive spindle, withdraw the spindle.
8. Remove the sump, oil pump and oil pump drive shaft.
9. Disconnect the engine revolution indicator drive, remove the securing nuts and washers and withdraw the indicator drive gear.
10. Take out the three set screws and shakeproof washers which secure the camshaft locating plate to the cylinder block, and withdraw the camshaft.
11. If the camshaft bearing clearances are excessive new bearings should be fitted. To do this, the engine should be removed from the car. Drift out the old bearing towards the rear of the engine and press in a new one. Ensure that the oil holes in the bearing line up with the oil passages in the cylinder block. The front bearing must be reamed to give .001 to .002 in. diametrical clearance.

Replacement of the camshaft is a reversal of the above procedure.

Note that the three set screws securing the camshaft thrust plate are not evenly spaced to ensure the correct alignment of the oil hole supplying the timing gear.

Refitting the Distributor Drive Gear
1. Turn the engine until No. 1 piston is at T.D.C. on its compression stroke. When the valves on No. 4 cylinder are 'rocking' (i.e. exhaust just closing and inlet just opening), No. 1 piston is at the top of its compression stroke. If the engine is set so that the notch in the crankshaft pulley is in line with the long pointer on the timing chain cover, or the 'dimples' in the crankshaft and camshaft gears are in line, the piston is exactly at T.D.C.
2. Turn the engine back so that the notch in the pulley is 7° before the long pointer on the timing cover. This is the correct ignition setting giving a 7° advance. As a guide to the 7° position the two short points on the timing cover are 5° and 10°

Replacing the distributor drive gear. Notice the slot angle. The large offset is uppermost.

B.T.D.C. respectively.

3. Screw one of the tappet cover bolts into the threaded end of the distributor drive gear and, holding the drive gear with the slot just below the horizontal and the large offset uppermost, enter the gear.

4. As the gear engages with the camshaft the slot will turn in an anti-clockwise direction until it is approximately in the one o'clock position.

5. Remove the bolt from the gear, insert the distributor housing and secure it with the special bolt and washer. Ensure that the correct bolt is used and that the head does not protrude above the face of the housing.

Refit the distributor, referring to Ignition Section for retiming instructions if the clamp plate has been released.

Removing and Replacing the Oil Pump

1. Remove the sump and oil sump strainer.
2. Two bolts secure the oil pump cover and three studs secure the pump to the crankcase. Unscrew the stud nuts and remove the pump and drive shaft.

When refitting the pump use a new joint washer.

Dismantling and Reassembling the Oil Pump

1. Remove the oil pump from the engine.
2. The oil pump cover is attached to the body of the pump by two bolts and spring washers, and when these bolts are removed the oil pump cover, the outer rotor and the combined

oil pump shaft and inner rotor may be extracted.

Removing and Replacing the Flywheel
1. Remove the clutch by unscrewing the six bolts and spring washers securing it to the flywheel. Release the bolts a turn at a time to avoid distortion of the cover flange. Two dowels locate the clutch cover on the flywheel.
2. Unlock and remove the six nuts and three lock plates which secure the flywheel to the crankshaft and remove the flywheel.
3. When replacing the flywheel, ensure that the 1 and 4 timing mark on the periphery of the flywheel is in line with and on the same side as the first and fourth throws of the crankshaft. To assist correct location of the flywheel, the depression in the crankshaft flange face is stamped with a similar timing mark which should be in line with the one on the flywheel periphery.
5. To release the special flywheel bolts the engine sump and rear main bearing cap must also be removed.

Removing and Replacing the Crankshaft
1. Take off the clutch and the flywheel, the timing cover, the timing wheels and chain, the sump and the oil pump strainer, and the rear engine mounting plate.
2. Remove the big-end bearing caps and then take off the main bearing caps.
3. **Mark each big-end bearing cap and bearing to ensure that it is reassembled to the correct journal, taking care, in the case of the bearings, that they are not damaged or distorted when marking. Punches should not be used for this purpose.**
4. Lift the crankshaft out of the bearings.

Replacement of the crankshaft is a reversal of the above operations.

Before replacing the crankshaft, thoroughly clean out all oilways.

Note that each main bearing cap is stamped with a common number which is also stamped on the center web of the crankcase near the main bearing.

Remember to fit the packing washers behind the crankshaft chain wheel.

For the correct functioning of the oil return thread it is imperative that it should be concentric with the bore of the housing and have between .003 and .006 in. clearance measured from the crest of the thread to the housing. This may be checked with the aid of a long feeler gauge and a mandrel.

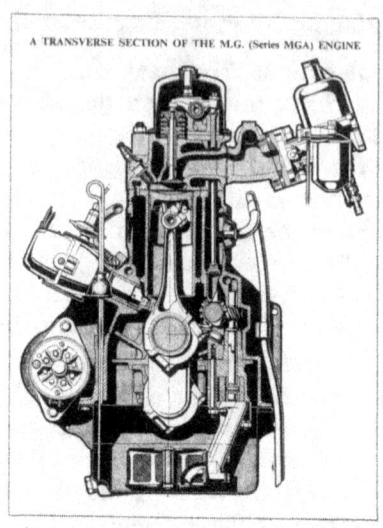

A TRANSVERSE SECTION OF THE M.G. (Series MGA) ENGINE

Modified Piston and Pin

Commencing at Engine No. 15GB/U/H28484, a new piston (Part. No. 1H1114) with a modified pin (Part No. 1H1113) is introduced, the pin having a reduced internal diameter to give increased strength.

The later pistons and pins are interchangeable with the originals but only as complete sets.

Modified Oil Pump and Strainer

On later engines a modified oil pump (Part No. 1H1191) and an oil strainer assembly of simplified construction (Part No. 1H1192) are fitted. The oil suction pipe position is now moved forward towards the front of the engine to eliminate any possibility of oil starvation during cornering or braking.

The new units are interchangeable as complete assemblies with the oil pumps and strainers previously used. The three oil pump to crankcase studs, however, have been lengthened to accommodate the greater thickness of the oil pump bottom cover, their part number now being 51K267.

These modifications were introduced at Engine No. 15GB/U/H46045 to 46100 and then 46342 onwards.

Modified Pistons and Rings

New piston assemblies with compression and oil control rings of increased radial thickness (see **'GENERAL DATA'**) are introduced at Engine No. 15GB/U/H40824. The compression ring grooves are of reduced diameter. These changes have been made to reduce oil consumption.

The piston assemblies complete with pins and rings are interchangeable in sets with those previously used. The new and old oil control rings are also interchangeable in sets, and the earlier-type compression rings may be used with the later-type pistons. It is not permissible, however, to fit the new-type compression rings to the old-type pistons.

Modified Gearbox Mounting Plate

Commencing at Engine No. 3298, the gearbox mounting plate has an oil escape recess and groove machined in the front face to relieve the air depression around the rear main bearing oil seal and prevent oil being drawn into the clutch housing. The plate is interchangeable and retains the same part number.

Modified Tappets and Push-rods

Commencing at Engine No. 5504, the ball ends of the push-rods and the seats in the tappets are increased in spherical diameter. The tappets and push-rods are interchangeable in sets and the new part numbers are:

        Tappet 1H822
        Push-rod 11G241

Piston Rings with Chrome Periphery

At Engine No. 5682 the top compression ring on the piston is superseded by a piston ring with a chrome periphery to improve the life of the piston ring and to improve oil consumption.

The later piston ring is interchangeable with the old.

Modified Oil Filter

Commencing at Engine No. 15GB/U/H26661 to 15GB/U/H26700 then 26933 onwards, a new oil filter is fitted. The element may be removed from a later-type oil filter without disconnecting the oil pipe. Tecalemit and Purolator filters are used, and the elements, which are interchangeable, bear the B.M.C. Part No. 8G683 (Tecalemit and Purolator).

Modified Crankshaft

Originally the diameter of the oil return thread on the crankshaft was 2.139/2.1405 in., but at Engine No. BP15GB/6615 this was reduced to 2.138/2.1385 in.

Oil Cooler Kits

Oil cooler kits were fitted as standard equipment to all export cars from Car No. 102737.

For older cars the kits are available under Part No. 8G2282 for standard cars and Part No. 8G2325 for cars fitted with disc brakes all round.

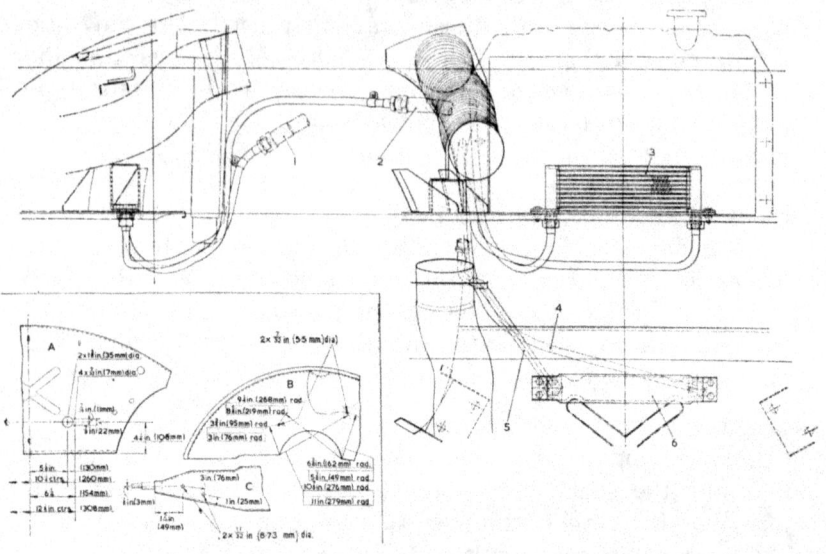

1. Flexible pipe—cooler to filter.
2. Flexible pipe—cooler to block.
3. Oil cooler.
4. Oil pipe—cooler to filter.
5. Oil pipe—cooler to block.
6. Oil cooler packing.

The oil capacity of the cooler is approximately ³/₄ pint and this quantity must be added to the sump when the cooler is fitted.

The fitting instructions, including the drilling of unmodified bodies, is as follows:

1. Jack up and support the front of the car and remove the front off-side wheel.
2. Remove the radiator case and grille to gain access to the horns and radiator duct panel.
3. Disconnect and remove the horns complete with their brackets.
4. Disconnect and remove the filter to crankcase pipe assembly.
5. Mark out and drill two ¹¹/₃₂ in. holes in each front suspension member for repositioning the horns as shown.
6. Mark out and drill four ⁹/₃₂ in. holes and cut two 1³/₈ in. holes in the radiator duct panel to accept the oil cooler.
7. Mark out and drill two ⁷/₃₂ in. holes in the front off-side wheel arch for the fitting of the oil cooler pipe clips.
8. Fit the packing-piece and oil cooler to the radiator duct panel and secure it with the **four** ¹/₄ in. UNF. hexagon-headed screws,

washers, and Aerotight nuts.

9. Fit the two oil pipes to the cooler and secure the pipes to the wheel arch with the two clips, No. 10 UNF. screws, plain washers, spring washers, and nuts provided.

10. Fit the two flexible pipes to the oil cooler pipes and then connect them to the oil filter and crankcase.

11. Refit, connect, and test the horns, replace the radiator grille and case, and refit the front road wheel. Remove the supports and jack.

12. Add ³/₄ pint of oil to the sump, run the engine, and check all pipe unions for leakage.

1600 Piston Sizes and Cylinder Bores

In production, pistons are fitted by selective assembly, and to facilitate this the pistons are stamped with identification figures on their crowns.

The number enclosed in a diamond, e.g. a piston stamped with a figure 2, is for use with a block having a stimilar stamp adjacent to the bore.

In addition to the standard pistons there is a range of four oversize pistons available for service purposes.

Oversize pistons are marked with the actual oversize dimensions enclosed in an ellipse. A piston stamped .020 is only suitable for a bore .020 in. larger than the standard bore; similarly, pistons with other markings are only suitable for the oversize bore indicated.

The piston markings indicate the actual bore size to which they must be fitted, the requisite running clearance being allowed for in the machining.

After reboring an engine, or whenever fitting pistons differing in size from those removed during dismantling, ensure that the size of the piston fitted is stamped clearly on the top of the cylinder block alongside the appropriate cylinder bore.

Pistons are supplied in the sizes indicated in the table below.

Piston marking	Suitable bore size
Standard	3-0011 in.
	3.0014 in.
Oversize +.010 in.	3.0111 in.
	3.0114 in.
+.020 in.	3.0211 in.
	3.0214 in.
+.030 in.	3.0311 in.
	3.0314 in.
+.040 in.	3.0411 in.
	3.0414 in.

MGB Piston Sizes and Cylinder Bores

In addition to the standard pistons there is a range of oversize pistons available for service purposes.

Oversize pistons are marked with the actual oversize dimensions enclosed in an ellipse. A piston stamped .020 is only suitable for a bore .020 in. (.508 mm.) larger than the standard bore; similarly, pistons with other markings are only suitable for the oversize bore indicated.

The piston markings indicate the actual bore size to which they must be fitted, the requisite running clearance being allowed for in the machining.

After reboring an engine, or whenever fitting pistons differing in size from those removed during dismantling, ensure that the size of the piston fitted is stamped clearly on the top of the cylinder block alongside the appropriate cylinder bore.

THE IGNITION SYSTEM

The automatic advance device is housed in the distributor unit, and it consists of a centrifugally and vacuum-operated mechanism by means of which the ignition is advanced in proportion to the engine speed and load.

Like the rest of the electrical equipment, the ignition is wired on the 'positive ground' system.

Locating the Cause of Uneven Firing
1. Start the engine and set it to run at a fairly fast idling speed.
2. Short-circuit each plug in turn by placing a hammer head or the blade of a screwdriver with a wooden or insulated handle between the terminal and the cylinder head. No difference in the engine performance will be noted when short-circuiting the plug in the defective cylinder. Shorting the other plugs will make uneven running more pronounced.
3. Having located the cylinder which is at fault, stop the engine and remove the cable from the terminal of the spark plug. Restart the engine and hold the end of the cable about $\frac{3}{16}$ in. from the cylinder head.
4. If the spark is strong and regular, the fault probably lies in the plug. Remove the plug, clean, and adjust the gap to the correct setting, or alternatively fit a new plug.
5. If there is no spark or if it is weak and irregular, examine the cable from the spark plug to the distributor. After a long period of service, the insulation may be cracked or perished, in which case the cable should be renewed.
6. Finally, examine the distributor moulded cap, wipe the inside and outside with a clean dry cloth, see that the carbon brush moves freely in its holder and examine the moulding closely for signs of breakdown. After long service it may become tracked, that is, a conducting path may have formed between one or more of the electrodes or between one of the electrodes and some part of the distributor in contact with the cap. Evidence of a tracked cap is shown by the presence of a thin black line in the places indicated. A replacement distributor cap must be fitted in place of one that has become tracked.

Testing the Low-tension Circuit
1. Spring back the securing clips on the distributor and remove the moulded cap and rotor. If the rotor is a tight fit, it can be levered off carefully with a screwdriver.
2. Check that the contacts are clean and free from pits, burns, oil or grease. Turn the engine and check that the contacts are opening and closing correctly and that the clearance is correct

when the contacts are fully opened to between .014 and .016 in.
3. Correct the gap if necessary.
4. Disconnect the cable at the contact breaker terminal of the coil and at the low-tension terminal of the distributor, and connect a test lamp between these terminals. If the lamp lights when the contacts close and goes out when the contacts open, the low-tension circuit is in order. Should the lamp fail to light, the contacts are dirty or there is a broken or loose connection in the low-tension wiring.

Locating a Low-tension Circuit Fault (MGA)

Having determined, by testing as previously described, that the fault lies in the low-tension circuit, switch on the ignition, and turn the engine until the contact breaker points are fully opened.

Refer to the wiring diagram and check the circuit with a voltmeter (0-20 volts) as follows.

NOTE — **If the circuit is in order, the reading on the voltmeter should be approximately 12 volts.**

1. **Battery to starter switch terminal.** Connect voltmeter to starter switch terminal and to ground. No reading indicates a faulty cable or loose connections.

2. **Starter switch to control box terminal 'A' (brown lead).** Connect a voltmeter to the control box terminal 'A' and to ground. No reading indicates a faulty cable or loose connections.

3. **Control box terminal 'A1'.** Connect a voltmeter to the control box terminal 'A1' and to ground. No reading indicates a fault in the series winding of the control box.

4. **Control box terminal 'A1' to terminal on ignition switch (brown with blue lead).** Connect a voltmeter to the ignition switch terminal and to ground. No reading indicates a faulty cable or loose connections.

5. **Ignition switch.** Connect a voltmeter to the second ignition switch terminal (white lead) and to ground. No reading indicates a fault in the ignition switch.

6. **Ignition switch to fusebox terminal 'A3' (white lead).** Connect the voltmeter to the fuse unit terminal 'A3' and to ground. No reading indicates a faulty cable or loose connection.

7. **Fuse unit terminal 'A3' to ignition coil terminal 'SW' (white lead).** Connect a voltmeter to the ignition coil terminal 'SW' and to ground. No reading indicates a faulty cable or loose connections.

8. **Ignition coil.** Connect a voltmeter to the ignition terminal 'CB' (white with black lead) and to ground. No reading indicates a fault in the primary winding of the coil and a new coil must be fitted.

9. **Ignition coil to distributor (white with black lead).** Connect a voltmeter to the distributor low-tension terminal and to ground. No reading indicates a faulty cable or loose connections.

10. **Contact breaker and capacitor.** Connect the voltmeter across the breaker points. No reading indicates a fault in the capacitor.

Locating a Low-Tension Circuit Fault (MGB)

Having determined, by testing as previously described, that the fault lies in the low-tension circuit, switch on the ignition, and turn the engine until the contact breaker points are fully opened.

Refer to the wiring diagram and check the circuit with a voltmeter (0-20 volts) as follows.

NOTE.—If the circuit is in order, the reading on the voltmeter should be approximately 12 volts.

1. **Battery to control box terminal 'B'.** Connect a voltmeter between control box terminal 'B' and ground. No reading indicates a damaged cable or loose connection.

2. **Control box terminal 'B' to ignition switch terminal (brown lead).** Connect a voltmeter between the ignition terminal and ground. No reading indicates a damaged cable or loose connections.

3. **Ignition switch (white lead).** Connect a voltmeter between the ignition switch terminal and ground. Turn the ignition key to the ignition position. No reading indicates a fault in the ignition switch.

4. **Ignition switch (white with red lead).** Connect a voltmeter between the ignition switch terminal and ground. Turn the ignition key to start position. No reading indicates a fault in the ignition switch.

5. **Ignition switch to fusebox terminal 'A3' (white lead).** Connect a voltmeter between the fuse unit terminal 'A' and ground. No reading indicates a damaged cable or loose connection.

6. **Fusebox terminal 'A3' to ignition coil terminal 'SW'.** Connect a voltmeter to the ignition coil terminal 'SW' and to ground. No reading indicates a fault in the primary winding of the coil and a new coil must be fitted.

High-tension Cables

The high-tension cables must be examined carefully and any which have the insulation cracked, perished or damaged in any way must be renewed.

To fit the cables to the terminal of the ignition coil, thread the knurled moulded terminal nut over the lead, bare the end

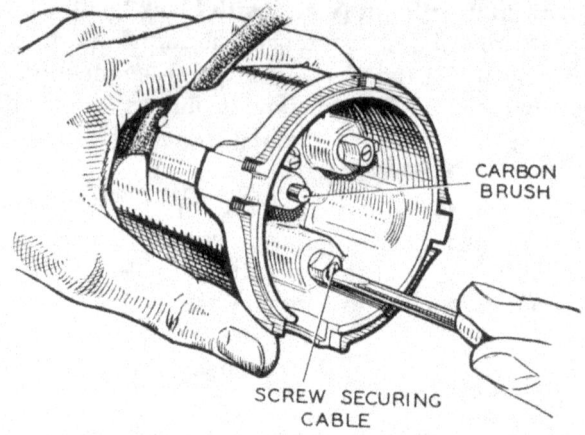

CARBON BRUSH

SCREW SECURING CABLE

of the cable for about ¼ in., thread the wire through the brass washer removed from the original cable and bend back the strands over the washer. Finally, screw the terminal into the coil.

To make the connections to the terminals in the distributor moulded cap, first remove the cap and slacken the screws on the inside of the moulding till they are clear of the cables. Fill the holes in the distributor cap with Silicone grease, then cut the new cables off to the required length, push them completely home and tighten the securing screws.

The cables from the distributor to the spark plugs must be connected up in the correct firing order, which is 1, 3, 4, 2. Screw them firmly to the suppressors.

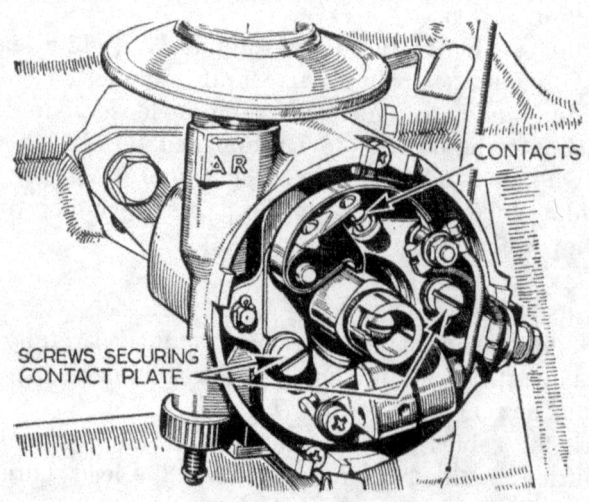

CONTACTS

SCREWS SECURING CONTACT PLATE

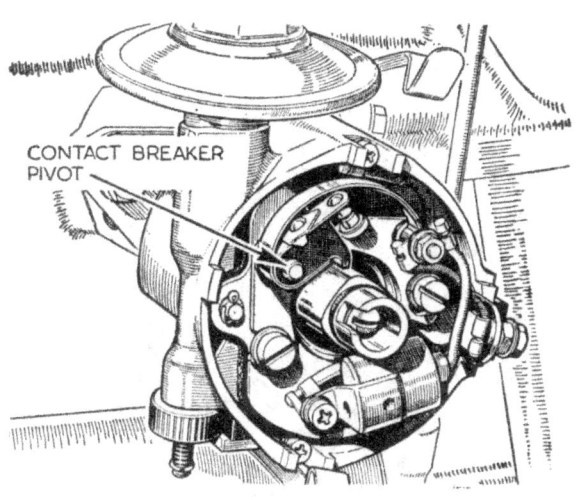

Contact Breaker

After the first 500 miles and subsequently every 6,000 miles check the contact breaker as follows:

1. Turn the crankshaft until the contact breaker points are fully opened and check the gap with a gauge having a thickness of from .015 to .016 in. If the gap is correct, the gauge should be a sliding fit. Do not alter the setting unless the gap varies considerably from the gauge thickness.

To adjust the setting, keep the engine in the position which gives maximum opening of the contacts and then slacken the two screws securing the fixed contact plate. Adjust the position of the plate until the gap is set to the thickness of the gauge and then tighten the two locking screws.

Remember that the cam only keeps the contact points fully open over a very small angle and that care must be taken to ensure that the points are in the fully open position.

2. If the contacts are dirty or pitted, they must be cleaned by polishing them with a fine carborundum stone, and afterwards wiping them with a cloth moistened with gasoline. The moving contact can be removed from its mounting in order to assist cleaning. Check and adjust the contact breaker setting after cleaning the contacts.

3. Check that the moving arm is free on its pivot. If it is sluggish, remove the arm and polish the pivot pin with a strip of fine cloth. Afterwards clean off all trace of emery dust and apply a spot of clean engine oil to the top of the pivot. The contact breaker spring tension should be between 20 and 24 oz. measured at the contacts.

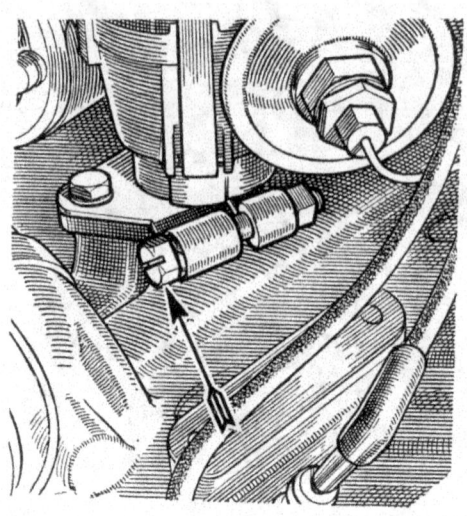

Removing and Replacing the Distributor (MGA)

The distributor can be removed and replaced without interfering with the ignition timing, provided the clamp plate pinch-bolt is not disturbed.

To facilitate the replacement of the distributor, turn the engine over until the rotor arm is pointing to the segment in the cover for No. 1 cylinder plug lead to provide a datum for replacement.

Remove the distributor cover, and disconnect the low-tension lead from the terminal on the distributor. Disconnect the vacuum advance pipe at the union on the distributor.

Extract the two bolts securing the distributor clamp plate to the distributor housing and withdraw the distributor.

To replace the distributor, insert it into the distributor housing until the driving dogs rests on the distributor drive shaft. The rotor arm should then be rotated slowly until the driving dog lugs engage with the drive shaft slots, both of which are offset to ensure correct replacement. Turn the distributor body to align the clamping plate holes with those in the housing. The remainder of the assembly is now in the reverse order to that of removal.

NOTE — Provided that the crankshaft has not been turned the rotor arm will be opposite the segment for No. 1 plug lead. The high-tension leads can then be replaced on their respective plug terminals in the order of firing, i.e. 1, 3, 4, 2, remembering that the distributor rotation is anti-clockwise when viewed from above.

Static Ignition Timing

Before timing the ignition refer to **'GENERAL DATA'** for the correct setting.

To set the distributor in the correct position for firing, the following procedure should be followed:

1. Turn the crankshaft in the direction of rotation until No. 1 piston is at T.D.C. on its compression stroke. This can best be effected by turning the engine and observing the valves. When the valves are 'rocking' (i.e. exhaust just closing and inlet just opening) on No. 4 cylinder, No. 1 piston is approximately at T.D.C. on its compression stroke. If the crankshaft is now rotated until the notch in the rear flange of the crankshaft pulley is in line with the long pointer on the timing cover or the dimples on the crankshaft and camshaft gears are in line, the piston is exactly at T.D.C.
2. Turn the engine back until the mark on the pulley is in the correct position (see **'GENERAL DATA'**). As a guide to this position the two short pointers on the timing cover are 5° and 10° before T.D.C.
3. Set the contact breaker points to .014 to .016 in. when in their position of maximum opening.
4. Insert the distributor into its housing, and engage the drive dog lugs with the drive shaft slots (both of which are offset) by slowly rotating the rotor arm.
5. Screw in the two bolts securing the distributor clamp plate to the distributor housing.
6. Position the distributor so that the vacuum control unit side of the body is to the front and the unit is vertical.
7. Rotate the distributor body anti-clockwise until the points are fully closed. Then slowly rotate it in a clockwise direction until the points just commence to open. Secure the distributor body in this position by tightening up the clamp late pinch-bolt and nut. Finally, check that the rotor arm is opposite the correct segment for the cylinder which is at the top of its compression stroke.

IMPORTANT — To obtain an accurate setting an electrical method should be used to determine the actual position at which the points break, and the following method can be used:

With the low-tension lead connected to the distributor, turn on the ignition switch and connect a 12-volt lamp in parallel with the contact breaker points (i.e. one lead from the distributor low-tension terminal and the other to ground) and turn the distributor as detailed above until the lamp lights, which indicates that the points have just opened.

NOTE — If the distributor drive gear assembly has been removed from the engine it should be refitted in accordance with instructions given previously before the above operation is carried out.

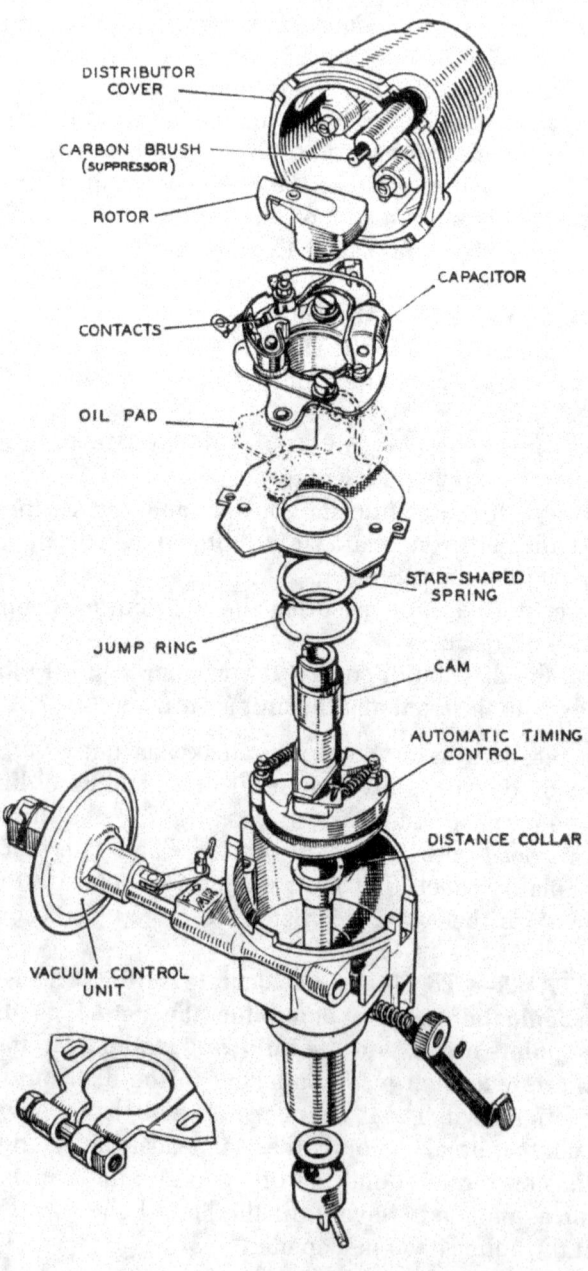

Dismantling the Distributor (MGA)

The contact breaker plate may be removed as an assembly to give access to the centrifugal weights without completely dismantling the distributor. To do this the rotor arm must first be removed and then the low-tension nuts slackened to enable the slotted connector to be withdrawn from between the head of the terminal bolt and the insulating washer. Next take out the spring clip securing the suction advance unit arm to the plate and release the plate assembly by extracting the two screws which secure it to the distributor body.

The following procedure is necessary if the distributor is to be completely stripped. Before dismantling make careful note of the positions in which the various components are fitted, so that they may be replaced correctly.

1. Spring back the clips and remove the moulded cap.
2. Lift the rotor off the top of the spindle. It it is a tight fit it must be levered off carefully with a screwdriver.
3. Remove the nut and washer from the moving contact anchor pin. Withdraw the insulating sleeve from the capacitor lead and low-tension lead connectors, noting the order in which they are fitted. Lift the moving contact from the pivot pin and remove the large insulating washer from the pivot pin and the small one from the anchor pin.
4. Take out the two screws, each with a spring and flat washer, securing the fixed contact plate, and remove the plate.
5. Take out the securing screw and remove the capacitor. Note that the grounding lead, which is attached to the same screw, passes under the capacitor to keep clear of the cams.
6. Remove the spring clip retaining the suction advance unit arm to the contact breaker base-plate. Extract the two screws securing the base-plate to the distributor body, noting that one also secures the grounding lead, and lift out the base-plate.

IMPORTANT — Note the relative position of the rotor arm drive slot in the cam spindle and the offset drive dog at the driving end of the spindle, to ensure that the timing is not 180° out when the cam spindle is re-engaged with the centrifugal weights during assembly.

7. Take out the cam retaining screw and remove the cam spindle.
8. Take out the centrifugal weights. These may be lifted out as two assemblies, each complete with a spring and toggle.
9. To release the suction advance unit, remove the circlip, adjusting nut and spring. Withdraw the unit. Take care not to lose the adjusting nut lock spring clip.

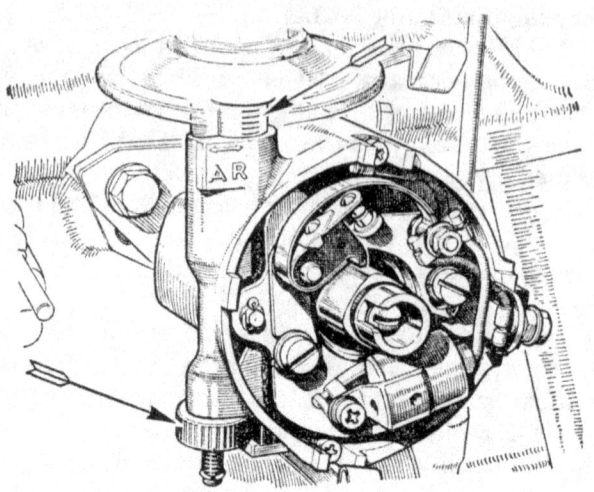

The vernier adjustment nut

10. To release the spindle from the body, drive out the parallel driving pin passing through the collar of the driving tongue member at the lower end of the spindle.

Capacitor

The best method of testing the capacitor is by substitution. Disconnect the original capacitor and connect a new one between the low-tension terminal of the distributor and ground.

Should a new capacitor be necessary, it is advisable to fit a complete capacitor and bracket, but should a capacitor only be available, use a hot iron to soften the solder securing the defective capacitor to the bracket. Care must be taken not to overheat the new capacitor when soldering it in position. The capacity of the capacitor is .2 microfarad.

Reassembling the Distributor

Reassembly is a direct reversal of the dismantling procedure, although careful attention must be given to the following points:
1. As they are assembled, the components of the automatic advance mechanism, the distributor shaft, and the portion of the shaft on which the cam fits must be lubricated with thin, clean engine oil.
2. Turn the vacuum control adjusting nut until it is in the halfway position when replacing the control unit.
3. When engaging the cam driving pin with the centrifugal weight, ensure that it is in the original position. When seen from above, the small offset of the driving dog must be on the right and the driving slot for the rotor arm must be downwards.

4. Adjust the contact breaker to give a maximum opening of .014 to .016 in.

Spark Plugs

Inspect, clean, adjust and renew spark plugs at the recommended mileage intervals

When plugs are removed from the engine their gaskets should be removed with them and replaced on the plugs, which should be placed in a suitable holder. It is advisable to identify each plug with the number of the cylinder from which it was removed so that any faults revealed on examination can be traced back to the cylinder concerned.

When examining the plugs, place a new plug of the same type beside the others to afford a ready comparison of the relative condition of the used plugs.

Examine for signs of oil fouling. This will be indicated by a wet, shiny, black deposit on the insulator. This is caused by oil pumping due to worn cylinders and pistons, oil from the cylinder walls is forced up past the rings on the suction stroke of the piston, and is eventually deposited on the plugs.

A permanent remedy for this cannot be effected, the only cure being the fitting of a new piston and rings, or, in extreme cases, a rebore may be necessary.

Next examine the plugs for signs of gasoline fouling. This is indicated by a dry, fluffy, black deposit which is usually caused by over-rich carburetion, although ignition system defects such as a run-down battery, faulty distributor, coil or condenser defects, or a broken or worn-out cable may be additional causes. If the plugs appear to be suitable for further use, proceed to clean and test them.

First remove the plug gaskets and examine them for condition. Gaskets in different conditions are illustrated. The upper left gasket was obviously not properly compressed, owing to the plug not having been tightened down sufficiently. A large proportion of the heat of the plug is normally dissipated to the cylinder head through the copper gasket between the plug and the head. Plugs not screwed down tightly can thus easily become over-heated so that they operate out of their proper heat range, thus producing pre-ignition, short plug life and pinging. On the other hand, it is unnecessary and unwise to tighten up the plugs too much. What is required is a reasonably good seal between the plug and the cylinder head.

The lower left-hand gasket clearly indicates that the plug was pulled down too tightly or has been in service too long.

Note its distorted condition and the evidence of blow-by, which is also a cause of plug overheating.

The upper right-hand gasket demonstrates a gasket in good condition, providing an adequate seal and a good path for heat dissipation.

For comparison a new gasket is shown at the lower right-hand corner of the photo. If gaskets are at all questionable they should be replaced by new ones.

If the plugs require cleaning it is preferable to make use of a proper plug cleaner of the type recommended by the plug manufacturers, and the makers' instructions for using the cleaner should be followed carefully.

Occasionally a blistered insulator or a badly burnt electrode may be noticed when examining the plugs.

If the plug is of the type normally recommended for the engine and it was correctly installed (down tightly on the gasket), this condition may have been brought about by a very lean mixture or an overheated engine. There is, however, a possibility that a plug of another type is required, but as a rule the recommended Champion plug should be adhered to (see 'GENERAL DATA').

After cleaning carefully, examine the plugs for cracked insulators and wear of the insulator nose due to excessive previous cleaning. In such cases the plugs have passed their useful life, and new plugs should be installed.

Examine the insulator for deposits underneath the side electrode which have possibly accumulated and which act as a 'hot spot' in service.

After cleaning the plugs in a special cleaner, blow all surplus abrasive out of the body recesses, and off the plug threads, by means of an air-blast. Next examine the threads for carbon.

Any deposits can be removed and the threads cleaned with a wire brush. A wire buffing wheel may also be utilized, but reasonable care must be used in both methods in order not to injure the electrodes or the tip of the insulator. The thread section of the plug body is often neglected when cleaning the

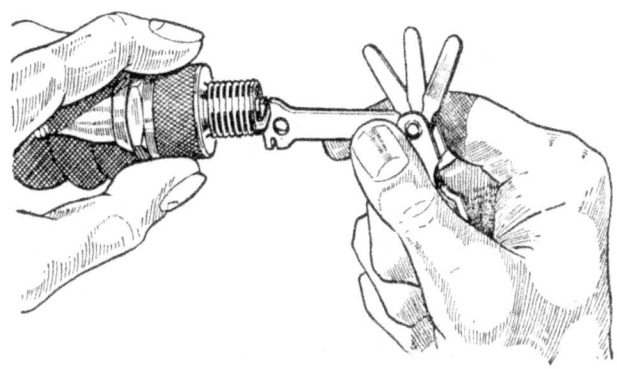

plugs, owing to the fact that it is not generally realized that, like the gaskets, the threads are a means of heat dissipation and that when they are coated with carbon it retards the flow of the heat from the plug, producing overheating. This simple procedure will also ensure absence of binding on the threads on replacement and also avoid unnecessary use of the plug spanner.

When replacing a plug, always screw it down by hand as far as possible and use the plug wrench for final tightening only.

Examine the electrodes for correct gap by inserting a feeler between them. Avoid an incorrect reading in the case of badly pitted electrodes. See **'GENERAL DATA'** for the correct clearance.

Remember that electrode corrosion and the development of oxides at the gap area vitally affects spark efficiency. The special cleaner can remove the oxides and deposits from the insulator, but the cleaner stream does not always reach this area with full effect owing to its location, and cannot necessarily deal with corrosion effectively as this sometimes requires too strong a blast for proper removal.

When plugs appear worthy of further use it is good practice to dress the gap area on both center and side electrodes with a small file before resetting them to the correct gap. The intense heat, pressure, explosion shock, and electrical and chemical action to which the plugs are submitted during miles of service are so intense that the molecular structure of the metal points is eventually affected. Plugs then reach a worn-out condition and resetting the points can no longer serve a good purpose. When points are burnt badly, it is indicative that the plug has worn to such an extent that its further use is undesirable and wasteful.

Before replacing the plug in the engine, test it for correct functioning under air pressure in a plug tester, following out the instructions issued by the makers of the plug tester. Generally speaking, a plug may be considered satisfactory for further service if it sparks continuously under a pressure of 100 lb. per sq. in. with the gap between the points set at .022 in. It is essential that the plug points should be reset to the correct gap (see **'GENERAL DATA')** before the plug is refitted to the engine.

While the plug is under pressure in the tester, it should be inspected for leakage by applying oil round the terminal. Leakage is indicated by the production of air bubbles, the intensity of which will serve to indicate the degree of leakage. The leakage gases have a 'blow-torch' effect when the engine is running which rapidly raises the temperature of the plug, raising it above its designed heat range, thus producing overheating, pre-ignition, and rapid electrode destruction.

The top half of the insulator is frequently responsible for poor plug performance due to the following faults: splashes; accumulation of dirt and dust; cracked insulators, caused by a slipping spanner; overtightness of the terminals.

Examine for a cracked insulator at the shoulder and the terminal post and remove any accumulations of dirt and dust.

Interference Suppressors

In order to reduce the interference with television reception to a minimum, all models are fitted with suppressors incorporated in the plug terminals of the high-tension leads.

Contrary to popular belief, these do not affect the ignition adversely.

DM2.P4 Pre-tilt Distributor

The DM2.P4 distributor fitted to later cars has a pre-tilted contact breaker unit. The moving contact breaker plate is balanced on two nylon studs and the angle through which the plate may be tilted is controlled by a stud riveted to the moving contact breaker plate locating in a slot in the base plate. The plate carrying the fixed contact is secured by one screw only on the new units.

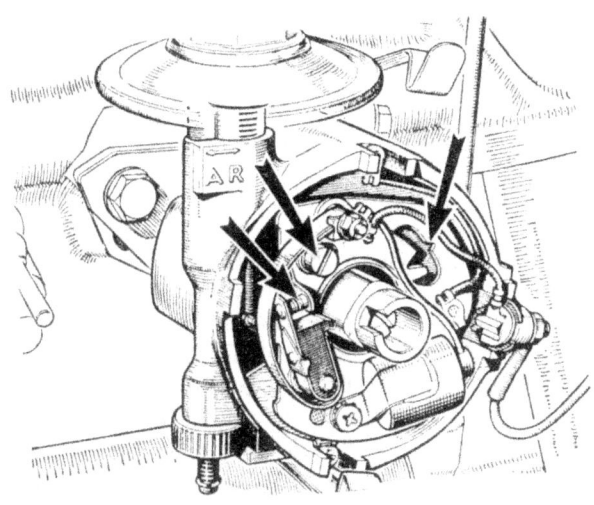

To adjust the contact breaker gap, turn the engine by hand until the contacts show the maximum opening. This should measure .014 to .016 in. If the setting is incorrect, slacken the securing screw and adjust the contact gap by inserting a screwdriver in the notched hole, and moving the plate carrying the fixed contact. Turn clockwise to reduce the gap and anti-clockwise to increase the gap. Tighten the securing screw.

The base plate components are assembled with a special lubricant and no further lubrication is necessary during the normal service life of the distributor.

An improved version of the metalized capacitor is fitted and the eyelets on the cables connected to the contact breaker terminal post are squared and slotted to prevent them twisting round and short-circuiting against the distributor. A flexible actuating link connects the diaphragm in the vacuum unit with the moving contact breaker plate.

The new contact breaker base plates are not interchangeable with those of the previous type and, to avoid confusion, distributors incorporating the new base plate are issued under a new part number — 1H811.

Ignition Vacuum Pipe Fuel Trap

At Engine No. 6625 a modified ignition vacuum pipe (Part No. 1H830) is fitted. A small trap which contains a fine-mesh gauze is incorporated in the pipe which will prevent fuel entering the vacuum control unit. The modified pipe may be fitted to earlier vehicles.

Modified Type DM2 Distributors

A modified Type DM2 distributor incorporating a rolling weight centrifugal advance mechanism superseding the standard toggle type was introduced at Engine Nos. 16GC/U/H101 and 16GC/U/L101.

The rolling weight mechanism consists of a shaft and action plate with two action cams and two spring pillars riveted to the plate. Two rolling weights, each located by a boss on the under side of the cam foot, roll round the action plate cams and thus alter the position of the contact breaker cam relative to the distributor driving shaft when the distributor is rotating within the speed limits of centrifugal operation.

The rate of advance is controlled by springs anchored between the pillars on the action plate and two pillars on the cam foot. The maximum amount of advance is governed by the cam foot, which strikes one of the spring pillars when maximum advance has been reached.

The modified distributor is interchangeable with the previous model and the instructions for dismantling and assembly are the same as given previously.

If it is desired to remove and replace the distributor without disturbing the timing proceed as follows:
1. Rotate the crankshaft until rotor arm is pointing to the segment in the cover for No. 1 cylinder plug lead. This will provide a datum for replacement.
2. Remove the distributor cover, L.T. lead, and the suction advance pipe union from the distributor.
3. Remove the two screws securing the split housing plate to the distributor housing. **Do not remove or disturb the split housing clamp bolt.**
4. Withdraw the distributor from its housing.
5. Insert the distributor into its housing until the driving dogs on the distributor drive shaft rest on the distributor driving spindle.
6. Slowly rotate the rotor arm until the driving dogs engage the slots in the drive spindle. Both the dogs and the slots are offset to ensure correct replacement.
7. Turn the distributor body to align the holes in the housing plate with those in the housing and secure the plate with the two screws.
8. Provided the crankshaft has not been rotated the rotor arm will be opposite the segment for No. 1 plug lead.
9. Refit the cap, plug leads, L.T. lead, and vacuum pipe union.

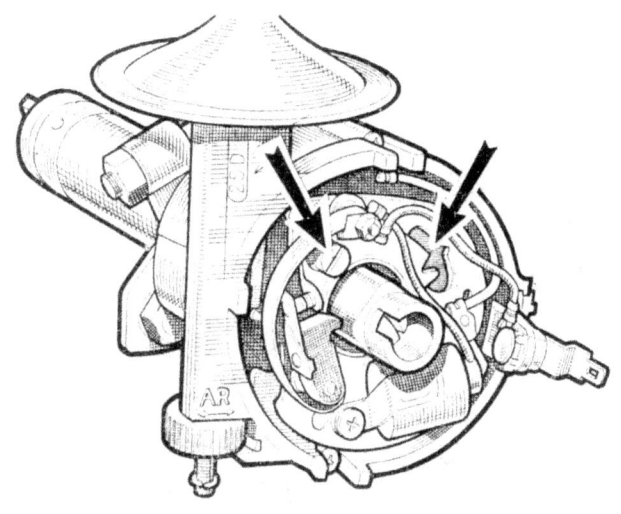

The distributor fixed plate securing screw and screwdriver notches

MGB Distributor

The Type 25D distributor incorporates a one-piece body shank casting which houses the distributor drive shaft, automatic advance mechanism, contact breaker plate assembly, capacitor, cam, rotor arm and their associated electrical connections. The direction of rotation is stamped on the body.

The upper end of the body is closed by a bakelite cap which houses the plug lead segments and the H.T. lead brush and spring.

The automatic advance mechanism comprises a centrifugally operated rolling weight mechanism and a vacuum-operated mechanism which together advance the ignition point in proportion to the engine speed and load. The vacuum-operated mechanism has a vernier adjustment screw to enable small adjustments to be made to suit varying grades of fuel or to satisfy tuning requirements. A double-headed arrow marked 'A' and 'R' is stamped on the body adjacent to the venier screw. A fuel trap is incorporated in the vacuum line from the induction manifold.

The contact breaker assembly is made up of a base plate secured to the distributor body, a moving contact breaker plate, a fixed contact breaker plate, the contact breaker points, and

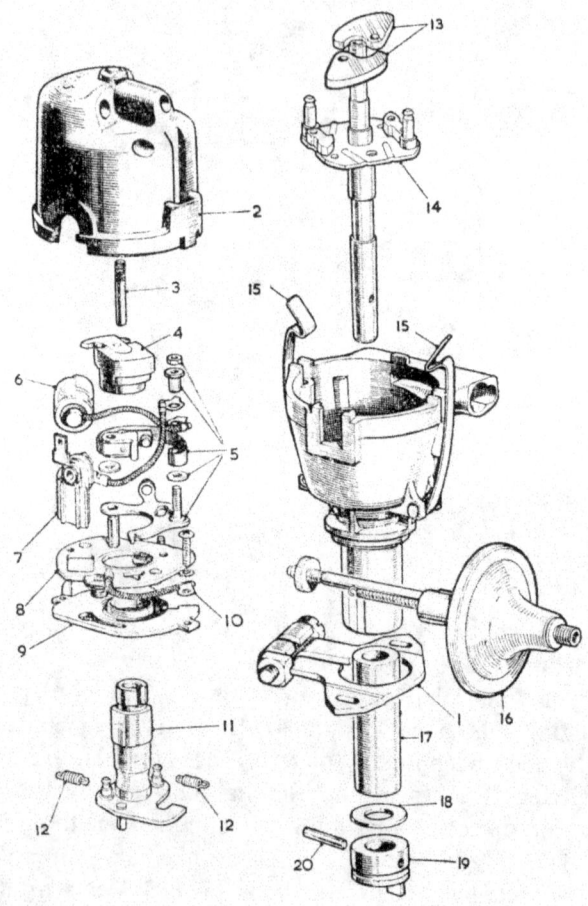

The distributor components

1. Clamping plate.
2. Moulded cap.
3. Brush and spring.
4. Rotor arm.
5. Contacts (set).
6. Capacitor.
7. Terminal and lead (low-tension).
8. Moving contact breaker plate.
9. Contact breaker base plate.
10. Earth lead.
11. Cam.
12. Automatic advance springs.
13. Weight assembly.
14. Shaft and action plate.
15. Cap retaining clips.
16. Vacuum unit.
17. Bush.
18. Thrust washer.
19. Driving dog.
20. Parallel pin.

a capacitor.

The moving plate is supported on the base plate by two nylon pads, which minimizes friction when the automatic advance moves the plate. A 'C' spring anchored to a vacuum control spring post bears against the under side of the base plate and so pre-tilts the moving plate. The pressure of the cam on the heel of the contact breaker points supplements this action and so minimizes rocking of the moving plate at high cam speeds.

A stud fixed to the under side of the moving contact plate engages a slot in the base plate and so limits the horizontal movement of the moving plate; the stud also limits the angle of tilt of the moving plate.

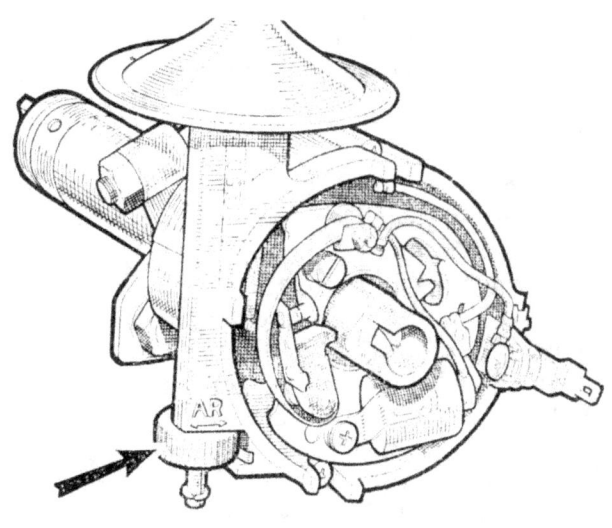

The vernier adjustment nut

The fixed contact breaker plate is secured by a screw which passes through a slot in the fixed plate. A notch cut in the free end of the plate permits the engagement of a screwdriver for adjustment purposes when setting the contact breaker points gap.

The distributor is secured to the engine by a split housing plate and clamp bolt. On some distributors the clamp bolt is trapped and the nut free and on others the nut is trapped and the bolt is free.

Servicing the 25D Distributor

The distributor should be checked and serviced periodically as detailed in **'Periodical Maintenance'**.

Contact Breaker Points

Examine the contact breaker points and if they are found to be burnt or blackened remove them with a fine carborundum stone or emery-cloth.

After cleaning remove all traces of dust and grease with a solvent moistened cloth. Lightly smear the contact breaker pivot pin with molybdenized non-creep oil or a suitable grease and refit the points.

It is important that no oil or grease is allowed to contaminate the contact breaker points.

Reset the gap by rotating the crankshaft until the contacts are at their maximum open position, slacken the fixed plate securing screw, insert a screwdriver between the notches in the fixed plate and adpust the gap until it is between .014 and .016 in. (.36 and .40 mm.). Tighten the securing screw and recheck the gap setting.

Distributor Cover

Thoroughly clean the moulded cover with a solvent moistened cloth, paying particular attention to the spaces between the electrodes. Examine the cover for cracks and signs of tracking.

Inspect the carbon brush for serviceability and ensure that it moves freely in its holder.

Check the H.T. leads for security and examine them for signs of deterioration. Cracked or perished leads must be renewed.

To fit new H.T. leads, remove the old leads, fill the holes in the distributor cap with Silicone grease, and cut the new leads off to required length. Push the ends of the leads fully home in the cap and secure them with the securing screws.

Remove the suppressors from the old leads and fit them to the new ones.

Vacuum Advance

To check the vacuum advance, fit a modified cap having a window cut in the side. Start the engine, operate the throttle sharply and observe the movement of the moving breaker plate.

Centrifugal Advance

Remove the distributor cover, grasp the rotor firmly, and turn it in the direction of rotation. Release the rotor when it should return to its original position without showing and tendency to stick.

Capacitor

If the capacitor is suspect it may be tested by substitution. Disconnect the suspect capacitor and connect a new one between the L.T. terminal and ground.

Should a new capacitor be necessary, remove the old one and fit the new.

Removing and Replacing the 25D Distributor

To remove the distributor for the engine disconnect the suction advance pipe union from the distributor, the H.T. leads from the spark plugs and the L.T. lead from the distributor. Remove the two screws securing the split housing plate to the engine and lift the distributor from its housing.

Replacement is a reversal of these instructions, after which the ignition timing must be set or re-checked.

Dismantling the 25D Distributor

To dismantle the distributor for overhaul remove it from the engine and then proceed as follows:
1. Remove the distributor cap and from it withdraw the carbon brush and its spring. Remove the rotor arm.
2. Lift the L.T. connector housing from the body, unscrew the two screws securing the contact breaker plates assembly, and disconnect the vacuum advance spring from its anchorage. Lift off the contact breaker plates assembly.
3. Unscrew the contact breaker spring anchorage nut and remove the nut, collar, L.T. lead and capacitor lead tags, moving contact breaker points, and the fiber washer.
4. Unscrew the fixed contact breaker plate securing screw and lift off the plate.
5. Remove the capacitor securing screw and the capacitor.
6. Rotate the moving plate and disengage the stud on it from the base plate. Disengage the base plate from the 'C' spring on the moving plate.
7. Remove the cam securing screw, the rolling weight springs, cam and action plate, and the weights.
8. Check the driving shaft end-float and clearance in the body bush.
9. Drive out the driving dog securing pin and remove the driving dog and thrust washer from the drive shaft. Withdraw the drive shaft from the body.
10. Remove the micro adjuster spring clip, unscrew the nut, and remove the spring and vacuum control from the body.

Assembling the 25D Distributor

Assembly is a reversal of the dismantling sequence, but at-

tention must be given to the following points during assembly.
1. Lubricate the components.
2. Set the micro-adjuster to the mid-way position.
3. Adjust the contact breaker points to the correct gap.
4. Leave the clamp plate securing bolt slack.
5. After fitting the distributor to its housing rotate the rotor arm until the driving dog engages the recess in the distributor drive from the camshaft. The lugs on the dogs are offset to ensure correct replacement.

THE COOLING SYSTEM

Description

The cooling system is sealed, and the water circulation is assisted by a pump attached to the front of the engine and driven by a belt from the crankshaft. The water circulates from the base of the radiator and passes around the cylinders and cylinder head, reaching the header tank of the radiator core via the thermostat and the top water hose. From the header tank it passes down the radiator core to the base tank of the radiator. Air is drawn through the radiator by a fan attached to the water pump pulley.

The thermostat is set to open between 70°C and 75°C (158°F and 167°F).

IMPORTANT — Never use a muff on the radiator grille to protect the cooling system in cold weather as this would seal the carburetor and heater unit air supply. The radiator must be protected by a blind such as the type available as an optional extra fitting.

Removing the Filler Cap

The cooling system is under appreciable pressure while the engine is hot after a run, and the radiator filler cap must be removed very carefully or left in position until the water has cooled.

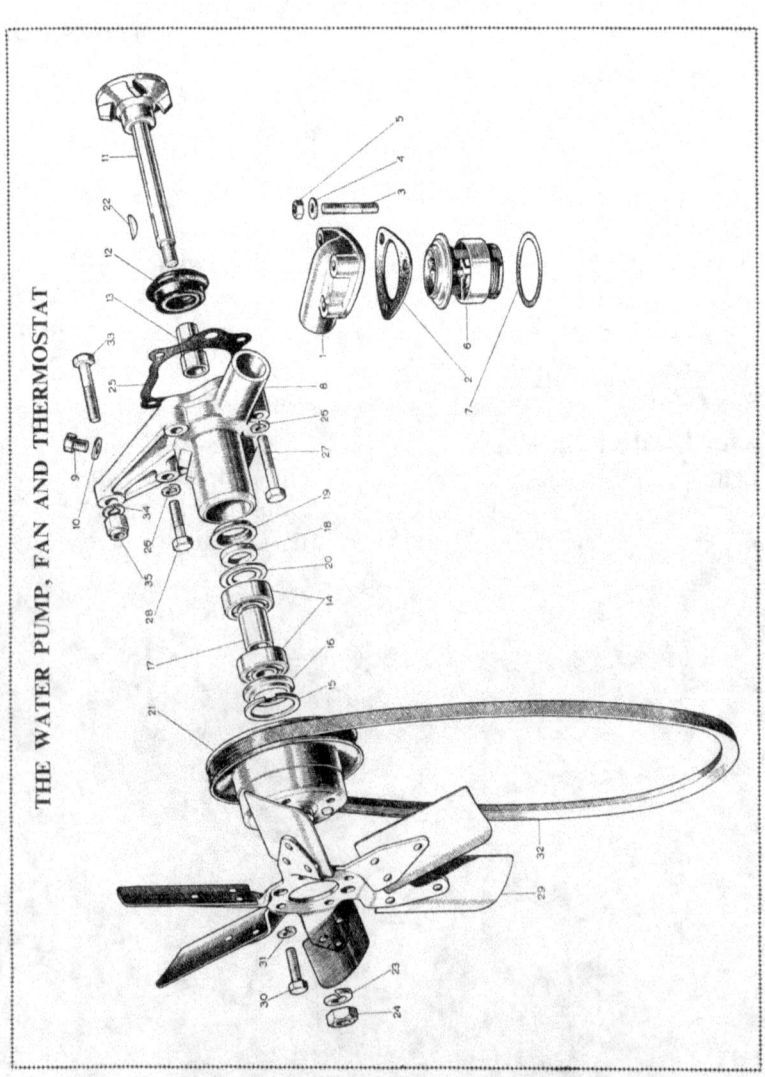

KEY TO THE WATER PUMP, FAN, AND THERMOSTAT

No.	Description
1.	Elbow—water outlet.
2.	Joint—elbow.
3.	Stud—elbow to cylinder.
4.	Washer—stud.
5.	Nut—stud.
6.	Thermostat.
7.	Joint—thermostat.
8.	Body.
9.	Plug.
10.	Washer—plug.
11.	Spindle with vane.
12.	Seal.
13.	Distance piece—gland.
14.	Bearing.
15.	Spring ring—bearing.
16.	Grease retainer—bearing.
17.	Distance piece—bearings.
18.	Washer—felt.
19.	Retainer—felt washer inner.
20.	Retainer—felt washer outer.
21.	Pulley and fan—water pump.
22.	Key—pulley.
23.	Spring washer.
24.	Nut—pulley to spindle.
25.	Joint—pump to block.
26.	Spring washer.
27.	Set screw—long—to block.
28.	Set screw—short—to block.
29.	Fan complete.
30.	Set screw—fan to pulley.
31.	Spring washer.
32.	Belt—wedge type—fan.
33.	Bolt—dynamo to water pump body.
34.	Spring washer.
35.	Nut—dynamo bolt.

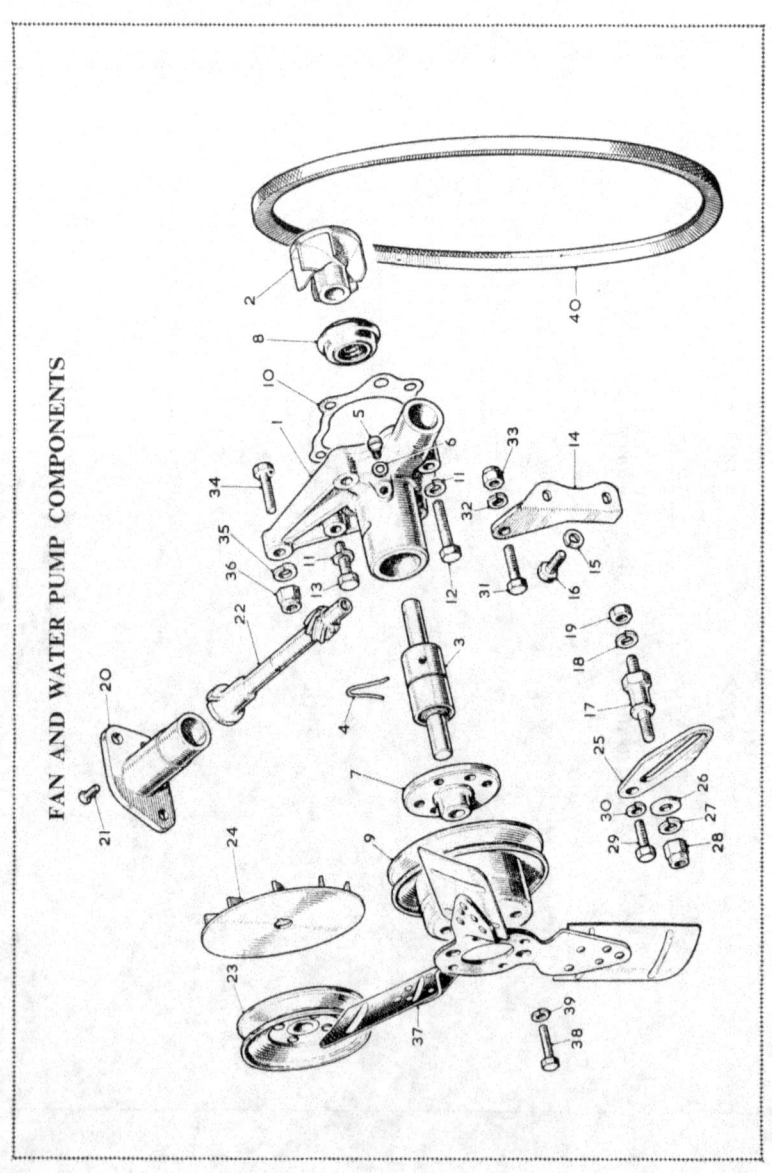

KEY TO THE FAN AND WATER PUMP COMPONENTS

No.	Description	No.	Description	No.	Description
1.	Pump assembly—water (with hub less pulley).	15.	Washer—spring—screw.	28.	Nut—adjusting link to pillar.
2.	Vane—water pump.	16.	Screw—dynamo bracket to crankcase.	29.	Screw—adjusting link to pillar.
3.	Bearing assembly complete with spindle.	17.	Pillar—dynamo adjusting link.	30.	Washer—spring—screw.
4.	Wire—bearing locating.	18.	Washer—spring—pillar.	31.	Bolt—dynamo to mounting bracket.
5.	Screw—lubricating point.	19.	Nut—dynamo pillar.	32.	Washer—spring—bolt.
6.	Washer—fibre—screw.	20.	Housing—distributor.	33.	Nut—bolt.
7.	Hub—pulley.	21.	Screw—housing to crankcase.	34.	Bolt—dynamo to water pump body.
8.	Seal—water pump.	22.	Spindle—distributor driving.	35.	Washer—spring—bolt.
9.	Pulley—fan and water pump.	23.	Pulley—dynamo.	36.	Nut—bolt.
10.	Joint washer—pump to crankcase.	24.	Fan—dynamo.	37.	Fan—washer pump (3-bladed)
11.	Washer—spring—screw.	25.	Link—dynamo adjusting.	38.	Screw—fan to pulley.
12.	Screw—long—water pump to crankcase.	26.	Washer—adjusting link to pillar.	39.	Washer—spring—screw.
13.	Screw—short—water pump to crankcase.	27.	Washer—spring.	40.	Belt—fan.
14.	Bracket—rear—dynamo.				

If it is necessary to remove the filler cap when the engine is hot it is absolutely essential to remove it gradually, and the filler spout in provided with a specially shaped cam to enable this to be done easily.

Unscrew the cap slowly till the retaining tongues are felt to engage the small lobes on the end of the filler spout cam, and wait until the pressure in the radiator is fully released before finally removing the cap.

It is advisable to protect the hand against escaping steam while removing the cap.

Draining the Cooling System
1. Remove the radiator header tank filler cap.
2. Open the two drain taps. One is fitted on the base of the radiator and the other at the rear of the cylinder block on the right-hand side.

NOTE — If anti-freeze mixture is being used it should be drained into a suitable container and carefully preserved for replacement.

Filling the Cooling System
1. Close the radiator and cylinder block drain taps.
2. Ensure that the water hose clips are tightened.
3. Fill up the system through the filler in the radiator header tank until approximately 1 in. of water is visible in the filler neck.
4. When possible, distilled water should be used for filling the system.
5. Avoid overfilling to prevent loss of anti-freeze due to expansion.
6. Screw the filler cap firmly into position.

7. The cooling system is unsuitable for use with anti-freeze mixtures having an alcohol base owing to the high temperatures attained in the top tank. Only anti-freeze mixtures of the ethylene glycol or glycerine type should be employed.

Removing and Replacing the Radiator
1. Drain the water from the cooling system.
2. Release the clips on the top and bottom water hoses and detach the hoses from their connections.
3. Remove the three bolts securing each side of the radiator to the body and lift out the radiator.
4. Replace the radiator core by reversing the above procedure, noting that there is a packing strip between the radiator flanges and the body.
5. Close the drain taps and refill the cooling system with clean water and check for leaks.

MGB Radiator and Diaphragm

The radiator block assembly is supported in a metal diaphram which is secured to the body by screws and washers. The diaphragm has two holes in the right-hand side to permit the oil cooler pipes to pass from the cooler to the engine. A rubber air seal is fitted across the top channel of the diaphragm.

The overflow pipe is secured by two clips that are retained by a radiator fixing screw and a diaphragm fixing screw respectively.

Removing

To remove the radiator drain the coolant, release the top and bottom hose clips, and detach the hoses from their connectors.

When an oil cooler is not fitted the radiator and diaphragm may be removed as a complete assembly by removing the top radiator to diaphragm screws to release the stays and then removing the screws securing each side of the diaphragm to the body.

If an oil cooler is fitted the pipe connection must be disconnected from the cooler and the engine before removing the radiator and diaphragm assembly.

To remove the radiator without the diaphragm undo the radiator to diaphragm securing screws, slacken the diaphragm to body securing screws, remove the screw retaining the overflow pipe clip, and then lift the diaphragm sufficiently to allow the radiator to be pulled forward and lifted from the car.

Replacing

Replacement is a reversal of the removal sequence, but en-

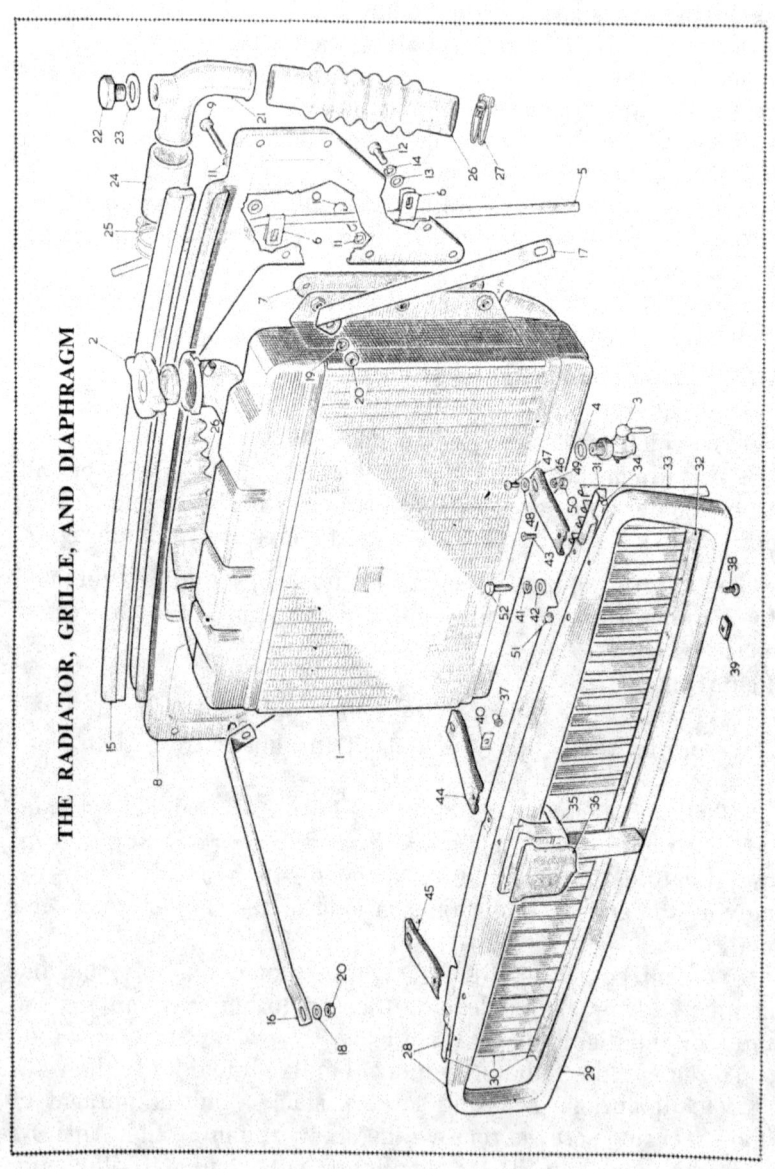

KEY TO THE RADIATOR, GRILLE, AND DIAPHRAGM

No.	Description
1.	Core assembly—radiator.
2.	Cap—filler.
3.	Tap—drain.
4.	Washer for tap.
5.	Tube—drain.
6.	Clip—drain tube.
7.	Packing.
8.	Diaphragm—radiator.
9.	Screw—long—radiator to diaphragm.
10.	Screw—short—radiator to diaphragm.
11.	Washer—spring—for screw.
12.	Screw—diaphragm to body.
13.	Washer—plain—for screw.
14.	Washer—spring—for screw.
15.	Rubber—radiator air seal.
16.	Tie—radiator—R.H.
17.	Tie—radiator—L.H.
18.	Washer—plain—radiator tie.
19.	Washer—spring—radiator tie.
20.	Nut—tie.
21.	Pipe—water pump connector.
22.	Plug—connector pipe.
23.	Washer—plug.
24.	Hose—connector.
25.	Clip—hose.
26.	Hose—top and bottom.
27.	Clip—hose.
28.	Case and grille assembly—radiator.
29.	Case assembly.
30.	Grille assembly.
31.	Bar—grille fixing—top.
32.	Bar—grille fixing—bottom.
33.	Slats—grille.
34.	Rivet—slat fixing.
35.	Bar and badge housing—centre.
36.	Badge.
37.	Fixing—blind badge.
38.	Screw—grille to case.
39.	Nut—spring.
40.	Fix—push-on—badge housing to case.
41.	Washer—spring.
42.	Washer—plain.
43.	Screw—grille to steady bracket.
44.	Bracket—steady grille centre assembly.
45.	Bracket—steady grille side assembly—R.H.
46.	Bracket—steady grille side assembly—L.H.
47.	Screw—steady bracket to bonnet lock platform
48.	Washer—plain.
49.	Washer—spring.
50.	Nut.
51.	Buffer—grille top rail.
52.	Screw—grille to radiator duct panel.

sure that the two packing pieces are correctly positioned either side of the radiator and that the over-flow pipe is secured.

Close drain taps, fill with coolant and check for leaks.

Fan Belt Adjustment

The adjustment of fan belt tension is effected by slackening slightly the two bolts on which the generator pivots, releasing the bolt securing it to the slotted link, and the nut securing the slotted link to the engine. Raise the generator bodily until the belt tension is correct. Tighten up the bolts with the generator in this position.

NOTE — A gentle hand pull only must be exerted or the belt tension will be excessive and undue strain thrown on the generator bearings.

To check the tension for correctness rotate the fan blades. If the generator pulley slips inside the fan belt, the tension is insufficient. When the tension is correct, it should be possible to move the belt from side to side to the extent of 1 in. at the center of the longest belt run.

Cold Weather Precautions

Before introducing anti-freeze mixture to the radiator it is advisable to clean out the cooling system thoroughly by swilling out the passages with a hose inserted in the filler cap, keeping the drain taps open. Only top up when the cooling system is at its normal running temperature, in order to avoid losing anti-freeze due to expansion.

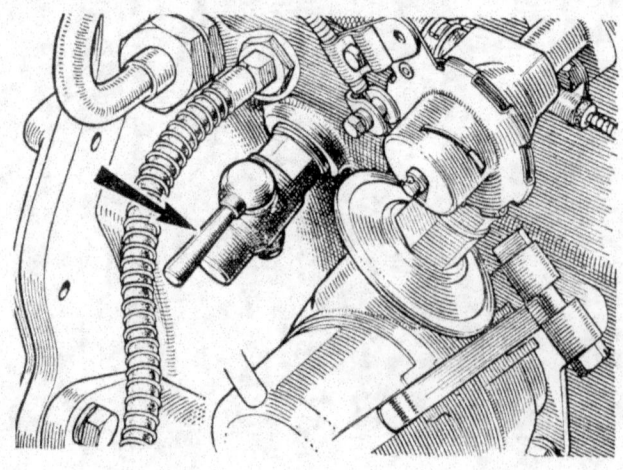

The engine drain tap on the right-hand side of the engine

Make sure that the cooling system is water-tight and examine all joints, replacing any defective rubber hose with new.

The capacity of the cooling system is 12 U.S. pints.

Removing the Water Pump

The water pump and fan assembly is attached to the front of the cylinder block by four bolts.

To remove the water pump it is first necessary to drain the water from the cooling system by opening the two drain taps as described, at the same time remembering to collect the water for re-use if it contains anti-freeze mixture.

1. Release the clips on the top and bottom water hoses and detach the hoses from their connections.
2. Remove the three bolts at each side securing the radiator core to the body and lift out the radiator.
3. Disconnect the generator leads, remove the generator attachment bolts and take off the generator.
4. Take out the four bolts securing the fan and pump assembly to the front of the cylinder block and withdraw the assembly.

Replacement of the fan and pump assembly is a reversal of this procedure, but care must be taken to see that the joint gasket between the pump body and the cylinder block is in good condition. It is always advisable to fit a new gasket.

Dismantling the Water Pump

When the fan and water pump assembly has been removed from the engine, the water pump may be dismantled for attention in the following way:

1. Unscrew the four set bolts which attach the fan and belt pulley to the hub and remove the fan blades and pulley.
2. Unscrew the nut and spring washer from the end of the pump spindle and pull off the fan hub with a suitable extractor.
3. Remove the Woodruff key from the spindle and remove any burrs from the keyway. Withdraw the dished oil seal washer after removing its circlip.
4. Gently tap the pump spindle rearwards out of the pump body. Withdraw the sealing gland.
5. Should it be necessary to withdraw the ball races, the front one can be withdrawn with an extractor.
6. When the front bearing is removed it releases the distance tube between the bearings and gives access to the rear bearing.
7. When the rear bearing is extracted it permits the withdrawal of the felt washer along with its inner and outer retainers. The rear distance piece now remains in the pump body and may be removed if required.

Reassembly is a reversal of the dismantling procedure, but care must be taken to see that the seal assembly is in good condition before proceeding. If it shows signs of damage, a new seal must be fitted.

Renew the felt oil seal washer for the rear ball race if it shows signs of damage.

Repack with grease.

Replacing Bearings

Support the body with the rear end downwards.

Assemble the driver, dummy front bearing, and pilot Position the rear bearing, the felt ring inner retainer, the felt ring and outer retainer, in that order, on the pilot and press them into the pump body

Position the distance tube and front bearing on the pilot and press the bearing into the pump body.

Modified Water Pump

A new water pump (Part No. 1H1149) which incorporates a one-piece bearing is fitted from engines numbered 15GB/U/H39365 to 15GB/U/H39400 inclusive, and 15GP/U/H39526 onwards. The pump is interchangeable with the original, but only as a complete unit.

Removing

1. Remove the radiator as detailed.
2. Remove the generator attachment bolts and take off the generator.
3. Unscrew the four bolts attaching the pump assembly to the front of the cylinder block and remove the fan and pump assembly.

Replacement of the fan and pump assembly is a reversal of the above procedure.

Dismantling

1. Unscrew the four set bolts which attach the fan and pulley to the hub and remove the fan and pulley.
2. Remove the fan hub with a suitable extractor.
3. Pull out the bearing locating wire through the hole in the top of the pump body.
4. Gently tap the pump bearing assembly rearwards out of the pump body. This will release the combined bearing and spindle assembly together with the seal and vane.
5. Remove the vane from the bearing assembly with a suitable extractor and remove the pump seal assembly.

Reassembly is a reversal of this procedure, but care must be taken to see that the seal assembly is in good condition. If there is any sign of damage the seal should be replaced by a new component. When the bearing assembly is fitted into the pump the hole in the bearing must coincide with the lubricating hole in the water pump body. Should the interference fit of the fan hub have been impaired when the hub was withdrawn from the spindle, a new hub should be fitted.

THE FUEL SYSTEM

Removing the Fuel Tank
1. Remove the hexagon drain plug and empty the tank.
2. Slacken the two clips on the filler neck hose and withdraw the filler extension.
3. Pull the hose from the tank. Take out the three screws and remove the tank filler neck seal and clamp plate.
4. Disconnect the fuel pipe at the union and the fuel gauge cable from the tank unit, each on the right-hand side of the tank.
5. Remove the two nuts from the bolts securing the rear of the tank to the anchorage brackets on the frame and remove the two bolts with spring washers which secure the front of the tank to the frame.
6. Withdraw the rear bolts and distance tubes.
   Replacement is a reversal of the above instructions.

Removing the Fuel Pump — MGA

1. Raise the top and remove the spare wheel.
2. Remove the top stowage compartment floor. This is secured by five quick-release screws and each requires only a quarter turn anti-clockwise to release the cover.
3. Disconnect the inlet and outlet pipe unions.
4. Disconnect the ground lead and the supply lead from the terminals on the pump.
5. Remove the two set screws securing the fuel pump to the bracket on the frame cross-member.

Removing the Fuel Pump—MGB

   The fuel pump is mounted on a bracket secured to the heelboard adjacent to the rear right-hand front spring mounting, and is accessible from beneath the car.
   Remove the ignition circuit fuse and disconnect the ground and supply leads from the terminals on the pump.
   Disconnect the inlet and outlet pipe unions.
   Remove the two bolts securing pump bracket to the heelboard.

Construction of the Fuel Pump

   The fuel pump is an S.U. Type HP high-pressure, 12-volt electric pump incorporating a radio suppressor.
   The pump consists of three main assemblies: the body, the magnet assembly and the contact breaker.

The body is composed of a hollow stamping or casting (8), into the bottom of which the filter (12) is screwed. The pump inlet union (1) is screwed in at an angle and tightens down on the delivery valve cage (5), which is clamped between the two fiber washers (2 and 6). In the top of the delivery cage is the delivery valve, a thin brass disc (4) held in position by a light spring on a seating machined in the body. Holes connect the space between the valves of the pumping chamber, which is a shallow depression on the forward face of the body. This space is closed by a diaphragm assembly (9) which is clamped at its outside edge between the magnet housing (27) and body (8) and its center between the retaining plate (11) and the steel arma-

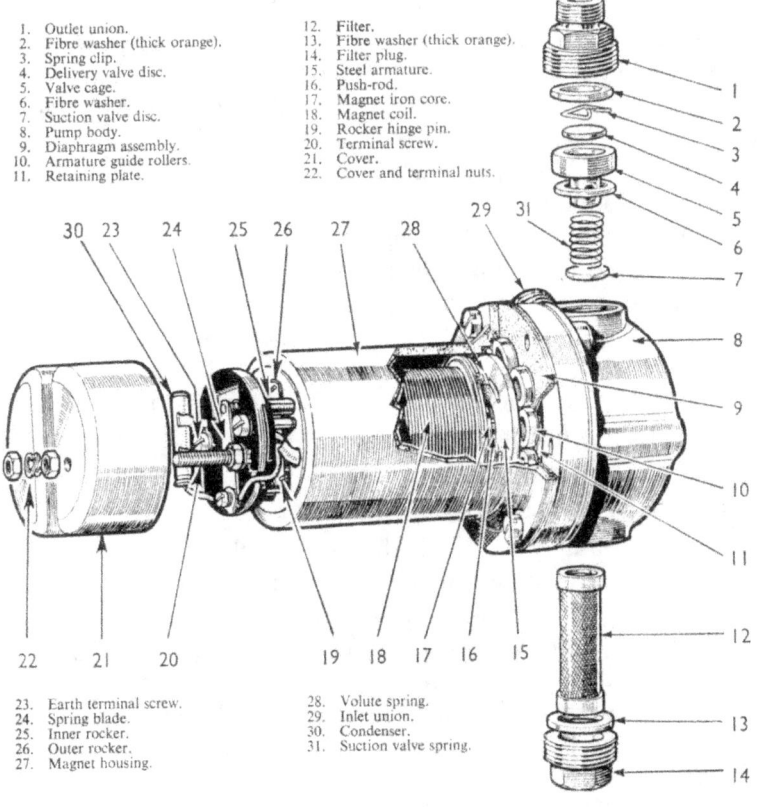

1. Outlet union.
2. Fibre washer (thick orange).
3. Spring clip.
4. Delivery valve disc.
5. Valve cage.
6. Fibre washer.
7. Suction valve disc.
8. Pump body.
9. Diaphragm assembly.
10. Armature guide rollers.
11. Retaining plate.
12. Filter.
13. Fibre washer (thick orange).
14. Filter plug.
15. Steel armature.
16. Push-rod.
17. Magnet iron core.
18. Magnet coil.
19. Rocker hinge pin.
20. Terminal screw.
21. Cover.
22. Cover and terminal nuts.
23. Earth terminal screw.
24. Spring blade.
25. Inner rocker.
26. Outer rocker.
27. Magnet housing.
28. Volute spring.
29. Inlet union.
30. Condenser.
31. Suction valve spring.

ture (15). A bronze rod (16) is screwed through the center of the armature, to which the diaphram is attached, and it passes through the magnet core to the contact breaker, which is located at the other end. A volute spring (28) is interposed between the armature and the end plate of the coil to return the armature and diaphram.

The magnet consists of a cast-iron pot having an iron core (17), on which is wound a copper wire which energizes the magnet. Between the magnet housing and the armature are fitted 11 spherical-edged brass rollers (10). These locate the armature centrally within the magnet at all times, and allow absolute freedom of movement in a longitudinal direction. The contact breaker consists of a small bakelite moulding carrying two rockers (25 and 26) which are both hinged to the moulding at one end by two small springs, arranged to give a 'throw over' action. A trunnion is fitted into the center of the inner rocker, and the bronze push-rod (16) connected to the armature is screwed into this. The outer rocker (26) is fitted with a tungsten point, which makes contact with a further tungsten point on a spring blade (24). This spring blade is connected to one end of the coil, and the other end of the coil is connected to the terminal (20).

A short length of flexible wire is connected to the outer rocker and to the other terminal (23), which also serves to hold the bakelite moulding onto the magnet housing.

The rocker mechanism is insulated by fiber bushes. Two fiber bushes are fitted to one of the spindles of the 'throw over' mechanism in order to silence the operation of the contact breaker.

The body is die-cast in two pieces, the joint between them being sealed by a gasket.

Action of the Fuel Pump

The action of the pump is as follows.

When the pump is at rest, the outer rocker lies in the outer position and the tungsten points are in contact. The current passes from the terminal through the coil back to the blade, through the points and to the earth return, thus energizing the magnet and attracting the armature. This comes forward, bringing the diaphram with it and sucking fuel through the suction valve into the pumping chamber. When the armature has advanced nearly to the end of its stroke the 'throw over' mechanism operates, and the outer rocker flies back, separating the points and breaking the circuit. The spring (28) then pushes the armature and diaphram back forcing fuel through the delivery valve at a rate determined by the requirements of the engine. As soon as the armature gets near the end of this stroke the 'throw over' mechanism again operates, the points again make contact, and the cycle of operations is repeated.

Dismantling and Reassembling the Fuel Pump

The first thing to do is to determine whether it has been in contact with gum formation in the fuel, resulting in the parts in contact with the fuel becoming coated with substance similar to varnish. These deposits cause the eventual destruction of the neoprene diaphram. The easiest way to identify this deposit is to smell the outlet union. If an unpleasant stale smell is noticed it indicates the presense of gum in the pump. The ordinary sharp, acrid smell of gasoline denotes that no gum is present.

Assuming that trouble with gum formation is indicated, the whole of the parts coming into contact with fuel will have to be dismantled. Those made in brass or steel should be boiled in 20 per cent caustic soda solution, given a dip in strong nitric acid and then washed in boiling water. Those made in aluminium should be well soaked in denatured alcohol and cleaned.

To Dismantle the Pump

1. Undo the filter plug and remove the filter plug washer and the filter. The latter may be found to be clogged completely with gum. Next the inlet union and its washer should be removed, followed by the outlet union, outlet union washer, valve cage washer and suction valve and spring. The valve cage should then be dismantled by removing the circlip retaining the delivery valve in place, and the valve itself can then be withdrawn.
2. Next undo the six screws holding the two main components of the pump together. All the components of the pump body—with the exception of the washer, but including the pump body itself—should now be cleaned to remove all trace of gum. New fiber washers should be used on replacement.
3. If there is no evidence of gum formation proceed as follows:
—First undo the six screws holding two parts of the pump together. The action of the valves can then be checked by blowing and sucking in the inlet union, to check the suction valve; and the outlet union to check the delivery valve. In the former case it should be possible to blow freely but not to suck air back, and with the latter to suck and not blow.
4. Clean the filter in fuel with a brush and swill out the body of the pump.
5. Next unscrew the diaphragm assembly from its trunnion in

the contact breaker. This is done by rotating the whole assembly in an anti-clockwise direction. Take care not to lose the brass rollers fitted behind the diaphram. The easiest method is to hold the body in the left hand and to rotate the diaphragm.

6. Now remove the contact breaker cover by taking off the nut which holds it in place on the terminal, and then undo the last nut on the terminal, which acts as a seating for the cover. Beneath this will be found a lead washer which is squeezed into the thread on the terminal. This should be cut away with a pocket knife, allowing the terminal to be pushed down a short way so that the tag on the coil end is free on the terminal.

7. Remove the 5 B.A. screw holding the contact blade in position, together with its spring washer and the contact blade.

8. Remove the two long 2 B.A. screws holding the bakelite pedestal in place, together with their spring washers. Take off the contact breaker assembly, using great care to get the coil end tag over the terminal without damaging the coil end.

9. Push out the hinge pin sideways and the pump is completely dismantled, since the rocker mechanism is supplied only as a complete assembly.

10. **Do not disturb** the core of the magnet; it can only be located correctly with special press tools.

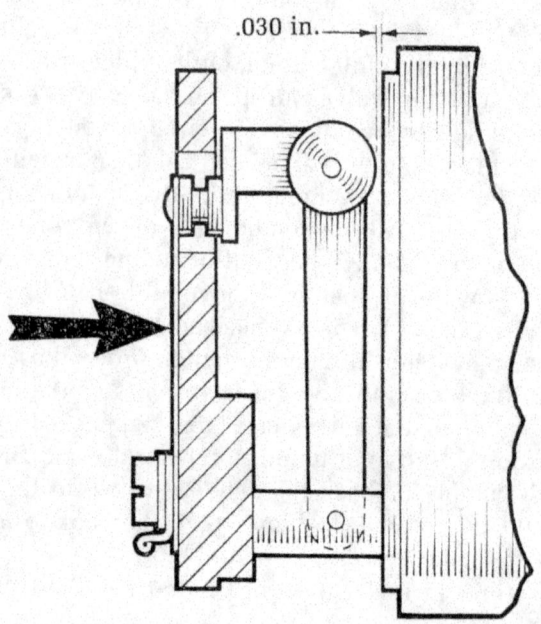

To Reassemble the Pump

When reassembling, see that all parts are clean. The valves (4 and 7) should be fitted with the smooth side downwards. Care should be taken that the valve retaining clip (3) in the delivery valve cage (5) is correctly located in its groove. The thin, hard fiber washer (6) should be fitted under the valve cage and a thick one (2) above the valve cage and above the filter plug. The washer on the inlet union (29) is a thick fiber one.

The contact breaker should be assembled on its pedestal in such a manner that the rockers are free in their mountings, without appreciable side-play. Any excessive side-play on the outer rocker will allow the points to get out of line, while excessive tightness will make the action of the contact breaker sluggish. To obtain the required freedom in cases of tightnesses, it may be necessary to square up the outer rocker with a pair of thin-nosed pliers. **The hinge pin is cased-hardened, and on no account should ordinary wire be used as a replacement. Always use the correct hardened pin.**

Should the spring contact breaker blade be removed it must always be replaced bearing diectly against the bakelite pedestal, i.e. underneath the tag.

When properly fitted the blade should rest against the ledge on the pedestal while the points are separated, and it should not be sufficiently stiff to prevent the outer rocker from coming right forward when the points are in contact. The points should make contact when the rocker is in its midway position. The simplest way to check this is to hold the blade in contact with the pedestal, taking care not to press on the overhanging portion, and see that you can get a .030 in. feeler between the white rollers and the cast-iron body of the pump. If necessary, the tip of the blade may be set to give the correct clearance.

Note.—**The spring washer on the B.A. screw to which the ground connection is made should be fitted between the tag and the pedestal. The spring washer is not a reliable conductor, and the brass tag must bear directly against the head of the screw.**

All four connections, namely the two ends of the ground tag and the two ends of the coil, should be soldered. The coil leading to the terminal should be soldered to its tag and not to the retaining nut. In the case of the terminal screw which holds the bakelite cover in position, similar considerations apply, the assembly being: spring washer (1), wiring tag (2), lead washer (3), and recessed nut (4). A lead washer has been found necessary at this point as some few cases of bad conection have been found. Under no circumstances must the spring washer be omitted, or the assembly shortened in any way. Any attempt to do so is likely to lead to breakage of the pedestal when the nut retaining the cover in position is tightened up.

The armature return spring should be fitted with its larger diameter towards the coil and its smaller diameter resting against the armature. This spring must not be stretched or otherwise interfered with, or the action of the pump will be affected.

Resetting the Diaphragm for Contact Breaker "Throw-Over"
If the armature and center rod have been unscrewed it will be necessary to reset as follows:—
1. **Swing to one side the spring blade which carries the contact points.**
2. Fit the impact washer in the recess of the armature.
3. Screw the armature into position.
4. Place the eleven guide rollers in position around the armature. **Do not use joining compound on the diaphragm.**
5. Hold the magnet assembly in the left hand, in an approximately horizontal position.
6. Screw the armature inwards until the "throw-over" ceases to operate, and then screw it back gradually, a sixth of a turn (or one hole) at a time, and press the armature in after each part of a turn until it is found that when it is pushed in slowly and firmly the "throw-over" mechanism operates. **Unscrew the armature a further two-thirds of a turn** (four of the six holes). When a new diaphragm is fitted it is probable that considerable pressure will be required to push the armature right home.
7. Place the cast-iron body in position on the main body, taking care to see that the drain hole in the cast-iron body is at the bottom in line with the filter plug in the main body, and all the rollers are still in their correct position.

Make sure that the cast-iron body is seating properly on the main body and insert the six securing screws. **Before tightening the screws down it is essential that the diaphragm should be stretched to its outermost position.**

Do this by inserting a match-stick behind one of the white fiber rollers on the outer rocker, thus holding the points in contact (after first re-positioning the spring blade into its noraml position). If a current is then passed through the pump the magnet will be energized and will pull the armature and diaphram forward, and while it is in this position the six screws should be tightened. Although the diaphragm-stretching opera-

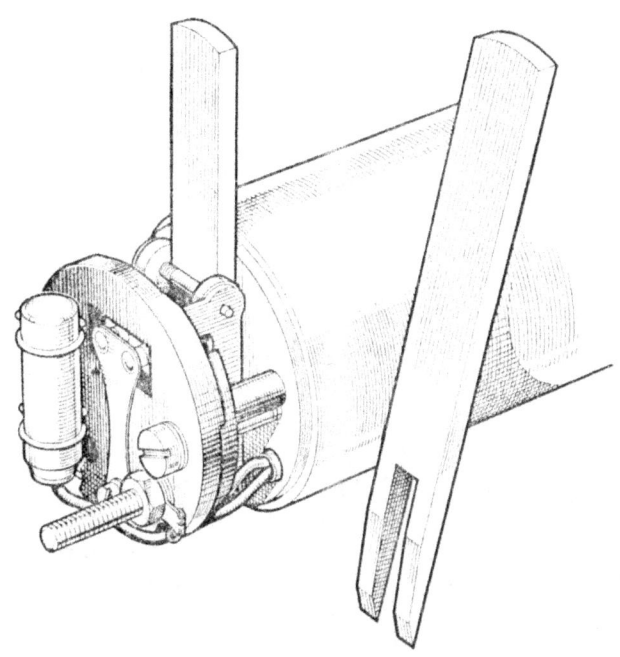

tion can be effected by the matchstick method, a special tool for the purpose is available from the S.U. Carburetter Co. or their Distributors. The tool is a steel wedge, to be inserted under the trunnion in the center of the inner rocker in order to stretch the diaphram to its outermost position before tightening the six flange screws.

8. Finally, check that when the spring blade is in its normal position the clearance hole in it is so positioned around the locking screw that each contact point, according to the operation of the outer rocker, **wipes over the center line of the other contact point,** and that this action is not to one side of the center on either contact. The width of the gap at the points is approximately .030 in.

Note.—There are three important points which are repeatedly overlooked by operators. These seriously affect the functioning of the pump; they are:—

1. To keep the contact breaker blade out of contact while obtaining the correct diaphragm setting.
2. To press firmly and steadily on the armature, instead of jerking it, while obtaining the setting.
3. Omission to stretch the diaphragm to the limit of its stroke while tightening up the body screws.

Tracing Fuel Pump Troubles

Should the pump cease to function, first disconnect the fuel delivery pipe from the pump. If the pump then works the most likely cause of the trouble is a sticking needle in the float-chamber of the carburetter. Should the pump not work, disconnect the lead from the terminal and strike it against the body of the pump after switching on the ignition. If a spark occurs it indicates that the necessary current is available at the terminals, and that the trouble arises with the pump mechanism. If no spark can be detected, then it is an indication that the current supply has failed and that attention should be given to the wiring and battery. If current is present, further investigation should be carried out by removing the bakelite cover which is retained by the terminal nut. Touch the terminal with the lead. If the pump does not operate and the contact points are in contact yet no spark can be struck off the terminal, it is very probable that the contact points are dirty and require cleaning. These may be cleaned by inserting a piece of card between them, pinching them together and sliding the card backwards and forwards.

It is possible that there may be an obstruction in the suction pipe, which should be cleared by blowing air through it, or that some irregularity in the pump itself is preventing the correct movement. This may be due either to the diaphragm having stiffened, or to foreign matter in the roller assembly which supports the diaphragm, in which case the diaphragm should be removed and the whole assembly cleaned and reassembled in accordance with the instructions.

On the other hand, if the points are not making contact, see that the tips of the inner rocker (25) are in contact with the magnet housing. If they are not, it is an indication that the armature has failed to return to the end of its normal travel.

To cure this, loosen the six screws, which attach the magnet housing to the pump body, and make sure that the diaphragm is not sticking to the face of the magnet housing by carefully passing a penknife between the two. The hinge pin (19) should then be removed and the six retaining screws tightened up again. The tips of the inner rockers will probably now be found to be making contact with the face of the magnet housing, but if they are not, it will be necessary to remove and dismantle the whole magnet assembly in order to ascertain if an accumulation of foreign matter has caused a jam. Remember that whenever the magnet housing is removed care should be taken to see that the guide rollers (10) do not drop out.

Pump Noisy

If the pump becomes noisy and works rapidly, it is usually an indication that there is an air leak on the suction side of the pump. Check the level of the fuel in the tank and see that it is not too low.

The simplest way to test for air leakage is to disconnect the fuel pipe from the carburetor and place its end in a glass jar (approximately 1 pint or half a litre) and allow the pump to deliver fuel into it. If air bubbles appear when the end of the pipe has become submerged in the fuel, it is a clear indication of an air leak on the suction side of the pump in the fuel feed pipe between the tank and the pump which should be found and cured. Check all the unions and joints, making sure that the filter union and inlet unions are all quite air-tight.

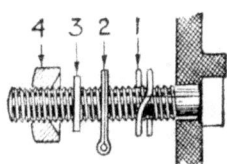

The correct sequence of assembly of the connecting components on the terminal screw.

Failure to Deliver Fuel

Should the pump continue beating without delivering fuel, it is probable that some dirt has become lodged under one of the valves, in which case they should be dismantled by unscrewing the top or delivery union and lifting out the valve cage, where they can be cleaned and reassembled. When replacing it see that the thin, hard red fiber washer is **below** the valve cage and the thick, orange one above.

If the pump struggles to operate and becomes very hot, it is probable that the filter has become clogged or there is an obstruction on the suction side. The filter is readily removed for cleaning by unscrewing its retaining plug at the bottom of the pump.

Fuel Pump Maintenance

Apart from keeping the contacts clean and removing the filter at regular intervals for cleaning, there is no maintenance required on the fuel pump.

The filter can be removed by unscrewing the hexagon plug at the bottom of the pump, where it can be cleaned in fuel with a stiff brush. Never use a rag to clean a filter.

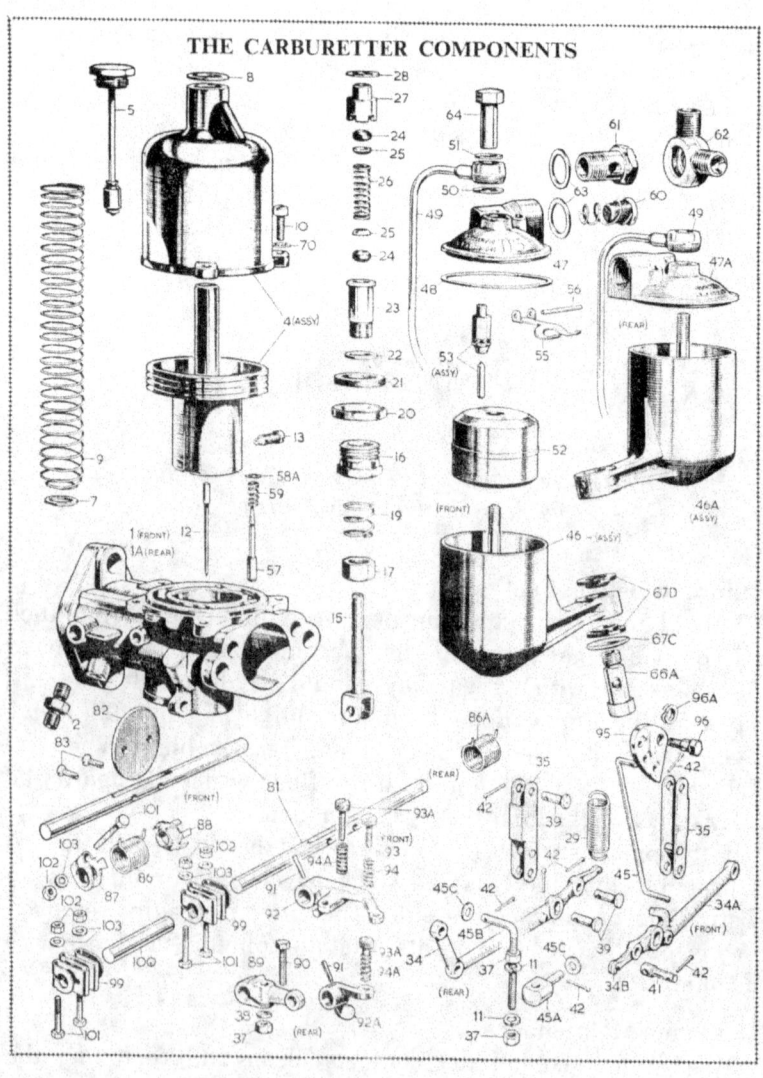

THE CARBURETTER COMPONENTS

KEY TO THE CARBURETTER COMPONENTS

No.	Description	No.	Description
1.	Body—front.	49.	Pipe assembly.
1A.	Body—rear.	50.	Serrated fibre washer.
2.	Auto-ignition union.	51.	Aluminium washer.
4.	Suction chamber and piston assembly.	52.	Float.
5.	Oil cap damper assembly.	53.	Float needle and seat.
7.	Thrust washer.	55.	Float hinged lever.
8.	Fibre washer—oil cap damper.	56.	Float hinged lever pin.
9.	Piston spring.	57.	Piston lift pin.
10.	Suction chamber securing screw.	58A.	Circlip—lift pin.
11.	2 B.A. spring washer—connecting rod.	59.	Spring—lift pin.
12.	Jet needle.	60.	Filter.
13.	Jet needle locking screw.	61.	Banjo bolt.
15.	Jet with head.	62.	Banjo union—double—rear.
16.	Jet screw.	63.	Fibre washer—banjo bolt.
17.	Jet adjusting nut.	64.	Cap nut.
19.	Jet adjusting lock spring.	66A.	Holding-up bolt—float-chamber.
20.	Jet sealing ring.	67C.	Washer—holding-up bolt.
21.	Jet sealing ring—neoprene.	67D.	Rubber grommet—holding-up bolt.
22.	Jet copper washer—bottom half.	70.	Shakeproof washer—securing screw.
23.	Jet bearing—bottom half.	81.	Throttle spindle—front and rear.
24.	Jet gland washer—cork.	82.	Throttle disc.
25.	Jet gland washer—brass.	83.	Screw—throttle disc.
26.	Jet gland spring.	86.	Return spring—throttle—front.
27.	Jet bearing—top half.	86A.	Return spring—throttle—rear.
28.	Jet copper washer—top half.	87.	Retainer clip.
29.	Return spring—jet lever.	88.	Anchor plate—throttle return spring.
34.	Jet lever—rear.	89.	Lever—throttle spindle.
34A.	Jet lever—front.	90.	2 B.A. bolt—throttle lever.
35.	Jet link.	91.	Taper pin—stop lever—front and rear.
37.	2 B.A. nut—connecting rod.	92.	Stop lever—front
39.	Pivot pin.	92A.	Stop lever—rear.
41.	Link pin.	93.	Stop adjusting screw—short.
42.	Split pin.	93A.	Stop adjusting screw—long.
45.	Link rod—intermediate jet and throttle.	94.	Stop adjusting screw spring—short.
45A.	Trunnion.	94A.	Stop adjusting screw spring—long.
45B.	Connecting rod.	95.	Cam.
45C.	Brass washer—connecting rod.	96.	Pivot bolt—cam.
46.	Float-chamber with stud—front.	96A.	Spring washer—pivot bolt.
46A.	Float-chamber with stud—rear.	100.	Connecting rod.
47.	Float-chamber lid—front.	101.	4 B.A. bolt.
47A.	Float-chamber lid—rear.	102.	4 B.A. nut.
48.	Oakenstrong washer—lid.	103.	4 B.A. washer.

The Carburetors—MGA

The S.U. H-4 carburetors are of the controllable jet type drawing air through oil wetted air cleaners.

A damper is provided in each unit, consisting of a plunger and non-return valve attached to the oil cap nut. The damper operates in the hollow piston rod which is partly filled with oil. Its function is to give a slightly enriched mixture on accelleration by controlling the rise of the piston, and also to prevent flutter.

Carburetor Adjustments

Slow running is governed by setting of the jet adjusting nuts and the throttle stop screws, all of which must be correctly set and synchronized if satisfactory results are to be obtained.

The two throttles are interconnected by a coupling shaft and spring coupling clips enabling them to be set and correctly synchronized when adjustments are being made.

The mixture control levers are also connected, between the carburetor, by a short adjustable link.

Before blaming the carburetor settings for bad slow running, make certain that the trouble is not caused by badly adjusted contact points, faulty plugs, incorrect valve clearance or faulty valves and springs.

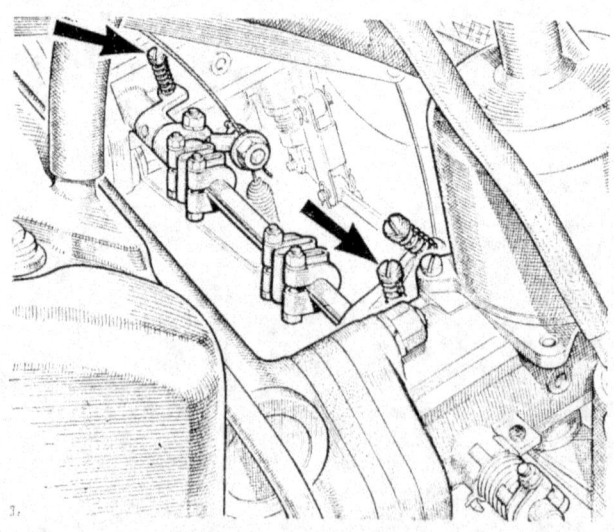

The slow-running adjustment screws are indicated by the arrows.

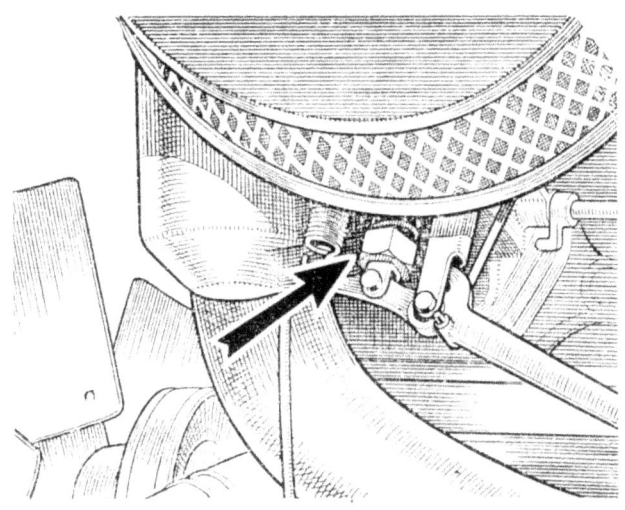

The arrow indicates the jet adjusting nut.

Adjusting the Jets

1. Run the engine until it attains normal running temperature.
2. Slacken off the pinch-bolt of one of the spring coupling clips locating the carburetor inter-connecting shaft to the throttle spindles so that each carburetor can be operated independently.
3. Disconnect the mixture control cable and the connecting link between the two jet adjusting levers.
4. Unscrew both throttle lever setting screws until the throttles are completely closed. Turn the adjusting screw of the rear carburetor in a clockwise direction approximately one turn to set the throttle for fast idling; lift the piston of the front carburetor $1/2$ in. to leave the carburetor out of action.
5. With the engine running, set the jet adjusting nut of the rear carburetor so that a mixture strength is obtained which will give the best running speed for this particular throttle opening, taking care to see that the jet head is in firm contact with the adjusting nut the whole time.

The correctness or otherwise of this setting can be checked by raising the suction piston about $1/32$ in. with the piston-lifting pin. This should cause a very slight increase in the speed of the engine without impairing the eveness of the running. If the engine stops, the mixture is too weak. If the speed increases and continues to increase when the piston is raised as much as $1/4$ in. the mixture is too rich.

6. When the setting of the mixture is correct for the rear carburetor, unscrew the throttle adjusting screw until the throttle is

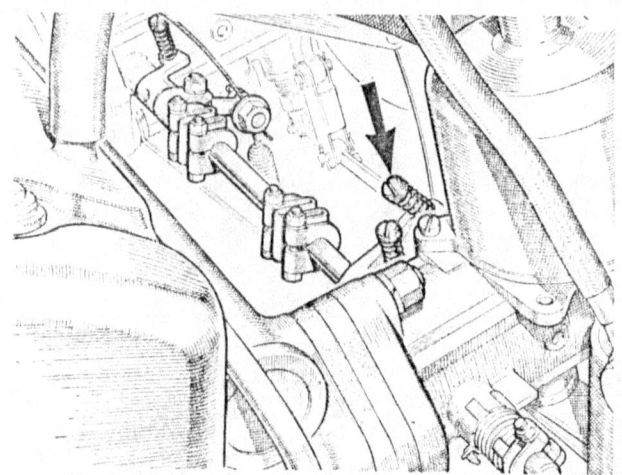

The screw indicated by the arrow is used to adjust the amount of throttle opening when the mixture control is in use

fully closed and lift the piston 1/2 in. to put it out of action. Repeat the adpustment operations on the front carburetor.

7. When both carburetors are correctly adjusted for mixture, set the throttle adjustment screw of each to give the required slow running. Adjust the link between the mixture levers so so that each lever is moved the same amount when the mixture control is used.

Slow-Running and Sychronization

1. Turn the throttle adjustment screw of each carburetor to give a fast idling speed, taking care to turn each screw the same amount. Now unscrew each throttle lever adjustment screw an equal amount, a fraction of a turn at a time until the desired slow-running speed is obtained.

2. Acuracy of synchronization can be checked by listening at each carburetor air intake in turn through a length of rubber tubing and noticing if the noise produced by the incoming air is the same at both. Any variation in the intensity of the sound indicates that one throttle is more widely open than the other.

3. When the same intensity of sound is given by both carburetors the coupling shaft clip should be tightened to ensure that the throttles work in unison.

4. Since the delivery characteristics when both carburetors are working together vary somewhat from those existing when each is working separately, it will be necessary to check again for correctness of mixture strength by lifting each piston in turn

as indicated in **'adjusting the jets'**, and adjusting as necessary.

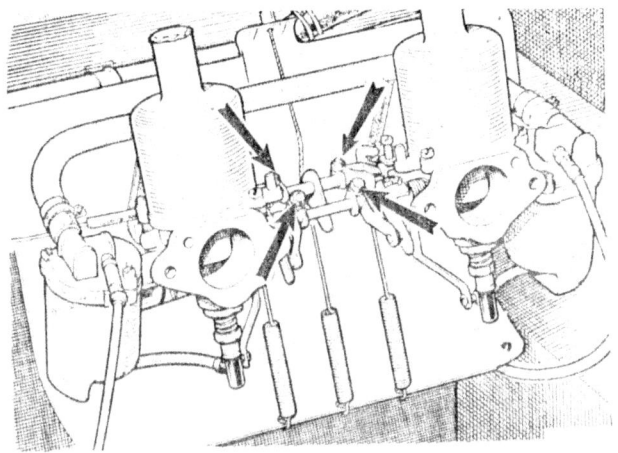

Locking nuts on the throttle and mixture control interconnecting levers

Removing the Carburetors
1. Release the spring clips and detach the breather hose from the air cleaner and rocker cover.
2. Disconnect the fuel supply pipe at the rear carburetor banjo union.
   Remove the split pin and flat washer and release the mixture cable and clevis pin from the mixture control linkage and release the mixture outer cable abutment from its bracket.
3. Detach the throttle return spring and release the throttle cable.
4. Unscrew the union nut and disconnect the ignition vacuum control pipe from the rear carburetor.
5. Remove the nut and flat washer to release the vent pipe from the top of each float-chamber.
5. Remove the four nuts securing the carburetor flanges and withdraw the carburetor and air cleaners as an assembly.
   Replacement is a reversal of the above instructions.

Centering the Jet H-4
1. First remove the clevis pin at the base of the jet which attaches the jet head to the jet operating lever; withdraw jet completely, and remove the adjusting nut and the adjusting nut spring. Replace the adjusting nut without its spring and screw it up to the highest position. Slide the jet into position until the jet head is against the base of the adjusting nut.
2. When this has been done remove the dashpot damper and

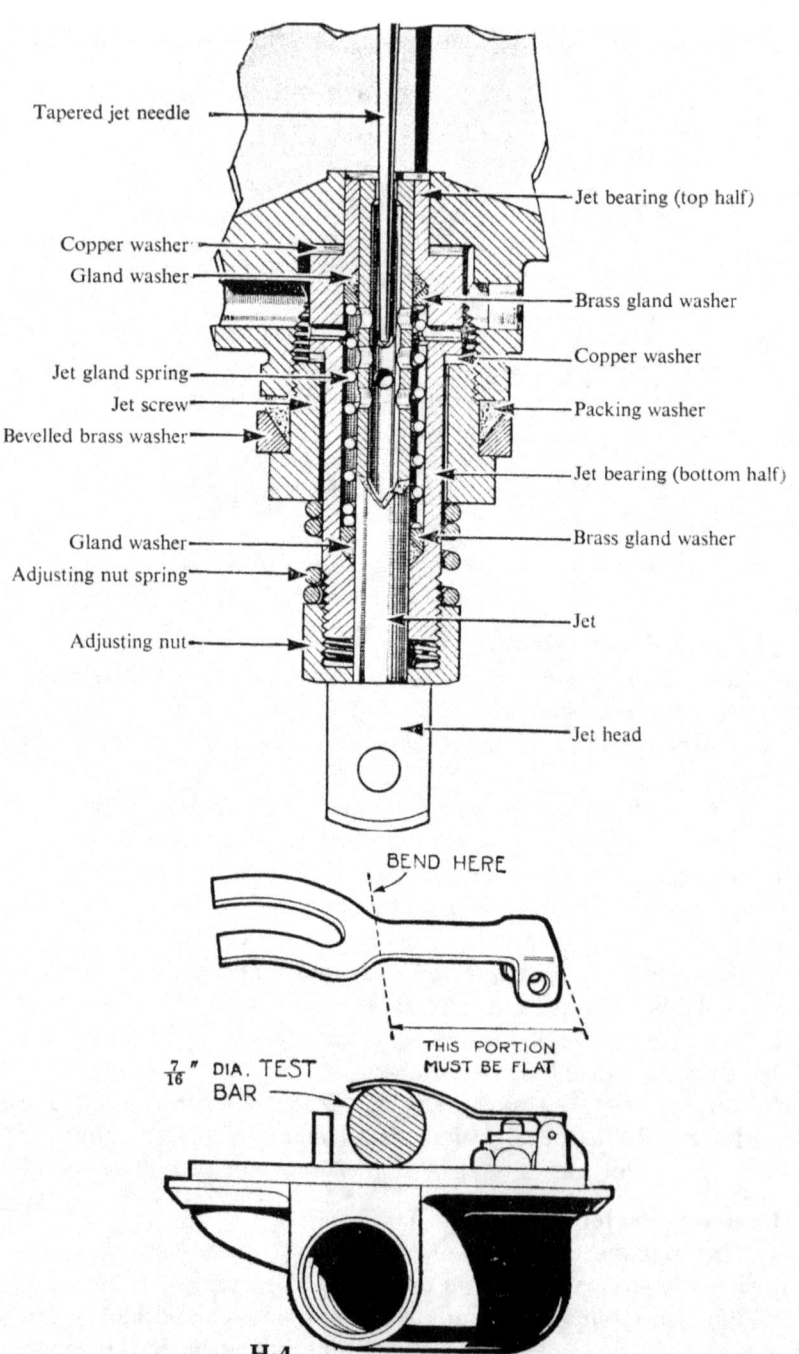

Showing the place where the float lever should be set and the method of checking the correct adjustment of the lever

test for free piston movement by lifting it with a finger. If it is not perfectly free, slacken the jet holding screw and manipulate the lower part of the assembly including the projecting part of the bottom half jet bearing, adjusting nut and jet head. Make sure that the assembly is now slightly loose. The piston should rise and fall quite freely as the needle is now able to move the jet into the required central position. Tighten the jet holding screw and check position again. If it is still not free, slacken the jet holding screw and repeat operation. When the piston is completely free-moving, remove the adjusting nut and replace its spring. Replace the nut, screwing it to its original position.

The Carburetors—MGB

The HS4 carburetor is of the automatically expanding choke type in which the size of the main air passage (or choke) over the jet, and the effective area of the jet, are variable according to the degree of throttle opening used on the engine against the prevailing road conditions (which may differ widely from light cruising to heavy pulling).

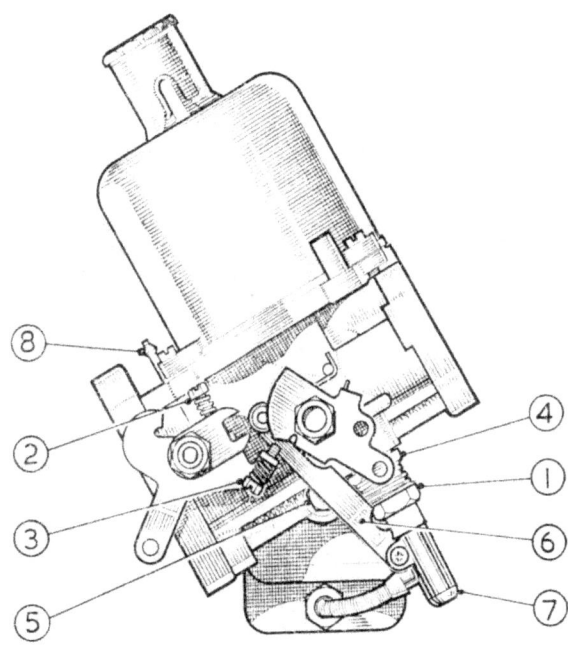

1. Jet adjusting nut.
2. Throttle stop screw.
3. Choke or fast-idle screw.
4. Jet locking nut.
5. Float-chamber securing nut.
6. Jet link.
7. Jet head.
8. Vacuum ignition take-off.

Therefore, to serve the complete throttle range a single jet only is used, being a simple metal tube sliding in a single bearing bush, fed by fuel along a small-diameter nylon tube leading direct from the base of a float-chamber. The jet is varied in effective area by a tapered fuel metering needle.

Float-Chamber—HS4

The position of the hinged float lever must be such that the level of the float (and therefore the height of the fuel at the jet) is correct.

To check the float level, hold the float-chamber lid and float assembly upside-down and place a 1/8 in. (3.18 mm.) diameter bar across the diameter of the machined lip of the float-chamber lid, parallel to the float lever hinge pin and under the float lever (see Fig. below). The face of the float lever should just rest on the bar when the float needle is held fully on its seating. If this is not so, carefully reset the angle made between the straight portion of the float lever and its hinge until the correct position is obtained.

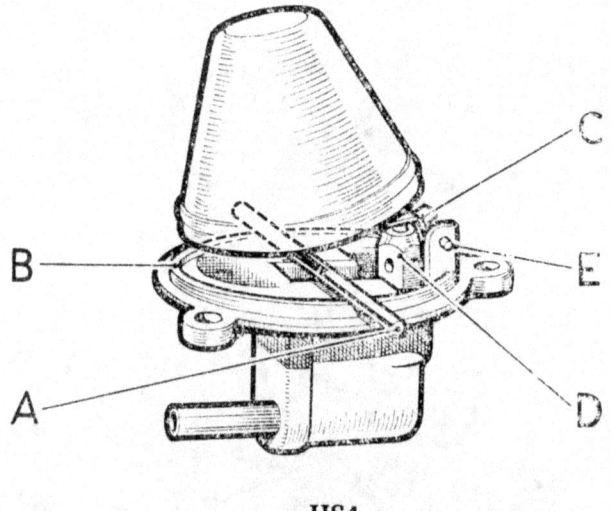

HS4

A. 1/8 in. (3·18 mm.) dia. bar.   C. Float lever resetting point.
B. Machined lip.   D. Needle valve assembly.
                   E. Hinge pin.

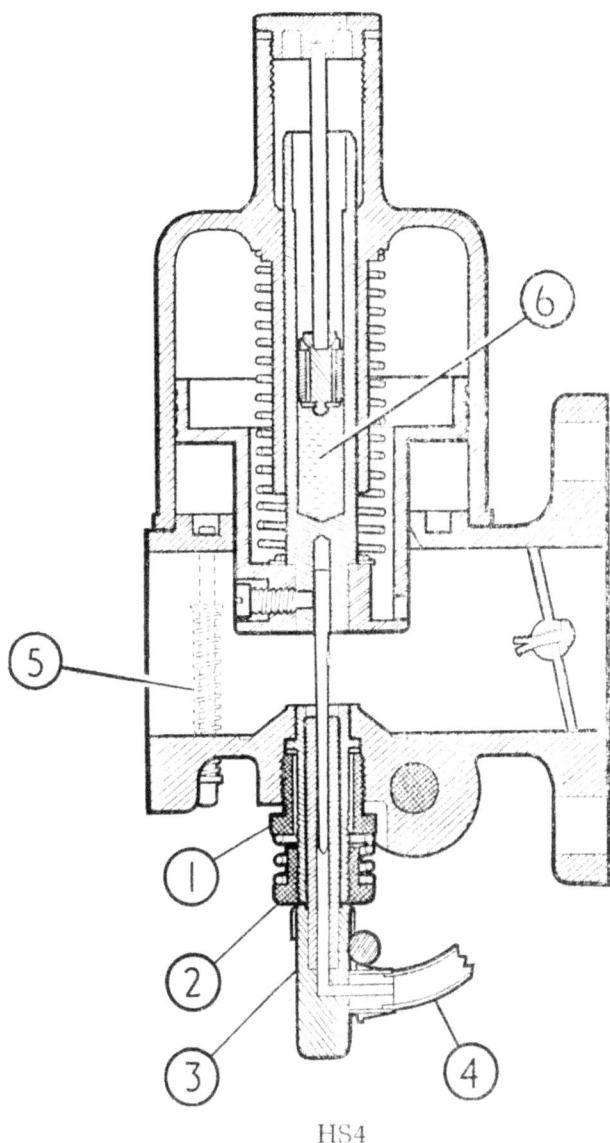

HS4

1. Jet locking nut.
2. Jet adjusting nut.
3. Jet head.
4. Feed tube from float-chamber.
5. Piston lifting pin.
6. Oil damper reservoir.

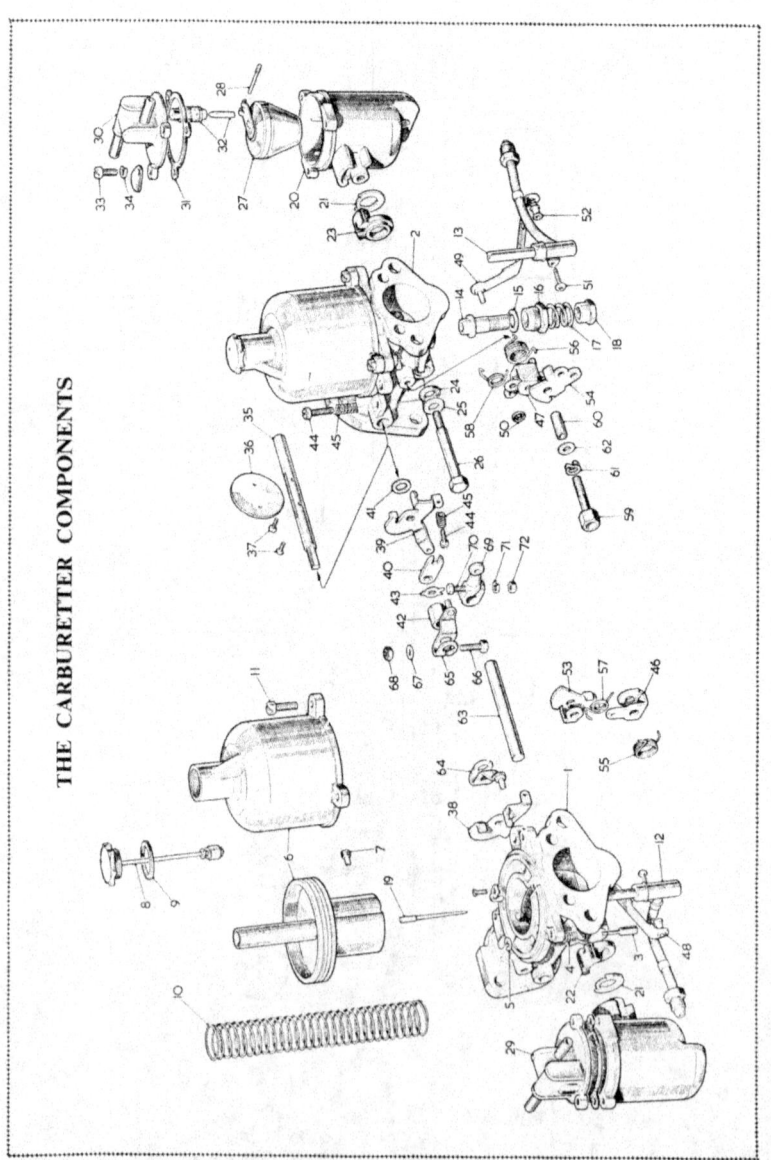

KEY TO THE CARBURETTER COMPONENTS

No.	Description
1.	Body—front carburetter.
2.	Body—rear carburetter.
3.	Pin—piston lifting.
4.	Spring—pin.
5.	Circlip—pin.
6.	Chamber and piston assembly.
7.	Screw—needle locking.
8.	Cap and dampers assembly.
9.	Washer—cap (fibre).
10.	Spring—piston (red).
11.	Screw—chamber to body.
12.	Jet assembly—front carburetter.
13.	Jet assembly—rear carburetter.
14.	Bearing—jet.
15.	Washer—jet bearing (brass).
16.	Screw—jet locking.
17.	Spring—jet locking.
18.	Screw—jet adjusting.
19.	Needle.
20.	Chamber—float.
21.	Washer—support.
22.	Grommet—front carburetter (rubber).
23.	Grommet—rear carburetter (rubber).
24.	Washer (rubber).
25.	Washer—plain.
26.	Bolt—float-chamber fixing.
27.	Float assembly.
28.	Pin—hinged lever.
29.	Lid—float-chamber—front carburetter.
30.	Lid—float-chamber—rear carburetter.
31.	Washer—lid.
32.	Needle and seat assembly.
33.	Screw—lid.
34.	Washer—spring—screw.
35.	Spindle—throttle.
36.	Disc—throttle.
37.	Screw—disc.
38.	Lever—throttle return—front carburetter.
39.	Lever—throttle return—rear carburetter.
40.	Lever—lost motion.
41.	Washer—spacing.
42.	Nut—lever.
43.	Washer—tab—nut.
44.	Screw—throttle stop.
45.	Spring—throttle stop screw.
46.	Lever—pick-up—front carburetter.
47.	Lever—pick-up—rear carburetter.
48.	Link—front carburetter.
49.	Link—rear carburetter.
50.	Washer—starlock—link.
51.	Screw—link to jet.
52.	Bush—screw.
53.	Lever—cam—front carburetter.
54.	Lever—cam—rear carburetter.
55.	Spring—pick-up lever—front carburetter.
56.	Spring—pick-up lever—rear carburetter.
57.	Spring—cam lever—front carburetter.
58.	Spring—cam lever—rear carburetter.
59.	Bolt—pivot.
60.	Tube—pivot bolt.
61.	Washer—spring—pivot bolt.
62.	Washer—distance.
63.	Rod—jet connecting.
64.	Lever and pin assembly—front carburetter.
65.	Lever and pin assembly—rear carburetter.
66.	Bolt—lever.
67.	Washer—bolt.
68.	Nut—bolt.

Centering the Jet—HS4

To check the jet for concentricity with the jet needle set the jet head and jet adjusting nut in the uppermost position, lift the suction piston with the piston lifting pin, and allow the piston to fall. It should fall freely, and a definite soft, metallic click will be heard as the base of the piston strikes the jet bridge.

If this does not happen with the jet raised, but does occur when the jet is lowered, the jet bearing and jet must be re-centered as follows:

1. Disconnect the lever between the interconnecting lever and the jet head.
2. Unscrew the union holding the nylon feed tube into the base of the float-chamber and withdraw the tube and jet together.
3. Unscrew the jet adjusting nut and remove the lock spring; screw up the nut to its fullest extent and refit the jet head and feed tube.
4. Slacken off the jet locking nut until the jet bearing is just free to rotate with finger pressure.
5. Remove the piston damper from the top of the suction chamber and gently press the piston down onto the jet bridge.
6. Tighten the jet locking nut, at the same time ensuring that the jet head is still in its correct angular position. Lift the piston and check that it falls freely and evenly, hitting the jet bridge with a soft, metallic click, with the jet in the raised and lowered position. If the result is not satisfactory and the piston is not sticking, the recentering operation must be repeated until the correct result is obtained.
7. When the operation is completed replace the adjusting nut lock spring and the jet operating lever.

This adjustment is best effected with the carburetors removed from the engine.

Source of Carburetor Trouble
Piston Sticking

The piston assembly comprises the suction disc and the piston forming the choke, into which is inserted the hardened and ground piston rod which engages in a bearing in the center of the suction chamber and in which is, in turn inserted the jet needle. The piston rod running in the bearing is the only part which is in actual contact with any other part, the suction disc, piston, and needle all having suitable clearances to prevent sticking. If sticking does occur the whole assembly should be cleaned carefully and the piston rod lubricated with a spot of thin oil. No oil must be applied to any other part except the piston rod. A sticking piston can be ascertained by removing the dashpot damper, inserting a finger in the air intake and lifting the piston, which should come up quite freely and fall back smartly onto its seating when released. On no account should the piston return spring be stretched or its tension altered in an attempt to improve its rate of return.

Float-Chamber Flooding

This is indicated by fuel dripping from the drain pipe, and is generally caused by grit between the float-chamber needle and its guide. This is cured by removing the float-chamber, washing the valve and float-chamber components and reassembling.

Float Needle Sticking

If the engine stops, apparently through lack of fuel, when there is plenty in the tank and the pump is working properly, the probable cause is a sticking float needle. An easy test for this is to disconnect the pipe from the electric pump to the carburetors and switch the ignition on and off quickly while the end of the pipe is directed onto a pad of cloth or into a container.

If fuel is delivered, starvation has almost certainly been caused by the float needle sticking to its seating, and the float-chamber lid should therefore be removed, the needle and seating cleaned and refitted. At the same time it will be advisable to clean out the entire fuel feed system, as this trouble is caused by foreign matter in the fuel and unless this is removed it is likely to recur. It is of no use whatever renewing any of the component parts of either carburetor, and the only cure is to make sure that the fuel tank and pipe lines are entirely free from any kind of foreign matter or sticky substance capable of causing this trouble.

H-4 Air Cleaner

Every 3,000 miles (4800 km.) or more frequently in dusty conditions the air cleaner should be serviced as follows.

Unscrew and remove the two bolts, remove outer cover and withdraw the element from the body of each cleaner. Wash the element thoroughly in gasoline, drain and dry. Wet the element with S.A.E. 20 engine oil and allow to drain before replacing.

Reassemble the front element with the corrugations clear of the breather spigot in the filter case.

HS4 Air Filters

The air intake filters are of the dry paper element type requiring no attention between filter replacement every 12,000 miles.

The air filter casings should be removed and cleaned out every 3,000 miles to remove any dust deposit.

Filter Replacement

Disconnect the engine rocker cover breather pipe from the front filter. Unscrew the bolts securing each air filter to the choke bracket and fixing plate respectively and remove the filters from the vehicle complete.

Remove the base plate and throw away the old paper element. Clean the inside casing and intake tubes thoroughly and re-assemble, using new paper elements.

Accelerator Return Spring

On later cars, commencing with Car No. 24954, an additional accelerator return spring was introduced as a safety precaution and the original spring replaced by a new spring.

The new parts may be fitted to earlier cars as a set as follows.
1. Remove the original accelerator return spring and fit the new spring (Part No. AHH5621).
2. Remove the accelerator cable and replace the anchor pin with the new anchor pin (Part No. AHH5625).
3. Fit the anchor bracket (Part No. AHH5623) to one of the accelerator cable guide screws and fit the auxiliary return spring (Part No. AHH5624).

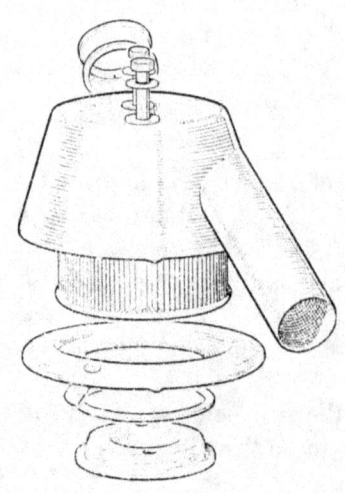

The SU Tool

One of the best, least expensive non-mechanical aids to the performance of the carburetor tuning process is the "SU Tool" (in reality a kit of tools) which greatly speeds up the functions of checking piston free movement, synchronization of two or three carburetors, testing mixture strength, adjusting float level and centering the jet needle. The SU Tool is distributed by Messrs. MG Mitten Co., 1163 E. Green St., Pasadena, California, USA and inquiries should be directed to that firm relative to purchase.

In principle, the SU Tool achieves synchronization at any rpm from idling to top speed without the necessity for removing air cleaners by making it possible to visually check the height of the pistons in two or more carburetors simultaneously. The test rods of the tool kit allow the pistons to be lifted and dropped accurately to check free movement or mixture strength. The rods are also precision made for use as gauges for float level setting. A jet pin, which is used to replace the needle permits accurate centering without danger of bending the needle itself. The jet wrench included in the kit is made specifically for the jet adjusting nut and is conveniently short for easy manipulation.

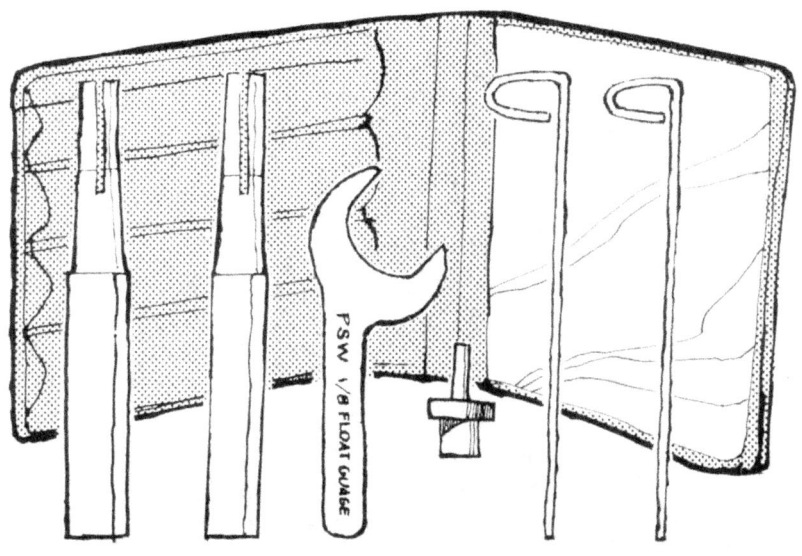

THE CLUTCH

MGA—Description

The clutch is of the single-plate dry-disc type operated hydraulically.

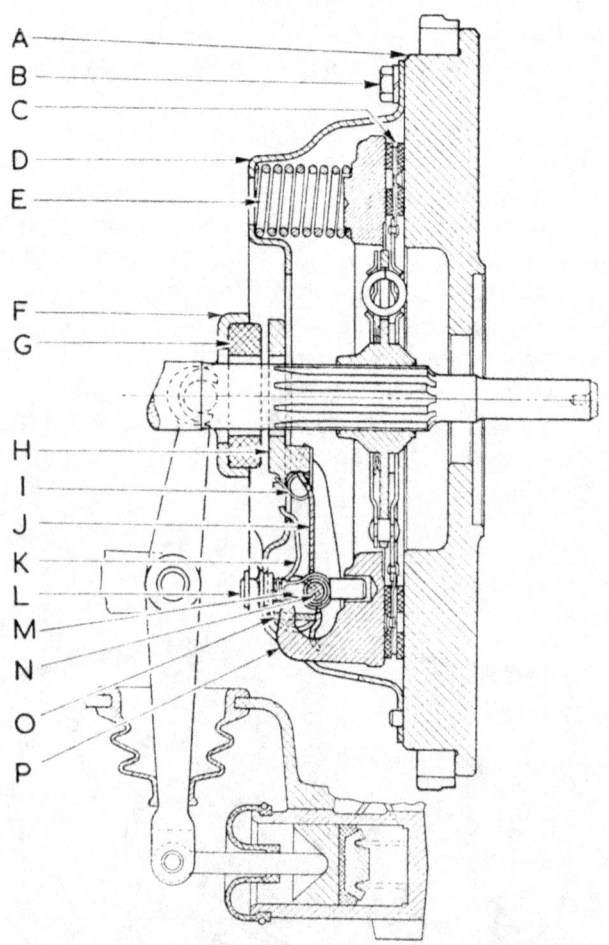

The Driven Plate Assembly

This consists of a splined hub and flexible steel driven plate (C), to the outer diameter of which are fixed the annular friction facings. This plate is attached to the splined hub by a spring mounting which provides a torsional cushion.

THE CLUTCH COMPONENTS

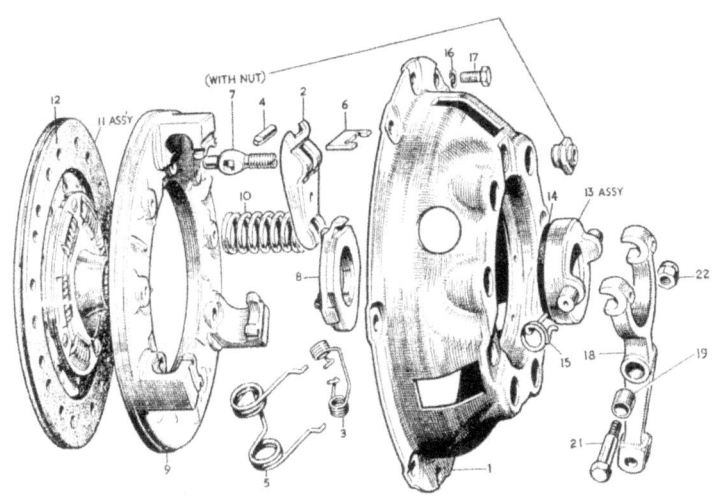

KEY TO THE CLUTCH COMPONENTS

No.	Description	No.	Description	No.	Description
1.	Cover—clutch.	8.	Plate—bearing thrust.	15.	Retainer.
2.	Lever—release.	9.	Plate—pressure.	16.	Washer—spring—cover screw.
3.	Retainer—lever.	10.	Spring—pressure plate.	17.	Screw—cover to flywheel.
4.	Pin—lever.	11.	Plate assembly—driven.	18.	Lever assembly—withdrawal.
5.	Spring—anti-rattle.	12.	Lining.	19.	Bush.
6.	Strut.	13.	Ring assembly—thrust.	21.	Bolt—lever.
7.	Eyebolt with nut.	14.	Ring—carbon.	22.	Nut—bolt.

Withdrawal Bearing Assembly

This comprises the graphite release bearing (G) mounted in a cup attached to the throw-out fork and a release plate (H) attached to the inner ends of the release levers (J) by means of the retainer springs (I). Release is accomplished by moving the release plate and thus applying pressure to the release levers.

Cover Assembly

Each release lever is privoted on a floating pin (N), which remains stationary in the lever and rolls across a short flat portion of the enlarged hole in the eyebolts extend through holes in the clutch cover and are fitted with adjusting nuts (L) by means of which each lever is located in its correct position. The outer or shorter ends of the release levers engage the pressure plate lugs by means of struts (O) which provide knife-edge contact between the outer ends of the levers and the pressure plate lugs, eliminating friction at this point. Thus the pressure plate (P) is pulled away from the driven plate (C), compressing the six thrust coil springs (E) which are assembled between the pressure plate and the clutch cover.

When the foot pressure is removed from the clutch pedal the clutch springs force the pressure plate forward against the driven plate, gradually and smoothly applying the power of the engine to the rear wheels.

Hydraulic Operation

A master twin-bore cylinder bolted to the chassis frame contains two pistons operated by the clutch and brake pedals. For clutch withdrawal, fluid pressure is transmitted to the slave cylinder bolted to the clutch housing., moving the piston, push-rod and clutch lever and disengaging the clutch.

The Master Cylinder

The assembly of the clutch master cylinder is similar to that of the brake master cylinder except that no combination inlet and outlet valve is fitted and therefore no pressure is maintained in the clutch line when the pedal is released.

The Slave Cylinder

This is bolted to the clutch housing and normally requires no maintenace; its assembly is similar to that of the front wheel brake cylinder, and the push-rod is not adjustable.

If the system is drained of fluid it will be necessary to bleed the cylinder after reassembly and refilling.

Adjustment

It is essential that there should be a clearance between the master cylinder push-rod and the piston when the clutch pedal is released. This clearance, 1/32 in., is adjusted by slackening the locknut and rotating the push-rod in the appropriate direction. Ensure that the pedal is not obstructed by the toeboard or by the floor covering. The free movement at the pedal pad must be sufficient to allow the piston fully to return in the cylinder and still retain the 1/32 in. clearance at the push-rod.

Excessive movement may indicate lack of fluid or the need for bleeding; whenever the system is drained, bleeding will be required after filling.

Removing the Clutch
1. Remove the engine and transmission.
2. Remove the clutch housing bolts and withdraw the gearbox from the engine, taking care to support the gearbox until the first motion shaft is clear of the driven plate and release lever plate.
3. Loosen each of the hexagon bolts securing the clutch to the flywheel by slackening them a turn at a time until spring pressure is released. The clutch cover can now be disengaged from the flywheel dowels and the whole assembly lifted from the flywheel.

Place the cover on the bed of a press with the presure plate resting on wood blocks so arranged that the cover is left free to move downwards. Place a block or bar across the top of the cover, resting it on the spring bosses.

Apply pressure to the cover with the spindle of the press and, holding it under compression, remove the three adjusting nuts. The pressure from the press may now be released gradually until the clutch springs are fully extended.

While stripping down the cover-plate assembly, the parts should be marked so that they may be reassembled in the same relative position to each other, to ensure that the correct balance is maintained. When a new pressure plate is fitted it is essential that the complete cover and pressure plate assembly be accurately balanced, for which reason it is not a practical proposition to fit new pressure plates unless balancing facilities are available.

All parts are available for inspection when the cover is lifted off.

To remove the release levers, grasp the lever and eyebolt between the thumb and fingers so that the inner end of the lever and the threaded end of the eyebolt are as near together as possible, keeping the eyebolt pin seated in its socket in the lever. The strut can then be lifted over the ridge on the end of the lever, making it possible to lift the eyebolt off the pressure plate. It is advisable to replace any parts which show signs of wear.

Asembling the Clutch

Lay the pressure plate on the wood block on the bed of the press and place the springs on it in a vertical position seating them on their small locating bosses. Thoroughly clean all parts and renew any which show appreciable wear.

Assemble the release levers, eyebolt and the inner end of the lever as close together as possible. With the other hand insert the strut in the slots of the presure plate lug sufficiently to allow the plain end of the eyebolt to be inserted in the hole in the pressure plate. Move the strut upwards into the slots in the pressure plate lugs, over the ridge on the short end of the lever, and drop it into the grooves formed in the lever.

Lay the cover over the parts, taking care that the anti-rattle springs are in position and the springs are directly under the seats in the cover. Also make sure if using the original parts, that the eyebolts, eyebolt nuts, pressure plate lugs and cover are fitted in their correct relative positions, as marked when dismantling, to ensure correct balance being maintained.

Compress the springs. Take care to guide the eyebolts and the pressure plate lugs through the correct holes in the cover. Make sure also that the thrust springs remain correctly in their seats.

Replace the eyebolt nuts on the eyebolts and release the pressure compresing the cover assembly.

Adjusting the Release Levers

Satisfactory operation of the clutch is dependent upon accurate adjustment of the release levers, so that the pressure plate face is maintained parallel to the flywheel face. This cannot be accomplished by setting the levers parallel to the face of the release bearings after the clutch has been assembled to the flywheel, because of the variations in the thickness of the driven plate.

For accurate adjustment a gauge plate must be used.

Place the gauge on the flywheel in the position normally occupied by the driven plate, and mount the cover assembly on the flywheel in the same position as before dismantling. Tighten the holding screws a turn or two at a time when pulling against the spring pressure, otherwise the cover may be distorted. Before the cover is tightened down be sure that the gauge plate is properly centered and the three flat machined lugs are directly under the levers. The release lever plate must be detached from the levers before the levers are adjusted.

After the cover assembly has been mounted, a short straight-edge should be laid across the center boss of the special gauge plate and one nut adjusted until the lever just makes contact with the straight-edge. The other levers can then be set in turn by the same method. If carefully done, this setting will be within the permissible tolerance of .005 in.

The adjusting nut is then locked in position by punching the protruding flange of the nut into the slot of the eyebolt, thereby definitely locking it in position. When carrying out this operation take care not to upset the adjustments previously made.

After adjustment is completed, loosen the holding screws a turn or two at a time until the spring pressure is released, which will allow the clutch assembly and the gauge plate to be removed.

Refitting the Clutch
1. Position the driven plate assembly on the flywheel, taking care to place the larger-chamfered spline end of the driven plate hub away from the flywheel.
2. Centralize the driven plate by means of the special alignment bar, Part No. 18G276, which fits the splined bore of the driven plate hub and the pilot bearing in the flywheel. As an alternative a spare first motion shaft can be used
3. Locate the cover assembly on the flywheel dowels and secure with the bolts, tightening them a turn at a time by diagonal selection. Do not remove the clutch alignment bar until all the bolts are securely tightened.
4. Remove the clutch alignment bar and refit the gearbox. The weight of the gearbox must be supported during refitting in order to avoid strain on the shaft and distortion or displacement of the release plate or driven plate assembly.

Servicing the Clutch
As the clutch facings wear, the pressure plate moves closer to the flywheel face, and the outer or shorter ends of the release levers follow. This causes the inner or longer ends of the levers to travel farther towards the gearbox. As the release bearing moves rearwards it must result in pushing the piston in the clutch slave cylinder inwards. The piston then forces the excessive fluid back into the master cylinder via the compensating orifice.

Provided that the minimum 1/32 in. free movement is maintained between the clutch pedal push-rod and the master cylinder piston, this automatic compensation for wear will always take place.

Should there be no free movement at this point the master cylinder piston will not be allowed to return fully to its stop and therefore the compensating orifice will be cut off.

Excessive pedal movement causes coil binding of the springs and imposes an undue load on the bearing and on the crankshaft, causing excessive and rapid bearing wear. It therefore follows that the required pedal travel is the sum of the two movements.

1.. **The free movement,** or travel necessary to take up the clearance between the master cylinder push-rod and the master cylinder piston, provided to ensure that the clutch is fully engaged when the foot is removed from the pedal.

2.. **The effective movement,** or travel necessary to release the clutch, i.e. the amount of effective pedal movement necessary to move the release plate the distance required to free the clutch completely.

If any difficulty is experienced in freeing the clutch when the correct release movement is provided, on no acount should efforts be made to improve matters by attempting to increase the effective pedal travel. The actual cause of the trouble must be ascertained and rectified.

To obtain a clean release, the release lever plate should move a distance of 5/16 in. towards the flywheel.

Spring Pressure

A tolerance of not more than 10 to 15 lb. pressure is allowable on the compression load of the operating springs when at their assembled height, and all clutch springs are tested for this before assembly.

The clutch operating springs are affected by high clutch temperatures, as the pressure plate absorbs heat rapidly, the springs have only line contact, and a draught is continually passing under them when the engine is running.

Tolerances

Wear on the working faces of the driven plate is about .001 in. per 1,000 miles under normal running conditions. The accuracy of the alignment of the face of the driven plate must be within .015 in.

Driven Plates

It is important that neither oil nor grease should contact the clutch facings.

Lubrication of the splines of the driven plate is provided

at assembly only, when CS881 graphite grease or zinc-based "Keenol" is used.

It is essential to install a complete driven plate assembly when renewal of the friction surfaces is required. If the facings have worn to such an extent as to warrant renewal, then slight wear will have taken place on the splines, and also on the torque reaction springs and their seatings. The question of balance and concentricity is also involved. Under no circumstances is it satisfactory to repair or rectify faults in clutch driven plate centers, and we do not countenace this as manufacturers.

Condition of Clutch Facings in Service

It is natural to assume that a rough surface will give a higher frictional value against slipping than a polished one, but this is not necessarily correct. A roughened surface consists of small hills and dales, only the "high spots" of which make contact. As the amount of useful friction for the purpose of taking up the drive is dependent upon the area in actual contact, it is obvious that a perfectly smooth face is required to transmit the maximum amount of power for a given surface area.

Since the non-metallic facings of the moulded asbestos type have been introduced in service the polished surface is common, but it must not be confused with the glazed surface which is sometimes encountered due to conditions to be discussed subsequently. The ideally smooth or polished condition therefore provide proper surface contact, but a glazed surface entire alters the frictional value of the facing, and will result in excessive clutch slip. These two conditions might be simply illustrated by comparison between a piece of smoothly finished wood and one with a varnished surface; in the former the contact is made directly by the original material, whereas in the latter instance a film of dry varnish is interposed between the contact surfaces and actual contact is made by the varnish.

If the clutch has been in use for some little time under satisfactory conditions, the surface of the facings assumes a high polish through which the grain of the material can be seen clearly. This polished facing is of light color when in perfect condition.

Should oil in small quantities gain access to the clutch and find its way on the facings, it will be burnt off as a result of the heat generated by the slipping occurred under normal starting conditions. The burning of this small quantity of lubricant has the effect of gradually darkening the facings, but provided the polish of the facing remains such that the grain of the material can be distinguished clearly it has little effect on clutch performance.

Should increased quantities of oil obtain access to the facing, then one of these, may arise, depending upon the nature of the oil.

1. The oil may burn off and leave a carbon deposit on the surface of the facings, which assume a high glaze, producing further slip. This is a very definite, though very thin deposit, and in general it hides the grain of the material.

2. The oil may partially burn and leave a resinous deposit on the facings. This has a tendency to produce a fierce clutch, and may also cause excessive "spinning" due to the tendency of the face of the linings to adhere to the surface of the flywheel or pressure plate.

3. There may be a combination of conditions (1) and (2) which produces a tendency to "judder" on such engagement.

Still greater quantities of oil produce a dark and soaked appearance of the facings, and the result will be further slip, accompanied by fierceness or "juddering."

If the conditions enumerated above are experienced, the clutch driven plate should be replaced by a new one. **The cause of the presence of the oil must be traced and removed.** It is, of course, necessary for the clutch and flywheel to be cleaned out thoroughly before assembly.

Where the graphite release bearing ring is badly worn in service, a complete replacement assembly should be fitted, returning the old assembly for salvage of the metal cup. These graphite rings are inserted into their metal cup by heating the metal cup to a cherry red, then forcing the graphite ring into position. Immediately the ring is forced into position, the whole should be quenched in oil. Alignment of the thrust pad in relation to its face and the trunnions should be within .005 in.

In almost every case of rapid wear on the splines of the clutch driven plate, misalignment is responsible.

Looseness of the driven plate on the splined shaft results in noticeable backlash in the clutch. Misalignment also puts undue stress on the driven member, and may result in the hub breaking loose from the plate, with consequence total failure of the clutch.

It may be responsible for a fierce chattering or dragging of the clutch, which makes gear changing difficult. In cases of persistent difficulty it is advisable to check the flywheel for truth with a dial indicator. The dial reading should not vary more than .003 in. anywhere on the flywheel face.

THE CLUTCH COMPONENTS

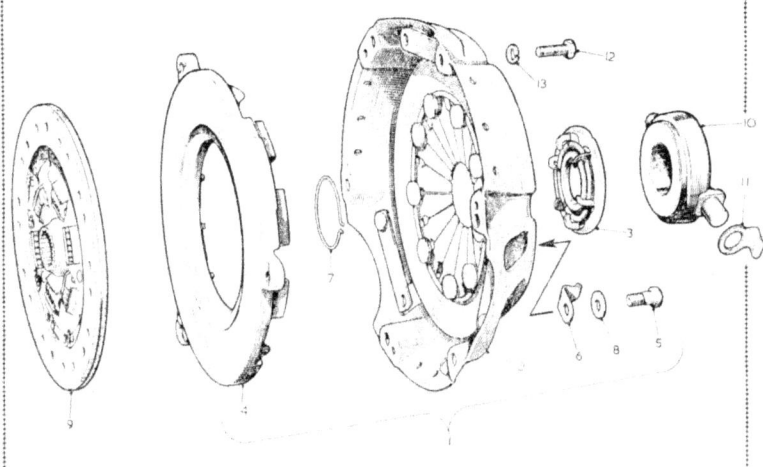

No.	Description	No.	Description
1.	Cover assembly.	8.	Washer—strap.
2.	Cover with straps and diaphragm spring.	9.	Plate assembly—driven.
3.	Plate—release.	10.	Bearing assembly—release.
4.	Plate—pressure.	11.	Retainer—bearing.
5.	Bolt—strap.	12.	Screw—clutch to flywheel.
6.	Clip—pressure plate.	13.	Washer for screw—spring.
7.	Circlip—release plate.		

THE CLUTCH CONTROL COMPONENTS

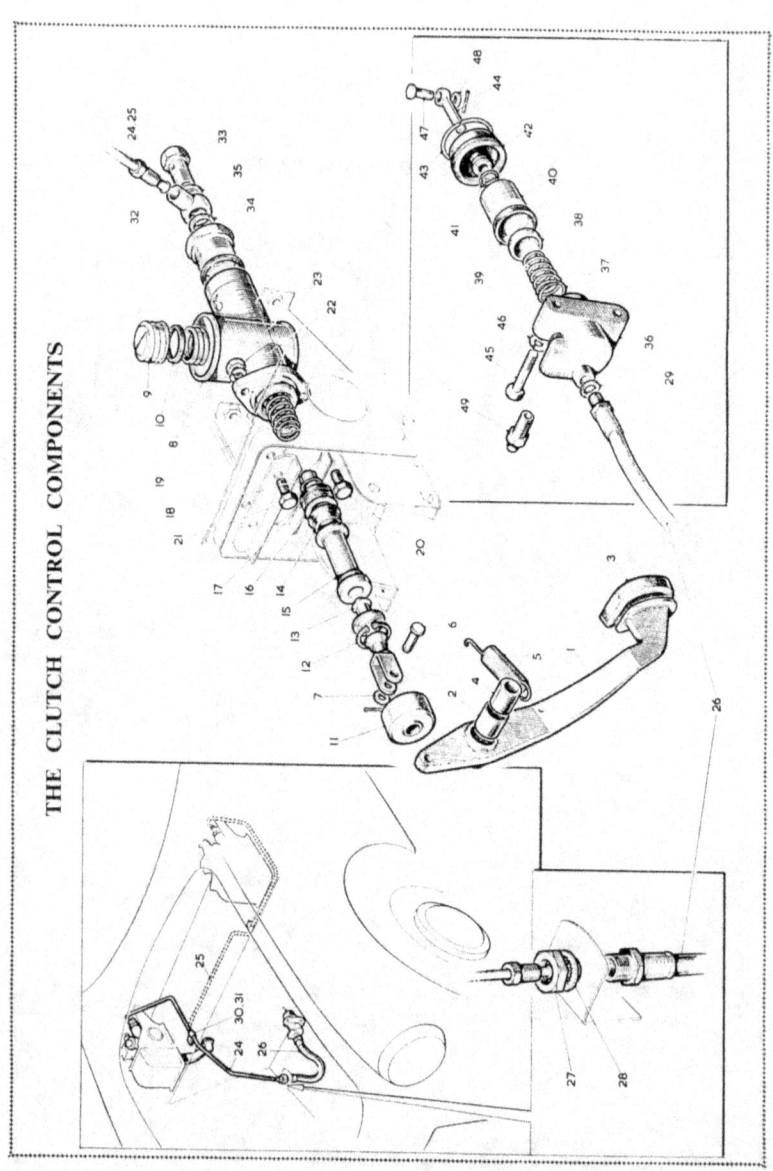

KEY TO THE CLUTCH CONTROL COMPONENTS

No.	Description
1.	Pedal—clutch.
2.	Bush.
3.	Pad—pedal (rubber).
4.	Tube—distance—clutch pedal.
5.	Spring—pedal pull-off.
6.	Pin—clevis—fork end to pedal.
7.	Washer—plain—for pin.
8.	Barrel and tank.
9.	Cap—filler.
10.	Seal—cap.
11.	Boot.
12.	Circlip.
13.	Rod—push.
14.	Cup—secondary.
15.	Piston.
16.	Washer—piston.
17.	Cup—main.
18.	Retainer—spring.
19.	Spring.
20.	Screw—cylinder to box.
21.	Screw—cylinder and stiffener to box.
22.	Washer—spring—for screw.
23.	Nut for screw.
24.	Pipe—master cylinder to hose.
25.	Pipe—master cylinder to hose.
26.	Hose—clutch.
27.	Locknut for hose.
28.	Washer—shakeproof.
29.	Gasket—hose to body.
30.	Clip—clutch pipe to bulkhead.
31.	Clip—clutch pipe to bulkhead.
32.	Connection—banjo.
33.	Bolt for banjo connection.
34.	Gasket.
35.	Gasket.
36.	Body.
37.	Spring—cup filler.
38.	Filler—piston cup.
39.	Cup piston.
40.	Piston.
41.	Clip—boot (small).
42.	Boot.
43.	Clip—boot (large).
44.	Rod—push.
45.	Bolt—cylinder to gearbox.
46.	Washer—spring—for bolt.
47.	Pin—clevis—cylinder to clutch fork.
48.	Washer—plain—for pin.
49.	Screw—bleeder.

Clutch Withdrawal Lever Pivot Bolt

On later types a modified clutch withdrawal lever pivot bolt (Part No. 11G3196) was fitted. The bolt was increased in diameter and has a shoulder to provide an abutment for the self-locking nut (Part No. LNZ.206) which supersedes the nut and spring washer previously fitted.

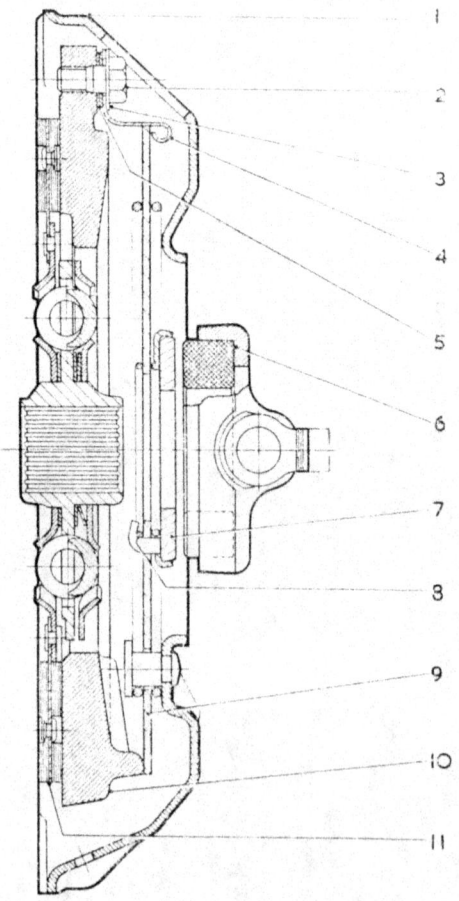

A section through the clutch

1. Cover.
2. Strap bolt.
3. Washer.
4. Clip.
5. Strap.
6. Release bearing.
7. Release plate
8. Circlip—release plate.
9. Diaphragm spring.
10. Pressure plate.
11. Driven plate.

A larger bearing bush for the withdrawal lever is needed and so a modified lever (Part No. 11G3193) complete with bush is fitted. The bosses on the front cover (Part No. 11G3197) are modified to take the larger diameter bolt.
The modified parts as a whole can be fitted to earlier vehicles.

MGB—Description
The clutch mechanism is hydraulically operated and consists of a driven plate, a pressure plate, and a diaphram spring and cover assembly. The cover is bolted to the flywheel and encloses the driven plate, pressure plate, and diaphram spring.
The hydraulic system comprises a master cylinder coupled to a slave cylinder which operates the clutch release mechanism

Clutch Assembly
The driven plate comprises a splined hub connected to a flexible steel plate by a spring mounting. The annular friction facings are riveted to the plate and damper springs are assembled around the hub to absorb power shocks and torsional vibration.
The diaphram spring is interposed between two annular rings which provide fulcrum points for the diaphram when it is flexed. The rings and the diaphram are located and secured to the cover by nine equally spaced rivets. Three clips that engage the outer edge of the diaphram are bolted to the pressure plate. The bolts pass through three straps which are riveted to the inside of the cover, the straps prevent the diaphram and the pressure plate from rotating in relation to the cover.
A release plate having an annular thrust ring is fitted to the outer face of the diaphram and is retained by a circlip. The release bearing is graphite and is mounted in a cup which fits into the fork of the clutch withdrawal lever. The cup is held in position by two spring retainers.

Removing.
Remove the engine.
Loosen each of the bolts securing the clutch assembly to the flywheel by slackening them a turn at a time until spring pressure is released. The clutch cover can now be disengaged from the dowels on the flywheel and the assembly removed.

Dismantling
1. Remove the circlip securing the release plate to the diaphram and lift the plate from the diaphram.
2. Unscrew the three screws securing the clips to the pressure plate, a turn at a time, until the diaphram contacts the cover. Remove the screws, clips, and washers and the pressure plate.

3. Rotate the release bearing spring retainers through 90 degrees and withdraw the bearing from the lever fork.

Assembling

Assemble is a reversal of the dismantling sequence, but ensure that the release bearing retainers are correctly located and that the spring clip bolts are tightened to the correct torque figure as given under **'GENERAL DATA'**.

Replacing

1. Position the driven plate assembly on the flywheel with the large end of the hub away from the flywheel.

Centralize the plate by using Service tool 18G680, which fits the splined hub of the driven plate and the pivot bearing in the flywheel. As an alternative a spare first motion shaft can be used.

2. Locate the cover assembly on the flywheel dowels and secure it with the bolts; tighten the bolts down a turn at a time by diametrical selection. Do not remove the centralizer until all bolts are securely tightened.

3. Remove the clutch centralizer and refit the engine. The weight of the gearbox must be supported during refitting in order to avoid strain on the first motion shaft and distortion or displacement of the release plate or driven plate assembly.

Driven Plates

It is important that neither oil nor grease should contact the clutch facings.

It is essential to install a complete driven plate assembly when the renewal of the friction surfaces is required. If the facings have worn to such an extent as to warrant renewal, then slight wear will have taken place on the splines, and also on the torque reaction springs and their seatings. The question of balance and concentricity is also involved. Under no circumstances is it satisfactory to repair or rectify faults in clutch driven plate centers.

Tolerances

Wear on the working faces of the driven plate is about .001 in. (.02 mm.) per 1,000 miles (1600 km.) under normal running conditions. The accuracy of the alignment of the face of the driven plate must be within .015 in. (.38 mm.).

Master Cylinder

The master cylinder has an integral-type supply tank in which the barrel passes through the tank. A piston contained within the barrel has a rubber main cup and is spring-loaded against its inner end; between the piston and cup is a thin washer which prevents the cup being drawn into the feed holes drilled around the head of the piston. The outer end of the piston carries a secondary cup and is formed with a depression to recieve the spherical end of the push-rod assembly. The push-rod has a piston stop that is retained in the body by a circlip. A rubber boot through which the push-rod passes is fitted to the end of the body.

At the opposite end of the barrel to the push-rod an end plug screws down against a gasket. This plug forms the outlet connection for the pipe line to the slave cylinder.

Removing
1. Remove the screws securing the brake and clutch master cylinder cover and take it off the cover.
2. Drain the fluid from the supply tank by attaching a rubber tube to the bleed screws in the clutch slave cylinder, opening the screw one full turn and then depressing the clutch pedal. Hold the pedal down and tighten the screw and then let the pedal return unassisted. Repeat this operation until the tank is empty.
3. Remove the split pin, washer, and clevis pin from the push-rod and disengage the clutch pedal lever.
4. Clean the pipe connection, disconnect the pipe line, and fit a plug to the end of the cylinder to prevent the entry of dirt.
5. Unscrew the fixing bolts and detach the master cylinder from the box assembly.

Dismantling
1. Detach the rubber boot from the barrel.
2. Depress the piston to relieve the load on the circlip then remove the circlip and the push-rod assembly.
3. Withdraw the piston, piston washer, main cup, spring retainer, and spring.
4. Remove the secondary cup by carefully stretching it over the end of the piston.

Examination.
Place all metal parts in a tray of clean Lockheed Super Heavy Duty Clutch and Brake Fluid. Dry them with a clean, non-fluffy cloth. Rubber components are to be examined for swollen or perished cups or other, signs of deterioration. Any suspect parts must be renewed.

Swill the main castings in industrial methylated spirit and thoroughly dry out before assembly.

Ensure that the by-pass ports are free of obstruction. The port is drilled with a 1/8 in. drill for half its length and then finished with a .028 in. drill.

Assembling

1. Dip all components in Lockheed Super Heavy Duty Clutch and Brake Fluid and assemble when wet.
2. Stretch the secondary cup over the piston with the lip of the cup facing the head of the piston. When the cup is in its groove work it round gently with the fingers to ensure that it is correctly seated.
3. Insert the return spring, largest diameter first, into the barrel and position the spring seat on the small-diameter end of the spring.

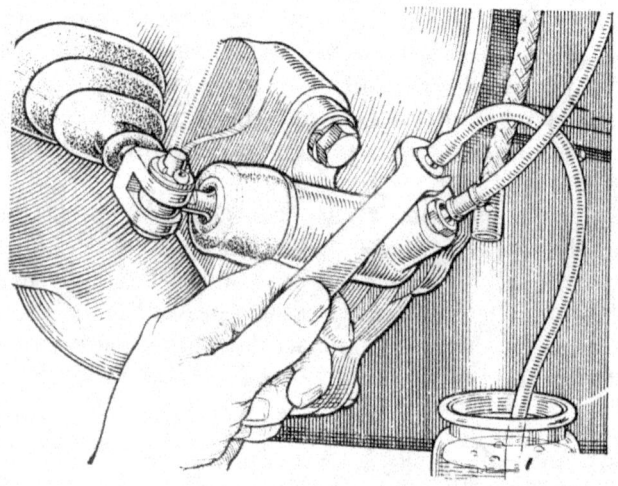

Bleeding the clutch hydraulic system at the slave cylinder

4. Assemble the main cup, piston washer, piston, and pushrod. When assembling the cups carefully enter the lip edge of the cups into the barrel first.
5. Depress the piston, position the piston stop, and retain it in the barrel with the circlip.
6. Place the rubber boot in position and fit the dust excluder.

Replacing

1. Refit the master cylinder to the master cylinder box and

secure it with the bolts. The long bolt passes through the stiffener plate.

2. Remove the dust excluder and fit the pipe connection to the master cylinder.

3. Refit the clutch pedal lever to the push-rod and secure it with the clevis pin, washer, and a new split pin.

4. Refit the master cylinder cover.

5. Fill the master cylinder and then prime and bleed the system.

Slave Cylinder

The slave cylinder incorporates two threaded connections for the feed hose and the bleed screw and accommodates in the body a piston, a cup, and a spring.

A rubber boot through which passes a push-rod is fitted to the body and is retained by two clips. The push-rod has an eye end which connects with the clutch withdrawal fork.

Removing

Drain the system.

Release the feed pipe from the cylinder and remove the two screws securing the cylinder to the clutch housing. The cylinder may be withdrawn, leaving the push-rod attached to the clutch withdrawal fork, or the rod may be detached from the fork.

Dismantling

Remove the rubber dust cover and with an air line blow out the piston and seal. Extract the spring and cup filler.

Examine all components and renew any that are suspect.

Assembling

Place the spring in the cylinder, followed by the filler, cup, and piston. Depress the piston with the push-rod and refit the rubber boot. Secure the boot to the rod with the small clip and then fit the boot to the cylinder and secure it with the large circlip.

Replacing

Fit the cylinder to the clutch housing and secure it with the two screws. Assemble the push-rod to the clutch withdrawal fork. Connect the feed line and fill, prime, and bleed the system.

Bleeding the Clutch System

Open the bleed screw on the slave cylinder three-quarters of a turn and attach a tube, immersing the open end in a clean receptacle containing a small quantity of the recommended hydraulic fluid. Fill the **master cylinder** reservoir with fluid. The use of Lockheed **Super Heavy Duty** Brake and Clutch Fluid is recommended.

THE GEARBOX

General Description MGA
The gearbox has four forward speeds and one reverse. Top gear is obtained by direct drive, third and second by gears in constant mesh, and first and reverse by sliding spur gears.

A sliding joint of the reverse spline type is fitted to the rear end of the third motion shaft and is lubricated from the gearbox.

Removing the Gearbox
1. Remove the engine and gearbox in unit.
2. Remove the starter motor and unscrew the bolts and nuts securing the bell housing and exhaust pipe support brackets and withdraw the gearbox and rear extension from the engine. Take care to keep the gearbox flange parallel with the crankcase face until the first motion shaft is clear of the clutch.

Dismantling the Gearbox
1. Extract the dipstick, drain plug and speedometer drive.
2. Unscrew the nuts and remove the gear lever remote control tower and point washer.
3. Unscrew and remove the six bolts and the rear extension cover and joint washer. Remove the interlock arm and bracket.
4. Remove the nut and seven set screws securing the gearbox extension to the gearbox. Pull the extension from the the gearbox, at the same time maneuvering the remote control shaft selector lever from the selectors.
5. Unscrew the three countersunk screws and the seven hexagon-headed set screws holding the gearbox cover; remove the cover and overshoot stop.
6. Cut the locking wire and unscrew the three change speed fork set screws.
7. Unscrew the two set screws and remove the shifter shaft locating block with shifter shafts from the gearbox; note the two dowels in the block; take care to catch the three selector balls and springs.
8. Withdraw the forks from the box in the following order—reverse, top and third, and first and second.
9. Unscrew the clutch lever pivot nut; screw out the pivot bolt and remove the lever with the thrust bearing.
10. Unscrew the nuts and remove the gearbox front cover; note the bearing shims between the cover and the bearing. Tap out the layshaft, allowing the gear cluster to rest in the bottom of the box

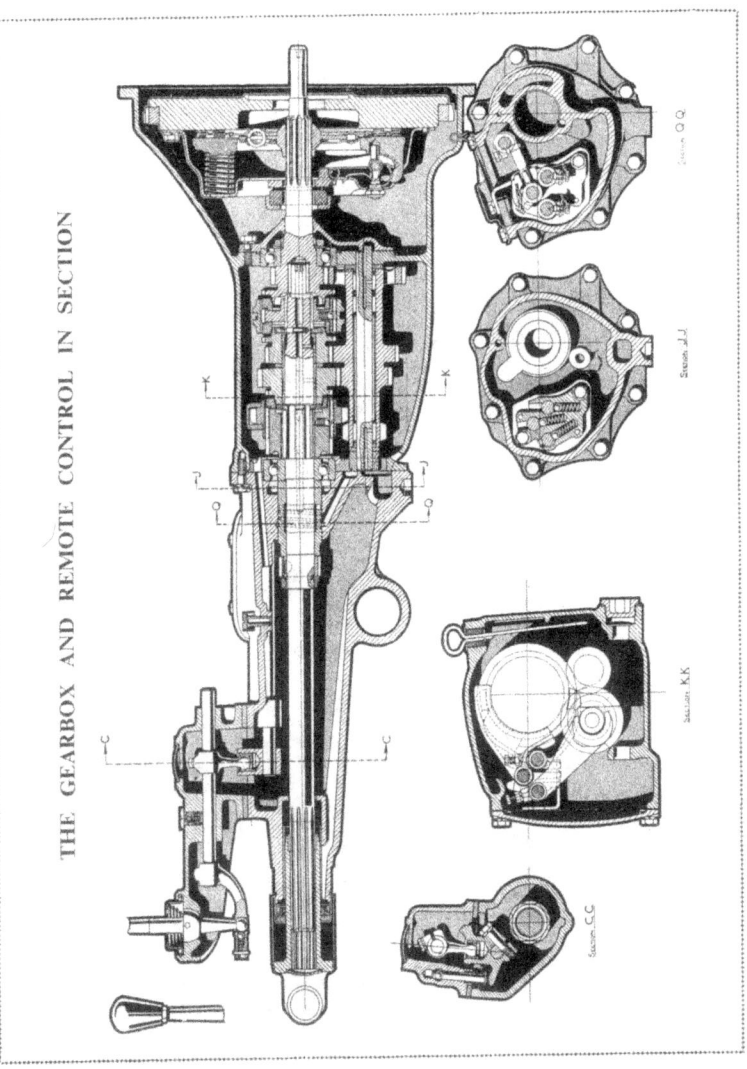

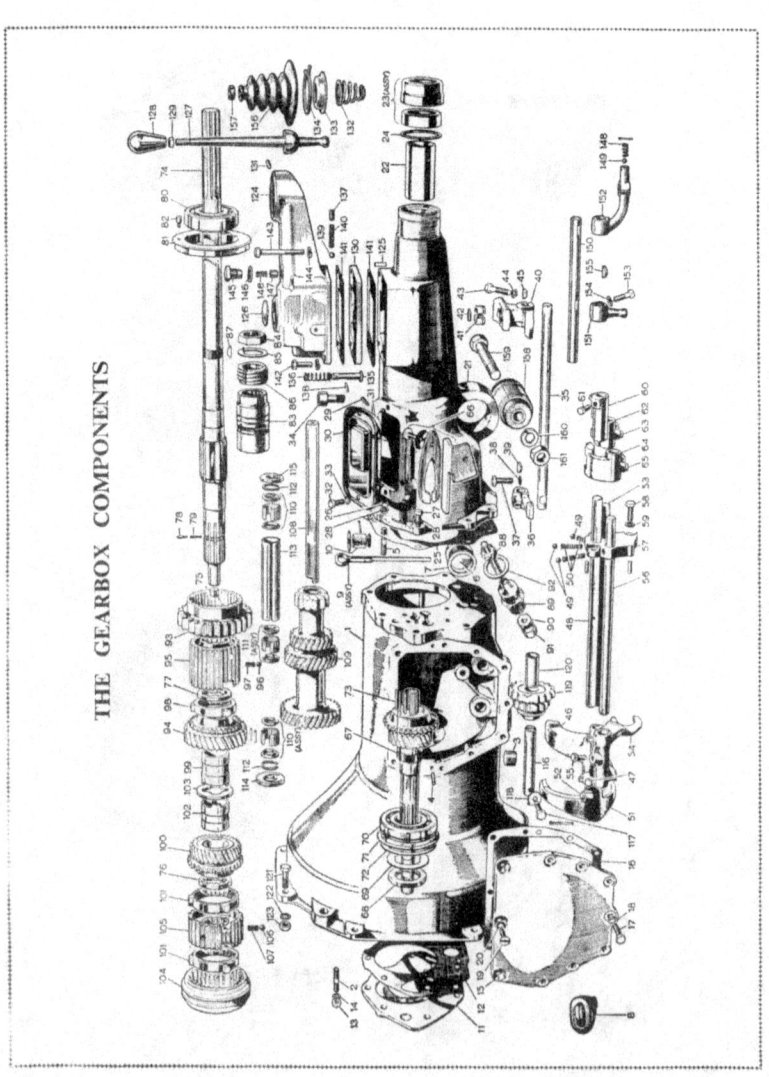

THE GEARBOX COMPONENTS

KEY TO THE GEARBOX COMPONENTS

No.	Description
1.	Casing—gearbox.
2.	Stud—front cover.
3.	Plug—drain.
4.	Dowel—side cover to gearbox.
5.	Stud—gearbox extension.
6.	Plug—blanking.
7.	Joint washer—blanking plug.
8.	Dust cover—clutch withdrawal lever.
9.	Dipstick.
10.	Felt.
11.	Cover—front.
12.	Joint—front cover.
13.	Nut—front cover studs.
14.	Spring washer—front cover stud.
15.	Cover—side.
16.	Joint—side cover.
17.	Set screw—side cover.
18.	Spring washer—side cover screw.
19.	Countersunk screw—side cover.
20.	Shakeproof washer—countersunk screw.
21.	Extension—gearbox.
22.	Bush.
23.	Oil seal.
24.	Joint washer—oil seal.
25.	Joint extension to gearbox.
26.	Nut—gearbox extension stud.
27.	Set screw—gearbox extension.
28.	Spring washer—stud and set screw.
29.	Plug—taper—gearbox extension.
30.	Cover—extension side.
31.	Joint—extension side cover.
32.	Set screw—extension side cover.
33.	Spring washer.
34.	Breather assembly.
35.	shaft—remote control.
36.	Lever—selector—front.
37.	Set screw—front lever.
38.	Spring washer—set screw.
39.	Key—selector lever.
40.	Lever—selector—rear.
41.	Bush—rear selector lever.
42.	Circlip—lever bush.
43.	Set screw—rear lever.
44.	Spring washer—set screw.
45.	Key—selector lever.
46.	Fork—1st and 2nd speed.
47.	Screw—fork locating.
48.	Shaft—1st and 2nd speed fork.
49.	Ball—shaft.
50.	Spring—ball.
51.	Fork—3rd and 4th speed.
52.	Screw—fork locating.
53.	Shaft—3rd and 4th speed fork.
54.	Fork—reverse.
55.	Screw—fork locating.
56.	Shaft—reverse fork.
57.	Block—shaft locating.
58.	Set screw—block to casing.
59.	Spring washer—block screw.
60.	Selector—1st and 2nd gear.
61.	Screw—selector locating.
62.	Selector—3rd and 4th gear.
63.	Screw—selector locating.
64.	Selector—reverse gear.
65.	Screw—reverse gear selector.
66.	Interlock arm complete.
67.	Shaft—1st pinion.
68.	Nut—shaft.
69.	Lock washer.
70.	Bearing—ball—shaft.
71.	Spring ring—bearing.
72.	Shim—bearing.
73.	Rollers—needle—shaft.
74.	Shaft—3rd motion.
75.	Restrictor—oil.
76.	Washer—thrust—front.
77.	Washer—thrust—front.
78.	Peg—thrust washer—front.
79.	Spring—peg.
80.	Bearing—rear—3rd motion shaft.
81.	Housing—bearing.
82.	Peg—locating.
83.	Distance-piece — speedometer gear.
84.	Nut—shaft and speedometer gear.
85.	Lock washer.
86.	Gear—speedometer drive.
87.	Key—gear.
88.	Pinion—speedometer drive.
89.	Bush—pinion.
90.	Oil seal—pinion.
91.	Ring—oil seal retaining.
92.	Joint—bush to rear cover.
93.	Gear—1st speed.
94.	Gear—2nd speed.
95.	Synchroniser—2nd speed.
96.	Ball—synchroniser.
97.	Spring—ball.
98.	Baulk ring—2nd speed gear.
99.	Bush—2nd speed gear.
100.	Gear—3rd speed.
101.	Baulk ring—3rd and 4th gear.
102.	Bush—3rd speed gear.
103.	Ring—interlocking—2nd and 3rd bushes.
104.	Coupling—sliding—3rd and 4th speed.
105.	Synchroniser—3rd and 4th speed.
106.	Ball—synchroniser.
107.	Spring—ball.
108.	Layshaft.
109.	Gear unit—layshaft.
110.	Bearing—needle roller—layshaft—outer.
111.	Bearing—needle roller—layshaft—inner.
112.	Spring ring—needle rollers.
113.	Distance-piece—bearing.
114.	Washer—thrust—front.
115.	Washer—thrust—rear.
116.	Shaft—reverse.
117.	Screw—locking—shaft.
118.	Lock washer—screw.
119.	Gear—reverse.
120.	Bush.
121.	Bolt—gearbox to mounting plate.
122.	Washer—spring.
123.	Nut—mounting plate bolt.
124.	Tower—remote control.
125.	Dowel—remote control tower.
126.	Core plug—tower.
127.	Lever—change speed.
128.	Knob—change speed lever
129.	Locknut—change speed lever knob.
130.	Stop plate.
131.	Snap—change speed ball.
132.	Spring—change speed lever
133.	Cover—ball spring.
134.	Circlip—ball spring cover.
135.	Plunger—reverse selector.
136.	Spring—reverse plunger.
137.	Plug—reverse plunger.
138.	Dowel—reverse plunger.
139.	Ball—reverse plunger.
140.	Spring—reverse plunger detent.
141.	Gasket—control tower.
142.	Bolt—short—tower.
143.	Bolt—long—tower.
144.	Spring washer.
145.	Plug—ball retaining—box cover.
146.	Washer—plug.
147.	Plunger.
148.	Spring—plunger.
149.	Ball—selector lever.
150.	Shaft—remote control.
151.	Lever—front—selector.
152.	Lever—rear—selector.
153.	Set screw—front and rear lever.
154.	Spring washer.
155.	Key.
156.	Draught excluder—rubber—gear lever.
157.	Ring—lever draught excluder.
158.	Flexible bush—rear engine mounting.
159.	Bolt—rear mounting bush.
160.	Washer—spring.
161.	Nut—rear mounting bush bolt.

11. Unscrew the retaining set screw and remove the reverse shaft and gear.
12. Withdraw the mainshaft assembly to the rear.
13. Withdraw the first motion shaft complete with 18 spigot needle rollers, using tool No. 68894 if necessary.
14. Lift out the layshaft gear cluster and the two thrust washers.

The arrow indicates the third speed thrust washer and locating peg. Note the hole in the gear cone

Rear Extension

Release the front and rear selector levers from the remote control shaft by removing the clamping screws and sliding the levers from the rod. Extract the keys from the shaft and withdraw the remote control shaft from the rear extension.

Dismantling the Third Motion Shaft

1. Remove the following items in this order: baulk ring; synchromesh sleeve and hub; second baulk ring. If the synchromesh sleeve is removed from the hub take care not to lose the three locating balls and springs which will be released in consequence.
2. Press down the third speed gear cone thrust washer plunger; rotate the thrust washer to align its splines with those on the

shaft and remove the washer.
3. Withdraw the third speed gear and its splined bush.
4. Withdraw the bush interlocking washer to release the second speed gear with its bush and baulk ring.
5. Remove the thrust washer from the splines on the shaft and withdraw the first and second speed hub and gear; if necessary slide the gear from the hub, taking care not to lose the three balls and springs.
6. Tap up the locking tab and unscrew the retaining nut; withdraw the washer, speedometer drive gear and key and the distance sleeve from the shaft.
7. Press the rear bearing and housing from the shaft.

Assembling the Third Motion Shaft
Assemble from the front end.
1. Locate the rear thrust washer on the front end of the splines, ground faces to the front.
2. Push the longer brass bush up to the splines with the dog towards the front.
Note.—This bush must be fitted so that the oil hole is in line with the one in the shaft and the cut-away portion of the third speed splined bush will be over the locating peg hole when the dogs of the two bushes are engaged with the bush interlocking washer.
3. Fit the second speed baulk ring and gear onto the bush with the plain side of the gear towards the front.
4. Slide on the bush interlocking ring and the shorter splined bush, locating the dogs of both bushes in the interlocking ring.
5. Insert the spring and locating peg into the holes in the shaft.
6. Fit the third speed gear onto the bush with the cone towards the front.
7. Thread on the front thrust washer, machined face towards the gear, while holding down the locating peg with a thin punch through the hole in the gear cone, and push the washer over it; turn the washer to allow the locating peg to engage in one of the splines.
8. Fit the three springs and balls to the third speed synchronizer and push on the synchronizer sleeve (striking dog).
9. Push on the top and third gear synchromesh assembly hub with its two baulk rings. The plain side of the hub faces the rear.
Assemble the following items from the rear:
1. Insert the three balls and springs in the second gear hub and push the synchronizer sleeve (striking dog) into position on the hub.

2. Fit the first speed gear and synchromesh hub assembly, and the baulk ring, to the splines on the shaft.

3. Press the rear bearing into its housing and fit it to the shaft, outer flange of the housing to the rear.

4. Push on the distance sleeve, speedometer drive gear and key, lock washer and nut.

Layshaft Gear

The assembly sequence of the layshaft bearings is as follows: a circlip at the rear, a needle race, a single long distance tube, a circlip, a needle race, a circlip, a needle race, a circlip, two races being fitted at the front end and one at the rear.

When assembling, fit a circlip to the innermost groove in the gear, pushing it in from the front, or large gear, end.

Hold the layshaft vertically in the vice, stepped end downwards.

Smear the shaft with grease and assemble a roller bearing on the shaft against the vice jaws and then slide the gear cluster over the shaft and the bearing with the large gear downwards.

Remove the shaft from the vice and push the bearing into the gear against the circlip. Fit a retaining circlip and follow with the end roller bearing assembly and retaining circlip.

Slide the distance tube into the other end of the gear, follow by the other end bearing and circlip. Withdraw the shaft from the gear.

Assembling the First Motion Shaft

Fit the bearing to the shaft with the spring ring away from the gear. Replace the lock washer and tighten the retaining nut; bend over the locking tab. Fit the shaft to the housing. Do not fit the front end cover until the layshaft has been fitted.

Assembling the Rear Extension

Locate the remote control shaft in the rear extension.

Fit the front and rear selector levers to the remote control shaft; note that they are secured and located by keys and set screws.

Fit the rear extension to the gearbox, locating the control shaft front selector lever in the shifter rod selectors.

Replace the interlock arm on the rear extension side cover flange and refit the cover.

Assembling the Gearbox

1. Place the layshaft gear in the box complete with end thrust washers but do not fit the shaft.

2. Assemble and replace the **first** motion shaft, and replace

the 18 needle-roller bearings.

3. Insert the third motion shaft from the rear; use the gasket fitted between the box and rear extension to position the dowel and bearing housing. Push home the shaft, the rear bearing and housing, and enter the spigot in the needle-roller race of the first motion shaft.

4. Fit the layshaft and thrust washers. Line up the cutaway portion of the front end with the layshaft locating groove in th front cover.

5. Fit the reverse gear and shaft; tighten and lock the set screw.

6. Refit the front end cover, replacing the bearing shims that were removed on dismantling.

7. Refit the clutch lever and fork.

8. Fit the selectors to the shifter shaft rear ends.

9. Bolt the shifter shaft locating block to the rear face of the gearbox; replace the balls and springs and insert the shifter shafts.

10. Position the gear change forks in the box in the following sequences: reverse first and second, third and top. Push the shifter shafts into the box and through the forks; insert, tighten, and wire up the set screws.

11. Position the selectors on the rear ends of the shifter shafts; insert, tighten, and wire up the set screws.

12. Refit the gearbox rear extension.

13. Locate the change speed gate in the gearbox and fit the side cover, using a new joint as necessary.

14. Screw in the speedometer drive gear assembly, plugs and breather.

15. The remote control assembly is fitted to the gearbox and the gearbox filled with oil, after the power unit is installed in the chassis.

Modified Gearbox Front End Cover

Commencing at Engine No. 7981, and a few earlier gearboxes, a modified gearbox front end cover was introduced. The new cover is fitted with an oil seal to prevent the possibility of oil leaking into the clutch housing. There is also a venting duct in the cover necessitating modified fork rods.

The parts may not be fitted to earlier cars.

The new part numbers are:

Gearbox front end cover 1H3137
Gearbox cover oil seal 1H3138
Reverse fork rod 11G3137
First and second fork rod 11G3079
Third and fourth fork rod 11G3140

Refitting the Front Cover

It is essential that the front cover should be concentric with the first motion shaft in order to avoid oil leaks. This is effected as follows.

Mount the cover, less oil seal, onto the gearbox, and push right home on the studs. Ensure that the cover is free to move in all directions on the studs. If not, the points at which the holes bind on the studs must be relieved until the cover is free to 'float'. Remove the cover and refit the oil seal, using Service tool 18G134 with adaptor 18G134Q.

Fit Service tool 18G598 to the bore of the front cover, and push it in until it is tight. Lightly oil the seal, and carefully fit the front cover, retaining the centralizer 18G598 firmly in position. Fit all spring washers and nuts and tighten them finger-tight only. Using a suitable socket spanner, tighten all nuts, by diametric selection, one half-turn at a time until the nuts are fully tightened. Remove the centralizer.

Modified Gearbox

Coincident with the introduction of the 15GD series power unit the following changes were incorporated in the gearbox.

The main gearbox casing was modified to accommodate the new high position of the starter motor on the engine. The gearbox extension was also changed to suit the new gearbox third motion shaft. The propeller shaft is bolted to a flange which is splined to the gearbox third motion shaft and secured by a nut and spring washer. This arrangement supersedes that of the splined sliding joint for the propeller shaft on the third motion shaft.

To remove the gearbox, remove the power unit and detach the gearbox from the engine as outlined previously.

The new gearbox is not interchangeable with that previously fitted.

Modified Gearbox Assemblies

Three modifications to the gearbox were introduced to prevent automatic disengagement of third gear. If trouble of this nature is experienced remove the gearbox from the car and check the following points:

1. Follow the gearbox dismantling procedure as far as removing the shift shaft locating block from the gearbox casing. Remove the third and fourth gear shifting rod from the locating block, being careful to catch the ball and spring that will be released. The free length of this spring should be between 18 and 20 lb. when the spring is compressed to .75 in. As these springs adopt

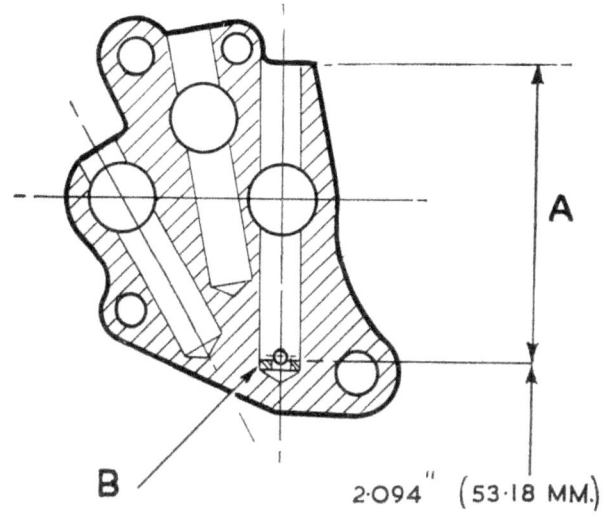

The fork locating block in section, showing a washer (B) ·063 in. (1·59 mm.) thick fitted to provide the revised bore depth (A) of 2·094 in. (53·18 mm.)

a permanent set in service without necessarily affecting the poundage, it is advisable to ensure that the spring is in order by checking its poundage.
2. Check the depth of the bore in the fork rod locating block, using a depth gauge micrometer. This dimension should be 2.094 in. On unmodified gearboxes the depth was 2:157 in. In such cases fit a packing washer .063 in. thick in the bottom of the bore.
3. Check the depth of the detent notches in the third and fourth speed selector fork rod. Give particular attention to the third speed notch nearest the center of the rod. It is not intended that the smaller central (neutral position) notch should be included in this check. Measure the diameter of the detent ball, using a micrometer. Place the ball in each of the deeper notches in turn and measure the distance (C). If this measurement is greater than .724 in. a new fork rod providing dimension (C) in both the third and fourth speed notches should be selected and fitted. The depth of these two detent notches was increased by .018 in. on later gear boxes to give the dimension shown.

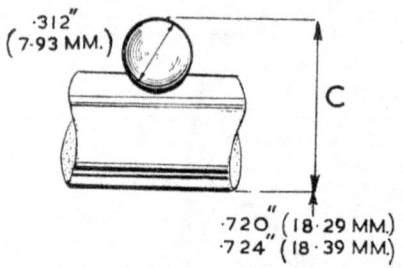

The third and fourth speed fork rod with detent ball
placed in a notch for measurement of distance (C)

4. Following the procedure given remove the third motion shaft (mainshaft) assembly from the gearbox. Remove the top and third gear synchromesh sleeve and hub with its baulk rings. Press down the third speed gear thrust washer locating plunger. Turn the thrust washer to align its splines with those on the shaft and remove the washer. Withdraw the third speed gear and its bronze bush and baulk ring. Check with a micrometer the outside diameter of the bronze bushes. This should be 1.3115 to 1.312 in. Ensure that this dimension is constant throughout the length of each bush. If the bushes are worn fit a new phosphor-bronze bushes (Part Nos. 11G3028 and 11G3029). These were reintroduced at Gearbox No. 24001 to replace the sintered bronze bushes used previously.

Reassemble the third motion shaft (mainshaft), and immerse the bronze bushes in warm oil to facilitate fitting.

Reassemble the gearbox.

MGB—General Description

The gearbox has four forward gears and a reverse gear. Top, third, and second gear engagement are affected by synchromesh hubs with direct drive for top gear and constant-mesh gears on the layshaft and main shaft for third and second gears. First and reverse are sliding spur gears.

A combined dipstick and filler plug is housed in the top of the gearbox and a drain plug in the bottom.

The bell housing is integral with the gearbox and accommodates the clutch release mechanism and the starter motor driving pinion.

An extension bolted to the rear end of the gearbox contains the gear selector mechanism.

The gearbox is bolted at the front end to the engine mounting plate and is supported at the rear by two rubber mountings that locate on the rear cross-member mounting brackets. An engine stay-rod attached to the under side of the rear extension is anchored to the rear cross-member.

Periodically inspect the gearbox for cleanliness, security, and external leakage. Leaks from the covers can normally be rectified by tightening the securing screws, or where the leakage is persistent, by renewing the cover gasket.

Excessive leakage from the bell housing or rear extension may be due to overfilling the gearbox or to faulty seals. If the seals are at fault they should be renewed.

Every 3,000 miles top up the oil level in the gearbox to the 'HIGH' mark on the dipstick. Do not overfill.

Every 6,000 miles remove the drain plug and drain off the old oil. Replace the drain plug and refill with fresh, clean oil.

The lubrication instructions are given in Section P.

Removing the Gearbox

1. Prepare the engine for removal from the car and take the weight off the engine.
2. Drain the oil from the gearbox.
3. Disconnect and remove the propeller shaft and disconnect the speedometer pinion drive.
4. Disconnect the clutch slave cylinder push-rod from the clutch withdrawal lever and the slave cylinder from the clutch housing. Tie the cylinder clear of the gearbox.
5. Remove the screws securing the rear cross-member to the body and lower the engine and gearbox until the gearbox rests on the fixed body cross-member.
6. Release the engine stay-rod bracket from the rear cross-member and remove the four nuts and washers securing the gearbox rear rubber mountings to the cross-member. Withdraw the rear cross-member from the body.
7. Remove the gear lever knob and the rubber cover from the tunnel. Remove the remote-control tower complete with gear lever from the gearbox.
8. Ease the assembly forward until it is clear of the fixed body cross-member and then tilt the assembly and lift it from the car.
9. Remove the screws securing the gearbox to the engine rear mounting plate and separate the gearbox from the engine.
10. Remove the stiffnut **and washer** from the clutch withdrawal

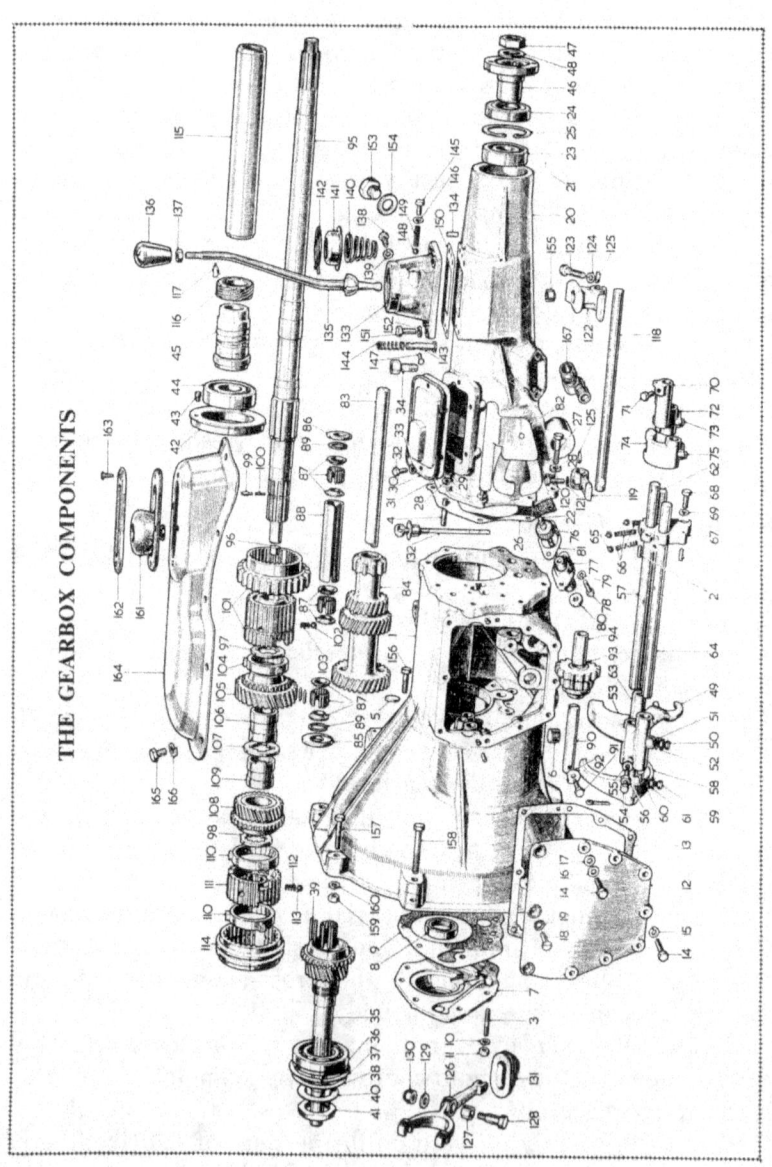

KEY TO THE GEARBOX COMPONENTS

No.	Description
1.	Casing assembly.
2.	Dowel—locating block to gearbox.
3.	Stud—front cover.
4.	Stud—rear extension.
5.	Plug—welch casing.
6.	Plug—drain.
7.	Cover assembly—front.
8.	Seal—oil.
9.	Joint washer—front cover to casing.
10.	Washer—spring—stub—front cover to casing.
11.	Nut—stud.
12.	Cover—gearbox side.
13.	Joint washer—side cover to casing.
14.	Screw—gearbox side cover.
15.	Washer—spring—screw.
16.	Washer—plain—screw.
17.	Washer—fibre—screw.
18.	Screw—countersunk—gearbox side cover.
19.	Washer—shakeproof—screw.
20.	Extension—rear.
21.	Plug—taper—rear extension.
22.	Button—thrust—speedometer.
23.	Bearing—rear extension.
24.	Seal—oil—rear extension.
25.	Circlip—oil seal.
26.	Joint washer—extension to casing.
27.	Screw—extension to casing.
28.	Washer—spring—screw.
29.	Nut—stud—rear extension.
30.	Cover—side—rear extension.
31.	Joint washer—side cover to extension.
32.	Screw—side cover to extension.
33.	Washer—spring—screw.
34.	Breather assembly.
35.	Shaft—first motion.
36.	Bearing.
37.	Ring—spring—bearing.
38.	Shim—first motion shaft—.002 in. (.051 mm.).
39.	Roller—needle—first motion shaft.
40.	Washer—locking—first motion shaft nut.
41.	Nut—first motion shaft.
42.	Housing—rear bearing.
43.	Peg—locating—rear bearing housing.
44.	Bearing—rear—third motion shaft.
45.	Distance piece assembly—speedometer gear to rear bearing.
46.	Flange—third motion shaft.
47.	Nut—third motion shaft flange.
48.	Washer—spring—nut.
49.	Fork—reverse.
50.	Screw—reverse fork locating.
51.	Washer—shakeproof—screw.
52.	Nut—screw—fork locating.
53.	Fork—first and second speed.
54.	Screw—fork locating.
55.	Washer—shakeproof—screw.
56.	Screw—fork locating.
57.	Rod—first and second speed fork.
58.	Fork—third and fourth speed.
59.	Screw—fork locating.
60.	Washer—shakeproof—screw.
61.	Nut—screw—fork locating.
62.	Rod—third and fourth speed fork.
63.	Distance piece—third and fourth speed fork rod.
64.	Rod—reverse fork.
65.	Ball—fork locating.
66.	Spring—locating ball.
67.	Block—sliding shaft locating.
68.	Screw—locating block to gearbox.
69.	Nut—screw—fork locating.
70.	Selector—first and second gear.
71.	Screw—selector locating.
72.	Selector—third and fourth gear.
73.	Screw—selector locating.
74.	Selector—reverse gear.
75.	Screw—selector locating.
76.	Pinion—speedometer.
77.	Bush—speedometer pinion bush.
78.	Screw—speedometer pinion bush.
79.	Washer—lock—screw.
80.	Seal—oil—speedometer pinion.
81.	Joint washer—speedometer pinion bush assembly—interlocking.
82.	Arm assembly—interlocking.
83.	Layshaft.
84.	Gear unit—layshaft.
85.	Washer—thrust—front—laygear.
86.	Washer—thrust—rear—.154 to .156 in. (3.912 to 3.962 mm.).
87.	Roller—needle bearing—layshaft.
88.	Tube—distance—laygear bearing.
89.	Ring—spring—layshaft.
90.	Shaft—reverse.
91.	Gear—reverse shaft.
92.	Washer—locking screw.
93.	Gear assembly—reverse.
94.	Bush—reverse gear.
95.	Shaft—third motion.
96.	Restrictor—oil.
97.	Washer—thrust—rear—third motion shaft.
98.	Washer—thrust—front—.1565 to .1575 in. (3.962 to 3.9837 mm.).
99.	Peg—thrust washer.
100.	Spring—peg.
101.	First speed wheel and synchronizer assembly.
102.	Ball—synchronizer.
103.	Spring—synchronizer ball.
104.	Baulk ring—second speed gear.
105.	Gear—second speed.
106.	Bush—second speed mainshaft gear.
107.	Ring—interlocking—second and third gear bushes.
108.	Wheel—third speed.
109.	Bush—third speed gear.
110.	Baulk ring—third and fourth speed gear.
111.	Synchronizer—third and fourth speed.
112.	Spring—synchronizer ball.
113.	Ball—synchronizer.
114.	Coupling—sliding—third and fourth speed.
115.	Distance piece—third motion shaft.
116.	Gear—speedometer.
117.	Key—speedometer gear.
118.	Shaft—remote-control (rear extension).
119.	Lever—selector—front.
120.	Screw—selector lever—front.
121.	Washer—shakeproof—screw.
122.	Lever—selector—rear.
123.	Screw—selector lever—rear.
124.	Washer—spring—screw.
125.	Key—selector lever.
126.	Lever—clutch withdrawal.
127.	Bush—withdrawal lever.
128.	Bolt—clutch withdrawal lever.
129.	Washer—bolt.
130.	Nut—stiff—bolt.
131.	Cover—dust—clutch withdrawal lever.
132.	Indicator—oil level—gearbox.
133.	Tower—remote-control.
134.	Dowel—remote-control tower.
135.	Lever—change speed.
136.	Knob—change speed lever.
137.	Locknut—change speed knob.
138.	Pin—locating—change speed lever.
139.	Washer—spring.
140.	Spring—change speed lever.
141.	Cover—ball spring.
142.	Circlip—ball spring cover.
143.	Plunger—reverse selector.
144.	Spring—reverse plunger.
145.	Screw—reverse plunger spring.
146.	Washer—spring—screw.
147.	Pin—locating—reverse plunger.
148.	Ball—reverse plunger.
149.	Spring—reverse plunger detent.
150.	Gearbox—control tower.
151.	Screw—tower to extension.
152.	Washer—spring—screw.
153.	Plug—reverse light switch hole.
154.	Joint washer—plug.
155.	Bush—change speed lever.
156.	Bolt—gearbox to mounting plate.
157.	Bolt—gearbox to mounting plate.
158.	Bolt—gearbox to mounting plate.
159.	Nut—bolt.
160.	Washer—spring—bolt.
161.	Grommet—gear lever.
162.	Retainer—gear lever grommet.
163.	Screw—retainer to cover.
164.	Cover—gearbox remote-control.
165.	Screw—cover to tunnel.
166.	Washer—spring.
167.	Box—speedometer drive adaptor.

lever bolt and take the dust cover and lever from the clutch housing.

11. Remove the nut, spring washer, and pin from the engine stay-rod and the stay-rod from the gearbox.

12. If the stay-rod and bracket are to be dismantled remove the rear nut and washer and slide off the plates, buffers, brackets, and distance tube. Separate the plates, buffers, and brackets from the distance tube.

Dismantling the Gearbox

1. Remove the dipstick, drain plug, and speedometer drive pinion.
2. Using Service tool 18G2, remove the propeller shaft flange.
3. Remove the remote-control tower, the gearbox extension side cover, and the interlock plate and bracket.
4. Slacken the locating screw on the remote-control front selector lever, unscrew the screws and nuts securing the extension to the gearbox, and remove the extension.
5. Retain the remote-control selector lever, which will fall free as the extension is withdrawn. Withdraw the shaft and rear selector lever from the rear extension and remove the selector lever from th shaft; withdraw the split bush and circlip from the selector.
6. Remove the three countersunk screws and seven hexagon headed screws from the gearbox side cover and lift off the cover and gasket.
7. Cut the locking wire, unscrew the three selector locating screws, and remove the selectors.
8. Unscrew the shift shaft locating block screws and remove the block from the rear face of the gearbox. Retain the three balls and springs which will be released when the block is withdrawn from the shafts. Two dowels on the block locate it on the rear face of the gearbox.
9. Release the locknuts and remove the fork locating screws and star washers from the change speed forks. Slide out the shafts and remove the forks in the following order: fourth and third speed, second and first speed.
10. If difficulty is experienced in removing the shafts remove the front cover and use a soft drift to tap the shafts out from the front of the box.
11. Remove the nuts and washers securing the front cover and then remove the cover, gasket, and the first motion shaft bearing shims. Do not remove the oil seal from the cover unless it has to be renewed.
12. Unscrew the reverse **shaft locating** screw and remove the

shaft and gear.
13. Using a soft drift, tap out the layshaft from the front of the box and allow the laygear to rest in the bottom of the box.
14. Ease the rear bearing housing from the rear of the gearbox and withdraw the third motion shaft assembly.
15. Withdraw the first motion shaft from the front of the gearbox. A soft drift may be used to tap the shaft from the inside of the box.
16. Reassemble the laygear on its shaft and check the end-float of the gear.
17. Remove the layshaft, laygear, and thrust washers.

Dismantling and Assembling the Control Tower

Do not dismantle the control tower unless worn or broken parts are to be renewed.
1. Remove the ball spring cover circlip to ease the tension on the spring and then remove the two change speed lever locating pins. Withdraw the lever, and from it remove the knob, cover, and spring.
2. From the rear of the control tower unscrew the reverse plunger detent screw and remove the reverse plunger detent spring and ball.
3. From the side of the tower remove the reverse plunger locating pin and retain the plunger and spring that will be released from inside the tower.

Assembly is a reversal of the dismantling sequence, but care must be taken to ensure that the front and rear selectors are correctly lined up and that the clinch bolts pass across the flats on the remote-control shaft.

When fitting a new pin to retain the reverse selector plunger ensure that the plunger is depressed sufficiently enough to permit the pin to engage the flats on the plunger.

Dismantling and Assembling the Rear Extension

1. Remove the rear selector lever clamp bolt, lever, and the Woodruff key and withdraw the shaft from the rear extension. Do not dismantle the rear extension any further unless the oil seal and/or bearing has to be renewed, in which case proceed as follows.
2. Using Service tool 18G389 and 18G389C, remove the rear oil seal.
3. Remove the rear extension bearing circlip and press out the bearing.

Assembly is a reversal of the dismantling sequence. If the bearing and/or seal have/has been removed, press in the new bearing and secure it with the **circlip, and,** using Service tool

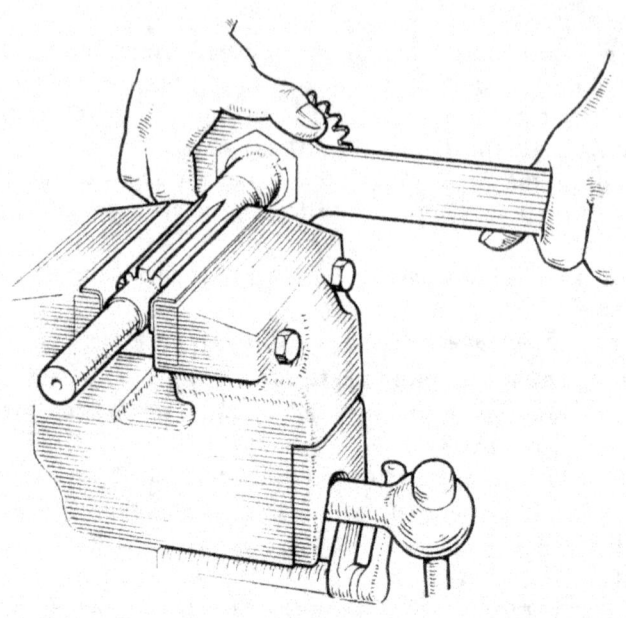

Using Service tool 18G2 to unscrew a first motion shaft nut. This nut has a left-hand thread

18G134 and adaptor 18G134N, fit the new oil seal.

Dismantling and Assembling the First Motion Shaft
1. Remove the needle rollers from the spigot bearing housing.
2. Secure the shaft in a soft-jawed vice, release the lock washer, and, using Service tool 18G5, unscrew the locknut.
    NOTE.—The locknut has a left-hand thread.
3. Press the bearing from the shaft and remove the spring ring from the bearing.
    Assembly is a reversal of the dismantling sequence.

Dismantling and Asembling the Laygear
Remove the circlips from the ends of the laygear and withdraw the needle-roller bearing assemblies and the distance tube.
    To asemble the laygear proceed as follows:
1. Hold the layshaft in a vice, stepped end downwards.
2. Smear the shaft with grease and assemble a bearing assembly, the distance tube, and the remaining two bearing assemblies to the shaft.

3. Fit a circlip to the front end of the laygear and place the laygear on the shaft.
4. Remove the laygear and shaft from the vice, fit the remaining circlip, and remove the shaft from the gear.

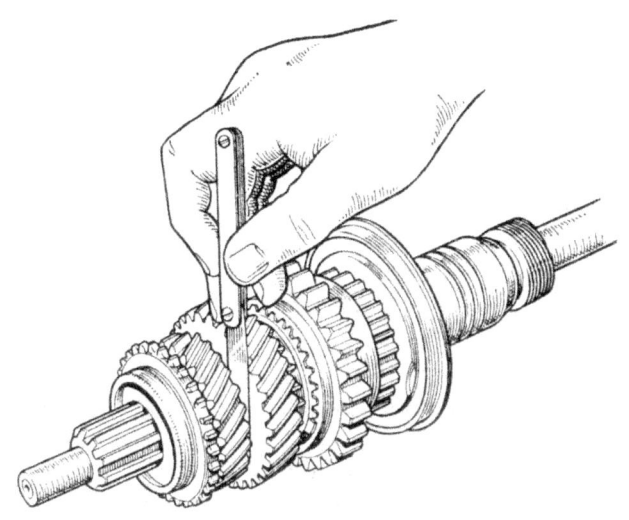

Checking the mainshaft third speed gear end-float

Dismantling the Third Motion Shaft

Before dismantling the third motion shaft check the end-float on the third speed mainshaft gear to ensure the fitting of the correct thrust washer during reassembly of the third motion shaft.
1. Remove the third and fourth speed gear front baulk ring, the synchromesh sleeve and hub, and the rear baulk ring. The synchromesh sleeve may be withdrawn from the hub, but care must be taken to retain the balls and springs that will be released when the sleeve is withdrawn form the hub.
2. Depress the front thrust washer retaining peg, rotate the washer to align its splines with those on the shaft, and remove the washer.
3. Withdraw the third speed gear and its bush and then remove the bush interlock ring to free the second speed gear. Remove the gear, baulk ring, bush, and thrust washer.
4. Withdraw the first and second speed synchromesh and gear. The first gear may be taken to retain the balls and springs that will be released when the gear is withdrawn from the hub.

5. Remove the speedometer drive gear and its Woodruff key and then slide the distance piece from the shaft.
6. Press the bearing from the shaft and then from its housing.

Examination of Components

Thoroughly clean, dry, and examine all components for wear, distortion, deterioration, and thread damage, paying particular attention to the following:
1. Bushes fitted to the clutch withdrawal fork, third motion shaft, and reverse speed gear. Worn or damaged bushes should be renewed.
2. Bearings fitted to the first motion shaft, third motion shaft, and rear extension.

Examine the bearings for looseness, pitting, security of cages, and fit in their housings and on their journals.

Examine also the needle rollers in the first motion shaft and the laygear.

Unserviceable bearings should be renewed.
3. Springs fitted to the synchromesh hubs, shaft locating block, and reverse plunger detent.

Comparisons may be made with new springs, but where facilities for test are available refer to the weights and lengths given under 'GENERAL DATA'.
4. The rubber gaiters for the clutch withdrawal fork and gear lever for cracks or signs of deterioration.
5. Ensure that all oilways are clear of obstruction, including the oil restrictor in the front of the third motion shaft.
6. Examine the interlock arm for burrs and for security of the rivet.

Assembling the Third Motion Shaft
1. Use Special tools 18G222 and 18G223 to assemble the second speed synchromesh hub and third and top gear synchromesh hub respectively.
2. Press the rear bearing into its housing and the bearing onto the shaft.
3. Fit the speedometer gear drive to the shaft with its key.
4. Fit the first gear and second gear synchromesh to the shaft, followed by the baulk ring and rear thrust washer.
5. Fit the second speed gear bush to the shaft and ensure that the lugs face forward and that the oil hole in the bush is in alignment with the oil hole in the shaft.
6. Assemble the second speed gear and the interlock washer so that the washer engages the lugs on the bush.
7. Fit the third speed gear bush, lugs first, and ensure that the lugs engage the interlock washer and that the oil hole and cut-

away in the bush are in alignment with the holes in the shaft.
8. Place the retaining pin spring and pin in the shaft and the third speed gear on the bush with the cone facing forward.
9. Position the gear so that the hole in the cone is in line with the retaining peg, depress the peg with a thin drift, fit the thrust washer to the shaft, then turn the washer to allow the peg to lock the washer in position.
    Thrust washers are available in four thicknesses as follows:
        .1565 to .1575 in.
        .1585 to .1595 in.
        .1605 to .1615 in.
10. Assemble the third and fourth speed gear rear baulk ring, synchromesh, and front baulk ring.

Assembling the Gearbox.
    Any gaskets or locking devices that are unserviceable or suspect should be renewed during assembly of the gearbox.
1. Place the laygear in the bottom of the gearbox together with the thrust washers and thread a piece of stiff wire through the laygear to allow Service tool 18G471 to pick up the thrust washers and laygear. The washers are available in four thicknesses as follows:
        .154 to .156 in.
        .157 to .159 in.
        .160 to .161 in.
        .163 to .164 in.
2. Fit the first motion shaft assembly to the gearbox.
3. Insert the third motion shaft from the rear of the box, use the gearbox extension gasket to align the dowel in the bearing housing, enter the spigot in the first motion shaft, and push home the shaft and bearing housing.
4. Using Service tool 19B471, fit the layshaft to the laygear and ensure that the cut-away end of the shift faces forward.
5. Assemble the reverse gear and shaft and secure the shaft with the locating screw and a new tab washer. Lock the screw with the washer.
6. Refit the first motion shaft bearing shims, align the step on the end of the layshaft with the inside edge of the front cover, and, using Service tool 18G598, fit the front cover.
7. Assemble the clutch withdrawal lever with its bolt and stiffnut.
8. Bolt the shaft locating block to the rear face of the gearbox and insert the three springs and balls into the block.
9. Assemble the selectors to the shafts and secure them with their locating screws. Lock the screw heads to the selectors

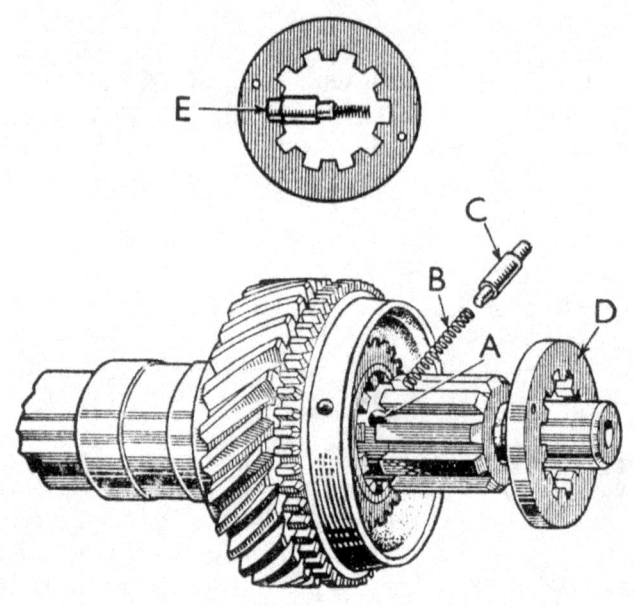

Securing the mainshaft gears

    A. Hole for spring.   C. Locating peg.
    B. Spring.   D. Locking washer.
    E. Peg located in the washer.

with new locking wire.
10. Using Service tool 18G41, depress the springs and balls in the locating block and pass the shafts through the block.
11. Position the gear change forks in the box in the following order: reverse, first and second speed, third and fourth speed.
12. Fit the distance piece to the third and fourth speed shaft, push the shaft through the forks, align the holes in the shaft and forks, and secure them with the fork locating screws. Tighten the locknut on each screw.
13. Replace the gearbox side cover and gasket.
14. Place the third motion shaft distance piece on the shaft and the extension gasket over the studs on the rear face of the gearbox.
15. Fit the rear extension to the gearbox and engage the rear extension remote-control shaft in the front selector and the dowel on the third motion shaft bearing housing with the hole in the extension.
16. Secure the selector with its Woodruff key and pinch-bolt and replace the extension side cover and gasket.

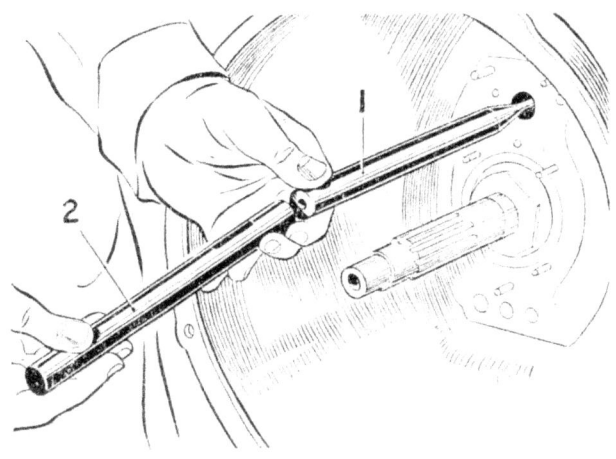

Using tool 18G471 as a pilot when installing the layshaft

1. Pilot.   2. Layshaft.

17. Refit the speedometer drive pinion, drain plug, dip-stick, and rear joint flange.
18. After refitting the gearbox to the vehicle replace control tower and its gasket and fill the box with clean oil.

Fitting Replacement Bushes

When fitting replacement bushes to the reverse gear, the clutch withdrawal fork, and the third motion shaft remove the old bushes and fit the new ones as follows.

Reverse gear

Press the new bush into the gear from the small end of the gear until the end of the bush is flush with the face of the small end.

Finish to an internal diameter of between .6255 and .6265 in. concentric with the gear teeth.

Clutch withdrawal fork

Press in the new bush and finish to an inside diameter of between .4996 and .5004 in.

Third motion shaft bushes

Heat the bushes to betwen 356 and 392° F. (180 and 200° C.), ensure that the locating tongues on the bushes are in line with the splines on the shaft and that the oil holes are in line, then assemble the second speed bush, interlock washer, and third speed bush.

Fitting the Gearbox Front Cover

To prevent oil leaking past the gearbox front cover oil seal the cover must be correctly fitted to ensure that the seal is concentric with the first motion shaft. When refitting the cover proceed as follows.

Clean off the cover and examine it carefully for burrs and bruising, particularly around the bore, stud holes, and machined surfaces. Check the flat surfaces for twist and warp, and correct it if necessary. If the condition is too bad to correct, fit a new cover.

Remove and discard the front cover to gearbox gasket and clean off the flat surfaces around the base of all studs.

Offer the front cover (less oil seal) to the gearbox and push it fully home on the studs. The cover should be free to move in all directions, and points at which the holes may be binding on the studs must be relieved until the cover is free to 'float.'

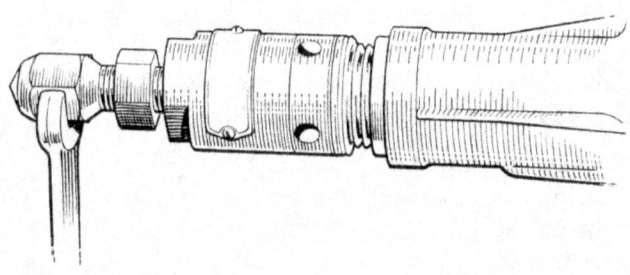

Removing a rear oil seal, using Service tools 18G389 *and* 18G389B

Remove the cover and, using Service tool 18G134 with adaptor 18G134N, fit the oil seal so that its lip faces inwards towards the gearbox front face, then fit a new gasket to the gearbox front face, then fit the centralizer (Service tool 18G598) to the bore of the front cover and push it in until it is tight. Lightly oil the seal and pass the cover over the first motion shaft, taking particular care not to cut or damage the knife edge of the seal.

Keep the centralizer firmly in position, push the cover onto the studs, and fit the **spring washers** and nuts, tightening the nuts finger tight only. Use a suitable socket spanner and long extension to tighten the nuts a half turn at a time by diametrical selection until all nuts are fully tightened.

Remove the centralizer and refit the clutch-operating components.

The propeller shaft and universal joints are of the Hardy Spicer type with needle-roller bearings.

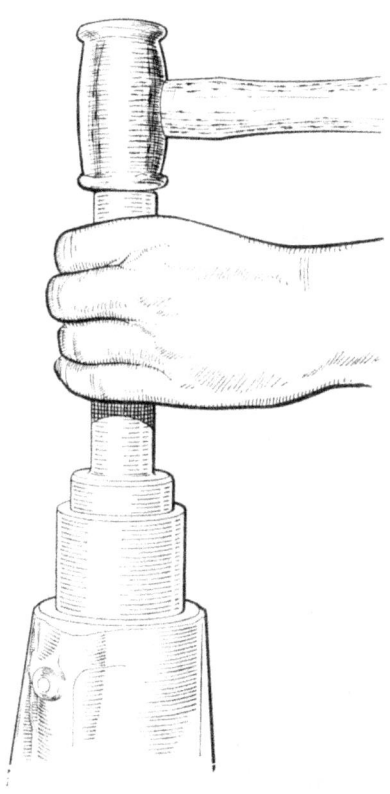

Installing a new rear oil seal, using Service tools 18G134 and 18G134N

THE PROPELLER SHAFT

A single shaft connects the rear axle and the gearbox. To accommodate fore and aft movement of the axle, a sliding joint of the reverse-spline type is fitted between the gearbox and the front universal joint flange. Each joint consists of a centre spider, four needle-roller bearing assemblies and two yokes.

Lubricating the Universal Joints

A lubricator is fitted to each front and rear spider and should be charged fully after overhauling and subsequently given three or four strokes with the gun every 1,000 miles.

If a large amount of lubricant exudes from the oil seal the join should be dismantled and new oil seals fitted.

The sliding joint is automatically lubricated from the gearbox.

Testing for Wear

Wear on the thrust faces is ascertained by testing the lift in the joint, either by hand or with the aid of a length of wood suitably pivoted.

Any circumferential movement of the shaft relative to the flange yokes indicates wear in the needle-roller bearings, or in the splined shaft in the case of the forward joint.

Removing the Propeller Shaft

Before removing the bolts and nuts securing the propeller shaft universal joint flange to the rear axle flange, carefully mark the flanges to assist in refitting them in their original positions. **This is important.**

Remove the bolts securing the propeller shaft to the rear axle flange. The shaft can now be removed from the car downwards and rearwards.

Dismantling the Propeller Shaft

Remove the enamel and dirt from the snap-rings and bearing races. Remove all the snap-rings by pinching their ears together with a pair of thin-nosed pliers and prising them out with a screwdriver.

If a ring does not slide out of its groove readily, tap the end of the bearing race slightly to relieve the pressure against the ring. Remove the lubricator from the journal and, holding the joint in one hand, tap the radius of the yoke lightly with a copper hammer. The bearing should begin to emerge; turn the joint over and finally remove with the fingers. If necessary, tap the bearing race from inside with a small-diameter bar, taking care not to damage the bearing face, or grip the needle bearing race in a vice and tap the flange yoke clear.

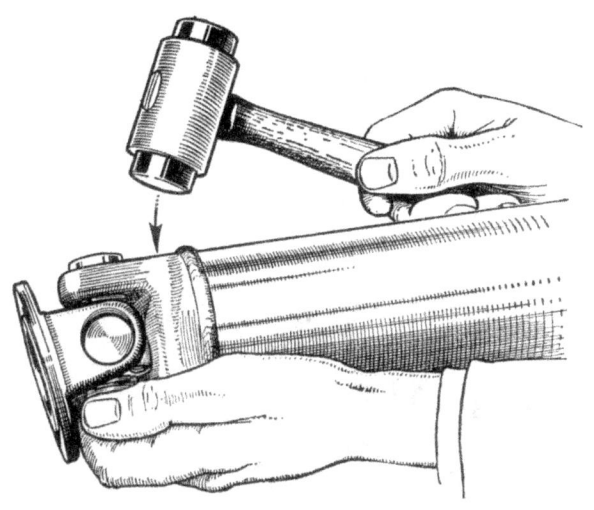

Where to apply light blows to the yoke after removing the retaining circlip

Be sure to hold the bearing in a vertical position, and when free remove the race from the bottom side to avoid dropping the needle rollers.

Repeat this operation for the opposite bearing.

Rest the two exposed trunnions on wood or lead blocks to protect their ground surfaces, and tap the top lug of the flange yoke to remove the bearing race.

Turn the yoke over and repeat the operation.

To Examine and Check for Wear

The parts most likely to show signs of wear after long usage are the bearing races and the spider journals. Should looseness, load markings, or distortion be observed, the affected part must be renewed complete; no oversized journals or races are provided.

It is essential that the bearing races are a light drive fit in the yoke trunnions. In the event of wear taking place in the yoke

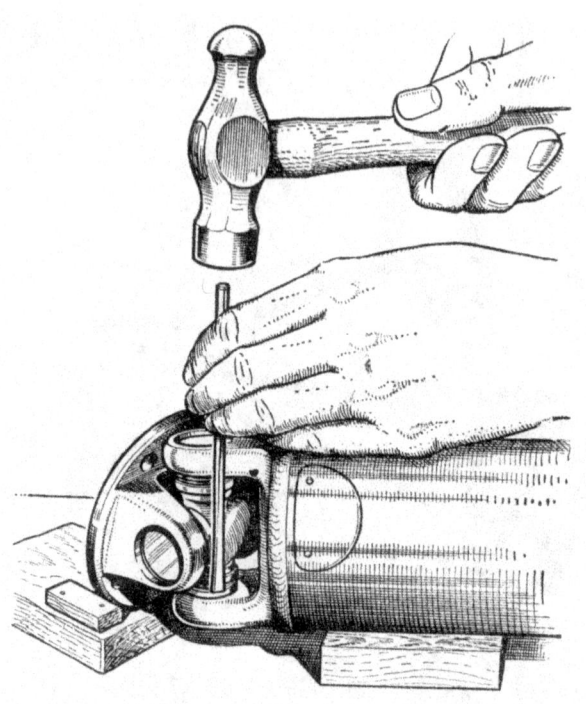

When dismantling a universal joint the bearings may be tapped out with a small-diameter rod from the inside as shown. Take care not to damage the roller races

cross-holes, rendering them oval, the yokes must be renewed. In case of wear in the cross-holes in the fixed yoke, which is part of the tubular shaft assembly, it should be replaced by a complete tubular shaft assembly.

Reassembling the Shaft

See that all the drilled holes in the journals are thoroughly cleaned out and free of grease or oil.

Assemble the needle rollers in the bearing races and fill with lubricant. Should difficulty be experienced in retaining the rollers under control, smear the walls of the races with lubricant to retain the needle rollers in position while reassembling.

Insert the spider in the flange yoke, ensuring that **the lubricator boss is fitted away from the yoke.** Using a soft-nosed drift, about 1/22 in. smaller in diameter than the hole in the yoke, tap

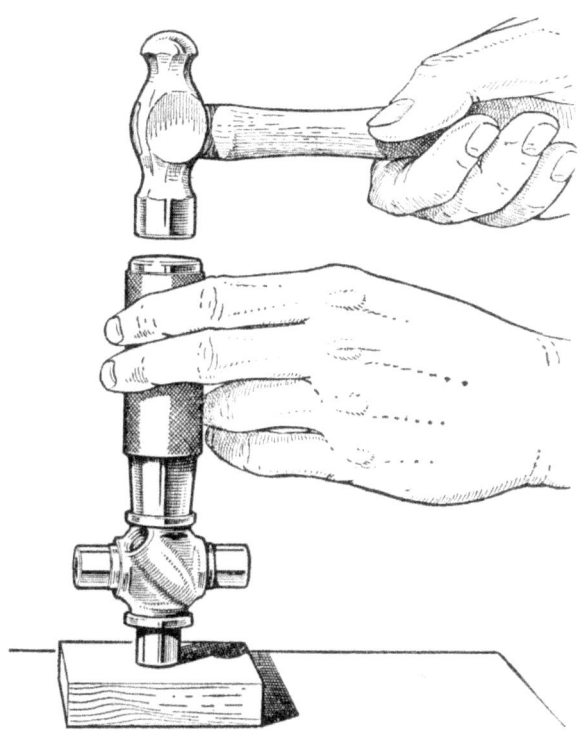

When replacing the gasket retainer, use should be made of a hollow drift to tap it into place without damage

the bearing into position. Repeat this operation for the other three bearings. Replace the circlips and be sure that these are firmly located in their grooves. If the joint appears to bind, tap lightly with a wooden mallet; this will relieve any pressure of the bearings on the end of the journals.

It is always advisable to replace the cork gasket and the gasket retainers on the spider journals by means of a tubular drift. The spider journal shoulders should be shellacked prior to fitting the retainers, to ensure a good oil seal.

Replacing the Propeller Shaft

Wipe the faces of the flanges clean, and place the propeller shaft in position on the car. Ensure that the flange registers engage correctly, that the components are replaced in exactly the same relation as before removal and that the joint faces bed down evenly all round. Insert the bolts and tighten the self-locking nuts.

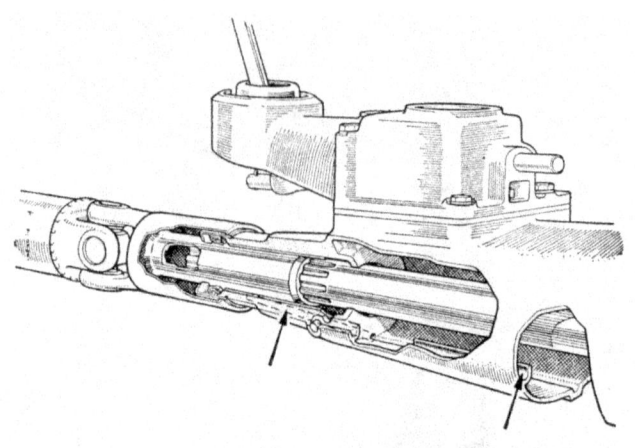

The sliding joint, showing the lubrication channels for the sliding joint bush

Modified Propeller Shaft

Coincident with the introduction of the modified power unit (15SD series) a propeller shaft incorporating a splined sliding joint at its front end was fitted.

In addition to the nipples fitted to each universal joint, a nipple is also provided on the sleeve yoke for the lubrication of the sliding joint splines. This nipple must receive attention every 1,000 miles.

Instructions given for the servicing of the earlier propeller shaft apply, in the main, to the modified propeller shaft. The following points, however, should be noted:

1. In order to remove the propeller shaft it is necessary to remove the four nuts and bolts securing the front universal joint flange to the gearbox flange, as well as those securing the rear flange to the rear axle flange.
2. Check the sliding splines for wear by attempting to turn the splined sleeve yoke in relation to the splined shaft. If excessive circumferential movement is present a reconditioned propeller shaft assembly will be required.
3. When fitting new universal joints it will be found helpful to separate the two parts of the propeller shaft at the sliding joint.
4. Before refitting the splined sleeve yoke to the shaft push the threaded dust cover, the metal washer, and the felt washer over the splines onto the splined shaft. When assembling the joint

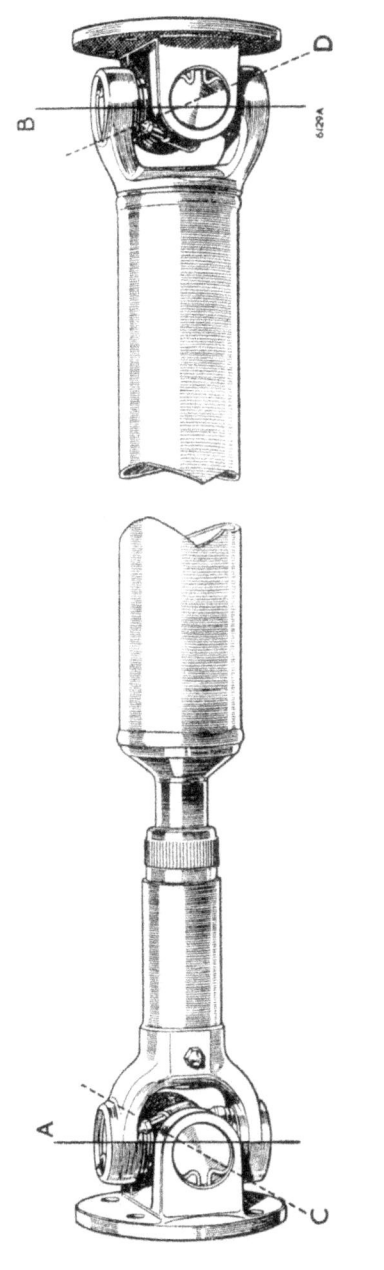

When the splined shaft is assembled to the drive shaft it is essential to see that the forked yokes on both shafts have their axes parallel to each other. In other words, the yoke (A) must be in alignment with the yoke (B), and the flange yoke (C) must be in alignment with the flange yoke (D)

ensure that the trunnions of the front and rear universal joints are in line. This can be checked by observing that the arrows marked on the splined sleeve yoke and the splined shaft are in line.

5. Fit the propeller shaft to the car with the sliding joint at the gearbox end.

THE REAR AXLE

The rear axle is of three-quarter-floating type, incorporating hypoid final reduction gears. The axle shafts, pinion and differential assemblies can be withdrawn without removing the axle from the vehicle.

The rear axle wheel bearing outer races are located in the hubs; the inner races are mounted on the axle tube and secured by nuts and lock washers. Wheel studs in the hubs pass through the brake-drums and axle shaft driving flanges.

The differential and pinion shaft bearings are pre-loaded, the amount of pre-load being adjustable by shims. The position of the pinion in relation to the crown wheel is determined by a spacing washer. The backlash between the gears is adjustable by shims.

Suspension is by semi-elliptic leaf springs, rubber-mounted, and the shackles are fitted with rubber bushes of the flexing type.

Lubrication

The axle is filled or topped up with oil through the filler plug in the rear cover by means of an oil gun with a special adaptor.

It is of the utmost importance that only hypoid oils of the approved grades and manufacture be used if satisfactory service is to be obtained from the hypoid gears.

Withdrawing an axle shaft. Note the bearing spacer which here is being replaced in the hub.

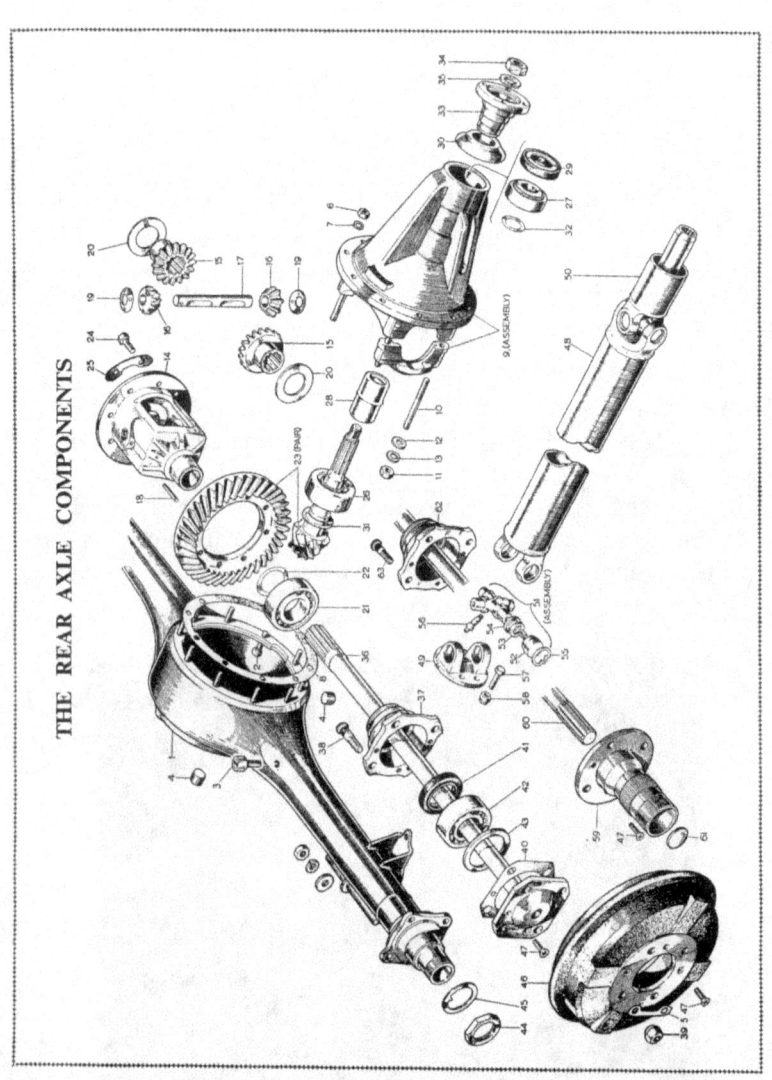

KEY TO THE REAR AXLE COMPONENTS

No.	Description
1.	Casing—rear axle. DW.
2.	Bolts—differential carrier.
3.	Breather assembly.
4.	Plug—oil—drain and filler.
5.	Washer—tab—drum retaining.
6.	Nut—differential carrier bolt.
7.	Washer—spring.
8.	Joint—carrier to case.
9.	Carrier.
10.	Stud.
11.	Nut.
12.	Washer—plain.
13.	Washer—spring.
14.	Case—differential.
15.	Wheel—differential.
16.	Pinion—differential.
17.	Pin—pinion.
18.	Peg—pin locating.
19.	Washer—pinion—thrust.
20.	Washer—wheel—thrust.
21.	Bearing—differential.
22.	Washer—packing—bearing (.002 in.).
23.	Crown wheel and bevel pinion 10/43.
24.	Bolt—crown wheel to case.
25.	Washer—lock—crown wheel bolt.
26.	Bearing—bevel pinion—rear.
27.	Bearing—bevel pinion—front.
28.	Spacer—bearing.
29.	Oil seal—bearing—front.
30.	Dust cover—oil seal.
31.	Washer—bevel pinion (.112 in.).
32.	Shim—front bevel pinion bearing (.004 in.).
33.	Flange—universal joint.
34.	Nut—flange.
35.	Washer—spring—flange nut.
36.	Shaft—rear axle. DW.
37.	Hub assembly—rear. DW.
38.	Stud—wheel. DW.
39.	Nut—wheel stud. DW.
40.	Gasket—shaft to hub housing.
41.	Seal—oil—rear hub.
42.	Bearing—rear hub.
43.	Spacer—bearing. DW.
44.	Locknut.
45.	Washer—tab—locknut.
46.	Drum—brake.
47.	Screw—drum hub—axle shaft. DW.
48.	Tubular shaft assembly.
49.	Yoke—flange.
50.	Yoke—sleeve assembly.
51.	Journal and needle—kit set.
52.	Bearing assembly—needle.
53.	Gasket.
54.	Retainer.
55.	Circlip.
56.	Lubricator—journal.
57.	Bolt—shaft flange yoke—rear.
58.	Nut—bolt.
59.	Hub extension R/H—rear. WW.
60.	Shaft—axle. WW.
61.	Welch plug—hub extension. WW.

Fig. H.2
Using the special service extractor on the rear hub

Inspect the oil level every 1,000 miles and top up as necessary to the level of the filler opening.

Every 6,000 miles drain off the old oil and refill with new. The capacity of the axle is 3.3 U.S. pints.

The hub bearings are lubricated from the axle and no provision is made for any other attention.

Removing and Replacing a Brake-drum and Axle Shaft
1. Jack up the car and place blocks under the spring as close as possible to the axle.
2. Remove the wheel.
3. Release the hand brake.
4. Unscrew and remove the two countersunk Phillips screws locating the drum and tap it from the hub. It may be necessary to slacken off the brake adjustment slightly if the shoes hold the drum.
5. Unscrew the countersunk Phillips locating screw in the axle shaft driving flange.
6. Withdraw the axle shaft by gripping the flange or carefully prising it with a screwdriver. If the latter method is used the paper washer may be damaged and must be renewed when reasembling.

To replace the shaft and drum, reverse the above sequence of operations but note that in some models the flange locating screw is shorter than the drum locating screws, and make sure that the bearing spacer is in position.

Removing and Replacing A Hub
1. Remove the drum and axle shaft.
2. Remove the bearing spacer.
3. Knock back the tab of the locking washer and unscrew the nut with a suitable spanner.
4. Tilt the lock washer to disengage the key from the slot in the threaded portion of the axle casing; remove the washer.
5. The hub can then be withdrawn with a suitable puller such as special tools Nos. 18G.304 and 18G.304B. The bearing and oil seal will be withdrawn with the hub.
6. The bearing is not adjustable and is replaced in one straightforward operation.

When reassembling it is essential that the outer face of the bearing spacer should protrude from .001 in. to .004 in. beyond the outer face of the hub and the paper washer, when the bearing is gripped between the abutment shoulder in the hub and the driving flange of the axle shaft.

Renewing the Bevel Pinion Oil Seal
1. Mark the propeller shaft and the pinion driving flanges so that they may be replaced in the same relative positions. Disconnect the propeller shaft.
2. Knock back the lock washer and unscrew the nut in the center of the driving flange. Remove the nut and washer and withdraw the flange and pressed-on end cover from the pinion shaft.
3. Extract the oil seal from the casing.
4. Press a new oil seal into the casing with the edge of the sealing ring facing inwards.
5. Replace the driving flange end cover, taking care not to damage the edge of the oil seal. Tighten the nut with a torque wrench to a reading of 140 lb. ft.

Reconnect the propeller shaft, taking care to fit the two flanges with the locating marks in alignment.

Removing the Differential Pinions
1. Drain the oil from the axle casing.
2. Remove the axle shafts.
3. Mark the propeller shaft and pinion shaft driving flanges so that they may be replaced in the same relative positions; unscrew the self-locking nuts and disconnect the joint.
4. Unscrew the 10 nuts securing the bevel pinion and gear carrier to the axle casing; withdraw the gear carrier complete with

the pinion shaft and differential assembly.
5. Make sure that the differential bearing housing caps are marked so that they can be replaced in their original positions, then remove the four nuts and spring washers. Withdraw the bearing caps and differential assembly.
6. Tap out the dowel pin locating the differential pinion shaft. the diameter of the pin is 3/16 in. and it must be tapped out from the crown wheel side as the hole into which it fits has a slightly smaller diameter at the crown wheel end to prevent the pin from passing right through. It may be necessary to clean out the metal peened over the entry hole with a 3/16 in. drill in order to facilitate removal of the dowel pin. Drive out the differential pinion shaft. The pinions and thrust washers can then be removed from the cage.

Replacing the Differential Pinions
1. Examine the pinions and thrust washers and renew as required.
2. Replace the pinions, thrust washers and pinion shaft in the differential cage and insert the dowel pin. Peen over the entry hole.
3. Reassembly is now a reversal of the instructions given previously.

Dismantling the Crown Wheel and Pinion
Remove the differential assembly.
1. Remove the differential bearings from the differential cage, using special tool 18G47C with adaptors 18G47T. Note that the word 'THRUST' is stamped on the thrust face of each bearing and that shims are fitted between the inner ring of each bearing and the differential cage.
2. Knock back the tabs of the locking washers, unscrew the nuts from the bolts securing the crown wheel to the differential cage, and remove the crown wheel.
3. Knock back the tab of the locking washer and unscrew the pinion nut; remove the driving flange and the pressed end cover.
4. Drive the pinion shaft towards the rear; it will carry with it the inner race and the rollers of the rear bearing, leaving the outer race and the complete front bearing in position.
6. The inner race of the front bearing may be removed with the fingers and the outer races of both bearings withdrawn with special tool 18G264, using adaptors 18G264E and 18G264F.
6. Slide off the pinion sleeve and shims; withdraw the rear bearing inner race from the pinion shaft with special tool 18G285, noting the spacing washer against the pinion head.

Assembling and Setting the Crown Wheel and Pinion

Apart from the fitting of components as detailed above it is not permissible to fit any new parts (e.g. crown wheel and pinion, pinion bearings, differential bearings, etc.) to the axle assembly without working through the procedure given in this Section. Furthermore, if a new crown wheel or a new pinion is needed, **a mated pair – crown wheel and pinion – must be fitted.**

Fitting a new crown wheel and pinion involves four distinct operations:
1. Setting the position of the pinion.
2. Adjusting the pinion bearing preload.
3. Setting the crown wheel position.
4. Adjusting the backlash between the gears.

The following special service tools are required to enable these operations to be carried out correctly:

Bevel pinion and differential setting gauge.
Bevel pinion inner race remover and replacer.
Bevel pinion outer race remover and replacer.
Bevel pinion preload gauge.

Setting the gauge to zero on the special block for determination of the pinion position. The arrow indicates the extension to the contact foot.

Setting the Pinion Position

1. Fit the bearing outer races to the gear carrier, using the special pinion race replacing tool.
2. Smooth off the pinion head with an oil-stone, but do not erase any markings that may be etched on the pinion head.
3. Assemble the pinion and rear bearings with a washer of known thickness behind the pinion head.
4. Position the pinion in the gear carrier without the shims, bearing spacer, and oil seal.
5. Fit the inner ring of the front bearing and the universal joint driving flange and tighten the nut gradually until a bearing pre-load of 10 to 12 lb. in. is obtained.
6. Remove the keep disc from the base of the magnet. Adjust the dial indicator to zero on the machined step 'B' of the setting block.
7. Clean the pinion head and place a magnet and dial indicator in position. Move the indicator arm until the foot of the gauge rests on the center of the differential bearing bore at one side and tighten the knurled locking screw. Obtain the maximum depth reading and note any variation from the zero setting. Repeat the check in the opposite bearing bore. Add the two variations together and divide by two to obtain a mean reading.
8. Take into consideration any variation in pinion head thickness. This will be shown as an unbracketed figure etched on the pinion head and will always be minus (—). If no unbracketed figure is shown the pinion head is of nominal thickness. Using the mean clock gauge reading obtained and the unbracketed pinion head figure (if any), the following calculation can be made:

a. **If the clock reading is minus** add the clock reading to the pinion head marking, the resulting sum being minus. **Reduce** the washer thickness by this amount.

Example:

Clock reading .... —.002 in.
Pinion marking .... —.005 in.
Variation from nominal .... —.007 in.

Reduce the washer thickness by this amount.

b. **If the clock reading is plus and numerically less** than the pinion marking **reduce** the washer thickness by the difference.

Example:

Pinion marking .... —.005 in.
Clock reading .... +.003 in.
Variation from nominal .... —.002 in.

c. **If the clock reading is plus and numerically greater** than the

pinion marking **increase** the washer thickness by the difference.
Example:
Clock reading ....+.008 in.
Pinion marking ....—.003 in.
Variation from nominal ....+.005 in.

Increase the washer thickness by this amount.

The gauge in position on the pinion with the dial indicating a variation from the standard setting

The only cases where no alterations are required to the washer thickness are when the clock reading is **plus** and **numerically equal** to the unbracketed pinion marking, or when the clock reading is zero and there is no unbracketed marking on the pinion head.

9. Allowance should then finally be made for the mounting distance marked on the pinion head in a rectangular bracket as follows.

If the marking is a **plus** figure **reduce** the washer thickness by an equal amount.

If the marking is a **minus** figure increase the washer thickness by an equal amount.

A tolerance of .001 in. is allowed in the thickness of the washer finally fitted.

Table of washer and shim thicknesses	
Pinion head washer thickness	·112 to ·126 in. in steps of ·002 in.
Pinion bearing preload shims	·004 to ·012 in. in steps of ·002 in., plus ·020 in. and ·030 in.
Crown wheel bearing shims	·002 in., ·004 in. and ·006 in.
Pinion bearing preload	10 to 12 lb. in. without oil seal; 13 to 15 lb. in. with oil seal
Crown wheel bearing pinch	·002 in. each side

Adjusting Pinion Bearing Preload
1. Fit the appropriate washer to the pinion head.
2. Assemble the pinion shaft, bearings, distance tube, and shims to the gear carrier; fit the oil seal and driving flange. Shims to a thickness of .008 to .011 in should be used as a starting-point for adjustment of the bearing preload.
3. Tighten the driving flange nut gradually with a torque wrench to 140 lb. ft. and check the preload on the bearings during tightening to ensure that it does not exceed 13 to 15 lb. in. i.e. 3 lb. in. greater than the recommended figure since the oil seal is now fitted. If the preload is too great, more shims must be added. If the preload is too small when the nut is tightened correctly, the shim thickness must be reduced.

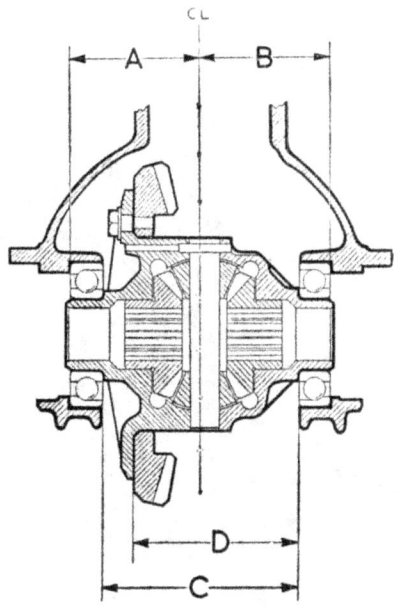

The dimensions referred to in the instructions for differential setting

Setting the Crown Wheel Position

1. Before fitting the crown wheel and differential assembly to the gear carrier it is necessary to calculate the shim thickness required behind each bearing to give the required pinch. To facilitate the calculation, machining variations are indicated by stamped numbers on the carrier adjacent to the bearing bores. The dimensions to be considered are shown in the drawing. (a) being the distance from the centre-line to the bearing register of the carrier on the left-hand side, and (b) the distance from the centre-line to the bearing register of the carrier on the right-hand side. The (c) dimension is from the bearing register on one side of the cage to the register on the other side, while the (d) dimension is from the rear face of the crown wheel to the bearing register on the opposite side. Any variation from normal

To measure variations in bearing thickness, first zero the gauge on the appropriate portion of the gauge block. Here the gauge is seen set for an 'A' type axle. Use the position marked 'B' for the 'MGA' axles

With the gauge set to zero, place the bearing on the surface plate with the outer ring thrust face down, and take a reading while the indicator foot contacts the inner ring

on the (a) dimension will be found stamped on the carrier adjacent to the bearing bore, and similarly with the (b) dimension. The variations from normal on (c) and (d) dimensions are stamped on the machined face of the differential cage.

It is possible to calculate the shim thickness required on the **left-hand** side by the use of the following formula:

$$A+D-C+.007 \text{ in.}$$

Substituting the actual variations shown, this formula gives the shim thickness required to compensate for the variations in machining plus the extra .002 in. to give the necessary bearing pinch. In addition, allowance must be made for variations in bearing thickness in the following manner.

Rest the bearing with the inner race over the recess and the outer ring thrust face downwards, on the small surface plate of tool 18G191B. Drop the magnet onto the surface plate and set the clock gauge to zero on the small gauge block on the step marked 'B.' This is the thickness of the standard bearing. Swing over the indicator until it rests on the plain surface of the inner race and, holding the inner race down against the balls, take a reading. Normally the bearing will be standard to —.003 in., though in some cases the tolerance may be from standard to —.005 in. A negative variation shown by this test indicates the additional thickness of shimming to be added to that side of the differential.

The formula for the **right-hand side** is:

$$B - D + .006 \text{ in.}$$

and here again final allowance must be made for variation in bearing thickness.

2. When a framed number is marked on the back of the crown wheel, e.g. +2, it must be taken into account before assembling the shims and bearings to the differential cage. This mark assists in relating the crown wheel with the pinion.

If, for example, the mark +2, then shims to the value of .002 in. must be transferred from the left-hand side (the crown wheel side) to the right-hand side. If the marking is —2, then shims to the value of .002 in must be moved from the right-hand side to the left-hand side.

Adjusting the Backlash

1. Assemble the bearings and shims as calculated to the differential cage.
2. Bolt the crown wheel to the differential case, but do not knock over the locking tabs. Tighten the nuts to a torque wrench reading of 60 lb. ft.

Fit the shims and differential bearings with the thrust faces outwards.

Mount the assembly on two 'V' blocks and check the amount of run-out of the crown wheel, as it is rotated, by means of a suitably mounted dial indicator.

The maximum permissible run-out is .002 in. and any greater irregularity must be corrected. Detach the crown wheel and examine the joint faces on the flange of the differential case and crown wheel for any particles of dirt.

When the parts are thoroughly cleaned it is unlikely that the crown wheel will not run true.

Tighten the bolts to the correct torque wrench reading and knock over the locking nuts.

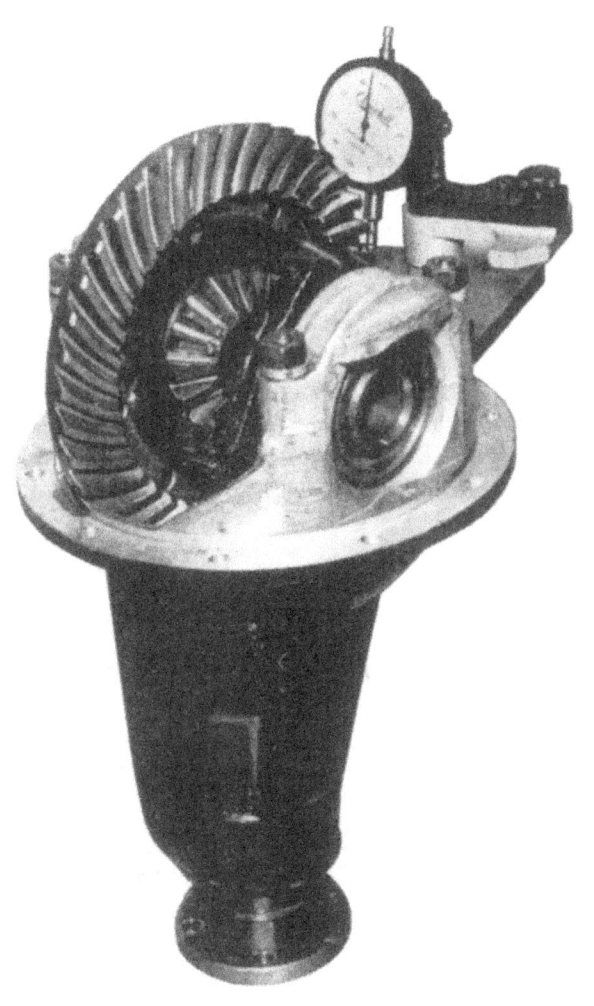

Measuring the crown wheel backlash

3. Fit the differential to the gear carrier. Replace the bearing caps and tighten the nuts to a torque wrench reading of 65 lb. ft. Bolt the special tool surface plate to the gear carrier flange and mount the clock gauge on the magnet bracket in such a way that an accurate backlash figure may be obtained. The minimum backlash allowed in any circumstances is .005 in. and the maximum is .007 in. The correct figure for the backlash to be used with any particular crown wheel and pinion is etched on the rear face of the crown wheel concerned and must be adhered to strictly.

NOTE.—To ensure adequate clearance when fitting a crown wheel and pinion to earlier axles it may be found necessary to use a pair of gears of which the crown wheel is unmarked.

A movement of .002 in. shim thickness from one side of the differential to the other will produce a variation in backlash of approximately .002 in. Thus it should be possible to set up the differential, even though the backlash is incorrect, by removing the bearings on one occasion only.

Great care must be taken to ensure absolute cleanliness during the above operations, as any discrepancies resulting from dirty assembly would affect the setting position of the crown wheel or pinion.

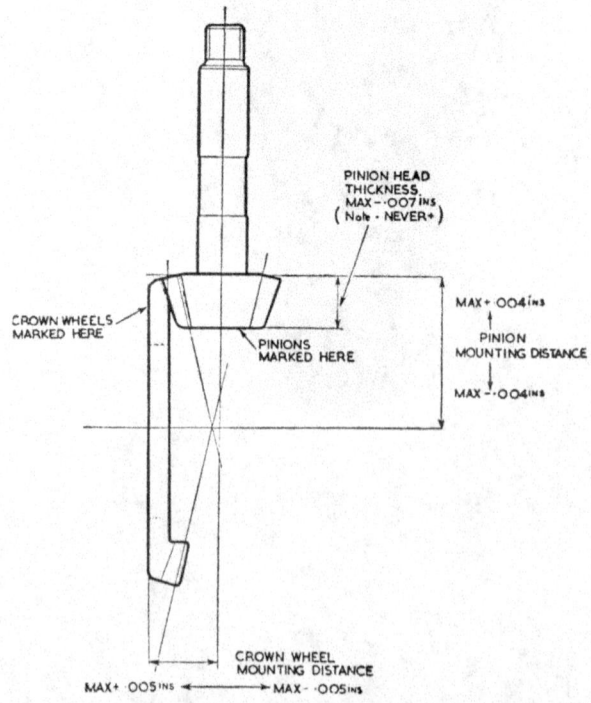

Removing and Refitting the Axle
1. Raise the rear of the car.
2. Mark the propeller shaft coupling flanges so that they may be replaced in the original relative positions. Remove the four bolts and self-locking nuts and release the rear end of the propeller shaft from the axle. Remove the nuts and spring and flat washers securing each end of each check strap to the anchor pins and remove the check straps.
3. Remove the split pin and clevis pin securing the brake cables to each brake operating lever. Remove the small nut and Phillips recessed-head screw securing the hand brake cable clip to the axle casing. Remove the self-locking nut and large flat washer securing the brake balance lever to the pivot on the axle casing.
4. Remove the nut and spring washer securing the lower end of each damper link to the rear spring clamp plate.
5. Unscrew the brake fluid supply pipe union and release the flexible pipe from the battery box support bracket.
6. Release the exhaust pipe from the exhaust manifold and the three supporting brackets and remove the exhaust pipe assembly.
7. Remove the nut and spring washer from the spring front anchor pin.
8. Support the axle casing and remove the rear shackle plates, brackets and rubbers. Lower the axle support until the axle and spring assembly rests on the road wheels. Withdraw the front anchor pins and roll the assembly from beneath the car.
9. Uncouple the propeller shaft at the rear flange by unscrewing the four self-locking coupling nuts and bolts. Support the tail end of the propeller shaft.
10. Remove the rear shackle nuts and bolts.
11. Remove the spring front anchorage bolts after removing the retaining nuts and spring washers.

The axle is now free to be withdrawn on the stand rearwards from the car.

Replacement is the reverse of the above sequence of operations.

Modified Axle Hub Bearing Nuts

This change introduced at:
Car No. 10917 on cars fitted with disc wheels.
Car No. 11450 on cars fitted with wire wheels.

The left-hand hub bearing nut on the rear axle now has a left-hand thread and is turned clockwise to unscrew. The right-hand hub nut is unchanged and retains the right-hand thread.

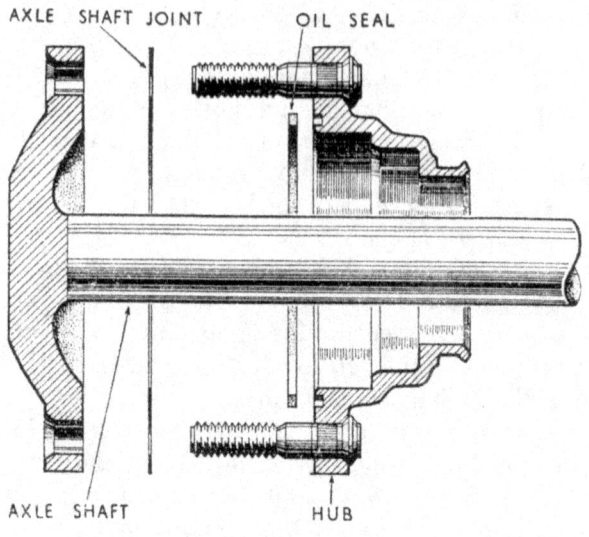

*The position of the additional hub oil seal
fitted on later models*

Rear Hub Oil Seal

On the rear axles fitted to later cars a modified rear hub was introduced with an additional oil seal. The hub assembly has a groove machined in the face and a rubber oil sealing ring is fitted in the groove, between the hub and the axle shaft to hub joint.

The oil seal may only be fitted to earlier axles together with the later-type hub.

This change was introduced at Axle No. 5225 on cars fitted with wire wheels and Axle No. 3725 on cars fitted with disc wheels.

Bevel Pinion and Differential Bearing Setting Gauge

In a modification to the bevel pinion and differential bearing setting gauge (Part No. 18G191B) a stepped gauge block and a small dial gauge with a $1/2$ in. extension to the contact foot replace the original cut-out block and large dial gauge

When in use this new block should be placed on the surface plate, together with the dial gauge and magnet assembly (with the keep disc removed), and the gauge set to zero on the appropriate step for the 'B' type axle with the later-type hub.

CARS WITH DUNLOP DISC BRAKES

Removing and Replacing a Hub Extension and Axle Shaft

1. Jack up the car and place blocks under the spring as close as possible to the axle.
2. Remove the wheel.
3. Release the hand brake.
4. Unscrew and remove the four self-locking nuts securing the hub extension driving flange to the hub.
5. Withdraw the hub extension and axle shaft by gripping the driving flange or the winged hub nut, which may be temporarily refitted for this purpose.
6. Remove the welch plug and apply pressure to the end of the axle shaft with a hand press to remove the hub extension from the spline on the shaft.

To replace the shaft and driving flange reverse the above sequence of operations. If the welch plug has been distorted on removal a new one should be fitted.

Unscrew and remove the four self-locking nuts to withdraw the hub extension

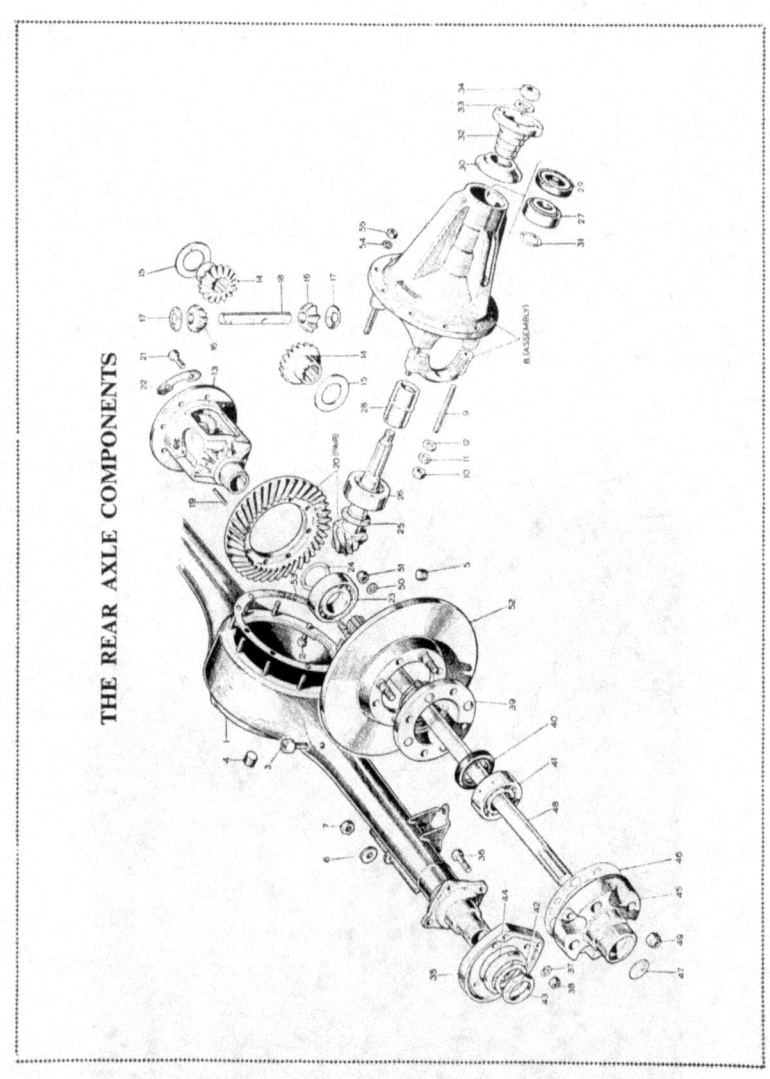

KEY TO THE REAR AXLE COMPONENTS

No.	Description	No.	Description	No.	Description
1.	Axle centre case.	20.	Crown wheel and pinion.	38.	Nut.
2.	Serrated bolt.	21.	Bolt.	39.	Wheel bearing housing.
3.	Breather.	22.	Lock washer.	40.	Oil seal.
4.	Filler plug.	23.	Differential bearing.	41.	Rear wheel bearing.
5.	Drain plug.	24.	Packing washer.	42.	Tab washer.
6.	Plain washer.	25.	Pinion head washer.	43.	Locknut.
7.	Nut.	26.	Pinion bearing.	44.	Dust cover.
8.	Gear carrier.	27.	Pinion bearing (outer).	45.	Hub extension.
9.	Stud.	28.	Pinion bearing spacer.	46.	Joint washer.
10.	Nut.	29.	Oil seal.	47.	Welch plug.
11.	Spring washer.	30.	Dust cover.	48.	Axle shaft.
12.	Washer.	31.	Pinion bearing shim.	49.	Pinnacle nut.
13.	Differential case.	32.	Flange.	50.	Plain washer.
14.	Differential wheel.	33.	Spring washer.	51.	Pinnacle nut.
15.	Thrust washer.	34.	Nut.	52.	Rear brake disc.
16.	Differential pinion.	35.	Adaptor plate.	53.	Differential joint.
17.	Thrust washer.	36.	Bolt.	54.	Spring washer.
18.	Pinion centre.	37.	Spring washer.	55.	Nut.
19.	Peg.				

Removing and Replacing a Hub
1. Remove the hub extension and axle shaft. Remove the wheel brake unit.
2. Knock back the tab of the hub nut locking washer, unscrew the nut, using spanner 18G152, and pull off the washer. The left-hand hub bearing nut has a left-hand thread and is turned in a clockwise direction to unscrew.
3. The hub and brake disc assembly can then be withdrawn, using rear hub remover 18G304 together with adaptors 18G304B and thrust pad 18G304J. The bearing and oil seal will be withdrawn with the hub.

The bearing is not adjustable and is replaced in one straightforward operation. Replace the hub and drift it into position with replacer 18G134 and adaptor 18G134P. The remainder is a reversal of the above sequence of operations.

THE REAR ROAD SPRINGS

The semi-elliptic leaf springs provided for the rear suspension are secured beneath the rear axle by "U" bolts.

The front ends of the springs are anchored in flexing rubber bushes and the rear ends are mounted in similar bushes in swinging shackles.

Rubber pads are fitted between the spring and the axle.

As the rear springs are mounted in rubber, spraying with oil should be strictly avoided.

Removal of Rear Road Springs

1. Raise the rear of the car and support the chassis with a sling attached to the rear bumper bolts, or channelled out or well-padded wood blocks forward of the rear springs. Support the axle on a suitable stand.
2. Remove the "U" clip locknuts and nuts and drive up the clips to release the hydraulic damper anchor plate, also removing the spring clamp plates and rubbers.
3. Remove rear shackles and front anchor pin and the spring.

Dismantling and Reassembling the Spring

1. Remove the locating plates and rubber pads.
2. Remove the locknut, nut and distance-piece from the spring center bolt, this will release the three bottom leaves. The remaining leaves are parted by prying open the clips on Nos. 3 and 4 leaves.
3. Clean each leaf, and examine for cracks or breakage. Check the center bolt for wear or distortion. This bolt forms the location for the spring on its axle pad and should be in good condition.

Important.—When fitting new leaves it is important that they are of the correct length and thickness, and have the same curvature as the remaining leaves.

It is advisable, even when no leaves are broken, to fit replacement springs when the originals have lost their camber due to settling.

The springs should be assembled clean, dry and free from any lubricant unless they are liberally coated with Shell Ensis 260 Fluid.

Place the leaves together in their correct order, locating them with the center bolt.

The dowel head of the bolt must be on top of the spring. Replace the distance-piece and clamp the leaves together.

Knock down the spring clips to close firmly round the main leaf.

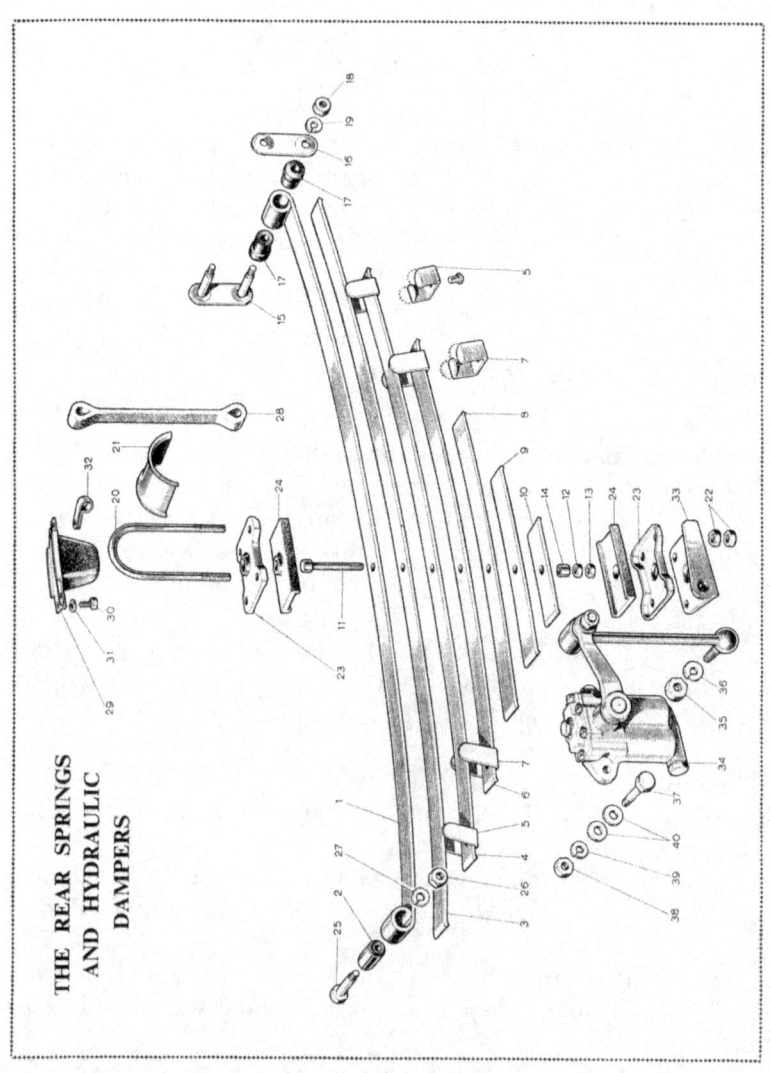

THE REAR SPRINGS AND HYDRAULIC DAMPERS

KEY TO THE REAR SPRINGS AND HYDRAULIC DAMPERS

No.	Description	No.	Description	No.	Description
1.	Leaf—main.	15.	Shackle plate and pins.	29.	Bump rubber.
2.	Bush.	16.	Shackle plate—inner.	30.	Screw—bump rubber to frame.
3.	Leaf—second.	17.	Bush—rubber.	31.	Washer—spring.
4.	Leaf—third.	18.	Nut—shackle plate.	32.	Clip—tail-lamp harness (on bump screw).
5.	Clip.	19.	Washer—spring.	33.	Bracket—shock absorber arm to rear spring—L/H.
6.	Leaf—fourth.	20.	" U " clip—rear spring.	34.	Shock absorber—rear—L/H.
7.	Clip.	21.	Plate—top " U " clip.	35.	Nut—arm to bracket.
8.	Leaf—fifth.	22.	Nut—" U " clip.	36.	Washer—spring.
9.	Leaf—sixth.	23.	Plate—spring locating.	37.	Bolt—shock absorber to frame.
10.	Bottom plate.	24.	Pad—spring seating.	38.	Nut—frame bolt.
11.	Bolt—locating.	25.	Bolt—spring front end.	39.	Washer—spring.
12.	Nut—locating bolt.	26.	Nut—front end bolt.	40.	Washer—plain.
13.	Locknut—locating bolt.	27.	Washer—spring.		
14.	Distance-piece—bolt.	28.	Rebound strap.		

Before replacing the shackle bolts, bushes and shackle plates they must be inspected for wear and, if necessary, replaced by new components.

Before tightening the spring bolts it is absolutely essential that the normal working load be applied to the springs so that the flexing rubber bushes are deflected to an equal extent in both directions during service. Failure to take this precaution will inevitably lead to early deterioration of the bushes.

THE STEERING GEAR

The steering gear is of the direct-acting rack-and-pinion type, providing light and accurate control under all conditions.

It consists of a rack bar and toothed pinion, both working in the plain bearings of the housing.

No adjustment for bearing wear in the box is provided, except by the fitting of the necessary new parts.

When in new condition the backlash in the tooth engagement is hardly perceptible, i.e. .001 to .003 in.

The steering mast is attached to the steering gearbox by a universal coupling.

All working parts are immersed in oil. An oil gun nipple is provided in the center of the box to replenish the oil, and a nipple on the pinion housing enables the upper end of the pinion shaft to be lubricated.

Felt bushes are fitted to the steering column. These are impregnated with oil and graphite, and no lubrication should be necessary, but if after long periods, a dry squeak develops, this may be cured by a small application of oil.

Removing and Replacing the Steering Wheel
1. Carefully pry the steering wheel cover from the hub of the wheel without chipping the material or the paintwork.
2. Unscrew the steering wheel nut and mark the wheel hub and column to ensure replacement in the original position. Pull off the wheel with a suitable tool.

When replacing the wheel, position it on the column splines in the original position to place the spokes equally about a horizontal datum line.

Tighten the nut to a torque wrench setting of 500 lb. in.

The steering wheel on a car fitted with the optional adjustable steering column may be removed complete with the column extension if necessary.
1. Remove the clamping nut and bolt from the telescopic adjustment clamp and extend the column as far as possible. Contract the plated helical sleeve and clamp collar towards the steering wheel and extract the key which engages the splined shaft.
2. Withdraw the steering wheel and column extension.

Removing the Steering Column
1. Withdraw the clamping bolt and nut securing the universal joint to the steering mast. Remove the nuts and clamp plate to release the draught excluding rubber from the toe-board at the lower end of the column.

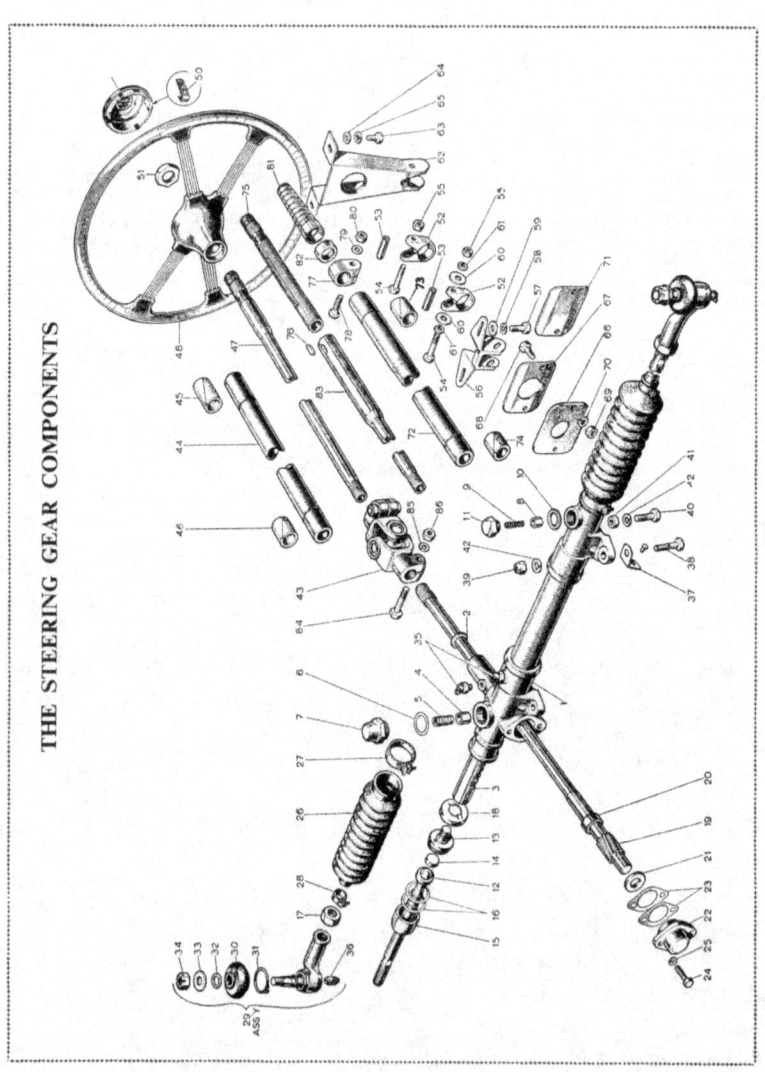

KEY TO THE STEERING GEAR COMPONENTS

No.	Description	No.	Description	No.	Description
1.	Housing assembly—rack. RHD.	30.	Boot—rubber.	59.	Washer—plain—bracket to frame.
2.	Seal—pinion shaft.	31.	Clip—boot.	60.	Washer—plain—lower bracket to clamp.
3.	Rack—steering.	32.	Ring—boot clip.	61.	Washer—spring—lower bracket to clamp.
4.	Pad—rack damper.	33.	Washer—ball socket.	62.	Bracket—upper—steering column.
5.	Spring—rack damper.	34.	Nut—ball socket.	63.	Screw—bracket to body rail.
6.	Shim—pad housing.	35.	Greaser—pinion/rack.	64.	Washer—plain.
7.	Housing—rack damper.	36.	Greaser—ball socket.	65.	Washer—spring.
8.	Pad—rack damper secondary.	37.	Shim—steering rack to brackets.	66.	Seal—rubber—column.
9.	Spring—rack damper secondary.	38.	Bolt—rack to bracket (front).	67.	Retainer—column seal.
10.	Washer—rack damper secondary.	39.	Nut—rack to bracket (Nylon).	68.	Screw—seal and retainer to dash.
11.	Housing—rack damper secondary.	40.	Bolt—rack to bracket (rear).	69.	Nut—seal/retainer screw.
12.	Rod—tie.	41.	Nut—rack to bracket (rear).	70.	Washer—spring—seal/retainer screw.
13.	Housing—male ball.	42.	Washer—spring—rack to bracket.	71.	Blanking plate.
14.	Seat—ball.	43.	Universal joint—steering column.	72.	*Tube—column outer.
15.	Housing—female ball.	44.	Tube—outer.	73.	*Bush—upper.
16.	Shim—ball housing .003 in.	45.	Bush—felt—upper end.	74.	*Bush—lower.
17.	Locknut—tie-rod.	46.	Bush—felt—lower end.	75.	*Top end—adjustable.
18.	Lock washer—tie-rod.	47.	Tube assembly—inner.	76.	*Key—top end.
19.	Pinion—steering.	48.	Wheel—steering.	77.	*Clamp—collar.
20.	Washer—thrust—upper pinion.	49.	Cover—steering wheel.	78.	*Bolt—clamp.
21.	Washer—thrust—lower pinion.	50.	Spring clip—cover.	79.	*Washer—spring—clamp bolt.
22.	Bearing—pinion tail.	51.	Nut—steering wheel.	80.	*Nut—clamp bolt.
23.	Shim .005 in.—tail bearing.	52.	Clamp—steering column.	81.	*Spring cover.
24.	Screw—bearing to steering box.	53.	Distance-piece—clamp.	82.	*Cup—spring cover.
25.	Washer—spring—bearing screw.	54.	Bolt—clamp.	83.	*Tube assembly—inner.
26.	Seal—rack.	55.	Nut—clamp bolt.	84.	Bolt—universal joint.
27.	Clip assembly—large—seal.	56.	Bracket (lower)—steering column	85.	Washer—spring.
28.	Clip assembly—small—seal.	57.	Screw—bracket to frame.	86.	Nut—universal joint bolt.
29.	Socket assembly—ball.	58.	Washer—spring—bracket to frame.		

* Optional equipment.

2. Withdraw the two clamping bolts, nuts, spring and flat washers and distance tube which support the steering column, and withdraw the column complete with steering mast and steering wheel.

Removing Steering Column Bushes

Remove the steering wheel and column assembly and withdraw the mast from the outer column. Pry out the felt bushes.

New bushes should be soaked in graphite oil before reassembly.

Removing the Steering Column Universal Joint

Bolts and nuts clamp the universal joint splines on the steering mast and steering pinion, and the bolts must be withdrawn completely to release the universal joint assembly.
1. Slacken the bolts supporting the steering column below the dash panel.
2. Withdraw the clamping bolts from the universal joint.
3. Move the steering column and steering mast assembly upwards to withdraw the steering mast from the universal joint.
4. Withdraw the universal joint from the steering pinion.

When replacing the universal joint see "Steering Column Alignment," below.

Dismantling the Universal Joint

The Hardy Spicer joint has four needle roller bearings retained on a center spider by circlips. The joints are packed with grease on assembly and there is no further provision for lubrication.
1. Remove any enamel and dirt from the snap rings and bearing races. Remove the snap rings by pinching the ears together and prying them out with a screwdriver.

If a ring does not slide readily from its groove, tap the end of the bearing race lightly to relieve the pressure against the bearing.
2. Hold the joint in one hand with the side of a yoke at the top and tap the radius of the yoke lightly with a copper hammer. The bearing should begin to emerge; turn the joint over and remove the bearing and needle rollers with the fingers. If necessary, tap the bearing race from the inside with a small-diameter bar, taking care not to damage the bearing face, or grip the needle bearing in a vice and tap the yoke clear.
3. Repeat this operation for the opposite bearing.
4. One yoke can now be removed. Rest the two exposed trunnions on wood or lead blocks to protect their ground faces, and tap the top lug of the flange yoke to remove the bearing race.

5. Turn the yoke over and repeat the operation.

When reassembling, replace the cork gasket and gasket retainers on the spider journals, using a tubular drift. The spider journal shoulders should be shellacked prior to fitting the retainers to ensure a good oil seal.

Smear the walls of the races with grease and assemble the needle rollers to the bearing races and pack with grease.

Insert the spider in one yoke and, using a soft-nosed drift slightly smaller in diameter than the hole in the yoke, tap the bearings into position. It is essential that the bearing races are a light drive fit in the yoke trunnions.

Repeat this operation for the other bearings and replace the circlips, making sure that they are firmly located in their grooves. If the joint appears to bind, tap lightly with a wooden mallet to relieve any pressure by the bearings on the ends of the journals.

Removing and Replacing the Steering Gearbox

The procedure detailed here will remove the steering rack from a completely assembled car. If the chassis frame front extension has been removed, the steering rack can be removed with the pinion in position.

1. Remove the steering rack damper and secondary damper assemblies.

2. Take out the two bolts and spring washers and withdraw the pinion tail bearing and shims and bottom thrust washer, placing a container to catch any oil that may drain from the steering rack. Support the front end of the car by placing jacks beneath the lower suspension arm spring pans, and remove the road wheels.

3. Remove the split pins and nuts and drive the tie-rod ball pins from the steering-arms. Turn the steering onto the left lock (R.H.D. cars) or right lock (L.H.D. cars). Withdraw the clamping nut and bolt from the universal joint on the pinion shaft and withdraw the pinion assembly. Remove the nuts and bolts securing the steering rack to the chassis frame, noting that the front bolts are fitted with self-locking nuts, and packing shims may be found between the rack and the frame brackets.

4. Move the steering assembly towards the center of the car until the steering tie-rod is clear of the front extension plate, and withdraw the assembly downwards.

Replacing

The steering gearbox is assembled to the car by reversing the above procedure although special attention should be given to the instructions in "Steering Column Alignment."

When re-engaging the pinion with the universal joint splines, ensure that the cut-away portion for the clamp bolt is aligned with the bolt hole.

Dismantling the Steering Gearbox

If the steering rack assembly is removed complete with the steering pinion in position, remove the pinion as follows.

1. Remove the damper housing, spring, pad and shims from above the pinion housing.
2. Unscrew the secondary damper housing and remove complete with washer, spring and damper pad.
3. Withdraw the pinion tail bearing and shims and the pinion bottom thrust washer, placing a container to catch any oil that may drain from the steering rack. The top thrust washer will remain trapped behind the steering rack.
4. Unlock the tie-rod ball-end locknuts and remove the ball end assemblies. Release the rubber gaiter seal clips and remove the seals.
5. Secure the rack housing between suitable clamps in a vice and tap back the washers locking the tie-rod ball housings. Unscrew the ball housings with special tool 18G313 and remove the lock washers.
6. The steering rack may now be withdrawn from the housing.

Screw the ball seat housing from the ball joint caps, using the special 'C' wrench previously mentioned together with the special tie-rod pin spanner 18G312.

The shims and ball seats are now free to be removed; ensure that they are kept to their respective sides.

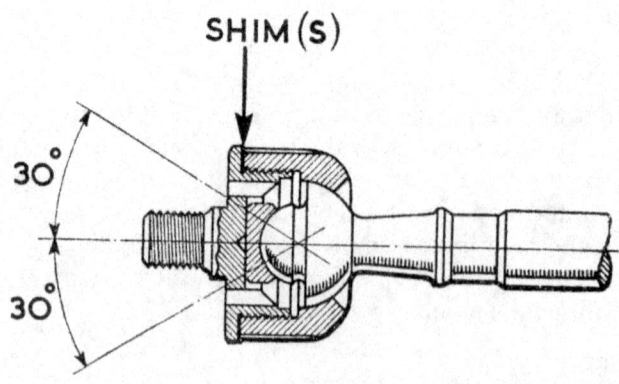

The assembly of a tie-rod ball joint

Reassembling the Steering Gear
1. Insert the ball end of the tie-rod in the female housing and assemble the ball seat, male seat housing and shims. Tighten the two housings together with special tools 18G312 and 18G313. The ball must be a reasonably tight sliding fit without play. Adjustment is carried out by varying the thickness of the shims between the ball housings. The shims are provided in thicknesses of .003 and .005 in. When correctly adjusted fit a new lock washer to one end of the steering rack, then replace and tighten the ball housing with special tool 18G313. The ball housing must be locked in three places by the flange of the lock washer.
2. Insert the top thrust washer (the thick one) with the slotted side away from the pinion and insert the rack in its housing. Refit and adjust the other ball seat.
3. Refit the rubber gaiters and clips.
4. Replace the ball end locknuts and joint assemblies in their approximate original positions.
5. Fit a new pinion shaft felt seal.
6. If the chassis frame front extension is in position, the steering rack assembly should be positioned on its mounting brackets before refitting the pinion.
7. Replace the smaller thrust washer on the plain end of the pinion shaft.
8. Replace the shims and the pinion tail bearing, and secure them in position. Check the end-play of the pinion shaft, which should be between .002 and .005 in. If necessary, the shims must be adjusted to give this degree of play.
9. To adjust the rack damper the plunger must be replaced in the cap and the cap screwed into position without the spring or shims until it is just possible to rotate the pinion shaft by drawing the rack through its housing. A feeler gauge is then used to measure the clearance between the hexagon of the plunger cap and its seating on the rack housing. To this figure must be added an additional clearance of .002 to .005 in. to arrive at the correct thickness of shims which must be placed beneath the damper cap. The shims are .003 in. thick.
10. Remove the damper cap and plunger and replace and tighten the assembly with the requisite number of .003 in. shims as defined in the previous paragraph.
11. Replace the secondary damper without shims.

Pump approximately $1/2$ pint of Hypoid oil into the rack housing through the nipple provided, or release one of the outer rubber gaiter clips and pour the oil in through a funnel. Move

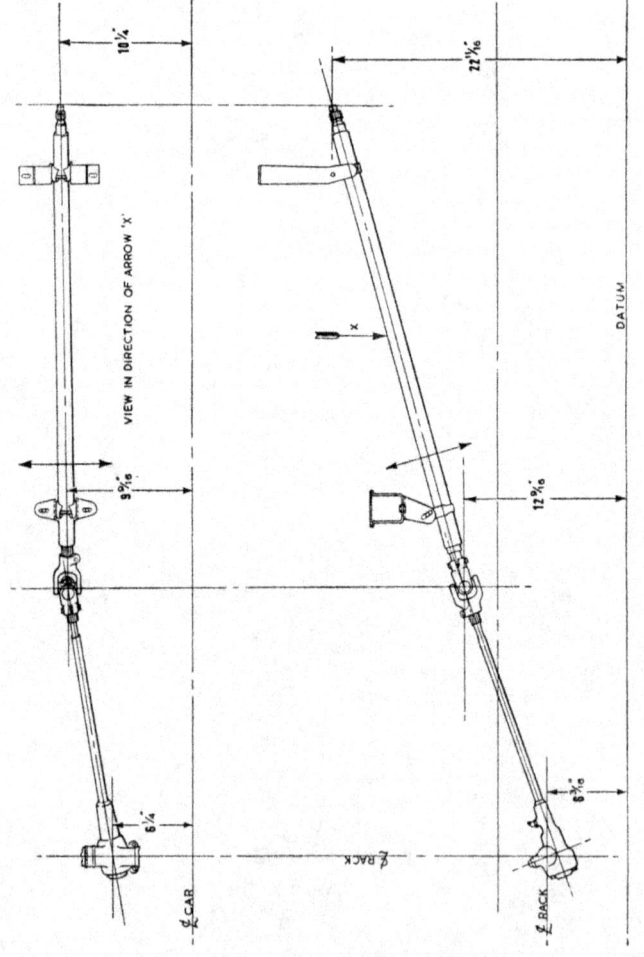

Steering-column alignment

the rack assembly backwards and forwards slowly to distribute the oil.

Steering Column Alignment

When assembling the steering column or steering gearbox assembly to the car, care must be taken to ensure a free condition at the universal joint before the column or gearbox securing bolts are tightened. For the universal joint to be completely unloaded, the center line of the steering column and the center line of the steering rack pinion must pass through the center of the universal joint spider when the assembly is viewed from above and from the side. Failure to ensure complete freedom at the universal joint will load the steering pinion upper bearing and cause extreme wear and steering stiffness.

To enable the assembly to be secured in the correct position, the attachment holes in the support bracket at the lower end of the steering column are slotted to permit up and down and sideways movement, and packing shims are fitted between the steering gearbox mounting bosses and the brackets on the front suspension member.

Tighten the universal joint clamp bolts.

With the steering column draught excluding rubber clamp plate and all column and rack securing bolts slack, position the universal joint and tighten the support bracket clamp bolts at the lower end of the column.

Should there be a gap between the gearbox bosses and mounting brackets, remove the bolts, pack with shims as required and replace and tighten the securing bolts.

To ensure complete alignment again slacken and retighten the steering column lower support bolt.

Tighten the upper support bracket bolt.

Checking and Adjusting Front Wheel Alignment — MGA

When checking the track width at the front and the rear of the front wheels, use a suitable trammel or any special proprietary alignment available.
1. The wheels should run parallel and have no toe-in.
2. See that the tires are inflated to the correct pressures.
3. Set the wheels in the straight-ahead position.
4. Set the arms of a suitable trammel to the height of the hub center on the outside of the wheels.
5. Place the trammel to the rear of the wheels and adjust the pointers to register with the wheel rims. Chalk the position of the pointers in each wheel rim and push the car forward one half-turn of the wheels. Take the front reading from the same

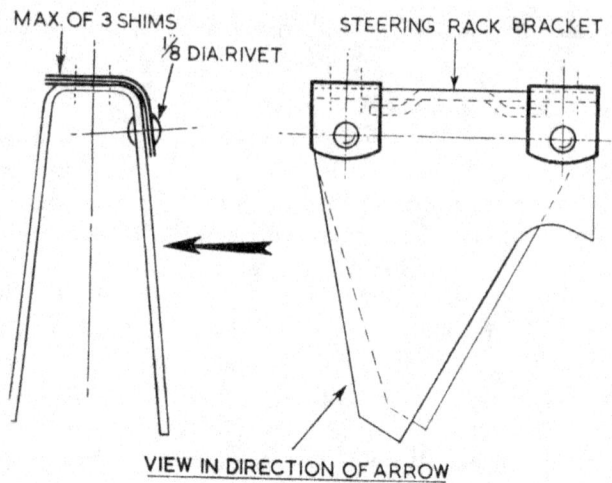

VIEW IN DIRECTION OF ARROW

The location of the steering gearbox mounting bracket shims which are used to position the gearbox and assist in obtaining correct steering column alignment. When the necessary thickness of shims has been determined they are riveted to the chassis frame to prevent their loss

marks on the rims. For the alignment to be correct the pointers should again register with the marks on the rims.
  If adjustment is necessary, proceed as follows.
1. Slacken the locknuts at the ends of the short tie-rods and the clips securing the rubber gaiters to the tie-rods.
2. Use the spanner flats on the rods to rotate each of the tie-rods **equally** in the desired direction. These both have right-hand threads.
  NOTE.—To ensure that the steering gearbox is in the central position and that the steering geometry is correct, it is important that the tie-rods are adjusted to exactly equal lengths. This can be ascertained by measuring from the end of the flats to the locknuts.
  After adjustment retighten the ball joint locknuts and rubber gaiter clips and ensure that the machined undersides of the ball joints are in the same plane.

Front Wheel Alignment — MGB
  When checking the track width at the front and the rear of the front wheels use a suitable trammel or any special proprietary alignment gauge available.

The wheels should toe in $\frac{1}{16}$ to $\frac{3}{32}$ in.

See that the tires are inflated to the correct pressures. Set the wheels in the straight-ahead position.

Set the arms of a suitable trammel to the height of the hub center on the outside of the wheels.

Place the trammel to the rear of the wheels and adjust the pointers to register with the wheel rims. Chalk the position of the pointers in each wheel rim and push the car forward one half-turn of the wheels. Take the front reading from the same marks on the rims. For the alignment to be correct the pointers should again register with the marks on the rims.

If adjustment is necessary, proceed as follows.

Slacken the locknuts at the ends of the short tie-rods and the clips securing the rubber gaiters to the tie-rods.

Use the spanner flats on the rods to rotate each of the tie-rods **equally** in the desired direction. These both have right-hand threads.

NOTE.—To ensure that the steering gearbox is in the central position and that the steering geometry is correct, it is important that the tie-rods are adjusted to exactly equal lengths. This can be ascertained by measuring from the end of the flats to the locknuts.

After adjustment retighten the ball joint locknuts and rubber gaiter clips and ensure that the machined under sides of the ball joints are in the same plane.

Fitting An Adjustable Steering Column

1. Remove the steering wheel.
2. Remove the steering column assembly.
3. Fit the steering column to the car and tighten the clamp bolts.
4. Fit the steering wheel, locating it on the splines to bring the center line of the spokes horizontal when the road wheels are in the straight-ahead position.

Nylon-seated Ball Joints

Nylon-seated ball joints, which are sealed in manufacture and therefore require no further lubrication, were progressively introduced as alternatives to the conventional types which need lubricating at regular intervals.

It is essential that no dirt or abrasive matter should enter the nylon ball joint; in the event of a rubber boot being torn or damaged in service it is probable that the ball joint has been left exposed, and it is therefore important to renew both the ball joint and the boot.

If damage to the boot occurs while the steering side- or cross-rod is being removed in the workshop, only a new rubber boot need be fitted, provided the ball joint is clean. Smear the area adjacent to the joint with a little Dextragrease Super G.P. prior to assembling the boot.

THE FRONT SUSPENSION

The independent front suspension is the wishbone type with coil springing. The front wheels follow the road surface without influencing each other, and each wheel is permitted to rise and fall vertically. The suspension gives perfect stability with riding comfort and, by the combination of the direct-acting rack-and-pinion steering gear, it also provides light and accurate control under all conditions.

The inner mountings of the lower wishbones are fitted with flexing rubber bearings which require no lubrication and form a silent and resilient connection to the robust box-section chassis frame cross-member.

The steering swivel pins are of a special design, with the top and bottom bearings threaded to provide large areas and absorb both thrust and journal loads. The swivel pin threads are of opposite hand on each side of the car and are therefore not interchangeable. The steering connection from wheel to wheel is provided by the steering gearbox rack bar and two short tie-rods, with ball joints at each end. The outer ball joints are fitted with grease gun nipples, but the inner ball sockets are enclosed in the telescopic rubber dust excluders and are automatically lubricated from the steering gearbox.

Removing the Front Suspension
1. Jack up the front of the car with a jack placed under the center of the front cross-member until the front wheels are just clear of the ground.
2. Remove the front wheels.
3. Place the jack under each spring pan and lift until the hydraulic damper arms are just clear of the rebound rubbers.
4. Disconnect the hydraulic brake hose.
5. Slacken the steering tie-rod nuts and screw the tie-rods out of the steering ball joints, using a spanner on the flats on the rods.
6. Remove the cotters and nuts from the two outer fulcrum bolts. Draw out the bolts and take away the front hub and swivel pin units complete. (Take care of the thrust washers, rubber seals, retainers and fulcrum pins.)
7. Release the jacks from under the spring pans.
8. Press down the lower wishbone assemblies and remove the coil springs.
9. Remove the four bolts holding the spring pan to the levers.
10. Remove the cotters, nuts and washers from the ends of the inner lower fulcrum pin and slide off the levers and the rubber bushes.

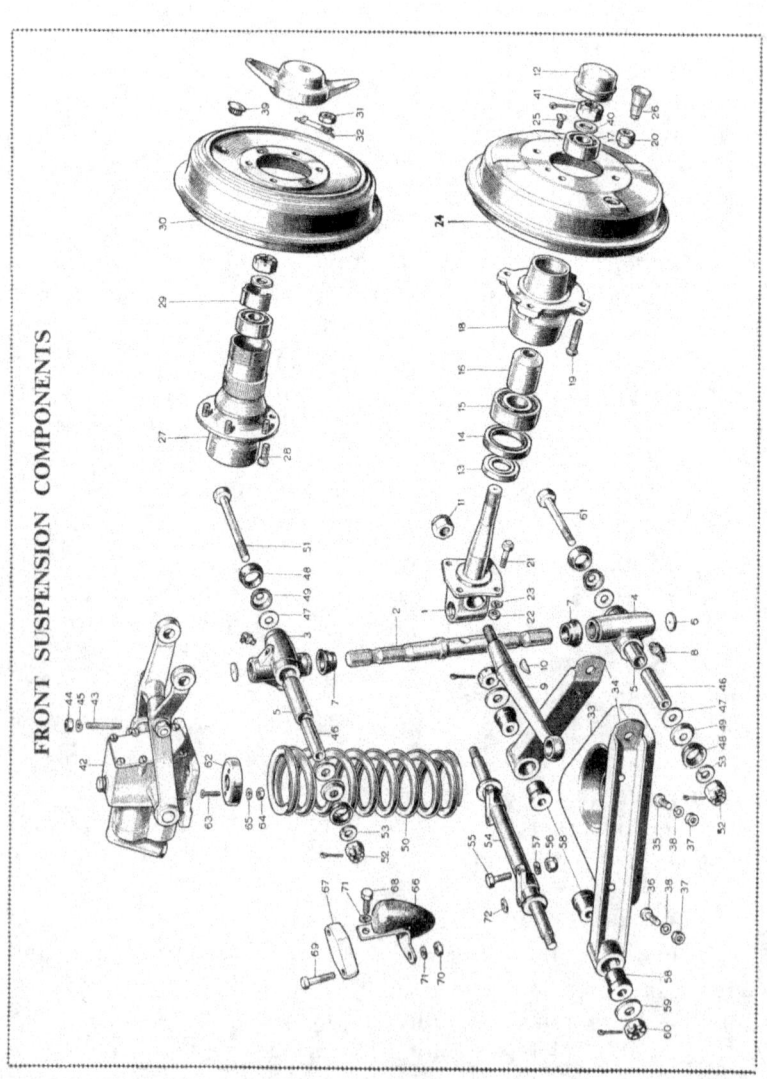

KEY TO FRONT SUSPENSION COMPONENTS (Disc or Wire Wheel)

No.	Description
1.	Steering knuckle—L/H.
2.	Swivel pin—L/H.
3.	Link—swivel pin—upper L/H.
4.	Link—swivel pin—lower L/H.
5.	Bush.
6.	Plate.
7.	Seal—swivel pin.
8.	Grease nipple—link.
9.	Steering lever—L/H.
10.	Key—Woodruff No. 8—steering lever.
11.	Nut—steering lever.
12.	Grease-retaining cup. DW.
13.	Distance washer—hub.
14.	Oil seal—hub.
15.	Bearing—large—hub.
16.	Distance piece—hub bearing.
17.	Bearing—small—hub.
18.	Hub assembly—front.
19.	Stud—wheel. DW.
20.	Nut—wheel stud. DW.
21.	Bolt—brake backplate.
22.	Nut—backplate bolt.
23.	Washer—spring—backplate bolt.
24.	Drum—brake. DW.
25.	Screw—countersunk—drum to hub. DW.
26.	Plug—large—brake-drum. DW.
27.	Hub assembly—front L/H. WW.
28.	Stud. WW.
29.	Grease retainer. WW.
30.	Drum—brake. WW.
31.	Nut—drum to hub. WW.
32.	Locking tab—drum to hub. WW.
33.	Spring pan assembly.
34.	Bottom wishbone assembly.
35.	Screw—spring pan to wishbone.
36.	Screw—spring pan to wishbone.
37.	Nut—spring pan to wishbone screw.
38.	Washer—spring pan to wishbone screw.
39.	Plug—brake-drum—large. WW.
40.	Washer.
41.	Nut—L/H thread.
42.	Hydraulic damper.
43.	Stud—hydraulic damper to cross-member.
44.	Nut—hydraulic damper to cross-member stud.
45.	Washer—spring—hydraulic damper to cross-member.
46.	Distance tube—link.
47.	Thrust washer—link.
48.	Seal—link.
49.	Support—link seal.
50.	Spring—coil.
51.	Bolt—wishbone to link.
52.	Nut—castle—wishbone to link.
53.	Washer—spring—wishbone to link.
54.	Wishbone pivot.
55.	Bolt—pivot to member.
56.	Nut—pivot to member bolt.
57.	Washer—spring—pivot to member bolt.
58.	Bush—bottom wishbone.
59.	Washer—wishbone pivot.
60.	Nut—slotted—wishbone pivot.
61.	Bolt—bottom wishbone to link.
62.	Spigot—spring.
63.	Screw—spigot to member.
64.	Nut—spigot to member screw.
65.	Washer—spigot to member screw.
66.	Check rubber.
67.	Distance piece—check rubber.
68.	Screw—check rubber to member.
69.	Bolt—check rubber to member.
70.	Nut—check rubber to member—bolt.
71.	Washer—spring—check rubber to member.
72.	Washer—plain—under front outer head pivot to member bolt.

201

11. Remove the bolts holding the lower fulcrum pins to the chassis cross-member.

12. Remove the nuts from studs securing the hydraulic dampers to the top of the suspension cross-member.

Inside the outer ends of the suspension cross-member will be found the coil spring locating plates. These are each attached by two bolts and nuts.

Dismantling the Swivel Pins

Unscrew the upper and lower links from the ends of the swivel pins. The left-hand swivel pin has a left-hand thread at each end.

The stub axle is located by a collar on the swivel pin and the stem of the steering lever engaging a groove in the pin. To separate the two, the steering lever must be withdrawn from the stub axle, but this procedure is not advised unless absolutely necessary.

Examining Parts For Wear

Examine the following parts before reassembling:—

Bushes for bottom wishbone

If these are split, perished, eccentric or oil-soaked, they should be renewed.

Bottom wishbone

Examine the end holes for elongation and the assembly for looseness. If there is any sign of slackness between the wishbone arms and the pan, separate the components and check the bolt holes for elongation. The bolt holes are $^{21}/_{64}$ in. diameter.

Coil spring

Examine for cracks and check for tension, if necessary, to details in the General Data Section. Renew the springs if they are defective.

Swivel link assemblies

Check the swivel links. The dimension across the thrust faces should be 2.237 in. If these are appreciably worn the assembly of link and bush should be renewed. If the bush only is worn, a new one should be pressed in and reamed and burnished to .750 in.

Note.—When pressing in this bush see that the hole in the bush faces the threaded bore.

Check the threaded bores of the links on the swivel pins. When new, these are a free turning fit without slack. An appreciable amount of slack is permissible in these threaded bearings and they do not require renewal unless they are very slack.

Check the fulcrum pin distance tubes for scoring or wear. These should be 2.337 in. long by .7480 in. diameter.

Examine the case-hardened thrust washers for ridges; the faces should be flat and parallel within .0005 in.

The thickness should be .068 to .065 in., the bore .510 to .505 in. and the outside diameter 1.25 in.

When the swivel links, distance tubes and thrust washers are assembled, the total end clearance between the link and the thrust washers should be .008 to .013 in.

Check that all grease nipples are clear.

Examine the rubber seals, and if these are perished or split, renew them.

Hub Ball Bearings

As far as possible, bearings which come under review during the overhaul of the car should be cleaned and inspected without being withdrawn from the housings to which they are fitted. Unnecessary withdrawal causes deterioration of the fitting surfaces, and may damage the bearing, whereas if bearings are examined in position and found still to be serviceable, they can be left undisturbed with advantage.

Rust on the exterior surfaces of the bearing is not detrimental unless the fit is affected, but if the tracks, balls or rollers are severely pitted, the running life of the bearing is at an end and a new one should be fitted.

Ball bearings should be cleaned thoroughly with paraffin. Bearings which have been washed in this manner should be rinsed thoroughly and dried, and should be immersed in mineral oil as soon as possible after they have been examined.

After cleaning, bearings should be examined for cracks in the races, chipped or broken balls, and worn or damaged tracks or cages.

If either race is cracked or chipped, or if the tracks have spalled or flaked, the bearing should be scrapped.

Replacing the Front Suspension

1. Bolt up the coil spring top locating plates inside the front cross-member.
2. Replace the hydraulic dampers.
3. The dampers are interchangeable from side to side.
4. Bolt up the lower fulcrum pins. The two front outer bolts have their nuts uppermost and the six other bolts have their nuts below.
5. Fit the rubber bushes into the lower levers. These bushes will be found to be a loose fit in the lever, but when clamped up by the nut and washer will expand into their housing. These

bushes do not rotate on their surfaces, the angular movement being taken up by the rubber itself flexing. Special care should be taken when assembling these bushes to maintain a central location, so that the expansion of each half of the bush is equal. To attain this, insert each bush so that it protrudes equally each side of the housing, and then clamp up with the washer and nut and fit the cotter pins. When central, the outer flanges of the bushes should all be of equal proportions.

It is essential to clamp up the bushes when the lower suspension levers are set parallel with the ground to ensure even stresses on the bushes in service.

6. Fit the spring pans between the levers, but with the heads of the bolts inside the spring pan. Do not tighten up the spring pan bolts solid, but leave them half a turn slack.
7. Press down the lower wishbone assemblies.
8. Smear each end of the coil springs with grease to prevent any slight squeaking in operation.
9. Push the coil springs up into the cross-member and over the locating plates.
10. Jack up the lower wishbone assemblies until they are approximately parallel to the ground.
11. Assemble the hub units and swivel pins.

   NOTE.—**The king pin bearing threads, the stub axles, and the stub axle nuts are right-hand-threaded on the right-hand side of the car and left-hand-threaded on the left-hand side.**
12. Fit the front hub units to the suspension levers.
13. Ensure that the thrust washers, rubber seals and retainers are assembled in the right order.
14. Lubricate these parts and the fulcrum pins during assembly and again afterwards with the grease gun, using the recommended lubricant.
15. Do not tighten up the top or the bottom slotted nuts solid, but leave them half a turn slack.
16. Connect up the hydraulic brake hoses. See correct method as explained in section on brakes.
17. Screw the steering tie-rods into the outer steering ball joints. Screw the rods right in and then slack off five complete turns. This will give a rough wheel alignment and render subsequent accurate alignment easier.
18. Adjust and bleed the front brakes.
19. Fit the front wheels.
20. Bounce the front end of the car up and down a few times. This allows the suspension fulcrums to settle down.
21. Now tighten the spring pan bolts and then tighten and cotter

up the outer fulcrum bolts.
22. Check and adjust the front wheel alignment.

Reassembling the Swivel Pins

The swivel pin assembly may be reassembled without difficulty by carrying out the removal instructions in the reverse order, provided the following points are given special attention:
1. The swivel pin and links fitted to the left-hand side of the car have left-hand threads at each end and those fitted to the right-hand side have right-hand threads.
2. The swivel pin links screw onto threads on each end of the swivel pin and the threads are waisted at their center to avoid fouling the pivot bolts passing through the links. Before the pivot bolt is replaced the link must be correctly positioned on the thread.

First screw the link onto the swivel pin until the waisted portion of the pin lines up with the pivot bolt hole.

Place the pivot bolt in position in the link and screw the link to the extent of its maximum travel on the swivel pin thread; this is about three revolutions total. Screw the link back approximately one and a half times to obtain the maximum clearances for the pivot pin in each direction.

If the brake plate has been removed from the swivel pin assembly, the lower link must also be centralized in a similar manner before the brake plate is replaced and before the swivel pin is fitted to the suspension arm.
3. Before the lower steering knuckle link is bolted in position ensure that both thrust washers and rubber seals are fitted correctly and make sure that the links have a total end clearance of .008 to .013 in. between the end faces of the link and the thrust washers.

NOTE.—Be sure to locate the lower link assembly correctly because it cannot be set once the brake back-plate is fitted.

Removing the Brake-drum and Hub
1. Slacken the wheel stud nuts.
2. Apply the hand brake and raise the car until the wheel to be operated on is clear of the ground.
3. Unscrew the stud nuts and remove the wheel.
4. Withdraw the two countersunk-headed screws and remove the brake-drum.
5. Remove the grease-retaining cap and withdraw the split pin from the stub axle nut and unscrew the nut, remembering that the axle on the left-hand side of the car has a left-hand thread.
6. Place a hub extractor (special tool 18G304 with adaptor bolts

18G304B in position and use the central extractor screw to withdraw the hub assembly.

IMPORTANT.—When the front hub has been removed the inner bearing, oil seal, and hub distance washer MUST be removed from the stub axle and replaced in the hub before it is refitted to the stub axle. If the hub is pressed on the shaft without first fitting the bearing and oil seal to it, the inner bearing will re-enter its housing but the oil seal will only be pushed farther from its correct position.

Replacing the Front Hub

If all grease has been cleaned from the hub and the bearings washed for examination, ensure that they are repacked with grease before the hub is reassembled.

Replace the bearing spacer with the chamfered side towards the small outer bearing and then press the large bearing into position. Replace the oil seal and distance washer. The metal face of the oil seal and the chamfered side of the distance washer are fitted away from the bearing.

Replace the hub on the stub axle shaft. Replace and tighten the hub nut, and replace grease-retaining cap.

Removing and Replacing the Front Coil Spring

1. Apply the hand brake and jack up the front end of the car until the wheels are clear of the ground, using a suitable jack placed under the center of the front cross-member.
2. Remove the front wheel on the side affected.
3. Place an additional jack under the lower spring pan and jack up until the hydraulic damper levers are clear of the rebound rubber.
4. Remove the lower fulcrum bolt.
5. Swing up the hub unit and rest on a suitable block.
6. Release the jack from under the spring pan, press down the lower wishbone assembly and remove the coil spring.

Replacement is carried out in the reverse manner to that detailed for removal.

NOTE.—Take care that the thrust washers, rubber seals, and retainers are assembled in the right order.

Lubricate these parts and the fulcrum pins during and after assembly.

Smear each end of the coil spring with grease and ensure that the upper end of the spring is correctly located.

Fitting New Rubber Bushes

1. Remove the coil springs.

2. Remove the four bolts holding the spring pan to the levers.
3. Remove the cotters, nuts and washers from the ends of the inner lower fulcrum pin and slide off the levers and the rubber bushes.
4. Fit the new rubber bushes into the levers. These will be found to be quite a loose fit in the lever, but when clamped up by the nut and washer will expand into their housing. These bushes do not rotate on their surfaces, and the angular movement being taken by the rubber deflecting torsionally in itself. Special care should be taken when assembling these bushes to maintain a central location, so that the expansion of each half of the bush is equal.

To attain this, insert each bush so that it protrudes equally each side of the housing, and then clamp up with the washer and nut. When central, the outer flanges of the bushes should be of equal proportions.

It is essential to clamp up the bushes when the suspension levers are set parallel with the ground to ensure even stresses on the bushes.

5. Now fit the spring pan between the levers, but with the heads of the bolts inside the spring pan.
6. Do not tighten up the spring pan bolts solid, but leave them half a turn slack.
7. Press down the lower wishbone assembly.
8. Smear each end of the coil spring with grease, and push the spring up into the front cross-member and over its top locating plate.
9. Jack up the lower wishbone assembly until it is approximately parallel to the ground.
10. Swing down the hub unit and fit the lower fulcrum bolt.

NOTE.—Take care that the thrust washers, rubber seals and retainers are assembled in the right order.

11. Lubricate these and the fulcrum pin during and after assembly with the grease gun.
12. Remove the jack from under the wishbone assembly.
13. Finally tighten up the spring pan bolts, and insert the split cotter pins in all castellated nuts.

Modified Front Coil Springs

Modified front coil springs were introduced at Car No. 15152. The new springs (Part No. AHH5546) are interchangeable on earlier cars in pairs only.

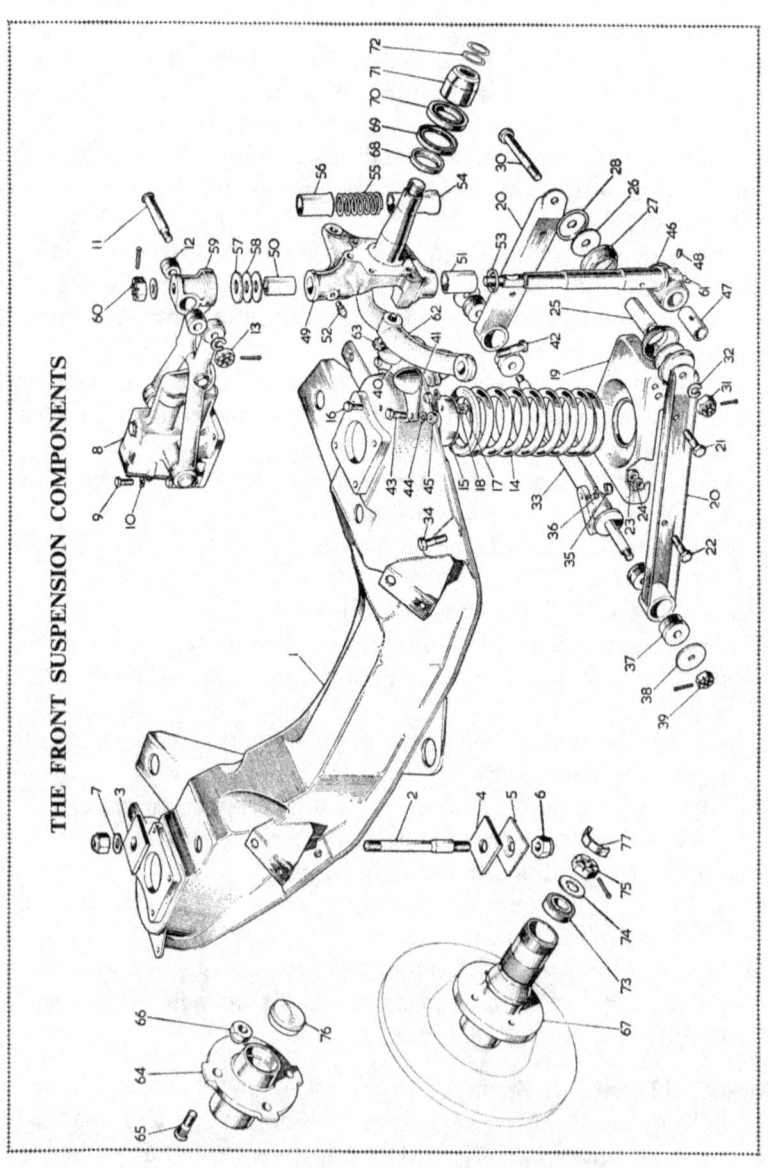

KEY TO THE FRONT SUSPENSION COMPONENTS

No.	Description
1.	Cross-member.
2.	Bolt—cross-member to body.
3.	Pad—mounting—upper (rubber).
4.	Pad—mounting—lower (rubber).
5.	Plate—clamp.
6.	Nut—mounting bolt.
7.	Washer—plain—nut.
8.	Absorber—shock.
9.	Screw—shock absorber to cross-member.
10.	Washer-screw—spring.
11.	Pin—fulcrum—top link to shock absorber arm.
12.	Bearing—link.
13.	Nut—fulcrum pin.
14.	Spring—coil.
15.	Spigot—spring.
16.	Screw—spigot to cross-member.
17.	Nut—screw.
18.	Washer—spring—nut.
19.	Pan assembly—spring.
20.	Wishbone assembly—bottom.
21.	Screw—spring pan to wishbone.
22.	Screw—spring pan to wishbone.
23.	Nut—screw.
24.	Washer—spring—nut.
25.	Tube—distance—link.
26.	Washer—thrust—link.
27.	Seal—link.
28.	Support—link seal.
29.	Nut—wishbone pivot.
30.	Bolt—wishbone to link.
31.	Nut—bolt.
32.	Washer—spring—nut.
33.	Pivot—wishbone.
34.	Bolt—pivot to member.
35.	Nut—bolt.
36.	Washer—spring—nut.
37.	Bush—wishbone.
38.	Washer—wishbone pivot.
39.	Nut—wishbone pivot.
40.	Buffer—rebound.
41.	Distance piece.
42.	Bolt—rebound buffer to cross-member.
43.	Screw—rebound buffer to cross-member.
44.	Washer—spring.
45.	Nut.
46.	Pin—swivel.
47.	Bush—swivel pin.
48.	Screw—grub—swivel pin.
49.	Axle assembly—swivel—R.H.
50.	Bush—swivel—top.
51.	Bush—swivel—bottom.
52.	Lubricator—swivel bush.
53.	Ring—swivel axle pin (cork).
54.	Tube—dust excluder—bottom.
55.	Spring—dust excluder.
56.	Tube—dust excluder—top.
57.	Washer—thrust.
58.	Washer—floating thrust—·052 to ·057 in. (1·32 to 1·44 mm.).
59.	Trunnion—suspension link.
60.	Nut—swivel axle pin.
61.	Lubricator—swivel pin.
62.	Lever—steering—R.H.
63.	Bolt—steering lever to swivel axle.
64.	Hub assembly.
65.	Stud—wheel.
66.	Nut—wheel stud.
67.	Hub assembly—R.H.
68.	Collar—oil seal.
69.	Seal—oil.
70.	Bearing for hub—inner.
71.	Spacer—bearing.
72.	Shim—·003 in. (·76 mm.).
73.	Bearing—hub—outer.
74.	Washer—bearing retaining.
75.	Nut—bearing retaining.
76.	Cup—grease-retaining.
77.	Cup—grease-retaining.

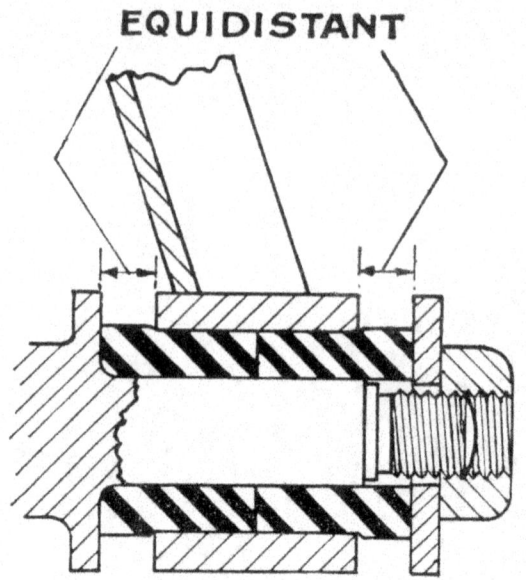

The correct method of clamping the rubber bushes of the lower suspension arm

LOCKHEED DISC BRAKED CARS

Removing and Dismantling a Front Hub

1. Apply the hand brake and raise the front of the car until the wheel to be operated on is clear of the ground.
2. Remove the road wheel.
3. Remove the brake unit.
4. Withdraw the grease retainer and extract the split pin from the stub axle nut and unscrew the nut, remembering that the stub axle on the left-hand side of the car has a left-hand thread.
5. Draw off the hub and brake disc assembly, using a puller as illustrated or special tool 18G363 (wire wheels) or 18G304 with adaptors 18G304B and 18G304J (pressed-steel wheels).
6. The brake disc can now be removed from the hub, if necessary, by removing the four nuts and spring washers.
7. Tap out the small bearing with a drift; remove the spacer tube and tap out the large bearing and oil seal.

   IMPORTANT.—If the inner bearing, oil seal, and distance washer remain on the stub axle as the hub is removed they must be replaced in the hub before it is fitted to the stub axle to ensure that the oil seal is in its correct position.

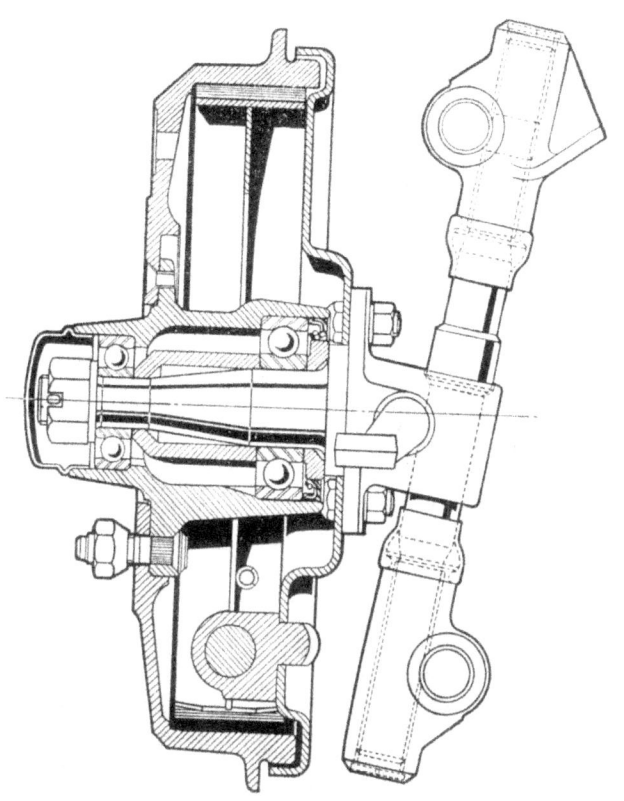

*A section through the front hub and brake drum
(disc wheel type).*

Reassembling and Replacing a Front Hub

If all the grease has been cleaned from the hub and the bearings washed for examination ensure that they are repacked with grease before the hub is reassembled.

Replace the outer bearing and the bearing distance piece with the chamfered side towards the outer bearing and then press the large (inner) bearing into position. Replace the oil seal and distance washer. The metal face of the oil seal and the recessed side of the distance washer are fitted away from the bearing.

Reassembly is then a reversal of the instructions given above.

NOTE.—The brake unit securing bolts must be tightened to the correct torque figure and reference should be made to brake section. If the brake disc has been disturbed the run-out must be checked.

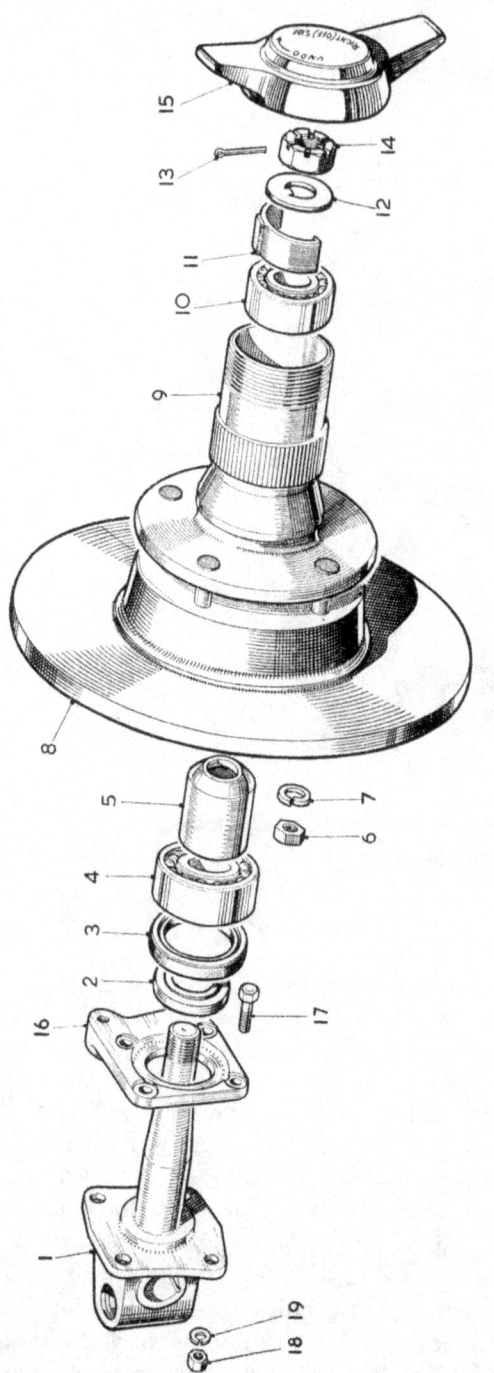

Fig. KK.3
The front hub components (wire wheel type)

1. Steering knuckle.
2. Distance washer.
3. Oil seal.
4. Large (inner) bearing.
5. Distance piece.
6. Disc securing nut.
7. Spring washer.
8. Brake disc.
9. Hub assembly.
10. Small (outer) bearing.
11. Grease retainer.
12. Washer.
13. Split pin.
14. Hub securing nut.
15. Hub cap.
16. Adaptor plate.
17. Adaptor plate bolt.
18. Nut for bolt.
19. Spring washer.

DUNLOP DISC BRAKED CARS

Removing and Dismantling a Front Hub
1. Apply the hand brake and raise the front of the car until the wheel to be operated on is clear of the ground.
2. Remove the wheel.
3. Remove the wheel brake unit as detailed in brake section.
4. Withdraw the grease retainer cap.
5. Extract the split pin from the stub axle nut and remove the nut, remembering that the stub axle on the left-hand side of the car has a left-hand thread.
6. Draw off the hub and brake disc assembly, using a hub puller or service too 18G304. The brake disc can now be removed from the hub by removing the four securing screws and spring washers.
7. Remove the distance washer, which will have remained on the stub axle.

Withdrawing a front hub (wire wheel type), using special tool 18G363. Special tool 18G304 should be used on vehicles fitted with pressed-steel wheels

Withdrawing the front hub, using tool 18G304

8. The center of the outer hub bearing may now be withdrawn together with the shims which are fitted between the bearing and the distance piece.
9. Remove the oil seal and draw out the center of the inner bearing and the bearing distance piece.
10. Place the hub on a press with the outer end downwards and press out the outer bearing ring. Press out the inner bearing ring in the same manner with the inner end of the hub downwards.

Reassembling and Replacing a Front Hub

If all grease has been cleaned from the hub and the bearings washed for examination, ensure that they are repacked with grease before the hub is reassembled.

Press the two bearing outer rings into the hub. Insert the bearing distance piece. Fit the inner bearing center, the oil seal, and the distance washer, with the metal face of the oil seal and the chamfered side of the distance washer away from the bearing.

Mount the assembly on the stub axle shaft and fit the adjusting shims and outer bearing center. Adjust the bearing end-float if necessary, and, finally, lock up as detailed below.

Pack the assembly with grease and replace the grease-retaining cap. Replace the wheel brake unit as detailed in brake section.

Adjusting the Front Hub Bearings

The end-float in the hub bearings must be checked and adjusted whenever the hub has been dismantled for attention or when the play in the hub bearings becomes excessive. The end-float is adjustable by means of shims situated between the outer bearing and the bearing distance piece.

Proceed as follows to obtain the correct setting:
1. Assemble the hub, **using no shims,** and mount the assembly on the stub axle. Fit the stub axle nut and washer and tighten the nut until the hub bearings bind. This will pull the outer rings of the bearings fully against their locating flanges inside the hub.
2. Remove the stub axle nut and washer and pull out the center of the outer bearing. Insert a sufficient thickness of shims **to produce an excessive amount of end-float** and note the total thickness of the shims used. Fit the bearing center, stub axle nut, and washer and tighten the nut.
3. Measure accurately the total amount of end-float in the bearings. Remove the stub axle nut, washer, and outer bearing center. Reduce the number of shims to a thickness which will give an end-float of between .002 and .004 in.
4. Replace the stub axle nut and washer and tighten the nut to a torque wrench reading of 40 to 70 lb. ft. Latitude for the torque wrench reading is given so that the nut can be tightened sufficiently to align a castellation with the stub axle split pin hole. Insert a new split pin.

Fitting the Anti-roll Bar

NOTE.—**Andrex Dampers and anti-roll bar equipment MUST NOT be used simultaneously.**

Place a jack under the center of the front cross-member and lift the front of the car; support the chassis side-members on stands. Remove the bumper bar and the front apron and the four body holding bolts on the front extension. Unscrew and remove the eight nuts and bolts securing the front extension to the chassis and remove the extension.

Locate the anti-roll bar, the split bushes, and the bush housings on the front extension cradles and ensure that the washers

THE ANTI-ROLL BAR COMPONENTS

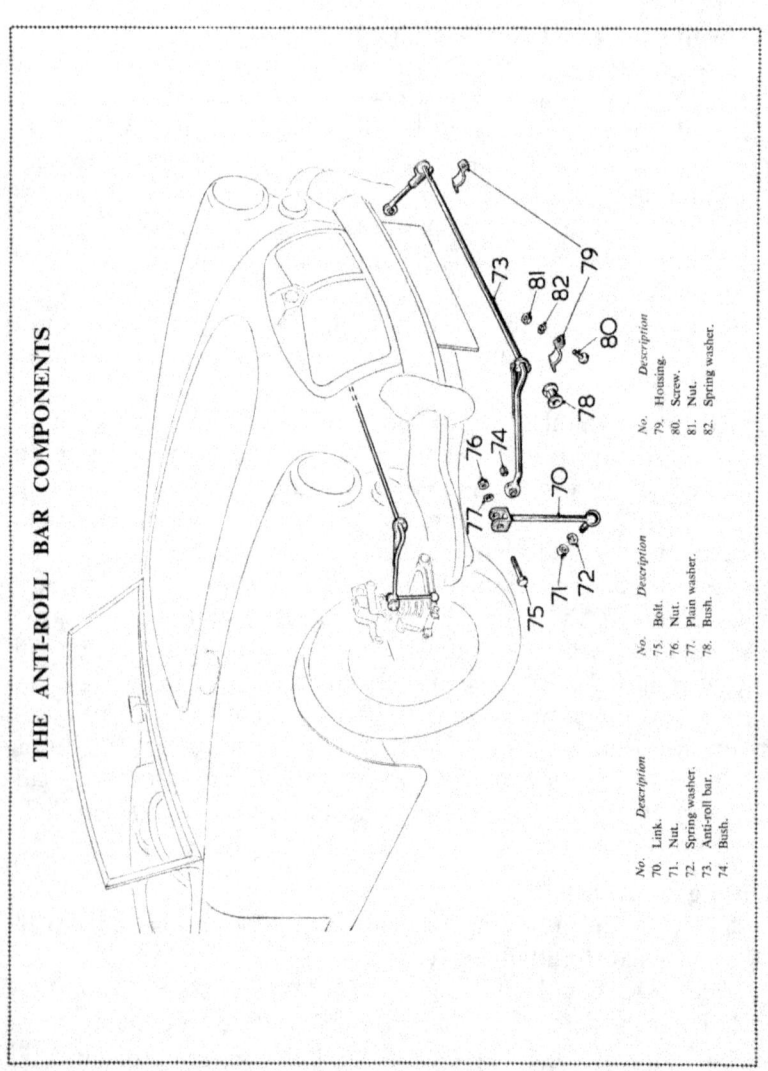

No.	Description	No.	Description	No.	Description
70.	Link.	75.	Bolt.	79.	Housing.
71.	Nut.	76.	Nut.	80.	Screw.
72.	Spring washer.	77.	Plain washer.	81.	Nut.
73.	Anti-roll bar.	78.	Bush.	82.	Spring washer.
74.	Bush.				

on the bar are interposed between the locating plates and the flange on the bushes. Secure the bush housings to the extension with the four $\frac{7}{16}$ in. bolts, spring washers, and nuts.

Refit the front extension to the chassis and secure the body to the body plates on the extension.

Fit the fork end of the left-hand link and the right-hand link to the appropriate ends of the anti-roll bar, insert a $\frac{7}{16}$ in. washer between each side of the Metalastik bushes and the fork ends, and secure the links with the $\frac{7}{16}$ in. clamp bolts and Aerotight nuts. Locate the ball end of each link in the appropriate wishbone and spring pan assembly and secure them with the $\frac{1}{2}$ in. spring washers and nuts.

Replace the front apron and the bumper bar.

THE HYDRAULIC DAMPERS

The maintenance of the hydraulic dampers, when in position on the vehicle, is confined to examination for leakage and examination of the anchorage to the chassis to ensure that the fixing bolts are tight. No adjustment of the hydraulic dampers is required or provided. They are accurately set before leaving the manufacturer to give the amount of damping most suitable for the car. **Any attempt to dismantle the assembly will seriously affect the operation and performance.**

Topping Up

Every 6,000 miles the front hydraulic dampers should be topped up by removing the filler plug and filling up to the bottom of the filler plug hole. **Use Armstrong Super (Thin) Shock Absorber Fluid No. 624.** (If this fluid is not available, any good quality mineral oil to specification S.A.E. 20/20W should be used, but this alternative is not suitable for low temperature operation).

Before removing the filler cap, which is located on the top of the damper, carefully wipe the exterior, as it is of utmost importance that no dirt whatever enters through the filler hole.

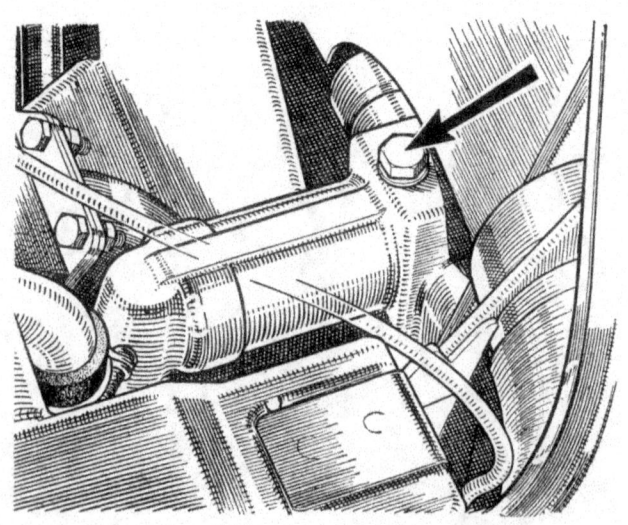

A front damper, showing the filler plug

On no account neglect the operation of topping up the damper fluid because if the low-pressure chamber of the unit is allowed to become empty, air will enter the pressure cylinders and the action of the damper will be impaired.

The rear dampers must be removed from the chassis frame every 12,000 miles for topping up of the fluid.

Removing and Replacing Rear Dampers

1. Jack up the rear of the car below the axle or rear springs and remove the rear wheel.
2. Remove the nut and spring washers securing the damper arm to the bracket on the rear spring.
3. Remove the nuts, spring and flat washers from the two bolts securing the damper to the chassis side-member, and withdraw the damper.

When replacing the damper, it is advisable to work the lever arm up and down a few times through its full stroke to expel trapped air from the pressure chambers.

Rear dampers must be removed by unscrewing the two securing bolts and disconnecting the lower end of the link from the rear spring bracket.

NOTE.—When handling hydraulic dampers that have been removed from the chassis for any purpose, it is important to keep the assemblies upright as far as possible, otherwise air may enter the operating chamber, resulting in free movement.

Removing a Front Damper
1. Jack up the car under the lower wishbone spring pan until the wheel is clear of the ground.
2. Remove the wheel and take out the swivel pin top pivot bolt. Swing out the hub unit clear of the upper wishbone and support it on a suitable stand to prevent straining the brake hose. Unscrew the four nuts holding the damper to the chassis frame.

Testing the Dampers

If the hydraulic dampers do not appear to function satisfactorily, the resistance may be roughly checked by bouncing each corner of the car up and down. A uniform movement indicates that no attention is required, but if the resistance is erratic or free movement of the car is felt, the damper should be removed for checking and topping up.

Indication of their resistance can be obtained by carrying out the following check.

Bolt the damper, in an upright position, to a plate held in a vice.

Move the lever arm up and down through its complete stroke. A moderate resistance throughout the full stroke should be felt. If the resistance is erratic, and free movement in the lever arm is noted, it may indicate lack of fluid.

While adding fluid the lever arm must be worked throughout its full stroke to expel any air that may be present in the operating chamber.

If the addition of fluid gives no improvement a new damper should be fitted.

Too much resistance, i.e. when it is not possible to move the lever arm by hand, indicates a broken internal part or a seized piston.

As it is essential for the dampers to apply the correct restraining action on the suspension, they should be checked whenever there is any doubt regarding their functioning.

The arms should not be removed from the dampers at any time as it is essential that they should be assembled to the damper shaft in the right relation to the damper cam lever so that there is the full range of movement on either side of the center line.

It must be clearly understood that there is no provision for adjusting the setting of the dampers, and if they are in any way defective they must be returned to the manufacturers for attention.

THE BRAKING SYSTEM

DRUM BRAKED CARS

General Description

The Lockheed hydraulic equipment includes a master cylinder and supply tank assembly in which two separate cylinders are supplied with fluid from a common supply tank. Hydraulic pressure generated in one of the cylinders operates the brakes through the wheel cylinders, which pressure in the other operates the clutch withdrawal mechanism through a slave cylinder, piston, and push-rod connected to the clutch lever.

The master cylinder and supply tank assembly is mounted on the engine side of the bulkhead just above the level of the pedal pads.

Steel pipe lines, unions and flexible hoses convey the hydraulic pressure from one of the master cylinders to each wheel cylinder and from the other to the clutch slave cylinder.

Each brake-shoe in the front drums has a separate wheel cylinder, thus providing two leading shoes. In the rear drums a single wheel cylinder, operated both hydraulically and mechanically, floats on the brake plate and operates the two shoes, giving one leading and one trailing shoe in either direction of rotation to provide adequate braking in reverse.

The master cylinder filler cap.

Maintenance

Periodically examine the quantity of brake fluid in the master cylinder. It should never be less than half-full or closer than $1/2$ in. to the bottom of the filler neck. The necessity of frequent topping up is an indication of over-filling or a leak in the system, which should at once be traced and rectified.

Adjust the brake-shoes to compensate for wear of the linings. The need for this is shown by the pedal going down almost to the floorboards before solid resistance is felt.

Adjustment of the brake-shoes in the manner indicated also adjusts the hand brake automatically, and no separate adjustment is required or permitted.

The Master Cylinder and Supply Tank Assembly
The brake master cylinder

Within the cylinder is a piston, backed by a rubber cup, normally held in the "off" position by a piston return spring. Immediately in front of the cup, when it is in the "off" position, is a compensating orifice connecting the cylinder with the fluid supply. This port allows free compensation for any expansion or contraction of the fluid, thus ensuring that the system is constantly filled; it also serves as a release for additional fluid drawn into the cylinder during brake applications. Pressure is applied to the piston by means of the push-rod attached to the brake pedal. The push-rod length is adjustable and should give a slight clearance when the system is at rest to allow the piston to return fully against its stop. Without this clearance the main cup will cover the by-pass port, causing pressure to build up within the system, and produce binding of the brakes on all wheels. The reduced skirt of the piston forms an annular space which is filled with fluid from the supply tank via the feed hole. Leakage of fluid from the open end of the cylinder is prevented by the secondary cup fitted to the flange end of the piston. On releasing the brake pedal, after application, the piston is returned quickly to its stop by the return spring, thus creating a vacuum in the cylinder; this vacuum causes the main cup to collapse and pass fluid through the small holes in the piston head from the annular space formed by the piston skirt. This additional fluid finds its way back to the reserve supply under the action of the brake return springs, when the system finally comes to rest, through the outlet valve and compensating orifice. If the compensating orifice is covered by the piston cup when the system is at rest, **pressure** will build up as a result of

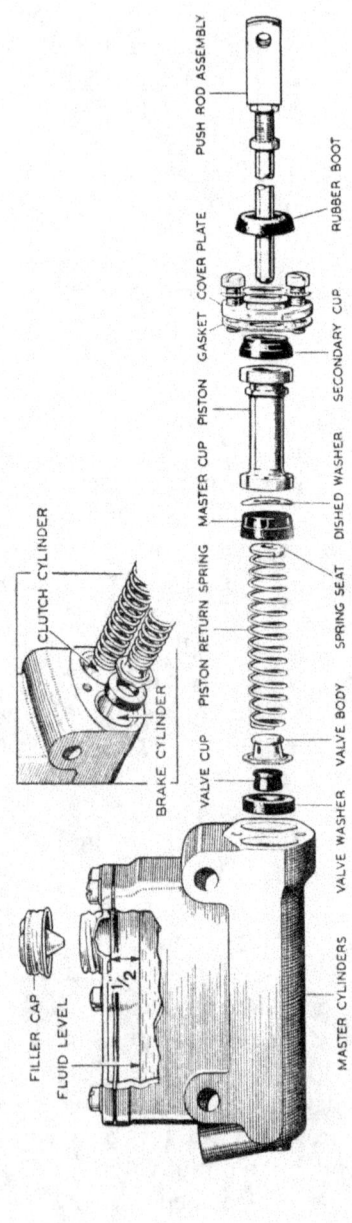

Illustrating the master cylinders for brake and clutch operation, and their components. Note that no valve is used in the clutch master cylinder

the brake application. The combination inlet and outlet check valve in the head of the cylinder is provided to allow the passage of fluid under pressure from the master piston into the pipe lines and control its return into the cylinder, so that a small pressure of approximately 8 lb. per square inch is maintained in the pipe lines to ensure that the cups of the wheel cylinder sare kept expanded; it also prevents fluid pumped out from the cylinder when "bleeding" from returning to the cylinder, thus ensuring a fresh charge being delivered at each stroke of the pedal.

The clutch master cylinder

The components and operation of the clutch master cylinder are, in the main, similar to those of the brake master cylinder, but with one important difference: the combination inlet and outlet check valve used in the brake cylinder is not incorporated in the clutch cylinder, and therefore no pressure is maintained in the clutch line when the clutch pedal is released.

A front brake assembly.

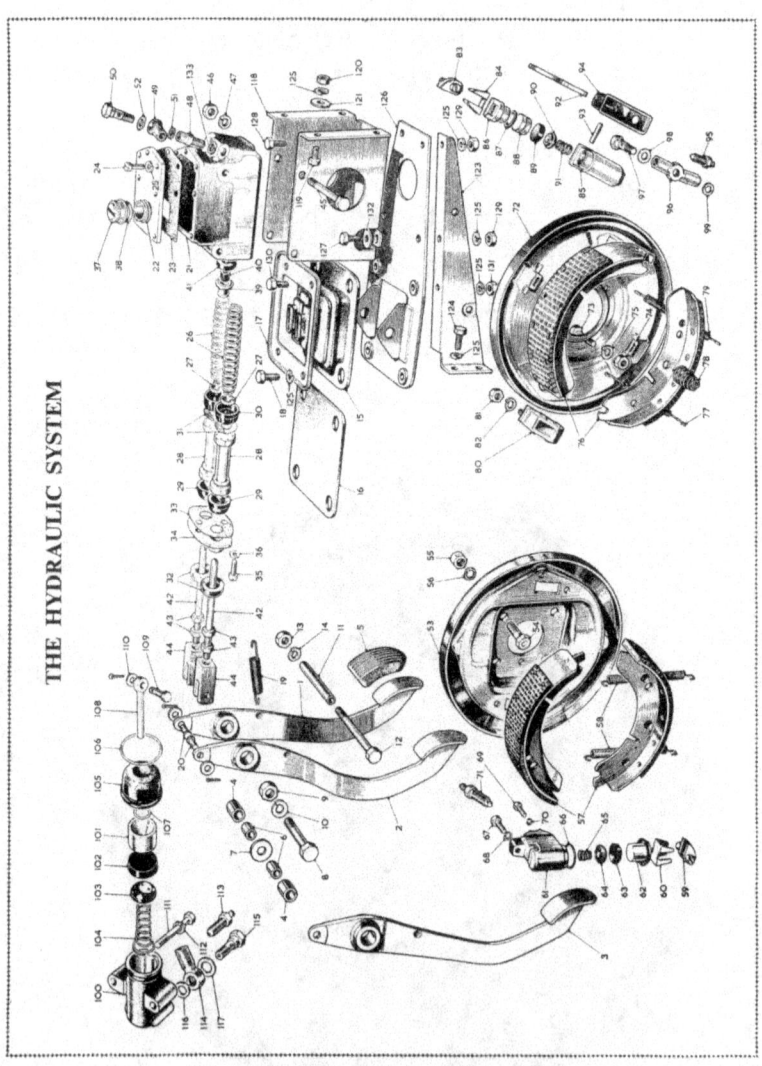

KEY TO THE HYDRAULIC SYSTEM

No.	Description
1.	Brake pedal.
2.	Clutch pedal—right-hand drive.
3.	Clutch pedal—left-hand drive.
4.	Bush.
5.	Rubber pad—pedal.
6.	Distance-piece—pedal.
7.	Distance washer—pedal.
8.	Bolt—pedal bracket.
9.	Nut—pedal bracket bolt.
10.	Washer—spring.
11.	Distance tube—pedal stop.
12.	Distance tube—bolt.
13.	Nut—distance tube bolt.
14.	Spring washer.
15.	Fume excluder—brake and clutch pedal.
16.	Rubber—blanking piece.
17.	Cover—blanking piece.
18.	Cover screw.
19.	Spring—pedal pull-off.
20.	Clevis pin.
21.	Body.
22.	Cover—body.
23.	Gasket—cover.
24.	Screw—cover to body.
25.	Washer—shakeproof.
26.	Spring—piston return.
27.	Retainer—spring.
28.	Piston.
29.	Cup—primary—piston.
30.	Cup—secondary—piston.
31.	Washer—primary clip to piston.
32.	Boot—push-rod.
33.	Gasket—boot fixing plate.
34.	Plate—boot fixing.
35.	Screw—plate.
36.	Washer—shakeproof.
37.	Cap—filler.
38.	Seal.
39.	Body—valve.
40.	Cup.
41.	Washer.
42.	Push-rod.
43.	Nut—locking.
44.	Yoke—push-rod—to pedal.
45.	Bolt—master cylinder to box.
46.	Nut—master cylinder to box bolt.
47.	Washer—spring.
48.	Adaptor—master cylinder.
49.	Banjo—master cylinder.
50.	Bolt—banjo.
51.	Gasket—banjo connection.
52.	Gasket—banjo connection.
53.	Plate—L/H front brake.
54.	Bolt—brake back-plate.
55.	Nut—brake back-plate.
56.	Washer—spring—brake back-plate.
57.	Shoe—lined—brake.
58.	Spring—shoe pull-off.
59.	Adjuster.
60.	Mask—adjuster.
61.	Body—L/H.
62.	Piston and dust cover.
63.	Cup—piston.
64.	Filler—piston cup.
65.	Spring—filler.
66.	Sealing ring.
67.	Bolt—cylinder to brake plate (⅜″).
68.	Spring washer—cylinder bolt.
69.	Bolt—cylinder to brake plate (¼″).
70.	Spring washer—cylinder bolt.
71.	Screw—bleeder.
72.	Plate—L/H rear brake.
73.	Bolt—brake back-plate.
74.	Nut—brake back-plate.
75.	Washer—spring—brake back-plate.
76.	Shoe—lined—brake.
77.	Spring—shoe pull-off.
78.	Spring—shoe steady.
79.	Spring—shoe tension.
80.	Abutment strip—brake-shoe.
81.	Nut—abutment strip.
82.	Washer—spring.
83.	Adjuster.
84.	Mask—adjuster.
85.	Body—with abutment strip.
86.	Piston—with dust cover.
87.	Seal.
88.	Piston—hydraulic.
89.	Cup—piston.
90.	Filler cup.
91.	Spring—filler.
92.	Lever—hand brake.
93.	Pin—lever.
94.	Boot—hydraulic cylinder.
95.	Screw—bleeder.
96.	Banjo connection—wheel cylinder.
97.	Bolt—banjo connection.
98.	Gasket—banjo connection—large.
99.	Gasket—banjo connection—small.
100.	Body.
101.	Piston.
102.	Cup—piston.
103.	Filler—piston cup.
104.	Spring—cup filler.
105.	Boot.
106.	Clip—large—boot.
107.	Clip—small—boot.
108.	Push-rod.
109.	Clevis pin—slave cylinder to clutch fork.
110.	Washer—plain.
111.	Bolt—slave cylinder to gearbox.
112.	Washer—spring.
113.	Bleeder screw.
114.	Banjo—slave cylinder.
115.	Bolt—banjo—slave cylinder.
116.	Gasket—banjo.
117.	Gasket—banjo.
118.	Master cylinder box.
119.	Screw box—master cylinder.
120.	Nut.
121.	Washer—plain.
123.	Support bracket—L/H master cylinder box.
124.	Screw—bracket to topping plate.
125.	Washer—spring.
126.	Base plate assembly.
127.	Screw.
128.	Screw—box to bracket rear.
129.	Nut.
130.	Screw—bracket to base plate.
131.	Nut—bracket to base screw.
132.	Plain washer.
133.	Gasket—adaptor.

227

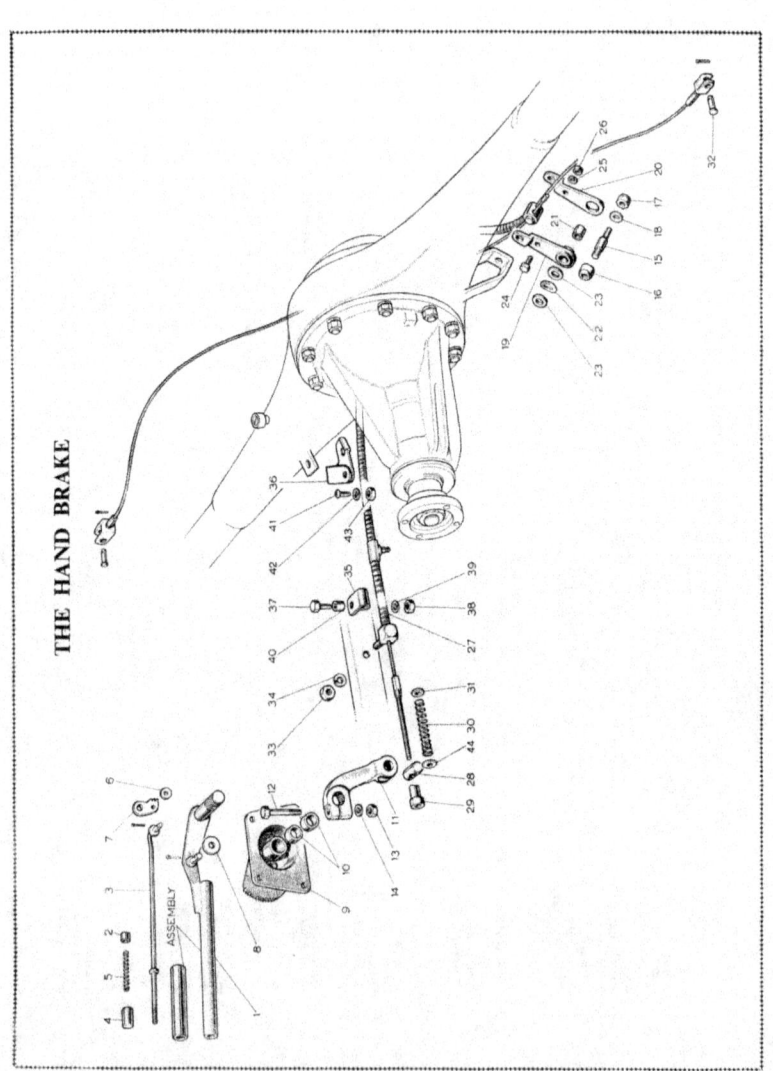

THE HAND BRAKE

KEY TO THE HAND BRAKE

No.	Description
1.	Handle plate and shaft assembly.
2.	Bush—handle plate and shaft.
3.	Pawl rod assembly.
4.	Knob—pawl rod.
5.	Spring—pawl rod.
6.	Washer—plain.
7.	Pawl.
8.	Washer.
9.	Fulcrum and ratchet assembly.
10.	Bush.
11.	Operating lever—hand brake.
12.	Bolt—operating lever.
13.	Nut—operating lever.
14.	Washer—spring.
15.	Fulcrum—hand brake compensator.
16.	Nut—fulcrum to axle.
17.	Nut—compensator to fulcrum.
18.	Washer—compensator to fulcrum.
19.	Lever—inner compensating.
20.	Lever—outer compensating.
21.	Bush—compensating lever.
22.	Washer—anti-rattle—compensating.
23.	Washer—plain—compensating lever.
24.	Screw—compensating lever.
25.	Washer—spring—compensating lever.
26.	Nut—compensating lever.
27.	Cable—hand brake.
28.	Trunnion—cable.
29.	Adjuster nut.
30.	Spring—cable.
31.	Washer—plain—cable spring.
32.	Clevis pin.
33.	Abutment nut.
34.	Washer—spring.
35.	Clip—cable to battery carrier.
36.	Clip—cable to 3-way piece—axle brackets.
37.	Screw—clip.
38.	Nut—clip screw.
39.	Washer—spring—battery carrier clip.
40.	Distance tube—battery carrier clip.
41.	Screw—clip—3-way piece.
42.	Washer—spring—3-way piece clip screw.
43.	Nut—3-way piece clip screw.
44.	Washer—plain—cable spring front.

Adjusting the Brake Pedal

The correct amount of free movement between the master cylinder push-rod and piston is set during assembly of the vehicle, and should never need alteration.

In the event of the adjustment having been disturbed, reset the effective length of the rod connecting the cylinder to the pedal until the pedal pad can be depressed approximately $1/2$ in. before the piston begins to move. The clearance can be felt if the pedal is depressed by hand.

Brake-shoe Adjustments

As the linings wear, the pedal will travel farther before the brakes come into action. When the travel becomes excessive the brake-shoes should be adjusted.

A hole sealed with a rubber plug is provided in the wheel and in the drum to allow adjustment without removal of the wheel. The hole in the drum is sealed by a neoprene tubular seal between the wheel and drum. When the wheel is replaced after removal for any purpose, take care to refit it with the holes in the wheel and drum in line and with both seals in position.

Front shoe adjustment

1. Jack up the front of the car and remove the wheel disc and rubber plug from the hole in the wheel.
2. Turn the wheel until one of the two adjustment screws is visible through the hole in the wheel and drum.
3. Insert a screwdriver and turn the adjustment screw in a clockwise direction until the drum is locked and then turn it anti-clockwise one notch. Rotate the drum until the other screw is visible and repeat the adjustment.
4. The drum should then be free to rotate without the shoes rubbing and the adjustment on that wheel is complete.

Rear shoe adjustment

The procedure is similar to that detailed for the front wheels except that there is only one adjuster controlling both shoes and hand brake.

Bleeding the System

Bleeding the system is not a routine maintenance job, and should only be necessary when some portion of the hydraulic equipment has been disconnected or the fluid drained off.

1. Fill the master cylinder with Lockheed Disc Brake Fluid and keep it at least half-full throughout the operation, otherwise air will be drawn into the system, necessitating a fresh start.
2. Attach the bleeder tube to the wheel bleeder screw and allow

the free end of the tube to be submerged in a small quantity of fluid in a clean glass jar.
3. Open the bleeder screw one full turn.
4. Depress the brake pedal quickly, and allow it to return without assistance. Repeat this pumping action with a slight pause before each depression of the pedal.

Watch the flow of fluid into the glass jar, and when air bubbles cease to appear, hold the pedal firmly against the floorboards while the bleeder screw is securely tightened.
5. Repeat the operation on each wheel.

NOTE.—Clean fluid bled from the system must be allowed to stand until it is clear of air bubbles before it is used again. Dirty fluid should be discarded.

Removing the Master Cylinder Assembly
1. Extract the push-rod split pins and clevis pins.
2. Unscrew the union nut and disconnect the clutch pipe from the rear end of the master cylinder.
3. Unscrew the brake pipe at the three-way union on the chassis side-member.
4. Remove the bolt securing the brake pipe clip to the front of the mounting plate.
5. Remove the two bolts passing through the bracket and master cylinder and lift out the assembly complete with the brake pipe and clip.

Dismantling the Master Cylinder and Supply Tank Assembly
1. Remove the filler cap and drain the Lockheed fluid from the unit.
2. Unscrew the two retaining screws and remove the end cover.
3. Withdraw the two pistons, piston cups, return springs and one valve cup assembly. Note that no valve assembly is fitted to the clutch cylinder.
4. To remove the secondary cups from the pistons, carefully stretch each one over the end flange of the piston, using only the fingers.

Assembling the Brake Master Cylinder
1. Clean all parts thoroughly, using Lockheed Genuine Brake Fluid for all rubber components. All traces of gasoline, kerosene, or trichlor-ethylene used for cleaning the metal parts must be removed before assembly.
2. Examine all the rubber parts for damage or distortion. It is usually advisable to renew the rubbers when rebuilding the cylinder. Dip all the internal parts in brake fluid and assemble them wet.

3. Stretch the secondary cup over the end flange of the piston with the lip of the cup facing towards the opposite end of the piston. When the cup is in its groove, work it round gently with the fingers to make sure it is correctly seated.

4. Fit the valve washer, valve cup and body onto the return spring, and insert the spring, valve first, into the cylinder. See that the spring retainer is in position.

5. Insert the master cup, lip first, taking care not to damage or turn back the lip, and press it down onto the spring retainer.

6. Insert the piston, taking care not to damage or turn back the lip of the secondary cup.

7. Push the piston down the bore and replace the end plate, rubber boots and push-rods.

8. Test the master cylinder by filling the tank and by pushing the piston down the bore and allowing it to return; after one or two applications fluid should flow from the outlet.

Assembling the clutch master cylinder

The procedure is similar to that for the brake cylinder, omitting the valve assembly.

Replacing the Master Cylinder and Supply Tank Assembly

The replacement procedure is the reverse of the removal instructions given previously with the following additions:

1. Replace the union in its correct position and fully tighten before replacing the master cylinder in its housing.

2. Check the shoe adjustment.

3. Connect the fluid pipes and bleed the system (including the slave cylinder).

4. Check the system for leaks with the brakes fully applied.

Brake Assembly

Two leading shoes are incorporated in the front wheel braking system and take the greater percentage of the braking load. The rear brakes are of the leading and trailing shoe type, giving the advantage of equal braking action when the brakes are used in reverse.

All the shoes have a floating anchorage, each front shoe utilizing the closed end of the other shoe actuating cylinder as its abutment. The two rear shoes share one common abutment stop.

The hand brake lever operates the rear brakes mechanically through a linkage operating on the piston of the rear wheel cylinder, which is made in two halves. The outer half of the piston applies the leading shoes when actuated by a lever pivoted in the cylinder body. The trailing shoes is applied by

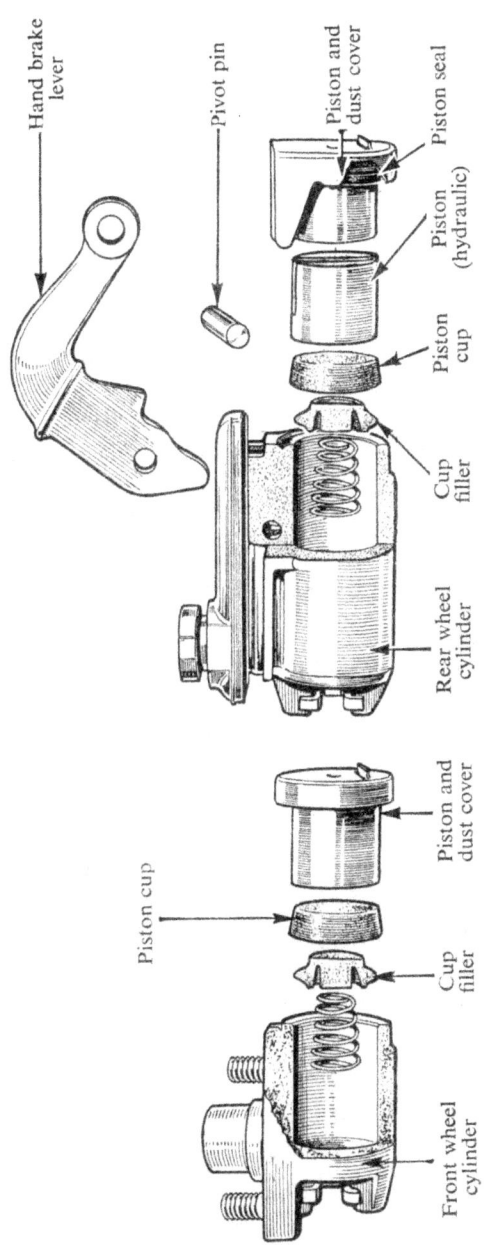

Front and rear wheel cylinder components.

the movement of the cylinder body, which slides on the brake plate as a result of the reaction of the mechanically operated lever on the pivot.

When operated hydraulically the inner half of the piston is forced outwards, carrying with it the outer half, thus applying the leading shoe, and the trailing shoe is applied by the floating cylinder body as a result of the reaction of the fluid pressure on the body.

Removing a Wheel Cylinder

Front cylinders

1. Raise the front of the car and remove the hub cap and road wheel.
2. Remove the brake-drum.
3. Draw the brake-shoes apart until the assembly can be removed from the back-plate.
4. Release the flexible hose.
5. Unscrew the hose from the wheel cylinder.
6. Unscrew the unions and remove the link pipe from both cylinders.
7. Unscrew the set bolts securing the cylinders to the back-plates and remove the cylinders.

Rear cylinder

1. Raise the rear of the car and remove the wheel.
2. Remove the brake-drum.
3. Turn and withdraw the brake-shoe steady springs.
4. Draw the brake-shoes apart until they can be removed from the brake-plate.
5. Unscrew the pipe union from the cylinder, noting the positions of the copper washers.
6. Remove the clevis pin from the hand brake cable yoke to disconnect the cable from the lever on the cylinder.
7. Remove the rubber boot.
8. Slide the cylinder upwards, push the lower end through the back-plate and slide the cylinder downwards and away from the back-plate.

Dismantling a Wheel Cylinder

Front cylinders

Withdraw the piston, the rubber cup, the cup filler and the spring.

Rear cylinders

Tap out the hand brake lever pivot pin and withdraw the

lever. Withdraw the upper half of the piston, the rubber cup, the cup filler and the spring.

Assembling a Wheel Cylinder
1. Clean all parts thoroughly, using only Lockheed hydraulic brake fluid for the rubber components. All traces of gasoline, kerosene or trichlorethylene used for cleaning the metal parts must be completely removed before assembly.
2. Examine the rubber cups for damage, wear, or distortion. Dip all parts in brake fluid and assemble wet.
3. Insert the cup filler and spring, and the rubber cup concave side first.
4. Replace the piston, and in the case of the rear cylinders insert the hand brake lever and its pivot pin.

Replacing a Wheel Cylinder
The procedure for replacing the wheel cylinder is a reversal of the sequence of operations given earlier, but attention must be given to the following important points:—

A rear brake assembly.

Front

The front brake wheel cylinders are interchangeable but the link pipe banjo unions must be fitted to them so that the flexible hose is connected to the rear cylinder and the bleeder screw to the forward cylinder. The link pipe must pass below the center line of the stub axle.

The brake-shoes are interchangeable but the recessed ends must engage the "Micram" shoe adjusters.

Rear

The wheel cylinders must be fitted on the rear side of the axle casing with the bleeder screw pointing downwards.

The brake-shoes are interchangeable but the recessed end of the upper or leading shoes must engage the "Micram" shoe adjuster. The other shoe should also be fitted with its recessed end against the wheel cylinder.

Removing the Flexible Hose

Do not attempt to release a flexible hose by turning either end with a wrench. It should be removed as follows:—

Unscrew the metal pipe line union nut from its connection to the hose.

Remove the locknut securing the flexible hose union to the bracket and unscrew the hose from the wheel cylinder. Note that a distance-piece is fitted at the rear of the bracket securing the front hoses.

Removing and Replacing Brake-shoe Assemblies

1. Jack up the car and remove the wheel. Remove the brake-drum.
2. Turn and withdraw the steady springs (rear only).
3. Draw the shoes apart until they can be removed from the back-plate.

Replacement is a reversal of the above procedure, but note the correct fitting of the shoes and springs.

Front springs

Both springs are fitted between the shoes and the back-plate. The shoes are fitted with the recessed ends on the adjusters. The rear spring is fitted to the rear hole in the upper shoe and the inner of the two holes in the lower shoe.

Rear springs

Both springs are fitted between the shoes and the back-plate. The lighter spring is fitted at the abutment end of the shoes. Both springs are fitted to the end holes in the shoes.

Relining the Brake-shoes

Owing to the need for the brake linings to be finished so that they are perfectly concentric with the brake-drums, special precautions must be taken when relining the shoes.

It is imperative that all brake linings should be of the same make, grade, and condition to ensure even braking.

When brake linings are in need of renewal they must always be replaced in axle sets, and the relining of the shoes in one brake-drum must be avoided.

Any variations from this will give an unequal and unsatisfactory braking performance.

After riveting the new brake linings to the brake-shoes it is essential that any high-spots should be removed before replacement of the backplate assembly.

When new shoes and linings are fitted it must be appreciated that considerable adjustment has to be made on the foot brake mechanism, and it is necessary to return the Micram adjusters to their fully anti-clockwise position before attempting to refit the brake-drums over the new linings. The hand brake must also be in the fully released position.

Do not allow grease, paint, oil or brake fluid to come into contact with the brake linings.

Do not clean the rubber parts with anything other than Lockheed hydraulic brake fluid. All traces of solvent or gasoline, used for cleaning metal parts must be removed before assembly.

Do not allow the fluid in the master cylinder and supply tank assembly to fall below the half-full mark. When full the fluid should be $1/2$ in. below the bottom of the filler neck, with the brakes in the 'off' position.

IMPORTANT.—Do not use any substitute for Lockheed Genuine Brake Fluid unless this is completely unobtainable: in such conditions use a fluid to Specification S.A.E. 70.R1.

Hand Brake Cable

The amount of slack in the cable and therefore the amount of movement of the lever is adjustable by means of the nut on the screwed end of the cable located beneath the car in the center.

To remove

1. Unscrew and remove the adjustment nut; withdraw the end of the cable from the lower end of the lever and remove the spring.
2. Disconnect the clips securing the cable assembly to the body.
3. Remove the clevis pins from the levers on the wheel cylinders.

4. Unscrew the two nuts on the axle balance lever; separate the two halves of the lever and remove the cable and trunnion.

Braking Irregularities and Their Causes

Pedal travel excessive (requires pumping)
1. Brake-shoes require adjusting.
2. Leak at one or more joints.
3. Master cylinder cup worn.

Pedal feels springy
1. System requires bleeding.
2. Linings not bedded in.
3. Master cylinder fixing loose.
4. Master cylinder cup worn.

Brakes inefficient
1. Shoes not correctly adjusted.
2. Linings not bedded in.
3. Linings greasy.
4. Linings wrong quality.
5. Drums badly scored.
6. Linings badly worn.
7. Wrongly fitted cup fillers.

Brakes grab
1. Shoes require adjusting.
2. Drums distorted.
3. Greasy linings.
4. Broken or loose road spring.
5. Scored drums.
6. Worn suspension linkage.

Brakes drag
1. Shoes incorrectly adjusted.
2. Shoe springs weak or broken.
3. Pedal spring weak or broken.
4. Hand brake mechanism seized.
5. Wheel cylinder piston seized.
6. Locked pipe line.
7. Filler cap vent hole choked.

Brakes remain on
1. Shoes over-adjusted.
2. Hand brake over-adjusted.
3. No free movement on pedal.
4. Compensator port in master cylinder covered by swollen rubber cup, or incorrect adjustment of push-rod.

5. Swollen wheel cylinder cups.
6. Choked flexible hose.

Unbalanced braking
1. Greasy linings.
2. Distorted drums.
3. Tires unevenly inflated.
4. Brake-plate loose on the axle.
5. Worn steering connections.
6. Worn suspension linkage.
7. Different types or grades of lining fitted.

LOCKHEED DISC-BRAKED CARS

General Description

The braking system consists of two Lockheed calliper-type disc brakes on the front wheels with conventional Lockheed drum brakes at the rear. The rear brakes are similar to those described and are serviced in the same way.

Front brake units

Each front wheel brake unit comprises a hub-mounted disc rotating with the wheel and a braking unit rigidly attached to the swivel pin. The brake unit consists of a calliper manufactured in two halves — the mounting half and the rim half — which are held together by three bolts. A cylinder in each calliper half houses a self-adjusting hydraulic piston, a fluid seal, a dust seal, and a seal retainer. Each piston is located on a guide post securely held in the back of each cylinder. A friction stop and a sleeve are interchangeable side for side.

The friction pad assemlies are fitted adjacent to the pistons and are retained in position by a retainer spring and pin.

Fluid pressure generated in the master cylinder enters the mounting half of each calliper and passes through the internal fluid ports into the rim half. An even pressure is therefore exerted on both hydraulic pistons, moving them along the cylinder bores until the friction pad assemblies contact the disc. In order to compensate for wear of the pads the pistons move progressively along each corresponding guide post, and the friction stops, which grip the posts, provide a positive datum to which the pistons return. The movement of the piston deflects the fluid seal in the cylinder bore, and on releasing the pressure the piston moves back into its original position, thus providing the required clearance for the friction pads.

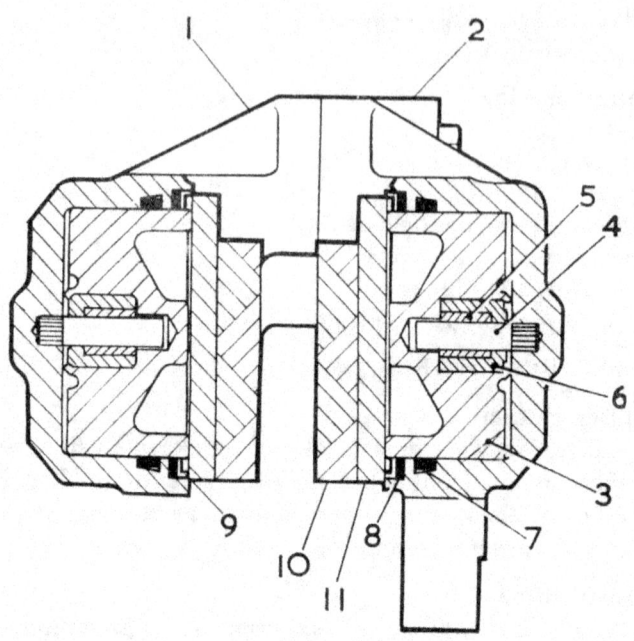

A disc brake in section

1. Calliper—rim half.
2. Calliper—mounting half.
3. Hydraulic piston.
4. Guide post.
5. Friction stop.
6. Sleeve.
7. Fluid seal.
8. Dust seal.
9. Dust seal retainer
10. Friction pad.
11. Pad backing plate.

Maintenance

Periodically examine the quality of brake fluid in the master cylinder. The correct level is $1/4$ in. below the bottom of the filler neck. The necessity for very frequent topping up is an indication of overfilling or of a leak in the system which should be traced and rectified at once.

Adjust only the rear brake-shoes to compensate for wear of the linings. The need for this will be indicated by excessive pedal travel. The front disc brakes automatically compensate for wear of the brake pads. The pads should be checked for wear every 3,000 miles by visual observation and measurement. When wear has reduced the pads to the minimum permissible thickness of $1/16$ in. the pads must be renewed.

Priming and Bleeding the Brake System

The following procedure should be adopted either for initial priming of the system or to bleed in service if air has been permitted to enter the system. Air may enter the system if pipe connections become loose or if the level of the fluid in the reservoir is allowed to fall below the recommended level. During the bleeding operation it is important that the reservoir is kept at least half-full to avoid drawing air into the system.

1. Check that all connections are tightened and all bleed screws closed.
2. Fill the reservoir with brake fluid. The use of Lockheed Genuine Brake Fluid is recommended, but if this is not available an alternative fluid conforming to Specification S.A.E. 70.R1 should be used.
3. Attach the bleeder tube to the bleed screw on the near-side rear brake and immerse the open end of the tube in a small quantity of brake fluid contained in a clean glass jar. Slacken the bleed screw and operate the brake pedal slowly backwards and forwards through its full stroke until fluid pumped into the jar is completely free from air bubbles. Close the bleed screw on a down stroke of the pedal. Release the pedal.
4. Repeat on the off-side rear brake.
5. Two bleeder screws are fitted to each front disc brake unit. Attach the bleeder tube to the inner bleed screw on the near-side brake unit. Slacken the bleed screw and bleed as described above. Repeat the operation on the outer bleed screw.
6. Bleed the off-side front brake in the same way.
7. Top up the fluid level in the reservoir.
8. If the disc brake callipers have been disturbed it will be necessary to pump the brake pedal several times to restore the automatic adjustment of the friction pad clearance.
9. Apply a normal working load on the brake pedal for a period of two or three minutes and examine the entire system for leaks.

NOTE.—**Clean fluid bled from the system must be allowed to stand until it is clear of air bubbles before it is used again. Dirty fluid should be discarded.**

Removing a Brake Unit

Apply the hand brake, place chocks under the rear wheels, and jack up the front of the vehicle. Remove the road wheel. Withdraw the brake friction pads.

Remove the two nuts and spring washers securing the brake hose support bracket and remove the bracket. Unscrew the two calliper securing bolts and swing the calliper clear of the disc.

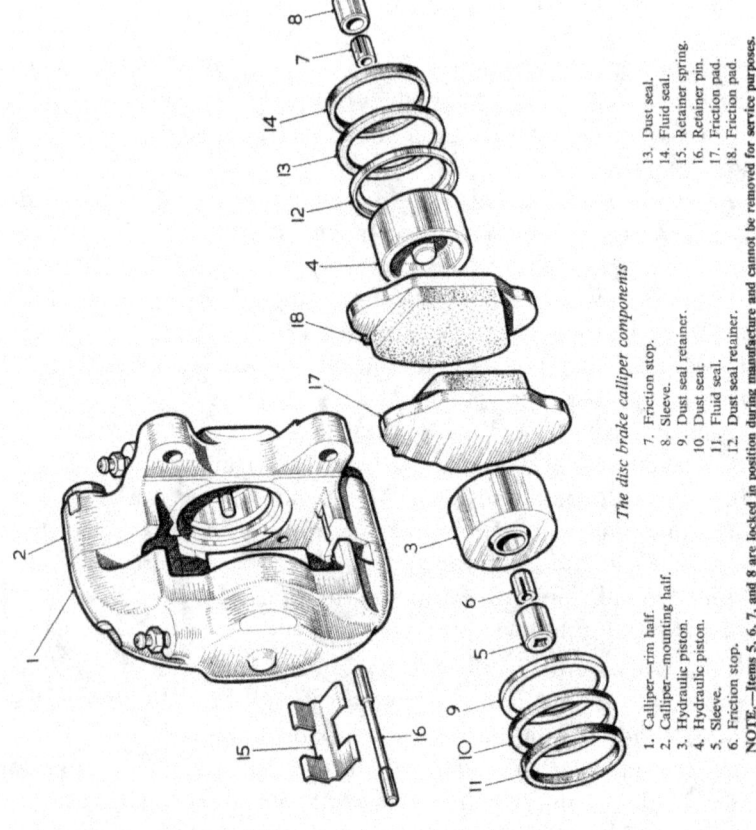

The disc brake calliper components

1. Calliper—rim half.
2. Calliper—mounting half.
3. Hydraulic piston.
4. Hydraulic piston.
5. Sleeve.
6. Friction stop.
7. Friction stop.
8. Sleeve.
9. Dust seal retainer.
10. Dust seal.
11. Fluid seal.
12. Dust seal retainer.
13. Dust seal.
14. Fluid seal.
15. Retainer spring.
16. Retainer pin.
17. Friction pad.
18. Friction pad.

NOTE.—Items 5, 6, 7, and 8 are locked in position during manufacture and cannot be removed for service purposes.

Do not disconnect the fluid hose if the calliper is to be subsequently dismantled. Support the brake unit carefully to avoid straining the hose.

Replacing a Brake Unit

The replacement procedure is a reversal of the instructions given. It is essential that the two calliper securing bolts are tightened to the correct torque figure of 45 to 50 lb. ft. If the unit has been dismantled or the brake hose uncoupled the system must be bled.

Dismantling a Brake Unit

1. Remove the brake unit from the swivel pin, leaving the brake hose in position to enable the pistons to be removed from the cylinders, using hydraulic pressure.
2. Only one piston can be removed at a time and this must be replaced before the other piston can be withdrawn. Using a suitable clamp, retain one piston in the calliper and remove the other piston by gently applying the foot brake until the piston has been pushed out far enough to allow removal by hand. It is advisable to carry out this operation over a receptacle to catch the fluid as the piston is withdrawn.
3. With the aid of a blunt-nosed tool remove the fluid seal from the cylinder bore, taking great care not to damage the base of the seal groove or cylinder bore.

Should the dust seal require renewal, the seal retainer can be removed by placing the blade of a screwdriver between the retainer and seal and carefully prying the retainer from the mouth of the bore.

4. After assembling the piston into its cylinder the other piston can be removed by the method described above.

IMPORTANT.—The two halves of the calliper should not be separated unless it is absolutely essential. If separation cannot be avoided then the following points must be borne in mind during assembly.

1. New bolts, lock plates, and fluid channel seal must be used. The bolts are manufactured from special high tensile steel and only the correct replacements should be employed. Failure to use the correct bolts could have serious results.
2. Ensure that the calliper faces are clean and that the threaded bolt holes are thoroughly dry. Make certain that the new fluid channel seal is correctly located in the recessed face before assembling the two calliper halves.

3. The bolt threads must be perfectly dry on assembly and they must be lightened to the correct torque reading detailed below.

Large bolts . . . . 65 lb. ft.
Small bolt . . . . 10 lb. ft.

Assembling a Brake Unit

1. Thoroughly lubricate a new fluid seal with Lockheed Disc Brake Lubricant (the seal must be dry before applying this lubricant) and locate it in its groove in the cylinder.
2. Gently work round the seal with the fingers to ensure correct seating.
3. Ensure that the piston and bore are quite clean; if it is necessary to clean either, use only alcohol or Lockheed Brake Fluid.
4. Coat the piston with Lockheed Disc Brake Lubricant. Open the appropriate bleed screw and offer up the piston to the calliper body. Turn the piston round until the portion which has been machined away from the outer face of the piston is adjacent to the lower end of the calliper (i.e. the end opposite the bleeder screws) and locate the piston squarely in the mouth of the bore. With the aid of a clamp press the piston fully home. **Great care must be taken to ensure that the piston is not allowed to tilt at any time during this operation.**

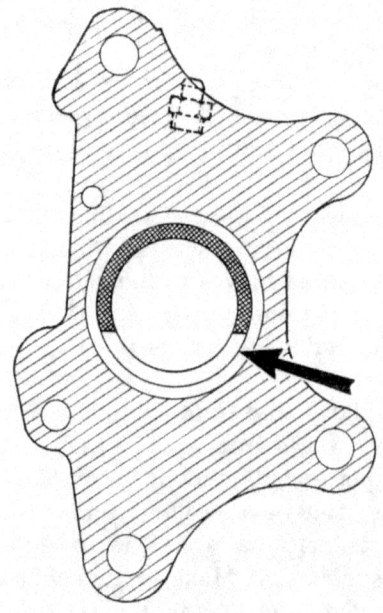

The cut-away portion of the piston (arrowed) must be located at the lower end of the calliper (i.e. the end opposite the bleeder screws)

5. Lubricate a new dust seal and dust seal retainer with Lockheed Disc Brake Lubricant (the seal must be dry before applying the lubricant). Fit the seal in the mouth of the bore, followed by the retainer (with the recessed side outermost). Press the retainer fully home, using a suitable clamp and disc. Earlier types of calliper are fitted with a dust seal which has a 'T'-shaped cross-section; this seal fits inside the retainer. The later seal is interchangeable with the earlier type. Place a suitable clamp on the piston and restore the fluid in the system by gently depressing the foot brake until the fluid flows from the open bleeder screw. Lock the bleeder screw.

6. Repeat the dismantling and assembling operations on the other piston if necessary. Replace the calliper, fit the friction pads and bleed the system.

NOTE.—Throughout the whole assembly operation it is essential that the clamp fitted to the opposite piston on dismantling is not removed.

Removing the Friction Pads

1. Jack up the front of the vehicle and remove the appropriate road wheel.
2. Push in the spring clip retaining the pads with a screwdriver and remove the locating pin.
3. The pads are now free to be withdrawn from the brake unit.
4. Thoroughly clean the surrounding area of the calliper.

Replacing the Friction Pads

Where the original friction pads are to be refitted it is only necessary to reverse the instructions given above.

If wear has reduced the pads to the minimum permissible thickness of $\frac{1}{16}$ in. the pads must be renewed. Press the piston assemblies with a suitable clamp to the base of the cylinder bores against the resistance offered by the friction stop and sleeve. The fluid level in the master cylinder must be observed at regular intervals throughout this operation as the displaced fluid returning to the reservoir may overflow.

Check that the portion which has been machined away from the outer face of each piston is correctly positioned. Insert the new friction pad assemblies (which are interchangeable side for side), replace the spring clip, and fit the locating pin.

Make certain that the clip is centrally located in the recessed portion of the pin. Pump the brake pedal several times to readjust the brake.

An improved type of brake pad was introduced on the 'MGA 1600' at Car No. 78144 (disc wheels). These pads are available

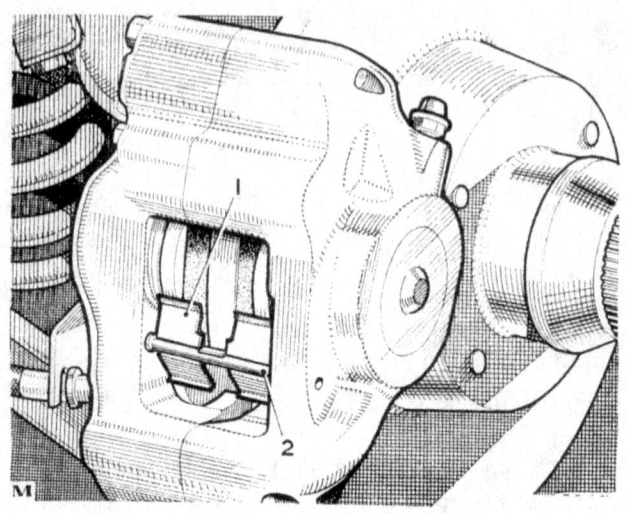

Depress the retainer spring (1) and withdraw the pin (2) to gain access to the friction pads

in sets only. If the improved pads are fitted to earlier cars it is essential that both right- and left-hand brakes are equipped. The later-type pads are color-coded red.

Removing a Brake Disc
Remove the brake unit and withdraw the hub.
The disc is separated from the hub by removing the four securing nuts and washers.

Replacing a Brake Disc
1. Assemble the brake disc to the hub and fit the assembly to the vehicle.
2. Check the disc for true rotation by clamping a dial indicator to a suitable fixed point on the vehicle with the needle pad bearing on the face of the disc. Run-out must not exceed .003 in., and in the event of the value being exceeded the components should be examined for damage and, if necessary, renewed.
3. Replace the brake unit.

A certain amount of concentric and even scoring of the disc faces is not detrimental to the satisfactory operation of the brakes.

If it is found necessary to regrind the disc faces they can be ground up to a maximum of only .040 in. off the original thickness of .380 to .370 in. This may be ground off equally each side, or more on one side than the other, provided that the total reduction does not exceed the maximum limit of .040 in. The reground surface must not exceed 63 micro-in.

After grinding, the faces must run true to within a total clock reading of .003 in. and the thickness must be parallel to within .001 in. clock reading.

Modified Calliper Units

A modified disc brake calliper dust seal and retainer was introduced at Chassis No. 103261 (disc wheels) and Chassis No. 103834 (wire wheels).

The new seal is 'U'-shaped in cross-section and is retained in the counterbore of the calliper by a retainer having an 'L'-shaped cross-section. The seal is carried within the retainer flange and abuts the face of the calliper counterbore.

Disc Brake Dust Covers

Disc brake covers which reduce inner pad wear were fitted to cars from Chassis No. 102589 (disc wheels). The covers may be fitted in sets to earlier cars.

To fit the covers proceed as follows:
1. Remove the front hub assembly.
2. Remove the adaptor plate from the steering knuckle and discard the adaptor plate bolts, washers, and nuts.
3. Refit the adaptor plate to the steering knuckle, using bolts (Part No. HBZ0611). Assemble the distance washers (Part No. BTB386) and cover (Part No. BTB384 [R.H.] or BTB385 [L.H.]) to the bolts and secure the bolts with spring washers (Part No. LWZ206) and nuts (Part No. FNZ506). Tighten the nuts to between 35 and 40 lb. ft.
4. Reassemble the front hub and ensure that the calliper securing bolts are tightened to between 45 and 50 lb. ft.

DUNLOP DISC BRAKED CARS

General Description

The braking system consists of four Dunlop calliper-type disc brakes hydraulically controlled by means of a foot-operated master cylinder.

Steel pipe lines, unions, and flexible hoses convey the hydraulic pressure from the master cylinder to each wheel cylinder.

The cable-actuated hand brake mechanism is entirely separate in operation from the hydraulic system and operates on the rear wheels only. Each brake consists of two carriers to which friction pads are riveted. The carriers are mounted on the top of the rear callipers, one each side of the disc, by means of hinge bolts.

Brake Units

Each wheel brake unit comprises a hub-mounted disc rotating with the wheel and a braking unit rigidly attached to the axle at the rear and to the swivel pin at the front. The brake unit consists of a calliper which straddles the disc and houses a pair of rectangular friction pad assemblies. Cylinder blocks bolted to the outer faces of each calliper accommodate piston assemblies keyed to the friction pad and securing plate assemblies. A spigot formed on the outer face of each piston locates in the bore of a backing plate with an integral boss grooved to accommodate the collar of a flexible rubber dust seal. When the piston is assembled to the cylinder block the seal engages a lip on the block face and so protects the assembly from intrusion of moisture and foreign matter. The central blind bore of the piston inner face accommodates the end of a retractor pin and its friction bush. A piston seal is located between the piston inner face and a plate secured to the piston by peen-locked screws. The piston assembly when pressed into the cylinder bore locates on the retractor pin assembly, which is peened into the base of the cylinder bore. This assembly comprises a retractor stop bush, two spring washers, a dished cap, and the retractor pin; it functions as a return spring and maintains the 'brake-off' working clearance of approximately .008 to .010 in. between the pads and the disc throughout the life of the pads.

Master Cylinder

The components of the master cylinder are housed within the bore of a cylinder body with an integral reservoir. The reservoir is fitted with a detachable cover which incorporates the filler orifice and is secured by means of six bolts and spring washers. A fluidtight joint is maintained by a cork gasket between the cover and reservoir faces. The enclosed end of the cylinder is bored to provide communication between the reservoir and the cylinder; a housing for an outlet connection is provided by an internally threaded boss integral with the cylinder. Formed around the opposite end of the cylinder is a flange with two holes for the master cylinder attachment bolts. In the unloaded condition a spring-loaded piston carrying a rubber 'O' ring in a groove is held against the under side of a dished washer retained by a circlip at the head of the cylinder. A hemispherically ended push-rod seats in a similarly formed recess at the head of

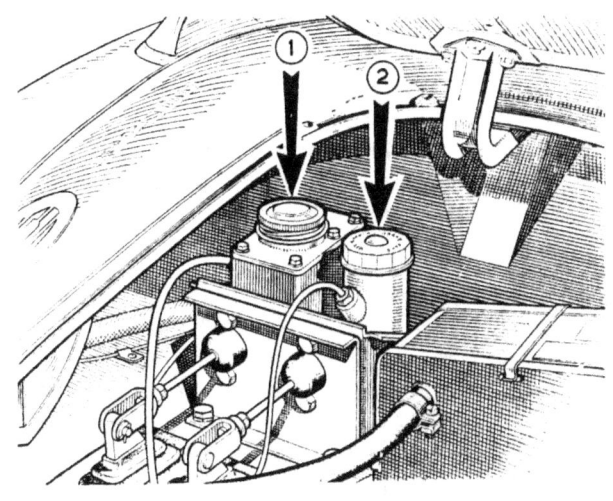

Periodically examine the quantity of fluid in the brake master cylinder reservoir (arrow 1). The clutch master cylinder reservoir is indicated by arrow 2

the piston. The head of the master cylinder is shrouded by a rubber dust excluded, the lip of which seats in a groove in the cylinder body.

A cylindrical spring support is fitted around the inner end of the piston and a small drilling in the end of the support is engaged by the stem of a valve. The larger-diameter head of the valve is located in a central blind bore in the piston. The valve passes through the bore of a vented spring support and protrudes into the fluid passage which communicates with the reservoir. Interposed between the spring support and an integral flange formed on the valve is a small coiled spring. A rubber seal is fitted between the end of the cylinder body and the under side of the valve flange. This assembly forms a recuperation valve which controls fluid flow to and from the reservoir.

When the foot pedal is in the 'off' position the master cylinder is fully extended and the valve is held clear of the base of the cylinder by the action of the main spring. In this condition the master cylinder is in fluid communication with the reservoir, thus permitting recuperation of any fluid loss sustained, particularly during the priming and bleeding operation of the brake system.

When a load is applied to the foot pedal the piston moves down the cylinder against the compression of the main spring. Immediately this movement is in excess of the valve clearance the valve closes under the influence of its spring and isolates the reservoir. Further loading of the pedal results in the discharge of fluid under pressure from the outlet connection via the pipe lines to the brake system.

Maintenance

Periodically examine the quantity of brake fluid in the master cylinder. It should never be less than half-full nor closer than $1/2$ in. to the bottom of the filler neck. The necessity for frequent topping up is an indication of overfilling or of a leak in the system which should be traced and rectified at once.

If the travel of the hand brake lever becomes excessive the mechanism should be adjusted.

The friction pads should be checked for wear at frequent intervals by visual observation and measurement. When wear has reduced the pads to the minimum permissible thickness of .250 in. the pads must be renewed.

Every 1,000 miles apply three or four strokes of the grease gun to the nipple provided on the brake cable.

Adjusting the Brake Pedal

The correct amount of free movement between the master cylinder push-rod and piston is set during assembly of the vehicle and should not require adjustment during normal service.

In the event of the adjustment having been disturbed a check should be made to ensure that there is no pre-loading of the master cylinder piston when the brake pedal is in the fully "off" position. In this position the piston should be held against the dished washer at the head of the master cylinder unit by the pressure of the piston return spring, thus forming a return stop, and a free axial movement of approximately .015 to .020 in. should be felt at the master cylinder push-rod. If necessary, the effective length of the push-rod should be reset to this figure.

Priming and Bleeding the Brake System

The following procedure should be adopted either for initial priming of the system or to bleed in service if air has been permitted to enter the system. Air may enter the system if pipe connections become loose or if the level of fluid in the reservoir is allowed to fall below the recommended level. During the bleeding operation it is important that the reservoir be kept at least half-full to avoid drawing air into the system.

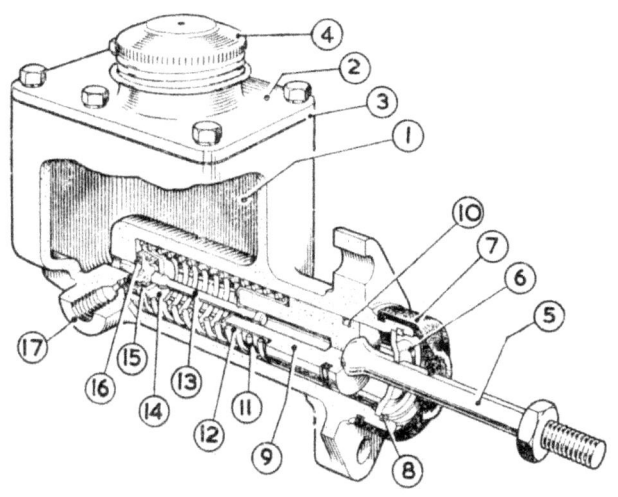

The brake master cylinder components

1. Reservoir.
2. Cover.
3. Cork gasket.
4. Filler cap.
5. Push-rod.
6. Dished washer.
7. Dust excluder.
8. Circlip.
9. Piston.
10. 'O' ring.
11. Return spring.
12. Spring support.
13. Valve.
14. Spring support.
15. Valve spring.
16. Seal.
17. Outlet connection.

1. Check that all connections are tightened and all bleed screws closed.
2. Fill the reservoir with brake fluid. The use of Wakefield Crimson Brake Fluid is recommended, but if this is not available an alternative fluid conforming to Specification S.A.E. 70.R1 should be used.
3. Attach the bleeder tube to the bleed screw on the near-side rear brake and immerse the open end of the tube in a small quantity of brake fluid contained in a clean glass jar. Slacken the bleed screw and operate the brake pedal slowly backwards and forwards through its full stroke until fluid pumped into the jar is reasonably free from air bubbles. Keep the pedal depressed and close the bleed screw. Release the pedal.
4. Repeat for each brake in turn.
5. Repeat the complete bleeding sequence until the brake fluid

pumped into the jar is completely free from air bubbles.
6. Lock all bleed screws and top up the fluid level in the reservoir.
7. Apply a normal working load on the brake pedal for a period of two or three minutes and examine the entire system for leaks.

NOTE.—**Clean fluid bled from the system must be allowed to stand until it is clear of air bubbles before it is used again. Dirty fluid should be discarded.**

Removing the Master Cylinder

Remove the split pin and washer and withdraw the clevis pin from the push-rod yoke. Remove the push-rod.

Remove the two bolts, nuts, and washers securing the front end of the master cylinder to the mounting plate and disconnect the brake pipe at the rear of the cylinder. On right-hand-drive vehicles this operation will be eased if the brake pipe securing clip on the bulkhead is released first.

Dismantling the Master Cylinder

Remove the master cylinder filler cap and drain the brake fluid from the unit.

Ease the dust excluder clear of the head of the master cylinder. Remove the retaining circlip with a suitable pair of pliers and withdraw the push-rod complete with dished washer. Draw out the piston and remove the rubber 'O' ring. The valve assembly complete with springs and supports can then be extracted and the valve sealing ring removed from the seal bush.

Assembling the Master Cylinder

Clean all parts thoroughly, using only the recommended brake fluid for all rubber components. All traces of gasoline, kerosene, or trichlorethylene used for cleaning the metal parts must be removed before assembly.

Examine all the rubber parts for damage or distortion. It is usually advisable to renew the rubbers when rebuilding the cylinder. Dip all the internal parts in brake fluid and assemble them wet. Fit the valve seal around the seal bush and the 'O' ring in the groove on the piston.

Place the seal bush in position on the valve stem and insert the piston into the spring support, ensuring that the head of the valve engages the piston bore. Slide the complete assembly into the sylinder body, taking particular care not to damage or twist the 'O' ring.

Position the push-rod and depress the piston sufficiently to allow the dished washer to seat on the shoulder at the head of

A front disc brake calliper

the cylinder. Fit the circlip and check that it fully engages in the groove.

Fill the dust excluder with Wakefield No. 3 Rubber Grease and reseat the excluder around the head of the master cylinder.

Replacing the Master Cylinder

The replacement procedure is the reverse of the removal instructions.

After replacement, bleed the brake system. Finally, check for leaks with the brakes fully applied.

Removing a Brake Unit
Front

Unscrew the brake pipe union nut below its support bracket and disconnect and blank off the pipe. Remove the two nuts securing the brake hose support bracket and remove the bracket.

Unscrew the two calliper retaining bolts and remove the calliper assembly complete with cylinders.

Take care not to misplace the shims which are fitted behind the mounting lugs on the calliper body. **The shims must be retained for reassembly and replaced in their original positions.**

Rear

Unscrew the fluid supply pipe union (below the inner cylinder block) and disconnect and blank off the pipe. Remove the split pin and clevis pin from the hand brake cable yoke to disconnect the cable from the calliper lever.

Tap back the tab washers and unscrew the two set screws securing the calliper to the mounting flange on the axle. The calliper complete with parking mechanism may now be removed from the vehicle.

The shims taken from behind the calliper body mounting lugs must be retained and **replaced in their original positions on reassembly.**

Dismantling a Brake Unit

The brake must be thoroughly cleaned before proceeding with the dismantling. It is recommended that a new dust seal should be fitted whenever the unit is dismantled.

1. Withdraw the brake pads. Disconnect and blank off the supply pipe (if the unit is being dismantled on the vehicle) and remove the bridge pipe.

A rear disc brake calliper with hand brake carriers

2. Remove the bolts securing the cylinder blocks to the calliper and withdraw the cylinder blocks.

3. Disengage the dust seal from the lip on the cylinder block face, connect the cylinder to a source of fluid supply, and apply pressure to eject the piston assembly. Remove the screws securing the plate to the piston, lift off the plate and piston seal, and withdraw the retractor bush from within the piston bore. Carefully cut away and discard the dust seal.

4. Support the backing plate on a bush of sufficient bore just to accommodate the piston; with a suitable tubular distance piece placed against the end of the piston spigot around the shouldered head press out the piston from the backing plate. Care must be taken during the operation to avoid damaging the piston.

Assembling a Brake Unit

1. Clean all components thoroughly, using only the recommended brake fluid for all rubber parts.

2. Engage the collar of a new dust seal with the lip on the backing plate on the piston spigot, and with the piston suitably supported press the backing plate fully home.

3. Insert the retractor bush into the bore of the piston. Lightly lubricate the piston seal with brake fluid (if there is any doubt about the condition of this component it should be renewed) and fit it to the piston face. Attach and secure the plate with the screws, and peen-lock the screws.

4. Check that the piston and the cylinder bore are thoroughly clean and show no signs of damage. Locate the piston assembly on the end of the retractor pin, and with the aid of a hand press slowly apply an even pressure to the backing plate and press the assembly into the cylinder bore. Ensure that the piston assembly is in correct alignment in relation to the cylinder bore and that the piston seal does not become twisted or trapped as it enters the cylinder bore. Engage the lip of the dust seal with the lip on the cylinder block face.

5. Reassemble the cylinder blocks to the calliper and fit the bridge pipe, ensuring that it is correctly positioned (with the near-vertical part of the pipe farthest from the wheel). If the complete brake unit has been removed it should be replaced.

6. Remove the blank, replace the supply pipe, and fit the friction pads.

7. Finally, bleed the system and check for leaks with the brakes fully applied.

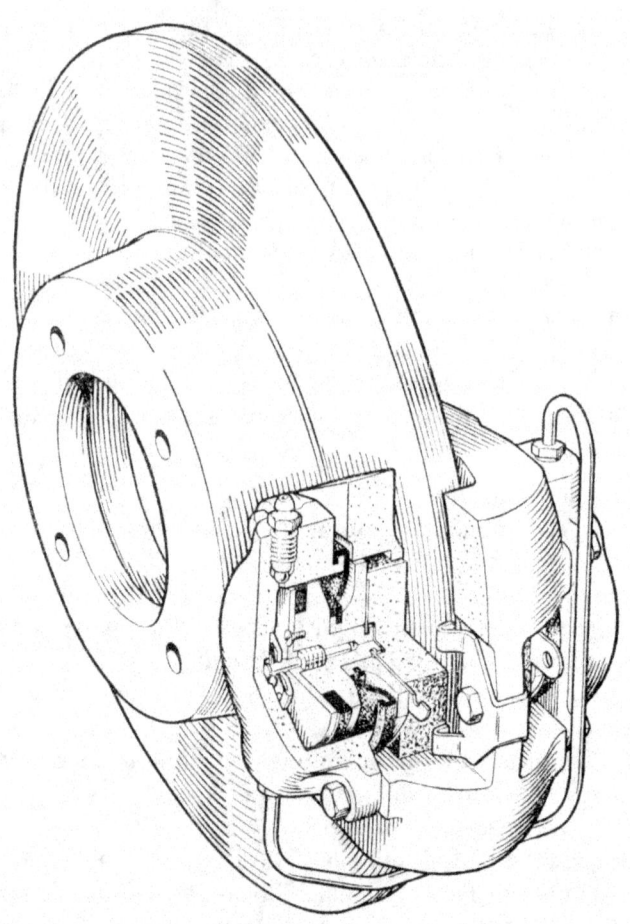

Sectioned view of a brake calliper

Replacing a Brake Unit

The replacement procedure is a reversal of the instructions given as to removing the unit, with the exception of the following details. Replace the brake pads. Check the gap between each side of the calliper and the disc. The difference should not exceed .010 in. and the shims may be altered to obtain this figure. Bleed the system and, finally, check for leaks with the brakes fully applied.

Removing the Friction Pads

Remove the nut, washer, and bolt securing the keep plate and withdraw the plate. Withdraw the pad assemblies with a suitable hooked implement engaged in the hole in the lug of the securing plate.

Thoroughly clean the backing plate, dust seal, and the surrounding area of the calliper.

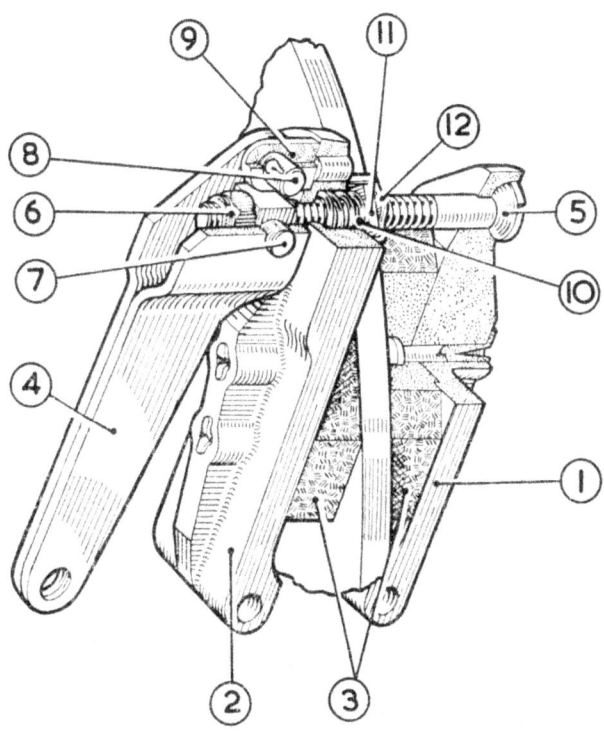

The hand brake carrier components

1. Pad carrier (outer).
2. Pad carrier (inner).
3. Pads.
4. Lever.
5. Adjuster bolt.
6. Locknut.
7. Trunnion.
8. Pivot pin.
9. Pivot seat.
10. Spring.
11. Spring retaining nut
12. Spring plate.

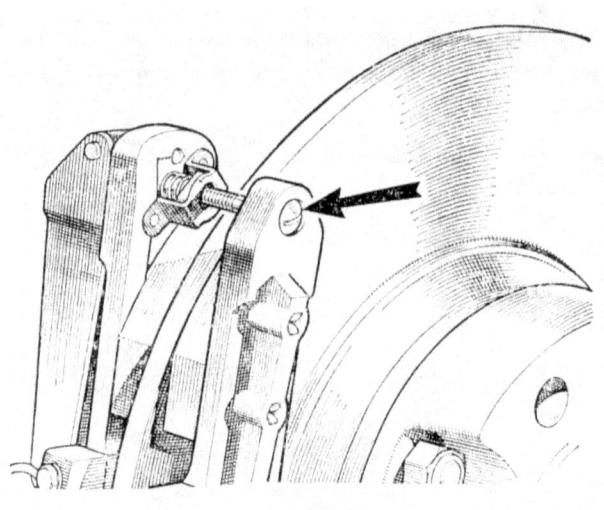

The arrow indicates the hand brake carrier pad adjusting bolt

Replacing the Friction Pads

Where the original friction pads are to be refitted it is only necessary to reverse the instructions given above.

If wear has reduced the pads to the minimum permissible thickness of .025 in. the pads must be renewed. Press the piston assemblies with a suitable lever to the base of the cylinder bores against the resistance offered by the retractor pin and bush. Insert the new friction pad assemblies, replace the keep plate, and secure it with the bolt, washer, and nut.

Relining the Hand Brake

Unscrew and remove the adjuster bolt and locknut and swing the pad carries away from the disc. Extract the split pin and withdraw the lever pivot pin.

Remove the bifurcated rivets from both carriers and pry off the worn linings. Place the new linings in position and secure them with new bifurcated rivets.

Place the lever in the position indicated in the drawing. Hold the locknut firmly against the outer face of the trunnion and screw in the adjuster bolt until three or four threads engage in the locknut. Align the holes in the lever and pivot seat, fit the pivot pin, and lock it with a split pin.

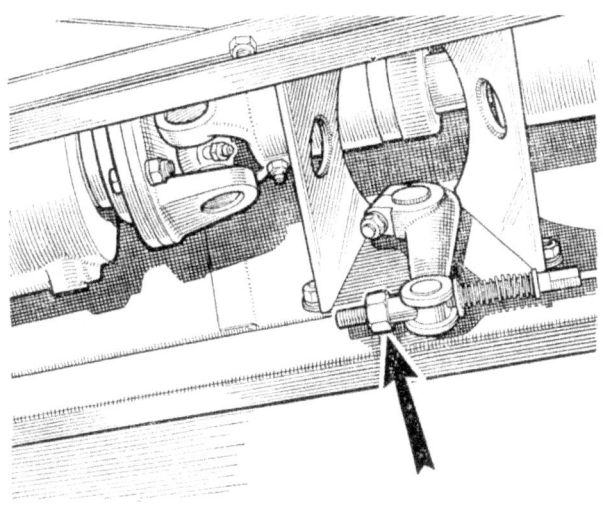

The arrow indicates the brass adjuster nut fitted to the cable relay lever

Adjusting the Hand Brake

Adjustment to compensate for pad wear must be made at the hand brake units and not on the relay lever adjuster. The adjustments should be made in the following manner when the travel of the hand brake lever becomes excessive.
1. Raise the rear of the car — making certain that the front wheels are suitably blocked to prevent the car running forward — and remove both rear wheels. The hand brake lever should be in the fully off position whilst the adjustments are made.
2. Slacken the brass adjuster nut fitted to the relay lever (located beside the front universal joint on the propeller shaft) so that the operating cable hangs loosely.
3. Tighten each adjuster bolt until the pads 'nip' the brake disc. Screw up the brass adjuster nut on the relay lever until all slackness is taken up, ensuring that there is no preload on the linkage.
4. Set the clearance between the pads and the brake disc by unscrewing each adjuster bolt approximately one-third of a turn. Make sure that the discs rotate freely.

Removing the Hand Brake Cable
1. Unscrew and remove the adjuster nut; withdraw the end of the cable from the lower end of the lever and remove the spring.
2. Disconnect the clips securing the cable assembly to the body.
3. Remove the clevis pins from the levers on the wheel brake units.
4. Unscrew the two nuts on the axle balance lever; separate the two halves of the lever and remove the cable and trunnion.

Removing a Brake Disc

Remove the brake unit and withdraw the hub by the methods described in front and rear suspension sections.

The rear disc is separated from the hub by a reversal of the instructions above and fit the assembly to the vehicle.

Check the disc for true rotation by clamping a dial indicator to a suitable fixed point on the vehicle with the needle pad bearing on the face of the disc. Run-out must not exceed .006 in., and in the event of the value being exceeded the components should be examined for damage and, if necessary, renewed.

Replace the brake unit.

Flexible Hoses

The flexible pipes must show no signs of deterioration or damage and the bores should be cleared with a jet of compressed air. No attempt should be made to clear a blockage by probing as this may result in damage to the lining and serious restriction to fluid flow. Partially or totally blocked flexible pipes should always be renewed. When removing or refitting a flexible pipe the end sleeve hexagon should be held with the appropriate wrench to prevent the pipe from twisting. A twisted pipe will prove detrimental to efficient brake operation.

Removing a rear hose

The front end of the rear flexible hose is held in a bracket mounted on the right-hand battery box. Unscrew the metal pipe union nut and release the pipe. Hold the hexagon on the flexible hose with a wrench and remove the large retaining nut and its shakeproof washer from the under side of the support bracket. The pipe may now be unscrewed at its rear end from the three-way piece on the rear axle.

Removing a front hose

Unscrew the metal pipe union nuts at each end of the front hose. Hold the hexagon on the flexible hose and remove the nut and shakeproof washer on the under side of the mounting brackets.

Refacing Brake Discs

Scoring of the brake discs is not detrimental, provided that the scoring is concentric, even, and is not excessive. The disc faces may be ground provided the following conditions are observed:
1. The final thickness of the disc must not be less than between .340 and .330 in.
2. The disc faces must run true to within .003 in.
3. The faces must be parallel to within .001 in.

ELECTRICAL SYSTEM

The 12-volt electrical equipment incorporates compensated voltage control for the charging circuit. The positive ground system of wiring is employed.

The two 6-volt batteries, mounted to the rear of the seats, are accessible for examination and maintenance attention.

The generator is mounted on the right of the cylinder block and driven by endless belt from the engine crankshaft. A rotatable mounting enables the belt tension to be adjusted.

The control box is sealed and should not normally need attention. The fuses and spare fuses are carried in external holders.

The starter motor is mounted on the flywheel housing on the right-hand side of the engine unit and operates on the flywheel through the usual sliding pinion device.

The headlamps employ the double-filament dipping system. Both lamps dip according to the regulations existing in the country concerned.

Battery Maintenance

In order to keep the batteries in good condition, a periodical inspection must be made.

Unscrew the five quick-release fasteners securing the panel immediately behind the seats and lift the panel away to obtain access to the batteries.

Topping up

Remove the filler plug from each cell and examine the level of the electrolyte. Add distilled water to bring the level of the electrolyte just above the separators.

NOTE.—Do not use tap-water and do not use a naked light when examining the condition of the cells. Wipe away all dirt and moisture from the top of the battery.

Testing the condition of the battery

Every 1,000 miles examine the condition of the batteries by taking hydrometer readings. The hydrometer contains a graduated float on which is indicated the specific gravity of the acid in the cell from which the same is taken.

The specific gravity readings and their indications are as follows:

Climates below 90°F. (32°C.)
    1.270 to 1.290   Cell fully charged.
    1.190 to 1.210   Cell about half-discharged.
    1.110 to 1.130   Cell fully discharged.

Climates frequently above 90°F. (32°C.)
1.210 to 1.230   Cell fully charged.
1.130 to 1.150   Cell about half-discharged.
1.050 to 1.070   Cell fully discharged.

These figures are given assuming an electrolyte temperature of 60°F. (16°C.). If the temperature of the electrolyte exceeds this, .002 must be added to hydrometer readings for each 5°F. rise to give the true specific gravity. Similarly .002 must be subtracted from hydrometer readings for every 5°F. below 60°F.

The readings of all the cells should be approximately the same. If one cell gives a reading very different from the rest it may be that the electrolyte has been spilled or has leaked from the cell or there may be an internal fault. Should a battery be in a low state of charge, it should be recharged by taking the car for a long daytime run or by charging from an external source of D.C. supply at a current rate of 5 amperes until the cells are gassing freely.

After examining the battery, check the vent plugs, making sure that the air passages are clear.

Storage

If a battery is to be out of use for any length of time, it should first be fully charged and then given a freshening charge about every fortnight.

A battery must never remain in a discharged condition, as the plates will become sulphated.

Generator
To test on vehicle
1. Make sure that belt slip is not the cause of the trouble. It should be possible to deflect the belt approximately $1/2$ in. at the center of its longest run between two pulleys with moderate hand pressure. If the belt is too slack, loosen the two suspension bolts and then the belt of the slotted adjustment link. A gentle pull on the generator outwards will enable the correct tension to be applied to the belt and all three bolts should then be tightened firmly.
2. Check that the generator and control box are connected correctly. The generator terminal 'D' should be connected to the control box terminal 'D' and the generator terminal 'F' connected to the control box terminal 'F'.
3. After switching off all lights and accessories, disconnect the cables from the generator terminals marked 'D' and 'F' respectively.
4. Connect the two terminals with a length of wire.

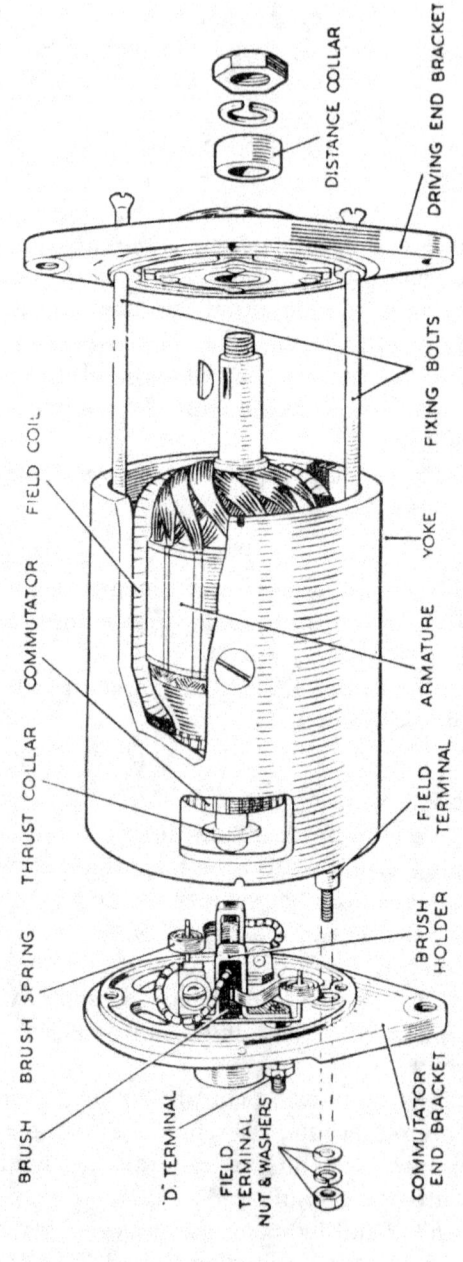

An exploded view of the dynamo.

5. Start the engine and set to run at idling speed.

6. Clip the negative lead of a moving-coil-type voltmeter, calibrated 0-20 volts, to one terminal and the other lead to a good ground point on the dynamo yoke.

7. Gradually increase the engine speed, when the voltmeter reading should rise rapidly and without fluctuation. Do not allow the voltmeter reading to reach 20 volts. Do not race the engine in an attempt to increase the voltage. It is sufficient to run the geenrator up to a speed of 1,000 r.p.m.

If there is no reading, check the brush gear.

If the reading is low (approximately 1 volt), the field winding may be faulty.

If the reading is approximately 5 volts, the armature winding may be faulty.

8. Remove the cover band and examine the brushes and commutator. Hold back each of the brush springs and move the brush by pulling gently on its flexible connector. If the movement is sluggish, remove the brush from its holder and ease the sides by lightly polishing on a smooth file. Always replace brushes in their original positions. If the brushes are worn so that they no longer bear on the commutator, or if the brush flexible lead has become exposed on the running face, new brushes must be fitted. If the commutator is blackened or dirty, clean it by holding a solvent-moistened cloth against it while the engine is turned slowly by hand-cranking. Re-test the generator; if there is still no reading on the voltmeter there is an internal fault and the complete unit should be renewed.

If the generator is in good order, leave the temporary link in position between the terminals and restore the original connections, taking care to connect the terminal 'D' to the control box terminal 'D' and the terminal 'F' to the control box terminal 'F'. Remove the lead from the 'D' terminal on the control box and connect the voltmeter between this cable and a good ground point on the vehicle. Run the engine as before. The reading should be the same as that measured directly at the generator. No reading on the voltmeter indicates a break in the cable to the generator. Carry out the same procedure for the 'F' terminal, connecting the voltmeter between cable and ground. Finally remove the link from the generator. If the reading is correct test the control box.

Removing and Replacing the Generator

To remove the generator, disconnect the leads from the terminals.

Slacken all four attachment bolts and pivot the generator towards the cylinder block to enable the fan belt to be removed from the pulley. The generator can then be removed by completely removing the two upper and one lower attachment bolts.

Replacement is an exact reversal of this procedure.

Dismantling the Generator
1. Take off the pulley.
2. Remove the cover band, hold back the brush springs and remove the brushes from their holders.
3. Unscrew the locknuts from the through-bolts at the commutator end. Withdraw the two through-bolts from the driving end.
4. Remove the nut, spring washer and flat washer from the smaller terminal (i.e. field terminal) on the commutator end bracket and remove the bracket from the yoke.
5. The driving end bracket, together with the armature, can now be lifted out of the yoke.
6. The driving end bracket which, on removal from the yoke, has withdrawn with it the armature and armature shaft ball bearing, need not be separated from the shaft unless the bearing is suspected and requires examination, in which event the armature should be removed from the end bracket by means of a hand press.

Servicing the Generator
Brushes

Test if the brushes are sticking. Clean them with gasoline and, if necessary, ease the sides by lightly polishing with a smooth file. Replace the brushes in their original positions.

Test the brush spring tension with a spring scale if available. The correct tension is 20-25 oz. Fit a new spring if the tension is low.

If the brushes are worn so that the flexible lead is exposed on the running face, new brushes **must** be fitted. Brushes are pre-formed so that bedding to the commutator is unnecessary.

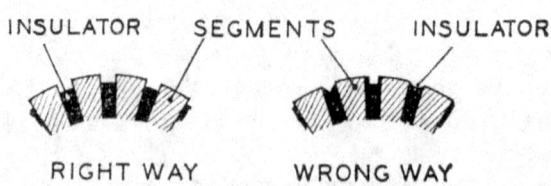

The correct method of undercutting the dynamo commutator.

Commutator

A commutator in good condition will be smooth and free from pits or burned spots. Clean the commutator with a solvent-moistened cloth. If this is ineffective, carefully polish with a strip of fine glass-paper while rotating the armature. To remedy a badly worn commutator, mount the armature (with or without the drive end bracket) in a lathe, rotate at high speed and take a light cut with a very sharp tool. Do not remove more metal than is necessary. Polish the commutator with very fine glass-paper. Undercut the mica insulation between the segments to a depth of $\frac{1}{32}$ in. with a hacksaw blade ground down to the thickness of the mica.

Field coils

Test the field coils, without removing them from the generator yoke, by means of an ohmmeter. The reading on the ohmmeter should be between 6.0 and 6.3 ohms. If this is not available, connect a 12-volt D.C. supply with an ammeter in series between the field terminal and the yoke. The ammeter reading

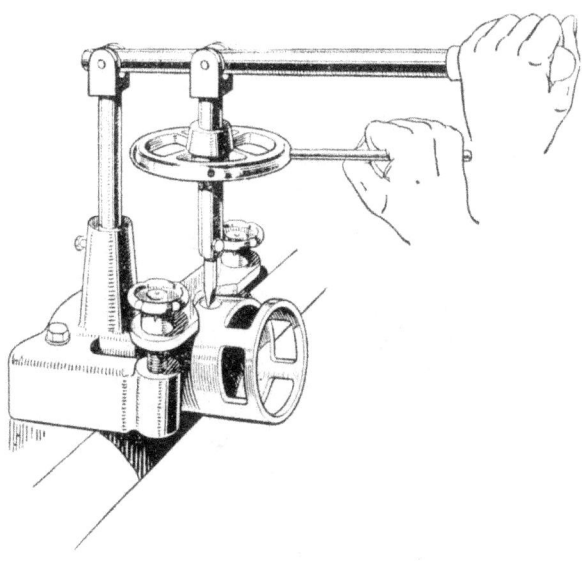

Showing the use of a wheel-operated screwdriver to remove the pole-shoe attachment screws

should be approximately 2 amps. If no reading is indicated the field coils are open-circuited and must be renewed. To test for grounded field coils, unsolder the end of the field winding from the ground terminal on the yoke and, with a test lamp connected from supply mains, test across the field terminal and ground. If the lamp lights, the field coils are grounded and must be renewed.

When fitting field coils, carry out the procedure outlined below, using an expander and wheel-operated screwdriver:

1. Remove the insulation piece which is provided to prevent the junction of the field coils from contacting the yoke.
2. Mark the yoke and pole-shoes in order that they can be refitted in their original positions.
3. Unscrew the two pole-shoe retaining screws by means of the wheel-operated screwdriver.
4. Draw the pole-shoes and coil out of the generator yoke and lift off the coils.
5. Fit the new field coils over the pole-shoes and place them in position inside the yoke. Take care to ensure that the taping of

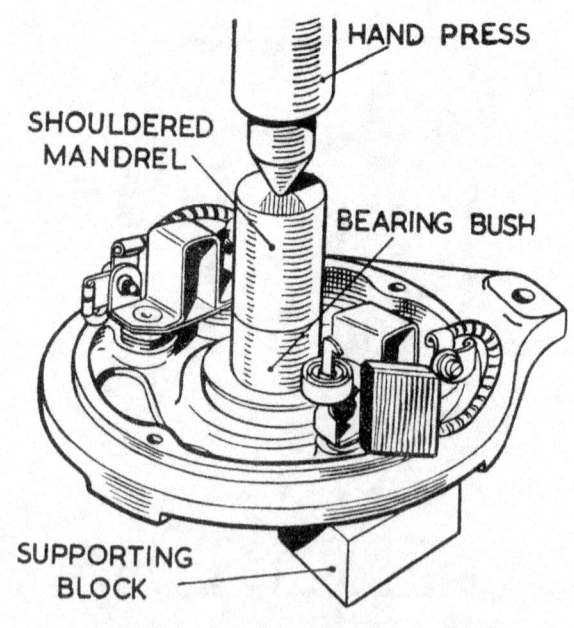

The method of pressing out the commutator end bracket bush is shown in this illustration

the field coils is not trapped between the pole-shoes and the yoke.
6. Locate the pole-shoes and field coils by lightly tightening the fixing screw.
7. Insert the pole-shoe expander, open it to the fullest extent and tighten the screws.
8. Finally tighten the screws by means of the wheel-operated screwdriver and lock them by caulking.
9. Replace the insulation piece between the field coil connection and the yoke.

Armature

The testing of the armature winding requires the use of a voltage drop test and growler. If these are not available, the armature should be checked by substitution. No attempt should be made to machine the armature core or to true a distorted armature shaft.

Bearings

Bearings which are worn to such an extent that they will allow side movement of the armature shaft must be replaced by new ones.

To fit a new bearing at the commutator end of the generator proceed as follows:
1. Press the bearing bush out of the commutator end bracket.
2. Press the new bearing bush into the end bracket, using a shouldered mandrel of the same diameter as the shaft which is to fit in the bearing.

Before fitting the new bearing bush allow it to stand completely immersed in thin engine oil for 24 hours, to fill the pores of the bush with lubricant.

The ball bearing at the driving end is renewed as follows:
1. Knock out the rivets which secure the bearing retaining plate to the end bracket and remove the plate.
2. Press the bearing out of the end bracket and remove the corrugated washer, felt washer and oil retaining washer.
3. Before fitting the replacement bearing see that it is clean and pack it with a high-melting-point grease.
4. Place the oil retaining washer, felt washer and corrugated washer in the bearing housing in the end bracket.
5. Locate the bearing in the housing and press it home by means of a hand press.
6. Fit the bearing retaining plate. Insert the new rivets from the inside of the end bracket and open the rivets by means of a punch to secure the plate rigidly in position.

Reassembly

The reassembly of the generator is a reversal of the operations described above.

If the end bracket has been removed from the armature in dismantling, press the bearing end bracket into the armature shaft, taking care to avoid damaging the end plate and armature winding.

Add a few drops of oil through the hole in the armature end cover.

Windowless Yoke Generator

Engines numbered 487 were fitted with a new generator (Part No. 11G220) without brush gear inspection windows. Access to the brush gear in these units is gained by undoing the two throughbolts and withdrawing the commutator end bracket. Every 12,000 miles the unit should be partially dismantled for the inspection of brush gear and commutator.

To check the brush spring tension, the yoke should be completely withdrawn from the armature and the commutator end bracket refitted to the shaft.

When reassembling a windowless yoke generator the brushes must first be held clear of the commutator in the usual way, i.e. by partially withdrawing the brushes from their boxes until each brush is trapped in position by the side pressure of its spring. The brushes can be released onto the commutator with a small screwdriver or similar tool when the end bracket is assembled to within about $1/2$ in. of the yoke. Before closing the gap between the end bracket and yoke, see that the springs are in correct contact with the brushes.

Coil steady plate, Part No. 11G221, should always be used with generator Part No. 11G220.

Lucas C40/1 Generator

From Engine No. 16GA6272 a later type of generator with increased output, Lucas type C40/1, was introduced, complete with Lucas connectors, modified Lucas type RB106/2 control box, and a new-type ignition coil bracket.

The modified control box must not be fitted with the earlier-type generator.

The instructions for dismantling the generator are basically the same as those given for the windowless yoke type.

Access to the brushes is obtained by removing the commutator end bracket.

Brushes:

The minimum permissible length of a worn brush is 5/32 in. Badly worn brushes must be renewed and the new brushes bedded to the commutator. The correct spring tension is 30 oz., maximum, on a new brush, and 13 oz., minimum, on a brush worn to 5/32 in.

Commutator:

The later type of commutators are moulded, and may be re-skimmed to a minimum diameter of 1.450 in. The undercut must conform to the following dimensions:

Width .... .040 in.
Depth .... .020 to .035 in.

It is important that the side of the undercut should clear the moulding material by a minimum of .015 in.

Field coil:

The resistance of the field coil is 6.0 ohms.

Bearings:

To remove the bearing bush in the commutator end plate screw a 5/8 in. tap squarely into the bush and withdraw the bush; then remove the felt ring and its retainer.

When refitting the bearing plate to the front bracket insert the rivets from the outer face of the bracket.

The part numbers of the new components are as follows:

Control box, Lucas, Type RB106/2....... 3H1836
Dynamo, Lucas type C40/1............. 13H219
Ignition coil bracket.................... 12H51

The Starter

To test on vehicle

Switch on the lamps and operate the starter control. If the lights do dim, but the starter is not heard to operate, an indication is given that current is flowing through the starter windings but that the starter pinion is meshed permanently with the geared ring on the flywheel. This was probably caused by the starter being operated while the engine was still running. In this case the starter must be removed from the engine for examination.

Should the lamps retain their full brilliance when the starter switch is operated, check that the switch is functioning. If the switch is in order, examine the connections at the battery, starter switch and starter, and also check the wiring between these units. Continued failure of the starter to operate indicates an internal fault and the starter must be removed from the

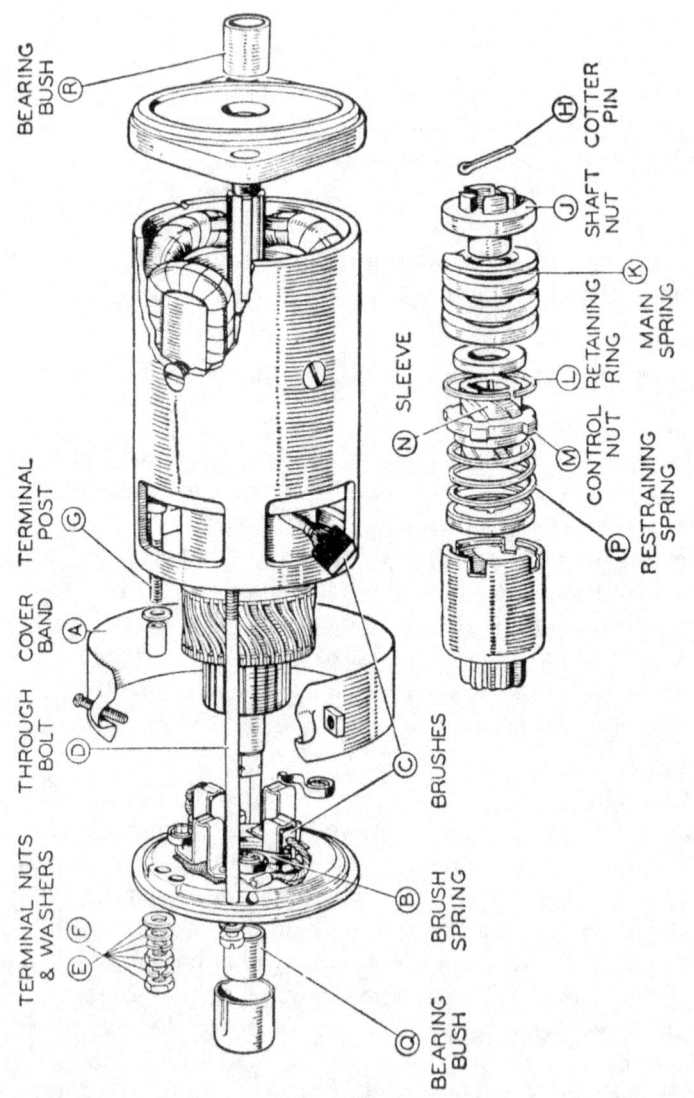

An exploded view of the starter and drive.

engine for examination.

Sluggish or slow action of the starter is usually caused by a poor connection in the wiring which produces a high resistance in the starter circuit. Check as described above.

Damage to the starter drive is indicated if the starter is heard to operate but does not crank the engine.

Removing and Replacing the Starter

Release the starter cable from the terminal and unscrew the two starter securing bolts. Maneuver the starter forwards below the oil filter, then rearwards and upwards.

Servicing the Starter
Examination of commutator and brush gear

Remove the starter cover band (a) and examine the brushes (c) and the commutator. Hold back each of the brush springs (b) and move the brush by pulling gently on its flexible connector. If the movement is sluggish remove the brush from its holder and ease the sides by lightly polishing with a smooth file. Always replace brushes in their original positions. If the brushes are worn so that they no longer bear on the commutator, or if the brush flexible lead has become exposed on the running face, they must be renewed.

If the commutator is blackened or dirty, clean it by holding a solvent-moistened cloth against it while the armature is rotated.

Secure the body of the starter in a vice and test by connecting it with heavy-gauge cables to a battery of the correct voltage. One cable must be connected to the starter terminal and the other held against the starter body or end bracket. Under these light load conditions the starter should run at a very high speed.

If the operation of the starter is still unsatisfactory, the starter should be dismantled for detailed inspection and testing.

Dismantling

Take off the cover band "A" at the commutator end, hold back the brush springs "B" and take out the brushes "C" from their holders.

Withdraw the jump ring and shims from the armature shaft at the commutator end and remove the armature complete with drive from the commutator end bracket and starter frame.

Remove the terminal nuts "E" and washers "F" from the terminal post "G" at the commutator end bracket and also withdraw the two through bolts. Remove the commutator end bracket and the attachment bracket from the starter frame.

Brushes

1. Test the brush springs with a spring scale. The correct tension is 30-40 oz. Fit a new spring if the tension is low.

2. If the brushes are worn so that they no longer bear on the commutator, or if the flexible connector has become exposed on the running face, they must be renewed. Two of the brushes are connected to terminals eyelets attached to the brush boxes on the commutator end bracket. The other two brushes are connected to tappings on the field coils.

The flexible connectors must be removed by unsoldering and the connectors of the new brushes secured in place by soldering. The brushes are pre-formed, so that bedding of the working face to the commutator is unnecessary.

Drive

1. If the pinion is tight on the sleeve, wash in kerosene; replace any worn or damaged parts.

2. To dismantle the drive, extract the split pin and remove the shaft nut "J"; withdraw the main spring and collar.

3. Rotate the barrel to push out the sleeve; remove the barrel and pinion.

4. The barrel and pinion are supplied as an assembly but the parts may be separated by extracting the retaining ring "L."

Note.—Should either the **control nut or screwed sleeve be damaged, a replacement assembly, consisting of a screwed sleeve and control nut, must be fitted. These components must not be fitted individually.**

Commutator

A commutator in good condition will be smooth and free from pits and burned spots. Clean the commutator with a cloth moistened with solvent. If this is ineffective, carefully polish with a strip of fine glass-paper, while rotating the armature. To remedy a badly worn commutator, dismantle the starter drive as described above and remove the armature from the end bracket. Now mount the armature in a lathe, rotate it at a high speed and take a light cut with a very sharp tool. Do not remove any more metal than is absolutely necessary, and finally polish with very fine glass-paper.

The mica on the **starter** commutator **must not be undercut.**

Field coils

The field coils can be tested for an open circuit by connecting a 12-volt battery, having a 12-volt bulb in one of the leads, to the tapping point of the field coils to which the brushes are

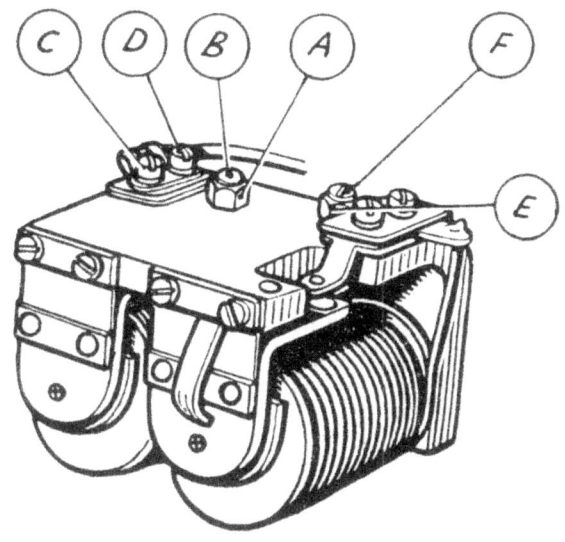

The cut-out and regulator assembly

connected, and the field terminal post. If the lamp does not light, there is an open circuit in the wiring of the field coils.

Lighting of the lamp does not necessarily mean that the field coils are in order, as it is possible that one of them may be grounded to a pole shoe or to the yoke. This may be checked by removing the lead from the brush connector and holding it on a clean part of the starter yoke. Should the bulb now light it indicates that the field coils are grounded.

Should the above tests indicate that the fault lies in the field coils, they must be renewed. When renewing field coils carry out the procedure detailed in the generator section.

Armature

Examination of the armature will in many cases reveal the cause of failure, e.g. conductors lifted from the commutator due to the starter being engaged while the engine is running and causing the armature to be rotated at an excessive speed. A damaged armature must in all cases be renewed — no attempt should be made to machine the armature core or to true a distorted armature shaft.

Bearings (commutator end)

Bearings which are worn to such an extent that they will

allow excessive sideplay of the armature shaft must be renewed. Press the new bearing bush into the end bracket, using a shouldered mandrel of the same diameter as the shaft which is to fit in the bearing.

The bearing bush is of the porous phosphor-bronze type, and before fitting, **new bushes should be allowed to stand completely immersed for twenty-four hours in thin engine oil in order to fill the pores of the bush with lubricant.**

Reassembly

The reassembly of the starter is a reversal of the operations described in this section.

The Control Box
Regulator adjustment

The regulator is carefully set before leaving the factory to suit the normal requirements of the standard equipment, and in general it should not be necessary to alter it. If, however, the battery does not keep in a charged condition, or if the generator output does not fall when the battery is fully charged, it may be advisable to check the setting and, if necessary, to readjust it.

It is important, before altering the regulator setting, when the battery is in a low state of charge, to check that its condition is not due to a battery defect or to the generator belt slipping.

How to check and adjust electrical setting

The regulator setting can be checked without removing the cover of the control box.

Withdraw the cables from the terminals marked 'A' and 'A1' at the control box and join them together. Connect the negative lead of a moving-coil voltmeter (0-20 volts full-scale reading) to the 'D' terminal on the generator and connect the other lead from the meter to a convenient chassis ground.

Slowly increase the speed of the engine until the voltmeter needle flicks and then steadies; this should occur at a voltmeter reading between the limits given below for the appropriate temperature of the regulator.

```
Setting at 10°C. (50°F.)    16.1-16.7 volts
   "      20°C. (68°F.)    15.8-16.4   "
   "      30°C. (86°F.)    15.6-16.2   "
   "      40°C. (104°F.)   15.3-15.9   "
```

If the voltage at which the reading becomes steady occurs outside these limits, the regulator must be adjusted.

Shut off the engine, remove the control box cover, release the locknut (a) holding the adjusting screw (b) and turn the screw in a clockwise direction to raise the setting or in an anti-clockwise direction to lower the setting. Turn the adjusting screw a fraction of a turn and then tighten the locknut.

When the generator is run at high speed on open circuit, it builds up a high voltage. When adjusting the regulator, do not run the engine up to more than 3,000 r.p.m. or a false voltmeter reading will be obtained.

Mechanical setting

The mechanical setting of the regulator is accurately adjusted before leaving the factory, and provided that the armature carrying the moving contact is not removed, the regulator will not require mechanical adjustment. If, however, the armature has been removed from the regulator for any reason, the contacts will have to be reset. To do this, proceed as follows:

1. Slacken the two armature fixing screws (e). Insert a .020 in. feeler gauge between the back of the armature (a) and the regulator frame.
2. Press back the armature against the regulator frame and down onto the top of the bobbin core with the gauge in position and lock the armature by tightening the two fixing screws.
3. Check the gap between the under side of the arm and the top of the bobbin core. This must be .012 to .020 in. If the gap is outside these limits correct by adding or removing shims (f) at the back of the fixed contact (d) or, in later types, by carefully bending the fixed contact bracket.
4. Remove the gauge and press the armature down, when the gap between the contacts should be between .006 in. and .017 in.

Cleaning contacts

To render the regulator contacts accessible for cleaning, slacken the screws securing the plate carrying the fixed contact. It will be necessary to slacken the upper screw (c) a little more than the lower screw (d), so that the contact plate can be swung outwards. Clean the contacts by means of fine carborundum stone or fine emery-cloth. Carefully wipe away all traces of dirt or other foreign matter. Finally tighten the securing screws.

Cut-out
Adjustment

If it is suspected that the cutting-in speed of the generator is too high, connect a voltmeter between the terminals marked 'D' and 'E' at the control box and slowly raise the engine speed. When the voltmeter reading rises to between 12.7 and 13.3 volts the cut-out contacts should close.

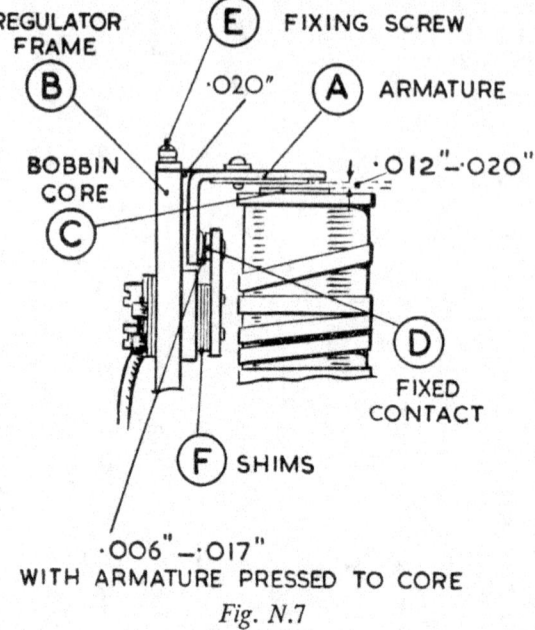

Fig. N.7
Mechanical regulator adjustment

If the cut-out has become out of adjustment and operates at a voltage outside these limits it must be reset. To make the adjustment, slacken the locknut (e) and turn the adjusting screw (f) a fraction of a turn in a clockwise direction to raise the operating voltage or in an anti-clockwise direction to lower the voltage. Tighten the locknut after making the adjustment.

Cleaning

To clean the contacts remove the cover, place a strip of fine glass-paper between the contacts and then, closing the contacts by hand, draw the paper through. This should be done two or three times, with the rough side towards each contact.

Modified Control Box

A modified C.V.C. control box, model RB106/2, with revised settings (Part No. AHH5356) was introduced on later cars. Servicing instructions remain as before, but adjustments must be made within 30 seconds, otherwise heating of the shunt winding will cause false settings to be made.

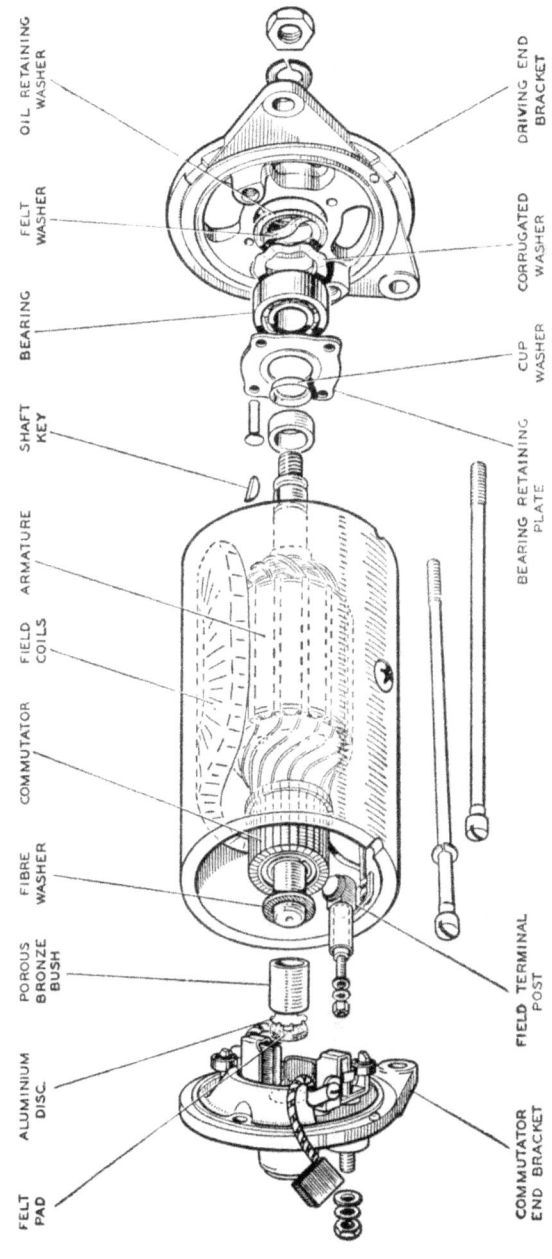

The windowless yoke dynamo

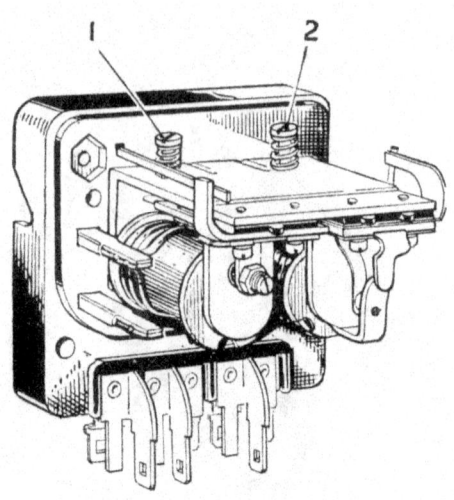

Al A F D E

Modified RB106/2 Control Box

The control box with cover removed

1. Regulator adjusting screw.
2. Cut-out adjusting screw.

Modified RB106/2 Control Box

The instructions for adjusting the modified Lucas Type RB106/2 control box are as follows.

Regulator adjustment:

The electrical setting of the control unit can be checked without removing the cover. Use a good-quality moving-coil voltmeter (0 to 20 volts).

Remove the cables from the control box terminals 'A' and 'A1' and connect the cables together.

Connect the negative lead of the voltmeter to the control box terminal 'D' and connect the other lead to the terminal 'E'.

Run the generator at 3,000 r.p.m., and watch the voltmeter reading, which should be between the limits given below, according to the ambient temperatures.

Ambient temperature	Open-circuit voltage
50°F. (10°C.)	16.1 to 16.7
68°F. (20°C.)	16.0 to 16.6
86°F. (30°C)	15.9 to 16.5
104°F. (40°C.)	15.8 to 16.4

An unsteady voltmeter reading may be due to dirty contacts, but if the reading is outside the appropriate limits the regulator must be adjusted.

Switch off the engine, remove the control box cover, restart the engine, and run the generator at 3,000 r.p.m. Turn the regulator adjusting screw in a clockwise direction to raise the setting, or in an anti-clockwise direction to lower the setting.

NOTE.—The operations of checking and adjusting the regulator should be completed within 30 seconds, otherwise false readings and settings, due to the heating of the shunt coil, will be made.

After adjustment a further check of the setting should be made by switching off and restarting the engine and then raising the generator speed to 3,000 r.p.m., when the open-circuit voltage must conform to the figures stated.

Refit the control box cover and restore the original connections.

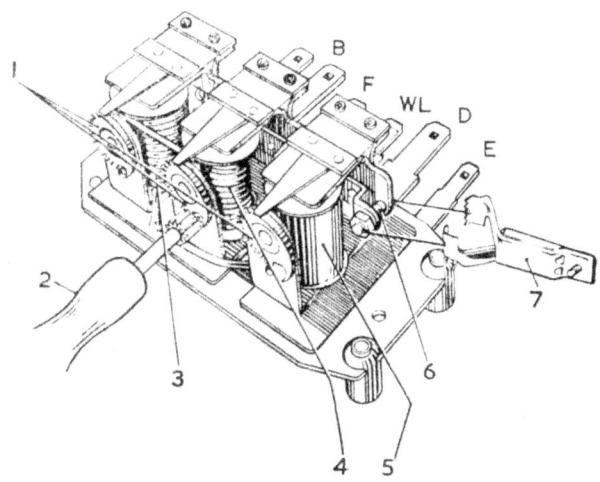

Model RB340

The control box with cover removed

1. Adjustment cams.
2. Setting tool.
3. Cut-out relay.
4. Current regulator.
5. Voltage regulator.
6. Voltage regulator contacts.
7. Bulldog clip.

Control Box Model RB340
General description

The RB340 control box operates on the current-voltage system of generator output regulation. Three units are housed in the control box: two separate vibrating armature-type single-contact regulators and a cut-out relay. One regulator is responsive to changes in current and the other to changes in voltage.

The voltage regulator and cut-out relay are temperature-compensated to allow for operating changes in the circuit resistance and for climatic variations in battery voltage. The effect of temperature fluctuation on control box settings is further minimized by the use of a swamp resistor connected in series with the shunt coils of the voltage regulator and cut-out relay.

For adjustment purposes toothed cams are carried on the front limb of each magnet frame to enable voltage and current settings to be made with a special tool.

The control box settings are accurately adjusted during manufacture and the cover should not be removed unnecessarily.

Preliminary checking of charging circuit

Before disturbing any electrical adjustments examine the items below to ensure that the fault does not lie outside the control box.
1. Check the battery by substitution or with a hydrometer and a heavy-discharge tester. Inspect the generator driving belt. This should be just taut enough to drive without slipping. Check the generator by substitution, or by disconnecting the cables from the generator terminals and linking the large terminal 'D' to the small terminal 'F', connecting a voltmeter between this link and ground and running the generator up to about 1,000 r.p.m., when a rising voltage should be shown.
2. Inspect the wiring of the charging circuit and carry out continuity tests between the generator, control box, and battery.
3. Check the ground connections, particularly that of the control box.

In the event of reported undercharging, ascertain that this is not due to low mileage.

Voltage regulator
Method of adjustment

Checking and adjusting should be completed as rapidly as possible to avoid errors due to heating of the operating coil. Withdraw the cables from the control box terminal blades 'B'. To enable the engine to be started it will be necessary to join the ignition and battery feeds together with a suitable lead.

Connect a first-grade 0-20 moving-coil voltmeter between control box terminal 'D' and a good grounding point. A convenient method of making this connection is to withdraw the ignition warning light feed from the control box terminal 'WL' and to clip the voltmeter lead of appropriate polarity to the small terminal blade thus exposed, this terminal being electrically common with terminal 'D'. Start the engine and run the generator at 3,000 r.p.m. The voltmeter reading should be steady and lie between the following appropriate limits according to the temperature.

Ambient temperature	Voltage setting
10°C. (50°F.)	14.9 to 15.5
20°C. (68°F.)	14.7 to 15.3
30°C. (86°F.)	14.5 to 15.1
40°C. (104°F.)	14.3 to 14.9

An unsteady reading may be due to dirty contacts. If the reading is steady but occurs outside the appropriate limits an adjustment must be made. Proceed as follows.

Stop the engine and remove the control box cover. Restart the engine and run the generator at 3,000 r.p.m. Using a suitable tool, turn the voltage adjustment cam until the correct setting is obtained. Turn the tool clockwise to raise the setting or anti-clockwise to lower it. Check the setting by stopping the engine and then again raising the generator speed to 3,000 r.p.m. Restore the original connections and refit the cover.

Current regulator
On-load setting

The current regulator on-load setting is equal to the maximum rated output of the geenrator, which is 22 amps.

Method of adjustment

The generator must be made to develop its maximum rated output whatever the state of charge of the battery might be at the time of setting. The voltage regulator must therefore be rendered inoperative, and to achieve this the bulldog clip is used to keep the voltage regulator contacts together.

Remove the control box cover and, using a bulldog clip, short out the contacts of the voltage regulator.

Withdraw the cables from the control box terminal blades 'B' and connect a first-grade 0-40 moving-coil ammeter between these cables and one of the terminal blades 'B'. It is important that terminal 'B' should carry only this one connection. All other load connections, including the ignition coil feed, must be made to the battery. Switch on **all lights and accessories**, start the

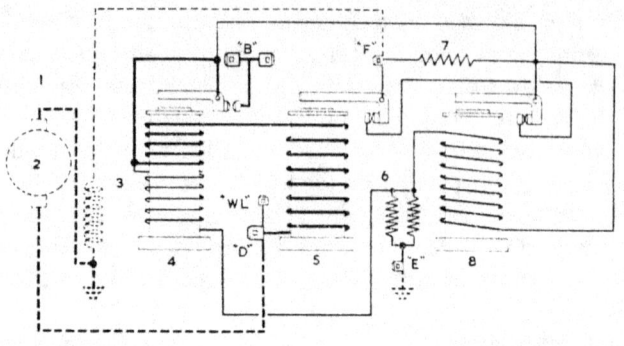

The charging circuit

1. Dynamo.
2. Armature.
3. Field.
4. Cut-out relay.
5. Current regulator.
6. Swamp resistor.
7. Field resistor.
8. Voltage regulator.

engine, and run the generator at 3,000 r.p.m. The ammeter pointer should be steady and indicate a current of 19-22 amps. An unsteady reading may be due to dirty contacts. If the reading is too high or too low an adjustment must be made. Proceed as follows.

Using a suitable tool, turn the current adjustment cam until the correct setting is obtained. Turn the tool clockwise to raise the setting or anti-clockwise to lower it. Stop the engine, restore the original connections, and refit the control box cover.

Cut-out relay
Cut-in adjustment

Checking and adjusting should be completed as rapidly as possible to avoid errors due to heating of the operating coil.

Connect a first-grade 0-20 moving-coil voltmeter between control box terminal 'D' and a good ground point. A convenient method of making this connection is to withdraw the ignition warning light feed from control box terminal 'WL' and to clip the voltmeter lead of appropriate polarity to the small terminal blade thus exposed, this terminal being electrically common with terminal 'D'. Switch on an electrical load such as the headlamps, start the engine, and gradually increase the engine speed. Observe the voltmeter pointer. The voltage should rise steadily and then drop slightly at the instant of contact closure. The cut-in voltage is that which is indicated immediately before the pointer drops back and should be within the limits 12.7 to 13.3 volts. If the cut-in occurs outside these limits an adjustment must be made. In this event proceed as follows.

Remove the control box cover. Using a suitable tool turn the cut-out relay adjustment cam until the correct setting is obtained. Turn the tool clockwise to raise the setting or anti-clockwise to lower it. Stop the engine, restore the original connections, and refit the cover.

Drop-off adjustment

Withdraw the cables from control box terminal blades 'B'. To enable the engine to be started it will be necessary to join the ignition and battery feeds together with a suitable lead. Connect a first-grade 0-20 moving-coil voltmeter between control box terminal 'B' and a good ground point. Start the engine and run up to approximately 3,000 r.p.m.

Slowly decelerate and observe the voltmeter pointer. Opening of the contacts, indicated by the voltmeter pointer dropping to zero, should occur between 9.5 and 11 volts. If the drop-off occurs outside these limits an adjustment must be made. Proceed as follows.

Stop the engine and remove the control box cover. Adjust the drop-off voltage by carefully bending the fixed contact bracket. Reducing the contact gap will raise the drop-off voltage and increasing the gap will lower it. Retest, and if necessary readjust until the correct drop-off setting is obtained. This should result in a contact 'follow through' or blade deflection of .010 to .020 in. Restore the original connections and refit the cover.

Adjustment of air gap settings

Air gap settings are accurately adjusted during manufacture and should require no further attention. If the original settings have been disturbed, it will be necessary to make adjustments in the manner described below.

Armature-to-bobbin core gaps of voltage and current regulators

Using a suitable tool, turn the adjustment cam to the point giving minimum lift to the armature tensioning spring (by turning the tool to the fullest extent anti-clockwise). Slacken the adjustable contact locking nut and screw back the adjustable contact. Insert a flat steel feeler gauge of .045 in. thickness between the armature and the copper separation on the core face, taking care not to turn up or damage the copper shim. Insert the gauge as far back as the two rivet heads on the under side of the armature. Retaining the gauge in position and pressing squarely down on the armature, screw in the adjustable contact until it just touches the armature contact. Retighten the locking nut and withdraw the gauge.

Carry out the electrical setting procedure.

Contact 'follow through' and armature-to-bobbin core gap of cut-out relay

Press the armature squarely down against the copper separation on the core face. Adjust the fixed contact bracket to give a 'follow through' or blade deflection of the moving contact of .010 to .020 in.

Adjust the armature back stop to give a core gap of .035 to .045 in.

Check the cut-in and drop-off voltage settings.

Cleaning contacts
Regulator contacts

To clean the voltage or current regulator contacts use fine carborundum stone or silicon-carbide paper, followed by denatured alcohol.

Cut-out relay contacts

To clean the cut-out relay contacts use a strip of fine glass-paper — never carborundum stone or emery-cloth.

Radio suppression

When it is desired to fit suppressors for radio equipment, make sure that this is done only in accordance with recommended practice. Suppressors and capacitors wrongly fitted may cause damage to the electrical equipment.

Fuses

The fuses are mounted in a separate fusebox and are therefore accessible without removing the control box cover.

Units protected

The units which are protected by each fuse can readily be identified by referring to the wiring diagram.

Blown fuses

A blown fuse is indicated by the failure of all the units protected by it, and is confirmed by examination of the fuse, which can easily be withdrawn from the spring clips. If it has blown, the fused state of the wire will be visible inside the glass tube. Before renewing a blown fuse, inspect the wiring of the units that have failed for evidence of a short circuit or other faults which may have caused the fuse to blow, and remedy the cause of the trouble.

The Electric Horn

If the horn fails or becomes uncertain in its action, it does not follow that the horn has broken down. First ascertain that the trouble is not due to a loose or broken connection in the wiring of the horn. If the fuse has blown, examine the wiring for the fault and replace with the spare fuse provided.

The performance of a horn may be upset by a loose fixing bolt, or by some component near the horn being loose. If after carrying out the above examination the trouble is not rectified, the horn may need adjustment.

Adjustment does not alter the pitch of the note: it merely takes up wear of moving parts. When adjusting the horn, short-circuit the fuse, otherwise it is liable to blow. Again, if the horn will not sound on adjustment, release the push instantly.

Adjustment

Remove the fixing screw from the top of the horn and take off the cover. Detach the cover securing bracket by springing it out of its location.

Slacken the locknut on the fixed contact and rotate the adjusting nut until the contacts are just separated (indicated by the horn failing to sound). Turn the adjusting nut half a turn in the opposite direction and secure it in this position by tightening the locknut.

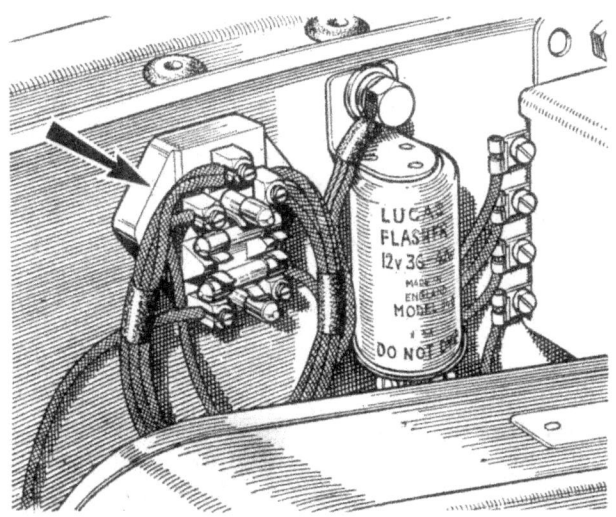

The fuses and flasher unit

Flashing Direction Indicators

The flashing direction indicators are operated by a pneumatic time switch through a flasher unit and a relay to the dual-filament bulbs in the side and tail lamps. In the event of failure, carry out the following procedure:
1. Check bulbs for broken filaments.
2. Refer to the wiring diagram and check over flasher circuit connections.
3. Switch on the ignition and check that terminal 'B' on the flasher is at 12 volts with respect to ground.
4. Connect together terminals 'B' and 'L' at the flasher unit and operate the direction indicator switch.

If the flasher lights now work, the flasher unit is defective and must be renewed.

If the lights do not work the relay is defective and must be renewed.

The length of time the flasher is operating can be altered by screwing up the adjusting screw located in the small boss at the back of the time switch. Screw in to lengthen the time of operation and out to shorten the period.

The Windshield Wiper

Normally the windshield wiper will not require any servicing apart from the occasional renewal of the rubber blades.

Should any trouble be experienced, first check for loose connections, worn insulation, etc., before dismantling the motor.

To detach the cable rack from the motor and gearbox:
1. Unscrew the pipe union nut.
2. Remove the gearbox cover.
3. Remove the split pin and washer from the crankpin and final gear wheel.
4. Lift off the connecting link.

Commutator dirty:

Remove the connecting leads to the terminals, and withdraw the three screws securing the cover at the commutator end. Lift off the cover. Clean the commutator with a cloth moistened with gasoline and carefully remove any carbon dust from between the commutator segments.

Brush lever stiff or brushes not bearing on commutator:

Check that the brushes bear freely on the commutator. If they are loose and do not make contact, a replacement tension spring is necessary. The brush levers must be free on their pivots. If they are stiff they should be freed by working them backwards

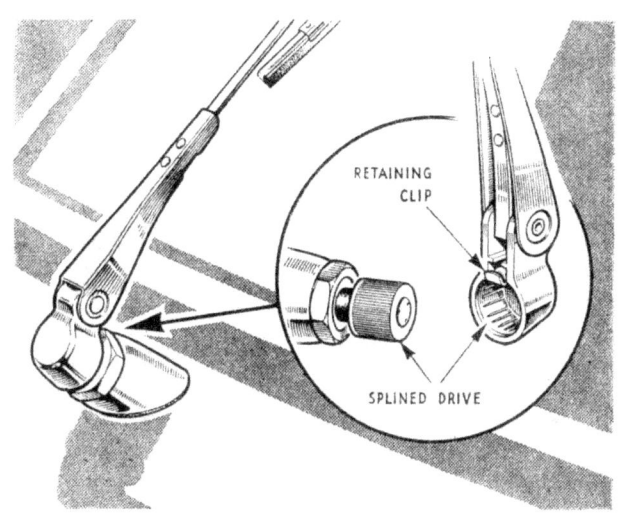

Fig. N.10
A windshield wiper arm and drive

and forwards by hand and by applying a trace of thin machine oil. Packing shims are fitted beneath the legs of the brush to ensure that the brushes are central and that there is no possibility of the brush boxes fouling the commutator. If the brushes are considerably worn they must be replaced by new ones.

Motor operates but does not transmit motion to spindles:

Remove the cover of the gearbox. A push-pull motion should be transmitted to the inner cable of the flexible rack. If the cross-head moves sluggishly between the guides, lightly smear a small amount of medium grade engine oil in the groove formed in the die-cast housing. When overhauling, the gear must be lubricated by lightly packing the gearbox with a grease.

Thrust screw adjustments:

The thrust screw is located on the top of the cross-head housing. To adjust, slacken the locknut, screw down the thrust screw until it contacts the armature and then turn back a fraction of a turn. Hold the thrust screw with a screwdriver and tighten the locknut.

To remove the motor:

Detach the cable rack from the motor and gearbox as de-

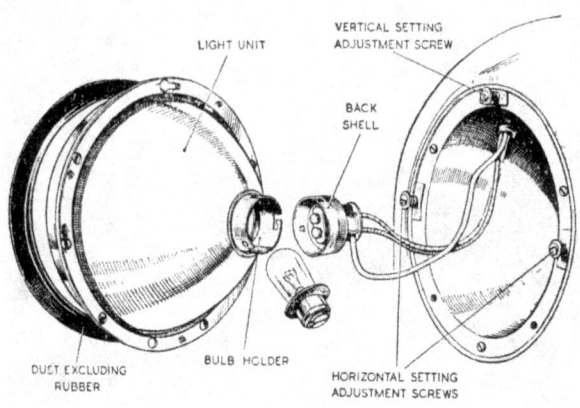

tailed above. Disconnect the lead. Remove the two screws securing the mounting bracket to remove the motor.

The Headlamps

The headlamps are fitted with double-filament bulbs. The design is such that the bulb is correctly positioned in relation to the reflector, and no focusing is required when a replacement bulb is fitted.

The anti-dazzle device

The double-filament bulbs are controlled by a foot-operated dipping switch deflecting both headlamp beams downward to avoid dazzle.

Certain countries have lighting regulations to which the foregoing arrangements do not conform, and cars exported to such countries have suitably modified lighting equipment, such as sealed beam units, described later.

The Light Units

The light units consist of a lamp glass, reflector, and a back shell. The light unit is located to the front wing by three spring-loaded attachment screws in a domed shield attached to the wing. The back of the lamp is therefore sealed to give complete protection.

A dust- and weather-excluding rubber is fitted in the recess of the rim of the light unit and a plated rim is fitted over this to complete the weather-sealing.

Removing the Light Units

To remove the light unit for bulb replacement, unscrew the retaining screw at the bottom of the plated lamp rim and lift the rim away from the dust-excluding rubber.

Remove the dust-excluding rubber, which will reveal the three spring-loaded screws. Press the light unit inwards against the tension of the springs and turn it in an anti-clockwise direction until the heads of the screws can pass through the enlarged ends of the keyhole slots in the lamp rim.

This will enable you to withdraw the light unit sufficiently to give attention to the wiring and bulbs.

Setting the Headlamps

The lamps should be set so that the main driving beams are parallel with the road surface or in accordance with your local regulations.

If adjustment is required, this is achieved by removing the plated rim and dust-excluding rubber.

Vertical adjustment can then be made by turning the screws at the top of the lamp in the necessary direction.

Horizontal adjustment can be effected by using the adjustment screws on each side of the light unit.

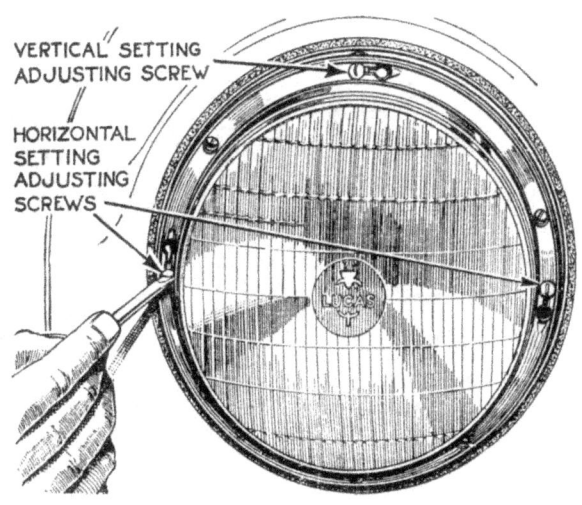

Headlamp Beam Setting

In the absence of specialized proprietary equipment the setting of the lamps can be carried out by placing the vehicle squarely in front of a blank wall at a distance of 25 ft. or more, taking care that the surface on which the car is standing is level and not sloping in relation to the wall. The vehicle should be loaded. It will be found an advantage to cover one lamp while setting the other.

Modified European Light Unit

Cars exported to Europe are now fitted with the new European-type headlamps. These lamp units are fitted with special bulbs and front lenses giving an asymmetrical beam to the right-hand side. This modification was introduced on the following cars:

From Car No. 58918 (Europe except France).
From Car No. 60340 (France).

Access to the bulb is gained in the same way as described. The bulb, however, is released from the reflector by withdrawing the three-pin socket and pinching the two ends of the wire retaining clip to clear the bulb flange.

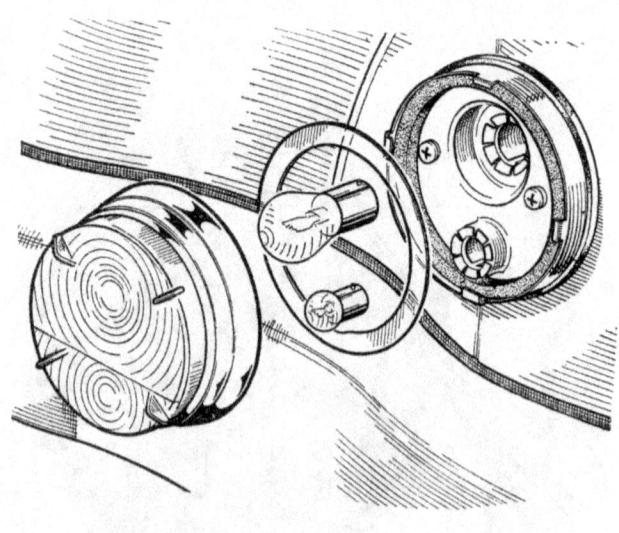

When replacing the bulb care must be taken to see that the rectangular pip on the bulb flange engages the slot in the reflector seating for the bulb.

Replace the spring clip with its coils resting in the base of the bulb flange and engaging in the two retaining lugs on the reflector seating.

The appropriate replacement bulbs are listed. They are not interchangeable with those used in conjunction with the Continental-type headlamps previously fitted.

1600 Front Pilot and Flashing Indicator Lamps

To gain access to the front pilot and flashing indicator bulbs press the front of the lamp inwards and turn it in a clockwise direction.

Both bulbs have single filaments and may be replaced either way round.

1600 Rear Flashing Indicator Lamps

Fold back the rubber lip surrounding the lamp rim and withdraw the rim and lens.

The bulb has a single filament and may be replaced either way round.

Mk. II Tail/Stop and Flasher Lamps

Each tail/stop flasher lamp is secured to the tail plinth by two screws. The plinths incorporate two studs that pass through the body shell and are secured by washers and nuts.

The tail/stop and flasher lamp is a combined unit and is enclosed in a two-piece cover that incorporates a sealed reflector. The tail/stop lamp cover is secured by a single screw; the flasher cover slides onto one end of the tail/stop lamp cover and is secured by two screws.

A 24-watt single-filament bulb is used in the flasher lamp and a 21/6-watt double-filament bulb is used in the tail/stop lamp bulb. To ensure that the stop light gives the brighter light the tail/stop lamp bulb has offset pegs and can only be fitted in one position.

To gain access to the flasher lamp bulb only, remove the two outer screws and slide off the flasher lamp cover. To gain access to the tail/stop lamp bulb remove all three screws and the two-piece cover complete.

1600 & Mk. II

Replacement Bulbs	B.M.C. Part No.	Watts	Volts
Headlamps (Home and Export R.H.D.—dip left)	13H140	50/40	12

Headlamps (Export and U.S.A. L.H.D.—dip right)	13H141	50/40	12
Headlamps Europe except France—dip vertical)	13H138	45/40	12
Headlamps (France L.H.D.—dip vertical)	13H139	45/40	12
Headlamps (Sweden R.H.D.—dip vertical)	3H921	45/40	12
Headlamps (Sweden R.H.D.—left dip, from Car No. 72040)	13H138	45/40	12
Stop/tail lamps	1F9026	6/21	12
Number-plate illumination lamp	2H4817	6	12
Flashing indicator lamps	1F9012	21	12
Panel lamps	2H4732	2.2	12

1600 Headlamps

From Car No. 70222 Mk. VIII headlamps with sealed-beam units were fitted to cars exported to U.S.A.

From Car No. 72040 cars exported to Sweden have special headlamps with asymmetrical left dip (Part No. BMK391). These are interchangeable with earlier types in pairs only.

Mk. X Sealed-beam Headlamps

Commencing at Chassis No. 103857, Mk. X sealed-beam light units were fitted to all cars exported to the U.S.A.

The lamp housing is secured by four screws and the back-shell is retained in the housing by a single coil spring. Two screws, each having a flange beneath its head, engage in slotted lugs on the rim of the back-shell and bear against the lamp housing; the screws are used to adjust the vertical and horizontal alignment. The lamp wiring passes through the housing and terminates in a three-hole socket.

Three pins at the back of the sealed-beam unit engage the holes in the socket, and the unit is retained in the back-shell by a lamp retaining plate that is secured to the back-shell by three screws. The lamp rim engages two lugs at the top of the housing and is retained in position by a screw.

To gain access to the lamp unit remove the rim retaining screw and lift the rim off the locating lugs. Slacken the three lamp retaining plate screws, turn the plate anti-clockwise, and remove it from the back-shell. Withdraw the lamp unit and disengage the three-pin plug.

To refit the lamp unit engage the three-pin plug and place the unit in the back-shell; ensure that the three lugs formed on the rear circumference of the unit engage the slots in the back-shell.

Refit the lamp retaining plate, press it firmly, and rotate it in a clockwise direction to the full extent of the slotted holes. Tighten the retaining plate screws. Fit the rim over the locating lugs, press the rim downwards and inwards, and secure it with its retaining screw.

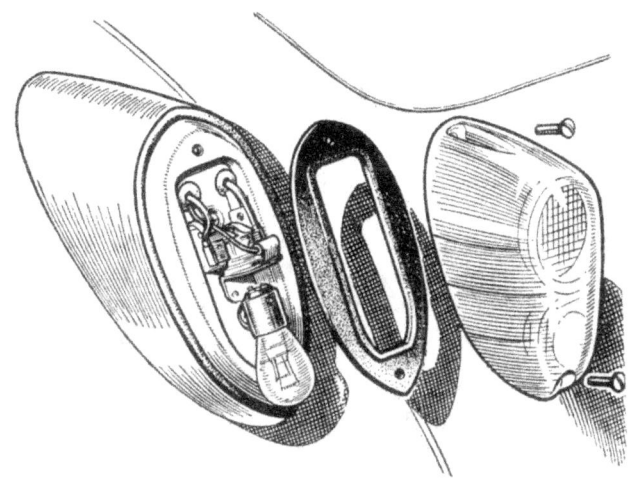

Replacing Headlamp Bulbs

Twist the back shell anti-clockwise and pull it off. Withdraw the bulb from the holder.

Insert the replacement bulb in the holder, making sure that the slot in the periphery of the bulb flange engages the projection in the holder.

Engage the projections on the back shell with the slots of the holder, press it on and twist it clockwise until it engages with its catch.

Replacing the Light Units

Position the light unit so that the heads of the adjusting screws coincide with the enlarged ends of the attachment slots. Push the light unit towards the wing to compress the springs and turn the unit to the right as far as it will go, that is, approximately $1/2$ in.

Replace the dust-excluding rubber on the light rim with its flanged face forward and refit the plated rim.

The Tail-lamps and Stop-lights

The tail-lamps are of the double-filament type, the second filament giving a marked increase in brilliance when the brakes are applied.

To obtain access to the bulbs, remove the glass by withdrawing the two screws. The bulbs are held in bayonet-type holders with offset pins to ensure correct fitting.

Cleaning the Lamps

Care must be taken when handling headlamp reflectors to prevent them from becoming finger-marked. If they do become marked a transparent and colorless protective covering enables any finger-marks to be removed by polishing with a chamois-leather or a very soft dry cloth. **Do not use metal polish on reflectors.**

Chromium-plated surfaces such as lamp rims should be washed with plenty of water, and when the dirt is completely removed they may be polished with a chamois-leather or soft dry cloth. **Do not use metal polishes on chromium plating.**

The Sidelamps

To obtain access to the bulb press the lamp front inwards and turn it anti-clockwise until it is free to be withdrawn. Reverse this movement to replace the front.

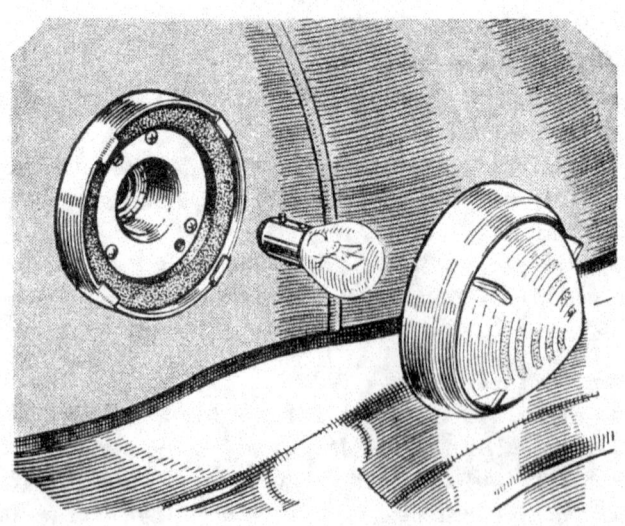

The locating pins on the bulbs are offset to ensure that it is fitted correctly to give increased brilliance when the flashing equipment is operating.

The Number-plate Illumination

The number-plate is illuminated by a separate lamp and the domed cover is removed for bulb replacement by unscrewing the slotted screw and withdrawing the cover.

Replacement Bulbs	B.M.C. Part No.	Watts	Volts
Headlamps (Home and Export R.H.D.—dip left)	13H140	50/40	12
Headlamps (Europe and U.S.A. L.H.D.—dip right)	13H141	50/40	12
Headlamps (Europe except France—vertical dip)	3H921	45/40	12

Headlamps (Europe except France—vertical dip) from Car No. 58918	13H138	45/40	12
Headlamps (France—vertical dip) from Car No. 60340	13H139	45/40	12
Sidelamp and stop/tail lamp	1F9026	6/21	12
Number-plate illumination lamp	2H4817	6	12
Panel lamps	2H4732	2.2	12

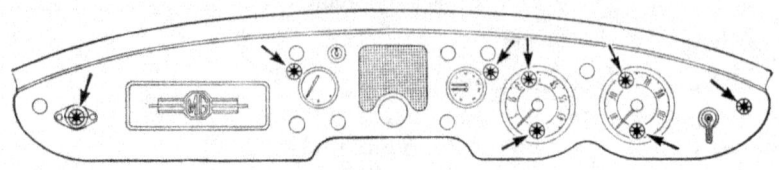

The panel and warning lights.

Fitting a Fog Lamp

A fog lamp is not fitted as standard equipment, but can be supplied as an optional extra. The necessary wiring together with the switch (marked 'F' on the instrument panel) is already provided to accommodate the fitment.

To fit a fog lamp bracket remove the over-rider and place the bracket in position. Mark off and drill a further hole through the bumper to accommodate an additional $\frac{5}{16}$ in. screw.

When mounted the lamp is connected up to the spare red and yellow lead located behind the radiator grille to the right-hand side.

The necessary parts are shown below, together with their part reference numbers.

ADH785	Fog lamp	2
AHH5454	Lead—fog lamp	2
AHH5521	Bracket—right-hand	1
AHH5520	Bracket—left-hand	1
RG103	Grommet—lead	4
HZS0506	Screw—bracket to blade—lower	2
FNZ105	Nut	2
LWZ205	Spring washer	2
PMP0518	Screw	2
PMP105	Washer	2

Location and Remedy of Faults

Although every precaution is taken to eliminate possible causes of trouble, failure may occasionally develop through lack of attention to the equipment, or damage to the wiring. The following pages set out the recommended procedure for a systematic examination to locate and remedy the causes of some of the more usual faults encountered.

The sources of trouble are by no means always obvious, and in some cases a considerable amount of deduction from the symptoms is needed before the cause is disclosed.

For instance, the engine might not respond to the starter switch; a hasty inference would be that the starter motor is at fault. However, as the motor is dependent on the batteries, it may be that the batteries are exhausted.

This, in turn, may be due to the generator failing to charge the batteries, and the final cause of the trouble may be, perhaps, a loose connection in some part of the charging circuit.

If, after carrying out an examination, the cause of the trouble is not found, the equipment should be checked by the nearest Lucas Service Depot or Agent.

Batteries in low state of charge:
1. This state will be shown by lack of power when starting, poor light from the lamps, and hydrometer readings below 1.200. It may be due to the generator not charging or giving low or intermittent output. The ignition warning light will not go out if the generator fails to charge, or will flicker on and off in the event of intermittent output.
2. Examine the charging and field circuit wiring, tightening any loose connections or replacing broken cables. Pay particular attention to the battery connections.
3. Examine the generator driving belt; take up any undue slackness by swinging the generator outwards on its mounting after slackening the attachment bolts.
4. Check the regulator setting and adjust if necessary.

Batteries overcharged:
This will be indicated by burnt-out bulbs, very frequent need for topping up the batteries, and high hydrometer readings. Check the charge reading with an ammeter when the car is running. It should be of the order of only 3-4 amperes.

If the ammeter reading is in excess of this value, it is advisable to check the regulator setting and adjust if necessary.

Starter motor lacks power or fails to turn engine:
1. See if the engine can be turned over by hand. If not, the cause of the stiffness in the engine must be located and remedied.
2. If the engine can be turned by hand, first check that the trouble is not due to a discharged battery.
3. Examine the connections to the batteries, starter and starter switch, making sure that they are tight and that the cables connecting these units are not damaged.
4. It is also possible that the starter pinion may have jammed in mesh with the flywheel, although this is by no means a com-

mon occurrence. To disengage the pinion, rotate the squared end of the starter shaft by means of a wrench.

Starter operates but does not crank engine:
This fault will occur if the pinion of the starter drive is not allowed to move along the screwed sleeve into engagement with the flywheel, due to dirt having collected on the screwed sleeve. Remove the starter and clean the sleeve carefully with solvent.

Starter pinion will not disengage from flywheel when engine is running:
Stop the engine and see if the starter pinion is jammed in mesh with the flywheel, releasing it if necessary by rotation of the squared end of the starter shaft. If the pinion persists in sticking in mesh, have the equipment examined at a Service Depot. Serious damage may result to the starter if it is driven by the flywheel.

Lamps give insufficient illumination:
1. Test the state of charge of the battery, recharging it if necessary from an independent electrical supply.
2. Check the setting of the lamps.
3. If the bulbs are discolored as the result of long service, they should be renewed.

Lamps light when switched on but gradually fade out:
1. As paragraph 1.
2. Examine the battery connections, making sure that they are tight, and renew any faulty cables.

WIRING DIAGRAM

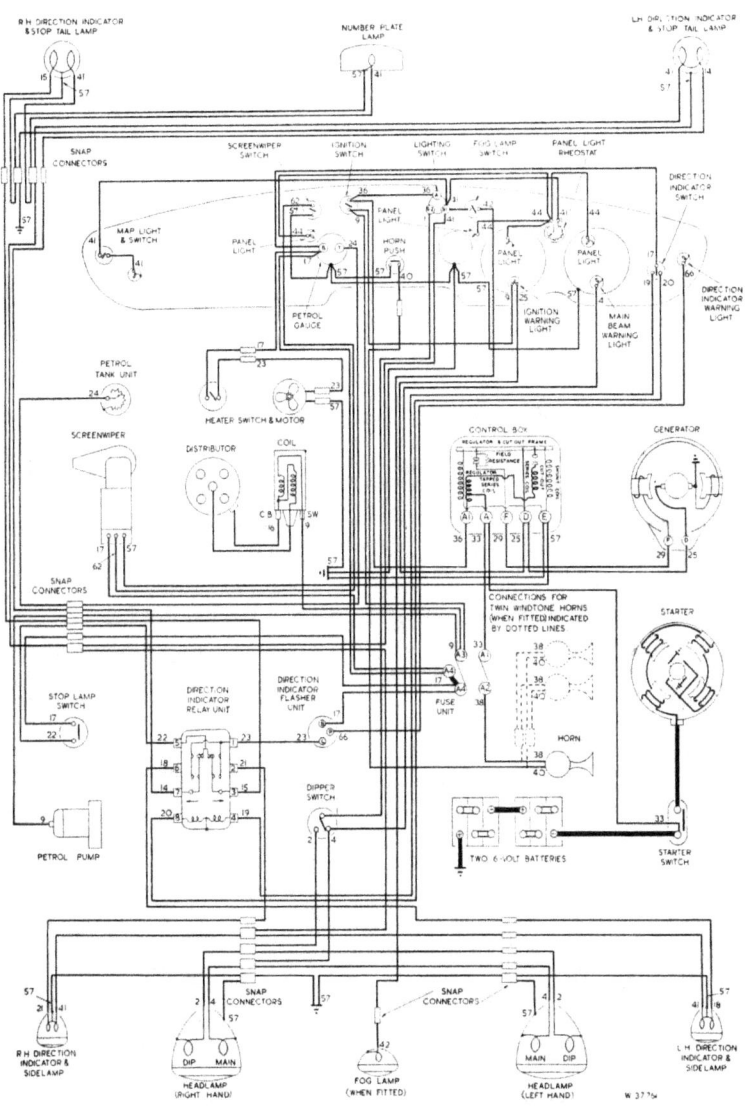

KEY TO CABLE COLOURS

1 Blue	23 Green with Brown	45 Red with Green
2 Blue with Red	24 Green with Black	46 Red with Purple
3 Blue with Yellow	25 Yellow	47 Red with Brown
4 Blue with White	26 Yellow with Red	48 Red with Black
5 Blue with Green	27 Yellow with Blue	49 Purple
6 Blue with Purple	28 Yellow with White	50 Purple with Red
7 Blue with Brown	29 Yellow with Green	51 Purple with Yellow
8 Blue with Black	30 Yellow with Purple	52 Purple with Blue
9 White	31 Yellow with Brown	53 Purple with White
10 White with Red	32 Yellow with Black	54 Purple with Green
11 White with Yellow	33 Brown	55 Purple with Brown
12 White with Blue	34 Brown with Red	56 Purple with Black
13 White with Green	35 Brown with Yellow	57 Black
14 White with Purple	36 Brown with Blue	58 Black with Red
15 White with Brown	37 Brown with White	59 Black with Yellow
16 White with Black	38 Brown with Green	60 Black with Blue
17 Green	39 Brown with Purple	61 Black with White
18 Green with Red	40 Brown with Black	62 Black with Green
19 Green with Yellow	41 Red	63 Black with Purple
20 Green with Blue	42 Red with Yellow	64 Black with Brown
21 Green with White	43 Red with Blue	65 Dark Green
22 Green with Purple	44 Red with White	66 Light Green

WIRING DIAGRAM
(MGA 1600)

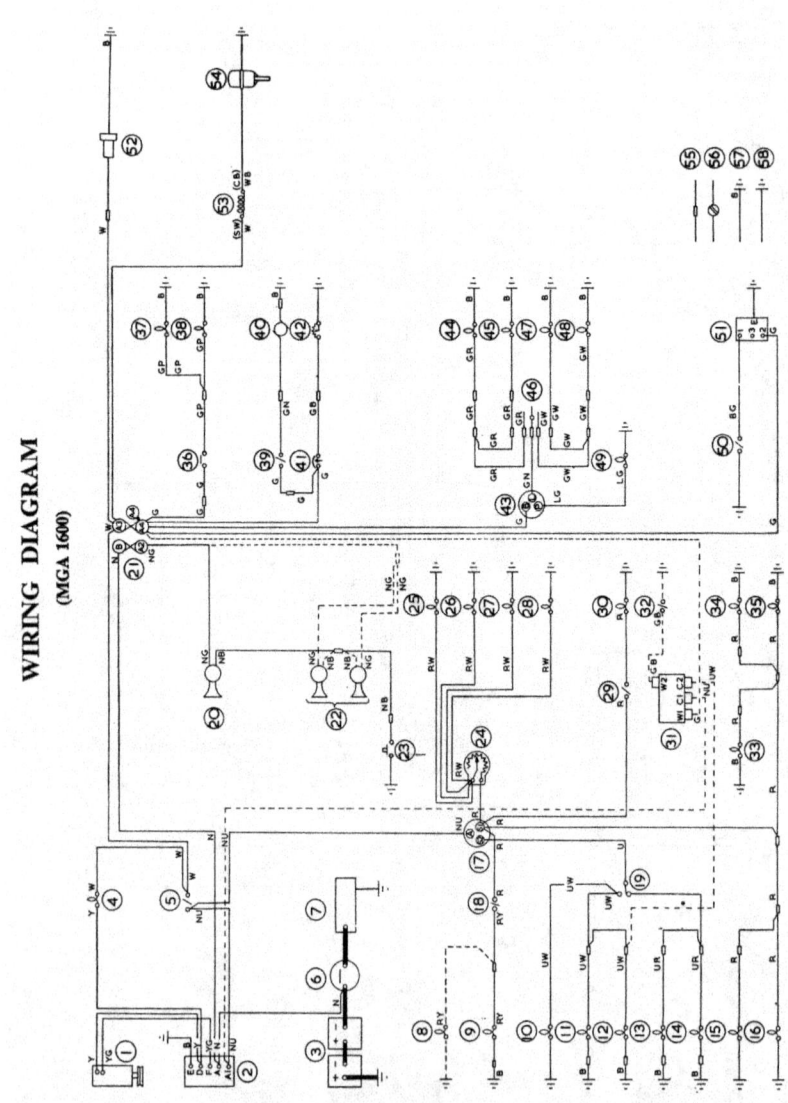

KEY TO WIRING DIAGRAM (R.H.D. AND L.H.D.)

No.	Description	No.	Description	No.	Description
1.	Generator.	21.	Fuse unit.	40.	Heater motor.
2.	Control box.	22.	Twin windtone horns (if fitted).	41.	Fuel gauge.
3.	Two 6-volt batteries.	23.	Horn-push.	42.	Fuel tank unit.
4.	Ignition warning light.	24.	Panel lamp rheostat.	43.	Flasher unit.
5.	Ignition switch.	25.	Panel lamp.	44.	L.H. rear flasher.
6.	Starter switch.	26.	Panel lamp.	45.	L.H. front flasher.
7.	Starter motor.	27.	Panel lamp.	46.	Flasher switch.
8.	R.H. fog lamp (if fitted).	28.	Panel lamp.	47.	R.H. front flasher.
9.	L.H. foglamp.	29.	Map lamp switch.	48.	R.H. rear flasher.
10.	Main beam warning light.	30.	Map lamp.	49.	Flasher warning light.
11.	R.H. headlamp main beam.	31.	Headlamp flick relay.	50.	Windshield wiper switch.
12.	L.H. headlamp main beam.	32.	Headlamp flick switch.	51.	Windshield wiper motor.
13.	L.H. headlamp dip beam.	33.	L.H. tail lamp.	52.	Fuel pump.
14.	R.H. headlamp dip beam.	34.	Number-plate lamp.	53.	Ignition coil.
15.	L.H. pilot lamp.	35.	R.H. tail lamp.	54.	Distributor.
16.	R.H. pilot lamp.	36.	Stop lamp switch.	55.	Snap connectors.
17.	Lighting switch.	37.	L.H. stop lamp.	56.	Terminal blocks or junction box.
18.	Fog lamp switch.	38.	R.H. stop lamp.	57.	Earth connections made via cable.
19.	Dipper switch.	39.	Heater switch (when fitted).	58.	Earth connections made via fixing bolts.
20.	Horn.				

CABLE COLOUR CODE

B	Black	P	Purple	Y	Yellow
U	Blue	R	Red	D	Dark
N	Brown	S	Slate	L	Light
G	Green	W	White	M	Medium
K	Pink				

When a cable has two colour code letters the first denotes the main colour and the second denotes the tracer colour

WIRING DIAGRAM

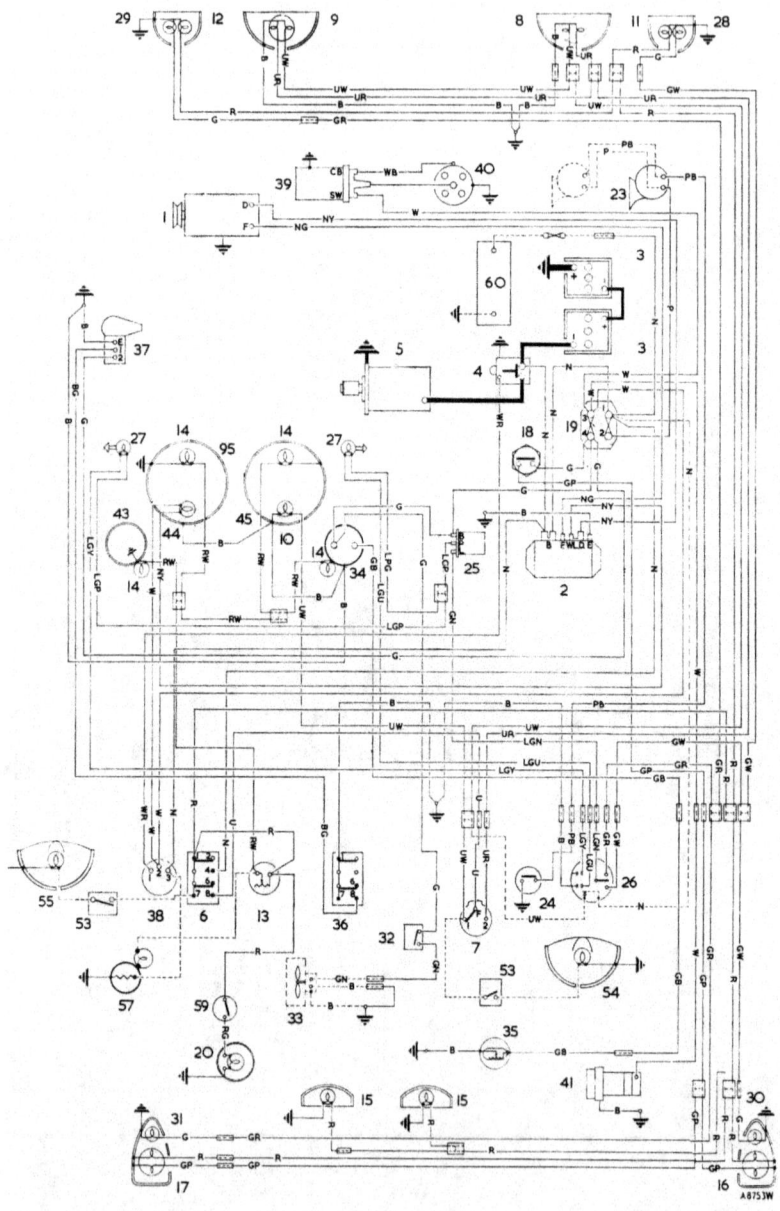

KEY TO THE WIRING DIAGRAM

No.	Description	No.	Description
1.	Dynamo.	28.	R.H. front flasher lamp.
2.	Control box.	29.	L.H. front flasher lamp.
3.	Batteries—6-volt.	30.	R.H. rear flasher lamp.
4.	Starter solenoid.	31.	L.H. rear flasher lamp.
5.	Starter motor.	32.	Heater or fresh-air motor switch.
6.	Lighting switch.	33.	Heater or fresh-air motor.*
7.	Headlamp dip switch.	34.	Fuel gauge.
8.	R.H. headlamp.	35.	Fuel gauge tank unit.
9.	L.H. headlamp.	36.	Windshield wiper switch.
10.	Main-beam warning lamp.	37.	Windshield wiper motor.
11.	R.H. sidelamp.	38.	Ignition/starter switch.
12.	L.H. sidelamp.	39.	Ignition coil.
13.	Rheostat—panel lamps.	40.	Distributor.
14.	Panel lamps.	41.	Fuel pump.
15.	Number-plate lamps.	43.	Oil pressure gauge.
16.	R.H. stop/tail lamp.	44.	Ignition warning lamp.
17.	L.H. stop/tail lamp.	45.	Speedometer.
18.	Stop lamp switch.	53.	Fog or driving lamp switches.*
19.	Fuse unit.	54.	R.H. fog or driving lamp.*
20.	Map light.	55.	L.H. fog or driving lamp.*
23.	Horn (twin when fitted*).	57.	Cigar-lighter—illuminated.*
24.	Horn-push.	59.	Map light switch.
25.	Flasher unit.	60.	Radio.*
26.	Direction indicator (and flasher*) switch.	95.	Revolution indicator.
27.	Direction indicator warning lamps.		

CABLE COLOUR CODE

N	Brown	P	Purple	W	White
U	Blue	G	Green	Y	Yellow
R	Red	LG	Light Green	B	Black

When a cable has two colour code letters the first denotes the main colour and the second denotes the tracer colour.

Items marked thus * may be fitted as optional extras. Their circuits are shown dotted on the **Wiring Diagram**.

LUBRICATION

NOTE: Lubrication chart, including overdrive and automatic transmission, will be found in the DRIVER'S HANDBOOK.

250 Miles — Engine

Inspect the oil level in the engine and refill if necessary to the 'MAX' mark on the dipstick. The oil filler cap is on top of the engine valve cover and is released by turning it anti-clockwise.

1,000 Miles Service
Steering Gear

Grease nipples are provided at the top and bottom of each swivel pin and on the steering tie-rods. The gun, filled to Ref. D, should be applied to the nipples and three or four strokes given.

Propeller Shaft

The joint at each end of the propeller shaft is provided with a nipple. Later cars have a third propeller shaft nipple on the sliding spine joint. Use lubricant to Ref. E.

Gearbox

Top up the oil level and ensure that the gearbox is not filled above the 'HIGH' mark on the dipstick. If the level is too high oil may get into the clutch case and cause clutch slip. The combined filler plug and dipstick are located beneath the rubber plug in the gearbox cover.

Rear Axle

The combined filler and level plug is reached from below the rear of the car. The oil level should be replenished if necessary to the level of the filler plug hole.

NOTE.—It is essential that only Hypoid oil be used in the rear axle.

Carburetor Dampers

Unscrew the oil cap at the top of each suction chamber, pour in a small quantity of thin engine oil and replace the caps. Under no circumstances should a heavy-bodied lubricant be used. Failure to lubricate the piston dampers will cause the pistons to flutter and reduce acceleration.

An oil indicated under Ref. F should be used.

Hand Brake Cable

The grease nipple on the hand brake cable should be given three or four strokes with a grease gun filled with grease to Ref. E.

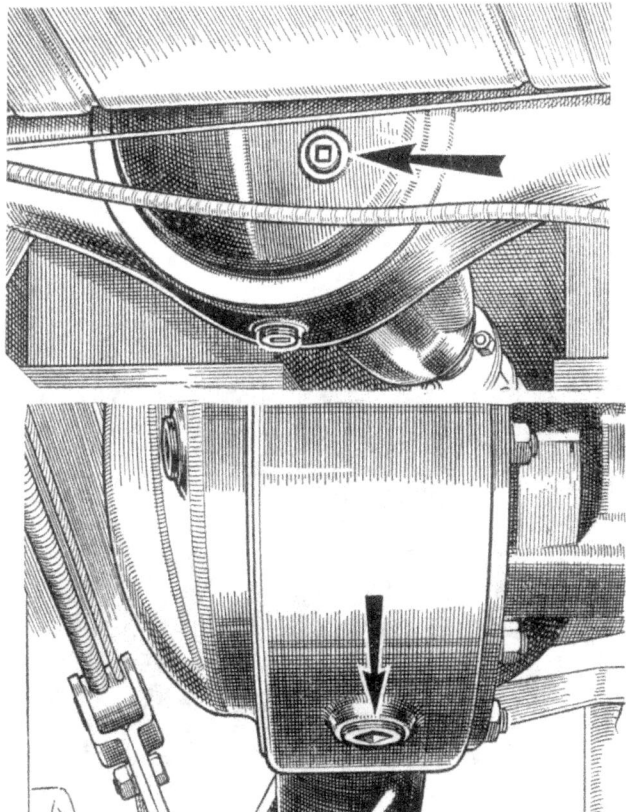

3,000 Miles Service

Carry out the instructions detailed above, except those under 'ENGINE', and continue with the following:

Engine Oil Change

Drain the oil from the engine sump after 3,000 miles. The drain plug is on the right-hand side of the sump and should be removed after a journey, while the oil is still warm and will drain easily.

The sump capacity is 9 U.S. pints. Refill the engine with new oil to Ref. A.

Air Cleaners

Wash the filter element in fuel and allow to dry. Re-oil the elements with S.A.E. 20 engine oil and allow to drain before reassembling.

It is only necessary to withdraw the two hexagon-headed screws and lift off the outer cover to release each corrugated element. Reassemble the front element with the corrugations clear of the breather spigot in the main filter case.

6,000 Miles Service
Distributor

Carry out the instructions detailed in above except those under 'GEARBOX' and 'REAR AXLE', and continue with the following:

Cam bearing

Lift the rotor off the top of the spindle by pulling it squarely and add a few drops of thin engine oil (Ref. F) to the cam bearing. Do not remove the screw which is exposed.

There is a clearance between the screw and the inner face of the spindle for the oil to pass.

Replace the rotor with its drive lug correctly engaging the spindle slot and push it onto the shaft as far as it will go.

Cam

Lightly smear the cam with a very small amount of grease (Ref. D), or if this is not available, clean engine oil can be used.

Automatic timing control

Carefully add a few drops of thin engine oil (Ref. F) through the hole in the contact breaker base through which the cam passes. Do not allow the oil to get on or near the contacts. Do not over-oil.

Contact breaker pivot

Add a spot of engine oil (Ref. F) to the moving contact pivot pin.

Gearbox Oil Change

Drain the gearbox oil.

When the gearbox has been drained completely 5.6 U.S. pints (2.56 litres) of oil are required to fill it. The oil should be poured in through the filler plug.

Rear Axle Oil Change

Remove the drain plug and drain out the oil. Refill with Hypoid oil (Ref. B) to the level of the filler plug hole.

Approximately 2.7 U.S. pints (1.28 litres) of oil are required to refill the axle.

Front Wheel Hubs

Remove the front wheel hub covers and pry off the grease-retaining cap from the end of each hub.

Refill with grease (Ref. C) and replace.

To lubricate the front hubs on cars fitted with wire wheels, the wheel retaining nuts must be unscrewed with the copper hammer in the tool kit and the hubs packed with grease (Ref. C).

Engine Oil Filter

Fit a new engine oil filter element. The filter is released by unscrewing the central bolt securing the filter body to the filter head. When fitting the new element, make sure that the seating washer for the filter body is in good condition and that the body is fitted securely to prevent oil leaks.

Care must also be taken to ensure that the washers below the element inside the bowl are fitted correctly. The small felt washer must be positioned between the element pressure plate and the metal washer above the pressure spring. It is essential for correct oil filtration that the felt washer should be in good condition and be a snug fit on the center-securing bolt.

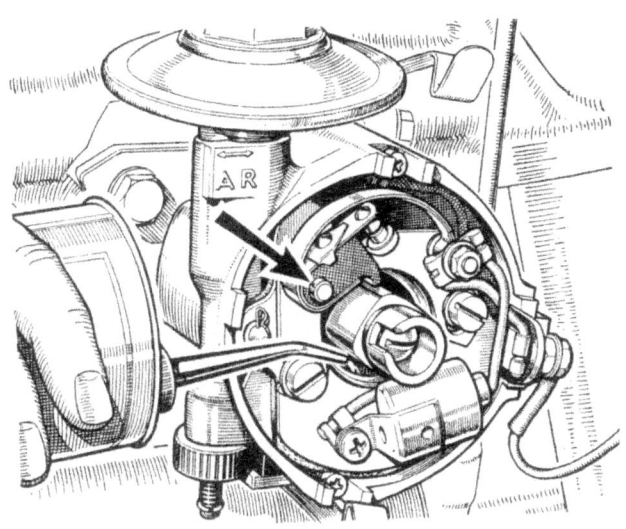

Generator

Add two drops of engine oil to Ref. F in the lubrication hole in the center of the rear end bearing plate.

Do not over-oil.

Where the later-type C40-1 generator is fitted inject a few drops of high-quality S.A.E. 30 engine oil into the hole marked 'OIL' at the end of the rear bearing housing.

12,000 Miles Service

Carry out the instructions detailed above in addition to the following.

Flushing the Engine

Flush the engine with a flushing oil supplied by one of the recommended manufacturers. This operation must be carried out prior to oil filter changing. Use approximately half the normal sump capacity and run the engine for $2^1/_2$ to 3 minutes at a fast tick-over, after which special care must be taken to ensure complete drainage of the flushing oil.

It is recommended that at 24,000 miles the sump and oil pump pick-up strainer should be removed for cleaning.

Water Pump

Remove the water pump plug on the water pump casing and add a small quantity of grease to Ref. C. The lubrication of the pump must be done very sparingly, otherwise grease will pass the bearings onto the face of the carbon sealing ring and impair its efficiency.

Steering Gearbox

The two nipples for the steering gearbox and pinion are reached from under the hood.

Give the gearbox nipple 15 strokes **only,** and the pinion nipple five strokes **only** at the same time, with a gun filled with oil to Ref. B.

Speedometer and Tachometer Cables

Unscrew the speedometer and tachometer drive cable outer casings from the instrument heads. Extract their inner cables and lubricate sparingly with grease to Ref. E. Oil must not be used. After replacing each cable in its outer casing withdraw the upper end approximately 8 in. and wipe off the surface grease before reconnecting it to the instrument head.

GENERAL DATA
(Series MGA)

ENGINE
Type .. .. 15GB.
(From Car No. 61504) .. .. 15GD.
Number of cylinders .. .. 4.
Bore .. .. 2·875 in. (73·025 mm.).
Stroke .. .. 3·5 in. (89 mm.).
Capacity .. .. 90·88 cu. in. (1489 c.c.).
Firing order .. .. .. 1, 3, 4, 2.
Compression ratio .. .. 8·3 : 1.
Capacity of combustion chamber (valves fitted) .. 2·3 to 2·4 cu. in. (38·2 to 39·2 c.c.).
Valve operation .. .. .. Overhead by push-rod.
B.M.E.P. .. .. 130 lb./sq. in. at 3,500 r.p.m.
Torque .. .. 77·4 lb. ft. at 3,500 r.p.m.
Cooling system .. .. Thermo-siphon, pump- and fan-assisted.
Oversize bore : 1st .. .. ·010 in. (·254 mm.).
Max. .. .. .. ·040 in. (1·016 mm.).

CRANKSHAFT
Main journal diameter .. .. 2 in. (50·8 mm.).
Minimum regrind diameter .. 1·96 in. (49·78 mm.).
Crankpin journal diameter .. 1·8759 in. to 1·8764 in. (47·65 to 47·66 mm.).
Crankpin minimum regrind diameter .. 1·8359 in. (46·64 mm.).
Main bearings
  Number and type .. .. 3. Shell-type.
  Material: Bottom half .. Steel-backed white metal.
  Top half .. Steel-backed white metal.
  Length .. .. .. 1·375 in. (34·925 mm.).
  End-clearance .. .. ·002 to ·003 in. (·051 to ·076 mm.).
  End-thrust .. .. Taken by thrust washers at centre main bearing.
  Running clearance .. ·0005 to ·002 in. (·0127 to ·0508 mm.).

CONNECTING RODS
Length between centres .. .. 6·5 in. (165·1 mm.).
Big-end bearings
  Material: Bottom half .. Steel-backed lead-indium or lead-tin.
  Top half .. Steel-backed lead-indium or lead-tin.
  Bearing side-clearance .. ·008 to ·012 in. (·203 to ·305 mm.).
  Bearing diametrical clearance .. ·0001 to ·0016 in. (·002 to ·04 mm.).

PISTONS
Type .. .. Aluminium alloy.
Clearances: Bottom of skirt .. ·0017 to ·0023 in. (·043 to ·051 mm.).
  Top of skirt .. ·0035 to ·0042 in. (·090 to ·106 mm.).
Oversizes .. .. .. +·010 in., +·020 in., +·030 in., +·040 in.
  (+·254 mm., +·508 mm., +·762 mm., +1·016 mm.).

PISTON RINGS
Compression: Plain .. .. Top ring.
  Tapered .. .. 2nd and 3rd rings.
  Width .. .. .. ·0615 to ·0625 in. (1·56 to 1·58 mm.).
  Thickness .. .. ·111 to ·118 in. (2·81 to 3·0 mm.) to Engine No. 40824.
  ·119 to ·126 in. (3·02 to 3·2 mm.) from Engine No. 40825.
Fitted gap .. .. .. ·008 to ·013 in. (·20 to ·33 mm.).
Clearance in groove .. .. ·0015 to ·0035 in. (·038 to ·089 mm.).

GENERAL DATA—continued

Oil control type	Slotted scraper.
Width	·1552 to ·1562 in. (3·94 to 3·99 mm.).
Thickness	·111 to ·118 in. (2·81 to 3·0 mm.) to Engine No. 40824.
	·119 to ·126 in. (3·02 to 3·2 mm.) from Engine No. 40825.
Fitted gap	·008 to ·013 in. (·20 to ·33 mm.).
Clearance in groove	·0016 to ·0036 in. (·040 to ·091 mm.).

GUDGEON PIN

Type	Clamped.
Fit	·0001 to ·00035 in. (·0025 to ·009 mm.). Hand push fit at 68° F. (20° C.).
Diameter	·6869 to ·6871 in. (17·447 to 17·4523 mm.).

VALVES AND VALVE GEAR

Valves

Seat angle: Inlet	45°.
Exhaust	45°.
Head diameter: Inlet	1½ in. (38·1 mm.).
Exhaust	1¼ in. (32·54 mm.).
Stem diameter: Inlet	·342 in. (8·68 mm.).
Exhaust	·342 in. (8·68 mm.).
Valve lift	·357 in. (9·06 mm.).
Valve stem to guide clearance: Inlet	·00155 to ·00255 in. (·0394 to ·0635 mm.).
Exhaust	·00105 to ·00205 in. (·027 to ·052 mm.) to Engine No. 4044.
	·002 to ·003 in. (·051 to ·076 mm.) from Engine No. 4045.
Valve rocker clearance: Running	·017 in. (·432 mm.) (hot).
Timing	·060 in. (1·52 mm.).
Timing markings	Dimples on timing wheels.
Chain pitch and number of pitches	⅜ in. (9·52 mm.), 52 pitches.
Inlet valve: Opens	16° B.T.D.C.
Closes	56° A.B.D.C.
Exhaust valve: Opens	51° B.B.D.C.
Closes	21° A.T.D.C.

VALVE GUIDES

Length: Inlet	1⅞ in. (47·63 mm.).
Exhaust	2¼ in. (57·94 mm.).
Diameter: Inlet: Outside	·5635 in. (14·31 mm.).
Inside	·3438 in. (8·73 mm.).
Exhaust: Outside	·5635 in. (14·31 mm.).
Inside	·3438 in. (8·73 mm.).
Fitted height above head	·625 in. (15·87 mm.).

VALVE SPRINGS

Free length: Inner	1 31/32 in. (50 mm.).
Outer	2 1/32 in. (51·99 mm.).
Fitted length: Inner	1 7/16 in. (36·51 mm.).
Outer	1 9/16 in. (39·69 mm.).
Number of working coils: Inner	6½.
Outer	4½.
Pressure: Valve open	Inner 50 lb. (22·7 kg.). Outer 105 lb. (47·6 kg.).
Valve closed	Inner 30 lb. (13·6 kg.). Outer 60¼ lb. (27 kg.).

GENERAL DATA—continued

TAPPETS
Type	Barrel with flat base.
Diameter: Body	$\frac{13}{16}$ in. (20·64 mm.).
Length	2·293 to 2·303 in. (58·25 to 58·5 mm.).

ROCKERS
Outside diameter before fitting	·751 in. (19·07 mm.).
Inside diameter (reamed in position)	·616 to ·620 in. (15·65 to 15·74 mm.).
Bore of rocker arms	·7485 to ·7489 in. (19·01 to 19·02 mm.).
Rocker ratio	1·426 : 1.

CAMSHAFT
Journal diameters: Front	1·78875 to 1·78925 in. (45·43 to 45·44 mm.).
Centre	1·72875 to 1·72925 in. (43·91 to 43·92 mm.).
Rear	1·62275 to 1·62325 in. (41·22 to 41·23 mm.).
End-float	·003 to ·007 in. (·076 to ·178 mm.).
Bearing: number and type	3. Thinwall steel-backed white metal.
Outside diameter (before fitting)	Front 1·920 in. (48·76 mm.), centre 1·860 in. (47·24 mm.), rear 1·754 in. (44·55 mm.).
Inside diameter (reamed in position)	Front 1·790 in. (45·47 mm.), centre 1·730 in. (43·94 mm.), rear 1·624 in. (41·25 mm.).
Clearance	·001 to ·002 in. (·0254 to ·0508 mm.).

ENGINE LUBRICATION SYSTEM

Oil pump
Type	Eccentric rotor.
Relief pressure valve operates	75 to 80 lb./sq. in. (5·3 to 5·6 kg./cm.²).
Relief valve spring: Free length	3 in. (76·2 mm.).
Fitted length	$2\frac{3}{16}$ in. (54·77 mm.) at 16 lb. (7·26 kg.) load.
Identification colour	Red spot.

Oil filter
Type	Tecalemit (element Part No. 1H779) or Purolator (element Part No. 1H1054) up to Engine No. 26932. Tecalemit or Purolator (element Part No. 8G683) from Engine No. 26933.
Capacity	½ pint (·28 litre).

Oil pressure
Normal running: Minimum	10 to 25 lb./sq. in. (·7 to 1·7 kg./cm.²).
Maximum	50 to 75 lb./sq. in. (3·5 to 5·2 kg./cm.²).

TORQUE WRENCH SETTINGS
Cylinder head nuts	50 lb. ft. (6·91 kg. m.).
Main bearing nuts	70 lb. ft. (9·7 kg. m.).
Connecting rod set screws	35 lb. ft. (4·83 kg. m.).
Clutch assembly to flywheel	25 lb. ft. (3·46 kg. m.).
Road wheel nuts	60 to 62·5 lb. ft. (8·3 to 8·65 kg. m.).
Gudgeon pin clamp	25 lb. ft. (3·45 kg. m.).
Manifold stud nuts	25 lb. ft. (3·45 kg. m.).
Water pump securing bolts	25 lb. ft. (3·45 kg. m.).
Clutch to flywheel bolts	35 to 40 lb. ft. (4·8 to 5·5 kg. m.).
Oil filter centre-bolt	15 lb. ft. (2·07 kg. m.).
Brake calliper securing bolts	45 to 50 lb. ft. (6·22 to 6·91 kg. m.).

GENERAL DATA—continued

FUEL SYSTEM
Carburetter
  Make and type .. .. S.U. twin H4 semi-downdraught.
  Diameter .. .. 1¼ in. (38·1 mm.).
  Needle .. .. GS.
  Jet .. .. ·090 in. (2·29 mm.).
  Piston spring .. .. Red.

AIR CLEANER
Make and type .. .. Vokes—oil-wetted.

FUEL PUMP
Make and type .. .. S.U. electric—high pressure.
Delivery test .. .. 10 gal. per hr. (45·4 litres per hr.).
Suction lift .. .. 33 in. (83·8 cm.).
Output lift .. .. 48 in. (121·9 cm.).

COOLING SYSTEM
Type .. .. Pressurized radiator. Thermo-siphon, pump- and fan-assisted.
Thermostat setting .. .. 70 to 75° C. (158 to 167° F.).
Quantity of anti-freeze: 15° frost .. .. 1 pint (57 litre).
                  25° frost .. .. 1½ pints (·85 litre).
                  35° frost .. .. 2 pints (1·1 litres).

IGNITION SYSTEM
Sparking plugs .. .. Champion N5, was NA8.
Size .. .. 14 mm.
Plug gap .. .. ·024 to ·026 in. (·625 to ·660 mm.).
Coil .. .. Lucas HA12.
Distributor .. .. Lucas. Type DM2. Later models DM2.P4.
Distributor contact points gap .. .. .. ·014 to ·016 in. (·35 to ·40 mm.).
Suppressors .. .. Lucas No. 78106A fitted on each H.T. cable.
Timing .. .. 7° B.T.D.C.

CLUTCH
Make and type .. .. Borg & Beck A6–G. Single dry plate.
Diameter .. .. 8 in. (20·3 cm.).
Facing material .. .. Wound yarn—Borglite.
Pressure springs .. .. 6.
  Colour .. .. Black and yellow.
                      Cream and light green: commencing Engine No. 16225.
Damper springs .. .. 6.
  Colour .. .. White with light-green stripes.
Release lever ratio .. .. 9 : 1.

GEARBOX
Number of forward speeds .. .. .. 4.
Synchromesh .. .. Second, third, and fourth gears.
Ratios: Top .. .. 1·0 : 1.
        Third .. .. 1·374 : 1.
        Second .. .. 2·214 : 1.
        First .. .. 3·64 : 1.
        Reverse .. .. 4·76 : 1.

Overall ratios: Top	4·3 : 1.
Third	5·908 : 1.
Second	9·520 : 1.
First	15·652 : 1.
Reverse	20·468 : 1.
Speedometer gears ratio	5 : 12.

STEERING

Type	Rack and pinion.
Steering-wheel turns—lock to lock	2⅔.
Steering-wheel diameter	16½ in. (419·10 mm.).
Camber angle	1° positive to ½° negative on full bump.
Castor angle	4°.
King pin inclination	9° to 10½° on full bump.
Toe-in	Wheels parallel.
Track: Front	Disc wheels 47½ in. (1·203 m.).
	Wire wheels 47⅞ in. (1·216 m.).
Rear	Disc wheels 48¾ in. (1·238 m.).
	Wire wheels 48¾ in. (1·238 m.)

FRONT SUSPENSION

Type	Independent coil.	
Spring detail:	*To Car No.* 15151	*From Car No.* 15152
Coil diameter (mean)	3·238 in. (82·24 mm.).	3·28 in. (82·25 mm.).
Diameter of wire	·498 in. (12·66 mm.).	·54 in. (13·72 mm.).
Free height	9·28 ± 1/16 in. (23·49 cm. ± 1·6 mm.).	8·88 ± 1/16 in. (22·55 cm. ± 1·6 mm.)
Number of free coils	7·5.	7·2.
Static laden length	6·60 ± 1/32 in. (16·76 cm. ± ·8 mm.).	
Static laden length at load of	1,095 ± 20 lb. (497 ± 9·1 kg.).	
Maximum deflection	4 in. (10·16 cm.).	
Dampers (front)	Piston type.	

REAR SUSPENSION

Type	Semi-elliptic.
Spring detail:	
Number of leaves	6.
Width of leaves	1¾ in. (44·45 mm.).
Gauge	7/32 in. (5·56 mm.).
Working load	450 lb. (203·7 kg.).
Free camber	3·60 in. (91·44 mm.).
Dampers (rear)	Piston type.

PROPELLER SHAFT

Type	Tubular. Reverse spline.
Make and type of joints	Hardy Spicer. Needle roller.
Propeller shaft length (between centres of joints)	31⅜ in. (79·69 cm.).
Overall length	38 13/32 in. (97·44 cm.).
Diameter	2 in. (50·8 mm.).
Type (with 15GD series power unit)	Tubular, incorporating sliding spline joint.
Overall length (fully extended)	32 11/16 in. (83·03 cm.).
Overall length (fully compressed)	31¾ in. (80·65 cm.).
Length between centres of joints (fully extended)	30 5/16 in. (77 cm.).
Length between centres of joints (fully compressed)	29⅜ in. (74·65 cm.).
Diameter (main tube)	2 in. (50·8 mm.).

GENERAL DATA—continued

REAR AXLE
- Make and type .. .. B.M.C. 'B' type, three-quarter-floating.
- Ratio: Standard .. .. 10/43.
-     Optional .. .. 9/41.
- Adjustment .. .. Shims.

ELECTRICAL EQUIPMENT
- System .. .. 12-volt. Positive earth.
- Charging system .. .. Compensated voltage control.
- Battery: Type .. .. Lucas SG9E.
-     Type (Export only) .. .. .. Lucas STGZ9E (dry-charged).
-     Voltage .. .. 6-volt (2 off).
-     Capacity (20-hr. rate) .. .. 58-amp.-hr.
- Starter motor .. .. Lucas 4-brush M35G.
- Dynamo .. .. Lucas C39PV2.
  Lucas C40/1 ('MGA 1600' after Engine No. 16GA6272).

BRAKES
- Type .. .. Lockheed hydraulic (front and rear).
- Size .. .. 10 in. × 1¾ in. (25·4 cm. × 44·45 mm.).
- Front .. .. 2 leading shoes.
- Rear .. .. Single leading shoe.
- Drum size .. .. 10 in. (254 mm.) (front and rear).
- Lining dimensions .. .. 9·6 in. × 1¾ in. (24·38 cm. × 44·45 mm.).
- Lining area: Front .. .. 67·2 sq. in. (433·55 cm.²).
-     Rear .. .. 67·2 sq. in. (433·55 cm.²).
- Material .. .. Ferodo DM12.

WHEELS
- Type: Ventilated disc .. .. 4J × 15.
-     Wire (optional) .. .. 4J × 15, 48-spoke.

TYRES
- Size .. .. 5·60—15.
- Tyre pressures: Normal: Front .. .. 17 lb./sq. in. (1·2 kg./cm.²).
-                         Rear .. 20 lb./sq. in. (1·4 kg./cm.²).
-             Fast motoring: Front .. 21 lb./sq. in. (1·48 kg./cm.²).
-                         Rear .. 24 lb./sq. in. (1·69 kg./cm.²).
-             Competition work and sustained high-speed motoring: Front .. 23 lb./sq. in. (1·62 kg./cm.²).
-                         Rear .. 26 lb./sq. in. (1·83 kg./cm.²).

CAPACITIES

	Imp.	U.S.	Litres
Engine sump (including filter)	7½ pts.	9 pts.	4·25
Gearbox	4½ pts.	5·4 pts.	2·56
Rear axle	2¼ pts.	2·7 pts.	1·28
Cooling system	10 pts.	12 pts.	5·67
Steering rack	½ pt.	·6 pt.	·28
Fuel tank	10 gal.	12 gal.	45·4
Brake system	1 pt.	1·2 pts.	·568

GENERAL DIMENSIONS
- Wheelbase .. .. 94 in. (238·8 cm.).
- Overall length .. .. 156 in. (396·2 cm.).
- Overall width .. .. 58 in. (147·3 cm.).
- Overall height .. .. 50 in. (127·0 cm.).
- Ground clearance .. .. 6 in. (15·24 cm.).
- Weight: fully equipped with tools, spare wheel, oil, water, and 2 gallons of fuel (2·5 U.S. gal., 9·1 litres) .. .. 1,988 lb. (901·81 kg.).
- Turning circles .. .. 28 ft. (8·534 m.).

GENERAL DATA
(MGA 1600)

ENGINE
Type	16GA.
Number of cylinders	4.
Bore	2·968 in. (75·39 mm.).
Stroke	3·5 in. (89 mm.).
Capacity	96·9 cu. in. (1588 c.c.).
Firing order	1, 3, 4, 2.
Compression ratio	8·3 : 1.
Capacity of combustion chamber (valves fitted)	2·36 cu. in. (38·7 c.c.).
Valve operation	Overhead by push-rod.
B.M.E.P.	135 lb./sq. in. (9·5 kg./cm.^{2}) at 4,000 r.p.m.
Torque	87 lb. ft. (12·03 kg. m.) at 3,800 r.p.m.
Cooling system	Thermo-siphon, pump- and fan-assisted.
Oversize bore: 1st	·010 in. (·254 mm.).
Max.	·040 in. (1·016 mm.).
Maximum b.h.p. (standard)	79·5 at 5,600 r.p.m.

CRANKSHAFT
Main bearings
Refer to Series MGA data on preceding pages.

CONNECTING RODS
Length between centres	6·5 in. (165·1 mm.).

Big-end bearings
Material: Top and bottom halves	Steel and lead-indium.
Bearing side-clearance	·008 to ·012 in. (·203 to ·305 mm.).
Bearing diametrical clearance	·0010 to ·0025 in. (·025 to ·063 mm.).
Undersizes	−·010 in., −·020 in., −·030 in., −·040 in. (−·254 mm., −·508 mm., −·762 mm., −1·016 mm.)

PISTONS
Refer to Series MGA data on preceding pages.

PISTON RINGS
Compression: Plain	Top ring.
Tapered	2nd and 3rd rings.
Width	·0615 to ·0625 in. (1·56 to 1·58 mm.).
Thickness	·141 to ·148 in. (3·57 to 3·76 mm.).
Fitted gap	·009 to ·014 in. (·229 to ·356 mm.).
Clearance in groove	·0015 to ·0035 in. (·038 to ·089 mm.).
Oil control type	Slotted scraper.
Width	·1552 to ·1562 in. (3·94 to 3·99 mm.).
Thickness	·135 to ·142 in. (3·43 to 3·61 mm.).
Fitted gap	·009 to ·014 in. (·23 to ·36 mm.).
Clearance in groove	·0016 to ·0036 in. (·040 to ·091 mm.).

GUDGEON PIN
Refer to Series MGA data on preceding pages.

VALVES AND VALVE GEAR
Valves
Seat angle: Inlet and exhaust	45°.
Head diameter: Inlet	1½ in. (38·1 mm.).
Exhaust	1$\frac{9}{32}$ in. (32·54 mm.).

GENERAL DATA—continued

Stem diameter: Inlet .. .. ·342 in. (8·68 mm.).
      Exhaust .. .. ·342 in. (8·68 mm.).
Valve lift .. .. ·350 in. (8·89 mm.).
Valve stem to guide clearance: Inlet .. .. ·00155 to ·00255 in. (·0394 to ·0635 mm.).
          Exhaust .. .. ·002 to ·003 in. (·051 to ·076 mm.).
Valve rocker clearance: Running .. .. .. ·015 in. (·38 mm.) (hot).
       Timing .. .. .. ·060 in. (1·52 mm.).
Timing markings .. .. Dimples on timing wheels.
Chain pitch and number of pitches .. .. .. ⅜ in. (9·52 mm.), 52 pitches.
Inlet valve: Opens .. .. 16° B.T.D.C.
    Closes .. .. 56° A.B.D.C.
Exhaust valve: Opens .. .. 51° B.B.D.C.
     Closes .. .. 21° A.T.D.C.

VALVE GUIDES
Length: Inlet .. .. 1⅞ in. (47·63 mm.).
   Exhaust .. .. 2 $\frac{13}{16}$ in. (55·95 mm.).
Diameter: Inlet and exhaust: Outside .. .. ·5635 to ·5640 in. (14·31 to 14·32 mm.).
        Inside .. .. .. ·34425 to ·34475 in. (8·744 to 8·757 mm.).
Fitted height above head .. .. ·625 in. (15·87 mm.).

VALVE SPRINGS
TAPPETS
ROCKERS Refer to Series MGA data on preceding pages.
CAMSHAFT

ENGINE LUBRICATION SYSTEM
Oil pump
 Type .. .. Eccentric rotor.
 Relief pressure valve operates .. .. .. 50 lb./sq. in. (3·5 kg./cm.²).
 Relief valve spring: Free length .. .. .. 3 in. (76·2 mm.).
      Fitted length .. .. .. 2 $\frac{9}{64}$ in. (54·77 mm.) at 16 lb. (7·26 kg.) load.
      Identification colour .. .. Red spot.
Oil filter
 Type .. .. Tecalemit or Purolator.
 Capacity .. .. 1 pint (·57 litre).
Oil pressure
 Normal running: Minimum .. .. 15 lb./sq. in. (1·05 kg./cm.²).
     Maximum .. .. 50 lb./sq. in. (3·5 kg./cm.²).

TORQUE WRENCH SETTINGS. Refer to Series MGA data on preceding pages.

FUEL SYSTEM
Carburetter
 Make and type .. .. S.U. twin H4 semi-downdraught.
 Diameter .. .. 1½ in. (38·1 mm.).
 Needle .. .. No. 6.
 Jet .. .. ·090 in. (2·29 mm.).
 Piston spring .. .. Red.

AIR CLEANER AND FUEL PUMP. Refer to Series MGA data on preceding pages.

COOLING SYSTEM. Data as for Series MGA on preceding pages except:
 Thermostat opening temperature: Crack open .. 68° C. (154° F.)⎫ from Engine No. 16GA4788.
        Fully open .. 83° C. (181° F.)⎭
 Filler cap spring pressure .. .. 7 lb. (3·18 kg.) from Car No. 71832.

GENERAL DATA—continued

IGNITION SYSTEM
Sparking plugs	Champion N5.
Size	14 mm.
Plug gap	·024 to ·026 in. (·625 to ·660 mm.).
Coil	Lucas HA12.
Distributor	Lucas Type DM2. Later models DM2.P4.
Distributor contact points gap	·014 to ·016 in. (·35 to ·40 mm.).
Suppressors	Lucas No. 78106A fitted on each H.T. cable.
Static timing	7° B.T.D.C.

CLUTCH
Make and type	Borg & Beck A6–G. Single dry plate.
Diameter	8 in. (20·3 cm.).
Facing material	Wound yarn—Borglite.
Pressure springs	6.
Colour	Black and yellow. Cream and light green: from Engine No. 16225.
Damper springs	6.
Colour	White with light-green stripes.
Release lever ratio	9 : 1.

GEARBOX
Refer to Series MGA data on preceding pages.

STEERING
Type	Rack and pinion.
Steering-wheel turns—lock to lock	$2\frac{2}{3}$.
Steering-wheel diameter	$16\frac{1}{2}$ in. (419·10 mm.).
Camber angle	1° positive to $\frac{1}{2}°$ negative on full bump.
Castor angle	4°.
King pin inclination	9° to $10\frac{1}{2}°$ on full bump.
Toe-in	Wheels parallel.

Track (MGA 1600):
Front	Disc wheels $47\frac{1}{4}$ in. (1·203 m.). Wire wheels $47\frac{7}{8}$ in. (1·216 m.).
Rear	Disc wheels $48\frac{3}{4}$ in. (1·238 m.). Wire wheels $48\frac{3}{4}$ in. (1·238 m.).

Track (MGA 1600 with Dunlop disc brakes):
Front	$47\frac{29}{32}$ in. (1·217 m.).
Rear	$48\frac{7}{8}$ in. (1·242 m.).

FRONT SUSPENSION
Type	Independent coil.
Spring detail:	
Coil diameter (mean)	3·28 in. (82·25 mm.).
Diameter of wire	·54 in. (13·72 mm.).
Free height	$8·88 \pm \frac{1}{16}$ in. ($22·55$ cm. $\pm 1·6$ mm.).
Number of free coils	7·2.
Static laden length	$6·60 \pm \frac{3}{32}$ in. ($16·76$ cm. $\pm ·8$ mm.).
Static laden length at load of	$1,095 \pm 20$ lb. ($497 \pm 9·1$ kg.).
Maximum deflection	4 in. (10·16 cm.).
Dampers (front)	Piston type.

GENERAL DATA—*continued*

REAR SUSPENSION
Type .. .. Semi-elliptic.
Spring detail:
  Number of leaves .. .. 6.
  Width of leaves .. .. 1¾ in. (44·45 mm.).
  Gauge .. .. 7/32 in. (5·56 mm.).
  Working load .. .. .. 450 lb. (203·7 kg.).
  Free camber .. .. .. 3·60 in. (91·44 mm.).
Dampers (rear) .. .. .. Piston type.

PROPELLER SHAFT
Type .. .. Tubular, flanged type.
Propeller shaft length .. .. 30¼ in. (77·47 cm.).
Overall length .. .. .. 32 11/16 in. (82·98 cm.).
Diameter .. .. 2 in. (50·8 cm.).
Make and type of joints .. .. Hardy Spicer needle roller.

REAR AXLE
ELECTRICAL EQUIPMENT } Refer to Series MGA data on preceding pages.

BRAKES
Type .. .. Lockheed hydraulic; disc front, drum rear.
Lining material .. .. .. DON24.
Disc material .. .. .. DON55.
Lining dimensions .. .. 9·63 in. × 1·7 in. (244·6 mm. × 43·2 mm.).
Total lining area (rear) .. .. 65·48 sq. in. (422·36 cm.^{2}).
Number of rivets (per shoe) .. 12.
Disc diameter .. .. .. 11 in. (27·9 cm.).

BRAKES (MGA 1600 with Dunlop disc brakes)
Type .. .. Dunlop disc (front and rear).
Disc diameter .. .. .. 11 in. (27·9 cm.).
Fluid .. .. Wakefield Crimson (S.A.E. 70.R3).

WHEELS
TYRES } Refer to Series MGA data on preceding pages for Series MGA 1600.

WHEELS (MGA 1600 with Dunlop disc brakes)
Type .. .. Ventilated disc, 4J × 15. Centre lock.

TYRES (MGA 1600 with Dunlop disc brakes)
Size .. .. 5·90—15. Road Speed.
Tyre pressures:
  Normal: Front .. .. .. 18 lb./sq. in. (1·27 kg./cm.^{2}).
         Rear .. .. 20 lb./sq. in. (1·4 kg./cm.^{2}).
  Fast motoring: Front .. .. 22 lb./sq. in. (1·55 kg./cm.^{2}).
         Rear .. 24 lb./sq. in. (1·69 kg./cm.^{2}).
  Competition work
  and sustained high- } Front .. 24 lb./sq. in. (1·69 kg./cm.^{2}).
  speed motoring   Rear .. 26 lb./sq. in. (1·83 kg./cm.^{2}).

GENERAL DATA—continued

CAPACITIES

	Imp.	U.S.	Litres
Engine sump (including filter)	7½ pts.	9 pts.	4·25
Gearbox	4½ pts.	5·6 pts.	2·56
Rear axle	2¼ pts.	2·7 pts.	1·28
Cooling system	10 pts.	12 pts.	5·67
Steering rack	½ pt.	·6 pt.	·28
Fuel tank	10 gal.	12 gal.	45·4
Brake system	1 pt.	1·2 pts.	·568
Oil cooler	¾ pt.	·9 pt.	·426

GENERAL DIMENSIONS

Wheelbase	94 in. (238·8 cm.).
Overall length	156 in. (396·2 cm.).
Overall width	58 in. (147·3 cm.).
Overall height	50 in. (127·0 cm.).
Ground clearance	6 in. (15·24 cm.).
Turning circles (MGA 1600)	30 ft. 6 in. (9·296 m.).
Turning circles (MGA 1600 with Dunlop disc brakes)	Right-hand 32 ft. 1 in. (9·78 m.). Left-hand 32 ft. 6 in. (9·91 m.).

WEIGHTS

Fully equipped with tools, spare wheel, oil, water, and 2 gallons (2·5 U.S. gal., 9·1 litres) of fuel	2,016 lb. (914 kg.).
Engine (dry)	359 lb. (162·84 kg.).
Gearbox (dry)	67¼ lb. (30·50 kg.).
Rear axle (dry)	117¼ lb. (53·32 kg.).

GENERAL DATA
(Series MGA 1600—Mk. II)

ENGINE
Type	16GC.
Number of cylinders	4.
Bore	3·0 in. (76·2 mm.).
Stroke	3·5 in. (89 mm.).
Capacity	99·5 cu. in. (1622 c.c.).
Firing order	1, 3, 4, 2.
Compression ratio: High	8·9 : 1.
Low	8·3 : 1.
Capacity of combustion chamber (valves fitted)	2·624 cu. in. (43·0 c.c.).
Valve operation	Overhead by push-rod.
Maximum horse-power (standard): High compression	90 at 5,500 r.p.m.
Low compression	85 at 5,500 r.p.m.
B.M.E.P.: High compression	148 lb./sq. in. (10·4 kg./cm.^{2}) at 4,000 r.p.m.
Low compression	140 lb./sq. in. (9·84 kg./cm.^{2}) at 3,000 r.p.m.
Torque: High compression	97 lb. ft. (13·1 kg. m.) at 4,000 r.p.m.
Low compression	92 lb. ft. (12·72 kg. m.) at 3,000 r.p.m.
Cooling system	Thermo-siphon, pump- and fan-assisted.
Oversize bore: 1st	·010 in. (·254 mm.).
Max.	·040 in. (1·016 mm.).

CRANKSHAFT
Refer also to Series MGA data on preceding pages.

Main bearings
Journal length: Front	1·528 to 1·544 in. (38·817 to 39·224 mm.).
Intermediate	1·471 to 1·473 in. (37·363 to 37·414 mm.).
Rear	1·494 to 1·498 in. (37·940 to 38·049 mm.).
Bearing length	1·25 in. (31·75 mm.).
Diametrical clearance	·001 to ·0027 in. (·0254 to ·0685 mm.).

CONNECTING RODS
Refer also to Series MGA data on preceding pages.
Small-end bore	·750 to ·7512 in. (19·05 to 19·08 mm.).

Big-end bearings
Diametrical clearance	·001 to ·0025 in. (·0254 to ·063 mm.).

PISTON RINGS
Compression: Top ring	Plain.
Second and third rings	Tapered.
Width	·0615 to ·0625 in. (1·56 to 1·58 mm.).
Thickness	·125 to ·132 in. (3·175 to 3·35 mm.).
Fitted gap	·009 to ·014 in. (·229 to ·356 mm.).
Clearance in groove	·0015 to ·0035 in. (·038 to ·089 mm.).
Oil control type	Slotted scraper.
Width	·1552 to ·1562 in. (3·94 to 3·99 mm.).
Thickness	·125 to ·132 in. (3·175 to 3·35 mm.).
Fitted gap	·009 to ·014 in. (·23 to ·36 mm.).
Clearance in groove	·0016 to ·0036 in. (·040 to ·091 mm.).

GENERAL DATA—continued

GUDGEON PIN
Type	Clamped.
Fit	·0001 to ·0006 in. (·0025 to ·0152 mm.). Hand push fit at 68° F. (20° C.).
Diameter: Outer	·7499 to ·7501 in. (19·047 to 19·050 mm.).
Inner	·3215 in. (7·94 mm.).
Length	2·693 to 2·703 in. (68·402 to 68·656 mm.).

VALVES AND VALVE GEAR
Valves

Seat angle: Inlet	45°.
Exhaust	45°.
Head diameter: Inlet	1·562 to 1·567 in. (39·6 to 39·8 mm.).
Exhaust	1·343 to 1·348 in. (34·11 to 34·23 mm.).
Stem diameter: Inlet	·342 in. (8·68 mm.).
Exhaust	·342 in. (8·68 mm.).
Valve lift	·350 in. (8·89 mm.).
Valve stem to guide clearance: Inlet	·00155 to ·00255 in. (·0394 to ·0635 mm.).
Exhaust	·002 to ·003 in. (·051 to ·076 mm.).
Valve rocker clearance: Running	·015 in. (·38 mm.) (cold)
Timing	·060 in. (1·52 mm.).
Timing markings	Dimples on timing wheels.
Chain pitch and number of pitches	$\frac{3}{8}$ in. (9·52 mm.), 52 pitches.
Inlet valve: Opens	16° B.T.D.C.
Closes	56° A.B.D.C.
Exhaust valve: Opens	51° B.B.D.C.
Closes	21° A.T.D.C.

VALVE GUIDES
Length: Inlet	$1\frac{5}{8}$ in. (41·275 mm.).
Exhaust	$2\frac{3}{16}$ in. (55·95 mm.).
Diameter: Inlet and exhaust: Outside	·5635 to ·5640 in. (14·31 to 14·32 mm.).
Inside	·34425 to ·34475 in. (8·744 to 8·757 mm.).
Fitted height above head	·625 in. (15·87 mm.).

VALVE SPRINGS
Free length: Inner	$1\frac{31}{32}$ in. (50 mm.).
Outer	$1\frac{29}{32}$ in. (48·8 mm.).
Fitted length: Inner	1·449 in. (36·8 mm.).
Outer	1·575 in. (40 mm.).
Number of working coils: Inner	$6\frac{1}{2}$.
Outer	$4\frac{1}{2}$.
Load: Full lift: Inlet and exhaust	Inner 50 lb. (22·7 kg.). Outer 113 lb. (51·2 kg.).
No lift: Inlet	Inner 28 to 32 lb. (12·7 to 14·51 kg.).
	Outer 53 to 57 lb. (24 to 25·8 kg.).
Exhaust	Inner and outer 53 to 57 lb. (24 to 25·8 kg.).

TAPPETS
ROCKERS } Refer to Series MGA data on preceding pages.
CAMSHAFT

GENERAL DATA—continued

LUBRICATION

Refer also to Series MGA data on preceding pages.

Normal pressure: Running .. .. 70 lb./sq. in. (4·9 kg./cm.^{2}) at 30 m.p.h.
Idling .. .. 15 lb./sq. in. (1·05 kg./cm.^{2}) at 500 r.p.m.

TORQUE WRENCH SETTINGS
FUEL SYSTEM } Refer to Series MGA data on preceding pages.
AIR CLEANER AND FUEL PUMP

COOLING SYSTEM

Thermostat opening temperature .. .. 150·8° F. (66° C.).

IGNITION SYSTEM

Static ignition timing: High compression .. .. 10° B.T.D.C. (up to Engine No. 4003).
5° B.T.D.C. (from Engine No. 4004).
Low compression .. .. 10° B.T.D.C.

CLUTCH

Make and type	Borg & Beck 8A6–G single dry plate.
Facing material	Wound yarn.
Friction plate damper springs	6. Maroon and light green.
Pressure springs	6. Light grey.
Minimum free length	2·27 in. (57·658 mm.).
Rate	282 lb. in. (3·24 kg. mm.).
Total spring load (mean)	1,200 lb. (544·3 kg.).
Test length	1·56 in. (39·624 mm.).
Load	195 to 205 lb. (88·45 to 92·98 kg.).

GEARBOX

Number of forward speeds	4.
Synchromesh	Second, third, and fourth gears.
Ratios: Top	1·0 : 1.
Third	1·374 : 1.
Second	2·214 : 1.
First	3·64 : 1.
Reverse	4·76 : 1.
Overall ratios: Top	4·1 : 1.
Third	5·633 : 1.
Second	9·077 : 1.
First	14·924 : 1.
Reverse	19·516 : 1.
Speedometer gears ratio	5 : 12.

STEERING
FRONT SUSPENSION
REAR SUSPENSION } Refer to Series MGA data on preceding pages.
PROPELLER SHAFT

GENERAL DATA—continued

REAR AXLE
Make and type .. .. B.M.C. 'B' type, three-quarter-floating.
Ratio .. .. 10/41.

ELECTRICAL EQUIPMENT
BRAKES } Refer to Series MGA data on preceding pages.
WHEELS

TYRES
Size .. .. 5·60—15 Gold Seal nylon (tubed).
Pressures:
  Normal use including motorways up to 100 m.p.h.: Front   21 lb./sq. in. (1·47 kg./cm.^{2}).
                                                Rear   24 lb./sq. in. (1·68 kg./cm.^{2}).
  Maximum or near-maximum performance: Front ..   24 lb./sq. in. (1·68 kg./cm.^{2}).
                                                Rear ..   27 lb./sq. in. (1·89 kg./cm.^{2}).
Size .. .. 5·90—15 Road Speed RS5 (tubed).
Pressures:
  Normal use: Front .. .. 17 lb./sq. in. (1·19 kg./cm.^{2}).
         Rear .. .. 20 lb./sq. in. (1·40 kg./cm.^{2}).
  Maximum or near-maximum speeds sustained for lengthy
    periods or for competition use: Front .. .. .. 24 lb./sq. in. (1·68 kg./cm.^{2}).
                                Rear .. .. .. 27 lb./sq. in. (1·89 kg./cm.^{2}).

CAPACITIES
GENERAL DIMENSIONS } Refer to Series MGA data on preceding pages.

WEIGHTS
Kerbside weight .. .. 2,016 lb. (914·4 kg.).
Shipping weight .. .. 1,987 lb. (901·2 kg.).
Engine and clutch (dry) .. .. 355 lb. (136·0 kg.).

MGB

GENERAL DATA
(18G/18GA)

ENGINE

Type	18G, 18GA.
Number of cylinders	4.
Bore	3·16 in. (80·26 mm.).
Stroke	3·5 in. (89 mm.).
Capacity	1798 c.c. (109·8 cu. in.).
Combustion chamber volume (valves fitted)	42·5 to 43·5 c.c. (2·59 to 2·65 cu. in.).
Firing order	1, 3, 4, 2.
Valve operation	Overhead by push-rod.
Compression ratio: H.C.	8·8 : 1.
L.C.	8·0 : 1.
Compression pressure: H.C.	160 lb./sq. in. (11·25 kg./cm.^{2}).
L.C.	130 lb./sq. in. (9·15 kg./cm.^{2}).
Torque: H.C.	110 lb. ft. (15·2 kg. m.) at 3,000 r.p.m.
L.C.	105 lb. ft. (14·5 kg. m.) at 3,000 r.p.m.
Engine idle speed (approx.)	500 r.p.m.
Oversize bore: First	·010 in. (·254 mm.).
Max.	·040 in. (1·016 mm.).

Crankshaft

Main journal diameter	2·1265 to 2·127 in. (54·01 to 54·02 mm.).
Crankpin journal diameter	1·8759 to 1·8764 in. (47·648 to 47·661 mm.).
Crankshaft end-thrust	Taken on thrust washers at centre main bearing.
Crankshaft end-float	·002 to ·003 in. (·051 to ·076 mm.).

Main bearings

Number and type	Three thinwall.
Material	Steel-backed copper-lead.
Length	1⅛ in. (28·5 mm.).
Diametrical clearance	·001 to ·0027 in. (·0254 to ·068 mm.).
Undersizes	—·010, —·020, —·030 and —·040 in. (—·254, —·508, —·762 and —1·016 mm.).

Connecting rods

Type	Angular-split big-end, split clamp small-end.
Length between centres	6·5 in. (165·1 mm.).

Big-end bearings

Type	Shell.
Material	Steel-backed copper-lead.
Length	·995 to 1·005 in. (25·2 to 25·52 mm.).
Diametrical clearance	·001 to ·0027 in. (·0254 to ·068 mm.).
Undersizes	—·010, —·020, —·030 and —·040 in. (—·254, —·508, —·762 and —1·016 mm.).
End-float on crankpin (nominal)	·008 to ·012 in. (·20 to ·30 mm.).

Pistons

Type	Aluminium solid skirt.
Clearance in cylinder: Top	·0036 to ·0045 in. (·091 to ·121 mm.).
Bottom	·0018 to ·0024 in. (·045 to ·060 mm.).
Number of rings	4 (3 compression, 1 oil control).
Width of ring grooves: Top	
Second	·064 to ·065 in. (1·625 to 1·651 mm.).
Third	
Oil control	·1578 to ·1588 in. (4·008 to 4·033 mm.).
Gudgeon pin bore	·7501 to ·7503 in. (19·052 to 19·057 mm.).

GENERAL DATA—continued
(18G/18GA—continued)

Piston rings

Compression
Type: Top .. .. Parallel ⎱ cast iron—molybdenum filled.
      Second and third .. .. Tapered ⎰
Width: Top .. .. ⎰ ·0615 to ·0625 in. (1·562 to 1·587 mm.).
      Second and third .. .. ⎱
Fitted gap: Top .. .. ⎰ ·012 to ·017 in. (·304 to ·431 mm.).
      Second and third .. .. ⎱
Ring to groove clearance: Top .. .. .. ⎰ ·0015 to ·0035 in. (·038 to ·088 mm.).
      Second and third .. .. ⎱

Oil control
Type .. .. Slotted scraper.
Width .. .. ·1552 to ·1562 in. (3·94 to 3·96 mm.).
Fitted gap .. .. ·012 to ·017 in. (·304 to ·431 mm.).
Ring to groove clearance .. .. ·0016 to ·0036 in. (·04 to ·09 mm.).

Gudgeon pin
Type .. .. Semi-floating.
Fit in piston .. .. Free fit at 20° C. (68° F.).
Diameter (outer) .. .. ·7499 to ·7501 in. (19·04 to 19·05 mm.).

Camshaft
Journal diameters: Front .. .. 1·78875 to 1·78925 in. (45·424 to 45·437 mm.).
                Centre .. .. 1·72875 to 1·72925 in. (43·910 to 43·923 mm.).
                Rear .. .. 1·62275 to 1·62325 in. (41·218 to 41·230 mm.).
Bearing liner inside diameter ⎰ Front .. .. 1·79025 to 1·79075 in. (45·472 to 45·485 mm.).
(reamed after fitting): ⎨ Centre .. .. 1·73025 to 1·73075 in. (43·948 to 43·961 mm.).
                     ⎱ Rear .. .. 1·62425 to 1·62475 in. (41·256 to 41·269 mm.).
Diametrical clearance .. .. ·001 to ·002 in. (·0254 to ·0508 mm.).
End-thrust .. .. Taken on locating plate.
End-float .. .. ·003 to ·007 in. (·076 to ·178 mm.).
Cam lift .. .. ·250 in. (6·35 mm.).
Drive .. .. Chain and sprocket from crankshaft.
Timing chain .. .. ⅜ in. (9·52 mm.) pitch × 52 pitches.

Tappets
Type .. .. Barrel with flat base.
Outside diameter .. .. ⁴⁹⁄₆₄ in. (20·64 mm.).
Length .. .. 2·293 to 2·303 in. (58·25 to 58·5 mm.).

Rocker gear
Rocker shaft
Length .. .. 14$\frac{1}{32}$ in. (356 mm.).
Diameter .. .. ·624 to ·625 in. (15·85 to 15·87 mm.).

Rocker arm
Bore .. .. ·7485 to ·7495 in. (19·01 to 19·26 mm.).
Rocker arm bush inside diameter .. .. .. ·6255 to ·626 in. (15·8 to 15·9 mm.).
Ratio .. .. 1·4 : 1.

Valves
Seat angle: Inlet and exhaust .. .. .. 45¼°.
Head diameter: Inlet .. .. 1·562 to 1·567 in. (38·67 to 38·80 mm.).
             Exhaust .. .. 1·343 to 1·348 in. (34·11 to 34·23 mm.).
Stem diameter: Inlet .. .. ·3422 to ·3427 in. (8·68 to 8·69 mm.).
             Exhaust .. .. ·3417 to ·3422 in. (8·660 to 8·661 mm.).
Stem to guide clearance: Inlet .. .. .. ·0015 to ·0025 in. (·0381 to ·0778 mm.).
                    Exhaust .. .. ·002 to ·003 in. (·0508 to ·0762 mm.).
Valve lift: Inlet and exhaust .. .. .. ·3645 in. (9·25 mm.).

GENERAL DATA—continued
(18G/18GA—continued)

Valve guides
- Length: Inlet .. .. 1⅝ in. (41·275 mm.).
-         Exhaust .. .. 2 11/64 in. (55·95 mm.).
- Outside diameter: Inlet and exhaust .. .. ·5635 to ·5640 in. (14·30 to 14·32 mm.).
- Inside diameter: Inlet and exhaust .. .. .. ·3442 to ·3447 in. (8·73 to 8·74 mm.).
- Fitted height above head: Inlet and exhaust .. .. ⅝ in. (15·875 mm.).
- Interference fit in head: Inlet and exhaust .. .. .. ·0005 to ·00175 in. (·012 to ·044 mm.).

(Later cars)
- Length : Inlet .. .. 1⅞ in. (47·63 mm.).
- Fitting height above head: Inlet .. .. .. ¾ in. (19 mm.).

Valve springs
- Free length: Inner .. .. 1 31/32 in. (50·0 mm.).
-              Outer .. .. 2 9/64 in. (54·4 mm.).
- Fitted length: Inner .. .. 1 7/16 in. (36·5 mm.).
-                Outer .. .. 1 9/16 in. (39·7 mm.).
- Load at fitted length: Inner .. .. 28 to 32 lb. (12·7 to 14·5 kg.).
-                        Outer .. .. .. 72 lb. (32·7 kg.).
- Load at top of lift: Inner .. .. 48 to 52 lb. (21·7 to 23·6 kg.).
-                      Outer .. .. 117 lb. (53 kg.).
- Valve crash speed .. .. 6,200 r.p.m.

Valve timing
- Timing marks .. .. Dimples on camshaft and crankshaft wheels.
- Rocker clearance: Running .. .. ·015 in. (·38 mm.) cold.
-                   Timing .. .. ·055 in. (1·4 mm.).
- Inlet valve: Opens .. .. 16° B.T.D.C.
-              Closes .. .. 56° A.B.D.C.
- Exhaust valve: Opens .. .. 51° B.B.D.C.
-                Closes .. .. 21° A.T.D.C.

ENGINE LUBRICATION
- System .. .. Wet sump, pressure-fed.
- System pressure: Running .. .. Between 50 and 80 lb./sq. in. (3·51 and 5·6 kg./cm.²).
-                  Idling .. .. Between 10 and 25 lb./sq. in. (·7 and 1·7 kg./cm.²).
- Oil pump .. .. Hobourn-Eaton or eccentric rotor.
-     Capacity .. .. 3¼ gal./min. at 2,000 r.p.m.
- Oil filter .. .. Tecalemit full-flow felt element.
- By-pass valve opens .. .. 13 to 17 lb./sq. in. (·9 to 1·1 kg./cm.²).
- Oil pressure relief valve .. .. 70 lb./sq. in. (4·9 kg./cm.²).
- Relief valve spring: Free length .. .. .. 3 in. (76·2 mm.).
-                      Fitted length .. .. 2 5/32 in. (54·7 mm.).
-                      Load at fitted length .. 15·5 to 16·5 lb. (7·0 to 7·4 kg.).

FUEL SYSTEM
- **Carburetters** .. .. Twin S.U. Type HS4.
-   Choke diameter .. .. 1½ in. (38·1 mm.).
-   Jet size .. .. ·090 in. (2·2 mm.).
-   Needles .. .. No. 5 (Standard), No. 6 (Rich), No. 21 (Weak).
-   Piston spring .. .. Red.

- **Air cleaners** .. .. Cooper paper element.

- **Fuel pump**
-   Type (Early cars) .. .. S.U. electric HP.
-   Minimum flow .. .. 7 gal./hr. (31·8 litres/hr., 8·4 U.S. gal./hr.).

GENERAL DATA—continued
(18G/18GA—continued)

Suction head	2 ft. 6 in. (76·2 cm.).
Delivery head	4 ft. (122 cm.).
Minimum starting voltage	9·5 volts.
Type (Later cars)	S.U. electric AUF 300.
Minimum flow	15 gal./hr. (68·2 litre/hr. 18 U.S. gal./hr.).
Suction head	18 in. (457 mm.).

COOLING SYSTEM

Type	Pressurized. Pump-impeller- and fan-assisted.
Thermostat setting	
Standard	74° C. (165° F.).
Hot climate	74° C. (165° F.).
Cold climate	82° C. (180° F.).
Pressure cap	7 lb. (3·175 kg.).
Fan blades	3 at 24°.
Fan belt: Width	$\frac{3}{8}$ in. (9·5 mm.).
Outside length	35$\frac{1}{2}$ in. (90·2 cm.).
Thickness	$\frac{5}{16}$ in. (7·9 mm.).
Tension	$\frac{1}{2}$ in. (12·8 mm.) movement.
Type of pump	Centrifugal.
Pump drive	Belt from crankshaft pulley.

IGNITION SYSTEM

Coil	HA.12 (oil-filled).	
Resistance at 20° C. (68° F.): Primary winding	3·1 to 3·5 ohms (cold).	
Consumption: Ignition switch on	3·9 amps.	
At 2,000 r.p.m.	1·4 amps.	
Distributor	25D4.	
Rotation of rotor	Anti-clockwise.	
Cam form	4-cylinder high-lift.	
Cam closed period	60°±3°.	
Cam open period	30°±3°.	
Automatic advance	Centrifugal and vacuum.	
	Serial Number 40897 (*H.C.*)	*Serial Number* 40916 (*L.C.*)
Automatic advance commences	400 r.p.m.	400 r.p.m.
Maximum advance (crankshaft degrees)	20° at 2,200 r.p.m.	24° at 4,400 r.p.m.
Vacuum advance (crankshaft degrees)	20° at 13 in. (33·3 cm.) Hg.	16° at 12 in. (30·5 cm.) Hg.
Decelerating check (crankshaft degrees, engine r.p.m.)	20° at 2,200 r.p.m.	24° at 4,400 r.p.m.
	15° at 1,600 r.p.m.	18° at 3,000 r.p.m.
	9° at 900 r.p.m.	9° at 1,000 r.p.m.
	6° at 700 r.p.m.	8° at 800 r.p.m.
	6° at 600 r.p.m.	6° at 600 r.p.m.
Contact point gap setting	·014 to ·016 in. (·35 to ·40 mm.).	
Breaker spring tension	18 to 24 oz. (510 to 680 gm.).	
Condenser capacity	·18 to ·24 mF.	
Timing marks	Pointer on timing chain case and notch on crankshaft pulley.	
Static ignition timing: H.C.	10° B.T.D.C. (98/100-octane fuel).	
L.C.	8° B.T.D.C. (95/97-octane fuel).	
Stroboscopic ignition timing: H.C.	14° B.T.D.C. at 600 r.p.m.	
L.C.	12° B.T.D.C. at 600 r.p.m.	
Suppressors	Lucas W55 Type L.2. Fitted in plug leads.	
Sparking plugs	Champion N-9Y.	
Size	14 mm. $\frac{3}{4}$ in. (19·0 mm.) reach.	
Gap	·024 to ·026 in. (·625 to ·660 mm.).	

GENERAL DATA—*continued*
(18G/18GA—*continued*)

CLUTCH

Make and type	Borg & Beck 8 in. DS.G diaphragm spring.
Diaphragm spring colour	Dark blue.
Clutch plate diameter	8 in. (20·32 cm.).
Facing material	Wound yarn.
Number of damper springs	6.
Damper spring load	110 to 120 lb. (49·8 to 54·3 kg.).
Damper spring colour	Black/light green.
Clutch release bearing	Graphite (MY3D).
Clutch fluid	Lockheed Disc Brake Fluid (Series II).

GEARBOX AND OVERDRIVE

Number of forward gears	4.	
Gearbox ratios: Reverse	4·76 : 1.	
First	3·64 : 1.	
Second	2·21 : 1.	
Third	1·37 : 1.	
Fourth	1·00 : 1.	
Overdrive ratio	·802 : 1.	
Overall gear ratios: Reverse	18·588 : 1.	
First	14·214 : 1.	
		Overdrive
Second	8·656 : 1.	4·306 : 1.
Third	5·369 : 1.	3·135 : 1.
Fourth	3·909 : 1.	
Top gear speed per 1,000 r.p.m.: Standard	17·9 m.p.h. (27·3 km.p.h.).	
Overdrive	22·3 m.p.h. (35·5 km.p.h.).	
Speedometer gear ratio: Standard	9/28.	
Overdrive	5/16.	
Synchromesh hub springs: Free length	½ in. (12·7 mm.).	
Fitted length	5/16 in. (7·9 mm.).	
Load at fitted length	4 to 5 lb. (1·8 to 2·2 kg.).	
Shaft and reverse plunger detent springs: Free length	1 3/16 in. (30·16 mm.).	
Fitted length	¾ in. (19·0 mm.).	
Load at fitted length	18 to 20 lb. (8·16 to 9·07 kg.).	
Reverse plunger spring: Free length	1 in. (25·4 mm.).	
Fitted length	13/16 in. (20·63 mm.).	
Load at fitted length	91½ to 92½ lb. (41·4 to 41·9 kg.).	
●Mainshaft second and third gear end-float	·004 to ·006 in. (·102 to ·152 mm.).●	
Laygear end-float	·002 to ·003 in. (·051 to ·076 mm.).	
Overdrive		
Pump spring: Free length	2·000 in. (50·8 mm.).	
Rate	11 lb. in. (12·7 kg. cm.).	
Clutch spring: Free length	1·510 in. (38·3 mm.).	
Rate	154 lb. in. (178 kg. cm.).	

PROPELLER SHAFT

Type	Open tubular, telescopic.
Universal joints	Hardy Spicer needle roller.
Angular movement	18° to 20°.
Overall length: Fully extended: Standard	30¾ in. (78·1 cm.).
Overdrive	31⅞ in. (81 cm.).
Fully compressed: Standard	29 1/16 in. (74 cm.).
Overdrive	30 1/8 in. (76·5 cm.).
Length of shaft assembly: Standard	25 5/16 in. (64·3 cm.).
Overdrive	26 13/16 in. (67 cm.).
Tube diameter	2 in. (50·8 mm.).

GENERAL DATA—continued
(18G/18GA—continued)

REAR AXLE

Type	Hypoid, three-quarter-floating.
Ratio	3·909 : 1 (11/43).
Differential bearing preload	·002 in. (·05 mm.) 'nip' per bearing.
Pinion bearing preload	7 to 9 lb. in. (·8 to 1·0 kg. m.).
Backlash adjustment: Crown wheel	Shims.
Pinion	Head washer.

STEERING

Type	Rack and pinion.
Steering-wheel diameter	16½ in. (419·10 mm.).
Turns—lock to lock	2·93.
Turning circle	32 ft. (9·75 m.).
Universal joint	Hardy Spicer KO518, GB166.
Pinion end float	·002 to ·005 in. (·05 to ·12 mm.).
Damper end-float	·0005 to ·003 in. (·012 to ·076 mm.) (unladen).
Toe-in	$\frac{1}{16}$ to $\frac{3}{32}$ in. (1·5 to 2·3 mm.) (unladen).
Angle of outer wheel with inner wheel at 20°	18°.

FRONT SUSPENSION

Type	Independent. Coil spring and wishbone.
Spring: Coil diameter (mean)	3·238 in. (82·2 mm.).
Free height	$9·9 \pm \frac{1}{16}$ in. (251·4 ± 1·5 mm.).
Static length at 1,030 lb. (467·2 kg.) load	$7 \pm \frac{1}{32}$ in. (178 ± ·8 mm.).
Number of free coils	7·5.
Camber angle	Nominal 1° positive $(+\frac{1}{4}°, -1\frac{1}{4}°)$
	$= 1\frac{1}{4}°$ positive, $\frac{1}{4}°$ negative
Castor angle	Nominal 7° $(+\frac{1}{4}°, -2°) = 5°$ to $7\frac{1}{4}°$ (unladen).
King pin inclination	Nominal 8° $(+1°, -\frac{1}{2}°) = 7\frac{1}{4}°$ to 9°
Dampers	Armstrong piston type.
Arm centres	8 in. (203·2 mm.).
Wheel bearing end-float	·002 to ·004 in. (·05 to ·10 mm.).

REAR SUSPENSION

Type	Semi-elliptic leaf spring.
Number of spring leaves	5 + bottom plate. Interleaving 1/2, 2/3, 3/4.
Width of spring leaves	1¾ in. (44·4 mm.).
Gauge of leaves	
Early cars	$\frac{7}{32}$ in. (5·56 mm.).
Later cars	3 at $\frac{7}{32}$ in. (5·6 mm.), 3 at $\frac{3}{16}$ in. (4·8 mm.).
Working load (±15 lb. [7 kg.])	
Early cars	400 lb. (181·5 kg.).
Later cars	450 lb. (204·1 kg.).
Dampers	Armstrong piston type.
Arm centres	5¼ in. (133 mm.).

ELECTRICAL EQUIPMENT

System	12-volt, positive earth.
Charging system	Current/voltage control.
Batteries—two 6-volt	Lucas SG9E or STGZ9E.
	Lucas BT9E or BTZ9E—later cars.
Capacity: 10-hour rate	51 amp.-hr.
20-hour rate	58 amp.-hr.
Plates per cell	9.
Electrolyte to fill one cell	1 pint (570 c.c.: 1·2 U.S. pints).

GENERAL DATA—continued
(18G/18GA—continued)

Regulator	RB.340.
Voltage setting at 3,000 r.p.m.: 10° C. (50° F.)	14·9 to 15·5 volts.
20° C. (68° F.)	14·7 to 15·3 volts.
30° C. (86° F.)	14·5 to 15·1 volts.
40° C. (104° F.)	14·3 to 14·9 volts.
Current setting at 4,000 r.p.m.	22 amps.
Cut-out relay: Cut-in voltage	12·7 to 13·3 volts.
Drop-off voltage	9·5 to 11·0 volts.
Reverse current	3·0 to 5·0 amps.
Current regulator	22 ± 1 amp.
Dynamo	C40/1. 12-volt two-brush.
Maximum output	22 amps.
Cut-in speed	1,585 r.p.m. at 13·0 volts.
Field resistance	6·0 ohms.
Brush spring tension	22 to 25 oz. (623 to 708 gm.).
Drive	Belt from crankshaft.
Drive adjustment	Swinging link on dynamo.
Starter motor	M418G four-brush inertia type.
Lock torque	15 lb. ft. (2·1 kg. m.) at 425 amps.
Torque at 1,000 r.p.m.	8 lb. ft. (1·11 kg. m.) at 250 to 270 amps.
Brush spring tension	32 to 40 oz. (907 to 1133 gm.).
Starter gear ratio	13·3 : 1.
Wiper motor	DR.3A single speed.
Drive to wheelboxes	Rack and cable.
Armature end-float	·008 to ·012 in. (·20 to ·30 mm.).
Running current	2·7 to 3·4 amps.
Wiping speed	45 to 50 cycles per minute.
Horns	
Type	9H 12-volt.
Maximum current consumption	3¼ amps.

BRAKES
Type	Lockheed hydraulic. Disc front, drum rear.
Brake fluid	Lockheed Disc Brake Fluid (Series II).

Front
Disc diameter	10¾ in. (27·3 cm.).
Pad material	Don 55—FF.
Swept area	203·2 sq. in. (1311 cm.²).

Rear
Drum diameter	10 in. (25·4 cm.).
Lining material	Don 24—FE.
Swept area	106·8 sq. in. (683·9 cm.²).
Lining dimensions	$9\frac{7}{16} \times 1\frac{3}{4} \times \frac{3}{16}$ in. (240 × 44·4 × 4·76 mm.).

WHEELS
Type	Ventilated disc, **4-stud fixing**. Wire (optional).
Size: Disc	4J × 14.
Wire	4½J × 14.

GENERAL DATA—continued
(18G/18GA—continued)

TYRES
Standard:
  Size .. .. 5·60—14 tubed C41.
  Rolling radius .. .. 11·65 in. (29·5 cm.) at 30 m.p.h. (48 km.p.h.)
Optional:
  Size .. .. 155—14 SP.
Standard tyres:
  Pressures (set cold)
    Front .. .. 18 lb./sq. in. (1·3 kg./cm.²).
    Rear .. .. 18 lb./sq. in. (1·3 kg./cm.²).
  Sustained speeds in excess of 90 m.p.h. (145 km.p.h.):
    Front .. .. 24 lb./sq. in. (1·7 kg./cm.²).
    Rear .. .. 24 lb./sq. in. (1·7 kg./cm.²).
Optional tyres (SP):
  Pressures (set cold):
    Front .. .. 21 lb./sq. in. (1·5 kg./cm.²).
    Rear .. .. 24 lb./sq. in. (1·7 kg./cm.²).
  Sustained speeds in excess of 90 m.p.h. (145 km.p.h.):
    Front .. .. 27 lb./sq. in. (1·9 kg./cm.²).
    Rear .. .. 31 lb./sq. in. (2·2 kg./cm.²).
  NOTE.—Rear tyre pressures may be increased by 2 lb./sq. in. (·14 kg./cm.²) with advantage when touring with a laden boot.

CAPACITIES
Fuel tank: Early cars .. .. 10 gallons (45·4 litres, 12 U.S. gallons).
        Later cars .. .. 12 gallons (54 litres, 14 U.S. gallons).
Cooling system .. .. 9¼ pints (5·4 litres, 11·4 U.S. pints).
Heater .. .. ½ pint (·28 litre, ·6 U.S. pint).
Engine sump .. .. 7½ pints (4·26 litres, 9 U.S. pints).
Oil cooler .. .. ¾ pint (·42 litre, ·9 U.S. pint).
Gearbox .. .. 4½ pints (2·56 litres, 5·6 U.S. pints).
Gearbox and overdrive .. .. 5⅞ pints (3·36 litres, 6 U.S. pints).
Rear axle .. .. 2¼ pints (1·28 litres, 2·75 U.S. pints).
Steering rack .. .. ⅓ pint (·19 litre, ·39 U.S. pint).

DIMENSIONS
Overall length .. .. 12 ft. 8½ in. (3·874 m.).
Overall length (with over-riders) .. .. 12 ft. 9⅞ in. (3·897 m.).
Overall width .. .. 4 ft. 11⅞ in. (152·3 cm.).
Overall height (hood erected) .. .. 4 ft. 1¾ in. (125·4 cm.).
Ground clearance (minimum) .. .. 5 in. (12·7 cm.).
Wheelbase .. .. 7 ft. 7 in. (231·1 cm.).
Track: Front (disc wheels) .. .. 4 ft. 1 in. (124·4 cm.).
      Rear (disc wheels) .. .. 4 ft. 1¼ in. (125 cm.).
      Front (wire wheels) .. .. 4 ft. 1¼ in. (125 cm.).
      Rear (wire wheels) .. .. 4 ft. 1¼ in. (125 cm.).

WEIGHTS
Unladen weight .. .. 1,920 lb. (871 kg.).
Engine (dry, with clutch) .. .. 358 lb. (163·3 kg.) approx.
Gearbox .. .. 78 lb. (35·5 kg.) approx.
Rear axle: Disc wheels .. .. 117¼ lb. (53·26 kg.) approx.
       Wire wheels .. .. 123 lb. (55·79 kg.) approx.

TORQUE WRENCH SETTINGS
Engine
  Main bearing nuts .. .. 70 lb. ft. (9·7 kg. m).
  Flywheel set screws .. .. 40 lb. ft. (5·5 kg. m.).
  Gudgeon pin clamp bolt .. .. 25 lb. ft. (3·4 kg. m.).
  Big-end bolts .. .. 35 to 40 lb. ft. (4·8 to 5·5 kg. m.).
  Cylinder head nuts .. .. 45 to 50 lb. ft. (6·2 to 6·9 kg. m.).

GENERAL DATA—continued
(18G/18GA—continued)

Rocker bracket nuts	25 lb. ft. (3·4 kg. m.)
Oil pump to crankcase	14 lb. ft. (1·9 kg. m.)
Sump to crankcase	6 lb. ft. (·8 kg. m.)
Cylinder side cover screws	2 lb. ft. (·28 kg. m.)
Second type—deep pressed cover	5 lb. ft. (·7 kg. m.)
Timing cover—$\frac{1}{4}$ in. screws	6 lb. ft. (·8 kg. m.)
Timing cover—$\frac{5}{16}$ in. screws	14 lb. ft. (1·9 kg. m.)
Rear plate—$\frac{5}{16}$ in. screws	20 lb. ft. (2·8 kg. m.)
Rear plate—$\frac{3}{8}$ in. screws	30 lb. ft. (4·1 kg. m.)
Water pump to crankcase	25 lb. ft. (3·5 kg. m.)
Water outlet elbow nuts	8 lb. ft. (1·1 kg. m.)
Rocker cover nuts	4 lb. ft. (·56 kg. m.)
Manifold nuts	25 lb. ft. (3·4 kg. m.)
Oil filter centre-bolt	15 lb. ft. (2·1 kg. m.)
Clutch to flywheel	25 to 30 lb. ft. (3·4 to 4·1 kg. m.)
Carburetter stud nuts	2 lb. ft. (·28 kg. m.)
Distributor clamp bolt (nut trapped)	4·16 lb. ft. (·57 kg. m.)
Distributor clamp nut (bolt trapped)	2·5 lb. ft. (·35 kg. m.)

Rear axle

Crown wheel to differential carrier	55 to 60 lb. ft. (7·6 to 8·3 kg. m.)
Differential bearing cap	60 to 65 lb. ft. (8·3 to 8·9 kg. m.)
Pinion bearing nut	135 to 140 lb. ft. (18·6 to 19·3 kg. m.)
Rear brake adjuster securing nuts	5 to 7 lb. ft. (·69 to ·97 kg. m.)
Bearing retaining nut	180 lb. ft. (24·8 kg. m.)

Rear suspension

●Rear shock absorber bolts	55 to 60 lb. ft. (7·6 to 8·3 kg. m.)●

Front suspension

Front shock absorber bolts	45 lb. ft. (6·2 kg. m.)
Brake disc to hub	40 to 45 lb. ft. (5·5 to 6·2 kg. m.)
Brake calliper mounting	40 to 45 lb. ft. (5·5 to 6·2 kg. m.)
Bearing retaining nut	40 to 70 lb. ft. (5·5 to 9·7 kg. m.)
Cross-member to body	55 lb. ft. (7·6 kg. m.)

Steering

Steering arm bolts	60 to 65 lb. ft. (8·3 to 8·9 kg. m.)
Steering-wheel nut	42 lb. ft. (5·8 kg. m.)
Steering tie-rod locknut	33·3 to 37·5 lb. ft. (4·6 to 5·2 kg. m.)
Steering lever ball joint nut	35 lb. ft. (4·8 kg. m.)
Steering universal joint bolt	20 lb. ft. (2·8 kg. m.)

Road wheels

Road wheel nuts	60 to 62·5 lb. ft. (8·3 to 8·6 kg. m.)

18GB SECTION
(second section)

This added section to the original handbook covers servicing of models with Engine Serial Number Prefix 18GB. The pages up to this added section still apply to prior models. Specify the engine serial number for ordering parts.

Floyd Clymer — Publisher

Beginning with engine serial No. prefix "18GB" and later, 5-main bearing crankshaft engines have been used and a number of chassis revisions have been made. Those changes in maintenance and repair procedures which apply are set forth in the following pages. If a part or method is not described herein, the techniques and components which apply to earlier models remain the same. For identification purposes, see the model chart at the front of this book.

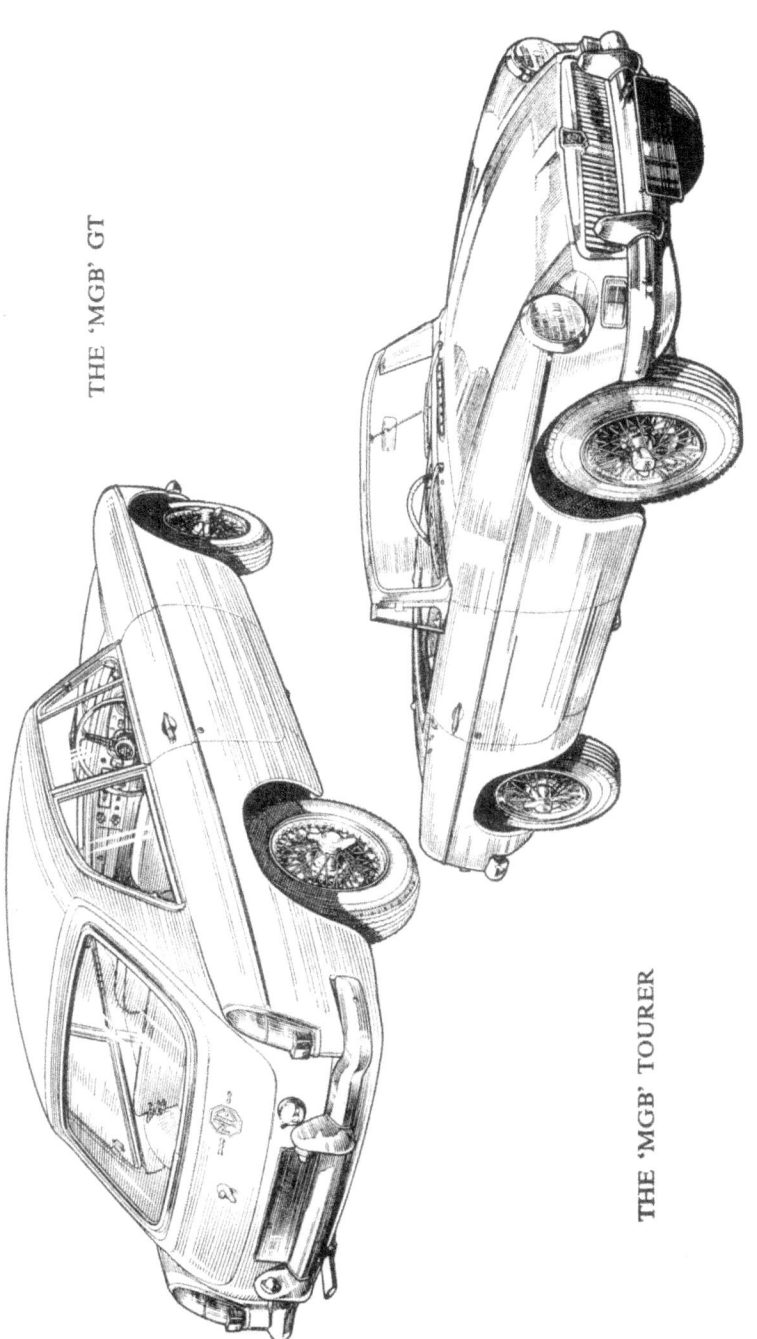

THE 'MGB' GT

THE 'MGB' TOURER

CONTENTS II

Engine	341
Crankcase Emission Control	350
Igniton System	352
Cooling System	354
Fuel System	356
Clutch	358
Gearbox	358
Overdrive	360
Propeller Shaft	372
Rear Axle	376
Rear Road Springs	379
Steering Gear	381
Front Suspension	385
Hydraulic Dampers	389
Braking System	390
Electrical System	404
Wiring Diagram	414
Exhaust Emission Control	416
General Data	427
Driver's Handbook	431

ENGINE

Oil Pressure
Under normal running conditions the oil pressure should not drop below 50 psi (3.5 kg./cm^2) on the gauge at normal road speeds, whilst about 15 psi (1.05 kg./cm^2) should be shown when the engine is idling. New engines with new oil will give considerably higher readings at low speeds.

Oil Pressure Relief Valve
The correct relief pressure of the valve is 70 psi, with the correct valve spring length of 3 in.

Removing and Replacing the Carburetors
1. Release the spring clips and detach the breather hose from the air cleaner and the rocker cover.
2. Disconnect the fuel supply pipe at the rear carburetor banjo union, then pull off the overflow pipes.
3. Loosen the bolt and nut securing the mixture and throttle cables respectively and withdraw the cables complete. Detach the throttle return springs.
4. Pull off the rubber connection for the vacuum ignition control pipe from the top of the rear carburetor body.
5. Remove the four nuts securing the carburetor flanges and withdraw the carburetors and air cleaners as an assembly.
6. To replace, be sure the center throttle return spring end eye is located between the flat washer and the throttle lever. The throttle linkage must be checked, and readjusted if necessary, after refitting.

Refitting the Cylinder Head
Follow the instructions in the previous ENGINE chapter, then switch on the ignition and check the fuel system for leaks. Start the engine and run it until the normal working temperature is reached. Remove the rocker cover and check the valve clearances. Replace the rocker cover and connect the breather hose.

Check the valve clearance again after the vehicle has run about 100 miles (160 km.) as the valves have a tendency to bed down. At the same time it is advisable to test the cylinder head nuts for tightness. Tightening the cylinder head nuts may affect valve clearances, although usually not enough to justify resetting.

Checking Valve Timing
1. Set No. 1 cylinder inlet valve to .055 in. (1.4 mm.) clearance with the engine cold, and then turn the engine until the valve

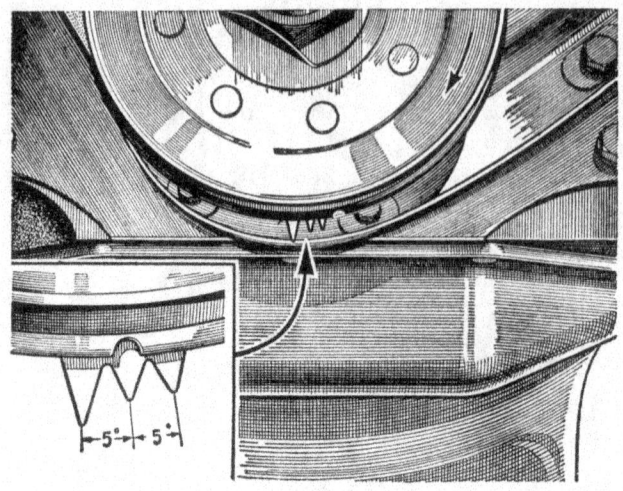

The notch in the pulley approaching the T.D.C. position for pistons 1 and 4. The inset shows the timing set at 5° B.T.D.C.

Static Timing

is about to open.

2. The indicating notch in the flange of the crankshaft pulley should then be opposite the longest of the three pointers on the timing cover, i.e. the valve should be about to open at T.D.C. and No. 4 piston will be at T.D.C. on its compression stroke.

3. **Note:** Be sure to reset the inlet valve clearance to the recommended clearance (see GENERAL DATA) when the timing check has been completed. The clearance of .055 in. (1.4 mm.) is necessary to bring the opening position of the valve to T.D.C. It is not possible to check the valve timing accurately with the normal running valve clearance.

Replacing Timing Chain Cover

After removing the cover as directed in steps (1) through (5) in the previous ENGINE chapter, replace as follows:

1. The oil seal in the cover must be renewed if it shows signs of damage. If it is the felt type seal, replace the whole cover assembly with a cover incorporating a rubber seal (Part No. 12H 2281), and the matching oil slinger (Part No. 12H 1740). **Both parts must be used together.**

2. If the timing cover gasket has been damaged, or the cover has been renewed, clean the face of the cover flange and the front engine mounting plate and fit a new gasket when reassembling.

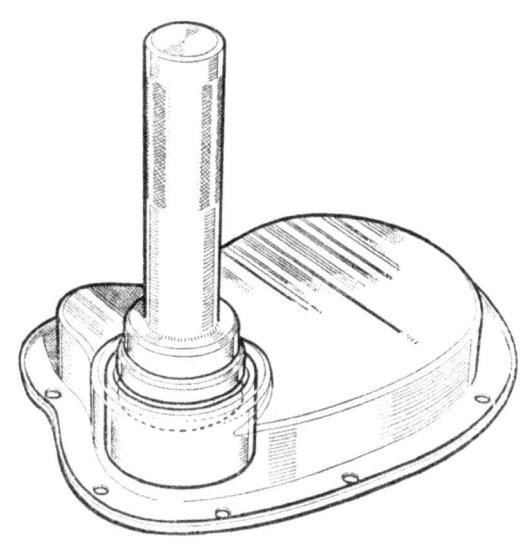

Replacing the oil seal in the crankcase front cover using Service tool 18G 134 and adaptor 18G 134 BD

Replacing oil seal

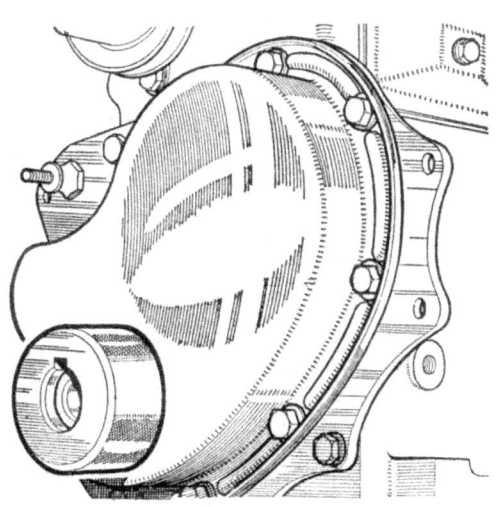

Install the securing screws finger tight and centralize the crankcase front cover with the crankshaft, using Service tool 18G 1046

Using Service tool 18G 1046

3. Be sure that the oil slinger behind the crankshaft pulley is fitted with the face marked 'F' or the concave side (early type) away from the engine.

4. When refitting the cover it is important to ensure that the seal is centralized on the crankshaft, and use Service tool 18G 1046 for this purpose.

NOTE: The early-type front cover and oil slinger must be used together. Use Service tool 18G 3 to centralize the rubber seal on the crankshaft, or use the crankshaft pulley as follows:

5. If a rubber seal is fitted fill the annular groove between the lips with grease. Lubricate the hub of the pulley and push it into the seal, at the same time turning it to avoid damaging the lips of the rubber seal. Slide the pulley onto the shaft with the keyway in line with the key in the crankshaft. Turn the cover as necessary to align the set screw holes with those in the crankcase, taking care not to strain the cover against the flexibility of the seal.

6. Insert the set screws and tighten up.

7. Refit and tighten the pulley securing screw.

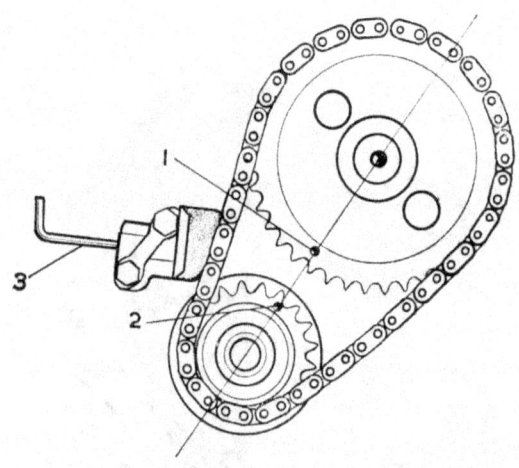

Crank the engine until the timing dimples (1) and (2) are opposite each other before removing the timing chain and chain wheels. The chain tensioner is retracted into the unloaded position by turning the Allen key (3) in a clockwise direction

Valve timing gear and chain tensioner

Replacing Timing Chain

Follow the instructions in the previous ENGINE chapter, being sure to replace the oil thrower, with the face marked 'F' or the concave side (early type) away from the engine, before replacing the rest of the components.

Timing Chain Tensioner

Before reassembling the tensioner (following Step (4) under this heading in the previous ENGINE chapter), perform the following tests:
5. Check the bore in the adjuster body for ovality.
6. If the ovality is greater than .003 in. (.076 mm.) when measured on diameters near the mouth of the bore, then a complete new adjuster must be fitted.
7. Be sure that dirt is not allowed to enter the adjuster, so ensure that all parts are clean before reassembly.

Note the following: After having installed the tensioner and the timing chain, and the tensioner is about to be released for operation (as per instructions in the previous ENGINE chapter under this heading), insert the key and turn it clockwise. DO NOT attempt to turn the key counterclockwise or force the slipper head into the chain by external pressure.

Removing and Replacing the Engine—MGB

Following Step (6) under the above heading in the previous ENGINE chapter, the following cautionary note should be inserted. The rest of the procedure remains the same:

NOTE: Great care must be taken during the following operation to ensure that no load is placed on the clutch release plate drive straps. Even slight damage to these may result in the clutch breaking up at high speed.

Main Bearings

NOTE: The MGB engine since Engine Serial No. Prefix 18GB is made as a five-main bearing model. The following instructions apply to this model only.
1. Remove the flywheel and clutch, the timing chain, the sump and strainer, and the rear engine mounting plate.
2. Note that a thrust washer is fitted on each side of the center main bearing to take the crankshaft end-thrust. These thrust washers each consist of two semicircular halves, one having a lug which is located in a recess in the detachable half of the bearing and the other being plain.
3. Before refitting the crankshaft check the end-float (see GENERAL DATA) and select and fit new upper and lower thrust washers as required. The washers are available in stand-

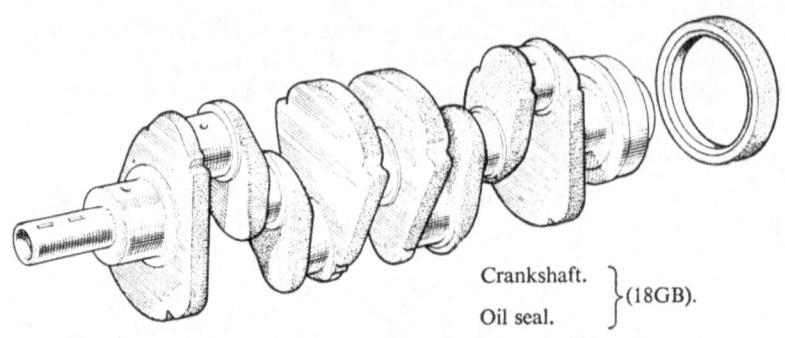

Crankshaft. ⎫
Oil seal. ⎬ (18GB).
           ⎭

5-Main bearing crankshaft and oil seal

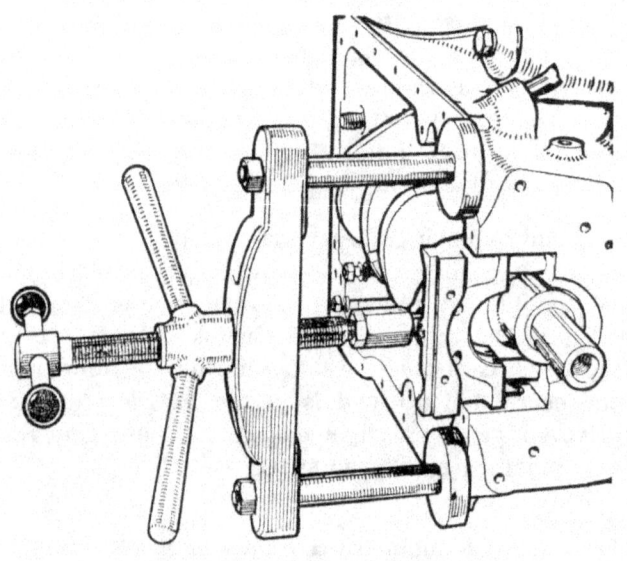

Withdrawing the front main bearing cap, using Service tool 18G42A *and adaptor* 18G42B

Front main bearing cap withdrawal

ard thicknesses and .003 in. (.076 mm.) oversize.

4. Remove the two bolts and locking plate securing the front main bearing cap to the engine front bearer plate.

5. Remove the main bearing cap retaining nuts and locking plates (early engines) or the self-locking nuts and plain washers (later engines).

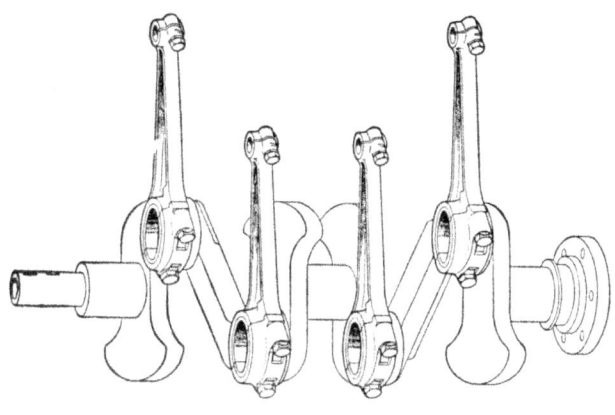

Assembly positions of the connecting rods, showing the offsets

Connecting rod offsets

6. When fitting new bearings no scraping is required as the bearings are machined to give the correct diametrical clearance of .001 to .0027 in. (.025 to .067 mm.).
7. In the case of a 'run' bearing, it is always essential to thoroughly clean out all the oilways in the crankshaft and block, wash out the engine sump with solvent or kerosene, and clean the oil pump and sump strainer to ensure that no particles of metal are left anywhere in the lubricating system.
8. The rear main bearing cap horizontal joint surfaces should be thoroughly cleaned and lightly covered with Hylomar Jointing Compound (or equivalent) before the cap is fitted to the cylinder block. This will ensure a perfect oil seal when the cap is bolted down to the block.
9. Refit each main bearing and cap, refitting the thrust washers in their correct positions at the center main bearing with the oil grooves away from the bearing.
10. Lubricate the main bearing cap joint seal liberally with oil before refitting.
11. When refitting the bearing caps on early and later engines, use flat washers and self-locking nuts. Check that the self-locking nuts lock to the stud threads securely.
12. Tighten the bearing cap nuts to the torque figure given in GENERAL DATA.

Removing and Replacing Pistons and Connecting Rods

This procedure is similar to the outline given in the prior ENGINE chapter, except for the following:

NOTE: The piston ring gaps should be set at 90° to each other.

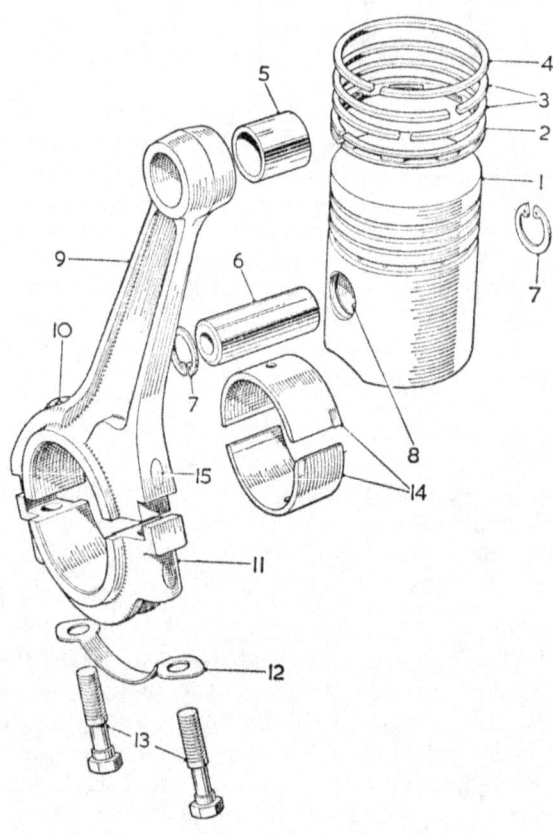

Piston and connecting rod

1. Piston.
2. Piston ring—scraper.
3. Piston rings—taper.
4. Piston ring—parallel.
5. Small-end bush.
6. Gudgeon pin.
7. Circlip.
8. Gudgeon pin lubricating hole.
9. Connecting rod.
10. Cylinder wall lubricating jet.
11. Connecting rod cap.
12. Lock washer.
13. Bolts.
14. Connecting rod bearings.
15. Connecting rod and cap marking.

Piston and connecting rod assembly

Dismantling and Reassembling Piston and Connecting Rod Assemblies

1. The gudgeon (wrist) pins are fully floating; remove the two circlips locating each pin and press out the pins.
2. It is essential that the piston assemblies should be replaced in their own bores and fitted the same way round: Mark them (along with the connecting rods and caps) with a prick punch (1 mark for the No. One Cylinder, 2 marks for the No. Two Cylinder, and so on) to facilitate this.
3. Assemble the pistons to the connecting rods with the gudgeon pin, which should be a hand fit at room temperature of 68°F. (20° C.). Secure each pin in its piston with two circlips, being sure that they fit well into their grooves.
4. Be sure the connecting rod is fitted so the 'short' side of the big end is toward the camshaft.

Removing and Replacing the Camshaft

Perform steps (1) through (6) as described previously under this heading in the previous ENGINE chapter. Continue as follows:

7. Take out the bolt securing the distributor housing to the cylinder block and withdraw the housing. Use one of the tappet cover bolts (5/16 in. UNF., $3^1/_2$ in. long) as an extractor. Screw it into the threaded end of the distributor drive spindle and, with the crankshaft at 90° B. or A.T.D.C. (pistons halfway up the bores), withdraw the spindle.
8. Remove the sump, oil pump and oil pump drive shaft.
9. Disconnect the engine revolution indicator drive, remove the securing nuts and washers, then withdraw the indicator drive gear.
10. Take out the three set screws and shakeproof washers which secure the camshaft locating plate to the cylinder block, then withdraw the camshaft.
11. While the camshaft is removed it is advisable to check the bearing liners for damage and wear. If these are not in good condition they must be removed and new ones fitted.
12. The old bearings can be punched out. The new ones must be tapped into position. These bearings are easily damaged and the use of Service tool 18G124A is recommended. This tool comprises a body with built-in thrust race, screw wing nut, stop plate, C washer and handle, which must be used in conjunction with the following adapters: 18G124B, 18G124C, 18G124F, and 18G124H. If the replacement cam bearings are not of the pre-reamed type, it will be necessary to in-line ream them to size.

13. Replacement of the camshaft is a reversal of the above procedure.
14. Note that the three set screws securing the camshaft thrust plate are not evenly spaced to ensure the correct alignment of the oil hole supplying the timing gear.

Refitting the Distributor Drive Gear
1. Turn the engine until No. 1 piston is at T.D.C. on its compression stroke. When the valves on No. 4 cylinder are 'rocking' (i.e. exhaust just closing and inlet just opening), No. 1 piston is at the top of its compression stroke. If the engine is set so that the notch in the crankshaft pulley is in line with the long pointer on the timing chain cover, or the 'dimples' in the crankshaft and camshaft gears are in line, the piston is exactly at T.D.C.
2. Withdraw the spindle to clear the camshaft gear and screw one of the tappet cover bolts into the threaded end, then holding the drive gear with the slot just below the horizontal and the large offset uppermost, re-enter the gear.
3. As the gear engages with the camshaft the slot will turn in a counterclockwise direction until it is about at the two o'clock position.
4. Remove the bolt from the gear, insert the distributor housing and secure it with the special bolt and washer. Ensure that the correct bolt is used and that the head does not protrude above the face of the housing.

Refit the distributor, referring to the IGNITION chapter for retiming instructions if the clamp plate has been released.

Removing and Replacing the Crankshaft

This procedure is similar to the outline given in the prior ENGINE chapter, except for the following:

NOTE: When replacing the crankshaft, renewal of the rear mounting plate oil seal is necessary.

Crankcase Emission Control

General Description: This system consists of a diaphragm control valve connected by hoses between the inlet manifold and the engine crankcase. The crankcase outlet connection has an oil separator to prevent oil being pulled over with the vapors leaving the crankcase. A filtered, restricted orifice (9/64 in. diameter) in the oil filler cap provides a supply of fresh air into the crankcase as vapors are withdrawn by inlet manifold vac-

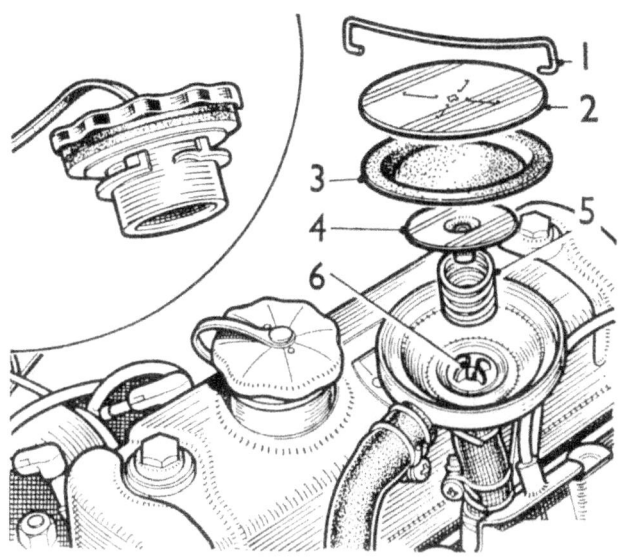

Closed-circuit breathing arrangement. (Inset) Oil filler cap with combined air filter and the breather control valve

1. Spring clip.
2. Cover.
3. Diaphragm.
4. Metering lever.
5. Spring.
6. Cruciform guides.

Crankcase closed-circuit breather

uum. The control valve diaphragm varies the opening to the inlet manifold according to the vacuum or pressure existing in the crankcase. With a decrease in crankcase vacuum or when the crankcase obtains a positive pressure the diaphragm opens the valve allowing the crankcase vapors to be drawn into the inlet manifold. During conditions of high crankcase vacuum, i.e. low engine speeds, the diaphragm closes the valve and restricts the flow into the inlet manifold, thus preventing a leaning-off of the air/fuel mixture to the cylinders.

Oil Filler Cap: An air filter is incorporated in the oil filler cap. The cap and filter are exchanged only as complete assembly. Replace every 12,000 miles or 12 months.

Breather Control Valve

1. **Testing procedure:** After warming engine to normal operating temperature, run it at idling speed.

2. If the engine speed rises by approximately 200 RPM as the oil filler cap is removed, the valve is functioning correctly.
3. If there is no audible change in engine speed as the oil filler cap is removed, the valve needs servicing.
4. **Servicing procedure:** Disconnect the hoses and renew the valve assembly, or clean, starting by removing the spring clip, then disassembling the valve.
5. Use solvent to clean all metal parts. If there are hardened deposits, immerse parts in boiling water before applying solvent. **Note:** Do not use any abrasives.
6. Use detergent or denatured alcohol to clean the diaphragm.
7. Replace any parts that are worn or damaged.
8. Assemble the valve, making sure the metering needle is in the cruciform guides and the diaphragm is seated correctly.

IGNITION SYSTEM

General Description

The ignition system is wired on the 12-volt positive ground system (prior to 1968), and in addition to the batteries (two 6-volt batteries connected in series) it comprises a combined ignition/starter switch, a fluid-filled HA.12 ignition coil, a Type 25D distributor, suppressed high tension leads, and Champion N5 spark plugs.

Ignition Coil

The ignition coil is mounted on a bracket bolted to the right-hand front engine mounting. To remove for testing, disconnect the switch, contact breaker and H.T. cables, loosen the securing bolts and remove the coil from its mounting bracket.

Static Ignition Timing

See the procedure under this heading in the previous IGNITION SYSTEM chapter, then add the following:
8. When securing the distributor body in its correct position, tighten the clamp plate nut or bolt to the torque tightening figure given in GENERAL DATA, then tighten the clamp plate set bolts.

NOTE: See the illustration in the ENGINE chapter of this section showing the valve timing.

9. If the static ignition timing figure is between T.D.C. and 5° B.T.D.C., or between 5° B.T.D.C. and 10° B.T.D.C., adjust the vacuum control adjusting screw to obtain the correct setting. About 55 clicks of the screw will move the vacuum control barrel one graduation on the scale, and each graduation is equal to about 5° of movement on the moving plate.
10. Check that the rotor is opposite the correct electrode in the distributor cap for No. 1 cylinder.

Distributor

See **MGB Distributor** in the previous IGNITION SYSTEM chapter, then add the following:

Distributor Lubrication

1. **Cam bearing:** lift the rotor off the top of the spindle by pulling it squarely, then add a few drops of thin oil to the cam bearing. Do not remove the securing screw which is exposed; there is clearance between the screw and the inner face of the spindle for the oil to pass.
2. Replace the rotor with its drive lug correctly engaging the spindle slot and push it onto the shaft as far as it will go.
3. **Cam:** Lightly smear the cam with a very small amount of grease or, if this is not available, clean engine oil may be used.
4. **Automatic timing control:** Add a few drops of thin oil through the hole in the contact breaker base through which the cam passes. Do not allow oil to get on or near the contacts. Do not over-oil.

Distributor Removal and Replacement

If it is desired to remove and replace the distributor without disturbing the timing, use the procedure outlined in **Modified Type DM2 Distributors** in the previous IGNITION SYSTEM chapter.

Distributor Examination

Examine all parts for wear, deterioration, thread damage, and the driving dog for indentation. Examine the 'O' ring oil seal (if fitted) on the shank for deterioration. Replace worn or unserviceable parts.

If the clearance between the action plate shaft and the body bush is excessive, the bush should be replaced.

COOLING SYSTEM

Description

The cooling system is pressurized, and a relief valve is incorporated in the radiator filler cap to control the pressure at seven pounds. The remainder of the system remains the same, except as noted below.

Draining the Cooling System

In the event of a drain tap becoming clogged, it is advisable to completely remove the tap from the cylinder block or radiator and then remove any foreign matter. The use of stiff wire to dislodge any obstruction will not always prove effective as the construction of the taps is such as to prevent complete penetration behind them.

NOTE: If a heater is fitted, under no circumstances should draining of the cooling system be resorted to as an alternative to the use of anti-freeze mixture, due to the fact that complete draining of the heater unit by means of the cooling system drain taps is impossible.

To ensure efficient circulation of the coolant and to reduce the formation of scale and sediment in the radiator, the system should be periodically flushed out with clear running water, preferably before putting in anti-freeze solution and again after taking it out.

The water should be allowed to run through until it comes out clear from the taps.

Cold Weather Precautions

Since the cooling system is pressurized, relatively high temperatures are developed in the radiator upper tank. For this reason anti-freeze solutions having an alcohol base are unsuitable owing to their high evaporation rate. Only anti-freeze solution of the ethylene glycol type incorporating the correct type of corrosion inhibitor is suitable for use in the cooling system.

Anti-freeze can remain in the cooling system for two years provided that the specific gravity of the coolant is checked periodically and anti-freeze added as required.

Removing and Replacing the Water Pump

1. Drain the cooling system and remove the radiator (previous COOLING SYSTEM chapter).
2. Remove the generator attachment bolts and take off the generator.
3. Unscrew the four bolts attaching the pump assembly to the

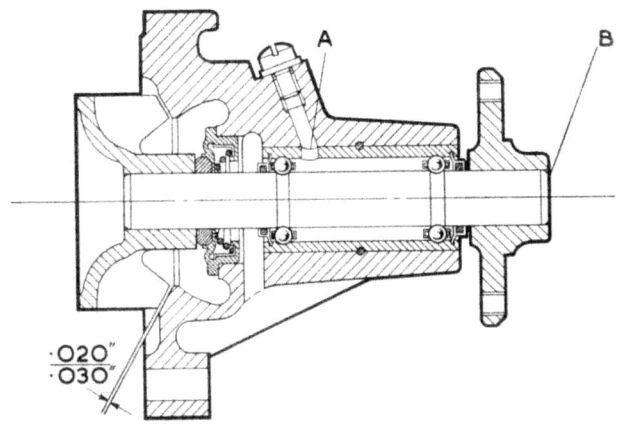

A section through the water pump. When assembled, the hole in the bearing (A) must coincide with the lubricating hole in the water pump, and the face of the hub (B) must be flush with the end of the spindle

Water pump section

front of the cylinder block and remove the fan and pump assembly.

4. Unscrew the four set bolts which attach the fan and pulley to the hub and remove the fan and pulley.

5. Replacement of the fan and pump assembly is a reversal of the above procedure.

FUEL SYSTEM

Description

The fuel system consists of a fuel tank mounted at the rear below the luggage compartment, an S.U. electric Type AUF 300 or HP fuel pump, twin S.U. semi-downdraught HS4 carburetors, and separate air cleaners and silencers. The level of the fuel in the tank is registered electrically by a meter on the instrument panel. See the previous FUEL SYSTEM chapter for procedures, except as noted below.

Fuel Gauge Tank Unit (later cars)
Removal and replacement

Remove the tank gauge locking ring with Service tool 18G 1001 and lift out the gauge assembly and rubber sealing ring. When replacing the gauge unit, a new rubber sealing ring should be fitted to ensure a fuel-tight joint.

Fuel Pump Removal and Replacement

1. The fuel pump is mounted on a bracket secured to the heelboard adjacent to the front mounting right-hand rear spring, and is accessible from beneath the car.
2. Disconnect the ground lead from the batteries and the ground and supply leads from the terminals on the pump.
3. Disconnect the inlet and outlet pipe unions.
4. Remove the two bolts securing the pump bracket to the heelboard.
5. When replacing, reverse the removal procedure.

Carburetor Removal and Replacement

1. Release the spring clips and detach the breather hose between the air cleaner and rocker cover.
2. Disconnect the fuel supply pipe at the rear carburetor or at each carburetor float-chamber.
3. Pull off the overflow pipes.
4. Loosen the bolt and nut securing the mixture and throttle cables respectively and withdraw the cables complete. Detach the throttle return springs.
5. Pull off the rubber connection for the vacuum ignition control pipe from the top of the rear carburetor body.
6. Remove the four nuts securing the carburetor flanges and withdraw the carburetors and air cleaners as an assembly.
7. When replacing, the center throttle return spring end eye is located between the flat washer and the throttle lever. The throttle linkage must be checked, and readjusted if necessary, after replacement.

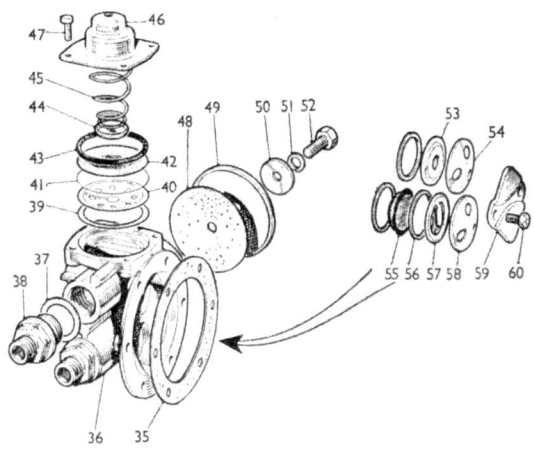

No.	Description
35.	Gasket.
36.	Pump body.
37.	Fibre washer.
38.	Outlet connection.
39.	Sealing washer.
*40.	Diaphragm plate.
41.	Plastic diaphragm barrier.
*42.	Rubber diaphragm.
43.	Rubber 'O' ring.
*44.	Spring end cap.
*45.	Diaphragm spring.
†46.	Delivery flow smoothing device cover.
47.	Set screw.
48.	Gasket
49.	Inlet air bottle cover.
50.	Dished washer.
51.	Spring washer.
52.	Set screw.
53.	Outlet valve.
54.	Valve cap.
55.	Filter.
56.	Sealing washer.
57.	Inlet valve.
58.	Valve cap.
59.	Clamp plate.
60.	Set screw.

† Delivery air bottle (later pumps).

* Early pumps.

S.U. AUF 300 type fuel pump

CLUTCH

WARNING: All B.M.C. cars use NATURAL RUBBER COMPONENTS in their clutch systems, NOT neoprene rubber components as do American makes. Therefore, it is extremely important that Castrol Girling Amber or Crimson Brake Fluid or BRITISH Lockheed Disc Brake Fluid be used in these systems, since they are the only brake fluids compatible with the natural rubber parts. Some American brake fluids are only suitable for all-neoprene rubber parts, and will cause natural rubber parts to swell and deteriorate, leading to eventual rupture.

Clutch Assembly

All components remain the same, except on later cars the release plate is secured directly to the diaphragm and is an integral part of the clutch cover assembly, rather than being retained with straps as on earlier models (both types are interchangeable). **NOTE:** It is extremely important that no load be placed on the clutch release plate drive straps during clutch removal or installation. Even slight damage to the straps may result in the clutch breaking up at high speed.

GEARBOX

Removing the Gearbox

Add the following caution upon performing step (9) under this heading from the previous GEARBOX chapter:

CAUTION: Great care must be taken during the separation of the gearbox from the engine to ensure that no load is placed on the clutch release plate drive straps. Even slight damage to these may result in the clutch breaking up at high speeds.

Dismantling and Assembling the Laygear

The **second-type laygear** has a larger diameter shaft and a pair of caged needle-roller bearings at each end.

Extract the two pairs of needle-roller bearings from the ends of the laygear and the distance tube from the small end.

To assemble the laygear, proceed as follows:

1. Dip the bearings in oil.
2. Hold the laygear in a vise and insert the distance tube and a

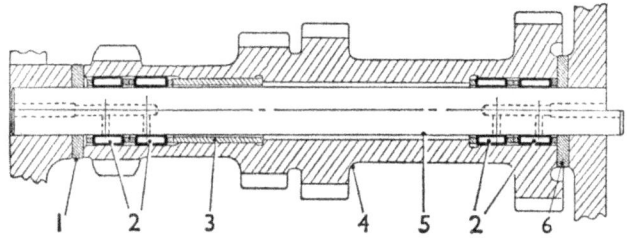

Laygear assembly—second type

1. Thrust washer—small.   4. Laygear.
2. Needle-roller bearing (pair).   5. Layshaft.
3. Distance tube.   6. Thrust washer—large.

Later laygear assembly

pair of bearings at the small end.
3. Insert a pair of bearings at the large end.

Assembling the Third Motion Shaft

Prior to assembling as outlined in the previous GEARBOX chapter, lubricate all contact surfaces with oil and smear the bore of the gears with Molycote, HRL Assembly Lube, or Duckham's Moly Disulphide Grease (max. size 5 microns).

Following step (9) under this heading, check the end-float of the second and third speed gear (see GENERAL DATA and the illustration in the previous GEARBOX chapter). The thrust washers listed under this heading should be used as needed.

Assembling the Gearbox
Step (4) should read as follows:
4. Using Service tool 18G 471, fit the layshaft to the laygear and ensure that the cut-away end of the shaft faces forward.

Fitting the Gearbox Front Cover
The fifth paragraph under this heading should read as follows:

Remove the cover and, using Service tool 18G 134 with adapter 18G 134 N, fit the oil seal so that its lip faces inwards towards the gearbox. Lightly grease and fit a new gasket to the gearbox front face, then fit the centralizer (Service tool 18G 598) to the bore of the front cover and push it in until it is tight. Lightly oil the seal and pass the cover over the first motion shaft, taking particular care not to cut or damage the knife edge of the seal.

OVERDRIVE

Description

The overdrive unit comprises a hydraulically controlled epicyclic gear housed in a casing which is directly attached to an extension at the rear of the gearbox.

The gearbox third motion shaft is extended and carries at its end the inner member of a uni-directional clutch. The outer ring of the clutch is carried in the combined annulus and output shaft.

Also mounted on the third motion shaft are the planet carrier and a freely rotatable sun wheel, and sliding thereon is a cone clutch member the inner lining of which engages the outside of the annulus while the outer lining engages a cast-iron brake ring sandwiched between the main and tail casings.

The cone clutch is held in contact with the annulus by compression springs, thus locking the sun wheel to the annulus so that the entire gear train rotates as a solid unit, giving direct drive. In this condition the drive is taken through the uni-directional clutch. Reverse torque or overrun is taken by the planet wheels, which being locked by the sun wheel, transmit the drive via the planet carrier and third motion shaft.

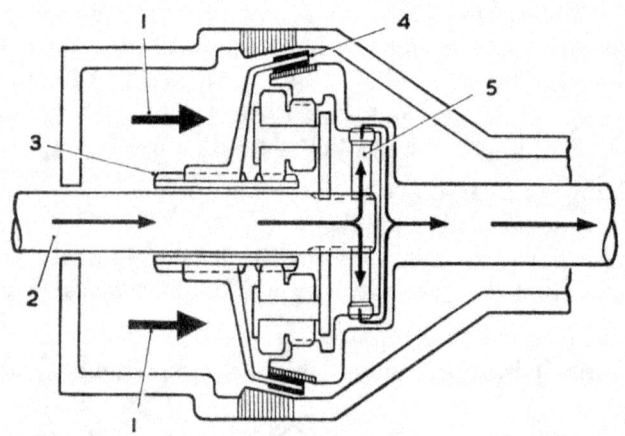

Direct drive

1. Spring pressure.
2. Third motion shaft.
3. Sun wheel.
4. Cone clutch.
5. Uni-directional clutch.

Overdrive operation (direct drive)

Hydraulic pressure produced when overdrive is selected forces two pistons in the unit housing against the cone clutch and overcomes the spring pressure, causing the cone clutch to engage with the stationary brake ring and bring the sun wheel to rest, allowing the annulus to overrun the uni-directional clutch and give an increased speed to the output shaft, i.e. OVERDRIVE.

When changing from overdrive to direct gear, if the accelerator pedal is released, the vacuum switch holds the OVERDRIVE until the engine takes up the drive. If the accelerator pedal is not released, when contact between the cone clutch and brake is broken, the unit still operates momentarily in its overdrive ratio as engine speed and road speed remain unchanged.

When the load on the engine is released it begins to accelerate, speeding up the sun wheel from rest until, just at the instant when its speed synchronizes with the speed of the annulus, the whole unit revolves solidly and the uni-directional clutch takes up the drive once more. The movement of the cone clutch is deliberately slowed down so that the unidirectional clutch is driving before the cone clutch contacts, ensuring a perfectly self-synchronized change.

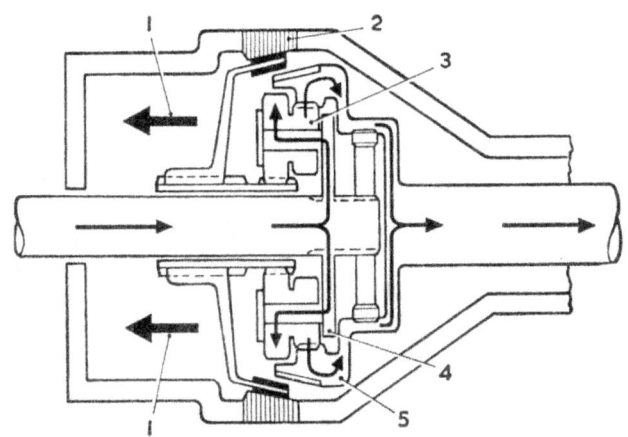

Overdrive engaged

1. Hydraulic pressure.
2. Brake ring.
3. Planet wheel.
4. Planet carrier.
5. Annulus.

Overdrive operation (engaged)

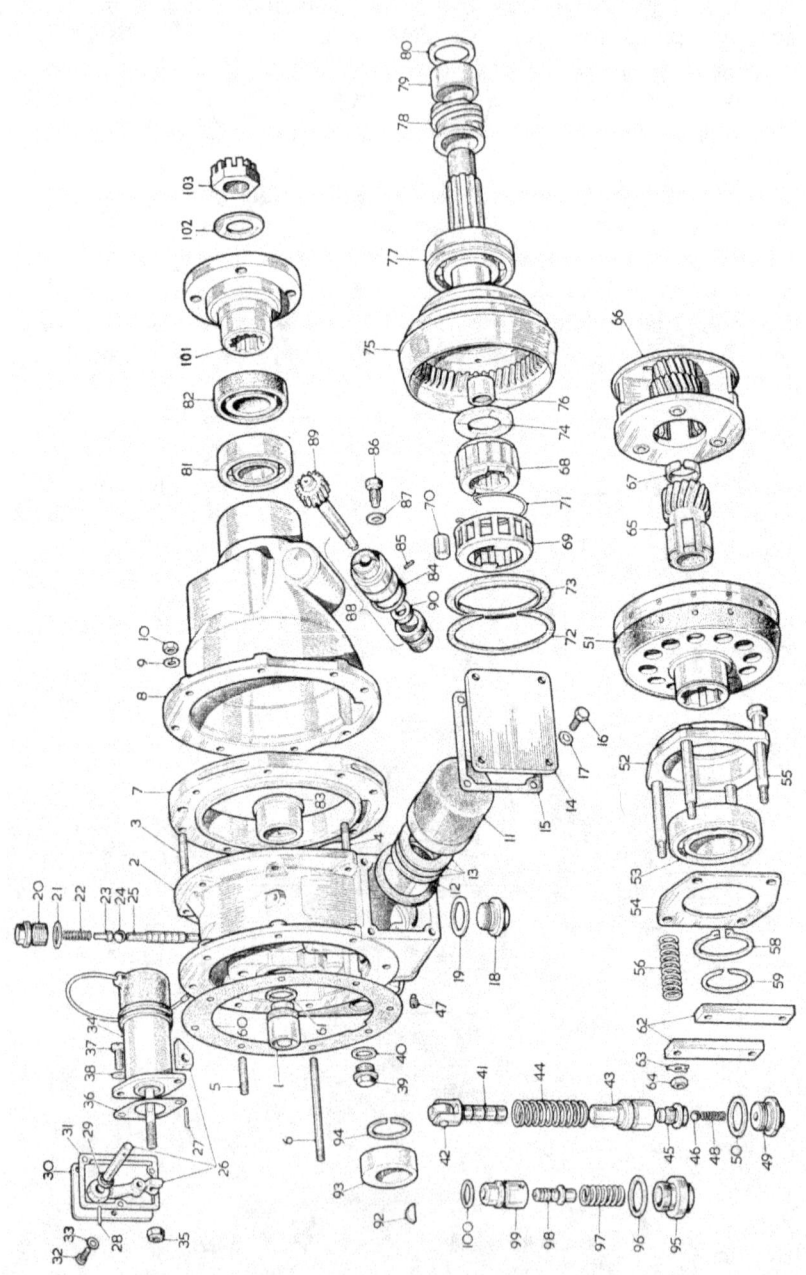

Overdrive components

KEY TO THE OVERDRIVE COMPONENTS

No.	Description
1.	Operating piston.
2.	Main casing assembly.
3.	Stud—main casing to rear casing.
4.	Stud—main casing to rear casing.
5.	Stud—main casing to gearbox adaptor.
6.	Stud—main casing to gearbox adaptor.
7.	Brake ring.
8.	Intermediate casing.
9.	Spring washer.
10.	Nut.
11.	Filter.
12.	Sealing plate.
13.	Magnetic rings.
14.	Side cover-plate.
15.	Joint for cover-plate.
16.	Set screw.
17.	Shakeproof washer.
18.	Drain plug.
19.	Washer for plug.
20.	Plug for operating valve.
21.	Washer for plug.
22.	Spring—operating valve.
23.	Plunger—operating valve.
24.	Steel ball.
25.	Operating valve.
26.	Operating valve lever assembly.
27.	Mills pin.
28.	Mills pin.
29.	'O' ring.
30.	Cover—solenoid.
31.	Joint for cover-plate.
32.	Set screw.
33.	Shakeproof washer.

No.	Description
35.	Self-locking nut.
36.	Joint for solenoid.
37.	Screw for solenoid.
38.	Shakeproof washer.
39.	Plug for solenoid bracket.
40.	Washer for plug.
41.	Pump plunger.
42.	Pin.
43.	Pump body.
44.	Pump plunger spring.
45.	Non-return valve body.
46.	Steel ball.
47.	Screw locating pump body.
48.	Spring—non-return valve.
49.	Plug—non-return valve.
50.	Washer for plug.
51.	Clutch assembly.
52.	Bearing housing.
53.	Bearing—thrust.
54.	Plate—retainer.
55.	Bolt for bearing housing.
56.	Spring—clutch return.
58.	Circlip—bearing retaining.
59.	Snap ring—sun wheel retaining.
60.	Joint for front cover.
61.	'O' ring.
62.	Bridge piece.
63.	Lock washer.
64.	Nut.
65.	Sun wheel assembly.
66.	Planet carrier.
67.	Locating ring—third motion shaft.
68.	Inner member—uni-directional clutch.

No.	Description
70.	Roller—uni-directional clutch.
71.	Spring for clutch.
72.	Snap ring.
73.	Oil thrower.
74.	Thrust bearing.
75.	Annulus assembly.
76.	Bearing—needle-roller.
77.	Bearing—inner.
78.	Speedometer driving gear.
79.	Bush.
80.	Thrust washer.
81.	Bearing.
82.	Oil seal.
83.	Steady bush—third motion shaft.
84.	'O' ring.
85.	Pin.
86.	Locking screw—speedometer bearing.
87.	Washer for locking screw.
88.	Speedometer drive bearing assembly.
89.	Speedometer driven gear.
90.	Oil seal—speedometer bearing.
92.	Key—third motion shaft cam.
93.	Cam—third motion shaft.
94.	Snap ring—third motion shaft.
95.	Plug—relief valve.
96.	Washer for plug.
97.	Spring—relief valve.
98.	Plunger—relief valve.
99.	Body—relief valve.
100.	'O' ring—relief valve.
101.	Flange—coupling.
102.	Washer—flange.
103.	Nut—flange.

Lubrication

The overdrive shares a common oil supply with the gearbox; it is filled and topped up through the gearbox dipstick hole and the oil level is checked with the gearbox dipstick.

Draining: When an overdrive is fitted, remove the overdrive drain plug marked DRAIN and the gearbox drain plug, and drain off the old oil.

Remove the overdrive filter cover-plate and gasket from the left hand side of the unit and withdraw the filter screen, together with the filter seal and magnetic rings. Wash the screen in fuel and clean out the filter housing. Clean the filter seal and remove all deposits from the magnetic rings.

Replace the filter seal (metal surface inwards) and place the magnetic rings in the filter location. Refit the filter, gasket, and cover-plate, replace the drain plugs, and refill with fresh oil. Check the filter cover-plate and drain plugs for leaks.

Guide to Service Diagnosis

1. **Overdrive does not engage:** Insufficient oil in the unit.
2. Solenoid not operating due to fault in electrical system.
3. Solenoid operating lever out of adjustment.
4. Insufficient hydraulic pressure due to pump non-return valve incorrectly seating (probably dirt on ball seat).
5. Insufficient hydraulic pressure due to sticking or worn relief valve.
6. Damaged gears, bearings, or moving parts within the unit requiring removal and inspection of the assembly.

1. **Overdrive does not release: NOTE: Do not attempt to reverse the car or damage may be caused within the overdrive unit.**
2. Fault in electrical control system.
3. Blocked restrictor jet in operating valve.
4. Solenoid operating lever adjustment.
5. Sticking clutch.
6. Damaged parts within the unit necessitating removal and inspection of the assembly.

1. **Clutch slip in overdrive:** As in (1), (3), (4), and (5) in **Overdrive does not engage.**

1. **Clutch slip in reverse or free-wheel condition or overrun:** Solenoid operating lever out of adjustment.
2. Partially blocked restrictor jet in operating valve.
3. Worn clutch linings.

Pump Non-Return Valve

Access to the pump non-return valve is gained through the center cap in the bottom of the main casing (see illustration).

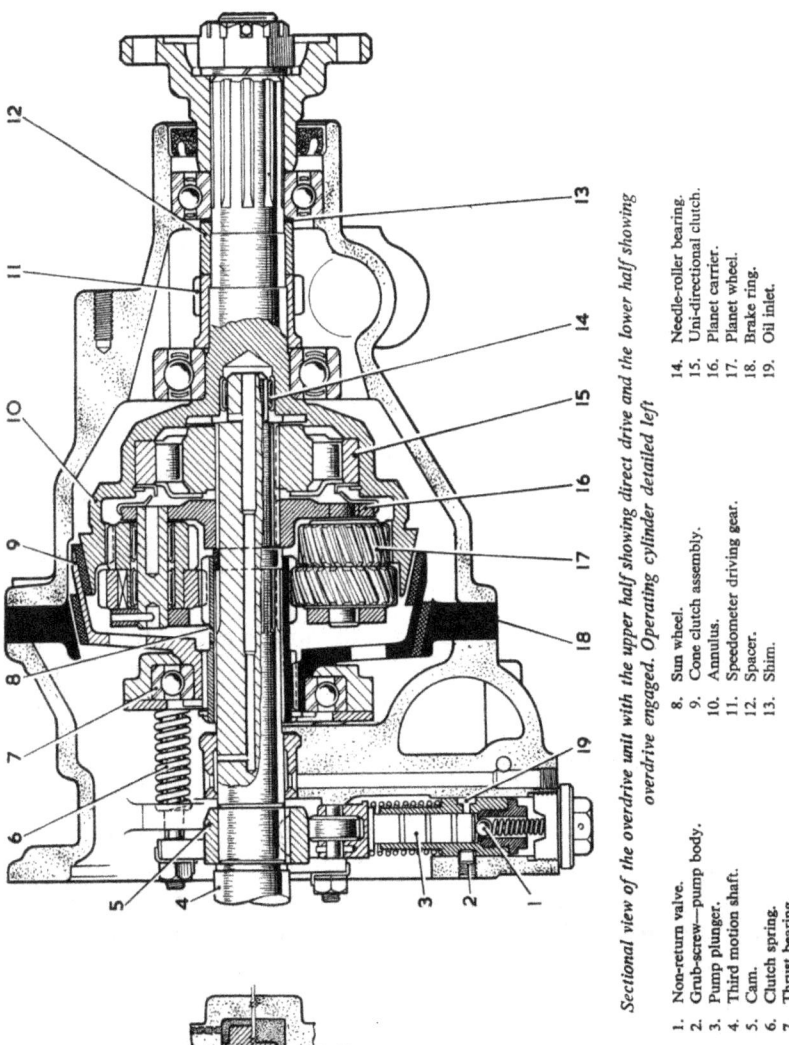

Sectional view of the overdrive unit with the upper half showing direct drive and the lower half showing overdrive engaged. Operating cylinder detailed left

1. Non-return valve.
2. Grub-screw—pump body.
3. Pump plunger.
4. Third motion shaft.
5. Cam.
6. Clutch spring.
7. Thrust bearing.
8. Sun wheel.
9. Cone clutch assembly.
10. Annulus.
11. Speedometer driving gear.
12. Spacer.
13. Shim.
14. Needle-roller bearing.
15. Uni-directional clutch.
16. Planet carrier.
17. Planet wheel.
18. Brake ring.
19. Oil inlet.

Overdrive sectional view

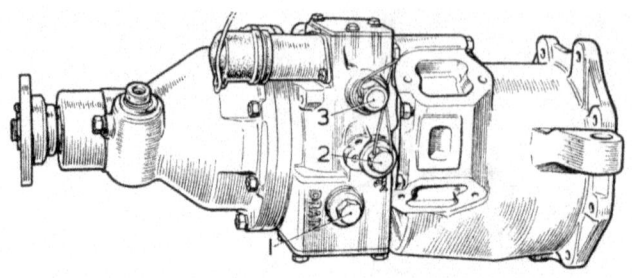

Bottom view of overdrive unit

1. Drain plug.
2. Non-return valve plug.
3. Relief valve plug.

Underside of overdrive unit

1. **Removal:** Remove the engine stay rod from the gearbox adaptor and the stay rod bracket from the rear cross member.
2. Remove the drain plugs and drain off the oil.
3. Unclip the locking wire. Unscrew the valve cap and take out the spring and ball and unscrew the non-return valve body from the pump body.

Inspection: Clean the components and examine the seating for pits, etc. If the ball valve is not seating correctly, the ball should be tapped sharply onto its seat in the non-return valve body, using a soft-metal drift.

Reassembly: Reassembly is the reverse of the above sequence. Position the ball on the spring with petroleum jelly. Ensure that the copper washer between the valve cap and main casing is fitted correctly over the step on the cap.

NOTE: The valve body must be removed from the pump body to reseat the ball valve, otherwise damage may be caused to the pump.

Relief Valve

Access to the relief valve is gained through the right-hand cap in the bottom of the main casing (see illustration).

1. **Removal:** Remove the engine stay rod from the gearbox adaptor and the stay rod bracket from the rear cross-member.
2. Remove the drain plugs and drain off the oil.
3. Unclip the locking wire. Unscrew the valve cap and remove the spring and piston.
4. Remove the relief valve body with circlip pliers, taking care

not to damage the piston bore.

5. **Reassembly:** This is the reverse of the above sequence. Ensure that the copper washer between the cap and main casing is fitted correctly over the step on the cap.

Hydraulic Lever Setting

1. The setting of the operating lever can be checked by means of a hole in the lever accessible from under the car after removal of the cover-plate on the right-hand side of the unit.
2. The controls are set correctly when a 3/16 in. (4.76 mm.) diameter rod can be passed through the hole in the lever into the hole in the casing with the solenoid energized, i.e. with the ignition switched ON, HIGH gear engaged, and the fascia switch in the OVERDRIVE position.
3. If the solenoid operates but does not move the setting lever far enough to allow the rod to be inserted, the solenoid plunger must be adjusted as follows:
4. Screw the self-locking nut on the plunger in or out, with the plunger pushed into the solenoid as far as it will go. The plunger must be held against rotation with a spanner (wrench) on two flats on the spindle. The operating lever fork should just contact the nut with the 3/16 in. (4.76 mm.) rod in position.

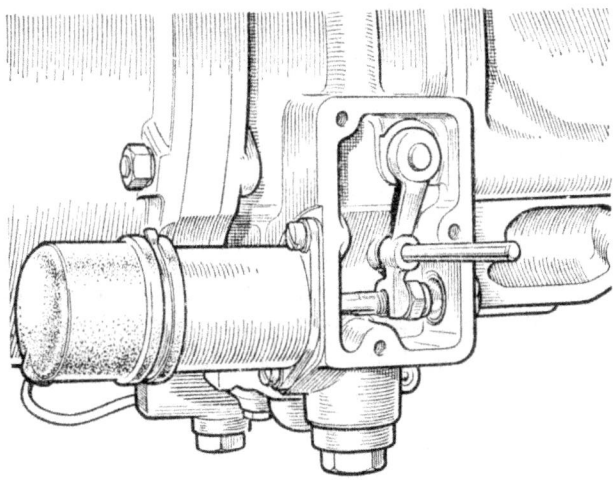

Align the operating lever to check the adjustment of the operating plunger

Hydraulic lever setting

5. Operate the overdrive several times and check that the setting rod can be inserted and that the solenoid current does not exceed 2 amperes.

6. If the current is maintained at about 17 amperes, it indicates that the solenoid plunger is not moving far enough to switch from the operating to the holding coil; the plunger must therefore be readjusted.

7. A new plunger must be fitted with a new solenoid. It will be necessary to check the setting for correct valve operation after replacement.

Operating Valve

1. Access may be gained to the operating valve after removing the gear selector remote control assembly from inside the car (see the next procedure, **Removing and Replacing**).

2. Having gained access, unscrew the plug and remove the spring and plunger. The ball valve will then be seen inside the valve chamber. The ball should be lifted 1/32 in.(.8 mm.) off its seat when the solenoid is operated.

3. If the ball does not lift, the fault lies in the control mechanism (see the previous procedure, **Hydraulic Lever Setting**).

4. Remove the ball with a magnet and pull out the valve, using a piece of 1/8 in. (3.175 mm.) dia. wire, taking care not to damage the seating at the top of the valve. Near the bottom of the valve will be seen a small hole breaking through the center drilling; this is the jet for restricting the exhaust of oil from the operating cylinders. Check the bore of the operating valve with a 1/8 in. (3.175 mm.) dia. drill and blow out the jet.

5. If the ball valve is not seating correctly the ball should be tapped sharply onto its seat in the casing, using a soft-metal drift.

6. If the unit fails to operate and the ball valve is seating and lifting correctly, check that the pump is operating as follows:

7. Jack up the rear wheels, then with the engine idling and the valve plug removed, engage top gear. Watch for oil being pumped into the valve chamber. If none appears, then the pump is not functioning.

8. Possible causes of trouble are:
  (a) Failure of the non-return valve due to foreign matter on the seat or to a broken valve spring.
  (b) Breakage of the spring holding the pump plunger in contact with the cam.

9. **Testing Oil Pressure:** Remove the operating valve plug, fit an adaptor (Service tool 18G 251D) in its place, and connect up a pressure gauge. Jack up the rear wheels and then with the

engine idling engage top gear. Operate the overdrive solenoid; a pressure of 540 to 560 psi (37.97 to 39.37 kg./cm.^{2}) should be recorded.

Removing and Replacing

To dismantle the overdrive further than already described necessitates removing the unit from the car.

It is not possible to lift out the overdrive alone from the car; The engine, gearbox, and overdrive must be removed complete.

1. **Removal:** Prepare the engine for removal from the car (see ENGINE chapter of the previous section), and hold the engine with lifting equipment.
2. Remove the retainer and pull the gear lever grommet clear of the remote control cover. Release the circlip and withdraw the gear lever from its housing.
3. Withdraw the four screws securing the speaker panel and remove the panel. Pull back the tunnel carpet and remove the gearbox remote control cover.
4. Pull the solenoid wire from the snap connector and disconnect the gear switch wires.
5. Drain the oil from the gearbox and overdrive.
6. Disconnect and remove the propeller shaft as detailed (see PROPELLER SHAFT chapter in this section), then disconnect the speedometer pinion drive.
7. Disconnect the clutch slave cylinder push-rod from the clutch withdrawal lever and the slave cylinder from the clutch housing. Tie the cylinder clear of the gearbox.
8. Remove the screws holding the rear cross-member to the body and lower the engine and gearbox until the gearbox rests on the fixed body cross-member.
9. Release the engine stay-rod bracket from the rear cross-member and remove the four nuts and washers securing the gearbox rear rubber mountings to the cross-member. Withdraw the rear cross-member from the body.
10. Ease the assembly forward until it is clear of the fixed body cross-member, then tilt the assembly and lift it from the car.
11. **Replacement:** Replacement is a reversal of the removal procedure. After refitting the overdrive, refill with fresh oil.

Drive Shaft Bearings and Seal

1. **Removal:** The drive shaft front bearing must be drawn from the shaft with a suitable puller.
2. The oil seal may be removed with the overdrive in position in the car after removing the propeller shaft and drive flange.

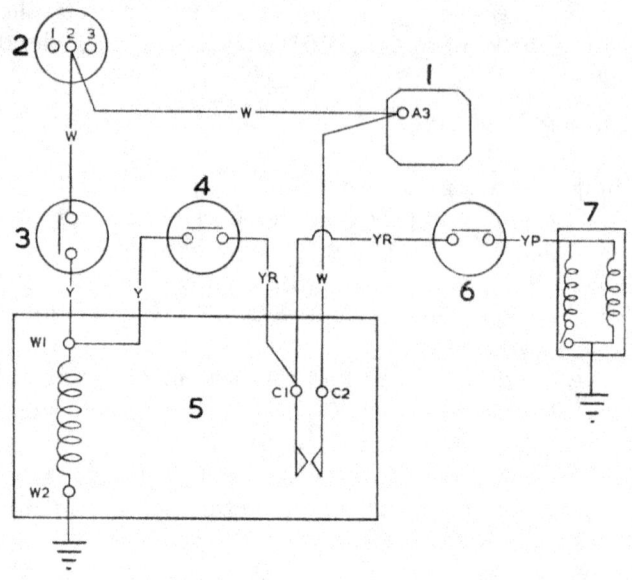

Diagram of the overdrive electrical circuit

1. Fuse block.
2. Ignition switch.
3. Driver's switch.
4. Vacuum switch.
5. Relay.
6. Gearbox switch.
7. Solenoid.

CABLE COLOUR CODE

When a cable has two colour code letters the first denotes the main colour and the second denotes the tracer colour.

P. Purple. R. Red. W. White. Y. Yellow.

Overdrive electrical circuit

3. The rear bearing should be pressed from its seating with a suitable spigot.

4. **Replacement:** A press should be used when replacing the bearings. Fit a new oil seal.

Overdrive Relay System

Description: Engagement of overdrive is controlled electrically through a manually operated toggle switch. The circuit is shown in the illustration and includes the following components:

1. **Relay:** An electro-magnetic switch used with item (2) to

enable an interlocking safeguard to be incorporated against changing out of overdrive with the throttle closed.

2. **Throttle switch:** A vacuum-operated switch to override the toggle switch under closed throttle conditions.

3. **Gear switch:** A small plunger-operated switch allowing overdrive to be engaged only in the two highest forward gear positions.

4. **Solenoid unit:** An electro-magnetic actuator to engage the overdrive mechanism by opening the hydraulic control valve.

Operation: When the driver engages OVERDRIVE by closing the contacts of the toggle switch, current is fed by way of the ignition switch and fuse unit supply terminal **A3** to energize the relay operating coil. Closure of the relay contacts connects terminal **A3** to the gear switch and, provided third or top gear is engaged, will energize the solenoid unit and effect a change from direct drive to overdrive.

Change from overdrive to direct drive is effected by selecting a low gear (when the gear switch contact will open) or by moving the toggle switch to NORMAL with the throttle open (when the vacuum will open).

If effected with the throttle closed (high manifold vacuum) the vacuum switch will over-ride the toggle switch, delaying the change until the engine takes up the drive.

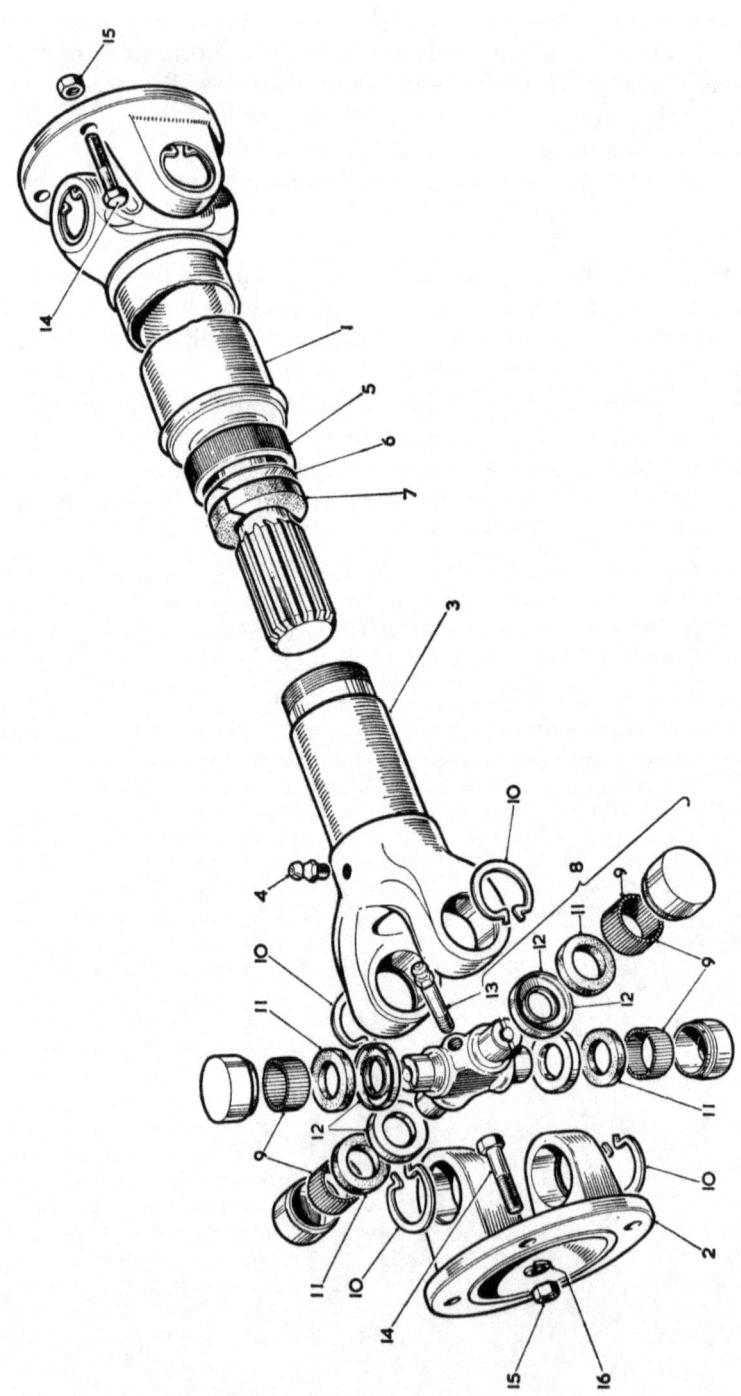

Propeller shaft components

KEY TO THE PROPELLER SHAFT COMPONENTS

No.	Description	No.	Description
1.	Shaft assembly—propeller.	9.	Bearing assembly—needle.
2.	Flange yoke.	10.	Circlip.
3.	Sleeve assembly—yoke.	11.	Gasket.
4.	Lubricator.	12.	Retainer—gasket.
5.	Cap—dust.	13.	Lubricator—journal.
6.	Washer—dust cap (steel).	14.	Bolt—shaft to pinion flange (front and rear).
7.	Washer—dust cap (cork).	15.	Nut for bolt.
8.	Journal assembly.	16.	Washer—spring—for front bolt.

PROPELLER SHAFT

General Description

The propeller shaft and universal joints are of the Hardy Spicer type with needle-roller bearings in the universal joints.

The rear end of the shaft is flanged and carries the rear universal joint flange yoke. The front end of the shaft is splined and engages a sleeve and yoke assembly. In the assembled condition a dust cap, steel washer, and cork washer seal the end of the sleeve and the sliding joint.

Each universal joint is made up of a spider and four gaskets, retainers, and needle bearing assemblies. Each needle bearing assembly is retained in its yoke by a circlip.

The yoke flanges are secured to the pinion and gearbox flanges respectively with eight bolts, springs, washers, and Aerotight or Nyloc nuts.

Removing and Replacing the Propeller Shaft

1. Mark the yoke flanges and the gearbox and rear axle flanges to assist in refitting them in their original positions. **This is most important.**
2. Remove the nuts, washers, and bolts securing the flanges and lower the propeller shaft.
3. Replacement is a reversal of the removal sequence, but be sure that the joint faces of the flanges are perfectly smooth and clean and that they are correctly aligned with the gearbox and rear axle flanges.

Dismantling the Propeller Shaft

Instructions pertaining to this procedure are in the preceding PROPELLER SHAFT chapter under this heading. However, prior to these instructions, unscrew the dust cap from the sleeve and slide the sleeve off the shaft. Remove the steel and cork washers.

Following the completion of the instructions in the preceding PROPELLER SHAFT chapter under this heading, remove the gaskets and their retainers from the spider journals.

Sealed Type Propeller Shaft

Dismantle as detailed in the preceding PROPELLER SHAFT chapter, except that no lubricators need to be removed. Then examine the shaft and check it for wear as previously detailed.

When reassembling the journals, it is of extreme importance that the operation be carried out under absolutely clean, dust-free conditions.

1. Fill the reservoir holes in the journal spider with the rec-

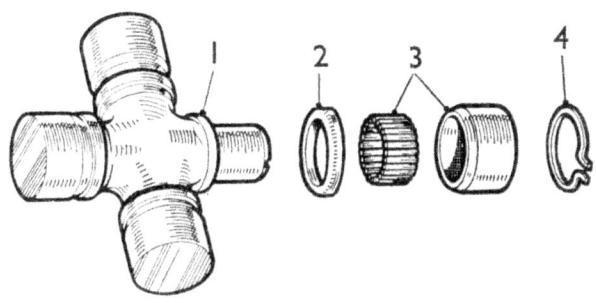

A universal joint bearing—sealed type
1. Journal spider. 3. Needle rollers and bearing.
2. Rubber seal.   4. Circlip.

Sealed type bearing

ommended grease, taking care to exclude all air pockets. Fill each bearing assembly with grease to a depth of $1/8$ in. (3.175 mm.).
2. Fit new seals to the spider journals and insert the spider into the flange yoke, tilting it to engage in the yoke bores.
3. Fit a bearing assembly into the yoke bore in the bottom position, then using a soft-nosed drift slightly smaller in diameter than the hole in the yoke, tap it into the yoke bore until it is possible to fit the circlip. Repeat this operation for the other three bearings starting opposite the bearing first fitted.
4. After assembly, carefully remove all surplus grease with a soft cloth. If the bearing appears to bind, tap lightly with a wooden mallet; this will relieve any pressure of the bearing on the ends of the journals.

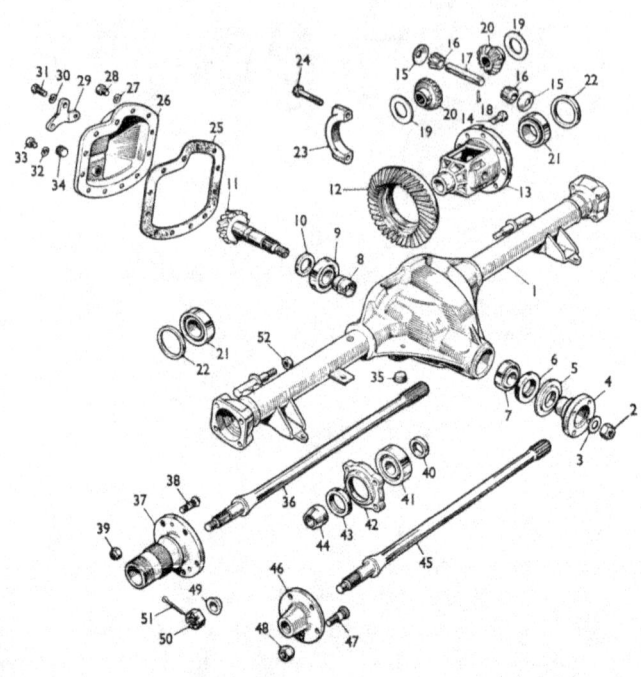

No.	Description	No.	Description	No.	Description	
1.	Case assembly	18.	Roll-pin.	35.	Drain plug.	
2.	Nut.	19.	Thrust washer.	36.	Axle shaft.	
3.	Plain washer.	20.	Differential wheels.	37.	Driving flange.	Wire wheels only.
4.	Universal joint flange.	21.	Differential bearing.	38.	Stud.	
5.	Dust cover.	22.	Distance collars.	39.	Nut.	
6.	Oil seal.	23.	Bearing cap.	40.	Bearing spacer.	
7.	Outer pinion bearing.	24.	Bolt.	41.	Bearing.	
8.	Bearing spacer.	25.	Joint washer.	42.	Bearing hub cap.	
9.	Inner pinion bearing.	26.	Axle case cover.	43.	Oil seal.	
10.	Pinion thrust washer.	27.	Spring washer.	44.	Oil seal collar.	
11.	Pinion.	28.	Set screws.	45.	Axle shaft.	
12.	Crown wheel.	29.	Compensating lever bracket.	46.	Driving flange.	Disc wheels only.
13.	Differential cage.	30.	Spring washer.	47.	Wheel stud.	
14.	Bolt.	31.	Set screw.	48.	Wheel nut.	
15.	Thrust washer.	32.	Spring washer.	49.	Axle shaft collar.	
16.	Differential pinions.	33.	Set screw.	50.	Axle shaft nut.	
17.	Pinion pin.	34.	Filler and level plug.	51.	Split pin.	

Semi-floating type rear axle components

REAR AXLE

Lubrication
Oil level: Check the level, and top up if necessary. The filler plug is located on the rear of the axle and also serves as an oil level indicator. After topping up allow time for any surplus oil to run out. This is most important; if the axle is overfilled, the oil may leak through to the brake linings and lessen their efficiency.

NOTE: It is essential that only Hypoid oil be used in the rear axle.

Draining: The most suitable time for draining is after a long journey while the oil is still warm. Clean the drain plug before it is replaced and tightened. Refill the axle with fresh oil.

Removing and Replacing a Brake Drum and Axle Shaft
Disc wheels: Follow the procedures (1) through (5) under this heading in the previous REAR AXLE chapter, then add the following:

6. Withdraw the axle shaft by gripping the flange or carefully prising it with a screwdriver. Note the gasket and bearing spacer between the axle flange and the hub (not illustrated).

7. **Replacing:** Reverse the above to replace the brake drum and axle shaft.

1. **Wire wheels:** Unscrew the four nuts securing the drum to the hub and tap the drum from the hub. It may be necessary to slacken off the brake adjustment to free the drum.

2. Unscrew the countersunk Phillips screw securing the hub extension flange to the hub.

3. Withdraw the hub extension and axle shaft. The extension flange has two threaded holes so that the shaft can be pulled out if it is tight. **Note the rubber ring oil seal between the hub extension flange and the hub (not illustrated).**

4. To replace the shaft and drum reverse the above sequence of operations.

Semi-Floating Type Rear Axle
General Description
The rear axle assembly is of the semi-floating type. Adjustment to the bearing is by means of spacers, as also is the position of the pinion in relation to the crown wheel and the backlash between the gears.

Lubrication
Oil level and draining instructions: See the preceding outline under these headings in this section.

Axle Unit

Removing and Refitting the Axle: Use the procedure under this heading in the previous REAR AXLE chapter.

Removing and Replacing Brake-drum and Axle Shaft: Follow procedures (1) through (4) under this heading in the previous REAR AXLE chapter, then add the following:

5. Remove the split pin, unscrew the slotted axle shaft nuts and withdraw the hub.
6. Remove the clevis pin securing the brake cable to the operating lever, and disconnect the hydraulic pipe from the wheel cylinder.
7. Remove the backplate.
8. Remove the oil seal housing and cone from the axle shaft.
9. Remove the axle shaft using impulse extractor 18G 284 with adaptor 18G 284 D and press the bearing from the shaft.

1. **Replacing:** Repack the bearings with grease before refitting.
2. Reverse the removal procedure, using tool 18G 1067 to drift the axle shaft into position.
3. Lubricate and fit a new seal, oil lip facing inwards.
4. Refit the seal housing and cone.
5. Tighten the axle nut shaft to the torque figure given in GENERAL DATA.
6. Bleed and adjust the brakes (see BRAKING SYSTEM chapter).

Renewing the Pinion Oil Seal

1. **Removal:** Mark the propeller shaft and pinion driving flanges so that they may be replaced in the same relative positions, and disconnect the propeller shaft.
2. Mark the pinion nut, pinion, and flange.
3. Hold the flange with wrench 18G 34 A and remove the nut and washer. Withdraw the flange by tapping it lightly with a leather hammer.
4. Remove the oil seal from the casing and press a new one into the casing with the lip facing inwards. Lubricate the seal and replace the driving flange, taking care not to damage the lip of the oil seal.
5. **NOTE: Align the marks on the pinion nut, pinion, and flange when refitting and tighten to give a torque figure of approximately 135 to 145 ft. lbs. (19 to 20 kg. m.).**
6. Reconnect the propeller shaft flanges after aligning the locating marks.

REAR ROAD SPRINGS

CAUTION: Note the part under IMPORTANT in the previous REAR ROAD SPRINGS chapter before proceeding.

Removal
1. Remove the road wheel adjacent to the spring to be removed.
2. Raise and support the body and support the axle with a hydraulic jack to enable the axle to be lowered to relieve the tension on the spring.
3. Disconnect the shock absorber link from its bracket and the rebound strap from the rebound spindle.
4. Remove the nuts and spring washers from the eyebolt and shackle plate pin alternately until the plate and pins are free of the spring and the mounting bracket.
5. Using a suitable drift, tap each shackle plate pin alternately until the plate and pins are free of the spring and the mounting bracket.
6. Withdraw the eyebolt from the front of the spring.
7. From the two U-clips remove the locknuts and nuts. Retain the shock absorber bracket, locating plate, and pad which will fall from the under side of the spring.
8. Remove the spring and retain the upper locating plate, pad, pedestal and U-clips.

Replacement
1. Place the front of the spring in its bracket and locate it with the front eyebolt.
2. Fit the shackle plate and pins to the rear eye and the body bracket.
3. Fit the upper locating plate and pad to the spring and locate the hole in the axle spring seat over the head of the center-bolt.
4. Place the pedestal over the axle, fit the lower pad, locating plate, and shock absorber bracket, then pass the U-clips over the axle and through the locating plates. Secure the U-clips with the nuts and locknuts.
5. Refit the road wheel, remove the axle and body supports, and refit the washers and nuts to the front eyebolt and the shackle plate, nuts, and washers to the rear shackle plate pins.
6. Refit the shock absorber link and rebound strap.

Dismantling
1. Remove the rear springs as previously detailed.
2. Straighten the ends of the clips on the third and fourth spring leaves.
3. Support the spring in a vise with the top and bottom leaves

against the vise jaws and the center-bolt just clear of the jaws.
4. Remove the locknut and nut from the center-bolt and withdraw the center-bolt and distance piece from the spring.
5. Slowly open the vise to relieve the tension in the spring leaves and remove the leaves from the vise.
6. Remove the two rubber bushes from the rear eye of the main leaf and then press out the Silentbloc bush from the front eye.
7. Remove and discard the spring clip rivets and clips.
8. Clean and examine each leaf for signs of cracks or fractures, particularly around the center-bolt holes.
9. Before assembly, cover each leaf with Shell Ensis 260 Fluid.

Reassembly
1. Press a new Silentbloc bush into the main leaf front eye and ensure that the outer bush is perfectly central in the eye.
2. Rivet new spring clips to the third and fourth leaves.
3. Use a tapered mandrel having the same maximum diameter as the center-bolt to align the holes in the spring leaves and assemble the leaves. The longest half of the spring faces the rear of the car.
4. Keep the leaves aligned and slowly compress them in a vise.
5. Remove the mandrel and assemble the distance piece and center-bolt. Secure the center-bolt with its nut and locknut.
6. Align the side of the spring and bend the spring clips over the main leaf.

STEERING GEAR

Lubrication
Early cars: Give the lubricating nipple on the steering gear housing up to 10 strokes of the oil gun, but no more. On R.H.D. cars the nipple is accessible from above the steering gearbox and on L.H.D. cars from below the car under the radiator.

Removing and Replacing the Steering Wheel
Release the three grub screws and remove the horn-button hub center. Then follow the instructions under this heading in the previous STEERING GEAR chapter. Note: Tighten the nut to a torque wrench setting of 42 ft. lbs. (5.8 kg. m.).

Steering-Column Removal and Replacement
1. Withdraw the clamping bolt and nut securing the universal joint to the inner steering-column.
2. Unscrew the four set screws from the direction indicator cowling and remove the indicator. Withdraw the clamping bolts, nuts, and spring and plain washers from the two brackets which support the column and remove the column complete.
4. **NOTE: Disconnect the wiring from the column lock when fitted and remove the ignition and auxiliary circuit fuses.**
5. **Bush removal:** Remove the steering wheel and column, then withdraw the inner column. Prise out the felt bush and pull out the polythene bush.
6. **Replacement:** Soak a new felt bush in graphite oil before fitting. To replace, reverse the removal procedure.

Rack and Pinion Removal and Replacement
1. Support the front end of the car by placing jacks beneath the lower suspension arm spring pans, then remove the road wheels.
2. Remove the locknuts and drive the tie-rod ball pins from the steering-arms. Turn the steering onto the left lock (R.H.D. cars) or right lock (L.H.D. cars).
3. Withdraw the clamping nut and bolt from the universal joint on the pinion shaft.
4. Remove the nuts and bolts securing the steering rack to the front suspension cross-member, noting that the front bolts are fitted with self-locking nuts, and packing shims may be found between the rack and the frame brackets.
5. The steering assembly can now be withdrawn downwards.
6. **Replacement:** The steering gear is assembled to the car by reversing the above procedure, although special attention should be given to the instructions under **Steering Column Alignment.**

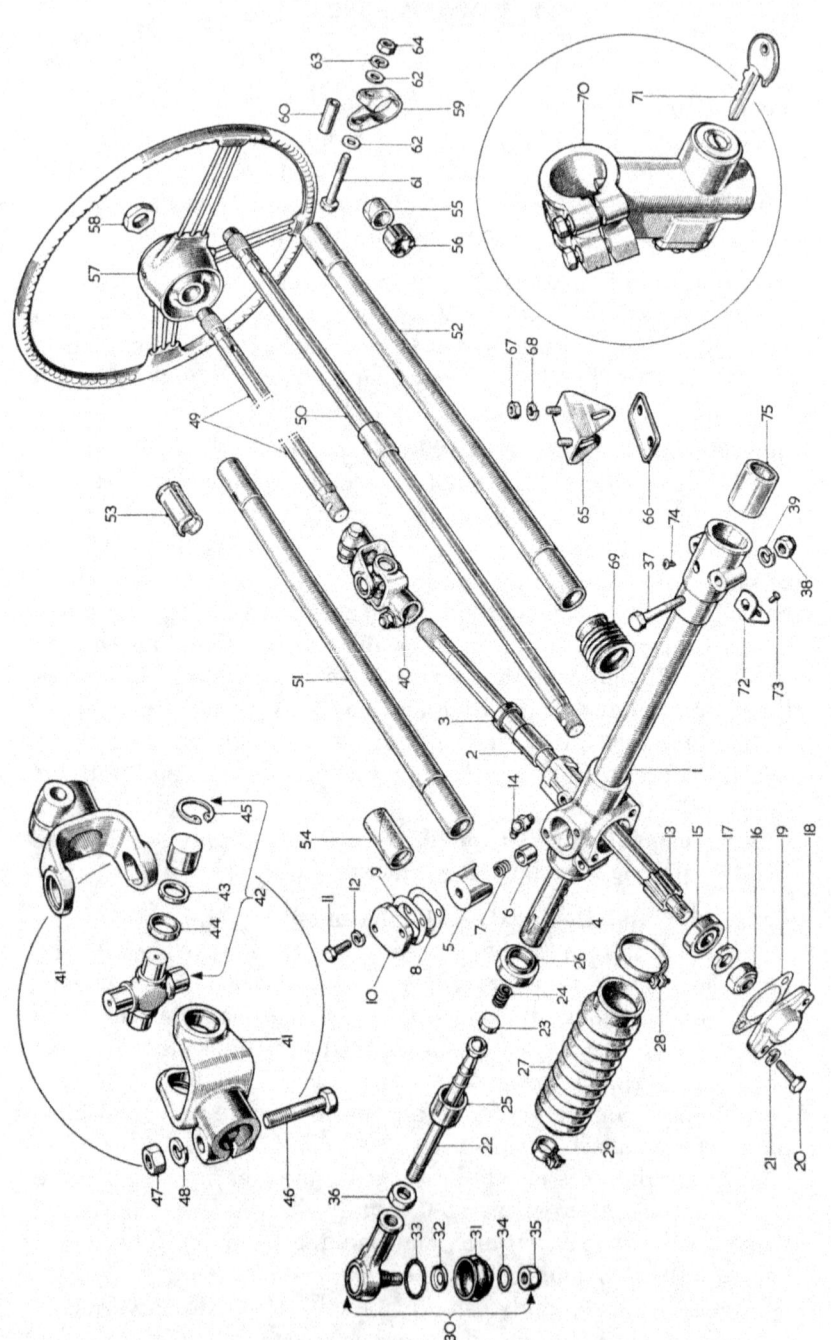

Steering gear components

KEY TO THE STEERING GEAR COMPONENTS

No.	Description
1.	Housing assembly.
2.	Bush—pinion.
3.	Seal—oil.
4.	Rack.
5.	Yoke—rack support.
6.	Pad—damper.
7.	Spring—damper pad.
8.	Shim—cover-plate.
9.	Joint—cover-plate.
10.	Plate—cover—yoke.
11.	Bolt—cover-plate.
12.	Washer—spring—bolt.
13.	Pinion.
14.	Lubricator—pinion shaft.
15.	Bearing—ball—pinion.
16.	Nut—pinion bearing.
17.	Washer—spring—nut.
18.	Cover—end.
19.	Joint—end cover.
20.	Bolt—end cover.
21.	Washer—spring—bolt.
22.	Rod—tie.
23.	Seat—ball.
24.	Spring—thrust—ball seat.
25.	Housing—ball.
26.	Locknut—ball housing.
27.	Seal—rack.
28.	Clip—inner—seal.
29.	Clip—outer—seal.
30.	Socket assembly—ball.
31.	Boot.
32.	Retainer—boot.
33.	Spring—garter.
34.	Washer—boot.
35.	Nut—ball pin.
36.	Locknut.
37.	Bolt—track to bracket.
38.	Nut—bolt.
39.	Washer—spring.
40.	Joint—universal—steering-column.
41.	Yoke.
42.	Journal—assembly.
43.	Joint—journal.
44.	Retainer—joint.
45.	Circlip.
46.	Bolt—universal joint.
47.	Nut—bolt.
48.	Washer—spring—nut.
49.	Column assembly—inner.
50.	Column assembly—inner—R.H.D.
51.	Tube—column—outer.
52.	Tube—column—outer—R.H.D.
53.	Bearing—upper—column.
54.	Bearing—lower—column.
55.	Bush (felt) ⎱ When steering lock
56.	Clip—retaining ⎰ is fitted.
57.	Wheel—steering.
58.	Nut—steering-wheel.
59.	Clamp—steering-column.
60.	Distance piece.
61.	Bolt—clamp.
62.	Washer—plain—clamp bolt.
63.	Washer—spring—clamp bolt.
64.	Nut—bolt.
65.	Bracket—lower—steering-column.
66.	Plate—blanking—bracket.
67.	Nut—bracket to body.
68.	Washer—spring—nut.
69.	Excluder—draught—column to bulkhead.
70.	Lock assembly—steering and ignition.
71.	Key.
72.	Shim—cross-member bracket.
73.	Rivet.
74.	Screw—retaining bush.
75.	Bush—rack housing.

383

Steering-Column Alignment

Set the steering in the straight-ahead position and check that the trafficator cancellation stud at the top of the column is in the correct angular position when the serrations on the coupling and column are aligned. Then follow the procedure outlined under this heading in the previous STEERING GEAR chapter.

Nylon-seated Ball Joints

Use the procedure outlined under this heading in the previous STEERING GEAR chapter, and note the following:

Early production cars are fitted with a plain washer under the steering ball joint nut.

Later production cars are fitted with steering levers having a reduced diameter taper hole. These levers have a longer ball joint pin, are fitted with a thicker nut and have no plain washer.

When early production cars with a plain washer under the steering ball joint nut are fitted with service steering levers, the plain washer must not be replaced.

Steering Lock Ignition Switch

On cars fitted with the lock a sleeve integral with the inner column is slotted to permit engagement of the lock tongue; the outer column is also slotted to allow the lock tongue to pass through. A hole drilled in the upper surface of the outer column locates the steering lock bracket. The bracket is secured by two bolts each waisted below the head to permit removal of the heads by shear action during assembly.

To remove the lock, disconnect the battery and the ignition/starter switch connection and turn the lock setting to GARAGE to unlock the steering. Free the steering-column assembly as described in **Steering-Column Removal and Replacement** and remove the lock securing bolts with an easy-out.

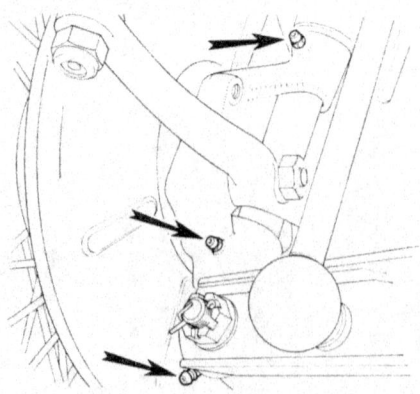

Steering gear lubrication

FRONT SUSPENSION

Removing the Hub (Lockheed Disc Braked Cars)
Follow instructions (1) through (6) under **LOCKHEED DISC BRAKED CARS — Removing and Dismantling a Front Hub** in the previous FRONT SUSPENSION chapter, then continue as follows:
7. From the hub withdraw the bearing retaining washer, outer bearings, shims, spacer, inner bearing, oil seal collar, and oil seal.
8. The outer bearing races should be left in the hub unless they are to be renewed.

Bearing Inspection
1. Wash the bearings in solvent and thoroughly dry them in an air blast or with a non-fluffy cloth.
2. Examine the rollers for chips, pitting, or other damage and for security in their cages. Examine also the inner and outer races. Replace any suspect or damaged bearings.
3. Immerse the bearings in mineral oil after examination.

Replacing the Hub
1. If the bearing outer races have been removed, refit the new ones by pressing them into the hub.
2. Fill each bearing with grease, ensuring a small protrusion either side of the bearing. Fill the cavity between the bearing and the oil seal, and lightly smear the spacer with grease. DO NOT fill the cavity between the bearings or the grease-retaining cap with grease.
3. Fit the inner bearing to its race, and the collar and seal to the hub, position the spacer and outer bearing, then assemble the hub to the axle.

Bearing Adjustment
Adjust the hub bearings to obtain the correct end-float of between .002 and .004 in. (.05 and .10 mm.) as follows:
1. Assemble the hub without the shims and mount the assembly on the axle. Fit the retaining washer and nut and tighten the nut until the bearings bind. This will pull the outer races fully against their locating flanges inside the hub.
2. Remove the nut and washer and pull out the roller race of the outer bearing. Insert sufficient shims to produce an excessive end float and note the thickness of shims used. Refit the bearing, washer, and nut and tighten the nut.
3. Using a dial indicator, measure accurately the end-float in the bearings. Remove the nut, washer, and outer bearing, and

reduce the number of shims to produce the required end-float. The shims are available in thicknesses of .003 in. (.076 mm.), .005 in. (.127 mm.), and .010 in. (.254 mm.).
4. Replace the bearing, washer, and nut, then tighten the nut to a torque loading of between 40 and 70 ft. lb. (5.3 and 9.6 kg. m.). Latitude for the torque wrench reading is given so that the nut can be tightened sufficiently to align a slot in the nut with the hole in the axle. Fit a new split pin.
5. Refit the hub caps.

Coil Spring Removal and Replacement

Each coil spring is located between a spring pan bolted to the lower wishbone arms and a spigot bolted to the underside of the cross-member assembly.
1. **Removal:** Fit a spring compressor (Service tool 18G 693) to the lower wishbone arms and compress the spring.
2. Remove the anti-roll bar link, if fitted, and the bolts securing the springpan to the wishbone arms.
3. Unscrew the spring compressor to release the tension in the spring, then remove the spring pan and spring.
4. **Replacement:** Reverse the removal sequence.

Swivel Axle Description

The swivel axles work on the swivel pins, which are supported at their upper ends by the trunnion links, which are bolted to the shock absorber arms, and at their lower ends by the fulcrum pins, which connect with the lower wishbone arms.

The center portion of the pins are protected by upper and lower spring-loaded dust shields.

The steering levers and the disc brake dust plates are bolted to the inside of the swivel axles.

Removing and Dismantling Swivel Axles

To remove the swivel axles, jack up and support the car, then proceed as follows:
1. Remove the front road wheel.
2. Detach the brake calliper and support it clear of the hub.
3. Remove the hub and brake disc assembly as previously described.
4. Remove the steering lever bolts and detach the lever and then the disc cover bolts and the cover.
5. Remove the coil spring as previously described.
6. Extract the split pins from the upper trunnion pin and fulcrum pin and remove the nuts.
7. Unscrew the clamp bolt and center bolt of the shock absorber arm, ease the arm outwards, and remove the swivel axle.
8. Extract the split pin from the swivel axle and remove the nut,

upper trunnion suspension link, steel and bronze thrust washers, swivel pin, and dust covers with their springs. From the swivel pin remove the cork washer.

Swivel Axle Examination, Assembling and Replacement

Wash all parts in solvent and thoroughly dry them with a non-fluffy cloth. Examine all parts for wear or damage, paying particular attention to the swivel pins, lower fulcrum pins, and all bushes. Check the pins for ovality. Worn or suspect pins or bushes must be renewed.

Reverse the dismantling procedures to assemble the axles, and if necessary, renew the thrust washers by selective assembly to produce a condition that will permit the swivel axle to rotate freely on the pin with a minimum amount of end-play. The maximum permissible end-play is .002 in. (.05 mm.).

The thrust washers are available in the following sizes: .052 to .057 in. (1.32 to 1.44 mm.), .058 to .063 in. (1.47 to 1.60 mm.), .064 to .069 in. (1.62 to 1.75 mm.). After assembly, reverse the removal sequence to refit the assembly to the hub.

Anti-roll Bar

Tourer: The front suspension units on later cars are interconnected by a rubber mounted anti-roll bar; this can also be fitted to early cars as follows:

1. Remove the coil springs as described previously.
2. Remove the lower wishbone arms as described in the previous FRONT SUSPENSION chapter.
3. Assemble the new right-hand and left-hand wishbone arms to the pivot and swivel pins.
4. Refit the coil spring, then fit the lower ends of the anti-roll bar links to the wishbone and spring pan.
5. Fit the two rubber bearings to the bar and loosely assemble the end location stops outboard of the bearings.
6. Fit the straps to the bearings and then secure the straps to the right-hand and left-hand body side-members respectively with the spring washers and screws.
7. Position the location stops so that their inner faces are $11\frac{1}{16}$ in. (28.1 cm.) from the center-line of the bar. Tighten the screw and nuts to secure the stops.
8. Place the ends of the bar into the fork ends of the links and secure them with the clamping bolts, washers, and stiff nuts. The Metalastik bushes are pressed into the ends of the anti-roll bar.

1. **(GT) Removal:** Raise the car to a workable height.
2. Remove the nuts and washers securing the anti-roll bar links to the bottom wishbones.
3. Remove the set screws securing the bearing straps to the

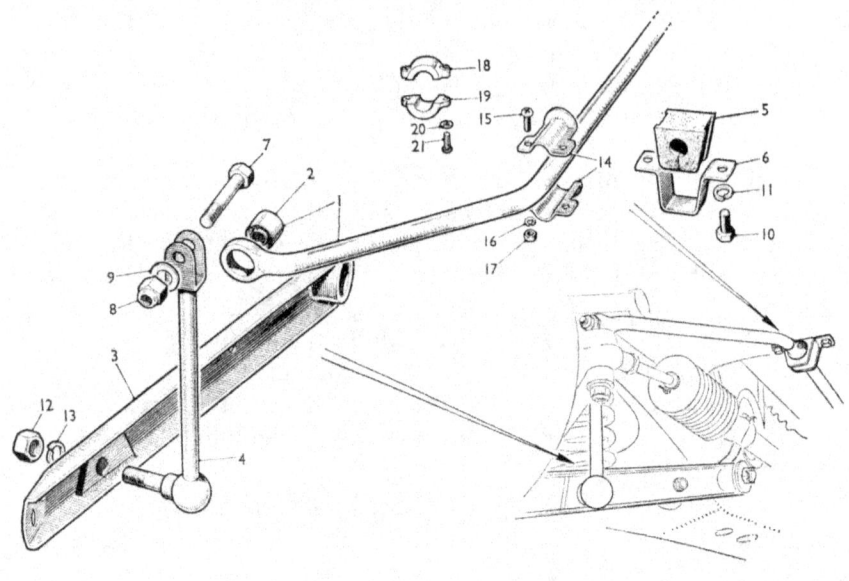

No.	Description	No.	Description
1.	Anti-roll bar assembly.	12.	Nut.
2.	Bush.	13.	Spring washer.
3.	Bottom wishbone assembly—RH.	14.	Location stop end.
4.	Anti-roll bar link—R.H.	15.	Screw.
5.	Anti-roll bar bearing.	16.	Spring washer.
6.	Bearing strap.	17.	Nut.
7.	Clamping bolt.		●
8.	Nut.	18.	Upper locator.
9.	Plain washer.	19.	Lower locator.
10.	Screw.	20.	Spring washer.
11.	Spring washer.	21.	Set screws.

GT only.

Anti-roll bar components

front longitudinal members and lift away the anti-roll bar assembly.

4. **Replacement:** Reverse the removal procedure.

HYDRAULIC DAMPERS

Topping Up

This procedure remains the same, except the rear dampers (shock absorbers) DO NOT need to be removed for topping up. Access to the rear dampers is obtained by removing the rubber plugs in the rear floor panel adjacent to the battery cover. Check every 12,000 miles.

Testing the Dampers

This procedure remains the same, except for the following additions:

Leakage from the damper lid may be rectified by fitting a new lid gasket and fully tightening the screws.

A weep from the valve screw may be stopped by gently tightening the screw.

BRAKING SYSTEM

WARNING: All B.M.C. cars use NATURAL RUBBER components in their brake systems, NOT neoprene rubber components as do American makes. Therefore, it is extremely important that Castrol Girling Amber or Crimson Brake Fluid or BRITISH Lockheed Genuine Brake Fluid be used in these systems, since they are the only brake fluids compatible with the natural rubber parts. Some American brake fluids are only suitable for all-neoprene rubber parts, and will cause natural rubber parts to swell, deteriorate, and rupture.

General Description

The outline under this heading in the **Lockheed Disc Braked Cars** part of the previous BRAKING SYSTEM chapter still applies, except there is no guide post to locate the piston anymore, the friction stop and sleeves are no longer used, and the pistons are interchangeable side for side.

Maintenance

NOTE: See the DRIVER'S HANDBOOK for preventive maintenance, the rear and hand brake adjustment, and the brake pedal adjustment. See the DRIVER'S HANDBOOK for fluid level checking (1968 and later cars), or this heading under Lockheed Disc Braked Cars in the previous BRAKING SYSTEM chapter (prior to 1968).

Front brake adjustment: Wear on the front pads is automatically compensated during braking, and manual adjustment therefore is not provided. In order to maintain peak braking efficiency and to obtain the maximum life from friction pads, they should be examined at the recommended periods, and if the wear on one pad is greater than that on the other, their operating positions should be changed over.

Priming and Bleeding the Brake System

See this heading under **Lockheed Disc Braked Cars** in the previous BRAKING SYSTEM for procedure, noting the following:

Fill the fluid reservoir with the fluid recommended at the beginning of this chapter (DO NOT rely on Specification S.A.E. 70. R1, since it also refers to American brands NOT compatible with natural rubber parts). Keep the reservoir at least half full throughout the bleeding operation, otherwise air will be drawn into the system, necessitating a fresh start.

Only ONE bleeder screw is fitted on the front disc brake units.

After completely bleeding the nearside rear brake cylinder,

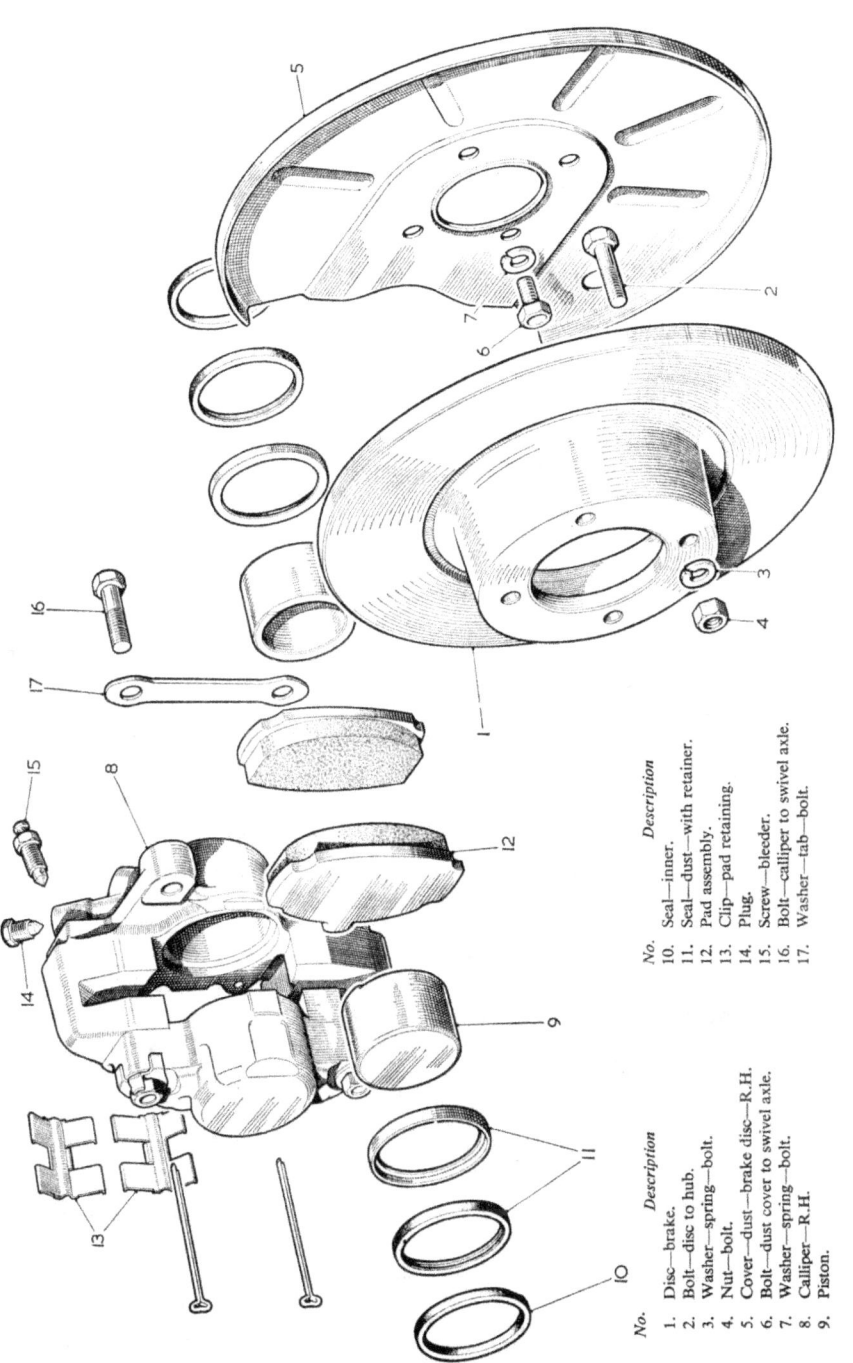

Disc brake components

repeat the process at each of the three remaining brake assemblies.

Renewing a Front Brake Unit

Use this procedure only when the calliper unit is to be renewed as a whole. If ONLY friction pad or piston renewal is needed, use the procedure under Removing a Brake Unit in **Lockheed Disc Braked Cars** in the previous BRAKING SYSTEM chapter. **NOTE: There should be no attempt made to dismantle the calliper. There is no need to dismantle the calliper for cleaning and inspection.**
1. Apply the hand brake, jack up the car, and remove the road wheel. Withdraw the brake friction pads.
2. Attach a bleeder tube to the bleed screw and drain the fluid by pumping the brake pedal.
3. Disconnect the flexible hose on the mounting half of the calliper and plug the end of the hose to prevent the entry of foreign matter.
4. Press back the ears of the locking washer, unscrew the two bolts securing the calliper to the swivel axle, and withdraw the calliper complete.

Replacing a Front Brake Unit

NOTE: Use the following instructions for either of the above procedures.

Reverse the previous instructions. Tighten the calliper securing bolts to a torque wrench reading of 40 to 45 ft. lbs. (5.6 to 6.2 kg. m.). Finally, bleed the system as described previously (if fluid has been lost or hose disconnected).

Removing the Calliper Pistons

1. Unscrew and remove the two bolts securing the calliper to the front hub and withdraw the calliper from the disc and hub.
2. Do not remove the rubber hose, and support the calliper to avoid straining the hose.
3. Remove the friction pads and clean the outside of the calliper, making sure that all traces of dirt and cleaning fluid are completely removed.
4. Clamp the piston in the mounting half of the calliper and gently apply the foot brake. This operation will force the piston in the rim half of the calliper to move outwards.
5. Continue with gentle pressure on the foot pedal until the piston has emerged sufficiently for it to be removed by hand. Have a clean receptacle ready to catch the fluid as the piston is removed.
6. With a suitable blunt-nosed tool remove the fluid seal from

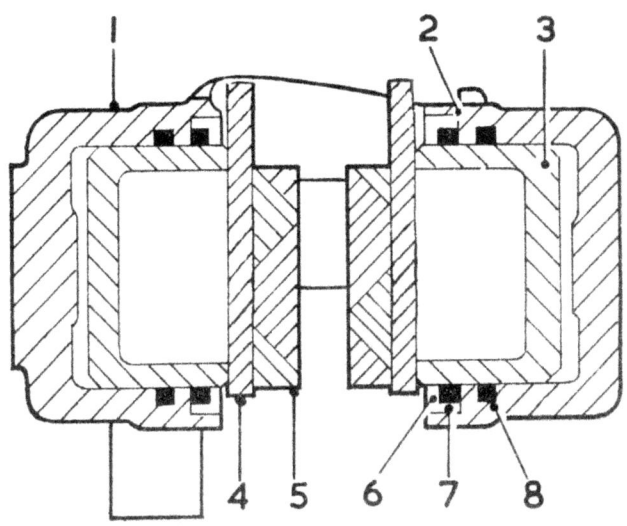

A disc brake in section

1. Calliper—mounting half.
2. Calliper—rim half.
3. Hydraulic piston.
4. Pad backing plate.
5. Friction pad.
6. Dust seal retainer.
7. Dust seal.
8. Fluid seal.

Disc brake section

its groove in the bore of the calliper, taking great care not to damage the bore of the calliper or the seal retaining groove.

7. The dust seal retainer can be removed by inserting a screwdriver between the retainer and the seal and gently prising the retainer from the mouth of the calliper bore. The rubber seal can then be detached.

8. Remove the clamp from the mounting-half piston. To remove the mounting-half piston from the calliper it is necessary to refit the rim-half piston first, and thereafter the procedure is as previously detailed.

9. When cleaning out the calliper it is essential that only alcohol or one of the recommended brake fluids be used as a cleaning medium. Other types of cleaning fluid may damage the internal rubber seal between the two halves of the calliper.

Servicing the Calliper

Further servicing of the calliper should be confined to removing the bleeder screw and the fluid pipe line and blowing the fluid passages clear with compressed air.

NOTE: There should be no attempt made to dismantle the calliper. There is no need to dismantle the calliper for cleaning and inspection.

Replacing the Calliper Pistons

1. Coat a new fluid seal with the recommended brake fluid or

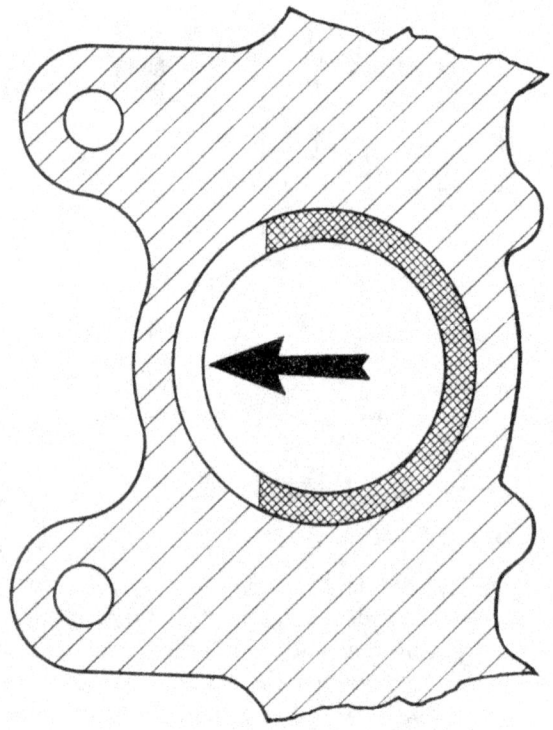

The cut-away portion of the piston (arrowed) must be located at the inner edge of the calliper, i.e. towards the hub

Piston placement

Lockheed Disc Brake Lubricant and locate the piston squarely in the mouth of the bore with the cutaway portion of the piston face correctly positioned (see illustration).

2. Press in the piston until approximately ⁵⁄₁₆ in. (7.94 mm.) of the piston is protruding from the bore. **Take great care to prevent the piston tilting during this operation.**
3. If the dust seal and retainer have been previously removed, take a new, perfectly dry dust seal, coat it with Lockheed Disc Brake Lubricant, and fit the seal into its retainer.
4. Position the seal assembly on the protruding portion of the piston with the seal innermost, ensuring that the assembly is square with the piston.
5. Press home the piston and seal assembly with the clamp. Retighten the bleeder screw.
6. The mounting-half piston is dealt with in the same manner as described for the rim-half piston. The rubber hose must be disconnected to allow the clamp to be used and the bleeder screw must be slackened.

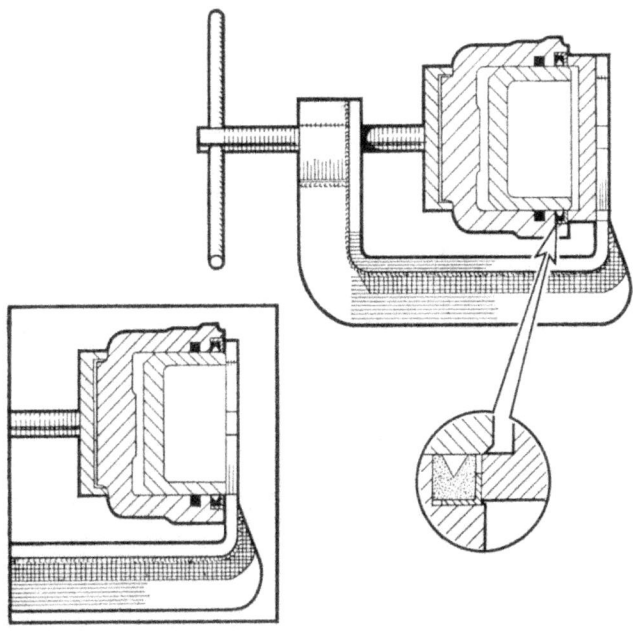

Using Service tool 18G590 to install the dust seal and retainer in the recessed mouth of the calliper cylinder. Shown inset is the tool, less the adaptor, being used to reset a piston

Using service tool 18G 590

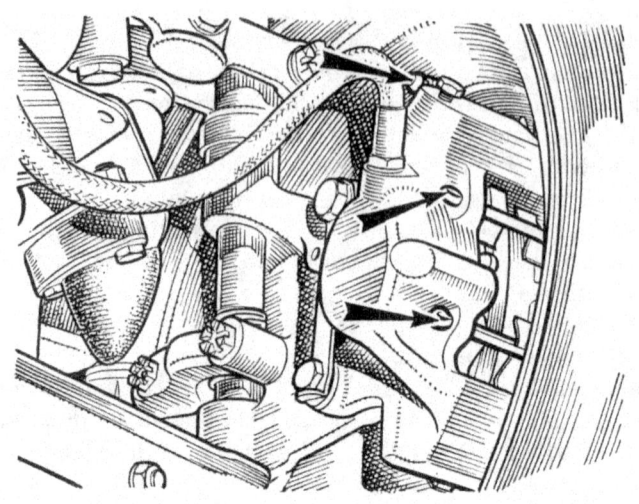

Friction pad retaining pins and bleed screw location

Calliper brake servicing points

7. Reconnect the hose and bolt the calliper to the hub. Do not depress the brake pedal.
8. Fit the friction pad assemblies, together with their retaining springs and split pins, and bleed the system.
9. After bleeding the system, operate the brake pedal several times to adjust the brake.

Removing the Friction Pads
1. Apply the hand brake, jack up the car, and remove the road wheel.
2. Depress the pad retaining springs and remove the split pins and the retaining springs; lift the pads out of the calliper.
3. When the lining material has worn down to a minimum permissible thickness of $\frac{1}{16}$ in. (1.59 mm.), the friction pads must be renewed.
4. Thoroughly clean the surrounding area of the calliper.

Replacing the Friction Pads
Follow the procedure in this heading under **Lockheed Disc Braked Cars** in the previous BRAKING SYSTEM chapter, but note the following:
Insert the friction pads (which are interchangeable side for side), replace the retaining springs, and fit the split pins. Ensure

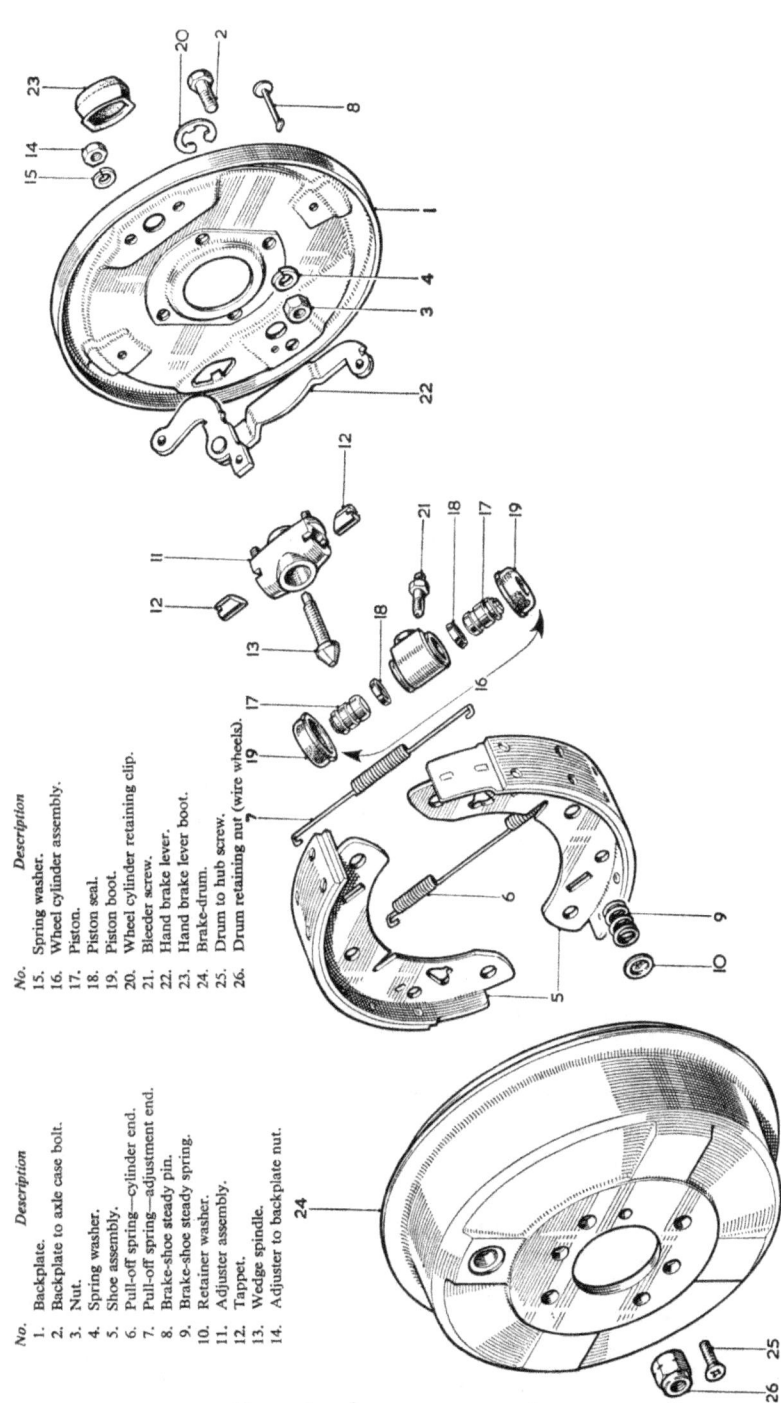

Rear brake components

No.	Description	No.	Description
1.	Backplate.	15.	Spring washer.
2.	Backplate to axle case bolt.	16.	Wheel cylinder assembly.
3.	Nut.	17.	Piston.
4.	Spring washer.	18.	Piston seal.
5.	Shoe assembly.	19.	Piston boot.
6.	Pull-off spring—cylinder end.	20.	Wheel cylinder retaining clip.
7.	Pull-off spring—adjustment end.	21.	Bleeder screw.
8.	Brake-shoe steady pin.	22.	Hand brake lever.
9.	Brake-shoe steady spring.	23.	Hand brake lever boot.
10.	Retainer washer.	24.	Brake-drum.
11.	Adjuster assembly.	25.	Drum to hub screw.
12.	Tappet.	26.	Drum retaining nut (wire wheels).
13.	Wedge spindle.		
14.	Adjuster to backplate nut.		

that the pad assemblies are free to move easily in the calliper recesses. Remove any high spots from the pad pressure plate by carefully filing.

Pump the brake several times to readjust the pistons and top up the fluid supply reservoir.

Replacing a Brake Disc

Follow the procedure under this heading in **Lockheed Disc Braked Cars** in the previous BRAKING SYSTEM chapter, but note the following:

If it is found necessary to regrind the disc faces they can be ground up to a maximum of only .040 in. (1.016 mm.) off the original thickness of .350 to .340 in. (8.89 to 8.63 mm.). This may be ground off equally each side, or more on one side than the other, provided that the total reduction does not exceed the maximum limit of .040 in. (1.016 mm.). The reground surface must not exceed 63 micro-in.

After grinding, the faces must run true to within a total dial indicator reading of .002 in. (.05 mm.) and the thickness must be parallel to within .001 in. (.0254 mm.) dial indicator reading.

Rear Brake Assembly Description

The rear brakes are of the leading and trailing shoe type, giving the advantage of equal braking action whether the car is travelling forwards or backwards.

The hand brake lever operates the brakes mechanically through linked levers which apply a force to each shoe. When the foot brake pedal is depressed, the master cylinder piston applies pressure to the fluid, thus causing the pistons in the wheel cylinder to operate on the tip of the leading and trailing shoes.

When pressure on the brake pedal is released, the brake-shoe springs return the shoes, thrust the pistons back into the wheel cylinders, and the fluid passes back to the master cylinder.

Removing Rear Brake Components

1. Jack up the car and remove the road wheel.
2. Remove the brake-drum as follows:
   a. **Disc wheels:** Unscrew and remove the two countersunk Phillips screws locating the drum and tap it from the hub. It may be necessary to slacken off the brake adjustment slightly if the shoes hold the drum.
   b. **Wire wheels:** Unscrew the four nuts securing the drum to the hub and tap the drum from the hub. It may be necessary to slacken off the brake adjustment slightly to free the drum.
3. Slacken fully the brake-shoe adjuster.

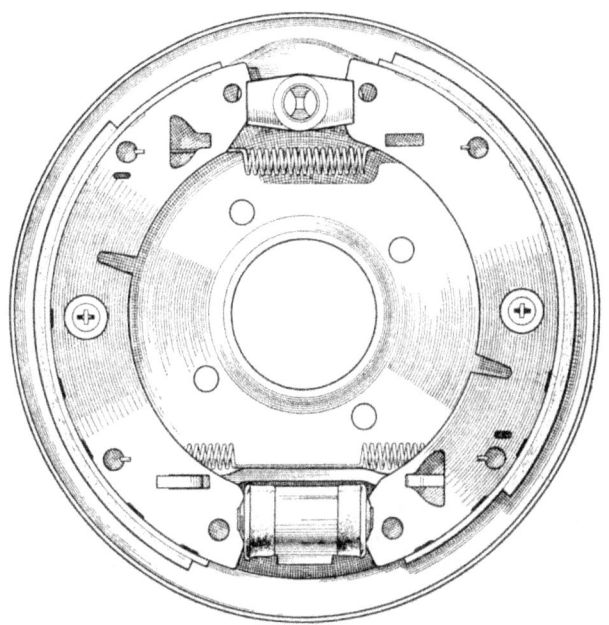

Rear brake assembly

4. Depress each shoe steady spring retaining washer and turn to release them from the anchor brackets on the backplate. Pull the trailing shoe against the load of the springs and disengage at each end; on releasing the tension on the springs the other shoe will fall away.
4. To remove the wheel cylinder, disconnect the brake fluid supply pipe, placing a clean container to catch the fluid.
5. Withdraw the circlip and retaining washer and remove the cylinder.
6. Extract the split pin and withdraw the clevis pin to release the hand brake cable from the lever. Detach the rubber dust cover from the brake lever at the rear of the backplate and withdraw the lever.
7. Withdraw the tappets from the spindle adjuster and screw the adjusting spindle inwards until clear of the threads.
8. Remove the two nuts and spring washers from the rear of the backplate to release the adjuster body.

Replacing Rear Brake Components
1. Thoroughly clean the adjuster body, tappets, and adjuster.

Smear the adjuster threads and tappets with Lockheed Expander Lubricant.

2. Screw the adjuster fully into the adjuster body and slide the tappets into the body, ensuring that the tapered portion on each is facing inwards.

3. Examine the rubber seals on both pistons and renew them should they appear damaged or distorted. It is usually advisable to renew the rubber parts when rebuilding the cylinders.

4. Smear all internal parts with fluid and reassemble. Replace the dust covers.

5. Hold the cylinder up against the backplate and replace the flat washer and circlip. Replace the fluid supply pipe.

6. Hold the brake lever against the backplate and replace the rubber boot. Reconnect the hand brake cable.

7. The brake shoes are interchangeable, but when replacing, the pull-off springs must be on the backplate side of the shoes and located in the shoes as shown in the illustration.

8. Replace the steady springs on the shoe web and locate them with the brackets on the backplate by depressing and turning the retaining washer.

9. Be sure that all adjustments are off and that the shoes are centralized. Fit the drum and road wheel, bleed the system, and adjust the brakes.

Hand Brake Cable

Lubrication: See the DRIVER'S HANDBOOK.

Adjustment: The rear brake-shoes should be adjusted as described in the DRIVER'S HANDBOOK before taking up brake cable stretch (shown by excessive movement of the hand brake lever). The amount of slack in the cable and therefore the amount of movement of the lever is adjustable by means of the nut on the screwed end of the cable located beneath the car in the center.

1. **Removal (lever and cable assembly):** Unscrew and remove the adjusting nut, withdraw the end of the cable from the lower end of the lever, and remove the spring and flat washers.

2. Remove the nut securing the brake lever to the hand brake spindle and withdraw the spring washer, forked lever, and plain washer. The hand lever may now be withdrawn from the inside of the car.

3. Remove the right-hand seat, then unscrew the three screws securing the ratchet plate to the floor tunnel.

4. Lift the carpet and remove the nut and spring washer securing the outer cable front abutment. Disconnect the clips secur-

ing the cable assembly to the body and rear axle.

5. Remove the bolt, nut, and spring washer connecting the two halves of the brake compensating lever to each other, slacken fully the self-locking nut securing the lever to the axle bracket, and release the cable abutment trunnion from the lever.

6. Extract the split pins and withdraw the clevis pins to release the cable yokes from the levers on the brake backplates.

7. **Replacement:** Reverse the removal procedure, then check and adjust the hand brake lever as detailed previously.

Master Cylinder Description

The master cylinder and fluid supply reservoir assembly is mounted on the engine side of the firewall above the brake pedal.

The piston is backed by a rubber cup normally held in the OFF position by a piston return spring. Immediately in front of the cup, when it is in the OFF position, is a compensating orifice connecting the cylinder with the fluid supply. Pressure is applied to the piston by means of the push-rod attached to the brake pedal.

The reduced skirt of the piston forms an annular space which is filled with fluid from the supply tank. On releasing the brake pedal after application, the piston is returned quickly to its stop by the return spring. A small bleed hole is drilled in the side of the check valve body to prevent any fluid pressure being retained in the system.

Master Cylinder Removal

1. Remove the screws securing the brake and clutch master cylinder cover and take off the cover.

2. Drain the fluid from the supply tank reservoir by attaching a rubber tube to a brake calliper bleed screw, open the screw one full turn, then depress the brake pedal.

3. Hold the pedal down, tighten the bleed screw, then let the pedal return unassisted. Repeat this operation until the tank is empty.

4. Remove the split pin, washer, and clevis pin from the push-rod and disengage the brake pedal lever.

5. Clean the pipe connection, disconnect the pipe line, and fit a plug to the end of the cylinder to prevent the entry of dirt.

6. Unscrew the fixing bolts and detach the master cylinder from the box assembly.

Dismantling

1. Detach the rubber dust cover from the cylinder barrel and move it along the push-rod.

2. Depress the push-rod to relieve the load on the circlip, then

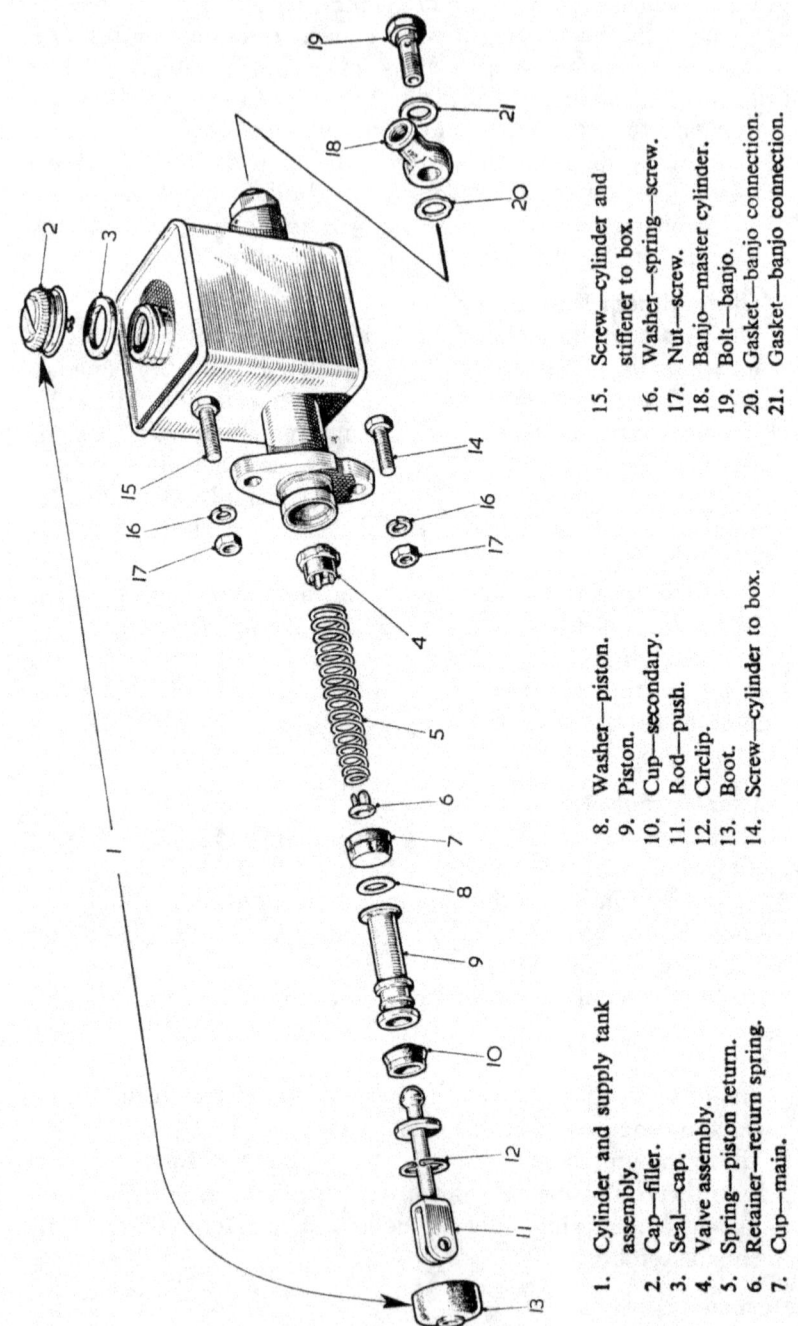

1. Cylinder and supply tank assembly.
2. Cap—filler.
3. Seal—cap.
4. Valve assembly.
5. Spring—piston return.
6. Retainer—return spring.
7. Cup—main.
8. Washer—piston.
9. Piston.
10. Cup—secondary.
11. Rod—push.
12. Circlip.
13. Boot.
14. Screw—cylinder to box.
15. Screw—cylinder and stiffener to box.
16. Washer—spring—screw.
17. Nut—screw.
18. Banjo—master cylinder.
19. Bolt—banjo.
20. Gasket—banjo connection.
21. Gasket—banjo connection.

Master brake cylinder

withdraw the circlip and the push-rod assembly.
3. Withdraw the piston, piston washer, main cup, spring retainer, and valve assembly.
4. Remove the secondary cup by carefully stretching it over the end of the piston.

Assembly
1. Clean all parts thoroughly, using the recommended brake fluid (see the WARNING at the beginning of this chapter) or alcohol. If alcohol is used, the rubber parts should not be allowed to soak, but should be dried and dipped in clean brake fluid.
2. The main casing, if cleaned with spirit, must be dried out before assembly. Be sure that the compensating port in the cylinder barrel is clear by probing with a piece of fine wire.
3. Examine all the rubber parts for damage or distortion. It is usually advisable to renew the rubber parts when rebuilding the cylinder. Dip all the internal parts in brake fluid and assemble them wet.
4. Stretch the secondary cup over the piston with the lip of the cup facing the head of the piston. When the cup is in its groove work it round gently with the fingers to ensure that it is correctly seated.
5. Fit the check valve assembly onto the large end and the retainer onto the small end of the return spring and insert the spring, check valve first, into the cylinder.
6. Insert the main cup, lip first, and press it down onto the spring retainer, taking care not to damage or turn back the lip.
7. Place the main cup washer in position with its concave face next to the main cup and insert the piston, taking care not to damage or turn back the lip of the secondary cup.
8. Place the push-rod in position, push the piston down the bore, and with the piston stop washer in the bore, refit the retaining circlip. Refit the dust cover.

Replacement of Master Cylinder
1. Refit the master cylinder to the master cylinder box and secure it with the bolts. The long bolt passes through the stiffener plate.
2. Remove the dust excluder and fit the pipe connection to the master cylinder.
3. Refit the clutch pedal lever to the push-rod and secure it with the clevis pin, washer, and a new split pin.
4. Refit the master cylinder cover.
5. Fill the master cylinder and then prime and bleed the system.

ELECTRICAL SYSTEM

NOTE: Previous to 1968 MGB cars used POSITIVE GROUND electrical systems. 1968 and later cars used NEGATIVE GROUND electrical systems. Wiring diagrams for 1968 and later cars will be found in the electrical section of the DRIVER'S HANDBOOK at the back of this publication.

Battery

Recharging from an external source: The length of time for a used battery to remain on charge before it can be accepted as fully charged depends entirely on the specific gravity before charging commences and the charging rate. The charging should continue at 5 amperes until all cells are gassing freely and evenly at the specific gravity in each of the six cells has reached a maximum, i.e. has shown no further rise in four hours. The specific gravity at the end of charging should be within the limits given and should not vary .005 from the values given.

Generator Servicing

Use the procedure under **Lucas C40/1 Generator** in the previous ELECTRICAL SYSTEM chapter, noting the following changes:

Test the brush spring tension, using a spring scale. The tension of the springs when new is 18 to 24 ozs. (510.7 to 681 gm.). In service it is permissbile for this value to fall to 15 ozs. (425 gm.) before performance may be affected. Fit new springs if the tension is low.

When undercutting one of the MOULDED TYPE generator commutators, cut it to a depth of ONLY .020 in. (.51 mm.).

The most common armature faults are usually confined to open or short-circuited windings. Indications of an open-circuited armature winding is given by burnt commutator segments. A short-circuited armature winding is easily identified by discoloration of the overheated windings and badly burnt commutator segments.

If the current reading (when testing the field coils) is much more than 2 amperes, or the ohmmeter reading much below 6 ohms, it is an indication that the insulation of one of the field coils has broken down.

Prior to renewing the field coils, drill out the rivet securing the field coil terminal assembly to the yoke and unsolder the field coil connections. Then continue with the steps. Add the following after step (9).

10. Resolder the field coil connections to the field coil terminal tags and re-rivet the terminal assembly to the yoke.

After servicing the bearings, note the following:

NOTE: When fitting a drive end bracket to the armature shaft the inner journal of the bearing MUST be supported by a mild-steel tube; DO NOT use the drive end bracket.

Generator Reassembly

The reassembly of the generator is a reversal of the dismantling procedure. If the end bracket has been removed from the armature in dismantling, press the bearing end bracket onto the armature shaft, taking care to avoid damaging the end plate and armature windings. When assembling the commutator end bracket, the brushes must first be held clear of the commutator by partially withdrawing them from their boxes until each brush is trapped in position by the side pressure of its spring. The brushes can be released onto the commutator by a small screwdriver or similar tool when the end bracket is assembled to within about 1/2 in. (13 mm.) of the yoke. Before closing the gap between the end bracket and the yoke, see that the springs are in correct contact with the brushes. Add a few drops of engine oil through the hole in the armature end cover.

Generator Replacement

Reverse the removal procedure noting that on later cars plain washers are fitted under the heads of the two upper fixing bolts.

Starter Motor Removal

1. Disconnect the cable from the ground terminal on the battery and the cable from the terminal on the starter.
2. Remove the external oil filter, the ignition coil and bracket, and the distributor. Unscrew the two bolts securing the starter to the flywheel housing and engine rear plate and withdraw the starter upwards from the engine compartment.

Servicing the Starter

Examination of commutator and brush gear: Use the procedure under this heading in the previous ELECTRICAL SYSTEM chapter.

1. **Dismantling:** Take off the cover band at the commutator end, hold back the brush springs, and take out the brushes.
2. Remove the circlip from the outer end of the drive head sleeve and take off the front spring anchor plate, the main spring, and the rear spring anchor plate.
3. Withdraw the pin securing the drive head sleeve to the armature shaft, push the sleeve assembly down the shaft, and re-

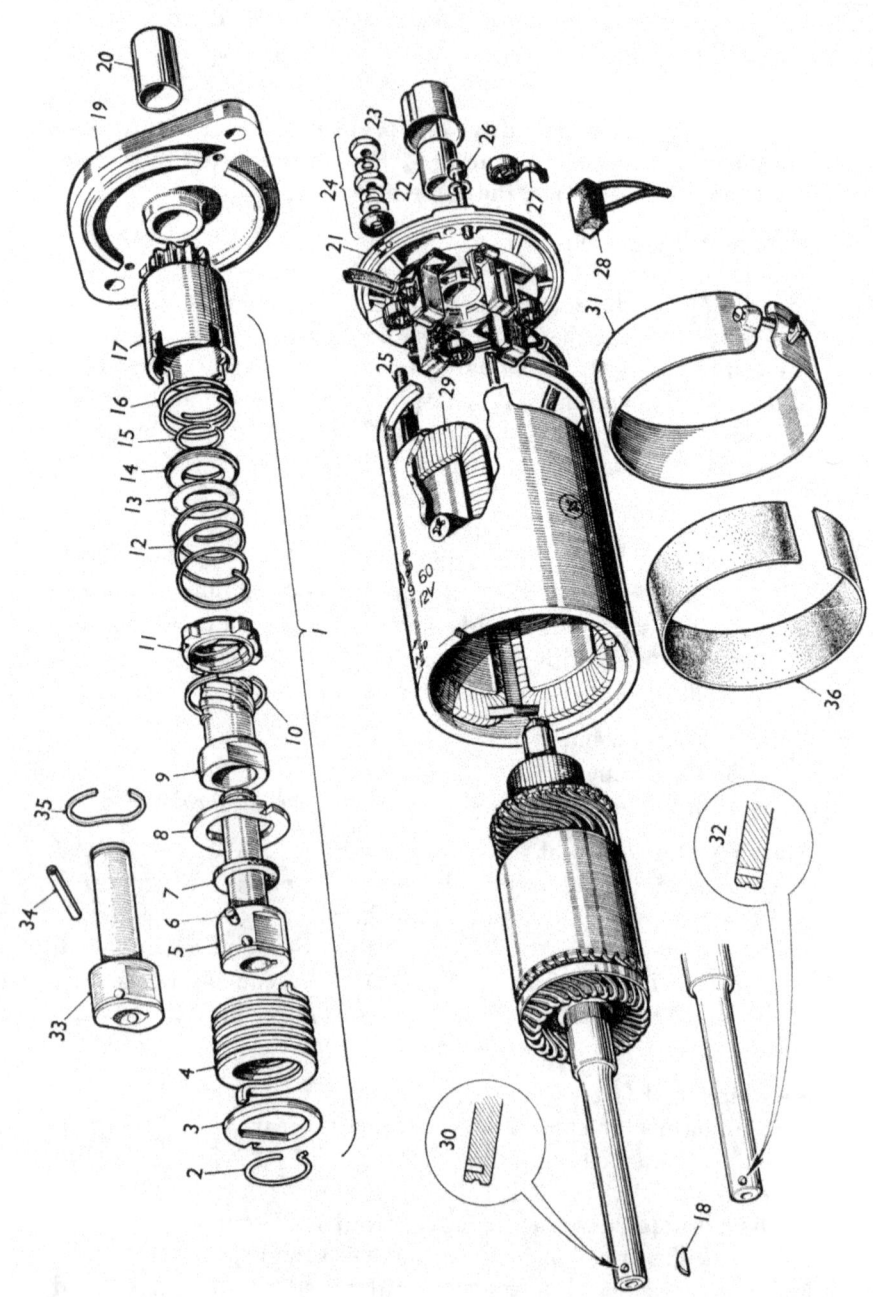

Starter motor components

KEY TO THE STARTER MOTOR COMPONENTS

No.	Description
1.	Drive assembly.
2.	Retaining ring.
3.	Anchor plate—front.
4.	Main spring.
5.	Centre sleeve.*
6.	Retaining pin.*
7.	Thrust washer (fibre).
8.	Anchor plate—rear.
9.	Screwed sleeve.
10.	Retaining ring.*
11.	Control nut.
12.	Restraining spring.
13.	Thrust washer—control nut.
14.	Locating collar.
15.	Retaining ring.
16.	Spring.
17.	Pinion and barrel.
18.	Woodruff key.*
19.	Drive end bracket.
20.	Bush—driving end.
21.	Commutator end bracket.
22.	Bush—commutator end.
23.	Shaft cap.
24.	Terminal nuts and washers.
25.	Terminal post.
26.	Through-bolt.
27.	Brush tension spring.
28.	Brush.
29.	Field coils.
30.	Armature.*
31.	Cover band.
32.	Armature.†
33.	Centre sleeve.†
34.	Spiral pin.†
35.	Waved circlip.†
36.	Cover band seal.†

* For starter motors Serial No. 25555.
† For starter motors Serial No. 25598.

move the woodruff key. Slide the complete drive assembly from the armature shaft.

4. Remove the barrel retaining ring from the inside of the barrel and pinion assembly, then withdraw the barrel and antidrift spring from the screwed sleeve.

5. From the inner end of the drive head sleeve remove the circlip, locating collar, control nut thrust washer, cushioning spring, control nut, screwed sleeve and the drive head thrust washer.

6. Remove the terminal nuts and washers from the terminal post and screw out the two through-bolts.

7. Remove the commutator end bracket, the drive end bracket, and the armature.

1. **Field coils:** Use the procedure under this heading in the previous ELECTRICAL SYSTEM, adding the following:

2. **NOTE: When carrying out this test, the brushes connected**

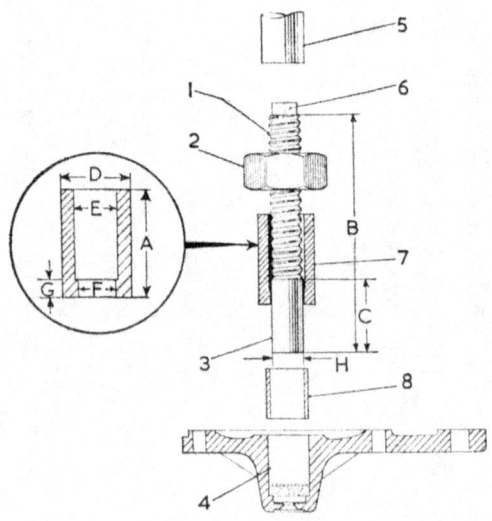

Using a self-extracting-type tool to fit an end bracket bush

1. ⅜ in. B.S.F. truncated thread.
2. Extracting nut.
3. Fitting pin.
4. Bearing housing.
5. Hand press.
6. Squared end.
7. Sleeve.
8. Bush.

A. 1½ in. (38 mm.).
B. 4 in. (10·2 cm.).
C. 1¼ in. (31·8 mm.).
D. 1 ₁₆ in. (33·3 mm.).
E. ·625 in. (15·87 mm.).
F. ·605 in. (15·37 mm.).
G. ¼ in. (6·35 mm.).
H. ·5924 in. (15·05 mm.).

Fitting end bracket bush

to the field coils must not be in contact with the starter yoke.

Control Box Model RB340
Adjustment of air gap settings

Air gap settings are accurately adjusted during manufacture and should require no further attention. If the original settings have been disturbed, it will be necessary to make adjustments in the manner described below:

Armature-to-bobbin core gaps of voltage and current regulators

Disconnect the battery. Using a suitable tool (see illustration), turn the adjustment cam of the regulator being adjusted to the point giving minimum lift to the armature tensioning spring (by turning the tool to the fullest extent counterclockwise). Loosen the appropriate contact locking nut and unscrew the contact. Insert a feeler gauge of .056 in. (1.42 mm.) thickness between the armature and the regulator head as far back as the two rivet heads on the underside of the armature. With the gauge in position, press squarely down on the armature, then screw in the contact until it just touches the armature contact. Tighten the locknut and withdraw the gauge. Repeat this procedure on the remaining regulator.

Horn and Horn-Button

Removing the horn: Disconnect the electrical connections, remove the screws and washers securing the horn to the hood lock platform or from the wing valance, then withdraw the horn.

Check the current consumption, which should be 3 to $3^{1}/_{2}$ amperes, when the horn is operating correctly.

After making a thorough external check, remove the horn cover and examine the cable connections inside the horn. Examine the contact breaker contacts. If they are burnt or blackened, clean them with a fine file, then wipe with a fuel-moistened cloth.

Flashing Direction Indicators

Checking Faulty Operation: During this procedure, be sure the ignition switch is turned on and check the appropriate fuses.

Maintenance: Flasher units cannot be dismantled for subsequent reassembly. A defective unit must therefore be renewed. During this installation, it is advisable to test the circuits before connections to flasher terminals are made. When testing, join the cables normally connected to those terminals (green, green with brown, and light green) together and operate the direction indicator switch. In the event of a wrong connection having been made, the ignition auxiliaries fuse will blow but no damage will be done to the flasher unit.

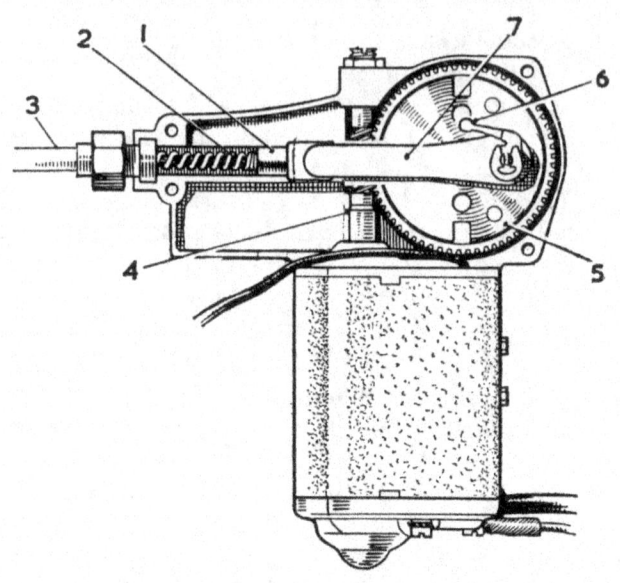

Windshield wiper drive components

1. Cross-head.
2. Cable rack.
3. Outer casing.
4. Armature.
5. Final gear.
6. Park switch.
7. Connecting rod.

Windshield wiper drive

Windshield Wiper
Resetting the limit switch

If the wiper fails to park or parks unsatisfactorily, the limit switch in the gearbox cover should be checked. Unless the limit switch is correctly set, it is possible for the wiper motor to overrun the open-circuit position and continue to draw current.

Loosen the four screws securing the gearbox cover and observe the projection near the rim of the limit switch. Position the projection in line with the groove in the gearbox cover. Turn the limit switch 25° in a counterclockwise direction and tighten the four securing screws.

Testing on vehicle

If the wiper fails to operate, or performs sluggishly, connect a 0-15 moving-coil ammeter in the wiper circuit, switch on the wiper, and note the current being supplied to the motor. The normal running current should be 2.7 to 3.4 amps.

Switches

Always disconnect the batteries before removing any switches and refer to the wiring diagram and switch contact numbers when refitting switches.

To remove the switches, depress the spring loaded plunger in the switch knobs and withdraw the knobs. Disconnect the Lucar connectors and, using Service tool 18G 670, unscrew the bezel lock rings. Remove the switches from the rear of the instrument panel. Reverse this sequence to refit the switches.

Bi-Metal Resistance Instrumentation
General description

The bi-metal resistance equipment for fuel and temperature gauges consists of an indicator head and transmitter unit con-

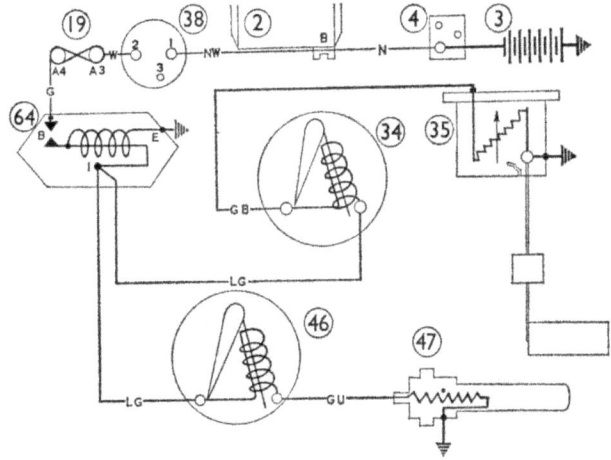

The bi-metal resistance instrumentation circuit

2.	Control box.	38.	Ignition switch.
3.	Batteries (12-volt).	46.	Coolant temperature
4.	Starter solenoid.		gauge.
19.	Fuse (A3–A4).	47.	Coolant temperature
34.	Fuel gauge.		transmitter.
35.	Fuel tank unit.	64.	Voltage stabilizer.

Instrumentation circuit

nected to a common voltage stabilizer. The system by which the equipment functions is voltage-sensitive, and the voltage stabilizer is necessary to ensure a constant supply of a predetermined voltage to the equipment.

Fault analysis

For rapid diagnosis of a faulty unit use Smiths Automotive Instrument Tester (which incorporates a thermal sensitive voltmeter).

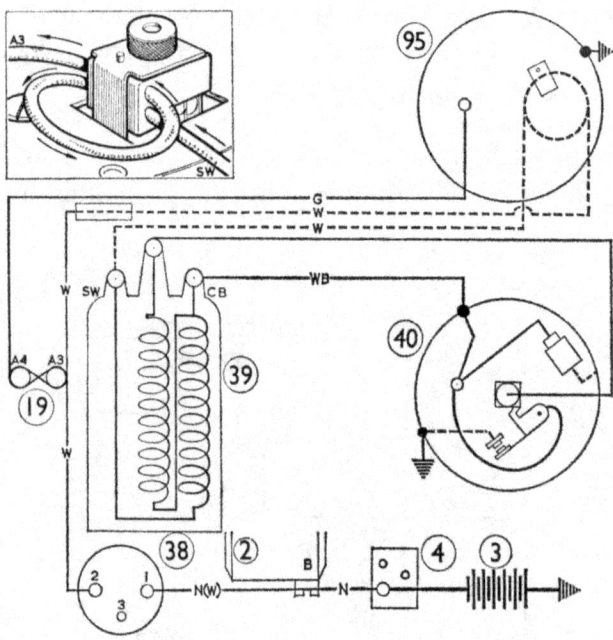

Impulse tachometer circuit

2. Control box.
3. Batteries (12-volt).
4. Starter solenoid.
19. Fuse—A3–A4.
38. Ignition switch.
39. Ignition coil
40. Distributor.
95. Tachometer

Inset: symmetrical loop of pulse lead

Impulse tachometer circuit

Battery voltage: Connect voltmeter to control box terminal **B** and ground:
  a. Engine stationary: 12 volts, approx.
  b. Engine running at 1,000 r.p.m. and ignition warning light out, 12-13 volts approx.

Wiring: Check for continuity between each unit and check for short to ground. Check for short-circuits in wiring to each transmitter. Check that voltage stabilizer and transmitters are grounded.

Voltage stabilizer: Ignition on; after two minutes check the main voltage between the output terminal **I** and ground, which should be 10 volts.

NOTE: If the voltage stabilizer is removed, it is essential to ensure that, when replacing, B and E are uppermost and not exceeding 20° from the vertical.
Substitute voltage stabilizer if faulty.

Gauges: Check for continuity between terminals with wiring disconnected. **NOTE: The gauges must not be checked by short-circuiting to ground.**
Substitute gauge if faulty.

Transmitter: Check for continuity between terminal and case with leads disconnected.
Substitute transmitter if faulty.

Impulse Type Tachometer

The equipment consists of an indicator head and pulse lead. The pulse lead is connected in series between the ignition switch and the ignition coil, and transmits voltage pulses to the indicator head.

Faulty operation

Check wiring connections to the indicator head and continuity of the circuit. Poor connections may result in faulty readings.

The pulse lead should form a symetrical loop and not be tight against the plastic forms as shown in the inset.

Cigar-Lighter
Removal
1. Disconnect the cigar-lighter feed wire from the ignition switch terminal.
2. Disconnect the ground wire from the cigar-lighter.
3. Press in the sides of the illumination lamp cover and withdraw the lamp unit from the lighter shell.
4. Unscrew the lighter shell from the lighter base.
5. Withdraw the switch base and glow ring from the front of the instrument panel.

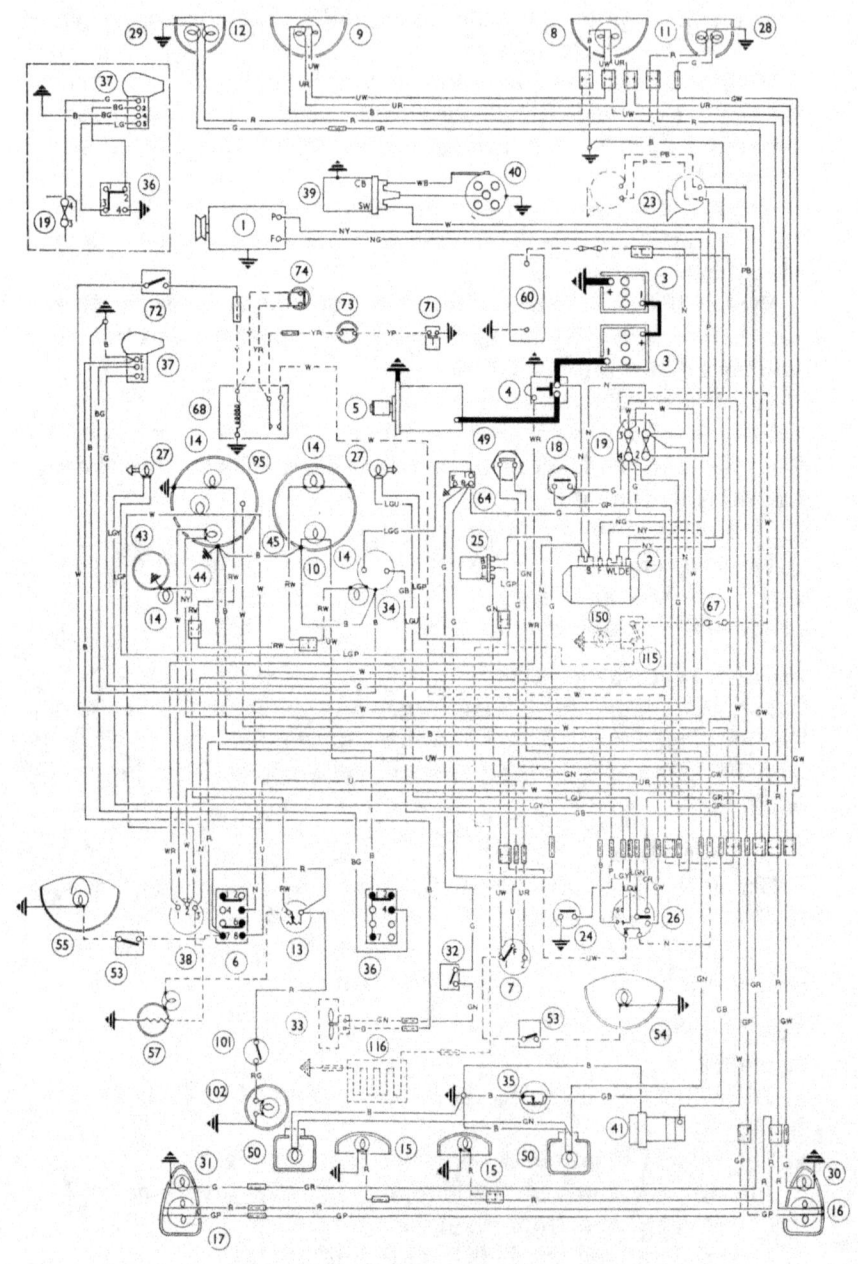

Wiring diagram (prior to 1968)

No.	Description	No.	Description
1.	Dynamo.	38.	Ignition/starter switch.
2.	Control box.	39.	Ignition coil.
3.	Battery—6-volt.	40.	Distributor.
4.	Starter solenoid.	41.	Fuel pump.
5.	Starter motor.	43.	Oil pressure gauge.
6.	Lighting switch.	44.	Ignition warning lamp.
7.	Headlamp dip switch.	45.	Speedometer.
8.	R.H. headlamp.	49.	Reverse lamp switch.
9.	L.H. headlamp.	50.	Reverse Lamps.
10.	Main-beam warning lamp.	53.	Fog or driving lamp switch (when fitted).
11.	R.H. sidelamp.	54.	R.H. fog lamp or R.H. driving lamp (when fitted).
12.	L.H. sidelamp.	55.	L.H. fog lamp or L.H. driving lamp (when fitted).
13.	Rheostat—panel lamps.		
14.	Panel lamps.	57.	Cigar-lighter—illuminated (when fitted).
15.	Number-plate illumination lamps.	60.	Radio (when fitted).
16.	R.H. stop and tail lamp.	64.	Bi-metal instrument voltage stabilizer.
17.	L.H. stop and tail lamp.	67.	Heated backlight line fuse—GT (when fitted).
18.	Stop lamp switch.	68.	Overdrive relay unit.
19.	Fuse unit.	71.	Overdrive solenoid.
23.	Horn (twin horns when fitted).	72.	Overdrive manual control switch. } when fitted.
24.	Horn-push.	73.	Overdrive gear switch.
25.	Flasher unit.	74.	Overdrive throttle switch (vacuum operated).
26.	Direction indicator switch (and flasher switch) (when fitted).	95.	Tachometer.
27.	Direction indicator warning lamps.	101.	Map light switch.
28.	R.H. front flasher lamp.	102.	Map light.
29.	L.H. front flasher lamp.	115.	Heated backlight switch.
30.	R.H. rear flasher lamp.	116.	Heated backlight. } GT (when fitted)
31.	L.H. rear flasher lamp.	150.	Heated backlight warning light.
32.	Heater or fresh-air motor switch.		
33.	Heater or fresh-air motor (when fitted).		
34.	Fuel gauge.		INSET
35.	Fuel gauge tank unit.	19.	Fuse unit.
36.	Windshield wiper switch. } Tourer	26.	Windshield wiper switch. } GT
37.	Windshield wiper motor.	37.	Windshield wiper motor.

CABLE COLOUR CODE

N. Brown.   P. Purple.   W. White.
U. Blue.   G. Green.   Y. Yellow.
R. Red.   LG. Light Green.   B. Black.

When a cable has two colour code letters the first denotes the main colour and the second denotes the tracer colour.

Key to wiring diagram (prior to 1968)

TUNING DATA

MODEL: MGB

ENGINE

Type	18GF
Firing order	1, 3, 4, 2
Capacity	1798 c.c. (109·8 cu. in.)
Compression ratio	8·8 : 1
Compression pressure	160 lb./sq. in. (11·25 kg./cm.^{2})
Idle speed (manual transmission)	900 r.p.m.
Fast idle speed (manual transmission)	1,300 to 1,400 r.p.m.
Valve rocker clearance	·015 in. (·38 mm.) set cold
Stroboscopic ignition timing	20° B.T.D.C. at 1,000 r.p.m. (vacuum pipe disconnected)
Static ignition timing	10° B.T.D.C.
Timing mark location	Pointer on timing case, notch on crankshaft pulley

DISTRIBUTOR

Make	Lucas
Type	25D4
Serial number	40897
Contact breaker gap	·014 to ·016 in. (·35 to ·40 mm.)
Rotation of rotor	Anti-clockwise
Dwell angle	57° to 63°
Condenser capacity	·18 to ·24 mF

Centrifugal advance

Crankshaft degrees (vacuum pipe disconnected)	0° at 400 to 600 r.p.m.
	14° at 1,500 to 1,750 r.p.m.
	20° ± 2° at 3,000 r.p.m.

Vacuum advance

Starts	5 in. Hg
Finishes	13 in. Hg
Total crankshaft degrees	10° ± 2°

SPARKING PLUGS

Make	Champion
Type	N-9Y
Gap	·024 to ·026 in. (·625 to ·660 mm.)

IGNITION COIL

Make	Lucas
Type	HA12
Resistance—primary	3·1 to 3·5 ohms at 20° C. (68° F.)

Consumption

Ignition on—standing	3·9 amps.
at 2,000 r.p.m.	1·4 amps.

CARBURETTER(S)

Make	S.U.
Type/Specification	Twin HS4/AUD 265
Choke diameter	1½ in. (38·1 mm.)
Jet size	·090 in. (2·2 mm.)
Needle	FX●
Piston spring	Red
Initial jet adjustment	14 flats from bridge

EXHAUST EMISSION

Exhaust gas analyser reading:

At engine idle speed	4·5 to 5·5% CO (provisional)
Air pump test speed	1,000 r.p.m. (engine)

SERVICING

General

The efficient operation of the exhaust emission control system is dependent on the engine being in good mechanical condition and correctly tuned to the settings given in 'TUNING DATA'.

Tuning and test procedure for the carburetters, ignition system, and engine are given at the end of the manual. These procedures are the quickest and surest way of locating engine faults or maladjustments and are the only methods that should be used for engine tuning.

Fault diagnosis

After tuning the engine to the correct settings, check for indications of the following symptoms:

Symptoms	Causes	Cure
Backfire in exhaust system	1. Leak in exhaust system	Locate and rectify leak
	2. Leaks in hoses or connections to gulp valve or vacuum sensing pipe	Locate and rectify leak
	3. Faulty gulp valve	Test gulp valve, and renew if faulty
	4. Leak in intake system	Locate and rectify leak
	5. Faulty carburetter limit valve	Fit new throttle plate and limit valve assembly
Hesitation to accelerate after sudden throttle closure	1. Leaks in hoses or connections to gulp valve or vacuum sensing pipe	Locate and rectify leak
	2. Faulty gulp valve	Test gulp valve, and renew if faulty
	3. Leak in intake system	Locate and rectify leak
Engine surges (erratic operation at varying throttle openings)	1. Leaks in hoses or connections to gulp valve or vacuum sensing	Locate and rectify leak
	2. Faulty gulp valve	Test gulp valve, and renew if faulty
Erratic idling or stalling	1. Leaks in hoses or connections to gulp valve or vacuum sensing pipe	Locate and rectify leak
	2. Faulty gulp valve	Test gulp valve, and renew if faulty
	3. Faulty carburetter limit valve	Fit new throttle plate and valve assembly
Burned or baked hose between air pump and check valve	1. Faulty check valve	Test check valve, and renew if faulty
	2. Air pump not pumping	Test air pump, service or renew if faulty
Noisy air pump	1. Incorrect belt tension	Adjust belt tension
	2. Pulleys damaged, loose or misaligned	Tighten loose pulleys, renew damaged pulleys
	3. Air pump failing or seizing	Test air pump, service or renew if faulty

ENGINE SPEED	TEST	COMPONENT CONDITION	READ/OBSERVE
START (cranking)	Cranking voltage	Battery; starting system	Voltmeter
	Cranking coil output	Coil; ign. primary circuit	Scope trace
	Cranking vacuum	Engine	Vacuum gauge
	Positive crankcase ventilation	Crankcase emission equipment	Vacuum gauge
IDLING	Idle speed	Carburetter idle setting	Tachometer
	Dwell	Distributor/drive; points	Dwell meter; scope
	Initial timing	Spark timing setting	Timing light
	Fuel mixture	Carburetter setting	Exhaust gas analyser
	Manifold vacuum	Engine idle efficiency	Vacuum gauge
CRUISE (1,000 r.p.m.)	Dwell variation	Distributor mechanical	Dwell meter
	Coil polarity	Ignition circuit polarity	Scope trace
	Cam lobe accuracy	Distributor cam	Scope trace
	Secondary circuit	Plugs; leads; cap; rotor	Scope trace
	Coil and condenser condition	Coil windings; condenser	Scope trace
	Breaker point condition	Points closing/opening/bounce	Scope trace
	Spark plug firing voltage	Fuel mixture; compression; plug/rotor gaps	Scope trace
	Fuel mixture	Carburetter	Exhaust gas analyser
ACCELERATE	Engine/cylinder balance/power drop	Cylinder compression	Tachometer (150 r.p.m. scale)
	Spark plugs under load	Spark plugs	Scope trace
	Carburetter open/close action	Carburetter	Exhaust gas analyser
TURNPIKE (2,500 r.p.m.)	Timing advance	Distributor mech./vacuum advance	Timing light/advance meter
	Maximum coil output	Coil; condenser; ignition primary	Scope trace
	Secondary circuit insulation	H.T. cables, cap, rotor	Scope trace
	Charging voltage	Regulator; cut-out	Voltmeter
	Fuel mixture	Air cleaner, carburetter	Exhaust gas analyser
	Exhaust restriction	Exhaust system	Vacuum gauge

CORRECT READINGS	CHECK SEQUENCE—FAULT LOCATION	
9·6 volts minimum at the battery	Battery—starter motor—connections/cables—dynamo/alternator—regulator	
17 KV. minimum	Ignition coil	
10—15 in. Hg even pulse	Hoses and connections—Valve rocker clearance—Gulp valve—Servo (if fitted)—Inlet manifold leaks—Valves or seats—Piston rings	
6—10 in. Hg	Oil filler cap—Pipes and connections—Emission valve—Oil separator	Pattern 1
See 'TUNING DATA'	Carburetter adjustment—Hoses and connections—Gulp valve—Servo (if fitted)—Carburetter limit valve or mechanical condition	
4-cyl. : 57 to 63°; 6-cyl. : 34 to 37°. See pattern 1	Breaker points—Distributor and drive mechanical condition	
See 'TUNING DATA'	Distributor adjustment	
See 'TUNING DATA'	Carburetter adjustment—Hoses and connections—Gulp valve—Crankcase emission valve—Servo (if fitted)—Carburetter limit valve or mechanical condition—Air pump—Check valve—Spark plugs	Pattern 2
18 to 20 in. Hg	Hoses and connections—Gulp valve—Inlet manifold leaks—carburetter limit valve—Valves or seats—Piston rings	PRIMARY WAVE FORM
Variation of 2° maximum	Distributor and drive mechanical condition	
See Pattern 2	Ignition circuit connections—Ignition coil	
2° max. variation. See pattern 3	Distributor mechanical condition (cam)	
Standard pattern	Spark plugs and leads—Breaker points—Carburetter adjustment—Hoses and connections—Gulp valve—Servo (if fitted)	Pattern 3
See Pattern 4	Ignition coil—Condenser	
See Pattern 1 (inset)	Breaker points—Condenser	
See Pattern 5; voltage 6—10 kV	Spark plugs and leads—Breaker points—Distributor cap and rotor—Carburetter adjustment—Hoses and connections—Gulp valve—Servo (if fitted)	
See 'TUNING DATA'	Carburetter adjustment—Hoses and connections—Gulp valve—Servo (if fitted)—Crankcase emission valve—Air pump—Check valve—Injectors	Pattern 4
Max. variation/cylinder 40 r.p.m.	Valve rocker clearance—Valves and seats—Piston rings	
See Pattern 6; 10 kV/plug maximum	Spark plugs and leads—Carburetter adjustment—Hoses and connections—Gulp valve—Servo (if fitted)	
Initial rich, lean off at throttle closure	Carburetter limit valve and mechanical condition—Hoses and connections—Gulp valve—Air pump	
See 'TUNING DATA'	Distributor mechanical condition, vacuum unit, centrifugal weights and springs	Pattern 5
Standard pattern; minimum reserve 2/3 more than requirement	Ignition coil—H.T. circuit insulation	
Standard pattern	H.T. leads—Distributor cap and rotor	
14·5 volts; steady reading	Cut-out—Voltage regulator—Dynamo/Alternator	
See 'TUNING DATA'	Hoses and connections—Carburetter adjustment—Air cleaners—Gulp valve—Air pump—Check valve—Injectors	
No variation in reading at constant speed for 10 sec.	Exhaust system	Pattern 6

EXHAUST EMISSION CONTROL

DESCRIPTION

Air is pressure-fed from an air pump through an injection manifold to the cylinder head exhaust port of each cylinder. The check valve in the air delivery pipe prevents blow-back from high pressure exhaust gases. The pump also supplies air through a gulp valve to the inlet manifold to provide air during conditions of deceleration and engine over-run.

Air Pump

The rotary vane type air pump is mounted on the front of the cylinder head and is belt driven from the water pump pulley. Air is drawn into the pump through a dry-type renewable element

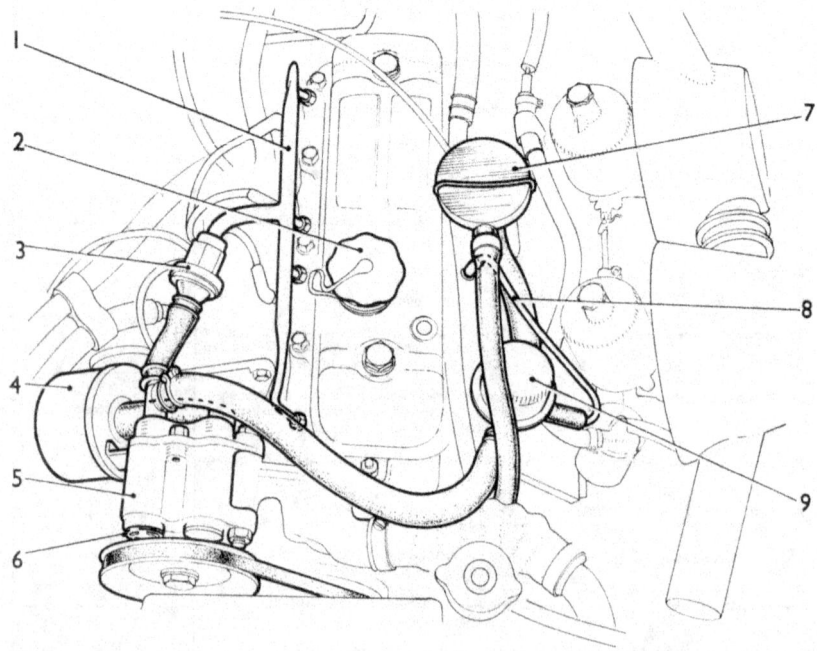

1. Air manifold.
2. Filtered oil filler cap.
3. Check valve.
4. Emission air cleaner.
5. Air pump.
6. Relief valve.
7. Crankcase emission valve.
8. Vacuum sensing tube.
9. Gulp valve.

Exhaust emission control

filter. A relief valve in the pump discharge port allows excess air pressure at high engine speeds to discharge to the atmosphere.

Check Valve

The check valve's function is to protect the pump from the backflow of exhaust gases. It is fitted in the pump discharge line to the injection manifold. The valve shuts if the air pressure ceases while the engine is running; i.e., if the pump drive belt should break.

Gulp Valve

The gulp valve, fitted in the pump discharge line to the inlet manifold, controls the flow of air for leaning-off the rich air/fuel mixture present in the inlet manifold immediately following throttle closure after running at full throttle opening, otherwise known as engine over-run.

A sensing pipe connected between the inlet manifold and the gulp valve transmits manifold vacuum directly to the underside of the diaphragm and through a bleed hole to the upper side. Sudden increases in manifold vacuum which occur immediately following throttle closure act on the underside of the diaphragm which opens the valve and admits air to the inlet manifold. The bleed hole allows the differences in vacuum acting on the diaphragm to equalize and the valve closes.

On some engines a restrictor is fitted in the air pump discharge connection to the gulp valve, which prevents surging when the gulp valve is operating.

Carburetter

The carburetters are manufactured to a special exhaust emission control specification and are tuned to give optimum engine performance with maximum emission control.

A limit valve is incorporated in the carburetter throttle disc which limits the inlet manifold vacuum to a maximum of 20.5 in. Hg, ensuring that under conditions of high inlet-manifold vacuum the mixture entering the cylinders is at a combustible ratio.

AIR PUMP

Drive Belt Tensioning

With proper tensioning, a total deflection of $\frac{1}{2}$ in., using moderate hand pressure, should be possible at the midway point of the longest belt run between the pulleys. To tension the belt:
    (1) Loosen the air pump mounting bolt and adjusting link bolts as shown in the illustration.
    (2) Using hand pressure only, pull the pump in the required direction until the correct tension is obtained.
    (3) Tighten the mounting and adjusting bolts to a torque figure of 10 ft. lbs.

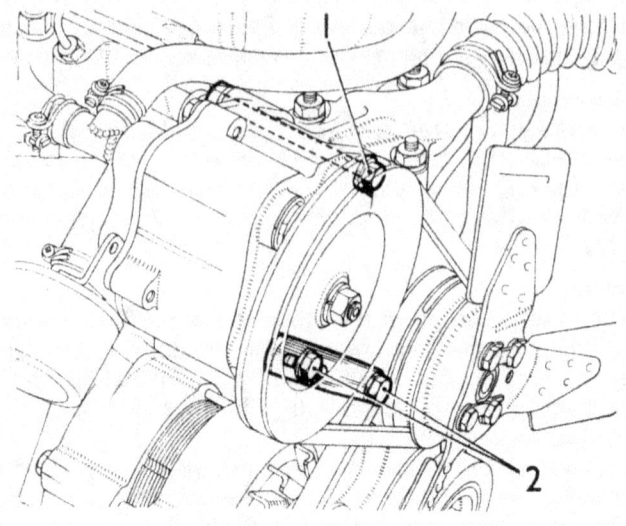

1. Pump mounting bolt.   2. Adjusting link bolts.

Drive belt tensioning

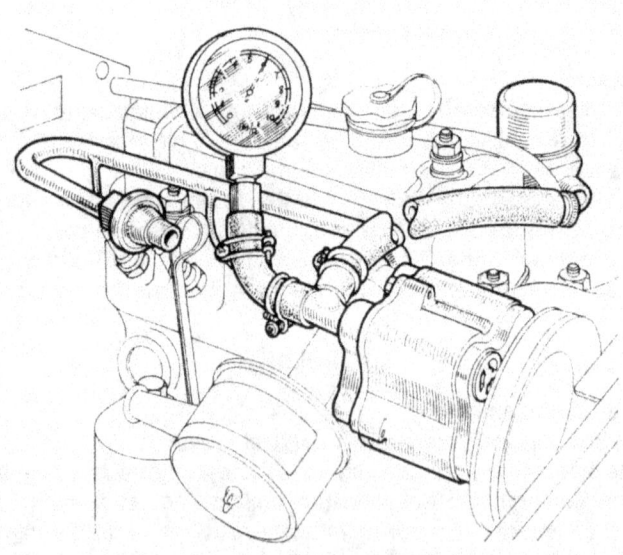

The pressure gauge connected

Air pump testing

Testing

(1) Check the drive belt for correct tensioning.
(2) Connect a tachometer to the engine in accordance with the instrument-maker's instructions.
(3) Disconnect the gulp valve air supply hose at the gulp valve and securely plug the valve.
(4) Disconnect the air manifold supply hose at the check valve, and connect a pressure gauge to the hose (see illustration).
(5) Run the engine at the air pump test speed given in TUNING DATA: a gauge reading of not less than 3 psi should be registered.
  (a) If the correct reading is not obtained, remove, dismantle and clean the pump air cleaner. Re-assemble using a new element, refit the air cleaner, and repeat the test.
  (b) If the reading is still unsatisfactory, check the relief valve for leakage. Renew the relief valve if faulty and repeat the test.
  (c) If a satisfactory reading is still unobtainable, remove and have the air pump serviced.
(6) Increase the engine speed to 3,000 rpm. When a gauge reading of between 4 and 5 psi is registered, the relief valve should operate. If the relief valve fails to function, remove the pump and renew the relief valve.

Removal

(1) Disconnect the air hoses from the pump connections and remove the air cleaner.
(2) Loosen the mounting and adjusting link bolts and slip the belt drive from the pump pulley.
(3) Remove the top adjusting link bolt and the nut securing the pump mounting bolt.
(4) Support the pump, withdraw the mounting bolt, then lift the pump from the engine.

Replacement

(1) Position the pump in the mounting bracket then fit, but do not tighten, the pump mounting bolt.
(2) Replace, but do not tighten, the adjusting link bolt.
(3) Fit and tension the drive belt.
(4) Reconnect the hoses and refit the air cleaner.

Relief Valve Replacement

(1) Remove the air pump.
(2) Remove the pump pulley.
(3) Place a ½ in. diameter soft metal drift through the pump discharge connection so that it registers against the relief valve, then drive the valve from the pump.

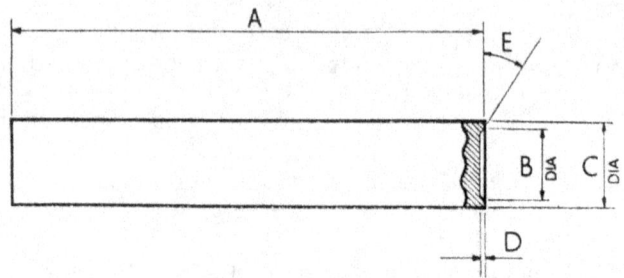

The dimensions of the relief valve replacing tool

A = 5 in.   B = ·986 in.   C = 1·062 in.
D = ·05 in.   E = 30°.

Relief valve tool

(4) Fit a new copper seating washer to the new relief valve and place the valve into the pump body.
(5) Using a tool made to the dimensions shown in the illustration, drive the valve into the pump body until the copper seating washer is held firmly, but not compressed, between the valve and the pump body.
(5) Refit the pulley, then replace the air pump.

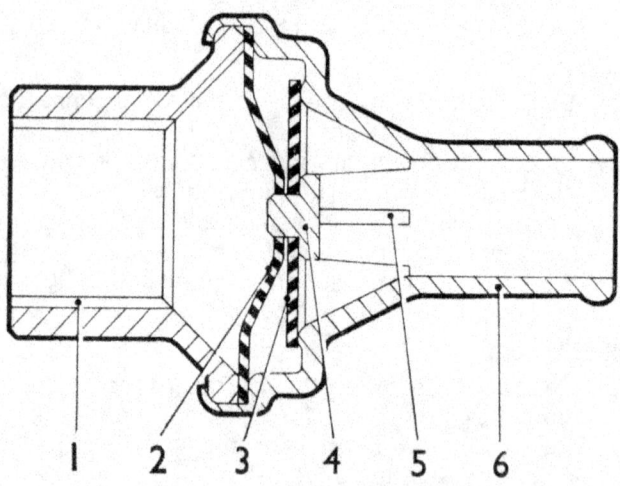

A section through the check valve

1. Air manifold connection.   4. Valve pilot.
2. Diaphragm.   5. Guides.
3. Valve.   6. Air supply connection.

Check valve

CHECK VALVE

Removal
(1) Disconnect the air supply hose from the check valve connection.
(2) Hold the air manifold connection to prevent it twisting and unscrew the check valve.

Testing
(1) Blow with the mouth through the valve, in turn from each connection.
   Note: Never use the high-pressure air hose for this test.
(2) Air should pass through the valve when blown from the air supply hose connection.
(3) Should air pass through when blown from the air manifold connection, replace the check valve.

Replacement
(1) Hold the air manifold connection to prevent it twisting, then screw in and tighten the check valve.
(2) Reconnect the air supply hose to the check valve.

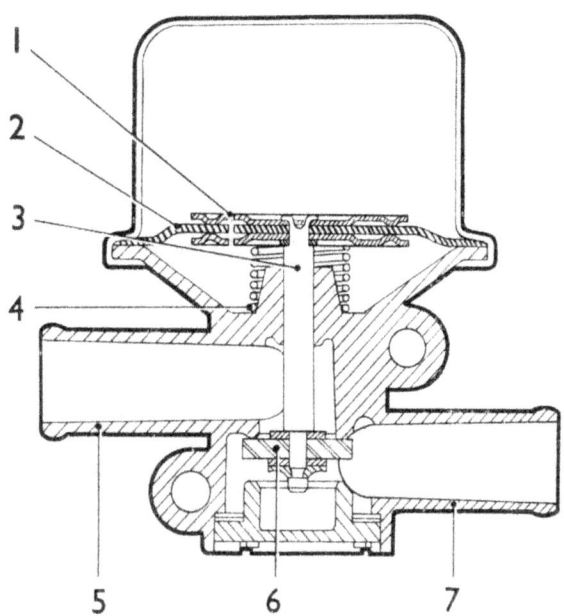

A section through the gulp valve

1. Metering balance orifice.
2. Diaphragm.
3. Valve spindle.
4. Return spring.
5. Inlet manifold hose connection.
6. Valve.
7. Air pump hose connection.

Gulp valve

GULP VALVE

Testing
(1) Disconnect the air supply hose at the gulp valve, then securely plug the disconnected hose end.
(2) Connect a vacuum gauge to the air supply connection of the gulp valve.
(3) Run the engine at idling speed and at operational temperature.
(4) A zero vacuum reading should be registered on the gauge indicating that the valve is seating correctly. If a vacuum is registered, replace the gulp valve.
(5) Operate the throttle from closed to open in rapid succession; The gauge should register a vacuum, then return slowly to zero. Repeat the test several times observing the gauge reaction; if the gauge fails to respond as above, renew the gulp valve.

Removal and Replacement
(1) Disconnect the air hoses.
(2) Unscrew the mounting screw and remove the gulp valve.
(3) To replace, reverse the removal procedure.

CARBURETTERS

The carburetters are adjusted and tuned to give optimum engine performance with efficient engine emission control. Adjustments to the carburetter settings must ONLY be performed by a licensed Pollution Control Service Station.

CRANKCASE EMISSION CONTROL

Refer to the ENGINE chapter in Section II for the description and the testing and servicing procedures.

GENERAL DATA
(18GB)

The following information is applicable to the 18GB-engined cars and should be used in conjunction with the preceding specification for the 18G/18GA-engined car.

ENGINE
- Type .. 18GB.

Main bearings
- Number and type .. 5 thin-wall.
- Length: Front, centre and rear .. 1⅛ in. (28·5 mm.).
- Intermediate .. ⅞ in. (22·23 mm.).

Connecting rods
- Type .. Angular-split big-end, bushed small-end.

Big-end bearings
- Length .. ·775 to ·785 in. (19·68 to 19·94 mm.).

Pistons
- Gudgeon pin bore .. ·8126 to ·8129 (20·610 to 20·617 mm.).

Gudgeon pin
- Type .. Fully floating.
- Fit in piston .. ·0001 to ·00035 in. (·0025 to ·007 mm.).
- Diameter (outer) .. ·8124 to ·8127 (20·608 to 20·615 mm.).

FUEL SYSTEM
- Carburetter needles .. FX.

REAR AXLE (GT)
- Type .. Hypoid, semi-floating.

FRONT SUSPENSION (GT)
- Spring coil diameter (mean) .. 3·28 in. (83·3 mm.).
- Free height .. 9·1 ± 1/16 in. (231 ± 1·6 mm.).
- Number of free coils .. 7·2.
- Static length at load of 1,193 lb. (541·5 kg.) ± 20 lb. (9·1 kg.) 6·6 in. (168 mm.).

REAR SUSPENSION (GT)
- Spring detail
  - Working load (± 15 lb. 7 kg.) .. 510 lb. (321·6 kg.).

WHEELS (GT)
- Size: Disc .. 5J × 14 in.

TYRES (GT)
- Optional:
  - Size .. 165—14 SP.
- Standard tyres:
  - Pressures (set cold):
    - Front .. 20 lb./sq. in. (1·4 kg./cm.²).
    - Rear .. 24 lb./sq. in. (1·7 kg./cm.²).
  - Sustained speeds in excess of 90 m.p.h. (145 km.p.h.):
    - Front .. 26 lb./sq. in. (1·8 kg./cm.²).
    - Rear .. 30 lb./sq. in. (2·1 kg./cm.²).
- Optional tyres:
  - Pressures (set cold):
    - Front .. 21 lb./sq. in. (1·5 kg./cm.²).
    - Rear .. 24 lb./sq. in. (1·7 kg./cm.²).
  - Sustained speeds in excess of 90 m.p.h. (145 km.p.h.):
    - Front .. 28 lb./sq. in. (2·0 kg./cm.²).
    - Rear .. 31 lb./sq. in. (2·2 kg./cm.²).

GENERAL DATA
(18GB)

The following information is applicable to the 18GB-engined cars and should be used in conjunction with the preceding specification for the 18G/18GA-engined car.

ENGINE
- Type .. .. 18GB.
- **Main bearings**
  - Number and type .. .. 5 thin-wall.
  - Length: Front, centre and rear .. .. 1⅛ in. (28·5 mm.).
  - Intermediate .. .. ⅞ in. (22·23 mm.).
- **Connecting rods**
  - Type .. .. Angular-split big-end, bushed small-end.
- **Big-end bearings**
  - Length .. .. ·775 to ·785 in. (19·68 to 19·94 mm.).
- **Pistons**
  - Gudgeon pin bore .. .. ·8126 to ·8129 (20·610 to 20·617 mm.).
- **Gudgeon pin**
  - Type .. .. Fully floating.
  - Fit in piston .. .. ·0001 to ·00035 in. (·0025 to ·007 mm.).
  - Diameter (outer) .. .. ·8124 to ·8127 (20·608 to 20·615 mm.).

GENERAL DATA

(18GF WITH EXHAUST EMISSION CONTROL)

Engine
Bore .. .. 3·16 in. (80·26 mm.)
Stroke .. .. 3·5 in. (89 mm.)
No. of cylinders 4
Capacity .. .. 1798 c.c. (109·8 cu. in.)
Compression ratio .. .. .. 8·8 : 1
Firing order 1, 3, 4, 2
Valve clearance (cold) .. .. ·015 in. (·38 mm.)
Oil pressure: Idling .. .. .. 10 to 25 lb./sq. in. (·7 to 1·7 kg./cm.²)
Normal .. .. 50 to 80 lb./sq. in. (3·5 to 5·6 kg./cm.²)
Idle speed (manual transmission) .. 900 r.p.m.
Fast idle speed (manual transmission) 1,300 to 1,400 r.p.m.

Ignition
Stroboscopic ignition timing .. 20 B.T.D.C. at 1,000 r.p.m.
Contact breaker gap .. .. ·014 to ·016 in. (·36 to ·41 mm.)
Sparking plugs .. .. .. Champion N–9Y
Plug gap .. .. ·025 in. (·64 mm.)

Fuel system
Carburetters .. .. .. Two S.U. type HS4
Needle .. .. FX●
Fuel pump .. .. .. S.U. Type HP or AUF 300 electric

Gearbox and overdrive
Overdrive ratio .. .. ·82 : 1
Overall ratios: First .. .. 13·446 : 1
Second .. 8·47 : 1   Overdrive
Third .. 5·40 : 1   4·43 : 1
Fourth .. 3·909 : 1   3·20 : 1
Reverse .. 12·098 : 1
Top gear speed per 1,000 r.p.m.:
Standard .. .. 18 m.p.h.
Overdrive .. .. 22 m.p.h.

Wheels
Type   Tourer   GT
Ventilated disc .. .. ..   4J × 14   5J × 14
Wire (optional) .. .. ..   4½J × 14 (60-spoke)

Tyres
Standard size .. .. ..   5·60—14 (tubed C41)
                          Tourer   GT
Optional size .. .. ..   155—14 (SP)   165—14 (SP)
Standard tyres:
Pressures (set cold):   Tourer   GT
Front .. .. ..   18 lb./sq. in.   20 lb./sq. in.
                   (1·3 kg./cm.²)   (1·4 kg./cm.²)
Rear .. .. ..   18 lb./sq. in.   24 lb./sq. in.
                   (1·3 kg./cm.²)   (1·7 kg./cm.²)
Sustained speeds in excess of 90 m.p.h. (145 km.p.h.):
Front .. .. ..   24 lb./sq. in.   26 lb./sq. in.
                   (1·7 kg./cm.²)   (1·8 kg./cm.²)
Rear .. .. ..   24 lb./sq. in.   30 lb./sq. in.
                   (1·7 kg./cm.²)   (2·1 kg./cm.²)

GENERAL DATA—continued

(18GF — continued)

	Tourer	GT
Optional tyres (SP): Pressures (set cold):		
Front	21 lb./sq. in. (1·5 kg./cm.²)	21 lb./sq. in. (1·5 kg./cm.²)
Rear	24 lb./sq. in. (1·7 kg./cm.²)	24 lb./sq. in. (1·7 kg./cm.²)
Sustained speeds in excess of 90 m.p.h. (145 km.p.h.):		
Front	27 lb./sq. in. (1·9 kg./cm.²)	28 lb./sq. in. (2·0 kg./cm.²)
Rear	31 lb./sq. in. (2·2 kg./cm.²)	31 lb./sq. in. (2·2 kg./cm.²)

NOTE.—Rear tyre pressures should be increased by 2 lb./sq. in (·14 kg./cm.²) when touring with a full luggage compartment.

Capacities
Fuel tank	12 gallons (54 litres, 14 U.S. gal.)
Cooling system	9½ pints (5·4 litres, 11·4 U.S. pints)
Cooling system with heater	10 pints (5·6 litres, 12 U.S. pints)
Sump	7½ pints (4·26 litres, 9 U.S. pints)
Sump with oil cooler	8¼ pints (4·5 litres, 9·6 U.S. pints)
Gearbox	4½ pints (2·56 litres, 5·6 U.S. pints)
Gearbox and overdrive	5¼ pints (3·0 litres, 6 U.S. pints)
Automatic transmission	10½ pints (6 litres, 12·7 U.S. pints)
Rear axle	1½ pints (·85 litre, 2 U.S. pints)

Dimensions
Length	12 ft. 8½ in. (3·8 m.)
Length with over-riders	12 ft. 9 3/16 in. (3·89 m.)
Width	4 ft. 11 15/16 in. (152·3 cm.)
Height, hood erected	4 ft. 1 3/8 in. (125·4 cm.)
Ground clearance (minimum)	5 in. (12·7 cm.)
Track: Front: Disc wheels	4 ft. 1 in. (124·4 cm.)
Wire wheels	4 ft. 1¼ in. (125·0 cm.)
Rear: Disc wheels	4 ft. 1¼ in. (125·0 cm.)
Wire wheels	4 ft. 1¼ in. (125·0 cm.)
Wheelbase	7 ft. 7 in. (231·1 cm.)
Turning circle	32 ft. (9·75 m.)
Toe-in	1/16 to 3/32 in. (1·5 to 2·3 mm.)

	Tourer	GT
Weights (Standard car) Unladen	2,109 lb. (956 kg.)	2,369 lb. (1076 kg.)
Kerbside	2,149 lb. (974 kg.)	2,409 lb. (1093 kg.)
Max. permissible gross	2,574 lb. (1167 kg.)	2,834 lb. (1285 kg.)

On the following pages will be found an edited reprint of the Driver's Handbook issued with each MGB. The reader will note that there is much information that pertains to other sections of the book.

M G B

TOURER *(GHN4)* and GT *(GHD4)*

Handbook

FOREWORD

This Handbook provides an introduction to your car, together with information on the care and periodic maintenance required to combine trouble-free motoring with minimal running costs. The contents may include variations in the specification of some or all of the models shown on the front page. The Handbook does not in any way constitute a particular vehicle specification.

Safety features are embodied in the structure of your car. You are advised to consult your Distributor or Dealer regarding repairs or replacements.

Your BMC Distributor or Dealer is provided with the latest information concerning special service tools and workshop techniques. This enables him to undertake your service and repairs in the most efficient and economic manner.

You are recommended to use the Maintenance Voucher Scheme. A Passport to Service containing service vouchers is provided and regular use of the vouchers in sequence is the best safeguard against the possibility of abnormal repair bills at a later date. Failure to have your car correctly maintained could invalidate the terms of the Warranty.

Completed voucher counterfoils are proof of regular servicing and could well enhance the value of your vehicle in the eyes of a prospective buyer. A replacement Passport to Service voucher book is obtainable from Distributors or Dealers.

Please note that references to right- or left-hand in this Handbook are made when viewing the car from the rear.

 IMPORTANT.—Your car is fitted with engine emission control equipment in accordance with legislation requirements. All maintenance checks and adjustments showing this sign must be entrusted to your approved **pollution control service station.**

INSTRUMENTS AND SWITCHES

STEERING COLUMN
Fig. 1

Headlamp beam (1) With the headlamps switched on at the lighting switch, move the lever down to operate the high beam. Lifting the lever towards the steering-wheel from the low beam position will flash the headlamp high beams irrespective of whether the lighting switch is on or off.

Direction indicators (1) The switch is self-cancelling and operates the indicators only when the ignition is switched on.

Horn (1) The horn is sounded by pressing the knob on the end of the switch lever.

Windscreen wiper (2) With the ignition switched on, move the switch lever back towards the seat to operate the windscreen wipers at slow speed; further movement in the same direction will operate the wipers at fast speed. The wiper blades park automatically when the switch lever is returned to the off position.

Windscreen washer (2) Press the knob on the end of the switch lever to operate the windscreen washer. When the windscreen is dirty, operate the washer before setting the wipers in motion.

In cold weather the washer reservoir should be filled with a mixture of water and a recommended washer solvent to prevent the water freezing. On no account may radiator anti-freeze be used in the windscreen washer.

Overdrive (2) Move the switch lever towards the steering-wheel to engage overdrive; move the switch lever away from the steering-wheel to return to normal drive (see 'RUNNING INSTRUCTIONS').

Fig. 1

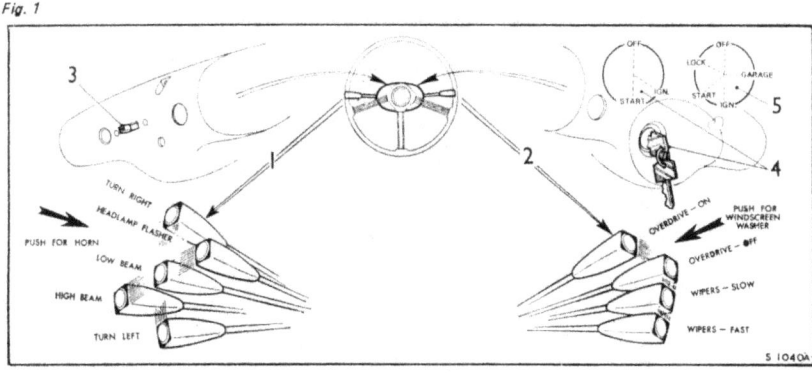

Instruments and Switches

Panel light switch (3) When the sidelights are switched on the instruments may be illuminated by moving the switch knob to the on position.

Ignition and starter switch (4) The ignition and starter are both controlled by a single switch operated by a removable key. To switch on the ignition, insert the key and turn it in a clockwise direction until a slight resistance is felt. Further movement in the same direction operates the starter motor. Release the key immediately the engine starts. If the engine fails to start the key must be returned to the off position before the start position can be re-selected.

The key can only be withdrawn when the switch is in the off position.

Ignition/ starter switch and steering lock (5) In addition to controlling the ignition and starter the switch also incorporates a steering-column lock. They key action for operating the ignition and starter is similar to that of the standard switch.

To lock the steering, turn the key to the 'LOCK' position and withdraw it, then turn the steering-wheel until the lock plunger is heard to click into engagement with the steering-column.

With the switch in the 'GARAGE' position the ignition is switched off and the steering lock disengaged. The key may be withdrawn in this position.

FASCIA
Fig. 2
Warning light (red) (1) Brake pressure. The light glows when the brake pedal is depressed if a loss of pressure has occurred in the front or rear hydraulic braking system.

To test the warning light bulb, press the test push on the right-hand side of the warning light mounting plate (see **'RUNNING INSTRUCTIONS'**).

Fig. 2

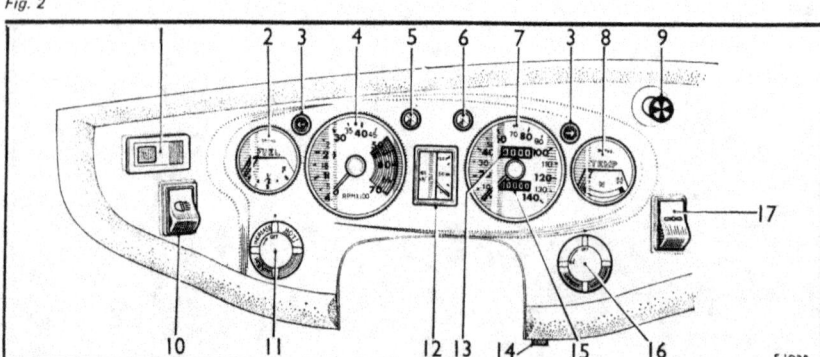

Fuel gauge (2)	When the ignition is switched on the gauge indicates approximately the amount of fuel in the tank. An important note on filling with fuel is given in **'RUNNING INSTRUCTIONS'**.
Warning light (green) (3)	Direction indicator. The arrow-shaped lights show the direction selected and operate with the flashing direction indicators.
Tachometer (4)	The instrument indicates the revolutions per minute of the engine and assists the driver to use the most effective engine speed range for maximum performance in any gear (see **'RUNNING INSTRUCTIONS'**).
Warning light (red) (5)	Ignition. The ignition warning light serves the dual purpose of reminding the driver to switch off the ignition and of acting as a no-charge indicator (see **'RUNNING INSTRUCTIONS'**).
Warning light (blue) (6)	Headlight high beam. The light glows when the headlights are switched on and the beam is in the raised position. The light goes out when the beam is lowered.
Speedometer (7)	In addition to recording the road speed this instrument also records the total distance (15) and the distance travelled for any particular trip (13). To reset the trip recorder, push the knob (14) upwards and turn it clockwise; it is important that all the counters are returned to zero.
Coolant temperature gauge (8)	The gauge is marked 'C' (cold); 'N' (normal); and 'H' (hot), indicating the temperature of the coolant as it leaves the cylinder head. An important note about temperature is given in **'RUNNING INSTRUCTIONS'**.
Mixture control (choke) (9)	Pull out the knob to enrich the fuel/air mixture to assist starting when the engine is cold. Notes on setting the control are given in **'RUNNING INSTRUCTIONS'**.
Lighting switch (10)	Press the lower end of the switch rocker to the first position to operate the parking lights, and fully in to operate the headlights.
Temperature control (11)	For operating instructions see **'HEATING AND VENTILATING'**.
Oil pressure gauge (12)	The gauge indicates the pressure of the oil in the engine lubrication system. Important notes on its indications are given in **'RUNNING INSTRUCTIONS'**.
Ventilation control (16)	For operating instructions see **'HEATING AND VENTILATING'**.
Blower switch (17)	The switch controls the booster blower for heating and ventilating and operates only when the ignition is switched on (see **'HEATING AND VENTILATING'**).

HEATING AND VENTILATING

FRESH AIR Fresh air is admitted to the car for cooling and ventilation through an adjustable vent mounted behind the speaker panel. The flow of air may be adjusted by moving the control knob (1, Fig. 1) to one of the three open positions; move the knob to the most forward position to close the vent.

HEATER The heating and ventilating system is designed to provide fresh air either heated
Fig. 1 by the engine cooling system or at outside temperature to the car at floor level and for demisting and defrosting to the windscreen.

Air distribution Air enters the car through the two doors located one each side of the gearbox tunnel in the foot wells. Close the spring-loaded doors (2) when full air flow is required for windscreen demisting or defrosting. Air distribution for heating is independent of the fresh-air system; the control knob (1) should be in the closed position when heated air is being distributed.

Controls **Heater.** Turn the knob (3) in the direction of the arrow to raise the air temperature.

Air flow. Turn the knob (4) in the direction of the arrow to direct the air distribution.

Booster. Press the lower end of the switch rocker (5) to boost the air flow.

Usage The heater and air flow controls may be set at the position marked on the control knobs or to any other intermediate positions. By varying the control settings, opening or closing the air distribution doors, and utilizing the booster blower, a wide range of settings can be obtained to suit prevailing conditions.

Fig. 1

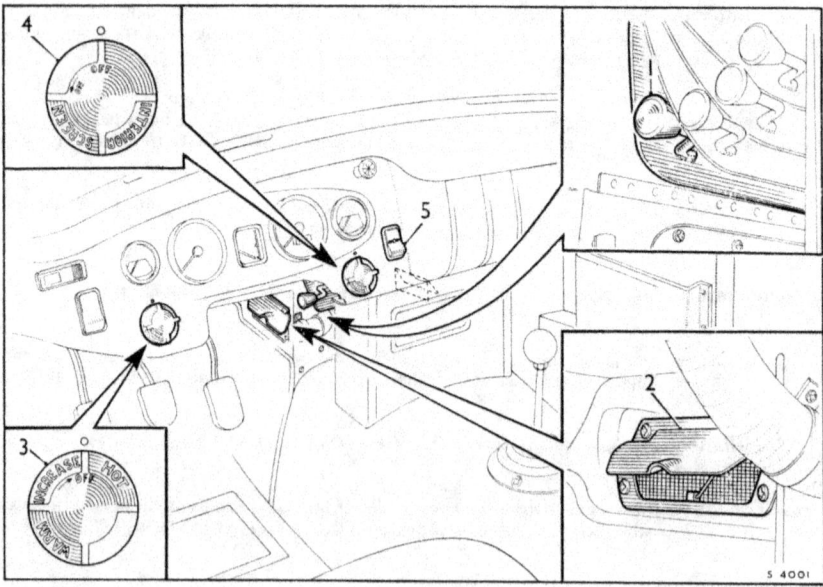

RUNNING INSTRUCTIONS

Choice of fuel The octane number of a motor fuel is an indication given by the fuel technicians of its knock resistance (pinking). High-octane fuels have been produced to improve the efficiency of engines by allowing them to operate on high compression ratios, resulting in better fuel economy and greater power. Owing to the high compression ratio of the engine, fuels with an octane rating below 98 are not suitable. Should it be necessary to use a fuel with a lower octane number, the car must be used very carefully until the correct fuel can be obtained.

It is necessary to use Premium grade fuels with octane ratings of 98 or above when optimum performance is required.

Filling up with fuel When filling up with fuel avoid filling the tank until fuel is visible in the filler intake tube. Should this be done and the car left in the sun, there will be a considerable risk of fuel leakage due to expansion, and consequent danger from exposed fuel. If inadvertently overfilled and the car is to be parked, take care to park it in the shade with the filler intake as high as possible.

Brakes The warning light on the fascia panel will glow when the brake pedal is depressed with the ignition switched on if an excessive difference in pressure exists between the front and rear hydraulic systems. To test, switch on the ignition and press the test push on the right-hand side of the light mounting plate; the light will glow if the bulb is functioning. Release the test push and depress the brake pedal; the light will remain off if the hydraulic system is satisfactory. The brake warning system should be checked daily.

If the warning light glows at any time other than when being tested, the car must be driven with extreme caution and the cause investigated by your Distributor or Dealer at the earliest possible opportunity.

Starting Check that the gear lever is in the neutral position.

If the engine is cold, pull out the mixture control (choke). In extremely cold conditions it may be necessary to pull the control out to its fullest extent.

Switch on the ignition, check that the ignition warning light glows and that the fuel gauge registers, then operate the starter.

As soon as the engine starts, release the ignition key and warm up the engine at a fairly fast speed (see **'Warming up'**). Check that the oil pressure gauge is registering and that the ignition warning light has gone out. Push in the mixture control (choke) completely as soon as the engine will run evenly without its use. **See page 23 when automatic transmission is fitted.**

Starter Do not operate the starter for longer than five to six seconds.

To prevent damage the starter cannot be operated while the engine is running. If the engine fails to start the ignition key must be returned to the off position before the starter can be operated again.

If after a reasonable number of attempts the engine should fail to start, switch off the ignition and investigate the cause. Continued use of the starter when the engine will not start, not only discharges the battery but may also damage the starter.

Running Instructions

Mixture control (choke) — Always use the minimum setting for the shortest possible time.

As soon as possible after the engine has started, push the control completely home.

To obtain a fast engine idling speed, set the control to within the first $\frac{1}{4}$ in. (6 mm.) approx. of its initial movement. The control may be locked in the required position by turning the knob a quarter of a turn to the left or right.

Ignition warning light — The light should glow when the engine is switched on, and go out and stay out at all times while the engine is running above normal idling speed. Failure to do so indicates a fault in the battery charging system. Check that the fan belt is correctly tensioned before consulting your Distributor or Dealer.

Oil pressure gauge — The gauge should register a pressure as soon as the engine is started up. The pressure may rise above 80 lb./sq. in., when the engine is started from cold and as the oil is circulated and warmed the pressure should then drop to between 50 and 80 lb./sq. in. at normal running speeds and to between 10 and 25 lb./sq. in. at idling speed.

Should the gauge fail to register any pressure, stop the engine immediately and investigate the cause. Start by checking the oil level.

Warming up — Research has proved that the practice of warming up an engine by allowing it to idle slowly is definitely harmful. The correct procedure is to let the engine run fairly fast, approximately 1,000 r.p.m., so that it attains its correct working temperature as quickly as possible. Allowing the engine to work slowly in a cold state leads to excessive cylinder wear, and far less damage is done by driving the car straight on to the road from cold than by letting the engine idle slowly in the garage.

For automatic transmission, see page 23.

Temperature gauge — When the engine is running the gauge indicates the temperature of the coolant leaving the cylinder head.

As overheating may cause serious damage, the readings should be noted and after the initial rise in temperature during the warming up period any sudden upward change in the reading calls for immediate investigation.

When the ignition is switched off the needle returns to the 'cold' position.

Running in — The treatment given to a new car will have an important bearing on its subsequent life, and engine speeds during this early period must be limited. The following instructions should be strictly adhered to.

During the first 500 miles:
DO NOT exceed 45 m.p.h.
DO NOT operate at full throttle in any gear.
DO NOT allow the engine to labour in any gear.

Tachometer For normal road work, and to obtain the most satisfactory service from your engine, select the appropriate gear to maintain engine speeds of between 2,000 and 4,500 r.p.m.

When maximum acceleration is required upward gear selections should be made when the needle reaches the yellow sector (5,500–6,000 r.p.m.). Prolonged or excessive use of the highest engine speeds will tend to shorten the life of the engine. Allowing the engine to pull hard at low engine speeds must be avoided as this also has a detrimental effect on the engine.

The beginning of the red sector (6,000 r.p.m.) indicates the maximum safe speed for the engine.

Never allow the needle to enter the red sector.

Wet brakes When the vehicle is being washed or driven through water the brake linings may become wet. To dry them, apply the brakes several times with the vehicle moving slowly. Driving with wet brakes is very dangerous.

Towing Should it become necessary to tow the car, use the towing eyes provided. (See 'AUTOMATIC TRANSMISSION'.)

Overdrive The overdrive unit, controlled by a switch on the steering column, provides a high erdriving ratio for use with third or fourth gear. To engage overdrive move the switch lever towards the steering-wheel, to disengage move the lever away from the steering-wheel. Do not depress the clutch pedal during engagement or disengagement.

Overdrive can be engaged at any throttle opening when in third or top gear. If increased acceleration is required the overdrive can be 'switched out' without alteration to the throttle setting. Do not 'switch out' the overdrive when travelling at speeds exceeding normal third or top gear road speeds.

In certain driving conditions while travelling in third gear, the overdrive can be switched in to provide a top gear ratio or out to provide third gear acceleration without the necessity of changing gear.

AUTOMATIC TRANSMISSION

Description   The usual flywheel and clutch are replaced by a fluid torque converter which is coupled to a hydraulically operated planetary gearbox providing three forward ratios and reverse. All forward ratios are automatically engaged in accordance with accelerator position, speed of the car, and road load.

Automatic selection may be over-ridden by manual selection of first or second using the selector lever when engine braking or increased acceleration is desired.

Driving features   The automatic transmission has many advantages over a manually selected gearbox. These will soon become apparent in time saved, safer driving, and less driving fatigue.

The technique of driving a car fitted with automatic transmission to its fullest advantage is very soon mastered. The following points, however, must always be observed.

DO NOT select 'P' or 'R' while the car is moving; always apply the hand brake before selecting 'P'.

DO NOT select 'D', 'L2', 'L1', or 'R' when the engine is running at high speed with the car stationary.

DO NOT select 'L2' at speeds above 68 m.p.h.

Selector positions   The positions for manual selection are marked 'P', 'R', 'N', 'D', 'L2', 'L1', on the selector lever quadrant plate.
Fig. 1

The stop (1) provided between 'N' and 'R' is to minimize inadvertent selection of 'P' or 'R' while the car is moving.

To select 'P' or 'R' from any of the other positions, move the lever forward raising the spring-loaded slide (2) sufficiently to clear the stop. The slide must also be raised when selecting the other positions with the lever at 'P' or 'R'.
DO NOT raise the slide when the car is in motion.

P   **Park.** In this position the transmission is mechanically locked. Use this position when parked, starting, or when the car is stationary with the engine running for tuning or adjustment.

DO NOT select 'P' when the car is moving, and always apply the hand brake before selecting 'P'.

R   **Reverse. DO NOT** select 'R' when the car is moving forward.

N   **Neutral.** The hand brake must be applied at all times when the lever is in 'N'. Use this position for starting.

D   **Drive.** This position is used when driving in normal traffic and road conditions. Changes of all forward ratios are automatic.

L2   **Lock-up second ratio.** Automatic changes are confined to first and second ratios only. This position is used when rapid acceleration or engine braking is required.

DO NOT select 'L2' at speeds above 68 m.p.h.

L1   **Lock-up first ratio.** In this position the transmission is locked to provide first ratio only.

Automatic Transmission

Starting the engine The procedure given in **'RUNNING INSTRUCTIONS'** for starting the engine also applies to cars fitted with automatic transmission. The following points, however, should be noted.

The starter will only operate when the selector lever is in the 'P' or 'N' positions. When the engine has been started from cold, warm it up using the mixture control (choke) fast idle position (see page 21), until the engine will run without its assistance, before driving off. Driving with the mixture control in the fast idle position can be dangerous due to sudden acceleration when the brake pedal is released after a drive position has been selected; driving with a cold engine may result in stalling.

Driving **Selecting a driving position.** Always release the accelerator pedal and apply the foot brake before moving the selector lever to the required position. This will prevent the car from creeping (i.e. a tendency for the car to move very slowly forward if 'D', 'L1', or 'L2' are selected or backwards when 'R' is selected. This creep feature can be used to advantage when manœuvring in a confined space.

Moving off. The selector can be in any one of the forward driving positions 'D' 'L1', or 'L2', selection of the position being dependent on prevailing circumstances. After releasing the brakes the take-off will be smooth regardless of how much the accelerator pedal is depressed. Discretion in the use of the accelerator must be exercised when in slippery road conditions or if optimum fuel economy is to be achieved.

Selector in 'D'. The automatic selection of all forward ratios takes place progressively up or down in accordance with changes in road speed, accelerator position, and road load.

The effect of the engine acting as a partial brake (engine braking) when the accelerator is released, as with a manual gearbox, is not present when driving with the selector in 'D'.

Fig. 1

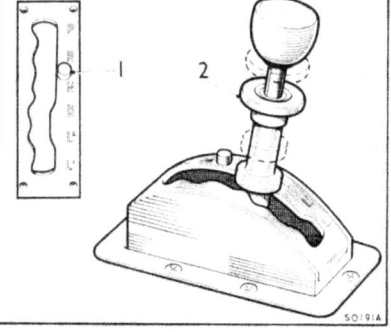

Fig. 2

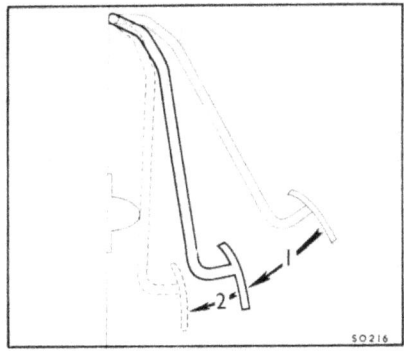

Selector in 'L2'. Selection of first and second ratios only will occur automatically in accordance with changing conditions. Appropriate engine braking is available when the accelerator pedal is released. Manual selection of 'L2' can be made when driving in 'D' at any speed below 68 m.p.h. and will provide a smooth down-change to second ratio. Use 'L2' when road conditions demand rapid acceleration or full engine braking; for example, when overtaking, approaching or negotiating bends, or gradients. It is recommended that 'L2' is used when towing a caravan or other vehicles at speeds up to 40 m.p.h.

Selector in 'L1'. The transmission will remain in first ratio irrespective of changes in road or driving conditions. This position provides full engine braking and full engine power, for example, when starting off on or ascending, very steep gradients. **Avoid overspeeding the engine.**

Stopping. Release the accelerator and apply the brakes.

Soft surfaces. When the rear wheels fail to grip in conditions such as mud or snow, the car may be rocked backwards and forwards by alternately selecting 'R' and 'D' while using light accelerator pressure.

Increased acceleration
Fig. 2

When lower gear acceleration is required for overtaking or hill-climbing, etc., down changes of gear can be made by depressing the accelerator pedal. The maximum down-change speeds are preset to give optimum performance without overspeeding the engine.

At speeds up to 30 m.p.h. in top gear, depression of the accelerator pedal within the limits of its normal travel (1) will produce a down-change to second gear. Fully depressing the pedal beyond its normal travel (2); this is termed 'kick-down', will produce a down-change to first gear.

At speeds above 30 m.p.h. within the 'kick-down' speed range, down-changes may be made by depressing the pedal to the 'kick-down' position. The speeds below which 'kick-down' changes can be made are:
From third to second gear, 52 to 56 m.p.h.
From second to first gear, 28 to 32 m.p.h.

Towing

For recovery the car may be towed with the selector lever at 'N', provided the automatic transmission is operating satisfactorily and the fluid is at its correct level.

If the transmission is inoperative, remove the propeller shaft or lift the rear wheels.

NOTE.—The car cannot be tow-started.

COOLING SYSTEM

Radiator filler cap
Fig. 1 (1)
The system is pressurized to 10 lb./sq. in. when hot, and the pressure must be released gradually when the filler cap is removed. It is advisable to protect the hands against escaping steam and turn the cap slowly anti-clockwise until the resistance of the safety stops is felt. Leave the cap in this position until all pressure is released. Press the cap downwards against the spring to clear the safety stops, and continue turning until it can be lifted off.

Draining the cooling system
There are two drain taps provided, one (2) on the radiator bottom tank and the other (3) on the right-hand side of the cylinder block. To drain the coolant, stand the car on level ground and open both taps.

When draining in freezing weather, do so when the engine is hot. Run the engine slowly for one minute when the water has ceased flowing to clear any water from the pump and other places where it might collect. Finally, leave a reminder on the vehicle to the effect that the cooling system has been drained.

If the system contains anti-freeze, remember to collect it in a clean container for future use.

Filling the cooling system
To avoid wastage by overflow add just sufficient coolant to cover the bottom of the header tank. Run the engine until it is hot and add sufficient coolant to bring the surface to the level of the indicator positioned inside the header tank below the filler neck.

NOTE.—The heater control must be set to 'HOT' when draining or filling the cooling system.

Fig. 1

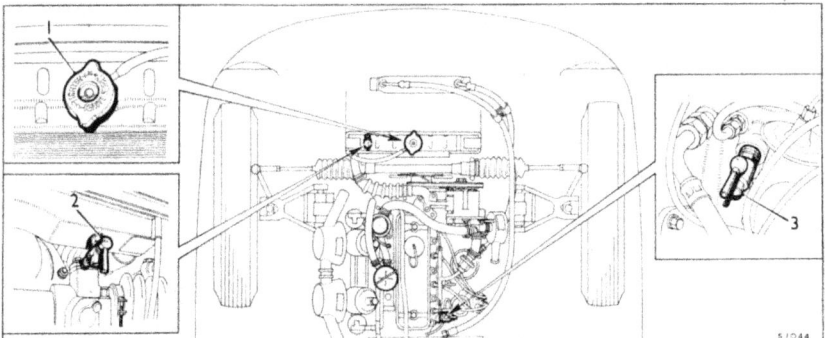

Cooling System

Frost precautions Water when it freezes, expands, and if precautions are not taken there is considerable risk of bursting the radiator, cylinder block, or heater. Such damage may be avoided by adding anti-freeze to the water.

Do not use radiator anti-freeze solution in the windscreen washer.

Anti-freeze solutions Before adding anti-freeze mixture to the radiator it is advisable to clean out the cooling system thoroughly by flushing out the passages with a hose inserted in the filler hole while keeping both drain points open.

Only top up when the cooling system is at its normal running temperature in order to avoid losing anti-freeze due to expansion.

Make sure that the cooling system is water-tight, examine all joints, and replace any defective rubber hose with new.

Anti-freeze can remain in the cooling system for two years provided that the specific gravity of the coolant is checked periodically and anti-freeze added as necessary. This operation should be carried out by an authorized Distributor or Dealer.

After the second winter the system should be drained and refilled with fresh water, and the appropriate amount of anti-freeze added when required.

Only anti-freeze of the ethylene glycol or glycerine type is suitable for use in the cooling system. We recommend owners to use Bluecol Anti-freeze (non-corrosive) in order to protect the cooling system during frosty weather and reduce corrosion to a minimum. We also approve the use of any anti-freeze which conforms to Specification B.S.3151 or B.S.3152.

The correct quantities of anti-freeze for different degrees of frost protection are:

Anti-freeze	Commences to freeze		Frozen solid		Amount of anti-freeze		
%	°C.	°F.	°C.	°F.	Pts.	U.S. Pts.	Litres
25	−13	9	−26	−15	$2\frac{3}{4}$	3	1·5
$33\frac{1}{2}$	−19	−2	−36	−33	$3\frac{1}{2}$	4	2
50	−36	−33	−48	−53	$5\frac{1}{2}$	6	3

WHEELS/TYRES

Jacking up
Fig. 1
The jack is designed to lift one side of the car at a time. Apply the hand brake, and place a wedge against each side of one of the wheels on the opposite side of the car to the one being jacked.

Remove the plug from the jacking socket located in the door sill panel and insert the lifting arm of the jack into the socket. **Make certain that the jack lifting arm is pushed fully into the socket and that the base of the jack is on firm ground.** The jack should lean slightly outwards at the top to allow for the radial movement of the car as it is raised.

Jack maintenance
If the jack is neglected it may be difficult to use in a roadside emergency. Examine it occasionally, clean off accumulated dust, and lightly oil the thread to prevent the formation of rust.

WHEELS
pressed type
Removing the wheel discs
Fig. 2
Insert the wheel disc lever in the recess provided in the road wheel and lever off the disc, using a sideways motion.

To refit the hub disc, place the rim over two of the buttons on the wheel centre and give the outer face a sharp blow with the hand over the third button.

Removing and refitting
Fig. 3
Slacken the four nuts securing the road wheel to the hub; turn anti-clockwise to loosen and clockwise to tighten. Raise the car with the jack to lift the wheel clear of the ground and remove the nuts. Withdraw the road wheel from the hub. When refitting the road wheel locate the wheel on the hub, lightly tighten the nuts with the wheel nut spanner (securing nuts must be fitted with the **taper side towards the wheel**), and lower the jack. Fully tighten the wheel nuts, tightening them diagonally and progressively, at the same time avoid over-tightening.

Replace the wheel disc and jack socket plug.

Fig. 1

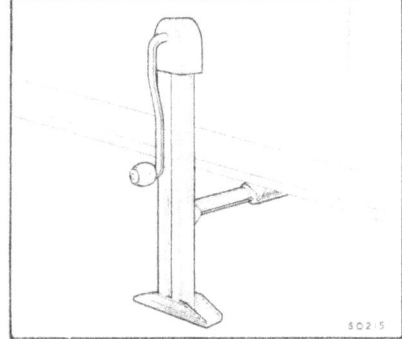

Fig. 2

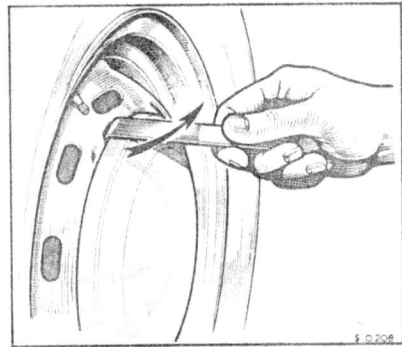

Wheels/Tyres

Wire type Removing and refitting Fig. 4
Use the spanner to slacken the octagonal hub nuts.

Always jack up a wheel before using the hammer, and always hammer the nuts tight.

Locknuts are marked 'LEFT' or 'RIGHT' to show to which side of the car they must be fitted, and also with the word 'UNDO' and an arrow.

Before replacing a wheel wipe all serrations, threads, and cones of the wheel and hub and then lightly coat them with grease. If a forced change is made on the road, remove, clean, and grease as soon as convenient.

Maintenance
When the car is new, after the first long run or after 50 miles of short runs, jack up the wheels and hammer the nuts to make sure that they are tight.

Once a year remove the wheels for examination and regreasing.

Tyre maintenance Fig. 5
To obtain the best tyre mileage and to suppress the development of irregular wear on the tyres the wheels can be interchanged diagonally bringing the spare wheel into use (see **Radial-ply tyres (SP)**).

Excessive local distortion as a result of striking a kerb, a loose brick, a deep pot-hole, etc., may cause the casing cords to fracture.

Tyres, including the spare, must be maintained at the pressures recommended (see **'GENERAL DATA'**); check with an accurate tyre gauge at least once a week, and regulate as necessary. Pressures should be checked when the tyres are cold; do not reduce the pressure in warm tyres where the increase above the normal pressure is due to temperature.

See that the valve caps are screwed down firmly by hand. The cap prevents the entry of dirt into the valve mechanism and forms an additional seal on the valve, preventing any leakage if the valve core is damaged.

Fig. 3

Fig. 4

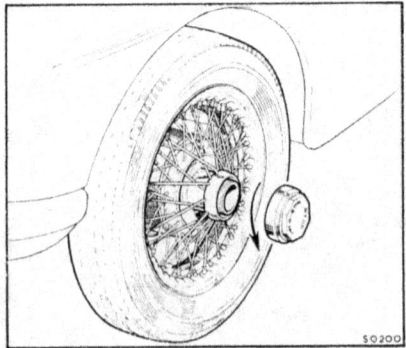

Flints and other sharp objects should be removed with a penknife or similar tool. If neglected, they may work through the cover.

Any oil or grease which may get onto the tyres should be cleaned off by using fuel sparingly. Do not use paraffin (kerosene), which has a detrimental effect on rubber.

When repairing tubes have punctures or injuries vulcanized. Ordinary patches should only be used for emergencies.

Vulcanizing is absolutely essential in the case of tubes manufactured from synthetic rubber.

Radial-ply tyres (SP) Radial-ply tyres (SP) should only be fitted in sets of four, although in certain circumstances it is permissible to fit a pair on the rear wheels; tyres of different construction must not be used on the same axle. A pair must never be fitted to the front wheels with conventional tyres at the rear. Consult your Distributor or Dealer before changing to radial-ply tyres.

The positional changing of wheels must not be undertaken if radial-ply tyres have been fitted to the rear wheels only.

Spare wheel The spare wheel is secured to the floor of the luggage compartment on tourer cars and below the luggage compartment floorboard on GT cars. To gain access to the spare wheel on GT cars (Fig. 6) turn back the luggage compartment floor covering, unscrew the two quick-release screws and lift the floorboard.

Wheel and tyre balancing Unbalanced wheel and tyre assemblies may be responsible for abnormal wear of the tyres and vibration in the steering. Consult your Distributor Dealer.

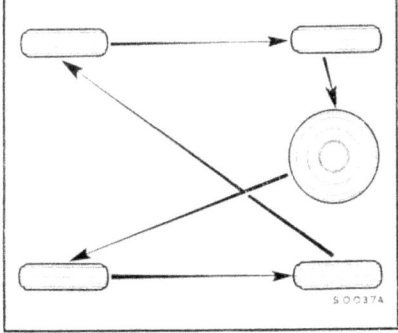

Fig. 5

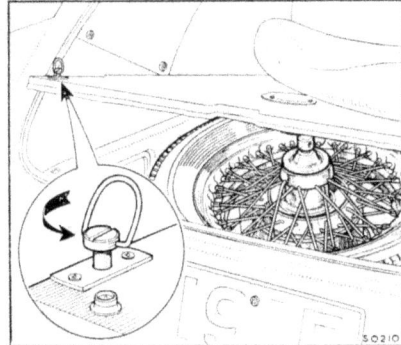

Fig. 6

BRAKES

Brake and clutch master cylinder
Fig. 1
The level of the fluid in the brake master cylinder reservoir is visible through the plastic reservoir (1); the level must be maintained up to the position marked (2) on the side of the reservoir.

To check the level of the fluid in the clutch master cylinder reservoir (3), remove the plastic filler cap. The fluid level must be maintained at the bottom of the filler neck. Use only **Lockheed Disc Brake Fluid (Series II) or Castrol Girling Brake Fluid Amber** for topping up. Before refitting the filler caps check that the breather holes (indicated by the arrows) in the caps are clear. The centre disc (4) of the brake reservoir cap may be removed for cleaning.

Brake pedal
Fig. 2
A free movement of $\frac{1}{8}$ in. (A), measured at the pedal pad must be maintained on the pedal. To adjust the free movement, slacken the stop light switch locknut (1) and turn the switch (2) clockwise to decrease or anti-clockwise to increase the clearance. Tighten the stop light switch locknut.

Front brakes
Fig. 2
Wear of the disc brake friction pads is automatically compensated for and manual adjustment is therefore not required. Before the lining material has worn down to the minimum permissible thickness of $\frac{1}{16}$ in. (1·6 mm.) the brake pads must be renewed. Special equipment is required, and new pads should be fitted by an authorized Distributor or Dealer.

Rear brakes
Excessive brake pedal travel is an indication that the rear brake-shoes require adjusting. The brakes on both rear wheels must be adjusted to regain even and efficient braking.

Adjusting
Fig. 3
Block the front wheels, fully release the hand brake and jack up each rear wheel in turn. Turn the adjuster (arrowed) in a clockwise direction (viewed from the centre of the car) until the wheel is locked, then turn the adjuster back until the wheel is free to rotate without the shoes rubbing. Repeat the adjustment on the other rear brake.

Inspecting rear brake linings
Block the front wheels, release the hand brake, and jack up each rear wheel in turn. Remove the road wheel and slacken off the brake-shoe adjuster fully. Remove the two countersunk screws (pressed wheels) or the four nuts (wire wheels) and withdraw the brake-drum.

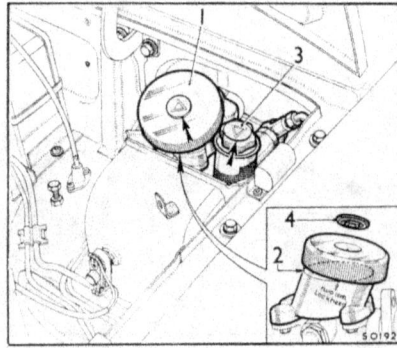

Fig. 1

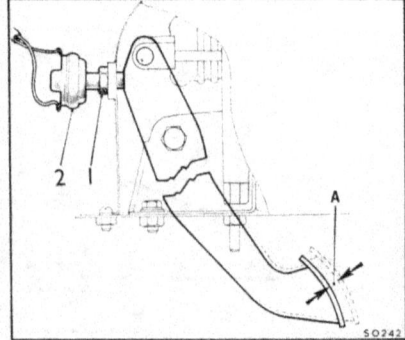

Fig. 2

Inspect the linings for wear, and blow out the dust from the backplate assembly and drum.

Refit the drum and road wheel and adjust the brake-shoes.

Hand brake The hand brake is automatically adjusted with the rear brakes. If there is excessive movement of the hand brake lever, consult your Distributor or Dealer.

Lubrication
Fig. 4 Charge the nipple on the hand brake cable with one of the recommended greases.

Preventive maintenance In addition to the recommended periodical inspection of brake components it is advisable as the car ages, and as a precaution against the effects of wear and deterioration, to make a more searching inspection and renew parts as necessary.

It is recommended that:
(1) Disc brake pads, drum brake linings, hoses, and pipes should be examined at intervals no greater than those laid down in the Passport to Service.
(2) Brake fluid should be changed completely every 18 months or 24,000 miles (40000 km.) whichever is the sooner.
(3) All fluid seals in the hydraulic system and all flexible hoses should be examined and renewed if necessary every 3 years or 40,000 miles (65000 km.) whichever is the sooner. At the same time the working surface of the pistons and of the bores of the master cylinder, wheel cylinders, and other slave cylinders should be examined and new parts fitted where necessary.

Care must be taken always to observe the following points:
(*a*) At all times use the recommended brake fluid.
(*b*) Never leave fluid in unsealed containers. It absorbs moisture quickly and this can be dangerous.
(*c*) Fluid drained from the system or used for bleeding is best discarded.
(*d*) The necessity for absolute cleanliness throughout cannot be over-emphasized.

Fig. 3

Fig. 4

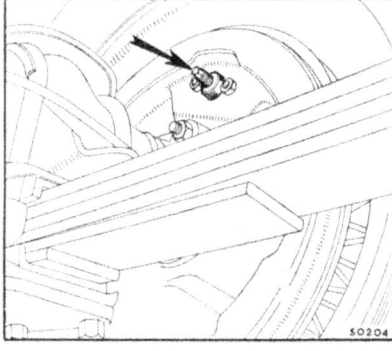

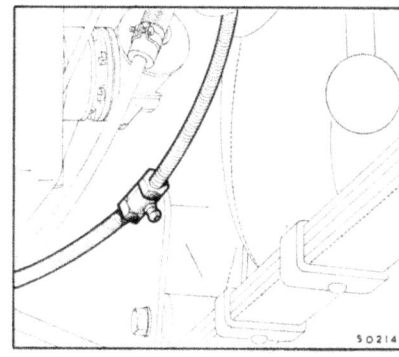

ELECTRICAL

POLARITY The electrical system is **negative** ground.

The following precautions must be observed to prevent inadvertent damage to the alternator and its control equipment.

Do not run the engine with the battery or any of the charging circuit cables disconnected. Ensure that all electrical connections in the generating and charging circuits are maintained tight at all times. If for any reason the engine is to be run with the charging circuit incomplete, disconnect the car wiring cables from the alternator and wire the main terminals on the alternator together using an external bridging wire.

Ensure that the correct battery polarity (**negative ground**) is maintained at all times.

If electric arc welding equipment is to be used on the car, all electric cables must be disconnected from the alternator and control box terminals.

BATTERIES
Checking To gain access to the batteries, remove the carpet covering the rear cockpit floor
Fig. 1 panel, release the five panel-retaining screws and remove the panel (1).

Remove the filler plugs (2) and check the electrolyte level in each cell.

DO NOT USE A NAKED LIGHT WHEN CHECKING THE LEVELS.

Topping up The electrolyte levels must be checked weekly and maintained so that the separator guards (3) are just covered. Top up the cells as necessary with distilled water only.

In hot weather or when long daily journeys are made more frequent topping up may be necessary.

After topping up, wipe all dirt and moisture from the top of the batteries.

NOTE.—Do not leave the batteries in a discharged condition for any length of time. When not in regular use, have the battery fully charged, and every fortnight give a short refresher charge to prevent permanent damage to the battery plates.

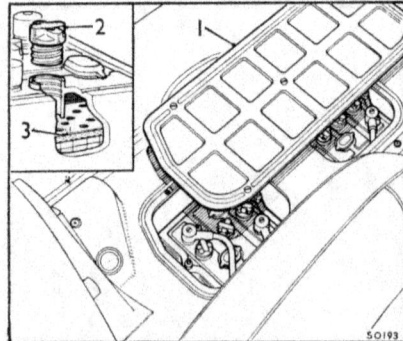

Fig. 1

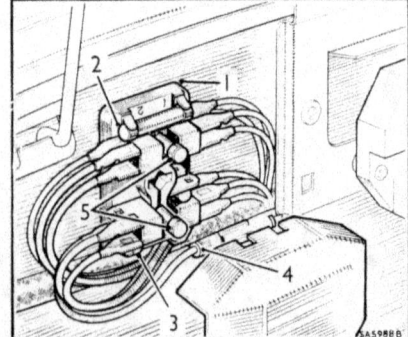

Fig. 2

FUSES
Fig. 2
The fuses are housed in a block (1) mounted on the right-hand wing panel in the engine compartment.

Fuse 'A1'–'A2' The 35-amp. fuse (2) protects the ancillary circuits which operate irrespective of whether the ignition switch is 'on' or 'off'; horns, interior light (GT).

Fuse 'A3'–'A4' The 35-amp. fuse (3) protects the ancillary circuits which operate only when the ignition is switched on; windscreen wipers, heater blower motor, instruments, direction indicators, reverse and brake stop lights.

Line fuse The 25-amp. line fuse (4) protects the electrically heated back-light on GT models when fitted.

Blown fuses The units which are protected by the fuses can be identified from the wiring diagram. A blown fuse is indicated by the failure of all the units protected by it, and is confirmed by examination of the fuse when withdrawn.

Before renewing a blown fuse inspect the wiring of the units that have failed for evidence of a short-circuit or other fault.

Two spare fuses (5) are provided and it is important to use only the correct replacement fuse. The fusing value is marked on a coloured slip of paper inside the glass tube of the fuse.

Accessories If an electrical accessory is being fitted and is required to operate irrespective of the ignition circuit it should be connected to terminal 'A2' on the fuse block; if it is required to operate only when the ignition is switched on, connect to terminal 'A4'. Radios must be further protected by their own fuse rated in accordance with the radio maker's instructions.

WINDSCREEN WIPER

Arms
Fig. 3
To reposition a wiper arm, hold the spring clip (1) clear of the retaining groove in the spindle and withdraw the arm. Place the arm in the required position and press it onto the spindle (2) until it is secured by the clip.

Fig. 3
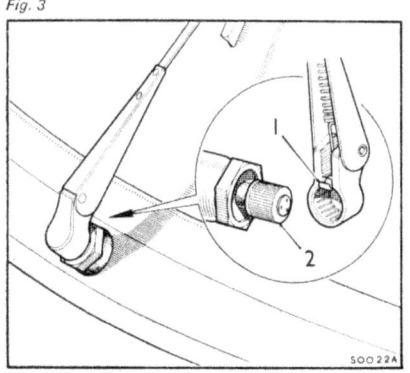

Fig. 4
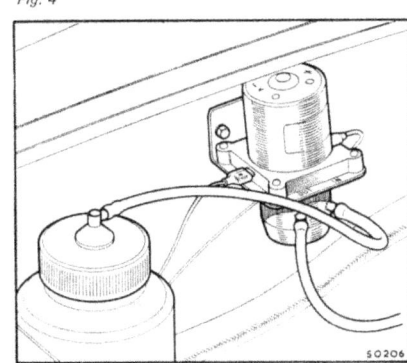

Electrical

Blades To ensure efficient wiping it is recommended that blade rubbers are renewed annually.

To remove a wiper blade rubber, withdraw the retaining rubber stop from one end of the blade and slide the rubber from the retaining clips.

Washer The pump for the windscreen washer is mounted on the right-hand wing panel
Fig. 4 in the engine compartment in the position as illustrated. The fluid flow is indicated on the pump just above the fluid connections.

HEADLAMPS

Light unit To remove a light unit, ease the bottom of the outer rim (1) forward away from
Fig. 5 the lamp. Unscrew the three inner rim retaining screws (2), remove the inner rim (3), withdraw the light unit (4), and disconnect the three-pin plug (5).

To fit a light unit, connect the three-pin plug, position the light unit in the headlamp body ensuring that the three lugs formed on the outer edge of the light unit engage in the slots formed in the body, and fit the inner retaining rim. Position the outer rim on the retaining lugs with the cut-away portion of the rim at the bottom of the lamp, press the rim downwards and inwards.

Beam setting Two adjusting screws are provided on each headlamp for setting the main beams. The screw (6) is for adjusting the beam in the vertical plane, and the screw (7) is for horizontal adjustment. The beams must be set in accordance with local regulations; resetting and checking should be entrusted to your Distributor or Dealer, who will have special equipment available for this purpose.

LAMPS

Parking and To gain access to the parking (1) and direction indicator (2) bulbs, unscrew the
direction two retaining screws (3) and withdraw the rim and lens.
indicator
Fig. 6

Fig. 5

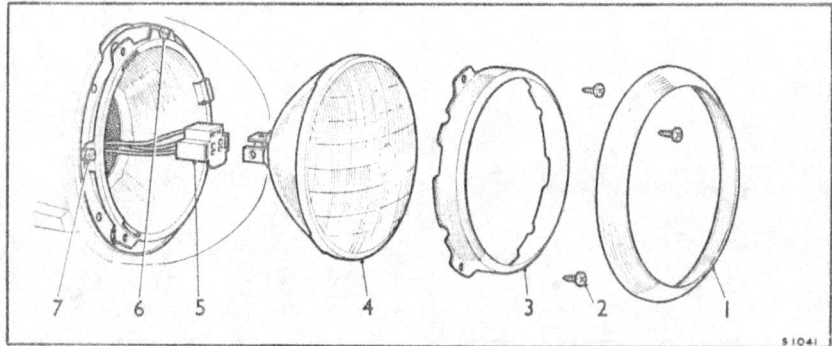

Stop, tail, and direction indicator
Fig. 7
Remove the lens retaining screw (1) and slide the lens upwards to gain access to the direction indicator (2) and stop/tail (3) bulbs.

Number-plate
Fig. 8
To change a bulb, remove the two securing screws and nuts, and lift off the lamp hood (1) and lens (2). When refitting ensure that the wedge-shaped distance piece (3) is fitted with its thickest edge towards the rear.

Map
Fig. 9
Remove the two securing screws and nuts, and lift off the lamp hood and lens to gain access to the screw cap bulb.

Interior
Fig. 10
The lens is held in the lamp by four locating lugs. To gain access to the bulb, gently squeeze the sides of the lens together and withdraw it from the lamp. The bulb may then be withdrawn from its contacts.

Fig. 6

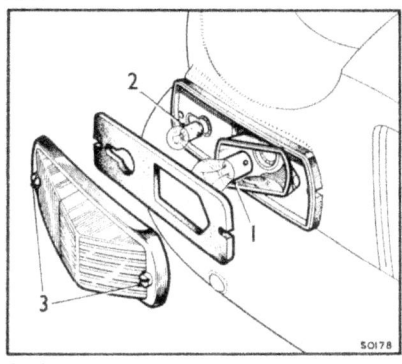

Fig. 7

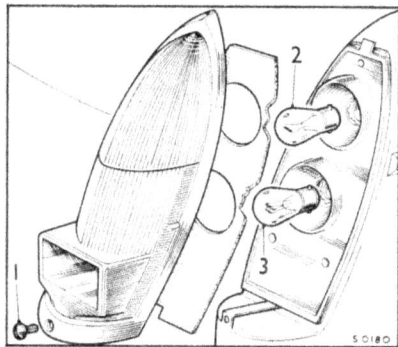

Fig. 8

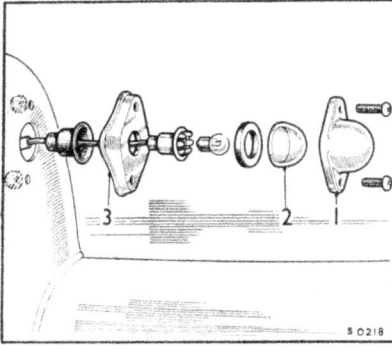

Fig. 9

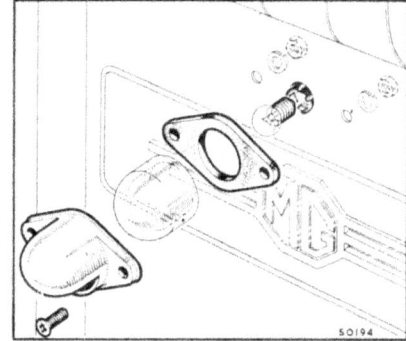

Electrical

Reverse To renew a bulb, remove the two securing screws and withdraw the lens. Press
Fig. 11   the bulb down towards the lower contact and withdraw it from the lamp. Fit one end of the new bulb into the hole in the lower contact, then press the top of the bulb into the lamp until the point of the cap engages in the hole in the upper contact.

WARNING AND PANEL LAMPS

Fascia The warning and panel illumination lamps are located in the back of the fascia
Fig. 12 in the positions shown. To gain access to the bulbs, unscrew the three screws securing the bottom panel and pull the panel forward from its retaining clips at the rear. The bulbs are housed in holders which are a press-fit into the back of the fascia panel.

Console To renew a bulb in the warning lamps fitted on the console, turn back the carpet covering the gearbox tunnel, remove the four console retaining screws and draw the console rearwards. The bulb holders can then be withdrawn from the warning lamps.

On cars fitted with a radio or ashtray these items will require removing before the console can be withdrawn.

Brake To gain access to the warning lamp bulb (inset, Fig. 12), withdraw the holder and test push assembly from the fascia panel. Gently press the switch rocker pivot lugs (arrowed) inwards and withdraw the rocker from the casing.

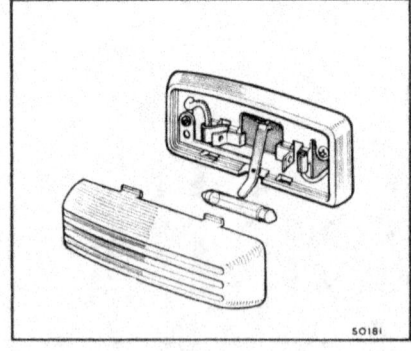

Fig. 10

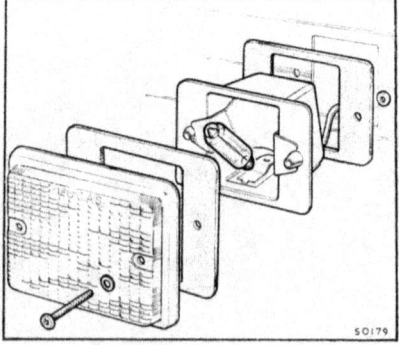

Fig. 11

CONTROL BOX	This is a sealed unit located on the right-hand wing panel in the engine compartment. This controls the charging rate of the alternator in accordance with the need of the batteries and requires no adjustment.
FUEL PUMP	The electric fuel pump is mounted on a bracket secured to the underside of the heelboard adjacent to the front of the right-hand rear spring.

Replacement bulbs

	Volts	Watts	BMC Part No.
Parking	12	6	BFS 989
Stop and tail lamps	12	6/21	BFS 380
Direction indicator lamps	12	21	BFS 382
Reverse lamp	12	21	27H 8814
Number-plate illumination lamp	12	6	BFS 989
Map light	12	2·2	BFS 987
Panel and warning lights	12	2·2	BFS 987
Interior light	12	6	BFS 254

Fig. 12

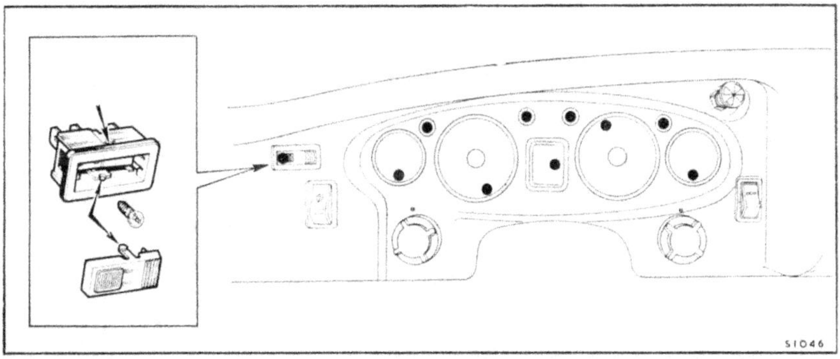

WIRING DIAGRAM

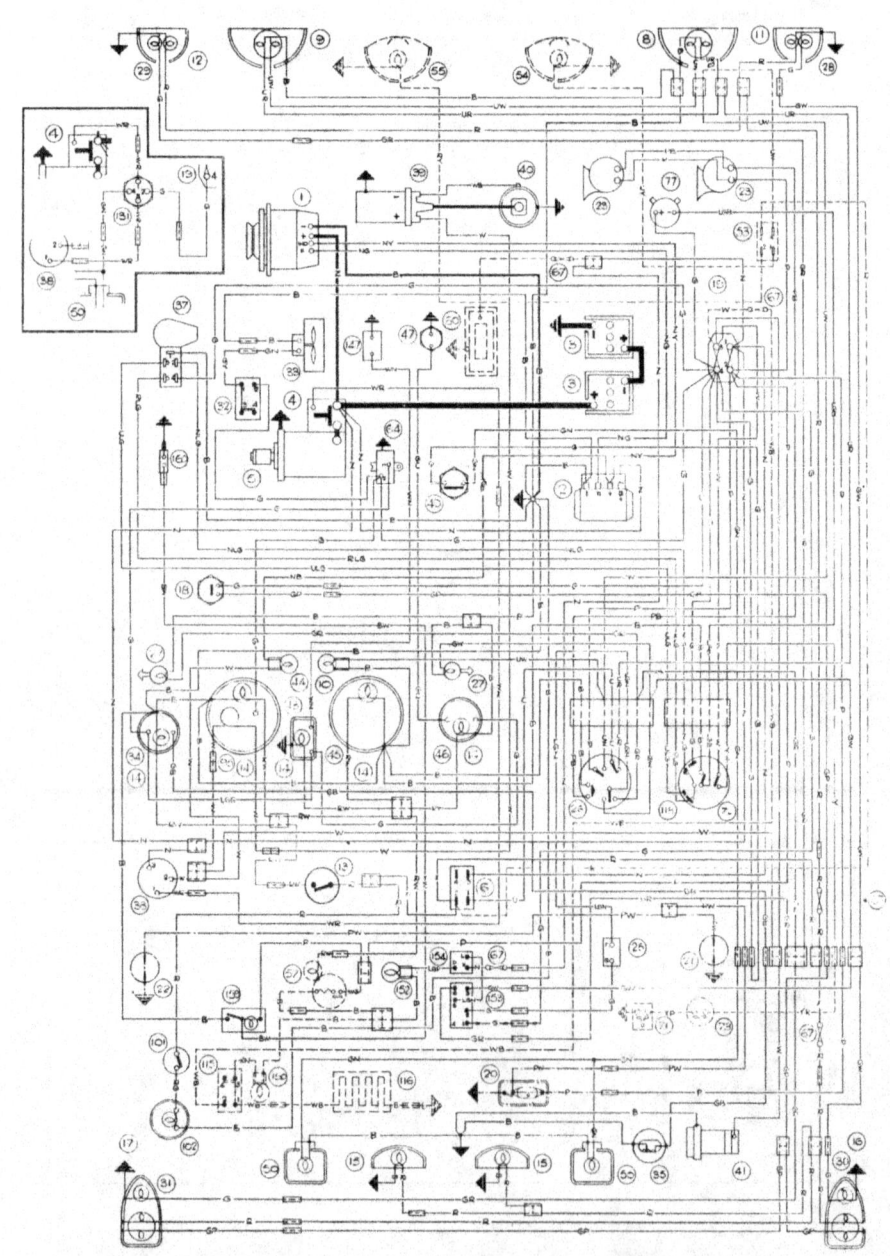

1. Alternator.
2. Control box.
3. Battery.
4. Starter solenoid.
5. Starter motor.
6. Lighting switch.
8. R.H. headlamp.
9. L.H. headlamp.
10. High-beam warning lamp.
11. R.H. parking lamp.
12. L.H. parking lamp.
13. Panel lamp switch.
14. Panel lamps.
15. Number-plate illumination lamp.
16. R.H. stop and tail lamp.
17. L.H. stop and tail lamp.
18. Stop lamp switch.
19. Fuse unit.
20. Interior lamp ⎫
21. R.H. door switch ⎬ GT only.
22. L.H. door switch ⎭
23. Horns.
25. Flasher unit.
26. Combined direction indicator/headlamp flasher/headlamp high-low beam/horn-push switch.
27. Direction indicator warning lamp.
28. R.H. front flasher lamp.
29. L.H. front flasher lamp.
30. R.H. rear flasher lamp.
31. L.H. rear flasher lamp.
32. Heater booster motor switch.
33. Heater booster motor.
34. Fuel gauge.
35. Fuel gauge tank unit.
37. Windscreen wiper motor.
38. Ignition/starter switch.
39. Ignition coil.
40. Distributor.
41. Fuel pump.
43. Oil pressure gauge.
44. Ignition warning lamp.
45. Speedometer.
46. Coolant temperature gauge.
47. Coolant temperature transmitter.
49. Reverse lamp switch.
50. Reverse lamp.
53. Fog and driving lamp switch.
54. Driving lamp.
55. Fog lamp.
57. Cigar-lighter—illuminated.
60. Radio.
64. Bi-metal instrument voltage stabilizer.
67. Line fuse.
71. Overdrive solenoid.
72. Overdrive manual control switch.
73. Overdrive gear switch.
77. Windscreen washer pump.
95. Tachometer.
101. Map light switch.
102. Map light.
115. Heated back-light switch ⎫ GT only.
116. Heated back-light ⎭
118. Combined windscreen washer and wiper switch.
131. Combined reverse lamp switch and automatic transmission safety switch.
147. Oil pressure transmitter.
150. Heated back-light warning lamp (GT only).
152. Hazard warning lamp.
153. Hazard warning switch.
154. Hazard warning flasher unit.
159. Brake pressure warning lamp and lamp test push.
160. Brake pressure failure switch.

CABLE COLOUR CODE

N. Brown. P. Purple. W. White.
U. Blue. G. Green. Y. Yellow.
R. Red. L.G. Light Green. B. Black.

When a cable has two colour code letters the first denotes the main colour and the second denotes the tracer colour.

IGNITION

Ignition timing — The ignition timing is set dynamically to give optimum engine performance with efficient engine emission control. Adjustments to the ignition timing setting must be carried out by your approved pollution control service station.

DISTRIBUTOR — Check the functioning of the automatic advance and retard mechanism as follows.

Centrifugal advance mechanism
Fig. 1 — Remove the distributor cap and grasp the rotor arm (1) firmly. Turn the rotor arm in the direction of rotation and release it. The rotor arm should return to its original position without showing any tendency to stick. Check that the moving plate (2) is free to move.

Contact breaker
Fig. 2 — Remove the distributor cap and turn the crankshaft until the contacts are fully open. Check the gap (1) with a feeler gauge (see '**GENERAL DATA**'); the gauge should be a sliding fit in the gap. If the gap varies appreciably from the gauge thickness, slacken the contact plate securing screw (2) and adjust the contact gap by inserting a screwdriver in the notched hole at the end of the plate (3) and turning clockwise to decrease and anti-clockwise to increase the gap. Retighten the securing screw.

If the contact breaker points are burned or blackened, clean them with a fine carborundum stone or with fine emery-cloth.

Cleaning the contacts is made easier if the contact breaker lever carrying the moving contact is removed. To do this unscrew the nut (4) securing the end of the spring, remove the spring washer, flat washer, and both lead terminals, and lift off the lever complete with spring. After cleaning refit the contact breaker and check the gap.

Lubrication
Fig. 3 — Remove the distributor cover and rotor arm and lightly smear the cam (1) and contact breaker pivot (2) with grease to Ref. B (page 60). Avoid overgreasing.

Fig. 1

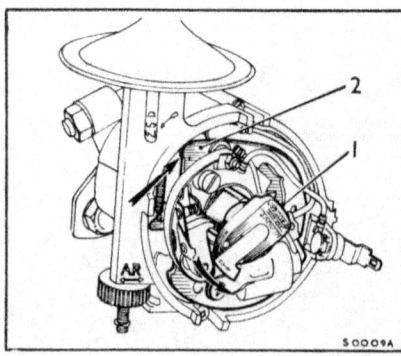

Fig. 2

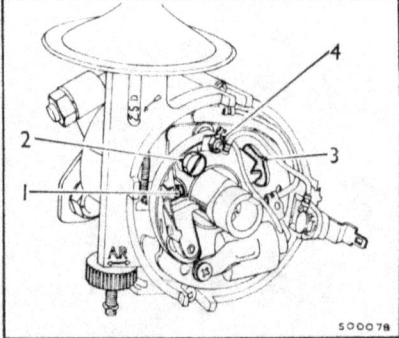

Drop a few spots of oil on to the automatic advance weights at (3) and on the screw (4) in the centre of the cam spindle after withdrawing the rotor arm. Do not remove this screw as clearance is provided for the oil to pass. Replace the rotor arm with its drive lug correctly engaging the spindle slot and push it onto the spindle as far as it will go.

Carefully wipe away all surplus oil and see that the contact breaker points are perfectly clean.

Ignition cables (high-tension) The high-tension cables connecting the distributor to the sparking plugs may, after long use, also show signs of perishing. They must then be replaced by the correct type of ignition cable. Cut the cables to length, fill the holes in the cap with silicone grease, push the cables well home in the cap, and secure with the pointed screws.

Sparking plugs
Fig. 1

The sparking plugs should be cleaned of all carbon deposit using a stiff brush dipped in paraffin (kerosene), or preferably with an air-blast service unit.

Check the plug gaps, and reset if necessary to the recommended gap (see **'GENERAL DATA'**). To reset, use a special Champion sparking plug gauge and setting tool; move the side electrode, never the centre one.

When refitting the plugs make sure that the copper washers are not defective in any way. If they have become worn and flattened, fit new ones to ensure a gas-tight joint. Screw the plug down by hand as far as possible, then use a spanner for tightening only. Always use a tubular box spanner to avoid possible damage to the insulator, and do not under any circumstances use a movable wrench. Never overtighten a plug, but ensure that a good joint is made between the plug body, washer, and cylinder head. Wipe clean the outside of the plugs before reconnecting the H.T. leads.

When fitting new sparking plugs ensure that only the recommended type and grade are used (see **'GENERAL DATA'**).

Fig. 3
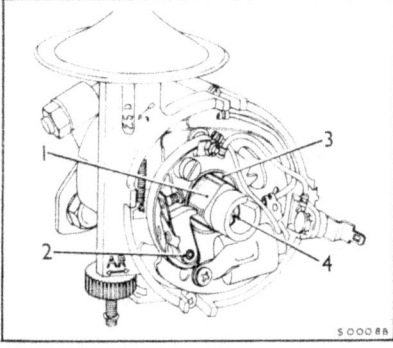

Fig. 4
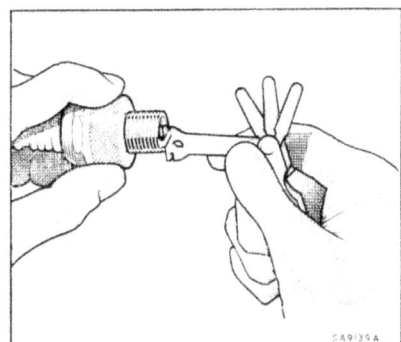

ENGINE

LUBRICATION
Checking
Fig. 1
The level of the oil in the engine sump is indicated by the dipstick (1) on the right-hand side of the engine. Maintain the level at the 'MAX' mark on the dipstick and never allow it to fall below the 'MIN' mark.

The filler (2) is on the forward end of the rocker cover and is provided with a quick-action cap. The filler cap also incorporates an intake filter for the crankcase emission control.

The oil level should always be checked before a long run.

Draining
To drain the engine oil, remove the drain plug (3) located on the right-hand side at the rear of the sump. This operation should be carried out while the engine is warm.

Clean the drain plug; check that its copper sealing washer is in a satisfactory condition, and refit.

Filling
Fill the engine with the correct quantity (see **'GENERAL DATA'**) of oil to Ref. A (page 60). Run the engine for a short while then allow it to stand for a few minutes before checking the level with the dipstick.

Fig. 1

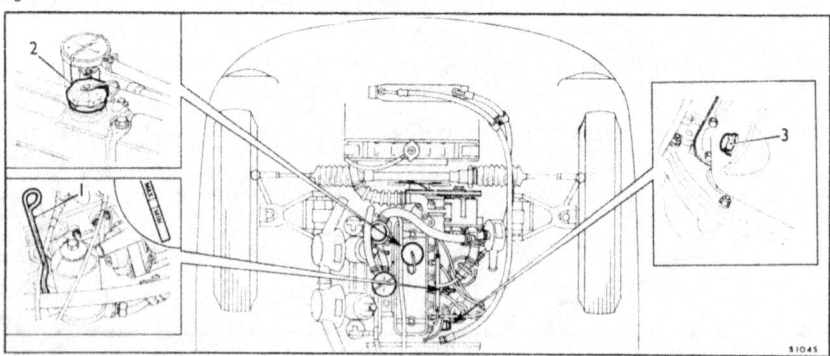

Fig. 2

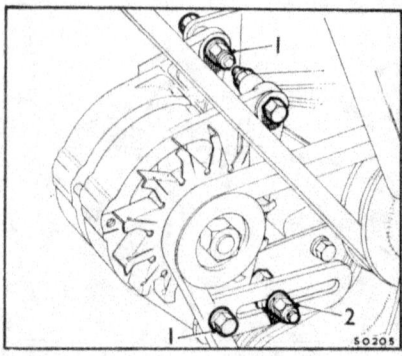

Fig. 3

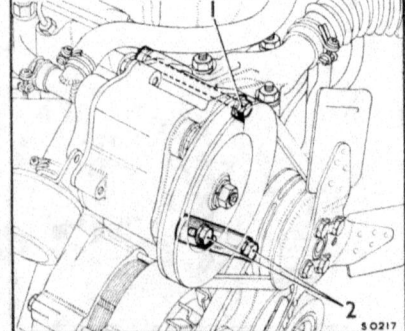

DRIVE BELTS

Belt tension — When correctly tensioned, a total deflection of ½ in., under moderate hand pressure, should be possible at the midway point of the longest belt run between the pulleys on the fan belt and the air pump drive belt.

Adjusting Fan belt
Fig. 2 — Slacken the three alternator securing bolts (1) and adjusting link nut (2), move the alternator to the required position using hand pressure only; avoid overtensioning. Tighten the securing bolts and adjusting link nut.

Air pump drive belt
Fig. 3 — The air pump drive belt is adjustable in the same manner as the fan belt after the pump mounting bolt (1) and the adjusting link bolts (2) have been slackened.

VALVE ROCKER CLEARANCE

Checking — Remove the rocker cover and insert a ·015 in. feeler gauge between the valve rocker arms and valve stems (inset). The gauge should be a sliding fit when the engine is cold. Check each clearance in the following order:

Check No. 1 valve with No. 8 fully open. Check No. 8 valve with No. 1 fully open.

```
 ,,  ,, 3 ,,    ,,  ,, 6 ,,  ,,    ,,   ,, 6 ,,  ,,  ,, 3 ,,  ,,
 ,,  ,, 5 ,,    ,,  ,, 4 ,,  ,,    ,,   ,, 4 ,,  ,,  ,, 5 ,,  ,,
 ,,  ,, 2 ,,    ,,  ,, 7 ,,  ,,    ,,   ,, 7 ,,  ,,  ,, 2 ,,  ,,
```

Adjusting
Fig. 4 — Slacken the adjusting screw locknut on the opposite end of the rocker arm and rotate the screw clockwise to reduce the clearance or anti-clockwise to increase it. Retighten the locknut when the clearance is correct, holding the screw against rotation with a screwdriver.

Fig. 4

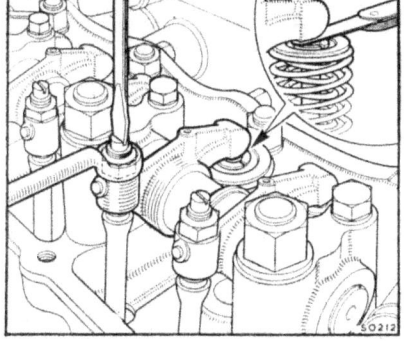

Fig. 5

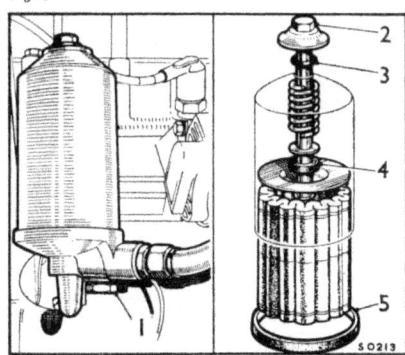

Engine

Oil filter The external oil filter is of the renewable-element type and is located on the right-
Fig. 5 hand side of the engine.

To renew the element, drain the filter by removing the plug (1); unscrew the filter body securing bolt (2) and lift off the body. Wash out the casing with gasoline (fuel) and dry it before fitting a new element. Check that the sealing rings (3) and (5) and the rubber washer (4) are in a satisfactory condition.

Reassemble the filter, ensuring that the components are correctly positioned.

CRANKCASE EMISSION CONTROL

Oil filler cap An air filter is incorporated in the oil filler cap (1). The cap and filter are renewed
Fig. 6 only as a complete assembly.

Control valve

Testing With the engine at normal operating temperature, run it at idling speed. Remove the oil filler cap. If the valve is functioning correctly the engine speed will rise slightly as the cap is removed, the change in speed being audibly noticeable. If no change in speed occurs, renew the valve or service it as follows:

Servicing Remove the spring clip (2) and dismantle the valve. Clean all metal parts with a solvent (trichlorethylene, fuel, etc.). If deposits are difficult to remove, immerse in boiling water before applying the solvent. Do not use an abrasive.

Clean the diaphragm (3) with detergent or methylated spirits.

Replace components showing signs of wear or damage.

Reassemble the valve, making sure the metering needle (4) is in the cruciform guides (5) and the diaphragm is seated correctly.

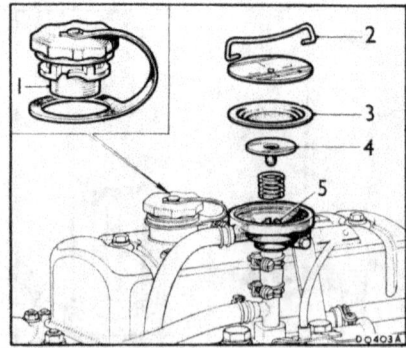

Fig. 6

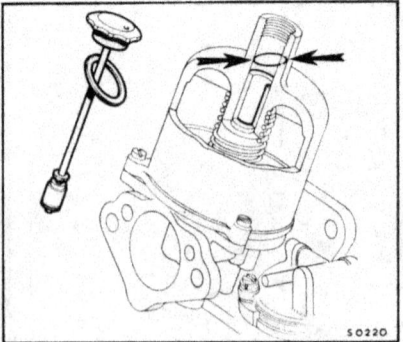

Fig. 7

CARBURETTERS

Adjustment The carburetters are adjusted and tuned to give optimum engine performance with efficient engine emission control. Adjustments to the carburetter settings must only be carried out by your approved pollution control service station.

Lubrication
Fig. 7
Each damper reservoir must be topped up periodically with thin engine oil to Ref. E (page 60). **Under no circumstances should heavy-bodied lubricant be used.** Unscrew the damper cap, withdraw the damper, and top up the reservoir until the oil level (arrowed) is $\frac{1}{2}$ in. (12 mm.) above the top of the hollow piston rod. Push the damper assembly back into position and screw the cap firmly into the reservoir.

AIR CLEANERS The elements of both the carburetters and the air pump air cleaners must be renewed every 12,000 miles or 12 months; more frequent changes may be necessary in dusty operating conditions.

Carburetter
Fig. 8
Unscrew the bolts (1) securing the air cleaner assembly to the carburretor and lift it from the car. Remove the base plate (2) and withdraw the element (3). Clean the inside of the casing (4) throughly and reassemble using a new element.

Air pump
Fig. 9
Unscrew the wing nut (1), withdraw the cover (2) and discard the element (3). Clean the inside of the cover thoroughly and reassemble using a new element.

Fig. 8
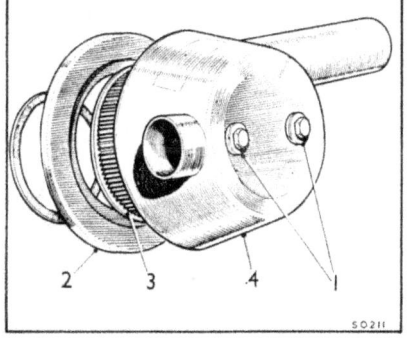

Fig. 9
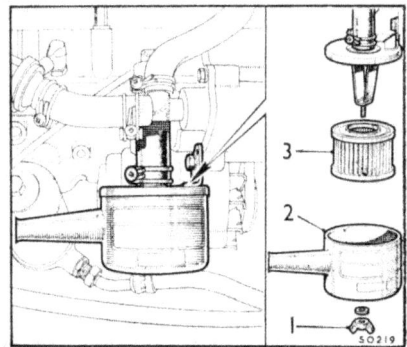

TRANSMISSION

GEARBOX
Checking To gain access to the gearbox combined oil filler and dipstick (1), lift the carpet
Fig. 1 on the right-hand side of the gearbox cover at the rear of the control console, and remove the rubber plug (2). Clean around the dipstick before removing it.

The oil level must be maintained at the 'HIGH' mark on the dipstick.

OVERDRIVE
Draining Remove the plug (3) to drain the oil from the gearbox and overdrive unit.

Sump filter Drain the gearbox and overdrive unit.

Clean the sump cover and its adjacent surroundings. Remove the cover securing screws, withdraw the cover (4) and the filter (5). Wash the magnets, cover, and filter in gasoline (fuel). Refit the filter and cover.

Relief valve filter Remove the plug and the seal (6); withdraw the relief valve approximately $\frac{1}{2}$ in. and remove the filter (7). Wash the filter, plug and seal in gasoline (fuel).

Fit the filter to the relief valve, push the valve fully home and refit the plug and seal.

Filling Fill the gearbox and overdrive unit through the combined oil filler (1) with the correct quantity (see **'GENERAL DATA'**) of one of the recommended oils. Run the car for a short distance, allow it to stand for a few minutes, then re-check the level with the dipstick.

Fig. 1

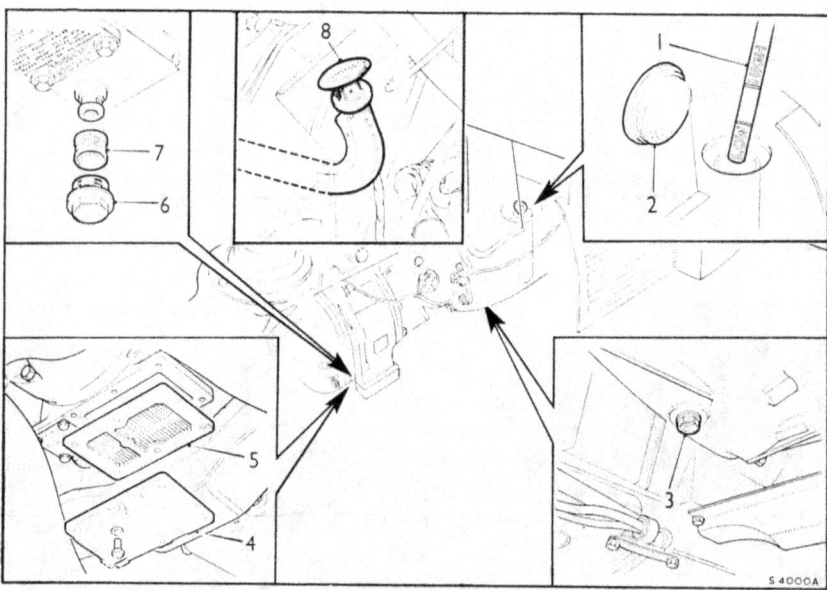

AUTOMATIC TRANSMISSION

Dipstick — The dipstick (8, Fig. 1) is housed in the filler tube located at the rear of the engine and is accessible when the bonnet is raised.

Checking — The fluid level must be checked only while the transmission is at normal running temperature. With the car standing level apply the hand brake and move the selector lever to 'P'. Run the engine at idling speed and normal operating temperature for at least two minutes. With the engine still idling in 'P', withdraw the dipstick from the filler tube and wipe it with a clean piece of paper or nylon material. Do not use rag.

Reinsert the dipstick, withdraw it again immediately and check the fluid level indication. The level must be maintained at the 'MAX' mark. The difference between the 'MAX' and 'MIN' marks on the dipstick is equivalent to 1 pint (1·2 U.S. pints)

Topping up — When topping up use only a recommended Automatic Transmission Fluid. **Observe scrupulous cleanliness; DO NOT OVERFILL.**

REAR AXLE

Checking
Fig. 2 — A combined oil filler and level plug (1) is located on the rear of the axle. The oil level must be maintained at the bottom of the plug aperture; ensure that the car is standing level when checking. After topping up the oil level, allow sufficient time for any surplus oil, which may have been added accidentally, to run out of the aperture before replacing the plug.

PROPELLER SHAFT

Lubrication
Fig. 3 — A nipple (1) is provided at the front end of the propeller shaft for lubricating the sliding yoke. To lubricate, give three or four strokes of a gun filled with grease to Ref. C (page 60).

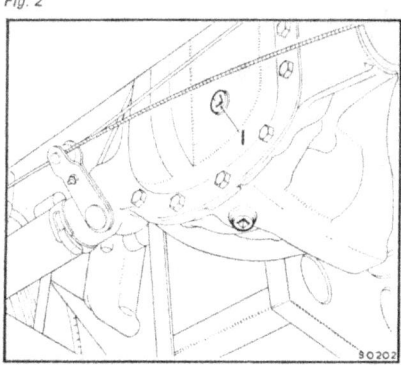

Fig. 2

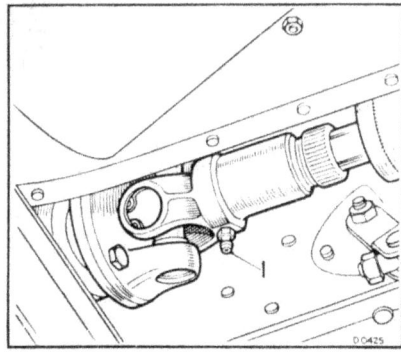

Fig. 3

BMC SERVICE

Identification When communicating with your Distributor or Dealer always quote the car and engine numbers. When the communication concerns the transmission units or body details it is necessary to quote also the transmission casing and body numbers.

Car number. Stamped on a plate secured to the left-hand inner wheel arch, under the bonnet.

Engine number. Stamped on a plate secured to the right-hand side of the cylinder block.

Gearbox number. Stamped on the left-hand side of the gearbox casing.

Rear axle number. Stamped on the front of the left-hand rear axle tube near the spring seating.

Warranty By keeping the Passport to Service, signed by the Distributor, Dealer, or vendor in the vehicle, you can quickly establish the date of purchase and provide the necessary details if adjustments are required to be carried out under warranty.

Claims for the replacement of parts under warranty must be submitted to the supplying Distributor or Dealer or, when this is not possible, to the nearest Distributor or Dealer, informing them of the vendor's name and address. Except in cases of emergency warranty work should always be carried out by a BMC appointed Distributor or Dealer.

Service Parts When Service Parts are required insist on **BMC GENUINE PARTS** as these are designed and tested for your vehicle and in addition have the full backing of the BMC Factory Warranty. ONLY WHEN GENUINE PARTS ARE USED CAN BMC ACCEPT RESPONSIBILITY.

ALL BMC GENUINE PARTS and APPROVED ACCESSORIES can be identified by this label on the packing.

Supplementary tool kit To supplement the tool kit a waterproof canvas roll containing the following is obtainable from all Distributors. Part No. AKF 1596 should be quoted.

6 spanners: $\frac{3}{16}$ in. × $\frac{3}{8}$ in. A.F.
$\frac{7}{16}$ in. × $\frac{1}{2}$ in. A.F.
$\frac{1}{2}$ in. × $\frac{9}{16}$ in. A.F.
$\frac{9}{16}$ in. × $\frac{5}{8}$ in. A.F.
$\frac{11}{16}$ in. × $\frac{13}{16}$ in. A.F.
$\frac{3}{4}$ in. × $\frac{7}{8}$ in. A.F.

1 pair 6 in. pliers.
1 7 in. × $\frac{3}{4}$ in. diameter tommy-bar.
1 $\frac{1}{2}$ in. × $\frac{9}{16}$ in. A.F. tubular spanner.
2 screwdrivers.

DISTRIBUTORS IN THE UNITED STATES FOR PRODUCTS OF
THE BRITISH MOTOR CORPORATION LIMITED

If any problem is encountered in obtaining service or parts in your local area please contact your nearest BMC Distributor. Always quote your vehicle's serial prefix and number and the name of your servicing dealer.

B & K Distributors, Inc.
1326 Hennepin Avenue
Minneapolis, Minnesota 55403
Phone: 612-336-2611

LeMans Sport Cars
15111 Hawthorne Blvd.
Lawndale, (Los Angeles)
California 90260
Phone: 213-772-4183

British Motor Car Distributors, Ltd.
1200 Van Ness Avenue
San Francisco, California 94109
Phone: 415-776-7700

Continental Cars Distributors, Inc.
5615 Pershing Avenue
St. Louis, Missouri 63112
Phone: 314-VO 3-2500

Crandall-Hicks Company
230 Worcester Turnpike
Wellesley Hills, Massachusetts 02181
Phone: 617-CE 5-7400

Falvey Motor Sales Co.
22600 Woodward Avenue
Detroit, Michigan 48220
Phone: 313-LI 3-5000

Great Lakes Car Distributors, Inc.
1301 Busse Road
Elk Grove Village, Illinois 60007
Phone: 312-439-6000

J. S. Inskip, Inc.
120 Commerce Road
Carlstadt, New Jersey 07072
Phone: 201-933-5533

Overseas Motors Corporation
2824 White Settlement Road
Fort Worth, Texas 76107
Phone: 817-ED 2-4181

Royston Distributors, Inc.
1601 Vine Street
Philadelphia, Pennsylvania 19103
Phone: 215-LO 3-6033

Shelly Motors, Ltd.
1017 Kapiolani Boulevard
Honolulu, Hawaii 96814
Phone: 808-504-437

Ship and Shore Motors
701 South Flagler Drive
West Palm Beach, Florida 33402
Phone: 305-TE 3-9661

A NATION-WIDE DEALER LIST IS AVAILABLE THROUGH YOUR DISTRIBUTOR

The British Motor Corporation Limited
BMC Service division
COWLEY · OXFORD · ENGLAND

Telephone: Oxford 77777   *Telegrams:* BMCSERV. Telex. Oxford
Telex: BMCSERV. Oxford 83145 and 83146
Overseas Cables: BMCSERV. Telex. Oxford. England

MAINTENANCE SUMMARY

Daily
Check brake pressure warning light.

Every week or before a long journey
Inspect engine oil level, and top up as necessary.
Check water level in radiator, and top up if necessary.
Check battery and top up to correct levels.
Test tyre pressures.

	Every 3,000 miles or 3 months	Every 6,000 miles or 6 months	Every 12,000 miles or 12 months	Every 24,000 miles or 24 months
Engine				
† Top up carburetter piston dampers.	X			X
‡ Check water level in radiator, and top up if necessary.	X	X	X	X
‡ Check fan and air pump belt tension.		X	X	X
‡ Fit new elements to carburetter and air pump air cleaners.			X	X
‡ Check exhaust emission.		X	X	X
‡ Oscilloscope tune-up.			X	X
‡ Check valve rocker clearances, and adjust if necessary.			X	X
‡ Crankcase closed-circuit breathing system; change engine oil filler cap, test and clean crankcase breather valve.	X	X	X	X
Top up windscreen washer bottle.			X	X
Ignition				
† Check functioning of automatic advance and retard mechanism.		X	X	X
† Check, and adjust if necessary, distributor contact points.		X	X	X
† Lubricate all parts as necessary.		X	X	X
‡ Fit new sparking plugs.				X
‡ Clean and adjust sparking plugs.		X	X	
Steering				
Check steering and suspension moving parts for wear.*		X	X	X
Check wheel alignment, and adjust if necessary.*		X	X	X
Check steering-column clamp bolts.*	X			
Clutch				
Check level of fluid in hydraulic clutch supply tank, and top up if necessary.	X	X	X	X

Gearbox and overdrive				
Clean overdrive filters.				X
Brakes				
Check brakes, and adjust if necessary.	X X	X X	X X	X X
Make visual inspection of brake lines and pipes	X		X X X	X X X
Check level of fluid in the hydraulic supply tank, and top up if necessary.		X		
Inspect disc brake friction pads and report if attention is required. *				X
Inspect and blow out brake linings and drums. *				X X X
Check brake pedal free movement *			X	
General				
Check rear road spring seat bolts.				X
Electrical				
Check battery cell specific gravity readings and top up to correct levels. *	X	X X	X X X	X X X
Check all lamps for correct functioning.	X			
Check headlamp alignment.				
Lubrication				
Check and top up engine oil level.	X X	X X X X	X X X X X	X X X X X X
Change engine oil (if using monograde only).				
Top up oil level in gearbox and rear axle.	X X	X X X X	X X X X X	X X X X X X
Fit new oil filter element.				
Change oil in engine.				
Lubricate all grease nipples.				
Lubricate door locks and hinges.				
Automatic transmission				
Check fluid level, and top up if necessary.	X	X	X	X
Wheels and tyres				
Check tyre pressures.	X	X	X	X

† These items must be entrusted to your approved pollution service station.

* These items should be entrusted to your Distributor or Dealer.

NOTE.—Take the advice of your Distributor/Dealer on:
1. The need for more frequent engine oil changes;
2. When to change around wheels;
3. When to check and adjust headlight beams.

LUBRICATION

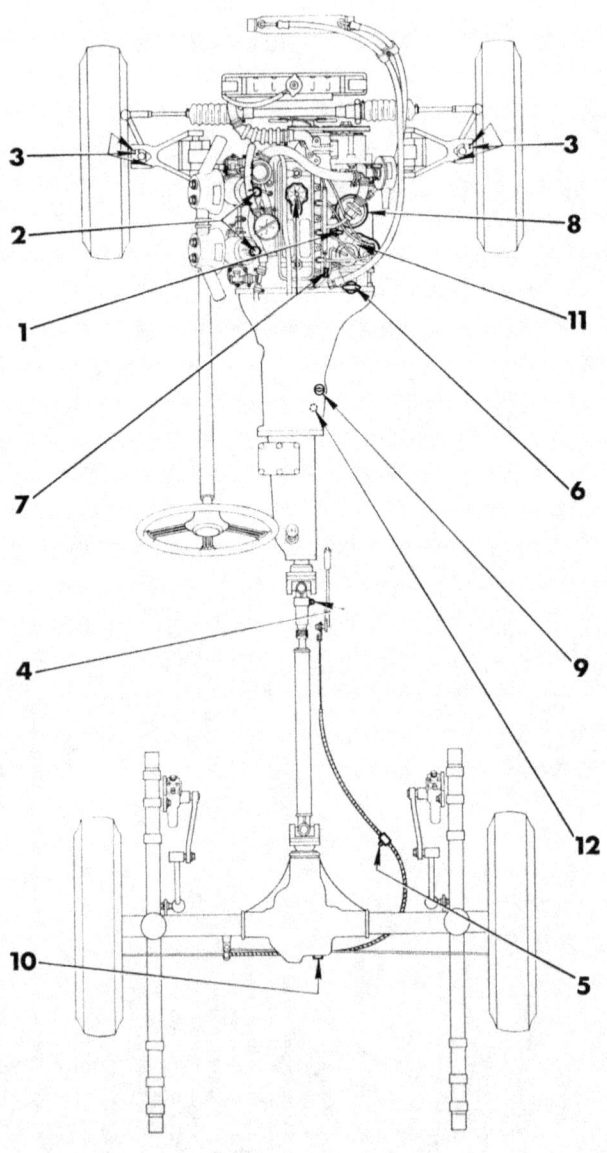

WEEKLY
(1) ENGINE. Check the oil level, and top up as necessary with oil to Ref. A.

Every 3,000 miles or 3 months
(2) CARBURETTERS. Top up damper reservoirs with oil to Ref. E.

(3) FRONT SUSPENSION (6 nipples). Give three or four strokes of a gun filled with grease to Ref. C.

(4) PROPELLER SHAFT (1 nipple). Give three or four strokes of a gun filled with grease to Ref. C.

(5) HAND BRAKE CABLE (1 nipple). Give three or four strokes of a gun filled with grease to Ref. C.

(6) AUTOMATIC TRANSMISSION. Check fluid level, and top up if necessary with fluid to Ref. F.

(7) ENGINE (if using monograde or single-viscosity oils only). Drain and refill with fresh oil.

Every 6,000 miles or 6 months
(7) ENGINE. Drain and refill with fresh oil to Ref. A.

(8) ENGINE OIL FILTER. Drain, wash the bowl in fuel and fit a new element.

(9) GEARBOX AND OVERDRIVE. Check oil level, and top up if necessary with oil to Ref. A.

(10) REAR AXLE. Check oil level, and top up if necessary with oil to Ref. B.

(11) DISTRIBUTOR. Lubricate all parts as necessary.

Every 24,000 miles or 24 months
(12) GEARBOX WITH OVERDRIVE. Drain, clean the overdrive filters and refill with fresh oil to Ref. A.

NOTE.—Oil and grease references are detailed.
   The engine oil change periods are those recommended when a multigrade oil is used. Monograde or single-viscosity oil should be changed at 3,000-mile or 3-month intervals.

LUBRICATION

KEY TO RECOMMENDED LUBRICANTS

Component		A – Engine and Gearbox			B – Rear Axle and Steering Gear			C – All Grease Points	D – Upper Cylinder Lubricant	E – Oilcan and Carburetter	F – Automatic Transmission
Climatic conditions predominating		Tropical and temperate down to 5° C. (41° F.)	Extreme cold temperatures between 5° C. (41° F.) and −12° C. (10° F.)	Arctic conditions temperatures consistently below −12° C. (10° F.)	All conditions down to −12° C. (10° F.)	Arctic consistently below −12° C. (10° F.)	All conditions	All conditions	All conditions	All conditions
STERNOL		Sternol W.W. 40 or W.W. Multigrade 20W/50	Sternol W.W. 20 or W.W. Multigrade 10W/40 or 20W/50	Sternol W.W. 10 or W.W. Multigrade 10W/40	Ambroleum E.P. 90	Ambroleum E.P. 80	Ambroline L.H.T.	Sternol Magikoyl	Sternol W.W. Multigrade 10W/40	Sternol Lynx Type A
MOBIL		Mobil Special 20W/40 Mobil A.F. Mobiloil Super 10W/40	Mobil Arctic or Mobiloil Special 10W/30 or Mobiloil Super 10W/40	Mobiloil Special 10W/30 Mobiloil 10W Mobiloil Super 10W/40	Mobilube G.X. 90	Mobilube G.X. 80	Mobilgrease M.P.	Mobil Upperlube	Mobiloil Special 10W/30 Mobiloil Super 10W/40	Mobil A.T.F. 200
ESSO		Esso Motor Oil 40/50 Esso Motor Oil 40 Esso Extra Motor Oil 20W/40	Esso Motor Oil 20 or 20W/30 Esso Extra Motor Oil 10W/30	Esso Motor Oil 10W Esso Extra Motor Oil 10W/30	Esso Gear Oil G.P. 90/140 or G.P. 90	Esso Gear Oil G.P. 80	Esso Multi-purpose Grease H	Esso Upper Cylinder Lubricant	Esso Extra Motor Oil 10W/30	Esso Automatic Transmission Fluid
FILTRATE		Filtrate Heavy Filtrate 20W/50	Filtrate Zero or Filtrate 10W/30	Filtrate Sub-Zero Filtrate 10W/30	Filtrate E.P. Gear 90	Filtrate E.P. Gear 80	Filtrate Super Lithium Grease	Filtrate Petroyle	Filtrate 10W/30 Multigrade	Filtrate A.T.F. Type A
BP		Energol S.A.E. 40 or Super Visco-Static 20W/50	Energol S.A.E. 20W Super Visco-Static 10W/40 or Visco-Static	Energol S.A.E. 10W Super Visco-Static 10W/40 or Visco-Static	BP Gear Oil S.A.E. 90 E.P.	BP Gear Oil S.A.E. 80 E.P.	Energrease L.2	BP Upper Cylinder Lubricant	Visco-Static or Super Visco-Static 10W/40	Automatic Transmission Fluid Type A
SHELL		Shell Super Motor Oil Shell X—100 40 Shell X—100 Multigrade 20W/40 or 20W/50	Shell Super Motor Oil Shell X—100 20W Shell X—100 Multigrade 10W/30 or 20W/40, or 20W/50	Shell Super Motor Oil or Shell X—100 10W Shell X—100 Multigrade 10W/30	Spirax 90 E.P.	Spirax 80 E.P.	Shell Retinax A	Shell Upper Cylinder Lubricant	Shell Super Motor Oil	Shell Domx T.6
CASTROL		Castrol X.L.	Castrolite or Castrol X.L.	Castrol Z or Castrolite	Castrol Hypoy	Castrol Hypoy Light	Castrolease L.M.	Castrollo	Castrolite	Castrol T.Q.
DUCKHAM'S		Q. 20,50	Q. 20,50 or Q. 5500	Q. 5500	Duckham's Hypoid 90	Duckham's Hypoid 80	Duckham's L.B. 10 Grease	Duckham's Adcoid Liquid	Q. 5500	Nolmatic A.T.F. Type A

www.ingramcontent.com/pod-product-compliance
Lightning Source LLC
Chambersburg PA
CBHW050133240426
43673CB00043B/1648